THE BOEING B-29 SUPERFORTRESS

The giant bomber of World War Two and Korea.'

By Graham M Simons

Pen & Sword
AVIATION

First published in Great Britain in 2012 by
Pen & Sword Aviation
An imprint of

Pen & Sword Books Ltd
47 Church Street
Barnsley
South Yorkshire
S70 2AS

Copyright © Graham M Simons 2012

ISBN 978 1 84884 753 8

First Published 1990 by Arms and Armour Press.
Revised and expanded by Pen & Sword Aviation 2012

The right of Graham M Simons to be identified as Author of this work has been asserted by him in accordance with the Copyright, Designs and Patents Act 1988.

A CIP catalogue record for this book is
available from the British Library

All rights reserved. No part of this book may be reproduced or transmitted in any form or by any means, electronic or mechanical including photocopying, recording or by any information storage and retrieval system, without permission from the Publisher in writing.

Printed and bound in England
by CPI Group (UK) Ltd, Croydon, CR0 4YY

Pen & Sword Books Ltd incorporates the Imprints of Pen & Sword Aviation, Pen & Sword Family History, Pen & Sword Maritime, Pen & Sword Military, Wharncliffe Local History, Pen & Sword Select, Pen & Sword Military Classics, Leo Cooper, Remember When, Seaforth Publishing and Frontline Publishing

For a complete list of Pen & Sword titles please contact
PEN & SWORD BOOKS LIMITED
47 Church Street, Barnsley, South Yorkshire, S70 2AS, England
E-mail: enquiries@pen-and-sword.co.uk

Website: www.pen-and-sword.co.uk

CONTENTS

Introduction	5
Origins	7
Birth Pains	25
Early Aircraft	49
China	61
Into the Pacific!	91
Operation Centreboard	109
Peace - and a 'Police Action'	145
Washingtons and Tankers	165
The B-50	179
The Tu-4 'Bull'	197
Specials	207
Operating the B-29	229
Bibliography	250
Index	251

ACKNOWLEDGEMENTS

A project of this nature could not be undertaken without considerable help from many organizations and individuals.

Special thanks must go to Marilyn Phipps of Boeing Archives, Col. Richard L Upstromm and Tom Brewer from the USAF Museum, now the National Museum of the USAF for the provision of many photographs and details.

Background to the development and procurement of all the B-29 projects, can be found in published and unpublished primary source research material in the form of memoranda, policy statements and other documents from the Army Air Corps, the Navy, and Carl L. Norden inc., provided to us by Lynn Gamma and all in the U.S. Air Force Historical Research Center at Maxwell Air Force Base, Montgomery, Ala. The same applies the valuable services provided by the History Office of the Air Technical Service Command, Wright Field, Dayton, Ohio. Much other primary source documentation is also located in the National Archives and Records Administration at College Park, Maryland.

The archives of the National Advisory Committee for Aeronautics provided access to all their relevant material, as did the archivesof the Institute of Aircraft Production provided much information and a number of photographs, as did the RAF Museum, the Imperial War Museum and the Science Museum in London.

The late Roger Freeman provided photographs, as did Simon Peters and Martin Bowman and Peter Green from their respective collections.

Personal thanks must also go to David Lee, the former Deputy Director and Curator of Aircraft of the Imperial War Museum at Duxford, John Hamlin and to Vince Hemmings, the former curator of the East Anglian Aviation Society's Tower Museum at Bassingbourn.

The author is indebted to many people and organisations for providing photographs for this book, many of which are in the public domain. In some cases it has not been possible to identify the original photographer and so credits are given in the appropriate places to the immediate supplier. If any of the pictures have not been correctly credited, the author apologises.

INTRODUCTION

The Boeing B-29 Superfortress, along with the fallback design of the Consolidated B-32 Dominator should the Superfortress prove unsuccessful, were two very heavy bomber designs that originated in the latter part of the 1930s which were intended to replace earlier, smaller four engined designs.

The B-29 was the progenitor of a series of Boeing-built bombers, reconnaissance aircraft, trainers and tankers and airliners including the B-50 Superfortress, the C-97 Stratofreighter the Model 377 Stratocruiser. Later jet-powered models from Boeing carried on the lineage.

The B-29 was one of the largest aircraft to see service during World War Two. It was a very advanced bomber for this time period that included features such as a pressurized cabin, an electronic fire-control system, and remote-controlled gun turrets. Though it was designed as a high-altitude daytime bomber, in practice it actually flew more low-altitude nighttime incendiary bombing missions. It was the primary aircraft in the American fire-bombing campaign against the Empire of Japan in the final months of World War Two, and carried the two atomic bombs that destroyed Hiroshima and Nagasaki. Unlike many other bombers from this era, the B-29 remained in service long after the war ended, with a few even being employed as flying television transmitters for the Stratovision company. The type

The classic image of the B-29 - high over Mount Fiji in Japan. *(USAAF)*

was finally retired in the early 1960s, with 3,970 aircraft in all built.

There were many early problems - The most common cause of maintenance headaches and catastrophic failures was the engine. Although the Wright R-3350 later became a trustworthy powerplant of large piston-engined aircraft, early models were beset with dangerous reliability problems. This problem was not fully cured until the aircraft was fitted with the more powerful Pratt & Whitney R-4360 'Wasp Major' in the B-29D/B-50 programme, which arrived too late for World War Two. Interim measures included cuffs placed on propeller blades to divert a greater flow of cooling air into the intakes, which had baffles installed to direct a stream of air onto the exhaust valves. Oil flow to the valves was also increased, asbestos baffles installed around rubber push rod fittings to prevent oil loss, and thorough pre-flight inspections made to detect unseated valves. This was as well as frequent replacement of the uppermost five cylinders for every 25 hours of engine time and the changing of entire engines every 75 hours!

This then is the story - of trials and tribulations to eventual success!

Graham M Simons
Peterborough
December 2011

In close at the moment of weapon release. A pair of 19th BG B-29s release their bombs. *(USAAF)*

ORIGINS

German troops had already marched into Vienna and Hitler proclaimed chief of the state when in March 1938 the US Army Air Staff, seeking an economical method for equipping the Air Corps, asked Boeing to submit ideas for pressurizing the cabin of the B-17 Flying Fortress.

Appropriations for purchase of military aircraft were extremely modest; all decisions were influenced by a need for economy. In 1938 only $62,602,727 had been appropriated for the overall support of Army aviation—aircraft, maintenance, operating cost and officer and personnel training—a sum less than the cost of one capital ship!

Six desirables were evident in aircraft design trends of the times. Boeing's spectacular pressurized-cabin Stratoliner had proved the wisdom of the first desirable. The bomber of the future must possess a pressurized cabin to provide improved comforts for the crew and permit the craft to fly above storms and flak. Secondly, it must have tricycle landing gear, to make for ease of handling on the ground and to improve landings – for many years this remained a moot point, for tricycle landing gear 'cost' the B-29 nearly two thousand pounds of extra weight. Thirdly, it must have greater speed; fourth, greater range; fifth, greater bomb capacity; and sixth, greater interchangeability between fuel and bombs. This meant larger fuselages.

Company design engineers set to work; their job was to conceive and prepare drawings of new aircraft believed to be of interest to the Air Corps and to prepare major revisions to existing designs. Their first task was to determine whether they had exploited to the fullest all the virtues of two existing designs: they studied the company's XB-15, then the world's largest land aircraft, of which only one had

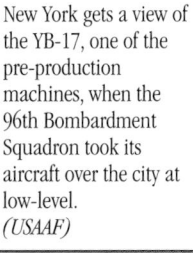

New York gets a view of the YB-17, one of the pre-production machines, when the 96th Bombardment Squadron took its aircraft over the city at low-level. *(USAAF)*

The Boeing XB-15 in flight, low over the Wright Brothers Kittyhawk memorial. (Simon Peters Collection)

been built and they studied, in parallel, the B-17 design. Could they 'squeeze' these aircraft into pressurized cabin models with tricycle landing gear, making them speedier, more far-ranging; could they make them carry more bombs?

From parallel studies made during the first half of 1938, two preliminary sketches emerged: Model 316, a modernized version of the XB-15, and Model 322, an improved version of the B-17 Flying Fortress. The ancestry of both Models 316 and 322 was above reproach. The XB-15 was to win world records for load-carrying to specified altitude. The B-17, then undergoing gruelling accelerated service tests, of which goodwill flights to Latin America were the most dramatic, and which had also broken world records for speed and altitude, was establishing the basic philosophy for the Air Corps heavy bombardment programme to come.

Model 316, A, B, C and D versions, offered variations of high and low-wing monoplanes. Model 322 was a mid-wing monoplane. Both the Model 316 series and Model 322 had pressurized cabins and tricycle landing gear. Both had good range, but they were not by any means the 'fastest and the mostest' aircraft Boeing designers believed were in the Air Corps' vision. And so, because improvements suggested in these designs were not convincingly beyond Flying Fortress performance of that day, and

Boeing only built ten Model 307 Stratoliners, but discovered one modification that was needed which changed the appearance of all subsequent B-17s - the extended fin that was to generate the nickname 'big-assed bird'. The change is evident in this photograph of a TWA 307 Stratoliner. (Real Aircraft Photographs)

Boeing executive Phillip Gustav Johnson (*b.* 5 November 1894, *d,* 13 September 1944)

because these marginal improvements promised would not be commensurate with cost, Boeing 316 and 322 designs never officially reached the Army.

A number of people and organisations played important rolés in the B-29 story. Philip G Johnson had returned to Boeing as president in September 1939. To Johnson fell the major task of contract negotiation with the Army for the aircraft to be known as B-29. This work was a role with which Johnson was familiar, for he was a man who had been reared in the Boeing organization. Upon graduation from the University of Washington in the spring of 1917, Johnson became draftsman for the Boeing company; five years later he had risen to vice president, general manager; in 1926 he was made president and general manager. In three years he was head of the sprawling Boeing aircraft and transport interests. He was president of United Aircraft and Transport Corporation, makers of the Pratt & Whitney engines, and president of United Air Lines. Resigning in July 1934, following the inquisitions of the Black Air Mail Committee at the time of the cancellation of the air mail, Johnson had entered the truck-manufacturing business. For a few years he took life easy. Then, in 1937, at invitation of the Canadian Government, he had established the operations of Trans-Canada Air Lines.

With him Johnson brought as executive vice president a man completely familiar with the requirements of aircraft production: H Oliver West. Boeing had also been West's Alma Mater. Joining the Boeing family in 1921 as an inspector of raw materials, he rose quickly to production chief; became superintendent of Boeing Air Transport's maintenance; retained the same job with United Air Lines and followed Johnson to Trans-Canada.

West's first act was to develop the plan for a new modern factory, to displace the old Plant One, by a sweeping expansion of the new Plant Two, a small portion of which had already been built. They must buy machine tools, millions of dollars worth, and get set to turn out Flying Fortresses in an efficient operation.

Later dubbed Multi-line Production, the West system called for the pre-completion of Fortresses in major sections or components and production lines which converged just before the factory door. These major sections were then hooked up, joined, and the aircraft was rolled out of the door. It was similar to what Consolidated and Fords were doing with the B-24.

On 17 June 1940 the Army had expressed its interest in substantiating wind tunnel data and with a mock-up of the XB-29, three major forces went into action: preliminary design engineers working closely with aerodynamicists, and with project engineers, advancing the design forwards.

The designers fell into two categories: research engineers and project engineers. Over a period of two years, preliminary design engineers and aerodynamicists had developed their design thinking to the promise stage. The heart of the bomber was the bomb bay, obviously built around the nature of the bombs, their sizes and number, the limiting fall angles and the hoisting clearances necessary for the bombs.

This determined the size of the fuselage. From there they drew the body design, the wing, the landing gear, the equipment and interior arrangement of the aircraft, its controls and control surfaces and its armament.

Remembering that the USAAF was the only customer for the embryonic Superfortress - it is not surprising that Wright Field and the Air Technical Service Command was constantly and closely involved with the B-29.

The War brought the AAF Materiel Command and Air Service Command - which merged in 1944 into the Air Technical Service Command (ATSC) with headquarters at Wright Field, Dayton, Ohio - into greater prominence than ever before. The Command's mission was three-fold: to conceive aircraft designs and put them through experimental development; purchase them in quantities and place them into production in minimum time.

The Air Technical Service Command was the branch of the Army Air Forces responsible for the engineering, procurement, production, supply and maintenance of all Army aircraft. To fulfill this responsibility ATSC had six divisions: Engineering, Procurement, Supply, Maintenance, Personnel and Base Services. It was the job of the Engineering Division to keep three years ahead of the then contemporary aviation by thinking in terms of the future. The B-29 was perhaps the most conspicuously successful example of the Army Air Forces' capacity for achieving long-range planning.

Throughout the conception, design, construction, flight test, programme-manufacturing and combat phases of the Superfortress story the Air Technical Service Command provided significant skills and thinking, vital to the successful completion and use of the B-29.

There were four very important players in the genisis of the B-29. 33 year-old Chief Engineer Wellwood E Beall was a product of University of Colorado and New York University. He had joined Boeing as instructor of drafting, mathematics, aerodynamics, structures, aircraft history and Air Commerce Regulations at the Boeing School of Aeronautics, Oakland, California; he later became Boeing's Far Eastern manager, selling pursuit planes to the Chinese Air Force. Returning in 1935, Beall was transferred to the engineering division, and as chief commercial project engineer played a major part in the design of the Clipper.

Edmund T Allen, 43, Chief of Boeing Flight Test and Aerodynamics staff, was at the time acclaimed as the world's greatest test pilot. Eddie Allen's life had been consecrated to the quest of aircraft stability and control. By 1940 his patience and pure scientific approach toward the flight-testing of aircraft had established him as the pre-eminent authority in the refinement of stability and control of heavy aircraft. His proved procedures for cruising operations of air transport craft had become the bible for practically all air transport operators in the world and his work with the Stratoliner and the B-17C and D Flying Fortress series had conquered for man's flight purposes, the thin, blue regions of the Stratosphere.

Working with Eddie Allen, as chief aerodynamicist, was George S Schairer, 27, graduate of Swarthmore and the Massachusetts Institute of Technology.

Edward Curtiss Wells, 29, a quiet genius with a lusty sense of humour so skillfully concealed it had a way of surprising even his closest friends. At twenty-three, this graduate of Stanford University had already

Wellwood E Beall, Boeing's Chief Engineer.(b. 1907, d. 1978)

Edmund T. 'Eddie' Allen (b.4 January 1896, d. 18 February 1943).

ORIGINS

The Model 316 of March, 1938.

Type: High-wing, pressurized cabin monoplane with tricycle landing gear, the main gear having double wheels.

Size: Wing span, 157 feet; length, 109 feet, two inches.

Design Gross Weight: 89,900 pounds.

Maximum Alternate Gross Weight: 89,900 pounds

Power Plant: Four Wright R-3350 developing 2,000 HP for take-off.

Wing Loading: 31 pounds per square foot.

Range with 2,000 lb of bombs: 4,000 miles.

Speed: 248 mph at 15,000 feet.

Armament: Seven .50 machine guns.

Maximum bomb load: 19,400 pounds. Crew: Nine

designed major portions of the Flying Fortress. As assistant chief engineer and spark plug of detailed design, Wells was to give expression to even greater talents in design of the B-29.

Overcoming the challenges

The overall design and evaluational problem facing Boeing at that time was: how to give an aircraft possessing twice the weight of the Flying Fortress thirty percent more speed with only eighty- three percent more horsepower? The magnitude of their problem could be stated in the cube-square law - to double the speed there had to be eight times as much power; for in doubling the speed ordinarily this produced four times the drag. Inasmuch as the power was fixed by the engines available, designers were relying on a big 'assist' from the aerodynamic cleanness they were giving the XB-29.

Aerodynamicists and powerplant engineers wrestled with the problem of propellers, their ideas moving toward the adoption of an entirely new propeller gear ratio for the Superfortress. For years scientists had known propeller tip speed must be kept as low as possible; where speeds approached the speed of sound a phenomena known as compressibility burble - a sudden high-drag action -

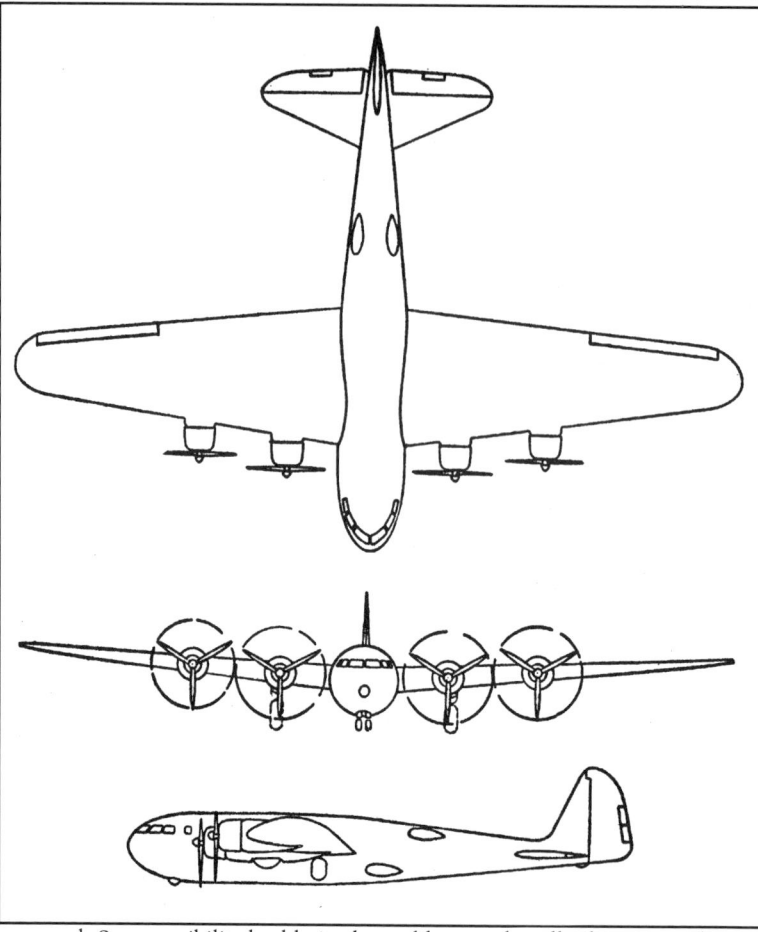

BOEING B-29 SUPERFORTRESS

The Model 322 from June, 1938.

Type: Mid-wing, pressurized cabin monoplane with single-wheeled tricycle landing gear.

Size: Wing span, 108 feet, seven inches; length, 75 feet, five inches

Design gross Weight: 40,000 pounds

Maximum Gross Weight: 53,100 pounds

Powerplant: Four Pratt and Whitney R-2180 developing 1,400 HP for take-off

Wing Loading: 35 pounds per square foot

Range with 2,000 pounds of bombs : 3,600 miles

Speed: 307 mph at 25,000 feet.

Armament: Four .50 machine guns

Maximum Bomb Load: 9,928 pounds.

Crew: Six

appeared. Compressibility burble is almost like a rock wall. Thus, it was known that the propellers must turn 'slowly.'

At the time propellers of most aircraft turned at 44% of engine speed. Engineers believed this would be too 'fast' for the B-29; this propeller speed would reduce high altitude performance of the aircraft. Furthermore, at this prop speed, sixteen mph would have to be be sacrificed. Wright Aeronautical engineers were asked for a propeller ratio enabling the B-29's propellers to turn more slowly. As a result Wright engineers proposed, and eventually achieved, a gear ratio which would turn the propeller at 35% of engine speed, making the B-29's propellers the slowest turning on any aircraft. After sweating out extensive propeller tests, the Hamilton Standard three-bladed propeller was initially adopted. Later another blade was added.

More and more tunnel models were built to sort through all aerodynamic unknowns - Where should the engines be placed? What shape of nacelle would cool the engines best? Model makers built up and scraped down, numerous clay nacelles in the constant hunt for that desirable shape which would accommodate the engines and accessories.

Structures, light of weight and adaptable to quantity production, were built

ORIGINS

The Model 333 of 26 January 1939)

Type: High-wing, pressurized cabin monoplane with single-wheeled tricycle landing gear

Size: Wing span, 109 feet; length, 80 feet, eight inches

Design Gross Weight: 41,000 pounds

Maximum Alternate Gross Weight: 48,600 pounds

Powerplant: Four Allison 1710 developing 1,150 HP for take-off

Wing Loading: 34 pounds per square foot

Range with 2,000 pounds of bombs: 3,420 miles

Speed: 307 mph at 15,000 feet

Armament: Five .50 machine guns and one .30.

Maximum Bomb Load: 5,800 pounds.

Crew: Six.

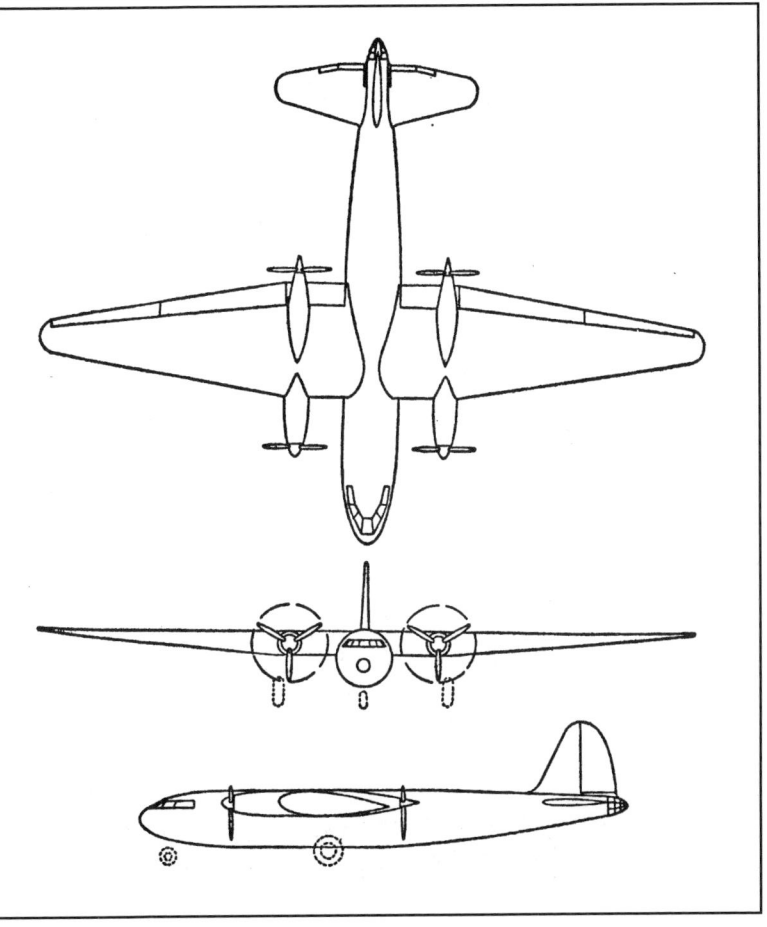

and proven. The research had to be right, and tests had to be comprehensive before the first XB-29s were built. If there had been time to place a small quantity of B-29s in the field long before Boeing had started engineering for production and long before the jigs and tools were built for production, then the job could have been done with less risks.

In January, 1939, Boeing engineers swept all existing design adaptation ideas from their heads and turned out Model 333. This design reflected the latest aerodynamic concepts of the times: the thought that the progressive aircraft must be aerodynamically cleaner and possess minimum size if it were to do a maximum job. Remarkably, they were not alone in their thinking – in the United Kingdom Geoffrey de Havilland and his chief designer Ronald Bishop were thinking along similar lines - what evolved from the drawing boards at Hatfield was the incredible De Havilland Mosquito.

These apparently diametrically opposed factors posed a challenging job of design refinement. Model 333 was a distinct break with tradition, an aircraft of substantial aerodynamic cleanness with four engines mounted in tandem arrangement, two Allison liquid-cooled V-type engines placed in tandem, one tractor and one pusher in each nacelle, one nacelle in each wing. Air observers returning from Europe described tail

14 **BOEING B-29 SUPERFORTRESS**

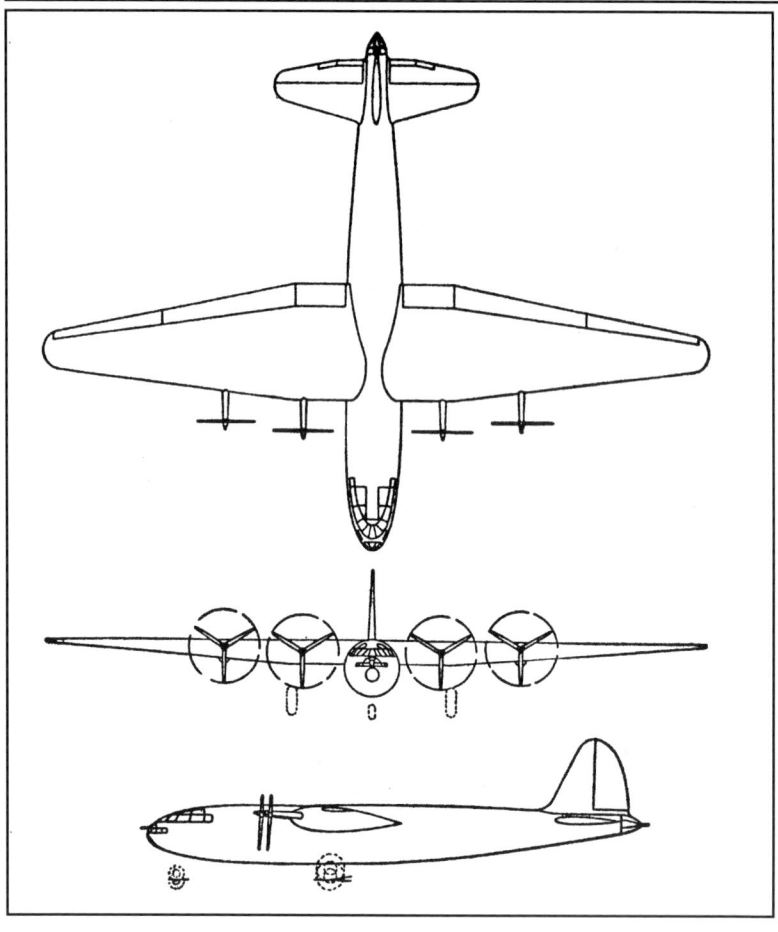

The Model 333-A from January 27, 1939.

Type: High-wing, pressurized cabin monoplane with single-wheeled tricycle landing gear

Size: Wing span, 108 feet, six inches; length, 80 feet, eight inches

Design gross Weight: 40,500 pounds

Maximum Gross Weight: 48,600 pounds

Powerplant: Four Allison 1710 developing 1,150 HP for take-off

Wing Loading: 34 pounds per square foot

Range with 2,000 pounds of bombs: 3,000 miles

Speed: 328 mph at 15,000 feet

Armament: Five .50 machine guns and one .30

Maximum bomb load: 5,800 pounds.

Crew: Six

guns as mandatory; and so, for the first time, tail guns appeared in a Boeing design. For the first time, too, double tandem bomb bays appeared.

But definite built-in disadvantages to the overall design of this machine appeared: rear engines would be difficult to cool; high, and therefore heavy landing gear would be required to ensure landing and take-off ground clearance for the pusher propellers. Because of the distribution of dead weight in the wing, wing tortional and vibration characteristics were involved.

There was also the problem of finding a wing that would promise unparalleled performance. The wing must possess low drag at high speeds; low drags at cruising and a high lift coefficient and good stall characteristics. A search undertaken by Eddie Allen and George Schairer's staff for a high performance wing for the B-29. Every worthy idea was thoroughly explored and evaluated with powered wind tunnel models, a practice which the Company had pioneered in the development of the Stratoliner. For two months they debated with David R Davis, the consulting aerodynamicist whose laminar flow wing that had been used on the Consolidated B-24 Liberator. After fruitless exploration to prove that the Davis wing could provide what was needed, Beall gave the official decision: Boeing aerodynamicists would develop their own wing.

ORIGINS

The 333-B of 21 February 1939.

Type: High-wing, pressurized cabin monoplane with single-wheeled tricycle landing gear

Size: Wing span, 111 feet; length, 80 feet, eight inches

Design Gross Weight: 46,000 pounds

Maximum Alternate Gross Weight: 52,180 pounds

Powerplant: Four Wright 1800 horizontal engines developing 1,850 HP for take-off

Wing Loading: 34 pounds per square foot

Range with 2,000 pounds of bombs: 2,500 miles

Speed: 364 mph at 20,000 feet

Armament: Five .50 machine guns and one .30.

Maximum bomb load: 5,800 pounds.

Crew: Six

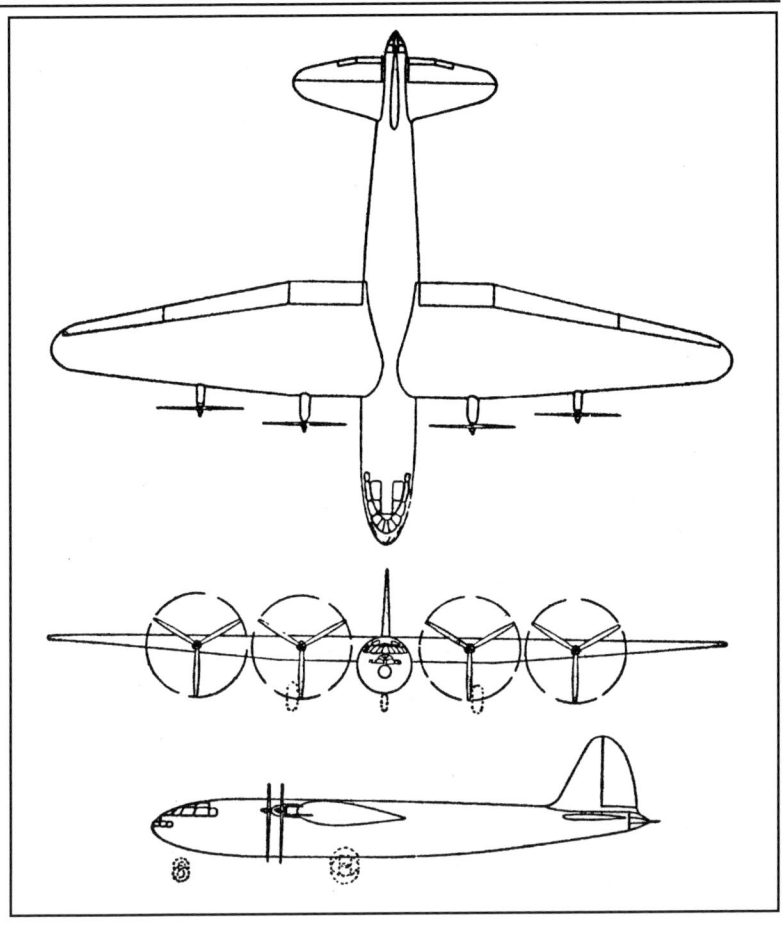

 And so, preliminary design engineers, making haste slowly in January, February and March, 1939, laid out Models 333-A, 333-B and 334, all high-wing pressurized cabin monoplanes with tricycle landing gear and each placing emphasis on submerged engine installations, engines which existed only in the minds of engine designers. At the time both Wright Aeronautical and Pratt & Whitney engine-makers were planning to develop horizontal-type, liquid-cooled engines to make these wing-installations possible. All these models were trying to do the same job: achieve maximum aerodynamic cleanness.

 After performing a myriad of calculations during March, April and May, Boeing designers came to the reluctant conclusion that the long propeller shafts required in Models 333-A, 333-B and 334 would introduce disadvantageous features; also that because of the thick, high-drag wing - brought about by the submerged engines - many of the aerodynamic gains of the submerged engines were more theoretical than real. Even those gains would be negated by the additional weight occasioned by cutting the wing structure to receive the engines. Added to these disadvantages were increased cooling problems, the major hazard in designing an aircraft completely around new engines of revolutionary and unproved design, and the fact that the range of the designs was crippled: there was too little room in the wings for fuel tanks. And so, in July, after

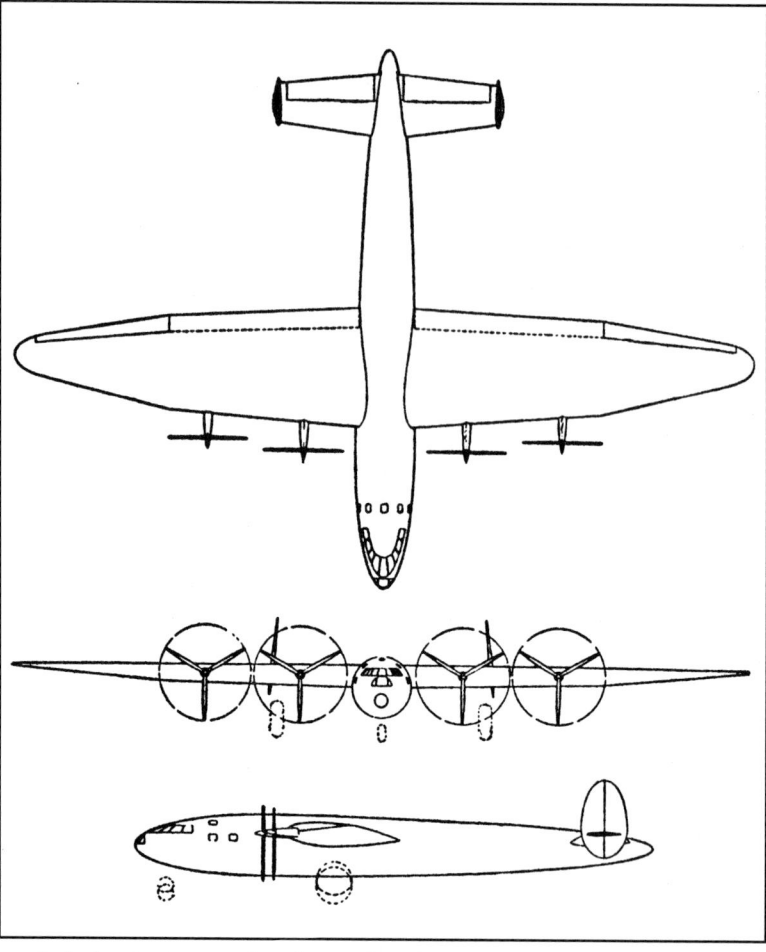

The Model 334 on 4 March 1939.

Type: High-wing monoplane with pressurized cabin, single-wheeled tricycle landing gear and twin tail

Size: Wing span, 120 feet; length, 83 feet, four inches

Design Gross Weight: 49,750 pounds

Maximum Alternate Gross Weight: 66.000 pounds

Poweplant: Four Pratt and Whitney 1800 Flat engines developing 1,850 HP for take-off

Wing Loading: 40 pounds per square foot

Range with 2,000 pounds of bombs: 4,500 miles

Speed: 390 mph at 20,000 feet

Armament: Five .30 machine guns and three .50

Maximum bomb load: 7,830 pounds.

Crew: Nine

much shadow-boxing over their drawing boards, engineers made another clean break with past thinking and designed Model 334A.

During all these design experiences, designers had sought to avoid committing themselves to any design which would involve increasing wing loading – that is the weight to be carried by each square foot of wing area. This dread of increasing wing loading, at that time, amounted almost to a phobia in the aircraft industry. The old adage of 'High wing loading means dangerously high landing speeds,' had been around for a long time. But before engineers had completely explored their next design. Model 334-A, they had convinced themselves that wing loading in a practical sense was largely a state of mind, all other things being equal. Their exploration persuaded them that once the highly loaded wing was safely air borne, high wing loading had wonderful virtues in low drag and great range. Their problem was to design a wing flap to assist the take-off and reduce the landing distance.

Conceived in July Model 334-A, the first 'blood ancestor' of the B-29 stemmed from this thinking. Of radical departure from previous models, the 334-A should not actually bear a 334 series identification.

ORIGINS

The Model 334-A of July 1939.

Type: High-wing, pressurized cabin monoplane with single-wheeled tricydt landing gear and single tail.
Size: Wing span, 135 feet; length, 80 feet.

Design Gross Weight: 55,000 pounds

Maximum Alternate Gross Weight: 66,000 pounds

Powerplant : Four Wright 3350 developing 2,200 HP for take-off.

Wing Loading: 47 pounds per square foot.

Range with 2,000 pounds of bombs: 5,333 miles.

Speed: 390 MPH at 16,000 feet

Armament: Five .30 machine guns and three .50.

Maximum Bomb Load: 7,830 pounds.

Crew: Nine

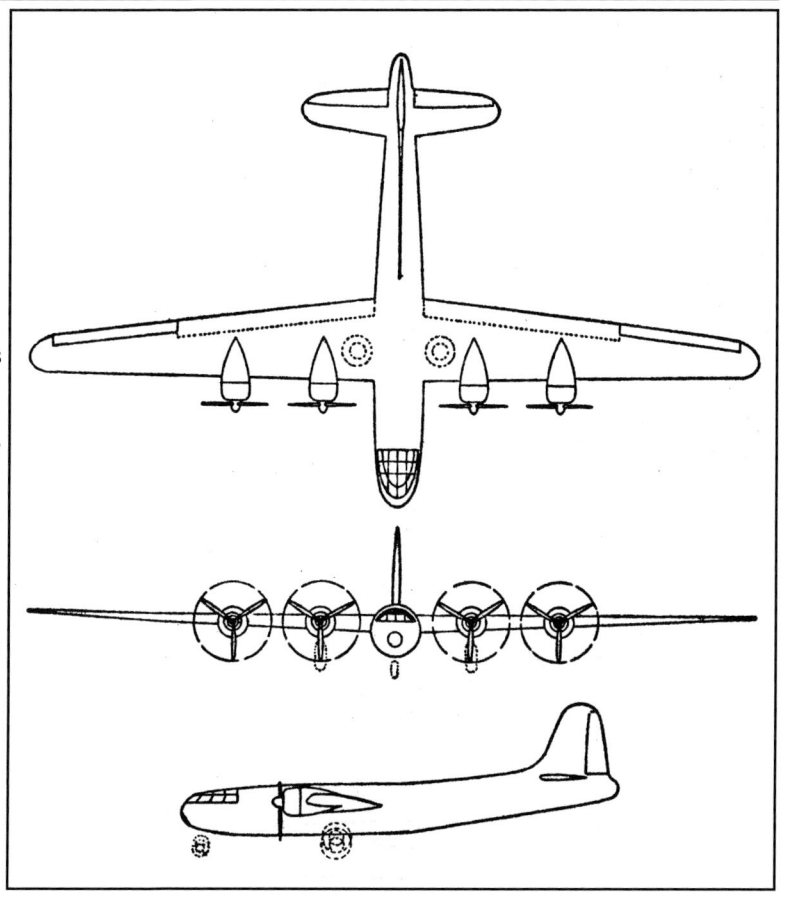

Almost immediately, designers realized that in Model 334-A they possessed a design of great promise. With the unprecedented wing load of forty-seven pounds. Model 334-A featured a long, narrow wing planform - indicative of long range - main landing gear retracting into the wings, a top speed of 390 m. p. h. at sixteen thousand feet, a maximum bomb load of 7,830 pounds, and a maximum range with two thousand pounds of bombs of 5,333 miles.

From the research work done, thousands of engineering hours invested in the design and evaluation of eight different wings, came the Boeing 115 wing - but now Wright Field was demanding that the XB-29 grow to one hundred thousand pounds design gross weight and one hundred and fourteen thousand pounds maximum alternate gross weight, an even greater performance wing was demanded. For these increased demands, the famous Boeing 117 wing was developed.

Beginning with this design—and because high wing loading had always caused opposition in the minds of pilots and designers - engineers set out on the long, hard trail to prove to themselves that a wing flap of sufficiently great size and effectiveness could be attached to highly loaded wings to facilitate take-off and reduce the distance required for landing.

After laborious months of design and wind tunnel evaluations, and of building

18 **BOEING B-29 SUPERFORTRESS**

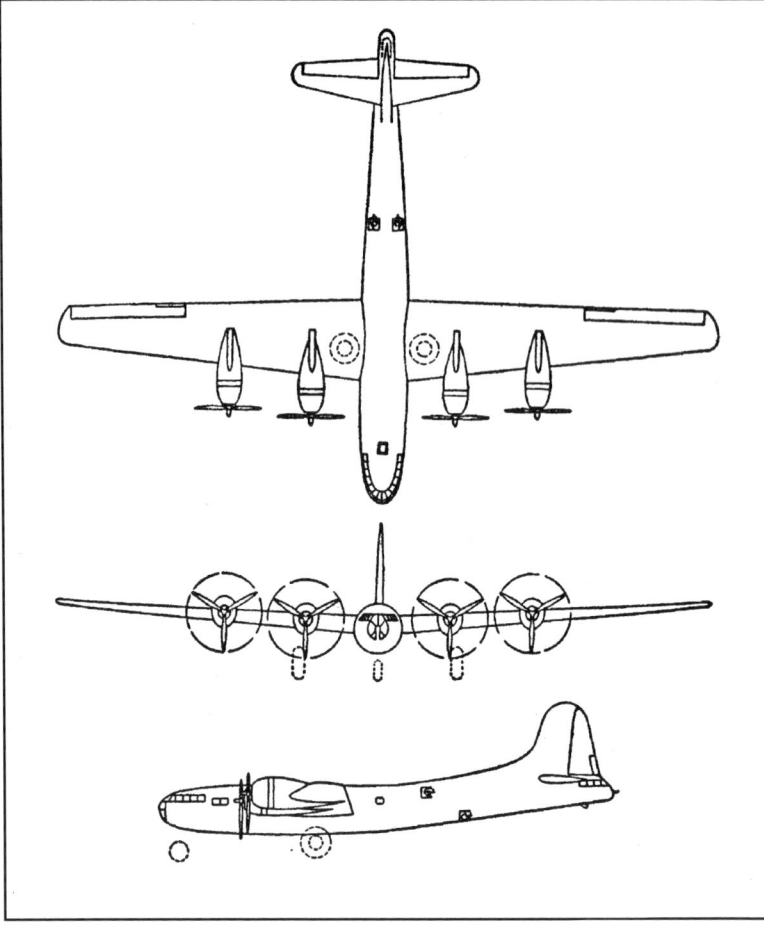

The Model 341 - designed August, 1939- March, 1940.

Type: Mid-wing, pressurized cabin monoplane with single-wheeled tricycle landing gear

Size: Wing span, 124 feet, seven inches: length, 85 feet, six inches

Design Gross Weight: 76,000 pounds

Maximum Alternate Gross Weight: 85,672 pounds

Powerplant: Four Pratt and Whitney R-2800 developing 2,000 HP for take-off

Wing Loading: 61 pounds per square foot

Range with 2.000 pounds of bombs: 5,533 miles at design gross weight and 7,000 miles at maximum alternate gross weight

Speed: 405 MPH at 2-25,000 feet

Armament: Six .50 flexibly mounted, manually-operated machine guns

Maximum Bomb Load: 10,000 pounds.

Crew: Twelve

scaled-down models of flaps and subjecting these to actual flight conditions, the Superfortress wing flap design emerged. They gave the flap 332 feet of area, equal to one-fifth of the B-29's wing area. Extended, this gave the wing one-third more lift. They extended it downward thirty degrees from its extendable position, increasing camber; thus giving the wing an additional one-third increased lift.

Throughout the summer of 1939 designers waged this battle with the many unknowns surrounding high wing loading. They battled the inhibition that said you cannot get optimum altitude performance with a highly loaded wing; they ferreted through extensive existing studies of high-load wing sections; they submitted their ideas to wind tunnel tests and they concluded, with great enthusiasm but not without a little trepidation, that they were on the right track.

Illustrative of the spectacular stride made in flap design, at that time, is this promise by the ingenious performance device: the wing flap would give the Superfortress, an aircraft ninety-four times the gross weight of a Cub and possessing only 9.4 times the wing area, a landing speed only three and one-half times that of the Cub!

Meanwhile, over the same period, explorative conversations continued with Wright Field on the nature of the superbomber the Army might seek when the

ORIGINS

Wind Tunnel Testing!

Boeing spent many thousands of hours testing different aerodynamic shapes and created literally hundreds of different wing designs from which they refined and eventually selected the best for the XB-29.

hour of need arrived. Participating in these germinating talks were Claire Egtvedt, Boeing President, Wellwood E Beall, chief engineer and Edward C Wells. In these huddles there were often such men as Gen H H Arnold, Air Corps chief Brig Gen Frank M Andrews, in command of General Headquarters Air Forces, Langley Field, Va, one of the earliest believers in the military effectiveness of the heavy, long-range, self-defensive bomber, whose philosophy had indoctrinated Air Corps planning; Col Oliver P Echols, in charge of Materiel Command; Maj William Irvine, Maj Turner A Sims, Jr. and Col William Craigie, technical assistants to General Arnold; Col Frank O Carroll, chief of the engineering division. Materiel Command, Lt. Col. Donald L Putt, of Materiel Command's experimental engineering, later to become the Air Forces project engineer for the XB-29 and Lt Col Frank Cook, later in charge of production engineering of the B-29.

It was known that engine cooling problems had plagued Martin engineers with their development of the Mars and Douglas engineers with the B-19 aircraft using the engine selected for the B-29. Boeing engineers gave exceeding care to this phase of the B-29, for unless the engines operated efficiently the Superfortress' performance might be critically compromised. Subjecting this problem to three explorative tests, engineers designed and built a complete mock-up of the duct system which would cool the engines. Driven by variable-speed electric motors, blower sections of turbo-superchargers were installed in the mock-up to simulate the two hundred and forty thousand cubic feet of air which would pour through the four engines per minute. A full section of a wing with one nacelle, complete with power plant, was built and fully tested. The duct system was to be fully evaluated, finally, in extensive flight tests of the Superfortress. But there still would be massive problems.

In its appraisal of the growing Superfortress design, the Army continued to be suspicious of the aircraft's high wing loading. At one time, Lt Gen George C Kenny summoned Wellwood Beall to his office at Wright Field, where he wrote on a blackboard behind his desk the gross weight, the wing loading and the ceiling of an aircraft later identified as the B-24 Liberator – an aircraft whose ceiling was considerably less than that of the B-17, which had less wing loading. General Kenny then wrote down the gross weight of the XB-29 and its wing loading: behind the word 'Ceiling' he placed a large question mark.

Beall argued that the turbo-supercharger installations of the Liberator differed radically from those of the B-17 and B-29, hence the cases were not comparable; that the altitude performance of the B-24 would always be compromised by these turbo-supercharger installations, thus the B-24's altitude performance limitations did not result from that aircraft's high wing loading. Boeing-Wright Field debates on this subject grew hot, so hot that on one occasion a technical commission with orders from Washington arrived at Seattle to demand that additional wing be given the B-29. This major change would compromise the entire performance of the aircraft, hence the company stuck to its guns.

Then there was the problem of the main gear - how to squeeze two wheels measuring fifty-six inches in diameter into the comparatively tiny nacelles. Overall design of the Superfortress was well under way when Wright Field armament engineers discovered that if the aircraft were to attain peak versatility, bomb bays should be lengthened. Elongation by sixty-two inches would allow greater interchangeability of bomb sizes - it would mean that as many 'small' bombs could be loaded as large bombs. It would double the number of five hundred pounders the B-29 could carry.

In August, 1939, Boeing placed the Model 341 on the drawing boards in old Boeing Plant One, a hallowed spot. Plant One had been the incubator of such aircraft as the Monomail, the 247 Transport, the Flying Fortress, the Stratoliner, and the Clipper. Beginning at that time design personnel - although the official

The men behind the engineering of the B-29 Left to right: George S. Schairer, chief aerodynamist; Edward C Wells, chief engineer; Wellwood E Beall. vice president in charge of engineering, N D Showalter, chief of flight test; and Lysle A A Wood, assistant chief engineer. From the munitions on the table, it looks as if they were discussing B-29 armament.

signal from Wright Field was still six months away - acquired the conviction that they were 'playing for keeps'. Personnel numbers were increased for the job at hand. Although the weight empty of Model 341, conceived at that historic time, was only six thousand pounds greater than that of Model 334-A, its useful load was more than twice that of 334-A. Its wing spread was less by ten feet, but its length was five feet more. Although Model 341 had a maximum alternate gross weight twenty thousand pounds greater than Model 334-A, it possessed a wing area less by seventy square feet, thus raising the wing loading from forty-seven to sixty-four pounds per square foot.

While retaining the same range, it carried 1,170 pounds more armament. Without the military armament weight the Model 341 would have made good a range of seven thousand miles!

Working in collaboration with the Flight Test and Aerodynamics staff, Boeing designers held themselves to exceedingly fine margins in the design of Model 341. All wing skin joints had to be smooth, all external rivets flush; turbo-superchargers had to be totally enclosed and none of the usual excrescences of aircraft would be allowed: they planned no drains, vents, no external air scoops. All lights, fuel system vents, thermometers and pitot tubes were to be flush, radio loop aerials streamlined; de-icers flush. Failure to meet these requirements defined for Model 341 would mean loss not only in speed but in range. Both speed and range were 'must have' requirements of the Army.

Believing strongly in the daring design philosophy exemplified in Model 341, Boeing implemented this belief. On 5 December 1939 at company expense, construction of a full-scale wooden mock-up of Model 341 was begun.

When, on 5 February 1940 the large brown envelope containing the official requirement arrived, the work of perfecting the design for presentation was intensified, for the presentation had to reach Wright Field by 5 March.

Over a lagging period of many indecisive months. Air Staff and Materiel Command had outlined the performance requirements needed in a superbomber. But history of the times was moving with giant strides. Ideas on the battle equipment of aircraft were changing rapidly. The phony war was four months old when, during the last days of March, after studying the Boeing Model 341 proposal. Air Staff officers' original ideas on a superbomber had been swept before the tides of war.

And so that month a supplementary specification went out from Wright Field saying, in brief: '...*Give us more airplane: greater bomb capacity, leakproof fuel tanks and more defensive armament*'.

Designing the armament

A huge problem facing Boeing engineers assigned to perfect defensive armament of the Superfortress was how to design powered gun turrets which could be operated by men working within a pressurized vessel.

Like all creations, the firepower system of the B-29 evolved. In December, 1941, all experience and most thinking had been in terms of manually operated guns mounted in such a manner that they could move through azimuth and elevation to cover the largest area possible. Battle experience in Europe had demonstrated that multiple guns mounted in power turrets were much to be preferred.

There were obvious disadvantages to manually operated guns for the B-29. If

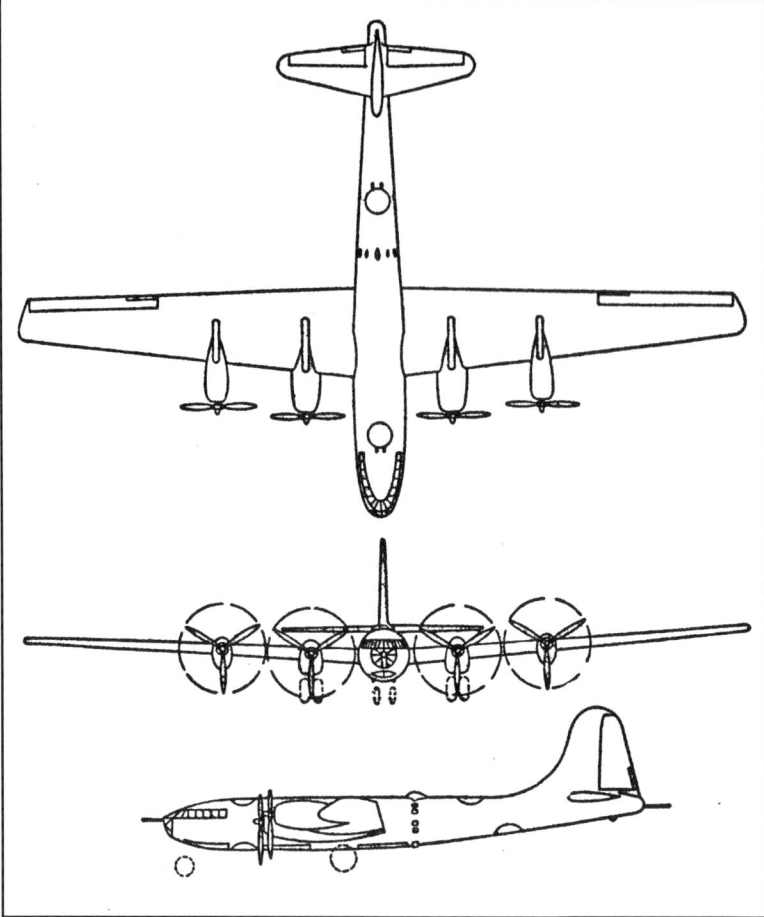

The Model 345 - designed in March-April. submitted to Wright Field: 11 May 1940.

Type: Mid-wing, pressurized cabin monoplane with double-wheeled tricycle landing gear, the main gear retracting into engine nacelles instead of in the wing as in previous models.

Size: Wing span, 141 feet, two inches; length, 93 feet

Design Gross Weight: 97,700 pounds.

Maximum Alternate Gross Weight: 112,300 pounds.

Powerplant: Wright R-3350 developing 2,200 HP for take-off.

Wing Loading: 65 pounds per square foot

Range with 2,000 pounds of bombs: 5,333 miles at design gross weight and 6,950 at maximum alternate gross weight.

Speed: 382 mph at 25,000 feet

Armament: Ten .50 machine guns and one twenty millimetre cannon, the latter mounted in the tail. Machine guns were mounted in four retractable turrets and one power tail turret. Guns were remotely controlled and sighted through periscope.

Maximum Bomb Load: 16,000 pounds.

Crew: Twelve

the guns were to be operated by hand, then it would be necessary to place gunners in great blisters outside the pressure vessel, the cabin. Such blisters would greatly reduce the aerodynamic cleanness of the aircraft, slow. The guns then, must be mounted outside the aircraft and controlled remotely, by gunners inside the pressurized vessel. If the computing sight, then in its infancy could be technically perfected and made psychologically acceptable to the gunners, would result in much more accurate firing. This compound design requirement was agreed to by Boeing and Air Technical Service Command engineers: the fire power system must possess computing sights, it must feature powered turrets operated by remote control by men inside the pressurized cabin.

Preliminary designers sweated out March and April to create Boeing's next design. Model 345, an aircraft reflecting the Air Forces' growing concern for making every military aircraft a fighting machine. The difference between Model 341 and 345 was the war.

With seventeen feet more wing span and eight feet more length, Model 345 could carry 7,600 pounds more useful load than Model 341. With a design gross weight of 97,700 pounds and a maximum alternate gross weight of 112,000 pounds, a speed of 382 m. p. h., Model 345 was to be powered by four Wright air-cooled engines developing 2,200 h.p. for take-off, two hundred more horsepower per engine than Model 341 had possessed. A different firepower arrangement was proposed: four remotely controlled retractable turrets housing eight .50 machine guns, one twenty millimetre gun and two .50 guns installed in a powered tail turret. This firing system was to be sighted through periscopes.

The war burden forced further changes in the design of the Model 345: leak-proofing the tanks had added three thousand pounds. Two thousand pounds more gasoline were needed to carry this tank weight alone if the range were to be kept constant. Likewise, when armament weight went from 1,646 pounds in Model 341 to 4,153 pounds in Model 345 more than 1,600 pounds of additional fuel was required to carry that added armament weight, if the range were to be kept constant. Summed up, this meant tankage capacity of Model 345 must be 5,440 gallons or 1,270 gallons above that of Model 341. This in turn meant Model 345 would grow larger to accomplish the bigger job: Result: Model 345 grew nearly 27,000 pounds heavier than the Model 341.

On 11 May 1940 Boeing submitted the Model 345 for War Department consideration. On 16 May President Roosevelt asked for an appropriation of one billion, one hundred million dollars for national defence, at a time when Americans were already concerned about the twenty-five billion dollar national debt.

The all-electric aircraft

Every piece of the B-29's equipment that moved - landing gear, wing flaps, bomb doors, the turbo-supercharger mechanism, the automatic pilot system - had be actuated by a powered, not manual, force. Hydraulic, pneumatic, mechanical and electrical systems were studied.

A hydraulic system would convey the required energy via fluids carried in pipes. An all-pneumatic system would transmit the energy by air in pipes. With an electrical system, energy would be created by generators and distributed through an intricate pattern of electric wires to points of utilization. Combat experience had proved that electric wires were less vulnerable to gunfire and flak than hydraulic and pneumatic

A full section of one wing was constructed, complete with engine nacelle in order to test its workings.

The Model XB-29 - developed from mid-1940 to early 1942

Type: Mid-wing pressurized cabin monoplane with tricycle landing gear

Size: Wing span, 141 feet, two inches; length, 98 feet, two inches

Design gross Weight: 100,000 pounds

Maximum Alternate Gross Weight: 114,500 pounds

Powerplant: Four Wright R-3350 developing 2,200 HP for take-off

Wing Loading: 66 pounds per square foot

Range with 2,000 pounds of bombs: 5.333 miles.

Speed: 382 mph at 25,000 feet

Armament: Ten .50 machine guns and one twenty millimetre cannon

Maximum Bomb Load: 20,000 pounds.

Crew: Twelve

tubes. Engineers therefore adopted, basically, an electric system to operate the B-29's functioning equipment, adapting it - where superior results could be obtained - to combinations of hydraulic and pneumatic mechanical apparatus. In the Flying Fortress, equipment was largely electrically operated.

On 14 June the War Department demonstrated its faith in Model 345 by authorizing the expenditure of $85,652, directing Boeing to assemble further design data, construct wind tunnel models. On 27 June Boeing was given contract and additional funds for the assembly of further data and construction of a full-scale wooden mock-up of Model 345.

The long labour and thought invested in the design of the company's interpretation of a superbomber had borne its first fruit. The Model 345, immediately given the Air Forces designation XB-29 - experimental, twenty-ninth bomber design purchased by the Army - was at last a project.

On 24 August just seventy days after authorizing Boeing to proceed with aerodynamic investigation of the XB-29, Wright Field was so impressed by substantiating wind tunnel data that a contract for two XB-29s, at a total cost of $3,615,095, was signed.

BIRTH PAINS

During the early part of May 1941 engineers began releasing their first drawings for guidance in construction of the first XB-29. Construction of the wooden mock-up, faithful to the metal aircraft-to-be, was begun. A wing, the nacelles, the fuselage
and all the equipment and the arrangement within the fuselage, were reproduced in the mock-up. Each item was be inspected by Wright Field's Mock-up Committee. It was the Committee's duty to live and work in the mock-up and to hand down final decisions on every aspect of the design arrangement recommended by the company. By this time, theoretically, all major decisions had been made by the various group engineers designing the craft.

In Plant I, Seattle, an old out-moded building, cruelly limited of space, the first Superfortress was to be born. Here the task of constructing what was at the time the world's largest aircraft was undertaken fully six months before all aerodynamic work had been completed and one year before all drawings of detailed parts were available. The aircraft had be completed by 3 August 1942.

On 4 May 1941 Boeing started with fifty mechanics assigned to the project; this staff was to grow to seven hundred before the aircraft rolled out of the factory doors. They cradled the first Superfortress in wooden jigs. The fuselage was built in one piece. They would build first those parts for which they had drawings, leaving vast 'holes' in the construction where drawings were not yet available. There was no time to build the aircraft logically and in sequence.

On 17 May Col W F Volandt, Air Forces contracting officer, dictated a letter to P G Johnson from his Wright Field:

'The War Department anticipates placing an order with you for approximately the following airplanes, funds for which in the amount of ten million dollars are available at this time:

250 B-29 type airplanes
335 Additional B-17 type airplanes

'Procurement is conditioned upon expansion of facilities at Boeing-Wichita to permit monthly productive capacity of sixty-five B-17s and twenty-five B-29 airplanes by July 1, 1942 and February 1, 1943, respectively.

'The Secretary of War advises that in the interest of national defense it is necessary that production be not delayed, awaiting the placing of the aforesaid order or orders. You will hereby be authorized to purchase such jigs, dies and fixtures (except machine tools and production machines) and such critical material and equipment as are necessary to the production of such aircraft and spare parts in anticipating of the placing of such order or orders'.

After the first four XB-29s, a further 14 service-test examples were ordered under the designation YB-29. These 250 B-29s were to be built in a new government-owned facility at Wichita, Kansas, that would be leased by Boeing for B-29 production.

After Pearl Harbor and the entry of the USA into the war, the contract was increased to 500 in February 1942. The next month, over a thousand more B-29s were ordered and the Army specified that three other corporations would also participate in B-29 production: the Bell Aircraft Company in a new plant in Marietta, Georgia, North American Aviation in a new plant at Kansas City, Missouri, and the Fisher Body Division of General Motors in its plant at Cleveland, Ohio.

In anticipation of the job ahead, Oliver West outlined plans for undertaking the task at Wichita, including the layout of a fully integrated factory facility and contracting for its construction. From Wichita came key production and engineering personnel to 'live with' the XB-29, to assimilate thoroughly every detail of its design and construction. On Beall and his staff fell the job of expanding the engineering department which would assume the major burden of engineering an aircraft to be constructed at Wichita, two thousand miles away.
One thousand engineers completed ten thousand drawings, costing 1,500,000 man hours and nearly three million dollars. At the height of B-29 production, 3,300 engineers would be working on the project and 80,000 Boeing men and women would be creating the aircraft.

Scarcity of materials and accessories and the snail's pace with which completed drawings were released added despair to the never easy task of building the first machine. Machining the spar chords, great lengths of duralumin almost as massive as railroad rails, was one of the most rugged tasks of those days. As many as thirty thousand manhours were invested in the machining of forgings, only to learn that the rough forgings, produced by new, inexperienced war companies, had cracked. Sometimes it was necessary to 'rob' a train of accessories in transit, to stop the train en-route, remove the accessories, load them on an aircraft and fly them to Seattle.

West's initial plan for B-29 production proposed that the body, inboard centre section and the main wing be built in the Seattle factory; that Wichita would manufacture only the outer wings and the tail surfaces of the aircraft. Seattle would ship Wichita its components and Wichita would complete the assembly job.

The Superfortress had be kept as 'small' as possible within the confines of the factory; this meant it had to be built in pre-completed sections. These sections had to then be joined just before the aircraft was ready to be rolled out of the factory door.

West and his staff broke the B-29's body into five sections. The joining-process of these sections would not be slowed down by splicing of beams or skin laps. They were joined by bolts with no drilling, reaming or riveting.

On 6 September 1941 the formal contract was signed for construction of 250 Superfortresses and 19,500,000 dollars' worth of spare parts. Strong rumours persisted that the War Department would order other companies to build the Superfortress; the grapevine said the Superfortress programme would be the

41-002, the first XB-29, seen during the early days with three-bladed propellers and no armament fitted. (USAAF)

BIRTH PAINS

greatest single industrial undertaking ever underwritten by the War Department.

At Wichita, a hastily assembled group of tool designers worked in a space measuring sixty by eighty feet, in an incompleted portion of the new factory rising over them. From a group of fifteen engineers and fifteen clerks, the staff grew to one hundred. Because there were no screens in the incompleted building through which the bursts of rivet guns still echoed, flies from the surrounding countryside swarmed in prodigious quantity. Two boys kept fly spray guns going constantly.

At the same time Seattle personnel-recruiters started their drive for manpower; to every major city west of the Mississippi went these seekers of skills with which to complete the engineering and the tooling for the B-29. To the towns and villages went the call *'Needed - men and women to build the B-29!'* Some of the men recruited in these drives were found working in bars, drug stores, grocery stores; some were working as garbage collectors, labourers or cowpunchers. Many of the men hired had been away from their engineering profession for five or six years.

Throughout the fall and winter months of 1941, the myriad- dimensioned struggle to complete aerodynamic research, the detailed design and engineering, the tool design and manufacturing and construction of the first XB-29, continued. The struggle carried men into far-reaching channels; into the rush-construction of Wichita's Plant II, to the building of roads, to the planning and erection of housing, to the seeking of hands to build the B-29, to the purchase of the machines for production.

Then, on 31 January 1942, America's Air Staff handed down its confidence decision in the B-29, with an order for a further five hundred Superfortresses and 53,000,000 dollars' worth of spare parts. Less than two weeks later, on 10 February a group of men who understood how to make automobiles and aircraft in quantity met in the General Motors Building, Detroit. They had assembled at the command of Major General Oliver P Echols, chief of the Materiel Center, Wright Field. Their assignment was stated simply, directly by Robert A Lovett, Under Secretary of War: General Arnold needed Air Forces with longer range and greater striking power, and the Boeing B-29 was the only answer. The Air Forces needed the B-29 quickly and by the thousands.

O E Hunt, vice president. General Motors Corporation, presided as chairman,

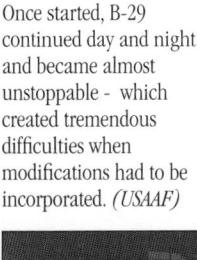

Once started, B-29 continued day and night and became almost unstoppable - which created tremendous difficulties when modifications had to be incorporated. *(USAAF)*

with, from the Air Force, Brig Gen George C Kenney, Col Kenneth B Wolfe and Col A M Drake. The War Department sent along Col E M Powers. From the Bell Aircraft Company came Lawrence E Bell, president; Ray Whitman and O L Woodson. Boeing Aircraft Company sent Fred B Collins, sales manager; Edward C Wells, Assistant chief engineer. From the Fisher Body Division of General Motors came Edward F Fisher, general manager, Detroit division; A J Fisher; Don R Berlin, director of aircraft development. North American Aviation, Inc sent J H Kindelberger, president and Ernest Breech, chairman of the board. Representing General Motors was Charles Wilson, president, and from the War Production Board came T B Wright, Aircraft Branch; E C Walton and Merrill C Meigs.

From this meeting eventually came the Superfortress Liaison Committee, established with headquarters at Seattle, fountainhead of all things B-29.

Before production actually began, rationalisation in production was made. North American Kansas City would concentrate on the B-25 Mitchell and its place in the B-29 pool would be taken by another Boeing plant, this one located at Renton in the state of Washington. The Boeing Renton plant had originally been built by the Navy for the manufacture of the Boeing PBB-1 Sea Ranger twin-engined patrol bomber seaplane. In an exchange between the Navy and the USAAF, it was agreed that the PBB-1 project would be cancelled and that the Renton plant would be reallocated to B-29 production in exchange for the delivery of land-based bombers such as the B-25 and the B-24 to the Navy.

The Fisher Corporation was to concentrate on the P-75 escort fighter plane, and its place in the B-29 production pool was taken by the Glenn L Martin company, which was allocated a contract to build the B-29 in a new government-owned plant at Omaha, Nebraska.

In addition to prime airframe assembly at these four plants, a complex sub-contracting programme was set up throughout the country for B-29 components and sub-assemblies. Companies such as Chrysler, Hudson, Goodyear, Briggs, Murray and Cessna were chosen to produce major B-29 airframe components.

Boeing's demonstration of how the sub-assembly 'kit of parts' for a B-29 was arranged. *(USAAF)*

BIRTH PAINS

An Air Corps Fairchild PT-19A trainer 41-20531 was modified and fitted with a scale B-29 wing and tail surfaces and was operated as a flying laboratory to aerodynamically evaluate the surfaces. *(USAAF)*

The Model 345 design that eventually emerged featured a high-aspect ratio wing that was mid-mounted on a circular-section fuselage. The B-29 wing was tested in flight by substituting quarter-sized B-29 wing mockups for the regular wings of a Fairchild PT-19A trainer.

Authored by West, the manufacturing system which had won the company top honours for building the most pounds of aircraft per man hour, per square foot of factory area with the B-17, was adopted for the B-29. It was a system of pre-completion of major sections of the aircraft on separate assembly lines before final assembly. Like the Seattle plant, the new Wichita plant was designed around this production philosophy. Tooling for B-29 quantity production was the first task, and a tough one, for work had just begun on construction of the first XB-29, and engineering of the aircraft was still one year from completion. This meant that tooling had to anticipate the job in many instances; in all cases it must be correct, adhering to finer tolerances than ever before. West and his staff first pictured the B-29 as a production article to determine how it could be broken down into component parts and finally assembled.

In this programme, production and tooling departments were ruled by one compelling consideration: to reduce fabrication and assembly to the simplest of operations so that hastily recruited, speedily trained personnel, many of them women, could build the aircraft in the least possible time. Critical labour shortages existed; it was known that most Superfortress builders would possess no previous experience in factory work.

Developing Defensive Armament

A remotely-controlled armament system had been adopted for the Model 345, since manned turrets were rejected as being impractical for the altitudes at which the B-29 would be operating. Four turrets were to be fitted, two on top and two underneath the fuselage, each with a pair of 0.5-inch machine guns. A fifth turret was in the tail and was under direct control of a tail gunner. It carried two 0.50-inch machine guns and one 20-mm cannon. Four companies competed for the contract to develop the armament system: Bendix, General Electric, Sperry, and Westinghouse. The Sperry system involved the use of retractable turrets that were aimed by periscopic sights, and this won the initial contract.

Air Technical Service Command proposed that the Sperry periscope sight be adopted. This feature required the operator of the gun computer to look through a periscope at his target. From the standpoint of eliminating gun blisters and keeping the aircraft aerodynamically clean, the periscope principle was good, but it had this major disadvantage: the periscope did not provide an adequate field of vision. The periscope sight had basic limitations, but the Command believed in it.

In December, two weeks before Pearl Harbor, Colonels T A Sims, Leonard 'Jake' Harman and Frank Wolfe, the latter in charge of Wright Field Armament Section, arrived in Seattle to discuss armament. They had come direct from the Air Staff, Washington, DC, and they were armed with explicit instructions to install locally controlled turrets in the B-29.

Boeing engineers resisted, convinced that locally controlled turrets would so compromise the B-29's aerodynamic cleanness that original performance goals would be fundamentally unattainable. Over the weekend Boeing engineers slaved over mock-ups of locally controlled turrets to substantiate their stand that such turrets would 'ruin' the aircraft. Boeing was asked to develop a plan for the use of retractable turrets comparable

Above: gunner working the side hatch controller. He had two knobs which were used to adjust the aiming graticule, the entire unit swivelling to give azimuth and elevation as he kept the sight on target.

Below: testing the top turret with the lid off. (both USAAF)

in size to the Sperry ball turret used on the belly of the Flying Fortress. But engineers showed that to retract the turrets would practically freeze crew members at their stations for the entire flight; there would not be sufficient room in the aircraft for both retracted turrets and crew.

Finally the issue was resolved: the General Electric fire control system, then definitely in its experimental phase, was adopted; the periscope system was abandoned.

Design work on the gunfire control system was undertaken in January 1942 and was developed jointly by General Electric, Boeing, and the Air Technical Service Command. The underlying philosophy of the B-29's firepower system was to obtain the maximum defensive action from the guns available – that is to use to a maximum all guns available against targets within the field of vision. This was accomplished by permitting several turrets to be controlled interchangeably from the various sighting stations. The system allowed any one gunner, except the tail gunner, to assume control of more than one of the Superfortress' turrets at one time. Individual gunners had primary control of certain turrets and secondary control of others. A gunner with primary control of a turret had first call on its services, which he could relinquish to gunners with secondary control. An intricate, but easy-to-operate signal system among the gunners permitted this exchange of turret control.

Many combinations of turret control were possible through this central control system, the upper and lower forward turrets, upper and lower rear turrets and tail turret being arranged to cover any possible angle of attack. As the bombardier had a greater range of vision than any other crew member, he could fire either of two forward turrets separately, or he could direct the fire of both simultaneously.

By shooting more bullets concentrated more accurately at a more distant target than any other aircraft ever built, it was hoped that the B-29 gunfire system enabled the aircraft to fly through enemy defences without fighter escort.

The system consisted of power turrets and multiple gun installations, and included computing gun sights which automatically corrected for various factors such as wind and aircraft velocity while putting the sight directly on the target. In an instant most of the aircraft's armament could be swung about to concentrate fire on one spot.

The brain of the fire control system was a small computer which enabled bullets to meet the enemy aircraft at a mathematically determined rendezvous. The computer was a combination of electric, electronic -valve, not transistor - and mechanical equipment engineered into a complete system. Nerve centre of the system was the 'selsyn' or more commonly known as a 'synchro', which resembled a small motor. The synchros was used to transmit angular information from guns and sights to an analogue fire control computer, and to transmit the desired gun position back to the gun location.

There were five sighting 'stations': one in the nose, one behind the tail, two in the waist position and one in the mid-upper location. The tail turret was the only position where the gunner was not remote from his guns. He operated the turret by control handles which energized an identical system to the other turrets, but with direct sighting. The other four turrets were all remotely controlled, as previously described. These turrets were fed from large curved ammunition boxes loaded with 925 rounds for each gun, the ammunition belts being pulled up into the guns by powered sprockets. The turrets were quite weighty, the four-gun front upper weighing 1,938 lb fully loaded, plus the gunner and his controls.

In common with many features of the B-29, the armament system had many teething troubles, mainly due to rushed production and inexperienced installation engineers. Gunners needed a four-month course to become competent, and even with such an advanced armament system many B-29s were shot down.

An aircraft's bomb bay is always located as near the centre of gravity as possible so that flight of the craft will not be unduly disturbed when bombs are dropped. To hold the diameter of the B-29 to minimum, thus reducing drag, two bomb bays arranged in tandem were given the machine; one bay forward of the wing, ahead of the centre of gravity, and the second, aft of the wing, behind the centre of gravity. This meant that one bay could not be emptied before the other without throwing the B-29 temporarily out of level flight. To cancel out this undesirable condition, an alternating system for dropping bombs - termed an intervalometer - was adopted. This mechanism was designed to drop a bomb alternately from one bay and then the other. A pneumatic actuating device was designed to snap open bomb bay doors in seven-tenths of a second and close them in three seconds.

The engine for the B-29 was the completely new 2200 hp Wright R-3350 Duplex Cyclone eighteen-cylinder twin row air-cooled radial. This was, at the time, the largest engine ever installed in an aircraft. Weighing 2,595 pounds without accessories and measuring fifty-five plus inches in diameter and seventy-six plus inches in depth, the engine offered the greatest masses over which air would be drawn of any aircraft engine.

Much development work was done on the B-29 powerplants and their nacelles.

Above: an engine in one of the test cells.

Left: a nacelle mock-up. Overheating problems arose through the cowlings being too-tightly fitted around the engines. This was never fully solved until the arrival of the B-50. (USAAF)

BIRTH PAINS

Components of the B-29 came together in sub-assemblies that were then brought together on the main assembly line.

Sub-assemblies were often slung from jigs in a manner that was best for workers to build them - be they on frames, or working from the inside out! *(USAAF)*

In the B-29 the principal design problem with the induction system was to reduce airflow to the minimum required to cool the engines. Airflow and heat transmission specialists had charge of constructing a mock-up of the system. The mock-up utilized a big powered blower to duplicate air conditions the B-29 would meet in flight, measure the distribution of air and survey all the eddies and irregularities in the duct system.

In order to duplicate conditions of flight, electric motors with special drives were installed in the mock-up to drive the turbines so as to simulate the manner in which they would act. It was necessary to determine the airflow used by each accessory, or each part of the whole system.

The B-29 induction system used only one air inlet for each engine, on the leading edge of the cowl. Engineers designed one big tunnel to pipe the air to positions behind the engine where it was distributed.

Development of a fuel system for the B-29 involved hydraulics and mechanical construction of pumps, valves, relief valves and controlling devices. The high-plus octane gasoline used by the B-29 was a low viscosity fluid. Lubricating oil is a high viscosity fluid affected by cold weather; it solidifies quite readily. Since the inception of high power engines, things had been discovered about oil that render design of an efficient system most difficult. There are two reasons for this: the air content within the oil and the cavitation of the pumps under altitude conditions, with this heavy viscosity. When the outside air pressure at high altitude is low enough, the pump refuses to function. Boeing's answer to this condition was to pressurize the oil tanks and re-design the lines leading to pumps to eliminate all possible pressure loss. This system reduced the 'altitude' inside the oil tank to a point where the pumps could still handle the oil. These problems were solved, theoretically, on the laboratory bench by equipment simulating conditions of high altitude flight, and, subsequently, in the aircraft operating at extreme altitude. The system was tested both for low pressures and temperatures in the Boeing's own Strato-Chamber.

Eight General Electric B-11 turbo-superchargers, two for each engine, were installed on the B-29. The dual turbo-supercharger arrangement was adopted because no single turbo-supercharger capable of putting out the volume of air required had been developed at that time. One of the major problems in this was the conflict between turbo-supercharger performance and the desired power for cruising. Because the B-29 was designed for long-range, low powers were required for cruising. All turbo-superchargers surge at certain low output. The problem was: how to obtain low enough powers at high altitude for cruising purposes without experiencing these surges.

Much was known concerning the turbo-supercharger's performance from long-term experience with it on the B-17, hence performance of the dual-turbo installation on the B-29 brought few surprises. Turbo-supercharger systems of the B-17 and the B-29 were broadly similar. The turbo-supercharger control for the B-29 was automatic. Supplied by the Minneapolis-Honeywell Company, this control was tested on the B-17, and had been developed to a point far beyond its experimental phase by the time it was installed on the B-29. The system incorporated provisions for shutting off one turbo so that when the B-29 cruised at certain altitudes one turbo per engine could be turned off.

The engine drove a three-bladed 17-foot diameter propeller. Special attention was paid to the nacelle designs to reduce aerodynamic drag. The oil coolers and the supercharger intercooler were mounted directly underneath the engine cooling air intake.

The construction of the B-29 was fairly conventional, being of all-metal throughout but with fabric-covered control surfaces. Each undercarriage unit had dual instead of single

Constructing the pressurised compartments - the pictures in this spread show the manufacture of the curved pressure bulkheads - complete with access holes to the bomb bay in the centre of the pressure dome and to the upper tube that connected the front and rear compartments.

The entire front fuselage was one complete pressurised sub-assembly that connected up to the B-29 centre-section.

The opposite page shows the front fuselage looking forward showing the hoops and stringers before cladding. The same process occurred in the bomb bay area. *(all USAAF)*

wheels. A retractable tail bumper was provided for tail protection during nose-high takeoffs and landings.

It was anticipated that the crew would vary from 10 to 14, but would normally consist of 12 consisting of two pilots, a navigator, a bombardier, a flight engineer, a radio operator, a radar operator, and five gunners. The bombardier sat in the nose with his bombsight and gunsight. The pilot and copilot sat side-by-side behind panels of armour and bulletproof glass. The flight engineer, radio operator, and navigator sat immediately behind the pilot's cockpit.

Pressurization of the B-29 was an outgrowth of the company's pioneering development of the pressurized Stratoliner transport in 1938. As in the Stratoliner, the cylindrical shape with similar hemispherical bulkheads was adopted for the Superfortress fuselage. But the B-29 posed many new problems. In the Stratoliner, the entire cabin except the tail area was pressurized. Of the B-29's five sections—the nose section, the bomb bays, the waist, the aft and the tail sections—only three sections would carry crewmen at high altitude, hence must be pressurized. These were the nose, waist and tail sections.

The problem of transferring crew members from the pressurized nose section through the unpressurized bomb bays to the pressurized waist section was solved by a cylindrical tunnel over the bomb bays to the nose and waist - a tunnel large enough for a man to crawl through. Aft of the pressurized waist section was a non-pressurized compartment separating it from the tail section. This design isolated the tail gunner in his small pressurized tail section during pressure flight. He could enter or leave the compartment only during unpressurized flight.

Turbo-superchargers were adopted to pressurize the B-29 cabin and an air conditioning system was incorporated. Compressed air from one of each of the superchargers on each outboard engine was ducted through this conditioning unit before entering the cabin. An automatic cabin temperature control valve controlled this function. When heat was needed in the cabin, hot air from the engine exhausts was directed to the unit to heat the supercharged air passing through it. When cooling was needed, cold air outside the aircraft was directed to the conditioning unit, cooling the supercharged air passing by.

Given the long missions planned for the B-29, sustained noise within the aircraft would jangle the nerves of crew members on the long missions, therefore aural annoyance had to be kept at a minimum. How was the sound of eight

Assemblies were supported by wheeled cradles to allow movement from one area to another, and workers used staging and custom-designed steps to reach specific areas. *(USAAF)*

BIRTH PAINS *37*

thousand eight hundred horses thundering just outside the fuselage to be reduced within the cabin? The problem inspired an intensive research programme for Boeing engineers assisted by various laboratories. The Cruft Laboratory of Harvard University, working under the auspices of the National Research Council Committee on Sound Control, provided reports used extensively by Boeing acoustics engineers. The total effect of these studies was to make the B-29 the quietest of all heavy aircraft.

A insulating blanket composed of animal hair, cotton and kapok in equal proportions was used to line the fuselage. The outboard side of this blanket was faced with a doped fabric impervious to air flow and inboard side with a porous, tough, trim fabric. Depth of the blanket ranged from half an inch to one and one and a half inches depending on the location in the aircraft. Blankets were installed by special fasteners allowing their removal for repair and conditioning in the field. To reduce heat losses - for the material had to serve as a thermal insulator as well - the side placed next to the skin of the B-29 was silver-colored. Soundproof blankets originally specified for the B-29 were composed of one-third kapok, one-third cotton and one-third animal hair, the entire installation weighing 398 pounds. After Pearl Harbor, the Japanese controlled the major sources of kapok, and so a substitute material had to be found. This was Fiberglas, manufactured by the Owens-Corning Fiberglas Corporation, a material far superior to kapok. The Fiberglas installation weighed only 167 pounds.

Engine nacelles were built in their own production area before moving across to the main line...

In the communication tunnel, connecting the forward and aft pressurized compartments, a carded blanket of sound-proofing material half an inch thick was placed. The blanket served three purposes: that of acoustic blanket, thermal insulator and carpet.

Structural Testing
The Army Air Force had ordered four B-29s; three XB-29 experimental, full-scale flying machines and a fourth, without engines, for test-to-destruction.

The work of the company's structural test group started as soon as structures proposed for the aircraft had been produced. Before any piece of the aircraft which was to carry a load was adopted as part of the fixed design, its maximum strength and its weight were carefully measured.

The engineers at Boeing could break a wing, crush a fuselage or flatten a landing gear with the greatest of ease. This destructive work had to be done to determine whether the aircraft was being built strong enough to support the loads it had to carry in manoeuvres which its specified performance demanded. They ran functional endurance tests on wing flap track and bearings to determine whether parts had been heat treated enough so that the metal would not disintegrate under loads. They wear-tested universal joints, gears, bearings, tubing. They subjected engine control rods, spot welds and joints to intense vibration. They operated all the electric motors that actuated the internal apparatus of the aircraft to study their endurance and reliability.

Testing to destruction assumed three phases on the B-29: the testing of component parts while the parts were held in special jigs, the testing of component parts in relation to others before they were installed on the aircraft, and the testing of the entire machine.

42-65275 - A B29-25-MO comes together. The nose section is brought to the centre fuselage. The cut-out of the wing is clearly visible. For some reason - possibly for publicity purposes the 'roof' of the wing cut out is show in position here...*(USAAF)*

BIRTH PAINS

...whereas in this picture it is clearly shown as an integral part of the centre-section that also has the outer engines and landing gear already installed before it was craned into the centre fuselage. *(USAAF)*

Because of the B-29's great size, it was necessary to erect a special building at Seattle to facilitate structural tests. This building was quickly dubbed 'The Cathedral' because of its size and shape but was nicknamed the 'Torture Chamber' because of its function.

Traditionally, aircraft were static tested by placing bags containing lead shot on the members being subjected to test. The bags were distributed to duplicate actual flight loads, until their weight breaks the member. When engineers remembered the handling of sixty five thousand pounds of lead in bags for the static testing of the XB-15 – a process that started at 7:30am and continued until 5.30 am the next morning - they determined that a better method of testing was needed for the XB-29. Three hundred thousand pounds of lead, or other weight force, would have to be used on the XB-29 wing.

The XB-15 test required a wing deflection of forty-eight inches; the wing deflection on the XB-29 was estimated at one hundred inches. This of itself ruled out the use of bags of lead shot, for how was this enormous weight to be held in place on the sloping wing?

Thoughts of the static test engineers turned to the use of hydraulic jacks. These pushing against the wing locked into place, would accomplish the test more quickly and with greater safety to personnel.

Almost a year of planning was invested in this phase of engineering the XB-29. Nobody had used jacks of the size required and, further, almost nobody in the hydraulic industry was interested in developing such equipment.

The jacks finally adopted and adapted for the test just slid in under the wire of requirements. They had barrels one hundred and fifteen inches in length and, in the final tests, the wing deflected somewhat under one hundred inches.

The wing centre-section is put into position, and the engine nacelles start to be fitted out ready to accept the powerplants. The rear fuselege is put into place, ready to be slid into the fuselage centre-section... (USAAF)

All control systems including the electric motors were tested: the bomb doors, wing flaps, nacelle doors, nose gear door, the main flight control systems. And here, with the electric motors, engineers experienced new dimensions of grief. While motor manufacturers supplying this equipment had tested for power output their tests did not proceed beyond that. When company engineers placed the motors on brake stands and tested for general performance characteristics from low load to maximum required load, under temperatures ranging from minus seventy-five degrees Fahrenheit to one hundred and twenty degrees, things began to go wrong. Low temperatures caused the motors to freeze up – the greases were too heavy. Clearances within the motors froze tightly; pinions broke; dog clutches struck. Not until the third XB-29 was ready to fly was a passable electric motor found.

Pressure testing the fuselage to 13.5 pounds per square inch was the next job. In this test the nose section blew up with a bang at 13.1 pounds per square inch, twice the actual pressure to which it would be subjected when flying. The nose section was reinforced where considered necessary. Subsequent pressure tests proved the reinforcing satisfactory.

The wing destruction test came next. In its first test the wing failed at ninety-seven percent of design load at high angle of attack condition. This test proved the wing could support four times the loads which the B-29 would ever likely be called on to haul.

The distribution of wing load around the cutout providing space for the landing gear retracting system was something engineers had not been able to calculate accurately when the B-29 was being designed. But now that destruction test had supplied the answer, structural and stress engineers beefed up that portion of the wing, strengthening it to a point proved to be sufficient.

Although the wing test itself was only of four hours' duration - and the results were obtained in twenty minutes - months had been invested in its preparation.

BIRTH PAINS
41

In this test, as in most structural tests, engineers were able to anticipate failure of a particular member of a section before failure had actually occurred; this was done by use of strain guages, wires placed at more than three hundred points on the wing. These wires actuated recording devices measuring the forces being applied and the structure's reactions to these forces. By forewarning engineers of imminent structural failure, the strain guage technique permitted engineers to halt tests long enough to reinforce a critical section, before pursuing the test to complete destruction.

The first XB-29, serialled 41-002, flew on 21 September 1942 at Boeing Field, Boeing's chief test pilot Edmund T 'Eddie' Allen being at the controls with Al Reed flying as copilot. Eddie climbed to 6,000 feet and checked lateral, directional and longitudinal stability and control. He checked controllability and general performance with the No.1 engine throttled back. Power off stalls were checked. Control response, forces and effectiveness were noted. Everything that should be checked on a first flight was satisfactorily accomplished in the one hour 15 minute flight. It was uneventful and first indications were certainly favourable, but everyone knew there was a great deal of work ahead.

There were to be very few additional uneventful flights. By this time, there were 1664 B-29 aircraft on order. No armament was initially fitted. The engines were four R-3350-12s with 17-foot diameter three-bladed propellers. Unfortunately, the early R-3350 engines were subject to chronic overheating and were specially prone to catching fire upon the slightest provocation. By December, Allen had been able to achieve only 27 hours in the air out of 23 test flights. Sixteen engines had to be changed, nineteen exhaust systems had to be revised, and twenty-two carburetors had to be replaced. There were also problems with the propeller

...where the engines were hung, and then each nose cowling and engine cooling gills were put into place. *(USAAF)*

The size of the main assembly line is shown in this picture and would be impressive even by Boeing's production facilities of today. *(USAAF)*

governors and fearthering mechanisms. On 28 December one of the R-3350 engines of the prototype caught fire during a test flight, forcing Allen to return immediately to Boeing Field. Aside from the engine problems, the performance and handling qualities of the B-29 were found to be excellent. Other than the rudder boost being removed, no significant aerodynamic changes were found to be necessary. The flight on 28 December was intended to check the service ceiling and set performance data. The No.1 engine failed at 6,800 feet and the flight was terminated after 26 minutes. Ground inspection of the No.2 engine showed metal chips in the sump - it, too, was about to fail. That was the last time Eddie Allen or Al Reed would fly the first XB-29.

On 30 December the second XB-29 - 41-003 - was ready for its initial flight. It too had engines that were cleared for only 35 hours in positions 1, 3 and 4. It was to be a thorough functional check of the aircraft and its extensive instrumentation The weather was marginal. The functional check proceeded normally until the No.4 propeller would not feather and governing was erratic. Eddie Allen elected to discontinue the flight and immediately headed hack to Boeing Field, at which time he was advised that the weather was deteriorating rapidly. About six minutes out, the No.4 engine caught fire, the propeller oversped to 3,500 rpm, the propeller would not feather and smoke, sparks and flame were coming from the exhausts. Shutting off the fuel and the use of fire extinguishers did nothing - the fire continued to worsen. About two minutes out the fire was burning fiercely in the accessory compartment. Flames were pouring from the nacelle access door and from the intercooler exit area. Heavy smoke and fingers of flame were trailing off the wing. In the meantime heavy smoke was pouring from the bomb bay into the cabin, making it increasingly difficult to see or breathe. Eddie landed downwind, choking, partially blinded, on the 5,200 foot long, 200 foot wide runway. The intense fire was put out by fire equipment on the ground. Eddie later received the Air Medal for his skill and bravery during that harrowing 32 minute flight. Ground inspection showed more trouble. A fire had just started in engine No.1 and engine No.3 was close to failure, too. Those three 35-hour engines each had less than three hours total ground and flight time. Because of engine shortages, two of the three engines had to be replaced with engines robbed from the XB-29 which was laid up for some modifications. In addition the fire in No.4 had been so severe that the No.4 nacelle had to be replaced with the No.4 nacelle also robbed from the first XB-29. At least the second XB-29 now had a full complement of so-called 'unlimited' engines.

Unfortunately, engine/nacelle fires similar to the No.4 fire continued to haunt production B-29s and caused at least nineteen B-29 accidents between February 1943 and September 1944. While Boeing and Wright tried to discover and then correct what was happening, there was a natural tendency for each to blame the other. It was fifteen months before there was proof that the R-3350 was susceptible to induction system fires which could very rapidly get out of hand and become uncontrollable magnesium fires which then destroyed evidence of the fire's origin. That proof came on 24 March 1944, when the first XB-29 suffered another induction system fire on the No.4 engine that was stopped before the fire reached the blower section or the intake pipes.. The partially burned magnesium impeller and interior of the blower case were irrefutable evidence. Wright then developed the fuel injection system to eliminate the potential for induction system fires.

It was almost a month before 41-003 flew again, on 29 January 1943. In the next three weeks emphasis was on engine, propeller, governing, and aircraft performance testing. Catastrophic engine failures eased up but that was about all. During descent for landing on 2 February there was a strong odour of fuel emanating from the bomb bay into the cabin. A thorough inspection uncovered nothing conclusive. On a flight on 17 February there was a bad fuel leak over the

The leading edges of much of the wing hinged up to allow access to control runs and services. *(USAAF)*

Another view of the production line, this time Martin Omaha - the aircraft is B-29-25-MO 42-65312. *(USAAF)*

wing from the No.4 fuel filler cap that was soon fixed.

The primary objectives of the 18 February flight were to measure climb and level flight performance and get engine cooling data with No.4 and No. 2 engines operating. Maximum altitude would be limited to 25,000 feet because of the excessive trouble that had been encountered with low engine oil pressures above that altitude. The effectiveness of fixes for some of the past problems would also be evaluated. Takeoff would be at the normal design gross weight of 105,000 pounds with full tanks - 5,410 gallons of fuel.

Eddie Allen took off southwards at 12.09 pm. Eight minutes later, while climbing through 5,000 feet with rated power, a fire was reported in the No.1 engine. Mixture and fuel to No.1 were cut off, propeller was feathered, cowl flaps were closed, a CO2 fire extinguisher bottle was discharged and a descent and return to Boeing Field was initiated. Since the fire appeared to have been put out and everything seemed under control, Allen elected to make a normal landing pattern and land from the north on runway 13 into the 5 mph wind rather than making a downwind landing on the 5,200 foot runway with a heavy aircraft. At 12:24 pm the radio operator routinely reported altitude at 1,500 feet at a point 4 miles NE of the field. They were on the downwind leg, headed NNW and starting a left turn onto base leg.

At 12:25 they had just completed turning onto base leg, had just crossed the heavily populated west shore of Lake Washington about five miles NNE of the field, were at about 1,200 feet altitude and were heading SW approaching the commercial and industrial south side of downtown Seattle. At that point ground witnesses heard an explosion that sounded like a loud backfire and a piece of metal fell from the aircraft. About that time the radio operator, who could see into the forward bomb bay and the wing centre section front spar, was overheard by the Boeing tower on an open microphone to say *'...Allen, better get this thing down in a hurry. The wing spar is burning badly'.*

BIRTH PAINS 45

41-002, the first XB-29 out on the flightline, having some work done on the vertical fin. Note the fuselage support just behind the rear underside turret. *(USAAF)*

He told Boeing Radio on a different frequency *'Have fire equipment ready. Am coming in with a wing on fire'*. About a mile down the flight path from the explosion, burned parts of a deicer valve, hose clamps, and instrumentation tubing were later found. They had come from an area normally inside the wing leading edge, ahead of the front spar, and just outboard of the No.2 nacelle near the No.2 fuel tank filler neck, which was rubber like the self sealing fuel cell.

The aircraft now turned south on an oblique final approach in a desperate effort to reach Boeing Field just four miles away. Allen was about 250 feet high and ground witnesses later reported that part of the wing leading edge between No.1 and No.2 engines was missing. In the next mile the flight engineer's data sheet was found and three of the forward compartment crew members left the aircraft - too low for their parachutes to open. At 12:26 pm, only three miles from Boeing Field, the second XB-29 crashed into the Frye Meat Packing Plant, killing pilots Eddie Allen, Bob Dansfield, and the other six crew members on board.

The crash and resulting fire killed a further 20 people on the ground and destroyed much of the aircraft and the plant. There was clear evidence that fire and dense smoke had gone through the bomb bay into the cockpit in the last moments before impact. Burns on the bodies and clothing of the three crew members who bailed out just before impact were a part of that evidence. In one minute the fire had gone from undetectable to catastrophic.

A very comprehensive investigation into the cause of the crash immediately got underway. Witnesses were interviewed, fallen bits and pieces along the flight path were collected and studied, debris from the crash site was sifted through for all the

BOEING B-29 SUPERFORTRESS

41-18335, the third XB-29 in flight, almost certainly close to Mount Rainier in Washington State. (USAAF)

evidence that could be found, the remains of engines and propellers were disassembled and examined and many, many ground tests and engineering analyses were run.

Extensive aircraft modifications resulted. Possible conditions which could cause fuel leaks were eliminated. Fuel filler necks were relocated, fire stop bulkheads were installed, better sealing in some places and better ventilation in other places was provided. Dams and overboard drains were also provided to get rid of any fuel which might leak. These and many other improvements were incorporated in the No.1 and No.3 XB-29s and all production aircraft.

Al Reed, Eddie's Chief of Flight Test and chief pilot, was now the only man alive who had ever piloted a B-29. He was not on board for this flight, but never flew again after the accident. He left Boeing a few weeks after Eddie's death and dropped from sight.

N D Showalter became the new Chief of Flight Test by the end of March. He had been Boeing Chief Military Projects Engineer and deeply involved in both the B-17 and B-29 programmes. He had flown with Eddie Allen on the testing of the second Stratoliner after Julius Barr had been killed in the crash of the first one.

There does not appear to be many surviving photographs of 41-003, the second XB-29, in which Eddie Allen and others lost their lives. This is the tail and rear fuselage sticking out of Plant II of Boeing Aircraft in Seattle. The aircraft has s few 'interesting' lumps and bumps. (USAAF)

BIRTH PAINS

N.D. was a good pilot but had not pursued that as a profession and did not have much opportunity to fly. Under his skillful guidance morale improved and flight test got back on its feet.

The crash caused ripples up the chain of command all the way to President Franklin Roosevelt, who was already unhappy about the delays in the B-29 programme. He wanted B-29s on their way to India by the end of 1943 so that they could begin bombing attacks against Japan. Senator Harry Truman's Special Committee to Investigate the National Defense Program, which had been established to expose fraudulent overcharging and other violations in defence acquisitions, looked into the B-29 programme and concluded that the problem lay with substandard or defective engines delivered by the Wright Aeronautical Company. The USAAF also came in for a share of the blame, by having put too much pressure on the Wright company to speed up engine delivery.

Shortly after the accident, Brigadier General Wolfe was directed by General Arnold to take over all aspects of the B-29 programme. One of his directives was that the Army Air Corps would take over the entire B-29 flight test programme and the first XB-29 flight test programme would be done at Wichita where conditions were much more favourable. The weather was better, runways were longer and wider, approaches were clearer and good alternate fields were relatively close. The Boeing Wichita plant would provide support. The XB-29 pilot and copilot would be Air Corps officers. Other than that the aircraft would be operated and maintained in accordance with Boeing flight test procedures and by Boeing people who were familiar with the large amount of highly specialized instrumentation. After 31 October the first XB-29 flight test programme was a 100% Boeing responsibility once again.

On 30 August 1943 the first XB-29 was flown from Seattle to Wichita by Col. Olson. Since the loss of the second XB-29, this was the only heavily instrumented B-29 in existence - a very valuable aircraft from which a lot of data was needed in a hurry. Col. H S Estes was the copilot.

The third prototype, 41-18335, flew for the first time in June 1943. It incorporated extensive powerplant and equipment revision as a result of

41-18335, the third XB-29, is seen here at Seattle and was clearly named *'Gremlin Hotel'*. Some sources state this was named *'The Flying Guinea-Pig'*, which was not the case - that name was given to the first XB-29. *(USAAF)*

48　　　　　　　　　　　　　　　　　　　　　　　　　　**BOEING B-29 SUPERFORTRESS**

experience with the first two. It was sent to Wichita to assist in the establishment of the production line and was soon handed over to the USAAF for armament and accelerated flight testing. It too eventually crashed, but not before verifying the potential of basic design.

By the end of October 1943 the initial testing with the the first XB-29 had been completed. In just under six weeks 24 flights in 72 hours of flying had been made. There had been no engine failures and no significant problems with large amounts of crucial performance and engine cooling data gained. Take-offs had been flown at 130,000 pounds weight. A 3,000 mile, 14-hour simulated bombing mission with a 10,000 pound simulated bomb load was made. It was time to take the first XB-29 back to Seattle for configuration and instrumentation changes before the next series of tests and to explore new ideas and potential improvements to make the B-29 fleet as safe and combat effective as possible.

The first XB-29 had earned the right to a name. After careful consideration and in view of its past and probable future of experimentation and exploration, it seemed right to call it *'The Flying Guinea Pig'*. To the end, it was an appropriate name.

Possibly out of sequence, but the end of a era. The old XB-29 Superfortress, 41-002, ordered in 1941 and first flown in 1943, was retired. Known as *The Flying Guinea Pig*, the aircraft had more than 500 hours of testing time in the air. Two of the crew, Clayton Scott (third from left), and Elliott Merrill (fourth from left), were thought to be two of the first pilots to ever land at Boeing Field. *(USAAF)*

EARLY AIRCRAFT

Fourteen service test aircraft were built at the Boeing plant at Wichita, Kansas as YB-29. The first YB-29 (41-36954) left the production line at Wichita on 15 April 1943, flying for the first time on 26 June 1943. Engines were four R-3350-21s, still driving three-bladed propellers.

On 1 June 1943, the first B-29 combat unit, the 58th (Very Heavy) Bombardment Wing, was activated at Marietta, Georgia in advance of delivery of the first YB-29s. By July, seven YB-29s had been delivered to the USAAF and were used to equip new training squadrons.

Periscopically-directed retractable turrets had been installed in early versions of the B-17 Fortress, the B-24 Liberator, and the B-25 Mitchell, but they had all been highly unsuccessful in actual combat, and were often removed in the field. After tests with the Sperry system of retractable turrets and periscopic sights on the first three XB-29 prototypes, the Sperry contract was withdrawn and given to General Electric. The General Electric system featured stationary, non-retractable turrets operated by remotely-situated gunners using computerized gunsights. There were five turret positions: upper-forward, upper-aft, lower-forward, lower-aft, and tail. Each turret contained two 0.50-inch machine guns, with the tail position containing an additional 20-mm cannon M-2 Type B cannon with 100 rounds. All guns except the tail gun were aimed and fired remotely by a set of gunners. There were four gunner sighting positions, one in the extreme nose operated by the bombardier, and three at the position in the waist where the rear pressurized compartment was located.

Reflector gunsights were placed at each of the four gunner sighting positions. Each gunsight was wired into the electrical system, and it sent electrical commands to direct and fire the guns. In order to direct the guns, the gunner operated the sight by grasping two round knobs on either side of the sight. The sight swiveled horizontally at the base and the upper section rotated

A pair of YB-29s seen in flight. Closest to the camera is 41-39950.

in elevation by a forward and backward twisting of the wrists. The sighting mechanism included an incandescent light source that projected a pattern of dots upward through a lens from inside the sight. This pattern was focussed onto a piece of clear glass as a circle of bright dots with one dot at the centre. By twisting the right-hand sight knob back and forth, the gunner could make the circle of dots shrink or expand. There was a dial on the back of the sight where the wingspan of the attacking aircraft could be set. With the computer switched on, a target could be tracked smoothly. Gyroscopes scanned the enemy plane's wingtips, and those electrical signals were sent to the turret, allowing it to lead the target and to elevate the guns to compensate for range. The right hand knob had a 'dead-man' switch which consisted of a metal flap which was spring-loaded to hold it out at a 30 degree angle. It had to be held down by the palm of the hand or else the turret would not activate.

The upper forward turret was normally operated by the bombardier, the upper rear turret by the upper waist gunner, and the bottom turrets by the two side waist gunners. However, the system could give control of turrets to more than one gunner. The bombardier and each gunner except the tail gunner could aim and fire up to two turrets simultaneously. The central fire control gunner located in the central gunner's section sat in an elevated seat between the two side gunners. Since he had a better overall view of the combat situation, he controlled the master gunnery panel which decided which gunner was to have control of which turret, and he could assign targets to gunners who had a better view of an attacking plane, thus increasing firepower when needed. However, the tail turret was operated exclusively by the tail gunner, and could not be 'handed off' to another gunner.

The General Electric gun system dispensed with the services of one turret gunner, reducing the crew to eleven. The crew members now consisted of a pilot (who was the aircraft commander), copilot, bombardier, navigator, flight engineer,

Many of the early aircraft were equipped with test equipment, like these Potentiometers for measuring temperature. (USAAF)

Three views of Boeing YB-29-BO 41-36957. Note the nose has an Erco ball turret with twin .50-cal. machine guns...

EARLY AIRCRAFT

radio operator, radar operator, central fire control gunner, left gunner, right gunner, and tail gunner.

This new remotely-controlled armament system was first installed in the third XB-29. Unfortunately, the new system required a lot more electrical power, necessitating the addition of several specially-designed generators. This delayed the onset of B-29 production still further, and brought the gross weight of the aircraft to over 105,000 pounds.

During the service test phase, the three-bladed propellers were replaced by four-bladed Hamilton-Standard propellers.

41-36954 - the first YB-29 - was turned over to General Motors for installation of liquid-cooled Allison V-3420 engines and further tests. The converted aircraft was later redesignated XB-39. The V-3420 engine was essentially a pair of Allison V-1710 twelve-cylinder liquid-cooled Vee engines coupled to a single propeller shaft. Normal output was 2100 hp at 25,000 feet. Aircraft speed increased to 405 mph at 35,000 feet, but the improvement in performance was not considered sufficient to justify production.

The basic model

The major production version of the Superfortress was the B-29, 2513 of which were built. 1620 B-29-BWs were built by Boeing at its Wichita, Kansas plant between September 1943 and October 1945, 536 B-29-BAs by Martin at its Omaha, Nebraska plant between February 1944 and January 1945, and 357 B-29-BOs by Bell Aircraft at its plant in Marietta, Georgia between January 1944 and September 1945.

....and the fuselage package guns just below and aft of the cockpit have twin .50-cal. machine guns mounted. (both USAAF)

The B-29 differed from the test models in having 16-foot 7-inch diameter fully-feathering four-bladed propellers. The engines were Wright R-3350-23, with a war emergency rating of 2300 hp. Only the very early Wichita-built models were delivered in olive drab and grey camouflage paint, the remainder being delivered unpainted.

B-29s began to roll off the production lines at Boeing-Wichita in September 1943. The first B-29s appeared on the production lines at Bell-Atlanta (Marietta) in February of 1944. The first Martin-

Omaha B-29 was delivered in mid-1944. The new Boeing plant at Renton built only the B-29A version.

Early models of the B-29 carried the Philco AN/APN-4 Loran (LOng RANge) constant- beam navigation aid. It was replaced by the more sophisticated RCA AN/APN-9 system later in World War Two.

The B-29 carried an AN/APQ-13 radar bombing/navigational aid set. This set was developed jointly by the Bell Telephone Laboratories and the Massachusetts Institute of Technology Radiation Laboratory and was manufactured by Western Electric, which was in those days the manufacturing arm of the Bell System. The radar antenna for this unit was housed inside a retractable 30-inch hemispherical radome located between the bomb bays and protruding below the fuselage a couple of feet when extended. Later in the war, the AN/APQ-7 Eagle radar unit was used, which was mounted in a wing-shaped housing installed underneath the forward section of the fuselage. The unit was also devised by Bell Labs and MIT, and was manufactured by Western Electric.

There were numerous variations within the production blocks. Boeing-Wichita models reached block number 100 in increments of five, and Martin and Bell reaching -60 and -65, respectively.

Early combat experience indicated that the B-29 needed more protection against fighter attacks coming from the front. The forward dorsal turret armament was increased to four 0.50-inch machine guns on Boeing-Wichita production block 40. Bell-Atlanta introduced this innovation on Block 10, and all Martin-built B-29s had four guns in the top turret from the beginning.

In the initial B-29 models, fuel was carried in fourteen outer-wing, eight inner-wing, and four bomb bay tanks, giving a maximum capacity of 8168 US gallons.

Boeing B-29-1-BW Superfortress 42-6242 in flight. *(USAAF)*

EARLY AIRCRAFT

An early modification added four tanks in the wing centre section, bringing total fuel capacity to 9438 US gallons. This extra fuel was first introduced on Block 25 aircraft from Boeing-Wichita, on Block 5 B-29s from Bell. Martin-built B-29s had these extra wing tanks from the beginning.

The R-3350-41 engine was introduced by Boeing on the Block 50 B-29. Both Martin and Bell followed suit on Block 20. The R-3350-41 had baffles and oil crossover pipes in an attempt to improve the cooling.

The trajectory of the shells fired from the 20-mm cannon in the tail was completely different from that of the bullets from the 0.50-inch machine guns, which made aiming difficult in combat conditions. Consequently, the 20-mm cannon was deleted from the tail position, beginning with Boeing-Wichita production block 55, Bell-Atlanta block 25 and Martin-Omaha block 25.

By the end of the production run, all three companies had begun to use the R-3350-57 engine.

Lingering doubts of about the efficacy of the remotely-controlled armament system resulted in the completion of one B-29-25-BW (42-2444) with manned turrets. This aircraft featured two manned power-operated dorsal turrets and two manned ventral 'ball' turrets, each with two 0.50-inch machine guns. There was a single 0.50-inch gun in each of two beam positions, and two additional 0.50 guns in a blister on each side of the fuselage nose. The remotely-controlled armament system of the standard B-29 proved to be adequate, and this unique armament scheme was not pursued any further.

Other test gear included manometers for measuring pressure. *(USAAF)*

The last standard B-29 was delivered by Boeing-Wichita in October 1945 and the last from Bell-Atlanta in January 1945, when it was replaced by the B-29B on the production line. The last B-29 was delivered by Martin-Omaha in September of 1945.

The Model A

The B-29A was the version of the Superfortress built by Boeing at the Navy-owned Renton plant between January 1944 and May 1946. It was essentially the same as the B-29, differing primarily in the wing centre structure.

The B-29 had employed a two-piece wing centre section that was bolted together at the centre line and installed as a single unit passing entirely through the fuselage and supporting the engine nacelles. The B-29A used a very short stub centre section that did not project beyond the fuselage sides, being only 47.75 inches wide on either side of the centre line or almost eight feet in total. Each pair of engine nacelles was fitted to a separate short section of wing. The outer wing panels were attached at the same point on B-29s and B-29As alike.

These wing changes were internal only, and there were no external differences visible in the wing root area, except for the overwing panelling on the fuselage. Contrary to what has been stated elsewhere, this change did not give the B-29A an additional foot of wingspan as compared to the B-29.

The B-29A was powered by four R-3350-57 engines. 1119 B-29As were built, with block numbers reaching BN-75. The 20-mm cannon was removed from the tail turret, beginning with production block 20, and a pair of 0.50-inch guns were added to the top forward turret to provide additional protection against fighter attacks coming from the front.

Revised engine nacelles were developed and tested and were to be used on late-model B-29As. These engine nacelles had the oil coolers and intercoolers moved further aft, which gave them a 'chinless' appearance. Because of this chinless appearance, these nacelles became known by the nickname 'Andy Gump', who was a famous cartoon character of the period.

Some early B-29As were fitted with pneumatically-operated bomb-bay doors which could be snapped shut in less than a second. The normal hydraulic doors took seven seconds to close. By early 1945, all B-29s were being manufactured with pneumatic doors as a standard fit.

The B-29 had always been somewhat underpowered for its weight, and in search of more power, one B-29A (42-93845) was handed over to Pratt & Whitney for conversion as a testbed for the four-row 28-cylinder Pratt & Whitney R-4360 air-cooled radial engine. This aircraft was later redesignated XB-44, and was readily recognizable by the new engine installation, with the oil cooler intake pulled further back on the lower part of the nacelle. The aircraft was initially ordered into production as the B-29D, but all contracts were cancelled at the end of the war. However, the B-29D project was later reinstated as B-50A.

42-2444, the experimental B-29-25-BW aircraft with manned turrets and powered cheek guns. One just has to wonder what the nickname of this machine was! (USAAF)

B Models

The B-29B was a lightened version on the Superfortress that was built exclusively by Bell-Atlanta. It had all but the tail defensive armament removed, since combat experience in the Pacific had shown that by that stage in the war the only

EARLY AIRCRAFT

significant enemy fighter attacks were coming from the rear.

The tail gun was aimed and fired automatically by the new AN/APG-15B radar fire control system that detected the approaching enemy aircraft and made all the necessary calculations.

Elimination of the turrets and the associated General Electric computerized gun system increased the top speed of the Superfortress to 364 mph at 25,000 feet and made the B-29B suitable for fast, unescorted hit-and-run bombing raids and photographic missions. Most of the weight saved by stripping off the defensive armament was devoted to additional bomb capacity. Right and left side gunners were not carried and the central fire control gunner occasionally acted as an observer and the bombardier's duties could often be performed by the radar operator. The aircraft could operate with a crew of seven to eight, since fewer gunners were now required. However, it often carried up to ten (commander, pilot, navigator, radar operator, bombardier, radio opperator, flight engineer, tail gunner, and two scanners). The scanners were supposed to look out for other aircraft, both friendly and enemy.

The B-29Bs were not ordered in a single large batch, but were ordered in small batches (sometimes singly) from B-29-BA production lines. It is often difficult to distinguish B-29Bs from 'ordinary' B-29s which had been stripped of their machine gun turrets to save weight during General LeMay's fire bombing campaign against Japan during 1945. However, they could be distinguished from

The 1,000th B-29 from Boeing-Wichita, along with the 10, 346th Boeing Kaydet from the same site. *(USAAF)*

Both manual and photo-recording was used for the test equipment, including monitoring the incredibly comprehensive engineers panel. (USAAF)

B-29s by their serial numbers and by the presence of the external radar antenna in the extreme tail.

A total of 311 B-29Bs were built between January and September of 1945, and most of them were issued to the 315th Bombardment Wing in the Marianas in 1945.

The Battle of Kansas

Brig Gen Orval Cook of the ATSC ordered all contractors responsible for modifying the B-29 to immediately assign personnel, accessories and materials to Salina, Pratt, Great Bend and Walker bases, and there complete changes on the aircraft. To the immediate job went Maj Gen B E Meyers; Col William Irvine; Col Pearl H Robey, chief of the technical staff; Colonels Harman and Olson of 20th Bomber Command and Col H A Shepard. On Maj Thomas Gerrity fell most of the load for expediting changes on the aircraft itself. Maj Gen B M ('Barney') Giles and Maj Gen C E Branshaw threw their skill, strength and authority into the overall job.

The programme was seriously hampered by the need to work in the open air in inclement weather, by delays in acquiring the necessary tools and support equipment, and by the USAAF's general lack of experience with the B-29. The four Kansas Air Force bases were out on the prairie, battered by

EARLY AIRCRAFT

mad March winds blowing snow and sleet around a dozen or so squat, prefabricated barracks, headquarters, mess halls and infirmary and four hangars that could only accommodate six aircraft. Outside was a lineup of thirty-four snowbound Superfortresses' awaiting modifications. To these fields came trainload after trainload of boxes containing accessories, ammunition, armament, and engines.

Army cargo aircraft of the ATC flew day and night bringing in men, accessories, and parts, operating a shuttle service between bases, bringing in war engines from San Antonio and Oklahoma City, returning with engines yet to be modified.

On 10 March a wing of the base hospital at Salina was set up as modification headquarters with General Meyers in charge. To this headquarters came superintendents responsible for completing aircraft at the various bases. Aircraft had to be modified in keeping with instructions. By 15 April every aircraft had to be completed, armoured, and fully equipped.

The work had be done in the open – only certain changes would be done in hangars. Every man was on his own. Every GI, modification technician and Army officer would eat and sleep when he felt he must; at all other times he would be on the job.

Legend has it that General Meyers personally served coffee and doughnuts at any hour of day or night to the workers. It was also said that one night a GI mechanic, head down, bracing himself against the brutal wind, ran into a propeller, cutting a gash in his head. General Meyers, passing by, picked the young man out of a snowbank, taking him to the infirmary for repairs. The men wore leather, sheepskin-lined, high-altitude flying suits against the cold of working outside. This became known as the 'Battle of Kansas'. Beginning in mid-March, technicians and specialists from the Wichita and Seattle factories

42-6208 *'Pioneer'* of the 793rd BS, 468th BG, 58th BW. The aircraft served in India as a fuel hauler. *(USAAF)*

were drafted into the modification centres to work around the clock to get the B-29s ready for combat.

The list of problems to be overcome was hundredfold. Reports of short-cutting the red-tape were legion. An order for a last-minute change in the gunfire interrupter mechanism required the insertion of a cam, or small disc, of a pattern which did not exist. General Electric field engineers on the spot phoned their Schenectady plant, where necessary tools were in operation. The tools, yes, but not the right man for the job; he was at a Bloomfield, New Jersey, plant. And so the tools were flown to Bloomfield where the cams were machined and flown to Salina.

Salina's Overseas Process quarters were converted overnight into a computer shop. Because these computers were delicate - this was in the days of radio valves, remember, not solid state 'chips' - ambulances were used to deliver re-worked computers through the blinding snow to the B-29s waiting on the line. The better riding quality built into the ambulances to minimize shocks was important here.

If you needed a part for a B-29, you grabbed a Jeep and chased after it yourself. Sometimes you phoned Detroit or Birmingham or Wichita or Marietta for it. Many a production man all over the nation was routed from bed by an Air Transport Command crew with orders to pick up parts, and now! On Easter Sunday Kermit Thompson, Service Manager at Wichita, was discovered at home. A cable assembly was needed and quickly; would Thompson supply one? Thompson answered by going to the Boeing factory and cannibalizing an aircraft on the line. He slipped the assembly under his jacket and walked past the guard.

As a result of superhuman efforts on the part of all concerned, 150 B-29s had been handed over to the 20th Bomber Command by 15 April 1944. Such was the urgency that the aircraft left Kansas with spare engines and a kit of spare parts in each of their bomb-bays.

First away, flying 41-36963, was Col Frank Cook, the former production engineering officer at Wright Field. Colonel Harman was next; he taxied his YB-29 to the end of the concrete ribbon at Salina, and took off for the wars. With the coming of April, more and more Superfortresses departed for the battle zones – four or five B-29s every dawn. Before each aircraft left, an engineering officer signed a statement saying the work ordered on this aircraft had been completed satisfactorily.

YB-29 41-36963 seen at Glatton airfield near Peterborough, England on 11 March 1944. *(USAAF)*

EARLY AIRCRAFT

Colonel Frank Cook's flight plan from Salina took him non-stop to Miami. Taking off at night, under secret orders, Colonel Cook flew south for one hour over the Atlantic, then he changed course and flew north, while still over the sea, on to Newfoundland. From there '963' flew non-stop at twenty thousand feet to a base in the UK. All this was according to plan. The appearance was supposedly to allow 8th Air Force Technical and Tactical staff to evaluate the machine, but in reality it was an attempt to mislead German Intelligence into believing that the B-29 was to be based in the UK. For the next two weeks, one thousand citizens, persons with vital war roles, inspected '963 at both Glatton and Knettishall. It was a feint and it worked, for at no time did enemy aircraft seek out and interfere with the 'air train' of Superfortresses which was to follow Colonel Harman across the Atlantic to Africa and on into India. Colonel Harman landed his Superfortress on the hot, dusty runway of his India base on 2 April. More B-29s were to follow him.

General Wolfe assigned the first B-29s to squadrons within the 58th Bombardment Wing and dispatched them immediately to India. This was a 11,530-mile journey, involving stops at Marrakech, Cairo, Karachi, and Calcutta.

Airo M Gonnella, a Boeing field service engineer, was ordered to take a team of Boeing B-29 field service engineers ahead of the Superfortresses. Their Air Transport Command transportation given top priority, Gonnella and his men - Warren Wilson, Richard H Steams, Leo F Hunt, Joseph A Zuber, Marvin P Hooker, Robert Schick and Edwin Whitney - flew direct to points where Superfortresses would stop to refuel enroute to India and would be on hand to help solve any problems that arose - and they were needed.

Olive drab and bare metal B-29s were stored at numerous airfields in the US until the modification programme could be correctly established.. *(USAAF)*

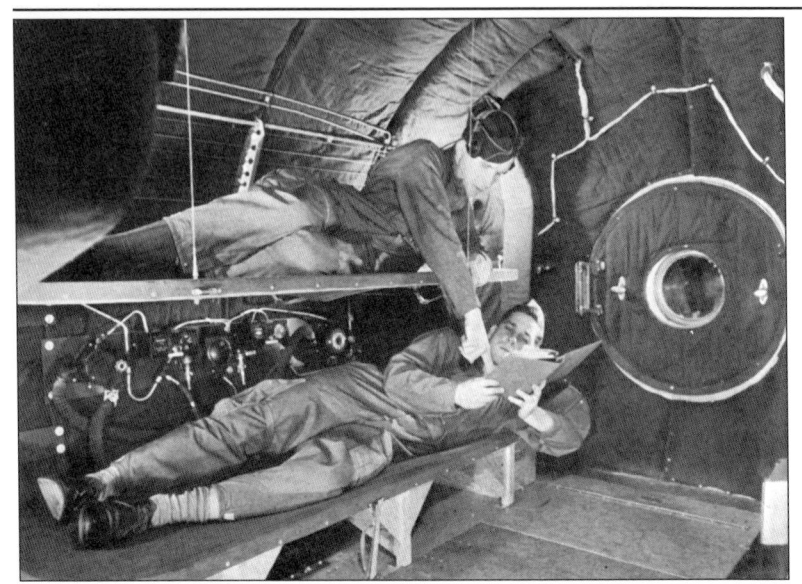

Early B-29s were equipped with crew rest areas and bunks, but many had this feature removed in a weight-saving exercise. *(USAAF)*

The most common cause of maintenance headaches and catastrophic failures was the engine. Though the Wright R-3350 later became a trustworthy workhorse in large piston-engined aircraft, early models were beset with dangerous reliability problems, many caused by demands that the B-29 be put in operation as soon as possible. It had an impressive power-to-weight ratio, but this came at a heavy cost to durability. Worse, the cowling Boeing designed for the engine was too close (out of a desire for improved aerodynamics), and the early cowl flaps caused problematic flutter and vibration when open in most of the flight envelope. The 18 radial cylinders, compactly arranged in front and rear rows, overheated because of insufficient flow of cooling air, which in turn caused exhaust valves to unseat.

During the week 15-22 April, five B-29s crashed near Karachi - a stop on the route to Calcutta - all from overheated engines. The entire B-29 fleet had to be grounded en route until the reason for the fault was found. The cause was traced to the fact that the R-3350 engine had not been designed to operate at ground temperatures higher than 115 degrees F, which were typically exceeded in Karachi. Wright engineers found that the exhaust valves on the rear row of cylinders were melting under the heat and pressure, and they designed new engine baffles to direct cooling air onto the affected areas. They also improved the flow of oil to the rear cylinders by installing crossover oil tubes from the intake to the exhaust port of the five top cylinders on both the front and rear rows. Modifications had also to be made to the cowl flaps. After these modifications, B-29 flights to India were resumed.

CHINA

The B-29 had been originally been designed with hemispheric defense in mind. Under such a plan, bombers would be able to operate out of bases inside the USA and would be able to hit any future enemy at long ranges to keep war well away from America's shores. However, in 1940, the War Department's contingency plan was changed to use 24 B-29/B-32 bomber groups to bomb Germany from bases in the United Kingdom and North Africa in case of war. But the B-29 was destined never to be used against Germany.

Even before Pearl Harbor, President Franklin D Roosevelt had been interested in providing military assistance to the Chinese leader, Generalissimo Chiang Kai-shek, so that he could retaliate against Japanese air attacks on Chinese cities. Roosevelt had even proposed to transfer some USAAC B-17s to China as early as December 1940 so that they could be used to bomb Japanese cities, but this plan had to be abandoned since there were not even enough B-17s to meet American needs. China had to be satisfied with 100 fighter aircraft instead.

Immediately following Pearl Harbor, the decision was made to place emphasis on defeating the European members of the Axis first, after which the Allies would turn their full attention to Japan. However, after the January 1943 Casablanca Conference, President Roosevelt decided to inform Chiang Kai-shek that all possible aid would be sent to prevent Japan from taking over all of China. In order to do this, Roosevelt wanted to send hundreds of heavy bombers to China so that they could bring the Japanese homeland under attack. Neither the B-17 nor the B-24 had the ranges to carry out such missions, and only the B-29 could do the job.

Chiang wanted the B-29s sent to China right away so that they could begin an air offensive against Japan. Both General Joseph W. Stilwell and General Claire L. Chennault supported this proposal, and exerted considerable pressure on the President to initiate such a plan.

Chiang Kai-shek was a political and military leader in China. He was an influential member of the nationalist party Kuomintang (KMT) and Sun Yat-sen's close ally. He became the Commandant of Kuomintang's Whampoa Military Academy and took Sun's place in the party when the latter died in 1925. In 1928,

Left to right: Lieutenant General Claire Lee Chennault (*b.* 6 September 1893, *d* 27 July 1958).

General Joseph Warren Stilwell (*b.* 19 March 1883, *d.* 12 October 1946)

Chiang Kai-shek (*b.* 31 October 1887, *d.* 5 April 1975)

Chiang led the Northern Expedition to unify the country, becoming China's overall leader. He served as chairman of the National Military Council of the Nationalist Government of the Republic of China (RoC) from 1928 to 1948. Chiang led China in the Second Sino-Japanese War, during which the Nationalist Government's power severely weakened, but his prominence grew.

Chiang's Nationalists engaged in a long standing civil war with the Chinese Communist Party (CCP). After the Japanese surrender in 1945, Chiang once again became embroiled in a bloody civil war with the Communist Party of China. Ultimately, with support from the Soviet Union, the CCP defeated the Nationalists, forcing the Nationalist government to retreat to Taiwan, where martial law was continued while the government still tried to take back mainland China.

Lieutenant General Claire Lee Chennault was something of a contentious officer - a fierce advocate of 'pursuit' or fight-interceptor aircraft during the 1930s when the U.S. Army Air Corps was focused primarily on high-altitude bombardment. Chennault retired in 1937, went to work as an aviation trainer and adviser in China, and commanded the 'Flying Tigers' during World War Two,

From the early days of the Pacific war it was evident that the B-17 Flying Fortresses and B-24 Liberator heavy bombers would not have the range to be used strategically against Japanese war industry. Therefore the new B-29 Superfortress, doubling the radius of action of the older and smaller bombers, figured in the plans to bomb the Japanese homeland.

By the spring of 1943, as production got under way, it appeared that the B-17 and B-24 would be adequate to the task in Europe and so consideration was given to using the Superfortress in the Pacific. Even with its 1,600 mile radius of action, suitable operating bases to reach Japan could then only be found in China. Since

Original Caption: 'The pilot and copilot of the first Boeing B-29 'Superfortress' to land In China are greeted by fighter pilots at an air base in west China. They are, left to right: Brig General Laverne G Saunders; Lt Colonel William Blanchard; Lt Colonel James F Whisenand, fighter pilot and Capt Nels A Anserson, fighter pilot. (USAAF)

CHINA

With no heavy machinery available in far off China, coolies band together pulling a 10 ton concrete roller to compact a runway for the big Boeing B-29 Superfortress. Chentu, China.

everything going into China for the air forces had to be flown over the Himalayas, there would be a large logistic problem.

An alternative to this was to re-capture Guam and take other islands in the Marianas group, lying 1,500 miles south-east of Japan in the central Pacific, but this would entail taking other enemy-held islands further east.

However, since the Japanese had cut off the Burma Road and the Lido Road overland routes to China, the effort would have to be supported entirely by air. General George C. Marshall was fully aware of the enormous supply problems involved in such an effort, and was wary about diverting effort from the European theatre, since the decision had already been made to win the war in Europe before diverting full effort against Japan. Nevertheless, President Roosevelt was insistent on getting help to Chiang, and suggested sending up to 300 US bombers to China.

Things became more definitive after the August 1943 Quadrant Conference in Quebec. At that time, General Henry H Arnold submitted a plan under which the newly-activated 58th Bombardment Wing (Very Heavy) would be stationed in the CBI Theatre by the end of 1943 and begin attacking Japanese targets by flying out of bases in China. It would be commanded by Brigadier General Kenneth B Wolfe and would consist of four groups of B-29s. It was envisaged that once sufficient numbers of B-29s were available, Japan could be forced out of the war within six months by the destruction of her war industries, making a costly seaborne invasion of the home islands unnecessary. It was projected that such a programme could defeat Japan by mid-1945.

The special B-29 project under the command of General Wolfe was given top priority in both men and materials, second only to the secret Manhattan Project. General Wolfe chose Colonel Harman as his deputy and General LaVerne Saunders was assigned as director of the B-29 crew training programme.

According to Arnold's original plan, the B-29s would be stationed permanently in China, at bases around Chengtu in the south-centre of the country. Supplies of fuel, ammunition, bombs, and spares would be flown in from India over the Hump. Although both the Joint Plans Committee and the Joint Logistics Committee had rejected Arnold's plan as being strategically infeasible, President Roosevelt was highly enthusiastic about the idea and passed it along to Lt Gen Stilwell, who was Chiang Kai-Shek's Chief of Staff. General Stilwell pointed out that it would be impractical to carry out all of the B-29 operations from China because of the length of the supply lines, and suggested instead that the B-29s be maintained at bases in eastern India, and only staged through Chengtu in the process or aftermath of the raids on Japan. This plan had the advantage in that a complex base facility would not be needed in China, and the supply problem would be simplified if the B-29s themselves could be used to carry some of the bombs and fuel needed to build up the dumps at Chengtu. Although the Joint Chiefs of Staff were still skeptical about the idea, President Roosevelt was still insistent, and since FDR was the Commander-in-Chief, they had to go along.

The British were brought into the plan, and on 10 November they agreed to provide bases for B-29 operations around Calcutta. At the same time, Chiang Kai-shek agreed to begin construction of five new airbases around Chengtu.

On 1 June 1943, the first Superfortress unit - the 58th Bombardment Wing (Very Heavy) - was activated at Marietta, Georgia, near Bell's Superfortress plant. On 15 September 1943, the

Maintenance was always a problem in the CBI theatre. Below: Men adjust a Norden Bomb Sight for a Boeing B-29 Superfortress somewhere in the India Burma Theatre of Operations.

Bottom: After the new engine has been installed on Boeing B-29 Superfortress 'Ouija Bird', the men work rapidly to connect wiring and engine lines.

CHINA

Boeing B-29-10-BW Superfortress 42-6331 with 'K-40' marked on the forward fuselage is seen having just landed in China. It is recorded that this machine had been attacked by Japanese Zeros en route and was the first B-29 to engage in actual combat. It was finally lost on 21 December 1944. *(USAAF)*

headquarters of the 58th BW was moved to Salina, Kansas, with some of its Groups near the Wichita factory. The first Superfortress Wing initially had five Groups, the 40th, 444th, 462nd, 468th, and 472nd BG. The 472nd BG was destined to remain at Smoky Hill Field, Salina as an operational training unit, and the others were to be deployed to India.

President Roosevelt wanted the B-29 bombing raids against Japan to start by January 1944. However, delays in the B-29 programme forced General Arnold to admit to the President that the bombing campaign against Japan could not begin until May 1944 at the earliest. The crews of the B-29 needed a degree of specialist training that was not required for crews of other, less complex aircraft. It usually took 27 weeks to train a pilot, 15 to train a navigator, and 12 to train a gunner. The complexity of the B-29 was such that a lengthy process of crew integration had to take place before combat deployment could begin. By the end of December 1943, only 73 pilots had qualified for the B-29 and very few crews had been brought together as a complete team.

Although 97 B-29s had been produced by the beginning of 1944, only 16 of them were really airworthy. Most of the others were in AAF modification centres, located near the Bell-Marietta and Martin-Omaha plants and at air bases in Kansas, undergoing a series of modifications and changes necessitated by the lessons of air combat over Europe. At that time, much of the equipment and components of the Superfortress had still not been perfected, and rather than delay production by stopping the assembly lines to incorporate modifications and add new equipment, it was decided to let the first production aircraft leave the lines at Wichita deficient in combat readiness and deliver them to these USAAF modification centres to bring them up to combat standards.

Engine fires were still plaguing the B-29 programme. Some of these problems were solved by the replacement of the original R-3350-13 engines by R-3350-21 engines, which did not really reduce the incidence of engine fires but at least reduced the risk of fires spreading to the aluminum-covered wings. The R-3350-23 was not ready in time to be fitted to aircraft as they rolled off the production line, so they had to be fitted at the modification centres.

In addition, the AN/APQ-13 bombing-navigational aid intended for the B-29 was a complex piece of equipment and was vulnerable to dirt and vibration and had to be carefully checked before each flight. Special schools had to be set up at Harvard, MIT and Boca Raton, Florida to train crews to operate the new radar set.

Alarmed at the slow pace of bringing adequate numbers of Superfortress into

Boeing B-29 Superfortress' 42-24471 of the 468th Bomb Group, XX Bomber Command, en route to its home base after bombing enemy targets at Anshan, Manchuria, China. *(USAAF)*

service, on 27 November 1943 General Arnold set up a new organization to take responsibility for the overall control of the Superfortress units. This was to be the XX (20th) Bomber Command, to be commanded by General Wolfe. It consisted of the 58th Bombardment Wing (the command of which was transferred from Wolfe to his deputy, Col Leonard 'Jake' Harman). At the same time, a new Wing, the 73rd, to be commanded by Colonel Thomas H Chapman, was added to the XX Bomber Command with four more Groups to absorb the second batch of one hundred and fifty Superfortresses.

Headquarters were set up close to the B-29 factory at Wichita, Kansas. Responsibility for crew training was assigned to Col Saunders of the Second Air Force. Four airfields in Kansas (Smoky Hill, Pratt, Great Bend, and Walker) were to handle this task.

The crew training programme was one of the more difficult aspects of the entire B-29 programme. Because of the complexity of the B-29 aircraft, a lengthy process of crew integration was required before combat operations could begin. There was no time to start from scratch, so volunteers were called for from B-24 crews returning from operations in Europe and North Africa. Crews began to arrive at Kansas bases in November 1943, but very few bombers were ready to receive them. At that time, there was only one Superfortress for every twelve crews, and most crews had to train on Martin B-26 Marauders or Boeing B-17 Fortresses. By the end of December, only 67 pilots had managed to fly a B-29 and very few crews had been brought together as a complete team. Many gunners did not even see their first B-29 until early 1944.

CHINA

Boeing B-29-10-BW Superfortress 42-6331 named 'Gone With the Wind' from the 45th BS, 40th BG, 20th AF. Aircraft was shot down by friendly-fire on a ferry mission from China to India on 1 December 1944. All but one man aboard was rescued, 1st Lt David M Lustig, the navigator, was KIA. (USAAF)

Men of Boeing B-29 Superfortress 42-24732 'K-304' check over the aircraft in preparation for the next mission. (USAAF)

In November 1943 the Army had established Marietta, Georgia, and Bechtol, McCone & Parsons, Birmingham, Alabama, as its major modification centres for the B-29. The Army had assumed full responsibility for modifying B-29; theoretically Boeing's responsibilities ended when aircraft left the Boeing factory and were accepted by the Army. At Marietta all changes on the aircraft itself were to be incorporated under direct Army supervision. By February Marietta was receiving more aircraft than could be handled, and so Col. Carl Cover from Wright Field assigned some B-29s to Glenn L Martin of Omaha, Nebraska, and to Continental Air Lines at Denver, Colorado in order to break the Marietta bottleneck. So called 'War engines' - engines with drilled rocker arms and oil sump changes - were to be installed at Air Force centres at Oklahoma City and San Antonio, working under ATSC supervision.

These organization changes made sense, for they brought more manpower than ever before to the modification process. By the end of February the backlog of B-29s yet to be modified was so great that it was obvious that concerted action would have to be taken if the quota of B-29s promised were to reach the CBI theatre on schedule. Material and accessory shortages, lack of developed skills with which to do the work, general organizational confusion, lack of a coordinated method of making the changes and the fact that modification centres were widely separated, were the cause of the debacle. Aircraft with highly non-standard equipment were emerging from modification centres. Modifications were being made hurriedly, and in some cases without complete inspection; commanding officers were refusing to accept the machines as being unsafe.

The list of changes was almost infinite; however, the major change items were: Flap switch link revision; emergency relief tank revisions; flux gate compass transmitter installation revisions; carburetor-air duct vane reinforcement; rudder rib revisions; fabric attachment revisions; side sighting dome revisions; fuel guage modifications; rudder tail rib revisions; flat glass installed in cockpit for navigation purposes; tail skid actuators modified; tail turret stops changed; all fuel guages recalibrated; turbo-supercharger radiation shields reinforced.

It was not until December 1943 that the decision not to use the B-29 against Germany was finally made, and to concentrate the B-29 exclusively against Japan.

Operation *Matterhorn*

The headquarters of the XX Bomber Command had been established at Kharagpur, India on 28 March 1944 under the command of General Wolfe. The first B-29 reached its base in India on 2 April. In India, existing airfields at Kharagpur, Chakulia, Piardoba and Dudkhundi had been converted for B-29 use. All these bases were located in southern Bengal and were not far from port facilities at Calcutta and had originally been established in 1942-43 for B-24 Liberators. Conditions were poor, and the runways were still in the process of being lengthened when the first B-29s arrived. The Headquarters of the 58th BW, together with the four squadrons of the 40th Bombardment Group (the 25th 44th, 45th, and 395th) were assigned to an airfield at Chakulia. The Headquarters was moved to Kharagpur on 23 April. The 444th Bombardment Group (676th, 677th, 678th and 679th Squadrons) went to Charra, arriving there on 11 April. The 462nd Bombardment Group (768th, 769th, 770th, and 771st squadrons) to Piardoba, arriving there on 7 April. The 468th Bombardment Group (792nd, 793rd, 794th and 795th Squadrons) arrived at Kharagpur on 13 April. The 444th Bombardment Group later moved to a permanent base at Dudhkundi, leaving Charra to become a transport base for the C-87s and C-46s which would support the effort.

On 4 April 1944, a special strategic command was established, to be known as the 20th Air Force, which would carry out the aerial assault against Japan. This was done at the insistence of General Arnold himself, mainly to avoid having the B-29s being diverted to tactical missions under pressure from CBI theatre commanders such as Major General Chennault or General Stilwell. The 20th Air Force would be commanded by General Arnold himself at Joint Chiefs of Staff (JCS) level. It would be completely autonomous and the B-29s would be completely independent of other

Carrying the traditional tandem baskets, a group of Chinese soldiers troop past a Boeing B-29 parked at a Western China base of the XX Bomber Command. *(USAAF)*

command structures and would be dedicated exclusively against strategic targets in Japan. For the first time, the B-29 offensive against Japan was given a name - Operation *Matterhorn,* which on 10 April 1944, the JCS informally approved Operation *Matterhorn*. The operational vehicle was to be the 58th Bombardment Wing (Very Heavy) of XX Bomber Command.

Before deployment from America, Saunders had taken over command of the 58th Bombardment Wing from Harmon. By 8 May 1944, 130 B-29s had reached their bases in India. For the next month, the four Groups flew a total of 2,867 hours of which 2,378 (83%) were on transport service, 50 on miscellaneous jobs, and only 439 in training activities, giving an average of less than 2 hours each for the 240 crews on hand.

Four sites in the Chengtu area of China were assigned to the B-29 operation - at Kwanghan, Kuinglai, Hsinching, and Pengshan. Construction work at these bases had begun as early as November 1943, but progress had been slow since much of the work had be done by hand. However, by May enough progress had been made that the four bases could actually be used, but conditions were far from ideal.

The primary flaw in the Operation *Matterhorn* plan was the fact that all the supplies of fuel, bombs, and spares needed to support the forward bases in China had to be flown in from India over the Hump, since Japanese control of the seas around the Chinese coast made seaborne supply of China impossible. Plans were made to use transport adaptations of the B-24 Liberator (known as the C-87) in support of the operation, and to even convert Liberators into special fuel transports under the designation C-109. Many of the supplies had to be delivered to China by the B-29s themselves. For this role, they were stripped of nearly all combat equipment and used as flying tankers each carrying seven tons of fuel. The Hump route was so dangerous and difficult that each time a B-29 flew from India to China it was counted as a combat mission, calling for the painting of a camel on the aircraft's nose.

By 8 May 1944, 148 B-29s had reached Marrakech and 230 were in India. The four bombardment Groups of the 58th BW were assigned to their bases.

The first action by the B-29 took place on 26 April 1944. Major Charles Hansen was flying a load of fuel to China when his aircraft was attacked by six Ki 43 Hayabusa fighters. The attack was beaten off, but one crew member was injured.

Original Caption: *The Army's huge new plane, the Boeing B-29 Superfortress bomber, is seen taking off for a flight.*

The aircraft is 42-6344. *(USAAF)*

The first B-29 bombing raid took place on 5 June 1944. Led by General Saunders himself, 98 B-29s took off from bases in eastern India to attack the Makasan railroad yards at Bangkok, Thailand. This involved a 2261-mile round trip, the longest bombing mission yet attempted during the war. The engines of the B-29 were still causing problems, and fourteen B-29s were forced to abort because of engine failures. The target was obscured by bad weather, necessitating bombing by radar. The formations became confused and dropped their bombs at altitudes between 17-27,000 feet rather than the planned 22-25,000 feet. Only eighteen bombs landed in the target area. Five B-29s crashed upon landing after the mission and 42 were forced to divert to other airfields because of a shortage of fuel. The B-29 campaign was off to a bad start, although none of the bombers was actually lost to enemy action.

On 6 June General Wolfe received an urgent message from Washington complaining that the JCS were getting impatient and that they wanted an immediate attack on Japan proper. This attack was needed to relieve pressure from Japanese forces in eastern China where General Claire Chennault's Fourteenth Air Force airfields were under attack and to assist an 'important operation' in the Pacific which was later revealed to be the invasion of Saipan. General Wolfe was caught flatfooted by this order and attempted to delay the mission until late June when he would have a larger force and more supplies in place at the forward bases in China. However, Washington demanded that he put a minimum of 70 B-29s over Japan by 15 June. One of the problems was that only 86 B-29s could be equipped with the bomb-bay tanks needed for the long flight to Japan, and, based upon previous experience, more than twenty of them would probably fail to leave their bases in China because of engine fires or other mechanical problems, while others would encounter problems along the

XX Bomber Command personnel examine the remains of Boeing B-29 42-24582, 40th Bomb Group at Chakulia, India, that was demolished as a result of an accident that occured when bombs were being unloaded on 14 January 1945. *(USAAF)*

CHINA

Boeing B-29-30-BW Superfortress 42-24504 named 'Gunga Din' from the 792nd BS, 468th BG, 20th AF. This machine crashed on 25 October 1944 approximately one minute after take-off for raid on Omura. All eleven men of the Maj Edward F Parsons crew were killed. (USAAF)

way and never reach the target. However, when your superiors give the orders, you do as you are told!

By mid-June, enough supplies had been stockpiled at Chinese forward bases to permit the launching of a single mission against targets in Japan. It was a night time raid to be carried out on the night of June 14/15, 1944 against the Imperial Iron and Steel Works at Yawata on Kyushu. This plant was considered to be the most important single objective within Japan's steel industry, and had long held top priority for the first strike. Intelligence estimated Imperial's annual production at 2.25 million tons of rolled steel - 24% of Japan's total. The secondary target was Laoyao harbor, an outlet for much coking coal, manganese, and phosphates. Because of the long distance - 3,200 miles - Washington had ordered a night mission with aircraft bombing individually. Bombing was to be done from two levels, 8,000 to 10,000 feet and 14,000 to 18,000 feet. Two pathfinder aircraft from each group were to illuminate the target. Takeoff was scheduled for 1630 local time, 15 June 1944, so permitting the aircraft to arrive over the target during darkness.

Staging at the forward bases in China began on 13 June 1944 and was completed shortly before H-hour on 15 June. The B-29s had left India fully loaded with bombs, requiring only refueling at the forward bases in China. Each aircraft carried two tons of 500-pound General Purpose bombs, considered powerful enough to disrupt the fragile coke ovens by either a direct hit or by blast. Of the 92 aircraft leaving India, only 79 had actually reached China, with one crashing enroute. Takeoffs from the forward staging bases in China began at 16:16 hrs early in the evening and two groups approximated the schedule of two-minute intervals between takeoffs. The other two Groups were slow in getting their aircraft airborne.

Of the 75 B-29s dispatched, one crashed and four were forced to return to base due to mechanical problems. At 23:38 hrs China time, the first B-29 over the target

BOEING B-29 SUPERFORTRESS

released its bombs. Of the 68 aircraft that had left China, only 47 attacked the intended target. One B-29 crashed in China (cause unknown), six jettisoned their bombs because of mechanical difficulties, two bombed the secondary target and five bombed targets of opportunity.

Unfortunately, the Japanese had been warned of the approaching raid and the city of Yawata was blacked out and haze and/or smoke helped to obscure the target. Only fifteen aircraft bombed visually while thirty-two bombed by radar. Only one bomb actually hit anywhere near the intended target, and the steel industry was essentially untouched. One B-29 was lost to enemy fire and six were lost in various accidents.

Although very little damage was done, the Yawata raid was hailed as a great victory in the American press, since it was the first time since the Doolittle raid of 1942 that American aircraft had hit the Japanese home islands.

General Wolfe was ordered to keep up the attacks even in spite of a shortage

Martin-Omaha B-29-5-MO Superfortress 42-65208 named 'Andy's Dandy' from the 794th BS, 468th BG. Local Indian labour was recruited for muscle! (USAAF)

Asian based USAAF B-29 Groups and their bases - April 1944.		
Group	Assigned to	Forward deployment
40th BG	Chakulia Airfield, India	Hsinching Airfield (A-1), China
444th BG	Dudhkundi Airfield, India	Kwanghan Airfield (A-3), China
462d BG	Piardoba Airfield, India	Kuinglai (Linqiong) Airfield (A-5), China
468th BG	Kalaikunda Airfield, India	Pengshan Airfield (A-7), China

CHINA

Martin-Omaha B-29-1-MO Superfortress 42-6232 named 'Kickapoo II' from the 792nd BS, 468th BG. Condemned due to battle damage on 20 June 1944. *(USAAF)*

It did not matter which theatre of war they were operating in, or how big the aircraft was, returning pilots often could not resist the temptation of an airfield beat-up! *(USAAF)*

of fuel and bombs at the Chengtu bases. He told his superiors that it was impossible to stage any more raids on Japan at the present time. Washington had to blame someone for the lack of progress, and General Wolfe was the most likely candidate. On 4 July, Arnold, impatient with Wolfe's progress, recalled him to Washington where he was promoted and re-assigned - and replaced temporarily with Brigadier General LaVern G Saunders, until Major General Curtis E LeMay could arrive from Europe to assume permanent command. Unfortunately, the three-week delay between the first and second missions reflected serious problems that prevented a sustained strategic bombing campaign from China against Japan. Each B-29 mission consumed tremendous quantities of fuel and bombs, which had to be shuttled from India to the China bases over the Himalayas, the world's highest mountain range. For every Superfortress combat mission, the command flew an average of six B-29 round-trip cargo missions over the Hump. Even after the Air Transport Command took over the logistical supply of the B-29 bases in China at the end of 1944, enough fuel and bombs never seemed to reach Chengtu.

Range presented another problem. Tokyo, in eastern Honshu, lay more than 2,000 miles from the Chinese staging bases, out of reach of the B-29s. Kyushu in southwestern Japan was the only one of the major home islands within the 1,600-mile combat radius of the Superfortress.

The aircraft still suffered mechanical problems that grounded some machines and forced others to turn back before dropping their bombs. Even those B-29s that reached the target area often had difficulty in hitting the objective, partly because of extensive cloud cover or high winds. Larger formations could have helped compensate for inaccurate bombing, but Saunders did not have enough B-29s to conduct such operations. Also, the Twentieth Air Force periodically diverted the Superfortresses from strategic targets to support theatre commanders in Southeast Asia and the southwestern Pacific. For these reasons, XX Bomber Command and the B-29s largely failed to fulfill their strategic promise.

On 7 July, while under temporary command of General Saunders, eighteen B-29s attacked targets at Sasebo, Nagasaki, Omura, and Yawata with ineffective results. Two days later 72 B-29s hit a steel-making complex at Anshan in Manchuria. Of the 72 aircraft, one crashed on takeoff and eleven suffered mechanical failures en route and had to abort. Four aircraft were lost. The plan had been to put a hundred bombers over the target for a daylight precision attack, but due to the usual pattern of malfunctioning aircraft and the poor condition of the Chinese airfields, barely half that number bombed the target. The bombing ignited the coke used for steel-making and at first it appeared that they had caused

A group of Chinese workers survey B-29 42-6323. It is recorded that on some airfields, 72,000 Chinese were supervised by just two US officers and three enlisted men. (USAAF)

Conditions in China were primitive, as this parking spot for 42-6279 Nashville Express shows. (USAAF)

CHINA

heavy damage, but later photographic reconnaissance showed that the Americans had caused little harm.

On the night 10-11 August, 56 B-29s staged through British air bases in Ceylon (now known as Sri Lanka) to attack the Plajdoe oil storage facilities at Palembang on Sumatra in present-day Indonesia. This involved a 4030-mile, 19 hour mission - the longest American air raid of the war. Other B-29s laid mines in the Moesi River. At the same time, a third batch of B-29s attacked targets in Nagasaki. These raids all showed a lack of operational control and inadequate combat techniques, drifting from target to target without a central plan, and were largely ineffective.

Many of the accidents which plagued the B-29s operating out of China and India were caused by engine fires, which were still a problem in spite of massive efforts to correct them. Cylinder head temperature gauges were red-lined at 270C. The combination of very high ambient ground temperatures (100 to 115F) and the inadequate cooling system of the engines would often result in head temperatures exceeding 310C during and immediately after takeoff. The high temperatures often resulted in the evaporation of valve stem lubrication, which could cause the valve to break off. The broken valve would then blow the cylinder off, which inevitably resulted in a fire.

Crews soon learned that the key to keeping the engine head temperature within tolerable limits was to have as much airspeed as possible when they became airborne on takeoff. During takeoff, they used the entire runway and reached a speed of 140-145 mph to become airborne in a fairly nose-low attitude. After takeoff, they would stay fairly low for a rather long time, with no effort to climb. This was done to attain the climbing speed of 200 mph as rapidly as possible. As the airspeed built up, the flight engineer would start to squeeze the large cowl flaps closed, since the key to controlling the head temperatures was airspeed, and as the speed got higher, cowling flaps in the extended position produced more drag than cooling.

Curious GIs look on as crew members of B-29 42-63395 of the 468th Bomb Group, XX Bomber Command, walk away from the aircraft which crashed and broke in half as it came in for a landing at an XX Bomber Command base in China. *(USAAF)*

Matters came to a head after the 20 August mission when the XX BC made its first daylight high-altitude mission to Japan to try again for the Yawata steel works. Seventy-two B-29s were greeted by the fiercest reception so far, anti-aircraft fire claiming one aircraft and three falling to fighters. The bombing was scattered and while the steel works took little hurt, substantial fires were started by incendiaries included in the bomb loads. Through combat damage and malfunctions, another ten B-29s failed to return, although one crew bailed out over Soviet territory. The gunners claimed seventeen enemy fighters and many others as probables or damaged, which helped to even the score, but the total of fourteen B-29s lost and ninety-five crewmen dead or missing was a stunning blow.

When word of the catastrophe reached Washington DC, Arnold immediately replaced General Wolfe - his replacement being Major General Curtis E LeMay, who arrived in India on 29 August. General LeMay was only 38 years old and was the youngest Major General in the Army and his arrival was intended to breathe new energy into the XX Bomber Command. The former Eighth Air Force Group and Wing commander had achieved remarkable success with strategic bombing operations in Europe, testing new concepts such as stagger formations, the combat box, and straight-and-level bombing runs. The youngest two-star General in the Army Air Forces was known as a tough, Patton-type of commander and had a 'take-charge' reputation. As a start, he stepped up the frequency of B-29 missions and intensified the training of combat crews. He replaced the four-plane diamond formation with one of twelve aircraft grouped in a defensive box. He introduced the concept of lead crews who would be responsible for finding and marking the target. In the future, both the bombardier and radar operator would control the

B-29 tail - This rear view of the huge new Boeing B-29 Superfortress bomber is the first to be released with armament undeleted and shows the mixed rear cannon and machine gun rear turret. Photograph was made in the China-Burma-India theatre. Note native workers in background (USAAF).

42-43529 of the 792nd BS, 468th BG unloads another load of bombs with another squadron aircraft behind. *(USAAF)*

bombing run, so that whoever had sight of the target at the critical moment in the bomb run could release the bombs. At the same time, the 58th Bombardment Wing was reorganized, and the junior squadron from each group (the 395th, 679th, 771st, and 795th) was disbanded. This left each group with three squadrons of ten B-29s each.

LeMay flew to Manchuria in one of the bombers launched on the next mission, another attempt at the Anshan steel works. In contrast to all the previous B-29 missions, this was a resounding success. Only fourteen of the bombers aborted and the ninety-five bombing was the highest number so far put over any target. The weather was clear and the bombing was good, with damage calculated to have cut production by a third. Although the bombers were contested, only one fell to fighters, and three others to operational causes.

To improve bombing accuracy LeMay formed and trained special lead crews. For daylight raids he replaced the four-aircraft flight used up to that time by the staggered twelve-aircraft, bomb-on-leader, formation that had been evolved in the 8th Air Force. It took a while for these changes to have an effect. Another raid against Anshan in Manchuria on 26 September was inclusive. An attack on 25 October on the Omura aircraft factory on Kyushu showed better results, particularly in the decision to use a two-to-one mixture of high-explosive and incendiary bombs. A raid was carried out on 11 November against the Chinese city of Nanking, which had been occupied by the Japanese since 1937. Supply problems and aircraft accidents were still preventing a fully effective concentration of force and effort. In addition, Japanese defensive efforts were becoming more

A sign of just why B-29s operating from China was such a problem. These drums once contained gasoline to fuel the Superfortresses for their onward journey to Japan...

effective. On 21 November six B-29s were destroyed by Japanese aircraft during a raid on Omura. A similar loss rate occurred on 7 December over the Manchurian Aircraft Company plant at Mukden. B-29 losses to accidents, enemy interception, and to Japanese air attacks on the Chengtu forward bases soon came to be prohibitive, and by the end of 1944 had reached 147.

Mechanical troubles with the B-29 were slowly overcome, but the average failure rate per operation was running at 17% and things did not improve appreciably until February 1945. The chief obstacle to bombing accuracy was the weather, which deteriorated as winter neared. As over Europe, clouds confounded the crews, yet on several occasions poor bombing was due to near hurricane force winds that buffeted, speeded up or slowed down the B-29s on their target approach. Nevertheless, LeMay was able to make a dramatic improvement in getting scheduled numbers airborne for a mission and in improving the accuracy of attacks.

So just what was it like flying Operation *Matterhorn?* 1st/Lt James J. O'Keefe USAAF recalls: *'Up forward at the bombardier's station of the B-29, things*

Some fuel arrived in bulk, flown in in converted B-24 Liberators but most arrived in drums and had to be manhandled around the forward air bases. *(both USAAF)*

CHINA

The fuel depot at a forward Chinese airfield. The caption states that '... *these are empty 50-gallon drums which accumulated during raids on Japanese territory, when getting fuel to continue operations imposed a logistical problem of considerable magnitude. Because of inadequate transportation on these bases they are rolled around by hand.* (USAAF)

A picture that eloquently describes the problems operated from remote fields in the CBI - Chinese refuel B-29 *O'Reillys Daughter* after an emergency landing at Liangsham, China. This plane had to be refueled by pouring gasoline from drums into five gallon cans and then poured directly into the tanks. (USAAF)

looked pretty tidy and efficient. When turned on, the Norden bombsight whirred away, ready to make all the intricate calculations and corrections for ground speed, altitude and drift. Peering through the electronic gun sight, which directed the fire of six .50-calibre machine-guns, I could see the crosshair reticle glowing brightly, and I knew that in there little electrons raced about making their own prodigious calculations of an enemy fighter's closing speed and wingspan.

So now, with confidence in our plane and equipment, we awaited the unveiling of the map in the Hsinching briefing room which would reveal the target for December 7, 1944. It was cold in China. For the first time we slept in our down sleeping bags, a novelty in 1944. Upon awakening in the unheated barracks, we slipped immediately into lined parkas, our uniform for the day. Looking down on the assembled crews, the briefing officer must have been reminded of a gathering of medieval monks, their faces obscured by hoods and clouds of vapor from their breath. Certainly there were a few silent prayers being said also.

Just the place for a quick cigarette break! Another method of fuel transfer is seen here - gasoline that had been flown 'over the hump' in 50 gallon drums was tipped into an open trough - from there it was pumped into a large storage tank. One can only imagine the fumes! *(USAAF)*

The target was an aircraft factory in Mukden, Manchuria. From a mysterious source we received a weather report - below freezing temperatures at ground level and a cloudless sky. Balanced against the advantage of a clear view of the target was the threat of frostbite, a serious crippler of aircrews of the 8th Air Force on their winter missions over Europe. Forty-eight hours earlier we had been enjoying the pleasant winter weather of India - suntan pants and shirts - the shirts were discarded for the afternoon ballgames. Now in the early morning we waddled to the planes. Long underwear, woollen shirts and sweaters, parkas, fleece-lined flying boots, heavy gloves. At about 9 a.m., over a small island in the Gulf of Po, the 40th Bomb Group began to assemble into formation. Major Weschler wheeled us into the No. 4 position of the lead element, which put us directly behind but below the lead plane. The formation began a slow climb to bombing altitude - 20,000 feet. A few minutes later we crossed the Manchurian coast, noting the iced-up bays and coves and the sprinkling of snow on the low hills. As predicted, the sky was clear, and from our altitude we could see for a hundred miles - but we could also be seen. The fighter defenses of Mukden were formidable. Because of distance, the Japanese

CHINA

Construction and airfield imrpovements was continuious - here a roller smooths the surface on a taxi strip during construction of an airfield in China while a B-29 undergoes engine runs. *(USAAF)*

With mountains just visible in the distance through the haze, a group of thirteen B-29s of the 444th Bomb Group, XX Bomber Command, are seen parked on an airfield in China sometime in December 1944. *(USAAF)*

air bases here were safe from strikes by General Chennault's 14th Air Force. Their planes then stood ready on the line, fresh and unscarred, the engines tuned by unhurried mechanics, the guns cleaned and oiled. Seeing little action, their pilots probably chafed and moped about from day to day and dreamed of what would happen to any American planes foolhardy enough to invade the Manchurian skies. We anticipated, correctly, that they would lack the caution and wariness of their embattled colleagues further south and would probably hurl their planes at our formations in reckless and uncoordinated attacks. Undoubtedly our adversaries saw themselves as warriors imbued with the true banzai spirit. Ours was a different view; we thought they were all a little crazy! On this morning we were glad for our unlimited visibility, for we would be able to see all of our attackers no matter from which direction they came at us and we could not be ambushed by planes suddenly darting out of the clouds.

Signs of battle appeared before us. A B-29 from the preceding formation had gone down, the burning wreckage marked only too clearly by the rising cloud of ugly, black smoke. It was not an easy victory for our enemy. Several smaller streams of flame and smoke - their fighters - spiralled down to crash around the downed bomber.

I swung the gunsight into position as the 40th Group prepared to run the

Groundcrew work on a B-29 'somewhere in China' while an armed Chinese soldier stands guard. *(USAAF)*

gauntlet of fighters and flak. We were still miles from Mukden. Rail lines leading to the city glistened far below us. All at once, a few miles ahead, a section of tracks disappeared in a cloud of exploding bombs. Inexplicably, an entire formation had released their bombs miles from the target. There was no time to puzzle further over this action, as fighters were now swinging into position to begin their runs on us.

As they bored in, those of us up front saw, to our horror, a film of ice forming on the inside of our windows. I shoved the gunsight to one side and brushed frantically at the ice with my gloved hands! It was a useless effort, and our view of the outside world and its perils quickly glazed over. From the navigator's spot, Clark Thomas saw the problem, thought quickly and seconds later came forward and thrust into my hands his set of plastic starfinders. Using them as scrapers, I cleared a panel for Major Weschler, then one for myself, then back to the Major's panel as the ice quickly reformed. Shelly Green, the co-pilot, peering through the glaze, called to my attention the opening switch, then passed the bomb toggle switch on its cord top to Clark. He would drop our bombs when the leader's bombs went away; I would carry on as ice-scraper.

I could not gain on the ice. My arms, enveloped in layers of clothing, became heavy. A lifelong concern with physical fitness now paid off thank God for the thousands of pushups ... the straining muscles ... the heaving lungs... the gallons of sweat.. .. I was aware of fighters hurtling by. Now and then I got off a frantic burst, but I doubt if I fired more than twenty rounds that day. Sturdy though my arms were, I began to tire, and the ice gained on me. But knowing we were close to the critical bomb release point, I gave another mighty effort, cleared the top panel and looked directly up into the bomb-bays of the lead plane. There above us hung twelve 500-pound general purpose bombs. Had there been time, I could have amused our crew by reading to them the obscene messages to the enemy scrawled in chalk on the underside of some

When 42-65252 from the 769th BS, 62nd BG was taking off from its base in India for a flight over The Hump, its electrical system blew out as a result of a sudden surge of power from the generators the pilot, 1st Lt William R Mcguire, circled the field for a landing, but given that it was fully loaded, the nosewheel gave way with predicable results. (USAAF)

bombs. I didn't bother with the intercom, I simply pointed upward. A split second later Major Weschler throttled back and, several seconds later, the twelve bombs left the lead plane on their way to the aircraft factory, clearing our nose by what was probably a few feet, but to my wide, blue eyes seemed to be no more than a few inches.

The turn for home swung the nose directly into the sun and the formation began to descend to a lower, somewhat warmer elevation. Within a few minutes the temperature climbed from -50 degrees F to a balmy -30 degrees F and the ice began to disappear from the windows. We pulled away from the flak zone and presently the fighters left. I slumped in my seat, suddenly aware of moist patches of sweat under my arms, ominous little patches should the cold penetrate the layers of clothes and freeze them. I took off my flak vest and felt with gratefulness the sun of my face and parka. It is perhaps a strain on the verb "to bask" if you are "basking in the sun" at -30 degrees F, but, however, as I absorbed the solar energy, the problem of the sweat patches soon disappeared.

After a while, I gathered up the shreds and mangled remains of the plastic starfinders. They would be of no further value for navigation; on them, the North Star was probably found somewhere over the Argentine. We now looked forward to landing back at Hsinching, where we would offer some suggestions to be forwarded to the factory which turned out our plane.

Ours was one of the older B-29s. We learned at the critique that most of the older models that went to Mukden that day had undergone the same ordeal. The nose of the lead plane of the formation (which had dropped its bombs so many miles short of the target) had become so iced over that the bombardier, desperately searching for the target through the glazed windows, had mistaken railyards for the factory.

Why, amidst the many intensive planning sessions which had resulted in America's most advanced bomber, had no one ever brought up the problem of solid condensation at low temperatures? Surely this had been a problem years earlier, one that had been dealt with by our 8th Air Force, the Royal Air Force and the German Air Force. The solution was a simple one. Two weeks later, when we returned to Mukden, all of the 40th Group planes had defroster tubes and ducts installed in their noses. 'We had a few problems that day but icing was not one of them'.

It was also on that same raid that a good friend of Jim O'Keefe's, Capt Ira Matthews, from the 45th Bomb Squadron of the 40th Bomb Group, had been piloting the *Eddie Allen,* a B-29 Superfortress which was one of the more well-known aircraft of World War Two. It bombed targets in seven countries before being badly damaged on 25 May 1945 over Tokyo and sent to salvage. The aircraft had been named after the Boeing chief test pilot who made the first flight of the experimental B-29, called the XB-29. Allen died shortly after in the crash of the second prototype.

'One by one the hazards expected on the seven-hour flight to the target in Manchuria were ticked off by the briefing officer. An early morning take-off would be followed by several hours of night flying in the company of other bombers, with none of them showing running lights. At daybreak we would cross into Japanese-occupied China, where we could expect vigorous resistance from enemy fighters. On the bombing run at 19,000 feet, the cold would be extreme, and the direction and velocity of the wind could only be guessed. A final admonishment from the briefing officer, "Men, be sure to wear your GI shoes, laced to the tops, in the event you are forced to bailout and have to walk to safety."

After making the usual feeble jokes about hailing a ricksha following a bailout, the crews compared notes. Yes, it had been a thorough briefing; no, we had been told nothing new or extraordinary.

The date, December 7, 1944; the place, an advanced Air Force base near Chengtu, in western China. We were members of the 40th Bombardment Group flying a handful of the first B-29s to go into action in World War II. In its six months of overseas operations the 40th had flown missions to targets ranging

The crew of the Boeing B-29, 42-24579 *'Eddie Allen'* of the 45th BS, 40th BG XX Bomber Command: left to right, back row: Major Ira V Matthews, Lafayette, AL, pilot; 1st Lt Robert A Winters, Wichita, KA, co-pilot; 1st Lt Herbert C Hirschfeld, navigator, Chicago, IL; 2nd Lt Charles Behrle, bombardier, New Haven, CT; Flight Officer Louis F Grace, engineer, S/Sgt John J Mahli, crew chief, Ambridge, PA, Sgt. Claude L Bolin of Newton, KA, assistant crew chief. Left to right, front row: T/Sgt Fred H Thompson, Ft. Worth, TX, radio operator; S/Sgt S V Sienkiewicz, Cook County, IL; S/Sgt L E McBride, Springfield, MA; S/Sgt Samuel P Winborne, top turret gunner, Raleigh, NC. *(USAAF).*

B-29 'Katie' - No. 298 - had this impressive nose art which was photographed at A-1 landing ground in China after it nosed over into a ditch alongside the runway when a tyre blew out as it landed. (USAAF)

from Sumatra, below the equator, to icy Manchuria. We had encountered a formidable number of meteorological hazards - cyclones (hurricanes), cold fronts, warm fronts, tornadoes, updrafts, downdrafts, winds of incredible velocity, heat, icing, dust, plus vagrant birds. The experience gained was precious insurance.

Tested and battle-hardened, the crews on this December morning were eager to get on with the mission, cope with whatever came up, and get it over with. In the early morning darkness planes began to rumble down the feebly-lit runway.

Shortly before dawn, B-29 the Eddie Allen neared Sian, in the Yellow River Valley. Close at hand was the northernmost airfield held by General Chennault's 14th Air Force. It was comforting knowledge that, in the event we were intercepted, friendly fighters could come to our aid.

At 14,000 feet the skies were clear and the air was smooth. Major Ira Matthews had the Eddie Allen on automatic pilot. The members of the veteran crew searched the sky for other planes, friendly or enemy. So far the flight had been uneventful. Without warning the plane swerved sharply left, the nose pitched downward, and the autopilot disconnected. Major Matthews and the co-pilot, Captain Alvin Hills, struggled to level the wings and raise the nose. Severe vibrations wracked the plane, and it pitched and rolled as if caught in a violent thunderstorm. An emergency interphone check found all crew members in position and strapped in. The gunners scanned the wings and tail, and reported that all surfaces appeared normal. Vibration and turbulence increased. Major Matthews considered alerting the crew for bailout, then reconsidered when he realized that no one could crawl to an escape hatch; vibration had reached a point where all movement was impossible. The flight instruments merged into a shimmering blur.

The frightening motion ceased abruptly. An interphone check found all crew members shaken but uninjured. Safety belts were unbuckled and scattered equipment was cautiously retrieved. Another scan of wing and tail surfaces showed nothing abnormal. How long had the turbulence lasted? The navigator, with admirable coolness, had timed it. His log entry read, "Five minutes of stark terror."

The Eddie Allen completed the mission. At debriefing, the crew members were as anxious to report the wild, completely unexpected turbulence as they were to report bombing results and the heavy fighter attacks over Manchuria. An Intelligence officer, politely sceptical, listened and recorded, then compared notes with other interrogators. No other crew reported the turbulence, although navigators' logs showed a number of planes near the Eddie Allen's position at that time.

The Eddie Allen was carefully checked by the ground crew. There was no evidence of structural damage. On the return flight to the 40th Group's home base in India, the flight crew put the plane through a number of flight checks while over the dangerous mountainous stretch known as the HUMP, an unlikely area for testing. The plane passed all tests, and the crew, sensing that to talk further about their unique experience would draw derisive comments and hints of "battle fatigue," resolved to say no more about it.

A possible explanation for the turbulence came several days later when survivors of a catastrophic earthquake in the Yellow River area streamed into Sian. The extent of the tragedy in terms of loss of life was never learned, nor was the quake's magnitude measured. An indubitable fact is that the quake occurred early on the morning of December 7th.

Some members of the 40th Group were trained in physics and meteorology. We don't recall that any of them offered an explanation of this atmospheric phenomenon. They had, in fact, no time to give to leisurely speculation about an isolated, unlikely-to-ever-occur-again incident. December 1944 was a grim, desperately busy month for the 40th Group.

But sometime in the 1950s a DC-7, flying at 20,000 feet near Arequipa, Peru, encountered severe clear air turbulence. The plane was badly damaged and several passengers were severely injured. After an emergency landing,

The scattered remains of Boeing B-29 42-24582 40th Bomb Group, XX Bomber Command, at Chakulia, India, that was demolished as a result of an accident that occurred when bombs were being unloaded on 14 January 1945. The B-29 *"LAST RESORT"*, parked in the same dispersal area, was riddled by fragments from the explosion. *(USAAF)*

CHINA

1st Lt Charles E Biehle, of North Vernon, Indiana is bombardier of *"Black Magic"*, aircraft No 276, of the 45th BS, 40th BG, 20th Bomber Command, which participated in the 21 November 1944 bombing raid on Omura, Japan.

The copilot's foot on the instrument panel shows wonderful disregard for government equipment! *(USAAF)*

the pilot learned he had flown over the site of a great Andean earthquake.

We know of no other incidents of this nature, and we know of no studies of these two.

So for those of us who flew over northern China on a cold December morning long, long ago, the questions remain: Was the heaving of the earth's surface under the passing B-29 responsible for the savage turbulence that rocked the Eddie Allen and terrified its crew? And if so, what were the physics of the interaction between surface and atmosphere?

During his first two months at XX Bomber Command, LeMay had little more success than Wolfe or Saunders. The command continued to average only about one sortie a month per aircraft against Japan's home islands. When Douglas

Sgt W J Yoder, radar operator of Richland, Iowa on *"Black Magic"* which participated in the 21 November 1944 bombing raid on Omura, Japan. *(USAAF)*

Sgt. Robert N. Archer of Medford, Oregon, is in charge of the scoreboard showing Japanese aircraft destroyed, probably destroyed or damaged by squadrons of the 40th Bomb Group. This chart and various wall panels on the War Room at this 20th Bomber Command base kept the men informed on the latest developments in all war theatres. *(USAAF)*

MacArthur invaded the Philippines in October 1944, LeMay diverted his B-29s from bombing Japanese steel facilities to striking enemy aircraft factories and bases in Formosa, Kyushu and Manchuria.

Meanwhile, LeMay gained the support of Communist leader Mao Zedong, who controlled parts of northern China. Willing to help against a common enemy, Mao agreed to assist downed American airmen and to locate in northern China a weather station that would provide better forecasts for the XX Bomber Command's raids on the Japanese in Manchuria and Kyushu. Hoping to gain American recognition of his own regime, Mao suggested that the Americans set up B-29 bases in northern China like those in Chiang Kai Shek's area of control in southern China. LeMay declined, however, because he found it difficult enough to supply the airfields at Chengtu.

LeMay gradually cut back on the number of missions flown out of the Chinese bases in favour of missions to Singapore, Borneo, Malaya, and Sumatra that could be flown from the bases in India where the supply situation was much more favourable.

The former European theatre bomber commander continued to experiment with new technologies and tactics and soon imported to China the incendiary weapons being used by the Royal Air Force against Germany. In late 1944, Japanese offensive (codenamed Operation Ichi-Go) in China probed toward the B–29 and Air Transport Command bases around Chengtu and Kunming. To slow the enemy advance, Maj Gen Claire L Chennault of the Fourteenth Air Force asked for raids on Japanese supplies at Hankow, and the Joint Chiefs directed LeMay to hit the city with firebombs. On 18 December LeMay launched the fire raid, sending eighty-four B-29s in at medium altitude with five hundred tons of incendiary bombs. The attack left Hankow burning for three days, proving the effectiveness of incendiary weapons against the predominantly wooden architecture of the Far East.

By late 1944, it was becoming apparent that B-29 operations against Japan

CHINA

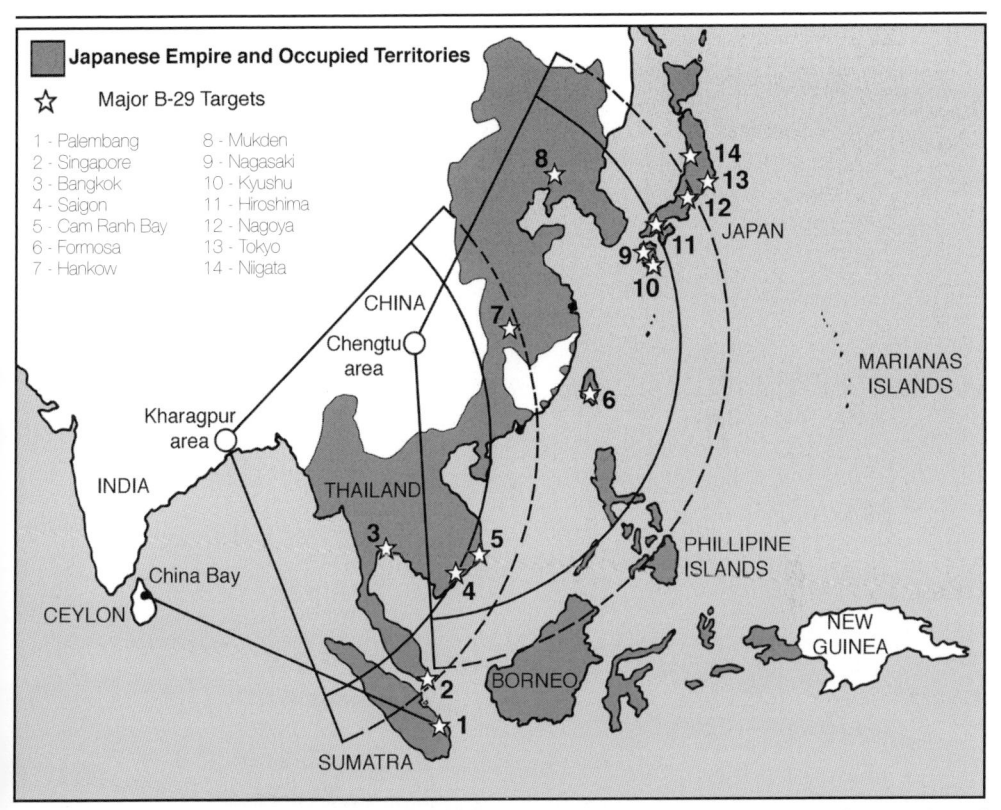

Japanese Empire and Occupied Territories

☆ Major B-29 Targets

1 - Palembang
2 - Singapore
3 - Bangkok
4 - Saigon
5 - Cam Ranh Bay
6 - Formosa
7 - Hankow
8 - Mukden
9 - Nagasaki
10 - Kyushu
11 - Hiroshima
12 - Nagoya
13 - Tokyo
14 - Niigata

Area of operations for the 20th Air Force from both India and China 1944-45.

The arcs show combat range, the 'normal' 1600 mile range being shown by solid lines, 'extreme combat range' of 1900 miles being denoted by dotted lines.

staged out of bases in Chengtu were far too expensive in men and materials and would have to be stopped. In December of 1944, the Joint Chiefs of Staff made the decision that Operation *Matterhorn* would be phased out, and the 58th Bombardment Wing's B-29s would be moved to newly-captured bases in the Marianas in the central Pacific.

The last raid out of China was flown on 15 January 1945, which was an attack on targets in Formosa. The 58th Bombardment Wing then withdrew to its bases in India and was redeployed to the Marianas in February.

During Operation *Matterhorn,* 49 separate missions had been flown involving 3058 individual aircraft sorties. Only 11,477 tons of bombs had been dropped. In spite of the massive effort, only insignificant damage had been done to targets in Japan.

After the war, the American Bomber Summary Survey stated that *"Approximately 800 tons of bombs were dropped by China-based B-29s on Japanese home island targets from June 1944 to January 1945. These raids were of insufficient weight and accuracy to produce significant results."*

Without doubt, XX Bomber Command had failed to achieve the strategic objectives that the planners had intended for Operation *Matterhorn,* largely because of logistical problems, the bomber's mechanical difficulties, the vulnerability of Chinese staging bases, and the extreme range required to reach key Japanese cities. Although the B-29s achieved some success when diverted to support Chiang

When Boeing B-29 42-63395 of the 468th Bomb Group was returning to its home base in China after bombing enemy installations at Muken, Manchuria, it stalled from about thirty feet up, breaking in half between the bomb bays. The aircraft was covered in ice, and so the pilot's visibility was impaired. (both USAAF)

Kai-shek's forces in China, MacArthur's offensives in the Philippines, and Mountbatten's efforts in the Burma Campaign, they generally accomplished little more than the B-17 Flying Fortresses and B-24 Liberators assigned to the Fourteenth, Fifth, Thirteenth, and Tenth Air Forces.

Chennault considered the Twentieth Air Force a liability and thought that its supplies of fuel and bombs could have been more profitably used by his Fourteenth Air Force. XX Bomber Command consumed almost 15% of the Hump airlift tonnage per month during *Matterhorn*. Lt Gen Albert C Wedemeyer, who replaced Lt Gen Joseph W Stilwell as American senior commander in the China theater, agreed with Chennault.

The supply problems proved to be insoluble, and the Chengtu bases in China were too far west, requiring long overflights of Japanese-occupied territory in China before the Japanese home islands could be reached. Even then, only the southernmost Japanese island of Kyushu was in range of the B-29s.

The two Generals were happy to see the B-29s leave China and India. Yet, despite those objections, *Matterhorn* did benefit the Allied effort. Using the China bases bolstered Chinese morale and, more important, it allowed the strategic bombing of Japan to begin six months before bases were available in the Marianas. The *Matterhorn* raids against the Japanese home islands also demonstrated the B-29's effectiveness against Japanese fighters and anti-aircraft artillery. Operations from the Marianas would profit from the streamlined organization and improved tactics developed on the Asian mainland.

INTO THE PACIFIC!

B-29 Wing Commanders - below: General Haywood Shepherd Hansell Jr., (b. 28 September 1903, d. 14 November 1988)

Bottom: General Emmett 'Rosie' O'Donnell, Jr. (b. 15 September 1906, d 26 December 1971) (both USAF)

The Marianas chain of islands, consisting primarily of Saipan, Tinian, and Guam, were considered ideal bases from which to launch B-29 operations against Japan. They form an arc-shaped archipelago made up by the summits of 15 volcanic mountains in the north-western Pacific Ocean between the 12th and 21st parallels north and along the 145th meridian east. They are south of Japan and north of New Guinea, and immediately to the east of the Philippine Sea. The islands are about 1500 miles from Tokyo, a range which the B-29s could manage.

In 1943, the Mariana chain was firmly under Japanese control. Plans for the conquest of the islands had been put forward as early as May 1943 by Admiral Ernest King at the Anglo-American Trident Conference in Washington, but little was done since the US Navy was locked in a bitter contest further south in the Solomons and New Guinea. It was not until September 1943 that the full potential of the Marianas as a B-29 base to attack Japan was realized. On 4 October 1943, General Henry H. Arnold approached the Joint Planning Staff with a proposal for the seizure of the Marianas at the earliest possible date as bases for the B-29. Much of the combat that followed in the Pacific for the next two years had as its major objective the seizure of B-29 bases that were ever closer to Japan.

The plan was approved at the Cairo Conference between President Franklin Roosevelt, Chinese President Chiang Kai-shek, and British Prime Minister Winston Churchill, held in November 1943. In command of the effort was Admiral Chester Nimitz.

First to be attacked was Saipan. On 11 June 1944 a four-day naval and air bombardment of the island began. On the 15th, Marine units went ashore, followed a day later by Army units. After several weeks of heavy fighting, during which over 3000 American and 24,000 Japanese lives were lost, the island was finally declared secure on 9 July. The seizure of Saipan enabled invasions of Guam and Tinian on 20 July and 23 July respectively. These islands were declared secure on 9 August. The US now had its bases - and more importantly these could be serviced by direct sea lanes from the USA.

Construction of B-29 airfields on Saipan began even while the fighting was still going on. Initial construction took place at a former Japanese airstrip called Aslito which was later renamed Isley Field, after Navy Commander Robert H Isely (unfortunately his name was misspelled and the incorrect version remained).

XXI Bombardment Command had been assigned the overall responsibility of the B-29 operations out of the Marianas bases. XXI BC had been activated at Smokey Hill on 1 March 1944. In August, Major General Haywood S Hansell Jr was directed to take over command of the XXI BC. The field on Saipan was to be occupied by the 73rd Bombardment Wing, made up of the 497th, 498th, 499th, and 500th Bombardment Groups, which had been formed at Salina, Kansas on 28 November 1943

B-29 fuselages were ideal for noseart - BIG noseart! Here US Marine Randall Sprenger puts the finishing touches on *Little Gem,* a pin-up adorning Boeing-Wichita B-29-40-BW B-29 42-24596 of the 869th BS, 497th BG, 73rd BW at Isley Field, Saipan during February 1945. *(USAAF)*

with Col Thomas H Chapman as the first commander. In March, Col. Chapman was replaced by Brigadier General Emmett 'Rosie' O'Donnell.

The 73rd BW was ordered to the Marianas, and the first B-29 arrived on Saipan on 12 October 1944, piloted by General Hansell himself. By 22 November over 100 B-29s were on Saipan. XXI BC was assigned the task of destroying the aircraft industry of Japan in a series of high-altitude, daylight precision attacks. However, General Hansell was fully aware that his crews still lacked the necessary experience to carry out such missions. In late October and early November 1944, a series of tactical raids were carried out as training exercises for the crews. On 27 October, 18 B-29s attacked Japanese submarine installations on Truk, some 630 miles away from the Marianas. Four Superfortresses had to abort because of the usual engine problems, and combat formations were scrappy. Truk was hit again by B-29s on 30 October and 2 November.

Japanese aircraft based on Iwo Jima staged a low-level raid on 2 November, when, in an attempt to counter the threat, nine or ten Imperial Japanese Navy G4M 'Betty' aircraft from Attack Hikotai 703 struck Isley Field and Kobler Field on Saipan. The raiders arrived over Saipan shortly after 01:30 and dropped their bombs from low altitude damaging several B-29s on the ground.

Retaliatory strikes were ordered on Iwo Jima on 5 and 11 November, but the results were poor. As with the *Matterhorn* campaign, the B-29s were in danger of being dissipated in tactical missions and even these were not all that successful.

On 24 November Marianas-based B-29s conducted their first raid against Japan, bombing targets in and around Tokyo. Three days later the Japanese mounted two raids against their bases. During the early hours of 27 November two G4Ms flying from Iwo Jima struck Isley Field from low altitude, and escaped after destroying one B-29 and damaging eleven others. This attack came as a surprise to the Americans, and construction lights were still on at Isley at the start of the raid. Later that day twelve Mitsubishi A6M 'Zero' fighters from the Imperial Japanese Navy 252nd Kokutai accompanied by two Nakajima C6N 'Myrt'

INTO THE PACIFIC!

Below: General 'Rosie' O'Donnell has a last word with Bob Morgan before departure from Saipan for the first attack on Tokyo since the Doolittle raid.

Bottom: Morgan's B-29 *Dauntless Dotty* - named after his third - or was it fourth? wife. *(both USAAF)*

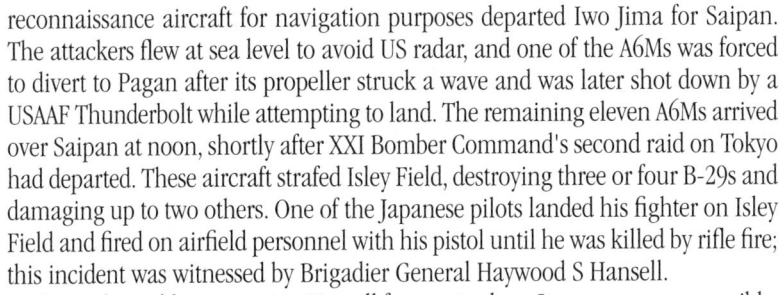

reconnaissance aircraft for navigation purposes departed Iwo Jima for Saipan. The attackers flew at sea level to avoid US radar, and one of the A6Ms was forced to divert to Pagan after its propeller struck a wave and was later shot down by a USAAF Thunderbolt while attempting to land. The remaining eleven A6Ms arrived over Saipan at noon, shortly after XXI Bomber Command's second raid on Tokyo had departed. These aircraft strafed Isley Field, destroying three or four B-29s and damaging up to two others. One of the Japanese pilots landed his fighter on Isley Field and fired on airfield personnel with his pistol until he was killed by rifle fire; this incident was witnessed by Brigadier General Haywood S Hansell.

General Arnold was pressing Hansell for an attack on Japan as soon as possible. Bad weather delayed the launch, but finally the first raid against Japan took place on 24 November 1944. The target was the Nakajima Aircraft Company's Musashi engine plant just outside Tokyo. It was the first attack on Tokyo since the Doolittle raid of over two years earlier. 110 B-29s took off, led by Brigadier General Emmett O'Donnell flying in *Dauntless Dotty,* the aircraft piloted by Robert K Morgan of *Memphis Belle* fame. Also on board from the *Memphis Belle* days was his old bombardier, Vince Evans.

Seventeen of the B-29s had to abort due to the usual spate of engine failures. The remainder approached the target at altitudes of 27-32,000 feet. For the first time, the B-29 encountered the jet stream, which was a high-speed wind coming out of the west at speeds as high as 200 mph at precisely the altitudes at which the bombers were operating. This caused the bomber formations to be disrupted and made accurate bombing impossible. In addition, the Nakajima plant was covered in patchy cloud at the time and only 24 of the B-29s dropped their bombs in even roughly the right place. The target was hardly damaged, and one B-29 was rammed by a Japanese fighter and destroyed. It was not a good start.

Bob Morgan became famous as 'The Man who flew the Memphis Belle', and indeed along with journalist Ron Powers he wrote a biography of the same name. In that work Morgan - or was it Powers? - reveals his earlier connection with the B-29 that occurred over the weekend of 1-3 August 1943 that has the distinct tinge of historical revisionism. At the start of Chapter 15 - pages 234 and 235 to be exact - they make a great deal about Bob Morgan being taken privately to one side during the War Bond Tour the B-17 *Memphis Belle* and crew made around the USA and asked if he would like to see a new, highly secret aircraft that was being kept away from prying eyes. According to their book, Morgan was escorted into a hangar during their stop-over at Boeing Wichita where he was given a guided tour of one of the B-29s then under high security test, and this it seems started him thinking about what he was going to do once the tour was over. This story is somewhat at odds with two of the pictures taken during the stop, for Bob Morgan

Two photographs taken at Boeing's Wichita plant during the *Memphis Belle's* tour in July and August 1943. The complex was thrown open to employees and public alike and clearly on display also was YB-29 41-36959 supposedly nicknamed *Amarillio's Flying Solenoid* which was fitted with the early 3-bladed props. Given the thousands of visitors that attended and the fact that the YB-29 was visible to all, it hardly seems the highly secret event as described by Bob Morgan.
(both via Harry Friedman)

INTO THE PACIFIC!

A photograph that is supposedly the first B-29 attack on Tokyo. Lead ship is B-29 42-24529 *Dauntless Dotty* of the 869th BS, 497th BG. Closest to the camera is B-29-40-BW 42-24594 *Bad Brew* (A-Square 6) from the 869th BS, 497th BG, *(USAAF)*

is recorded taxiing the *Memphis Belle* past Boeing-built YB-29 41-36959 parked out on the ramp for all to see!

It sounds very familiar - and for good reason - it is exactly the same as a scene in a 1955 Hollywood movie - substitute Bob Morgan for Jimmy Stewart and the B-29 for the B-47 and you have the exact sequence from *Strategic Air Command* where the Stewart character is introduced to the B-47 jet bomber!

But back to the Marianas. The Musashi plant was revisited ten more times over the next few weeks, but without any good results. Only 10% of the damage done by the bombs was actually inside the plant area. 40 bombers had been lost in these eleven raids, many to accidents caused by the same gremlins of engine failures.

In December there were a series of raids against the Mitsubishi engine plant at Nagoya. Although some 17% of the facility was gutted, Japanese defenses were becoming more effective and losses to enemy action were now reaching four or five B-29s per mission.

The Marianas operation was starting to go the same way as Operation *Matterhorn,* with losses being high and not much damage to the enemy being done. Hansell strove to improve the skill of his bombardiers and lead crews, who seemed to be far too eager to resort to radar when conditions were unfavourable. However, it could be said that they did have good reason - one hindrance to bombing was restricted vision through iced-up windows, necessitating new heating devices.

Though dissatisfied with the early performance of his Command, Hansell seems to have considered this as an experimental period. Not so Arnold, who was no doubt apprehensive of the Joint Chiefs of Staff view if the expensive programme did not soon produce tangible evidence of success. The war in Europe might soon be concluded, when the full weight of Allied power would be shifted to the Pacific with an invasion of the Japanese home islands. If the B-29s were to make this unnecessary by bombing Japan into submission, there was need of immediate improvement.

Firestorms...

In November Arnold and Major General Lauris Norstad - Hansell's successor as 20th AF Chief of Staff - had studied a report prepared by economic experts on the vulnerability of Japan's industrial communities. War industries were concentrated in the country's largest cities - Tokyo, Osaka, Nagoya and Kobe - and were located in areas with a high density of dwellings and other buildings constructed mainly of wood. Hundreds of small businesses sub-contracted for war work, these so-called home industries being widely dispersed in these combustible areas. The report clearly advocated the use of incendiaries against these areas and estimated their effect on the enemy's war economy that would, ton for ton, be five times greater than precision bombing of selected targets. This was area bombing, which the Army Air Force had disdained to practice, and had as far as possible avoided, in Europe.

This idea was contrary to all previous endeavours of US strategic bombing, but in the light of the largely unfruitful campaign of precision attack with the B-29s, 20th AF HQ decided to explore the effect of fire raids. In mid-December Hansell was directed to launch a full-scale incendiary attack on an industrial community area with the intent of causing wholesale destruction by fire. Burning out Japanese cities did not appeal to the XXI BC leader, a dedicated advocate of precision attack on selected industrial targets, and he seems to have remained unhappy, even after an assurance from Norstad that this was purely an experimental project. The experimental fire mission was flown on 3 January 1945 against Nagoya. This time the incendiaries were not aimed at the Mitsubishi plant but at a section of the city which it was hoped would burn and destroy or badly damage many small factories. The results were inconclusive, for despite a large fire being started and a textile mill destroyed, the bombing pattern was too small to start a major conflagration.

B-29s of the 29th BG, 314th BW, 20th AF on their new airbase, North Field, on the island of Guam. *(USAAF)*

A low-level view of part of Isley Field on Saipan in the Marianas. There are well over one hundred B-29s in this picture *(USAAF)*

At this point General Arnold recalled General Hansell and moved General LeMay from India to take over the XXI BC. LeMay arrived in the Marianas on 20 January 1945.

Before departure, General Hansell introduced reforms which were to have lasting effects. Engine failures were still a problem for the B-29 as late as mid-January of 1945, and the abort rate was running at 23% per mission. To reduce this, Hansell ordered a weight reduction programme for the B-29 in which one of the fuel tanks was taken out and some of the 0.50-inch machine gun ammunition was removed, shaving over 6000 pounds from the weight of each aircraft. Maintenance was centralized under Hansell's headquarters rather than having it

Japanese Empire and Occupied Territories

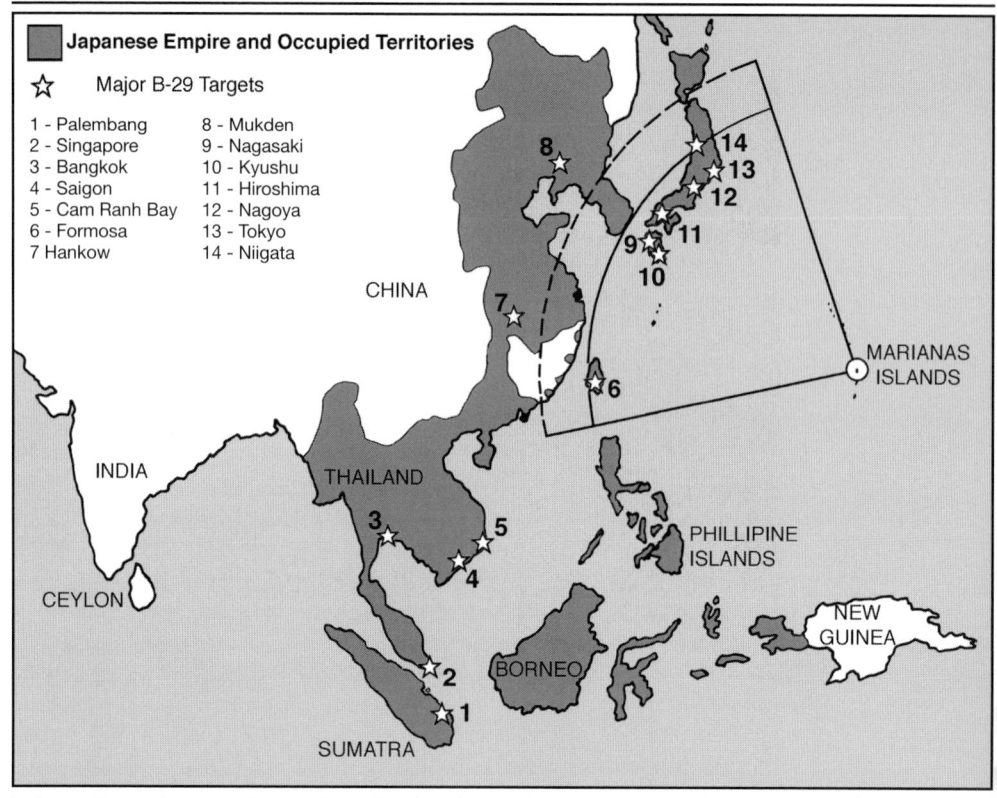

☆ Major B-29 Targets

1 - Palembang
2 - Singapore
3 - Bangkok
4 - Saigon
5 - Cam Ranh Bay
6 - Formosa
7 - Hankow
8 - Mukden
9 - Nagasaki
10 - Kyushu
11 - Hiroshima
12 - Nagoya
13 - Tokyo
14 - Niigata

Area of operations for of the USAAF B-29 fleets from the Mariana islands in 1945.

The arcs show combat range, the 'normal' 1600 mile range being shown by solid lines, 'extreme combat range' of 1900 miles being denoted by dotted lines.

being split up between the various Bombardment Groups. As a result B-29 endurance began to lengthen, engine life was extended from 200 to 750 hours, and the abort rate started to decline. By July 1945, it was down to less then 7% per operation.

In January 1945, the 313th BW, comprising the 6th, 9th, 504th, and 505th BG under the command of Brig Gen John H Davies took over the newly-built North Field on Tinian. Their first mission was a high-altitude daylight raid on Kobe on 4 February. This was the last of the raids on Japan for some time, for General LeMay's B-29s were diverted to the campaign to capture Iwo Jima, an island that was considered vital to the B-29 campaign.

The Battle of Iwo Jima took place from 19 February until 26 March 26, 1945 under the title Operation *Detachment*. The US invasion, charged with the mission of capturing the three airfields on Iwo Jima, resulted in some of the fiercest fighting in the Pacific Campaign of World War Two

Imperial Japanese Army positions on the island were heavily fortified, with a vast network of bunkers, hidden artillery, and eleven miles of underground tunnels. The Americans were covered by extensive naval and air support, capable of putting an enormous amount of firepower onto the Japanese positions. The battle was the first American attack on the Japanese Home Islands, and the Imperial soldiers defended their positions tenaciously. Of the more than 18,000 Japanese soldiers present at the beginning of the battle, only 216 were taken prisoner - the rest were killed or missing and assumed dead.

INTO THE PACIFIC!   99

In preparation for a bombing mission over Tokyo, Japan, an armourer moves a bomb dolly holding a 500 lb. Incendiary bomb cluster under the fuselage of a B-29 at Saipan, Marianas Islands. *(USAAF)*

General Curtis Emerson LeMay (*b.* 15 November 1906, *d* 1 October 1990). *(USAF)*

Iwo Jima was vital to the Americans for a number of reasons - the Japanese had radar and were therefore able to provide early warning to the Japanese mainland islands of incoming B-29 Superfortresses flying from the Mariana Islands. Before capture, Japanese fighter aircraft based on Iwo Jima sometimes attacked these attackers, which were especially vulnerable on their way to Japan because they were heavily laden with bombs and fuel. Although the island was used as an air-sea rescue base after its seizure, the traditional justification for Iwo Jima's strategic importance to the United States' war effort has been that it provided a landing and refueling site for American bombers on missions to and from Japan and also as a base for fighters capable of escorting the B-29s to Japan.

During one of the high-atltitude raids over Japan from Saipan, one gunner had a lucky escape. It was on a raid in February 1945 that Sgt James Krantz was blown out of 42-24593 *American Maid* when his observation blister was shot away. Home made straps he had designed saved him from plunging to death and he dangled for fifteen minutes over Nagoya before his fellow crew members could pull him back into the ship. An alert aerial photographer in another aircraft snapped the now-famous picture of the plucky gunner hanging by his straps from the *American Maid* while the fighting went on about him. *"We were struck by two twin engine Jap fighters that rushed our tail,"* Captain Bartlett said in describing the stirring incident. *"The tail gunner called up and said one of his fingers had been shot off but he dropped his cap over the blood stained stub on the floor and shot down one of the planes. The second one came in and blew the waist gunner out of the ship along with his gun-set. We were 27,000 feet up at the time and the temperature was about 45 degrees below zero. Krantz lost a few fingers from frostbite but other than that he came out all right."*

LeMay was concerned about the relative failure of the B-29 offensive to deal any crippling blows to Japan. He decided to continue to use incendiary bombs rather than purely high-explosive bombs,

Above: Original caption: *This remarkable photograph, taken on a Boeing B-29 strike over Tokyo, Japan, shows Sgt. J R Krantz, Hickory Point, Tenn., a waist gunner on a 21st Bomber Command Superfortress, dangling from his aircraft over Japan.*

The accuracy of this is suspect, for the report says Nagoya, the caption Tokyo - also the original print shows distinct signs of early photo-manipulation!

Right: another load of bombs are prepared to be loaded aboard 44-69684 on the Marianas. *(both USAAF)*

which would, it was hoped, cause general conflagrations in large cities like Tokyo or Nagoya, spreading to some of the priority targets.

LeMay had concluded that the effects of the jet stream, cloud cover, and high operating altitudes were to blame for the failure of the B-29 raids to do any significant damage to the Japanese war industry. The initial raids against Japan had taken place at high altitudes in order to stay above anti-aircraft fire and the effective altitude of defending fighters. LeMay believed that high-altitude, daylight attacks should be phased out and replaced by low-altitude, high-intensity incendiary raids at nighttime. The aircraft would attack individually, which meant that no assembly over the base at the start of the mission or along the way would be needed. Consequently, aircraft could go directly from the base to the target and return, maximizing the bomb load and saving substantially on fuel.

The main objection to this was the percieved hazard of anti-aircraft fire at lower altitudes which might bring increased losses. LeMay took the risk and decided to use the B-29s at between 5,000 to 6,000 feet, reasoning that it was beyond range of Japanese light anti-aircraft guns, while the larger calibre weapons would have laying difficulties for such relatively low altitudes. Using the B-29 force in this manner would be ideal for the fire raids that now had priority. LeMay already had some experience of the advantages of carrying out incendiary strikes at lower altitude. In November 1944, while commanding XX BC, he had been ordered to assist the theatre command in China by mounting a B-29 attack on Hankow, the inland port on the Yangtse river through which passed much of the war supplies for Japanese armies in that part of China. General Chennault, commanding the 14th AF, influenced LeMay in making maximum use of incendiaries and in attacking from a lower than normal altitude to improve accuracy. On 18th December the eighty-four B-29s involved dropped 511 tons of bombs, some four-fifths of which were incendiaries, from heights around 20,000 feet. Huge fires were started among the closely packed wooden buildings along the Hankow waterfront and many of them were still burning three days later. The damage and destruction to stores and port facilities were enormous.

This technique was essentially the same as the Royal Air Force had used in

Boeing B-29 Superfortresses of the 500th BG, 73rd BW dropping incendiary bombs on Japanese installations. *(USAAF)*

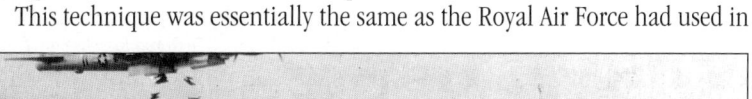

Sometimes close formations were flown! (USAAF)

their attacks on Germany and LeMay 'tested' his theories on 19 February, when 119 B-29s hit port and urban areas in Japan. This was followed on 25 February when 174 B-29s dropped incendiaries that destroyed an estimated 28,000 buildings in Tokyo.

LeMay then ordered that all the B-29s be stripped of their General Electric defensive gun systems, leaving only the tail gun. The weight of extra crew members, armament, and ammunition would translate into bombs, each B-29 being loaded down with six to eight tons of M69 incendiary bombs. These bombs would be dropped from altitudes of only five to six thousand feet. This strategy would enable the B-29s to escape the effects of the jet stream and would get the bombers below most of the cloud cover, for it was known that 120-180 knot winds at high altitude had caused drift on target approaches which in turn brought innacurate bombing. In addition, the B-29s would no longer have to struggle up to 30,000 feet, which would save both fuel and wear and tear to the engines.

The first raid to use these new techniques was on the night of 9-10 March against Tokyo. Another Wing - the 314th, comprising the 19th, 29th, 39th, and 330th BG and commanded by Brig. Gen. Thomas S Power, had arrived in the Marianas and was stationed at North Field on Guam. A large number of B-29s participated in the raid - some sources suggest 325 - with 279 arriving over the target. The raid was led by special pathfinder crews - again a concept pioneered by the Royal Air Force - who marked central aiming points. The raid - which lasted for two hours - was a success beyond General LeMay's wildest expectations. The weather was good and each aircraft was able to carry on average a 12,000lb bombload due to the weight-saving measures taken. Over 1,650 tons of petroleum-based incendiaries were dropped over the target area, with individual fires caused by the bombs joined to create a general conflagration known as a firestorm. Fierce fires took hold in the north-east section of the area, fanned by 20 mph winds, which precipitated a holocaust. When it was over, sixteen square miles of the centre of Tokyo had gone up in flames and nearly 84,000 people had been in the resulting firestorm, a higher figure than those immedately killed by either the Hiroshima or Nagasaki atomic bombs. The US Strategic Bombing Survey later estimated that nearly 88,000 people died in this one raid, 41,000 were injured, and over a million residents lost their homes. The Tokyo Fire Department estimated a higher toll: 97,000 killed and 125,000 wounded. The Tokyo Metropolitan Police Department established a figure of 124,711 casualties including both killed and wounded and 286,358 buildings and homes destroyed. Some historians put deaths at over 100,000, injuries at a million and homeless residents at a million. This one raid alone brought destruction on an almost unprecedented scale that rocked the Japanese nation; it is fair to say that public morale never recovered.During the raid fourteen B-29s were lost. The B-29 was finally beginning to have an effect.

Up to this point damage to Tokyo's heavy industry was slight until the firebombing destroyed much of the light industry that was used as an integral source for small machine parts and time-intensive processes. Firebombing also killed or made homeless many workers who had been taking part in war industry. Over 50% of Tokyo's industry was spread out among residential and commercial neighbourhoods; firebombing cut the whole city's output in half. The Imperial Palace was surrounded by areas destroyed by firebombing. The main Palace itself - home of the Imperial General Headquarters, took heavy damage by fire, even though bombing it was specifically prohibited by USAAF order.

It has been said that Emperor Hirohito's viewing of the destroyed areas of

The classic image of B-29s over Japan, three 19th BG Superfortresses fly past Mount Fujiyama. *(USAAF)*

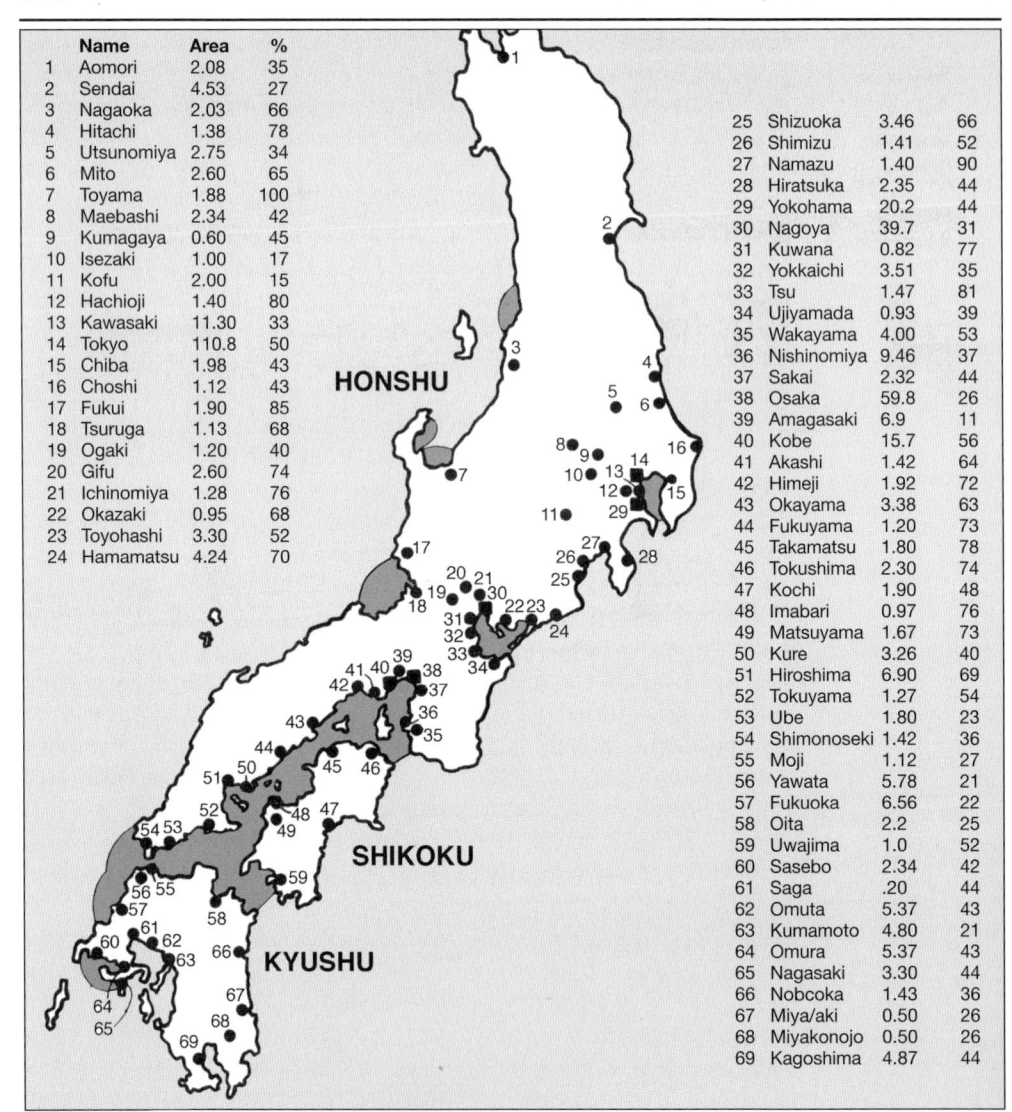

#	Name	Area	%
1	Aomori	2.08	35
2	Sendai	4.53	27
3	Nagaoka	2.03	66
4	Hitachi	1.38	78
5	Utsunomiya	2.75	34
6	Mito	2.60	65
7	Toyama	1.88	100
8	Maebashi	2.34	42
9	Kumagaya	0.60	45
10	Isezaki	1.00	17
11	Kofu	2.00	15
12	Hachioji	1.40	80
13	Kawasaki	11.30	33
14	Tokyo	110.8	50
15	Chiba	1.98	43
16	Choshi	1.12	43
17	Fukui	1.90	85
18	Tsuruga	1.13	68
19	Ogaki	1.20	40
20	Gifu	2.60	74
21	Ichinomiya	1.28	76
22	Okazaki	0.95	68
23	Toyohashi	3.30	52
24	Hamamatsu	4.24	70
25	Shizuoka	3.46	66
26	Shimizu	1.41	52
27	Namazu	1.40	90
28	Hiratsuka	2.35	44
29	Yokohama	20.2	44
30	Nagoya	39.7	31
31	Kuwana	0.82	77
32	Yokkaichi	3.51	35
33	Tsu	1.47	81
34	Ujiyamada	0.93	39
35	Wakayama	4.00	53
36	Nishinomiya	9.46	37
37	Sakai	2.32	44
38	Osaka	59.8	26
39	Amagasaki	6.9	11
40	Kobe	15.7	56
41	Akashi	1.42	64
42	Himeji	1.92	72
43	Okayama	3.38	63
44	Fukuyama	1.20	73
45	Takamatsu	1.80	78
46	Tokushima	2.30	74
47	Kochi	1.90	48
48	Imabari	0.97	76
49	Matsuyama	1.67	73
50	Kure	3.26	40
51	Hiroshima	6.90	69
52	Tokuyama	1.27	54
53	Ube	1.80	23
54	Shimonoseki	1.42	36
55	Moji	1.12	27
56	Yawata	5.78	21
57	Fukuoka	6.56	22
58	Oita	2.2	25
59	Uwajima	1.0	52
60	Sasebo	2.34	42
61	Saga	.20	44
62	Omuta	5.37	43
63	Kumamoto	4.80	21
64	Omura	5.37	43
65	Nagasaki	3.30	44
66	Nobcoka	1.43	36
67	Miya/aki	0.50	26
68	Miyakonojo	0.50	26
69	Kagoshima	4.87	44

Incendiary raids and minelaying operations on Japan mainland 1945.

Mined waters are shown in dark grey. In the table, 'area' shows the total in square miles of built-up area for a town/city, '%' shows the percentage of that built-up area that was destroyed by 20th AF bombing.

Tokyo in March 1945 was the the beginning of his personal involvement in the peace process, culminating in Japan's surrender five months later.

On the night of 11 -12 March the B-29s were in action against the city of Nagoya. This time, the scattered fires did not create a firestorm, and only two square miles of the city were destroyed. On the night of 13-14 March eight square miles of Osaka went up in flames. Two days later on 16-17 March three square miles of Kobe were destroyed, and on 19-20 March during a return visit to Nagoya, a further three more square miles were destroyed. This destructive week had killed over 120,000 Japanese civilians at the cost of only twenty B-29s lost. The strategic bombing campaign had at last been justified, despite the disapproval of a number of AAF leaders who prefered to take the moral high ground by being against the bombing of the civilian population and the concept of 'area bombing'. Many western observers thought it was not in the Japanese character to surrender, and

INTO THE PACIFIC!

No, not the result of an atomic bomb attack, but a graphic example of the destructive power of LeMay's incendiary raids on the built-up areas of Japan's cities - the few brick-built structures remain, while the rest is completely wiped out. *(USAAF)*

Boeing B-29 Bell-Atlanta B-29-15-BA Superfortress 42-63425 *"The Dragon Lady"* from the 497th Bomb Group undergoes maintenance on Saipan, Marianas. Note that two propellers have been removed. *(USAAF)*

so invading the home islands would be necessary to obtain victory. Such a venture was expected to cost at least half a million Allied lives, to say nothing of the casualties that Japan would incur, and so to many American leaders the onslaught of XXI BC was justified if it could force a surrender before the proposed invasion.

By 20 March XXI Bombardment Corps had run out of incendiaries, a development that forced a momentary pause. While waiting for new incendiary stocks to arrive, LeMay devoted his B-29s to flying tactical missions over the island of Kyushu in support of the invasion of Okinawa, with airfields and support facilities being the primary targets.

Eventually replacement stocks of incendiary bombs arrived in the Marianas, so General LeMay was able to order more fire raids - this time on the aircraft engine factories at Musashi and Nagoya along with urban areas of Tokyo, Nagoya, Osaka, Kawasaki, Kobe, and Yokohama. On 7 April, 153 B-29s struck the aircraft-engine complex at Nagoya, destroying about 90% of it. Five days later, 93 B-29s destroyed the Nakajima factory at Musashi, virtually wiping out the Japanese aircraft engine industry.

On 13 April 327 B-29s burned out another eleven square miles of Tokyo - a few days later the XXI BC received the 58th Bombardment Wing, which had been redeployed from the now-defunct XX BC in the CBI theatre to West Field on Tinian.

A month later - on 14 May - 472 B-29s attacked the area around the Mitsubishi engine factory at Nagoya. Two nights later, another visit to Nagoya devastated another four square miles of the city. Tokyo was hit again on 23 and 25 May - although these two Tokyo raids had cost 43 B-29s, over 50% of the city had now been destroyed.

Alarmed at the increasing B-29 losses, a change of tactics was ordered. In an attempt to confuse the enemy defences and to lure Japanese fighters into an air battle in which many of them would be destroyed, high-altitude daylight attacks were temporarily resumed. On 29 May, 454 B-29s appeared over Yokohama, but this time they were escorted by P-51 Mustangs from Iwo Jima. In the resulting dogfight, 26 Japanese fighters were destroyed as against the lost of four B-29s and three P-51s. Thereafter, the Japanese hoarded their surviving fighters for a last-ditch effort against the inevitable invasion force, and the air defence of cities became a lesser priority. By June 1945, Japanese interceptors were seen much less frequently and the B-29s had virtually free reign throughout all Japanese airspace.

On 5 June the B-29s attacked Kobe with such effectiveness that the city was crossed off the target list as not worth revisiting. By the end of the month, the six major cities on LeMay's list had all been effectively destroyed and so the XXI BC began a low-level fire campaign against the secondary cities of Japan, mainly those with populations of between one and two hundred thousand people. There were fifty-eight in this category, and during the next two months 72.5 square miles

Boeing B-29-40-BW 42-24603 'T-Square 7' from the 873rd BS, 498th BG, 20th AF seen low over the harbour at Saipan. (USAAF)

INTO THE PACIFIC!

of burned out urban districts were added to the total. Japanese opposition was so insignificant that LeMay began to announce his fire targets in advance, warning the people to evacuate the area. On 27 July 660,000 pamphlets were dropped on eleven cities giving warning of the forthcoming attacks. The following night six of these were bombed; casualties were much reduced through the inhabitants having heeded the warning and fled the localities. The Japanese people had more faith in their enemy's warning than their Government's ability to protect them.

There was a general weakening of fighter opposition that allowed more diverse operations in daylight. Enemy fighter strength in the Japanese home islands was estimated as a thousand aircraft. Interceptions on day raids were relatively few after June and fuel shortages further weakened fighter defences. Japanese tactics, too, were ill-conceived and poorly executed with individual head-on approaches predominating. Except when a vital part was struck, the armament of Japanese fighters was insufficiently heavy to destroy a large aircraft like a B-29 in a fleeting pass. Enemy pilots were, nonetheless, tenacious in their attempts to bring down the bombers and frequently resorted to ramming tactics.

The newly-arrived 315th Bombardment Wing (16th, 331st, 501st, and 502nd BGs) stationed at Northwest Field on Guam, was equipped entirely with the B-29B variant. This variant had been built by Bell Aircraft at Marietta, Georgia and had been manufactured without the General Electric gun system in order to save weight.

The 315th's aircraft were equipped with Eagle radar, a sophisticated development of H2X providing a vastly improved scope picture. Weight reductions and low-level operations enabled an average 18,000 lb load and on one occasion a record 22,800 lb was flown. Commanded by Brigadier General Frank Armstrong, the Wing was specially trained to operate at night employing Pathfinder

The devastation brought about by the B-29 raid on the Mitsubishi aero-engine plant at Nagoya. *(USAAF)*

Waist gunner of escort B-29 Superfortress watches a trio of North American P-51 Mustangs flying close-in during a fighter sweep to Japan. (USAAF)

techniques. Starting on 26 June they completely destroyed nine oil refining and storage plants in fifteen missions, depriving Japan of an estimated 6,055,000 barrels of storage tank capacity. A synthetic oil plant at Ube was not only demolished, it was submerged when bombs broke dykes protecting the reclaimed land on which it was built!

Mining Operations

In late March of 1945, the 313th Bombardment Wing began a series of mining operations against Japanese ports. Nearly 13,000 acoustic and magnetic mines were placed in the western approaches to the narrow Shimonoseki strait and the Inland Sea as well as in the harbours of Hiroshima, Kure, Tokyo, Nagoya, Tokuyama, Aki, and Noda. The mining operation was extremely successful and brought Japanese coastal shipping to a standstill by April. In May, merchant vessels were ordered to break through the line of mines, and 85 of them were sunk. These mining efforts were so effective that the postwar Strategic Bombing Survey credited the B-29 with 9.3% of the total Japanese shipping losses during the war.

By the end of June, the civilian population began to show signs of panic, and the Imperial Cabinet began to consider negotiating an end to the war. However, at that time, the Japanese military was adamant about continuing on to the bitter end.

During the Marianas operation, 25,500 individual aircraft sorties were flown, and 170,000 tons of conventional ordnance had been dropped. A total of 371 bombers had been lost.

OPERATION *CENTREBOARD*

It was shortly after one o'clock when we left 'Dogpatch Inn' and returned to our quarters long enough to pick up our flying gear. I had to gather my smoking equipment which, for a twelve hour flight, consisted of cigars, cigarettes, pipe tobacco, and pipes. Then the four of us jumped in a jeep and headed for the flight line, where a surprise awaited us.

There stood the Enola Gay, bathed in floodlights like the star of a Hollywood movie. Motion picture cameras were set up and still photographers were standing by with their equipment. Any Japanese lurking in the surrounding hills - and there were still some who had escaped capture - had to know that something very special was going on.

I had known, of course, that there would be some routine picture-taking before departure, but I was unprepared for this. For the next twenty minutes, we were put through a photo routine to which none of us was accustomed. These were official army photographers, of course, assigned to take pictures for the record of this most important bombing mission of the war.

The entire crew was photographed together beside the plane, and separately for use in hometown newspapers when announcement of the bombing would be made to the press. I was photographed waving from the cockpit, and I think the picture-taking would have continued all night if I hadn't called a halt shortly before two o'clock in order to complete preparations for takeoff.

The weather planes had already taxied away. Their takeoff was at 1:37 am.

General Farrell was among those on hand to wish us well. We shook hands and he gave me a few words of encouragement.

Meanwhile, I personally made all the external preflight checks. Although I don't remember the entire checklist today, I made sure that there were no open pieces of cowling, no pitot covers left hanging, and that the tires were inflated and in good condition. I also checked the pavement for telltale evidence of

Colonel Paul W Tibbets in his office on Tinian ahead of Operation *Centreboard.(USAAF)*

The famous picture of Colonel Paul Tibbets 'waving' - many have claimed that this was a friendly gesture of departure. The more likely reason was that he was waving the many spectators away from the propellers prior to engine start. *(USAAF)*

hydraulic leaks and looked into the bottom of the engine cowlings with a flashlight to be sure there was no excessive oil drip.

Twelve of us climbed into the B-29 for the flight. The others were Captain Robert A. Lewis of Ridgefield Park, New Jersey, the copilot; Major Thomas W. Ferebee, Mocksville, North Carolina, bombardier; Captain Theodore J. Van Kirk, Northumberland, Pennsylvania, navigator; Lt. Jacob Beser, Baltimore, Maryland, radar countermeasures officer; Navy Captain William S. Parsons, Santa Fe, New Mexico, weaponeer and ordnance officer; Second Lt. Maurice Jeppson, Carson City, Nevada, assistant weaponeer; Sgt. Joe Stiborik, Taylor, Texas, radar operator; Staff Sgt. George R. Caron, Lynbrook, New York, tail gunner; Sgt. Robert H. Shumard, Detroit, Michigan, assistant flight engineer; Pfc. Richard H. Nelson, Los Angeles, California, radio operator, and Tech. Sgt. Wyatt E. Duzenbury, Lansing, Michigan, flight engineer.

It is interesting that almost every part of the country—both coasts, the Midwest and the South were represented. All of us wore the loose-fitting belted coveralls that were customary for bomber flight crews. With two exceptions, we wore the standard long-peaked flight caps. George Caron was wearing the Brooklyn Dodger cap that had become his trademark. He was a fanatical Dodger fan. A preflight picture shows Dutch Van Kirk in an ordinary overseas cap.

Each of us was equipped with a standard service pistol. When Deak Parsons arrived at the plane without his weapon, he borrowed one from Nick Del Genio, a security officer. Our other gear, which we kept handy to wear only if needed, included parachute harnesses and the heavy flak suits that we kept within reach to wear only if there were signs of anti-aircraft fire when we approached our target.

Once aboard, I settled in the left-hand seat beside Bob Lewis and began to run through the checklist, with Lewis verifying each item. We checked all the instruments and radio equipment and turned on the auxiliary power unit to check the electrical system. Now it was time to start the engines.

First, it was our practice to have a ground crewman pull the engines through by hand. This meant that he turned each of the four propellers through twelve blades, or three revolutions.

I signaled for Duzenbury to start No. 3, the inboard engine on the right side. We always started it first because it was opposite from the side which anyone would approach the plane. Moreover, the two inboard engines were fitted with hydraulic pressure pumps.

Duzenbury ran the engine through twelve blades with the starter before switching on the ignition. It caught immediately. Next engine to be started was Number 4, the right outboard, then 1 and 2.

With all engines running smoothly, I checked the rise in oil pressure and made sure the fuel pressure was steady, also that the RPM gauges showed all performing at full efficiency. The entire checkout and starting procedure required about 35 minutes, and it was now 2:30. Making sure that the brakes were set, I signaled with both thumbs pointing outward for the ground crewmen to remove the wheel chocks. We were ready to taxi.

Waving to the crowd of almost a hundred well-wishers who were standing by, I gunned the engines and began our taxi jaunt of more than a mile to the southwest end of the runway from which we would take off. Behind me, having followed the same procedures, were Sweeney's Great Artiste and Marquardt's

The crew of *Enola Gay* receives last-minute instructions from Colonel Tibbets before taking off on the historic flight of dropping the first atomic bomb. It appears that all the crew were carrying side arms. *(USAAF)*

Original Caption: 'Flight Crew Of Enola Gay: L To R, kneeling: Ssgt George R. Caron, Sgt Joe S Stiborik, Ssgt Wyatt E Duzenbury, Pfc Richard H Nelson, Sgt. Robert H Shumard. L To R, Standing: Major Thomas W Ferebee, Group Bombardier; Captain Theodore Van Kirk, Navigator; Colonel Paul W Tibbets 509th Group CO and pilot: Captain Robert A Lewis, aircraft Commander. (USAAF)

No. 91, a plane with a number instead of a name. Following them was McKnight's standby plane, which would fly with us as far as Iwo Jima.

The possibility of mechanical trouble in takeoff is never completely outside the subconscious thoughts of a pilot, particularly when handling an airplane that is loaded considerably beyond its design limit, as ours was that night. Nevertheless, my insistence on thorough maintenance minimized my worry as I turned the Enola Gay into the runway and prepared for the final warm-up before releasing the brakes for takeoff. Destination: Hiroshima.

So wrote Colonel Paul Tibbets about the departure of B-29 44-86292 radio call-sign 'Dimples 82' and named *'Enola Gay'* after his mother, from the island of Tinian, one of the three principal islands of the Commonwealth of the Northern Marianas Islands in the Pacific.

General Leslie R Groves Jr (*b*. 17 August 1896, *d*. 13 July 1970).

The story of the Manhatten Project - the effort, led by the USA with participation from the UK and Canada which led to the development of the first atom bomb - is too long and complex to be told in detail here. From 1942 to 1946 the project was under the command of Major General Leslie R Groves Jr of the US Army Corps of Engineers. The Army component of the project was designated the Manhattan District or Manhattan Engineer District, but 'Manhattan' gradually superseded the official codename for the project. From the start it was divided into three 'spheres of influence' - Scientific and Technical, Political and Military.

As early as March 1944 General Groves met with Hap Arnold to discuss the delivery of the finished bombs to their targets, but it was not until early 1945 that those individual spheres of influence began

OPERATION CENTREBOARD   113

to come together in order to insert the Manhattan Project into the forward planning for the war in the Pacific.

The aerial component of the project was the delivery of both designs of the weapons, and the monitoring of their effects. If the Manhattan Project was to succeed, it had to do more than simply build atomic bombs - it also had to come up with a reliable means of delivering those bombs to the enemy. Overall management of atomic weapon delivery was given to Captain William S 'Deke' Parsons, USN, and Dr Norman F Ramsey. Parsons had previously been successful in getting the proximity fuse out to the fleet. Ramsey, a gifted physicist and engineer-organizer, would be the 'fixer' responsible for running day-to-day operations.

The first scale models of the plutonium gun bomb were fashioned by simply cutting a standard 500 pound bomb in half and splicing a length of sewer pipe in between. Test drops were made from a Grumman TBF beginning in August 1943 at the Naval Proving Ground range near Dahlgren, Virginia, but the ballistic characteristics of the 'sewer pipe bomb' were terrible. On release, the bomb went into a flat spin and broke up when it hit the ground broadside. Even as revised scale models of the plutonium gun continued to be flight-tested at Dahlgren, however, Norman Ramsey was beginning to scout out a suitable carrier aircraft for the full-sized weapon.

Captain William S 'Deke' Parsons (*b.* 26 November 1901, *d.* 5 December 1953) - seen here with the rank of Rear Admiral.

In 1943, there were no aircraft in the US inventory with a bomb bay that could contain a 17 foot bomb. Ramsey did consider modifying a B-24 Liberator for the purpose, only to abandon the idea when he discovered that the Navy had already tried to modify the B-24 for internal torpedo carriage and failed. That left the Boeing B-29 as the only other possible American candidate. During a field trip in August, Ramsey made surreptitious measurements of the Superfortress. He found that it could be adapted for the purpose by combining its two 12 foot bomb bays into one, but only if the bomb was no more than two feet in diameter. The reason was that the two bays were separated by the wing spar carry-through box, and the maximum distance between the lower side of the box and the bottom of the fuselage was no more than two feet.

Norman Foster Ramsey, Jr. (*b.* August 27, 1915)

By the autumn of 1943, the ballistic problems of the plutonium gun bomb had been largely solved with improved tail surfaces and a better weight balance. As its internal arrangements became more firmly established, the casing's layout was modified to follow suit. The final 'pod' featured a rounded, bulbous nose to house the fusing arrangements and the muzzle plug - the 'anvil' - that was to hold the plutonium target, and a long, slender body with an elongated box tail. The full-size models were eighteen feet long, and the design team estimated that the final product would weigh about 7,500 pounds.

Scale model air-drops continued on into the winter at Dahlgren, but it had become obvious that another site was needed. The air near Chesapeake Bay was hazy, and full-sized model testing would have to be conducted from as high as 30,000 feet; good visibility was important. But security was also a concern - there were too many curious eyes in eastern Virginia. Parsons and Ramsey began searching for an alternative test site. In the meantime, Los Alamos scientists and engineers had also made progress in working out the practicalities of an implosion bomb. Its arrangements would be quite different from the plutonium gun weapon, however, and that meant that the search for a suitable bomber had to be expanded. In September, Ramsey was instructed to find an aircraft with a bomb bay that could carry a weapon weighing as much as 9,500 pounds. Unlike the long, slender plutonium gun, this new bomb had to be ball-shaped to contain the bulky explosive charges; Los Alamos' best guess was that the new design could be up to six feet in diameter.

Ramsey quickly concluded that there were only two Allied bombers capable of carrying both weapons: a modified Boeing B-29 and the British Avro Lancaster. The Lancaster had ample room and was a prodigious weight lifter; it almost won the contest. Ramsey travelled to Canada in October 1943 to meet Roy Chadwick, the Lancaster's chief designer, who had crossed the Atlantic to view Lancasters being built at the Avro Canada works in Toronto, Ramsey seized the chance to show Chadwick some preliminary sketches of both the gun and the implosion weapon casings. Chadwick assured Ramsey that the Lancaster could accommodate either bomb and promised whatever support might be needed, but he was well used to wartime secrecy; Chadwick did not ask why the weapons had such unusual shapes.

When Ramsey returned to the US, he recommended to Parsons that the Avro Lancaster should be seriously considered as a good means of carrying the atomic bombs. Apparently General Groves had not yet asked for USAAF support however, and when he did a different kind of detonation took place when 'Hap' Arnold, received word of the proposal. Arnold had been personally briefed on the programme's importance by the Army Chief of Staff, but Arnold

Above: Roy Chadwick CBE, FRAeS (*b.*30 April 1893, *d.*23 August 1947) designer of the Lancaster, who was consulted about it carrying the atomic weapons.

Left: what might have been- an Avro Lancaster is serviced - the open bomb-bay doors show the load carrrying ability.

OPERATION CENTREBOARD

Casings for the *'Thin Man'* plutonium gun design weapons being developed during the Manhattan Project as part of Project *Alberta* at Wendover Field, Utah. The plutonium gun design was eventually abandoned as infeasible, as the spontaneous fission rate of reactor-bred plutonium was much higher than expected. These weapons appear to have two lugs - one on the nose, and one before the tail fins for suspension in the aircraft bomb-bay. (USAAF)

made it clear to Groves that, if any atomic bombs were to be dropped in combat, a USAAF-crewed B-29 would deliver them. With that proviso firmly established, Arnold willingly endorsed the Manhattan Project's request for USAAF assistance.

On 29 November 1943, a team of USAAF and Manhattan Project representatives met at Wright Field to work out the details for modifying a small number of B-29s to carry atomic weapons. The USAAF was to modify the first aircraft and turn it over to the Project by 15 January 1944; a small number of combat-ready aircraft would follow later. For its part, the Manhattan Project agreed to send technical representatives and two full-sized examples of the plutonium gun weapon (code-named *Thin Man*) and the implosion weapon (codenamed *Fat Man*) to Wright Field by mid-December. The following day, instructions were sent to the AAF Materiel Command to modify a B-29 at Wright Field for a project to be held in greatest secrecy, code-named *Silver Plated*. In turn, AAFMC's engineering Division issued the work a separate internal code name, *Pullman* and a classified project reference number, MX-469.

The word 'Pullman' had been chosen to fit the overall cover story devised on 29 November: British Prime Minister Churchill (the Fat Man) would visit the US to tour defence plants with President Roosevelt (the Thin Man) in a specially-modified (Silver Plated) B-29 (the Pullman). With usage, the overall code name was soon shortened to its more familiar form: *Silverplate*.

Boeing-Wichita completed its fifty-eighth B-29, AAF serial number 42-6259, on 30 November 1943. The aircraft was delivered to Salinas Field, Kansas that day, and it was in Wright Field's modification shop two days later. The revisions were done 'by hand,' and consumed over 6,000 man-hours. The belly skinning was removed between the two bomb bays to make one long opening, and the four 12-foot bomb bay doors were replaced by two 27-foot doors. The rear bay's forward bomb racks were fitted with a carrier frame and sway bracing, and hoists were mounted at each of the four corners of the frame. Dual release mechanisms were adapted from glider tow equipment and fitted fore-and-aft to the carrier frame, and motion picture camera mounts were added to the rear bay. The *Thin Man* shape fited

The headquarters area of the 509th on Tinian *(USAAF)*

but, as expected, with very little clearance: its 'pod' nose was 23 inches in diameter. The modification process took until early February, and engine troubles further delayed the aircraft's availability; it didn't arrive at Muroc Field - now Edwards AFB - California until 20 February 1944.

The first flight test drop at Muroc - a standard *Thin Man* - took place on 6 March, followed on 14 March by two *Fat Men* shapes fitted with circular tail shrouds designed by engineers at the National Bureau of Standards. The *Thin Man* worked well; its ballistics had been largely ironed out during the previous scale model tests at Dahlgren. On the other hand, the *Fat Men* shapes performed poorly, demonstrating yaw angles of as much as 19 degrees; the problem was attributed to poor workmanship and misalignment of the tail surfaces.

The use of glider tow releases also proved to be a major problem. All three bombs failed to release immediately, leading the calibration efforts completely awry. A fourth drop test, scheduled several days later, resulted in a premature release while the B-29 was still enroute to the test range. The *Thin Man* fell on the bay doors and severely damaged them; the aircraft had to be sent to San Bernadino for repairs. The consensus was that the twin release lugs were at fault, and the test team successfully argued that the project should adopt the British method of suspending heavy bombs by a single lug.

Testing resumed in mid-June, and twelve shapes were dropped from 42-6259 between the 14th and the 27th: three *Thin Men* and nine *Fat Men*. Various combinations of tail boxes and drag fins were tested on the implosion shape, all in an effort to dampen the device's persistent wobble. The solution that was finally adopted combined a box tail with internal drag plates set at 45 degrees to the line of flight; the test team called this arrangement a 'California Parachute.'

The *Thin Man* becomes *Little Boy*

Previous theoretical studies had identified a possible problem with gun-assembled plutonium weapons. When the first Hanford-produced plutonium samples arrived at Los Alamos in the spring of 1944, that 'possible problem' turned out to be a show-stopper. To make plutonium meant 'cooking' uranium in a nuclear reactor. Unfortunately, the same process that made plutonium also created impurities in it, and those impurities could not be removed by chemical means. The impurities raised the 'fissionability' of Hanford-produced plutonium to such a level that no 'gun' could shoot pieces of it together fast enough; they would begin to interact well before they could be fully joined. *Thin Man* was a dead end.

The failure of *Thin Man* was a blessing in disguise, for as a hedge against the failure of implosion - still not a sure thing in the spring of 1944 - the gun model was revamped to use U235 instead of plutonium. U235 fissions less efficiently than plutonium, but there was an advantage to this approach in that the assembly speed could be greatly reduced. By lowering the gun's muzzle velocity to 1,000 feet per second, the barrel length could be reduced to less than ten feet - and that would fit the gun weapon into a standard B-29 bomb bay. The new weapon was code-named *Little Boy*.

The two types of atom bombs dropped on Japan. The upper one is a *Little Boy,* the lower design is the *Fat Man.* (both USAAF)

Silverplate moves to Wendover.

As the summer of 1944 progressed, the expanding test programme and the need to form a combat unit argued strongly for the acquisition of more *Silverplate* aircraft. On 22 August, 24 *Silverplate*-modified B-29s were ordered from the Glen L Martin Modification Center at Omaha, Nebraska, with the first three aircraft to be delivered by 30 September, followed by eleven more by 31 December. These fourteen aircraft would be used for test and training purposes. The remaining ten were due 'as soon as possible' in 1945; outfitted with the latest changes, they would be reserved for combat.

Given that Muroc did not have the facilities necessary to support twelve to fourteen B-29s and the 500 to 650 people needed to operate and maintain them, the Project was persuaded to pick another site for training. It needed clear weather, and to be just as isolated for security purposes. Wendover, Utah fit the bill perfectly. In addition to a site selection, the combat unit was identified and its commanding officer selected: the 393rd Bomb Squadron, a part of the newly-activated 504th Bomb Group (Very Heavy). The 393rd was detached from the 504th without explanation and assigned to a new unit, the 509th Composite Group. Another flying outfit, the 320th Troop Carrier Squadron, was also assigned so as to provide the Group with its own internal airline. Because of their signature paint scheme - and after *The Green Hornet*, a popular radio programme of the day - the 320th's five C-54s were called the *Green Hornet Line*. Practice missions, strict security, and 'need to know' quickly became the 509th's daily bread. Only the Group's commander, Colonel Paul W. Tibbetts, Jr., knew its mission.

In mid-October, the first three of the new *Silverplate* aircraft batch (42-65209, -216, and -217) were accepted from the Martin-Omaha facility. Unlike 42-6529, the original *Pullman* aircraft, they were

Wendover Field, Utah, at the time of the 509th CG occupation. The sign above is a small example of the level of security applied. *(both USAAF)*

fitted with a single-point bomb release modelled after the British 'Type F' heavy bomb mechanism and mounted on an improved frame fitted in the forward bomb bay. Long range fuel tanks could be carried in the rear bay, and a new crew position, equipped with an elaborate monitoring system, was added to support the test programme, and to prepare the bomb for release and detonation during the actual combat drops. In recognition of these new, complex duties, the additional position was called a 'weaponeer station.'

Training and test work began in parallel at Wendover immediately upon arrival of the 509th and continued through the winter and on into spring. Long-range missions were flown to test facilities established at Naval Weapons Station Inyokern, California, and later to ranges south of Albuquerque, New Mexico. The *Fat Man* design evolved considerably in sophistication, although its ballistic characteristics still remained less than satisfactory. The new *Little Boy* design also underwent continued development, but it had far fewer teething problems than *Fat Man*.

One major consideration was the state of readiness of the strike aircraft. Although the original order for the 'replacement' aircraft had specified ten aircraft to be delivered at a rate of two per month, by January 1945 it was clear that a piecemeal approach would not serve the 509th very well. The 'state-of-the-art' had rapidly overtaken many of the planes delivered to Wendover in the fall, and Colonel Tibbetts had made sure they flew as many hours as maintenance would support. In short, the 509th's aircraft were worn out. In February, the standing order for modified aircraft was doubled from a total of 24 to 48, and in April, five more were added to the order. The delivery schedule called for thirteen aircraft to be delivered to the 509th in April, and two more per month for the next four months. (In all, 54 *Silverplate* aircraft were ordered before V-J Day, but only 46 were actually completed and delivered.)

These new aircraft included all of the latest technical changes made to recent B-29 aircraft, as well as special modifications added only to *Silverplate* aircraft. In addition to the special equipment related to carrying and dropping atomic bombs, the latest *Silverplate* batch received fuel-injected engines and reversible-pitch propellers. Given that the final versions of the *Fat Man* and *Little Boy* weapons each weighed about 10,000 pounds, significant efforts were made to reduce aircraft weight. All the turrets were removed, as was a substantial amount of armour plate. As a result, the *Silverplate* aircraft were slightly faster, achieved better fuel economy, and could carry a heavier payload at higher altitudes. Ramsey subsequently wrote that "...*the performance of* [the 509th aircraft] *was exceptional ... they were without doubt the finest B-29s in the theater.*"

Paul Tibbets explains the reasoning behind some of the changes: *'My experience with the B-29 at Wichita, Grand Island, and Alamogordo gave me a knowledge of the strengths and weaknesses of this newest and largest of all bombing planes.*

Although it would fly high and carry a heavy load, its engines had a tendency to overheat on a long flight at high altitudes. Also, in the thin upper air, the controls behaved badly when the plane was heavily loaded. Under those conditions, the B-29 was sluggish: it lacked maneuverability. These were serious problems since our mission to deliver the atomic bomb called for a long flight at high altitude, climaxed by a maneuver that required exacting control response.

The scientists had warned that it would be unsafe to drop the bomb from an altitude of less than 30,000 feet. Because of the combined weight of the bomb and the fuel required for the 14-hour round-trip flight, the plane had to operate beyond its design specifications.

The solution seemed obvious to me. I remembered my experience at Alamogordo with the bomber that came to us without armament. Why not fly it with only the tail guns? To do so would immediately save more than 7,000 pounds of installed weight, increase its operating altitude, and relieve some of the strain on the engines.

With our newly modified airplanes, we began intensive training at once over the vast open spaces of the western desert from Utah and Nevada to California. My first concern was for accuracy in dropping the bomb, and my next, for a maneuver that would put us as far as possible from the point of explosion.

Views of Tinian island in the Marianas. Tinian is one of the three principal islands of the Commonwealth of the Northern Marianas Islands. It is about 5 miles, southwest of its sister island, Saipan, from which it is separated by the Saipan Channel. It has a land area of 39 square miles. The island was transformed into the busiest airbase of the war, with two B-29 airfields (West and North) having eight 8,500 foot runways. *(both USAAF)*

OPERATION CENTREBOARD

A low-level view of part of the North Field Tinian. (USAAF)

Although the 393rd Squadron came to Wendover with its own airplanes, these were later replaced with newer models direct from the production line but modified to my specifications.

Since the potential power of the atomic weapon was only theoretical at the time, and its consequences open to speculation even by the most knowledgeable scientists, there was no assurance that we could escape the violent shock wave that would be created by the explosion.

The scientists had told me that the minimum distance at which we could expect to survive would be 8 miles. It takes a B-29 two minutes to fly 8 miles, whereas it would take the bomb only 43 seconds from the moment it left our airplane, flying at 31,000 feet, to the point of detonation less than 2,000 feet above the ground. The shock wave would race toward us at the speed of sound - about 1,100 feet a second - which meant that it would take approximately 40 seconds to travel 8 miles.

It was obviously impossible to reach a point over the earth 8 miles from the explosion in 1 minute and 23 seconds. However, we would be almost 6 miles away, vertically, at the time we released the bomb; hence a slant-line distance of 8 miles from the detonation to the plane at the time the shock waves reached us could be achieved by flying only a little more than 5 miles in the opposite direction after bomb release.

My strategy was to make a tight turn that, when completed, would have our plane flying almost directly away from the aiming point. Calculations convinced me that the most effective maneuver would be a sharp turn of 155 degrees. This would put considerable strain on the airplane and would require a degree of precision flying unfamiliar to bomber pilots. Nevertheless, it seemed our best bet for survival.

Once I had decided on this maneuver, the next requirement was to practice. I worked on this tactic before the new planes began to arrive. My immediate goal was to train all our pilots in the techniques required to make a fast diving turn of 155 degrees the moment their bombardiers released the practice bombs.

As for the bombardiers, their task was to drop the bomb from 30,000 feet onto a target on the ground that consisted of a circle 400 feet in diameter. We would accept a miss of no more than 200 feet from the aiming point.

A lot of nonsense was written during the war about the pickle-barrel accuracy of the Norden bomb sight. Many had the idea that a bomb could be dropped into a pickle barrel through the use of the sight. This was a figure of speech, of course, and the Norden sight was miraculously superior to any other that had ever been invented, but a miss of several hundred feet from high altitudes, where the wind factor could not be determined as accurately as we would have liked, was not unusual.

To begin with, we used conventional practice bombs. With the extreme accuracy essential to our mission, it soon became apparent that we should have a supply of dummy bombs the same size, shape, and weight as the real thing. Practicing with them would be useful in determining the ballistics. We wanted no aerodynamic surprises when the real one was dropped.

On one level Tinian Field was very 'rough and ready' - on others it had every facility, including this Sikorsky R-4 helicopter 43-46533 that was employed on search and rescue work.

Every available facility was needed, for problems brought about through operating the B-29 and the simple fact there was two airfields and eight runways on the island meant that accidents happened, as the lower picture of the Tinian scrapyard shows!*(USAAF)*

OPERATION CENTREBOARD

General Groves saw no need for the dummy bombs. He considered them a waste of time and money. I was supported by a number of the scientists, however, particularly Dr. Ernest O. Lawrence of the University of Southern California's radiation laboratory. Lawrence wanted to check their ballistic trajectory, just as I did, and we finally won out.

Because of the bulbous shape of the plutonium bomb, made necessary by its complicated firing mechanism, our practice shapes became known as 'pumpkins'. Altogether, we received about 200 of these dummies. Eventually, a few were filled with conventional explosive material for use against a number of selected objectives in Japan'.

Changes in markings

Many researchers have been puzzled by apparent changes of markings during the build up and aftermath of the atomic raids. The *Enola Gay* was a B-29-45-MO, serial number 44-86292, and was given a so-called 'victor number' 82.

This apparently originated from when the 73rd Bomb Wing began combat in October 1944 from Isley Field, and marked its aircraft similarly to that of the Fifteenth Air Force 55th CBW. A letter denoting the group was painted on the upper third of the tail fin, with a square symbol in the centre, and an aircraft identifier, known as the 'victor number,' in the lower third. Aircraft commonly used their tail identifiers as radio voice calls.

With the creation of the the 509th Composite Group its tail marking was a circle outline around an arrowhead pointing forward, but while flying combat missions its fifteen B-29s used the tail markings of other Groups and Wings as a security measure, for there were fears that Japanese survivors on Tinian were observing 509th operations, and reporting them by clandestine radio to Tokyo.

The 509th repainted the tail identifier with those of four XXI Bomber Command groups already in combat, and altered victor numbers to avoid misidentification with aircraft already bearing the numbers. New victor numbers 82, 89, 90, and 91 carried the markings of the 6th Bomb Group (Circle R); victors 71, 72, 73, and 84 those of the 497th Bomb Group (large A); victors 77, 85, 86, and 88 those of the 444th Bomb Group (triangle N); and victors 83, 94, and 95 those of the 39th Bomb Group (square P).

Enola Gay itself was built by the Glenn L. Martin Company at its Bellevue,

Enola Gay seen on Tinian sometime before the atom bomb mission, for it carries the 'circle and arrow tail markings of the 509th which Paul Tibbets had painted out and replaced with the 'Circle R' of the the 6th BG. *(USAAF)*

The 'rear end' of 44-27297 Bockscar, showing the false victor number and triangle N tail markings of the 444th Bomb Group. (USAAF)

Nebraska, plant and was one of fifteen B-29s with the *Silverplate* modifications necessary to deliver atomic weapons, which included an extensively modified bomb bay with pneumatic doors, special propellors, modified engines along with the deletion of protective armour and gun turrets. Famously, 44-86292 was personally selected by Colonel Paul W Tibbets, Jr on 9 May 1945, while still on the assembly line.

The second atomic bomber, *Bockscar*, B-29-36-MO 44-27297, victor number 77, was also built at the Glenn L Martin Aircraft Plant at Bellevue, Nebraska as a Block 35 aircraft. It was one of 10 modified as a *Silverplate* and re-designated Block 36. Delivered on 19 March 1945 to the USAAF, it was assigned to Capt Frederick C Bock and crew C-13 and flown to Wendover Army Air Field, Utah.

The aircraft left Wendover on 11 June 1945 for Tinian and arrived on 16 June. *Bockscar* was also used in 13 training and practice missions from Tinian, and three combat missions in which it dropped pumpkin bombs on industrial targets in Japan.

Target Planning and Politics.
The manufacture of the atom bomb had reached a point where its use was a strong possibility. Germany had been defeated, so its target would be Japan - but where?

In early May 1945 a series of meetings were held in Dr Robert Oppenheimer's office at Los Alamos. The end result was a memorandum sent to Major General Leslie R Groves, in which is was stated that:

'Dr. Stearns described the work he had done on target selection. He has surveyed possible targets possessing the following qualification: (1) they be important targets in a large urban area of more than three miles in diameter, (2) they be capable of being damaged effectively by a blast, and (3) they are unlikely to be attacked by next August. Dr. Stearns had a list of five targets which the Air Force would be willing to reserve for our use unless unforeseen circumstances arise. These targets are:

(1) Kyoto - This target is an urban industrial area with a population of 1,000,000. It is the former capital of Japan and many people and industries are now being moved there as other areas are being destroyed. From the psychological point of view there is the advantage that Kyoto is an intellectual

center for Japan and the people there are more apt to appreciate the significance of such a weapon as the gadget. (Classified as an AA Target)

(2) Hiroshima - This is an important army depot and port of embarkation in the middle of an urban industrial area. It is a good radar target and it is such a size that a large part of the city could be extensively damaged. There are adjacent hills which are likely to produce a focussing effect which would considerably increase the blast damage. Due to rivers it is not a good incendiary target. (Classified as an AA Target)

(3) Yokohama - This target is an important urban industrial area which has so far been untouched. Industrial activities include aircraft manufacture, machine tools, docks, electrical equipment and oil refineries. As the damage to Tokyo has increased additional industries have moved to Yokohama. It has the disadvantage of the most important target areas being separated by a large body of water and of being in the heaviest anti-aircraft concentration in Japan. For us it has the advantage as an alternate target for use in case of bad weather of being rather far removed from the other targets considered. (Classified as an A Target)

(4) Kokura Arsenal - This is one of the largest arsenals in Japan and is surrounded by urban industrial structures. The arsenal is important for light ordnance, anti-aircraft and beach head defense materials. The dimensions of the arsenal are 4100' x 2000'. The dimensions are such that if the bomb were properly placed full advantage could be taken of the higher pressures immediately underneath the bomb for destroying the more solid structures and at the same time considerable blast damage could be done to more feeble structures further away. (Classified as an A Target)

(5) Niigata - This is a port of embarkation on the N.W. coast of Honshu. Its importance is increasing as other ports are damaged. Machine tool industries

Original Caption: *At the briefing prior to the flight of the Enola Gay, Capt. William S. Parsons and Colonel Tibbets go over last-minute data.* (USAAF)

are located there and it is a potential center for industrial dispersion. It has oil refineries and storage. (Classified as a B Target)

(6) The possibility of bombing the Emperor's palace was discussed. It was agreed that we should not recommend it but that any action for this bombing should come from authorities on military policy. It was agreed that we should obtain information from which we could determine the effectiveness of our weapon against this target.

It was the recommendation of those present at the meeting that the first four choices of targets for our weapon should be the following:
> a. Kyoto
> b. Hiroshima
> c. Yokohama
> d. Kokura Arsenal

Admittedly not of the best quality, but nevertheless remarkable in its survival, a XXI BC target map of the Hiroshima area. *(USAAF)*

Dr. Stearns agreed to do the following: (1) brief Colonel Fisher thoroughly on these matters, (2) request reservations for these targets, (3) find out more about the target area including exact locations of the strategic industries there, (4) obtain further photo information on the targets, and (5) to determine the nature of the construction, the area, heights, contents and roof coverage of buildings. He also agreed to keep in touch with the target data as it develops and to keep the committee advised of other possible target areas. He will also check on locations of small military targets and obtain further details on the Emperor's palace.

The meeting went on to discuss the psychological aspects as to the weapon's use: *'It was agreed that psychological factors in the target selection were of great importance. Two aspects of this are (1) obtaining the greatest psychological effect against Japan and (2) making the initial use sufficiently spectacular for the importance of the weapon to be internationally recognized when publicity on it is released.*

In this respect Kyoto has the advantage of the people being more highly intelligent and hence better able to appreciate the significance of the weapon. Hiroshima has the advantage of being such a size and with possible focusing from nearby mountains that a large fraction of the city may be destroyed. The Emperor's palace in Tokyo has a greater fame than any other target but is of least strategic value.

Much has been written about the rights and wrongs of dropping both atomic bombs, mostly from the position of hindsight - which always has 20/20 vision - and from selected political viewpoints. However, the crux of the whole decision goes back to the

Detail from a USAAF map of Hiroshima, pre-bombing, circles drawn at 1,000 foot intervals radiating out from ground zero, the site directly under the explosion. *(USAAF)*

overall plan for the defeat of Japan, the strategy for the invasion of the mainland islands throughout late 1945 and into 1946 and the actual and projected loss of lives.

This was discussed in a Presidential meeting held at the White House at 1530 hrs on 18 June 1945. Also present was Fleet Admiral William D Leahy, General for the Army George C Marshall, Fleet Admiral J King, Lt. General Ira C Eaker (representing General of the Army H H Arnold, The Secretary of War Henry Stimson, The Secretary of the Navy James Forrestal, the Assistant Secretary of War John J Mcloy. The secretary of the meeting was Brigadier General A J McFarland.

General Marshall pointed out that the present situation with respect to operations against Japan was practically identical with the situation which had existed in connection with the operations proposed against Normandy. He then read, as an expression of his views a digest of a memorandum prepared by the Joint Chiefs of Staff for presentation to the President:

Likewise is the remarkable survival of this XX1 BC target map of Nakasaki. *(USAAF)*

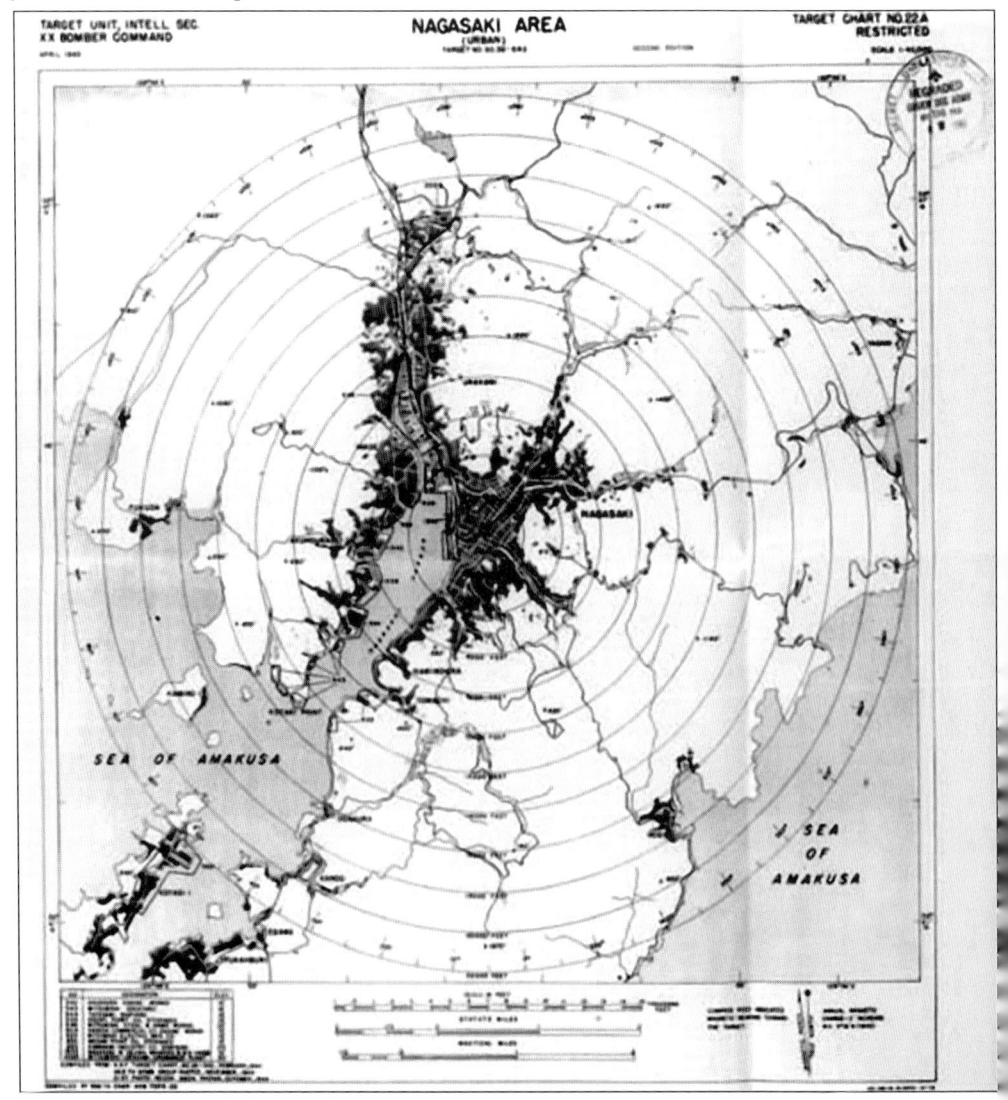

OPERATION CENTREBOARD

There is a certain amount of mystery regarding the target maps of Hiroshima and Nagasaki.

This Nagasaki map for instance is clearly pre-bombing, and yet is dated 27 September 1945, over a month after the raid, which is also erroniously recorded as being 5th August.

Although not proven, this picture could have been one of the photograpic reconnaissance mission images taken just before the Hiroshima raid on 6 August when all probable targets were surveyed - these were then put together on 27 September for a report. (USAAF)

27SEPT45 NAGASAKI, JAPAN BEFORE BOMBING 5AUG.

1. TATEGAMI SHIPYARD
2. MITSUBISHI DOCKYARD
3. AKUNOURA ENGINE WORKS
4. MITSUBISHI ELECTRIC MFG. CO.
5. NAGASAKI & DEJIMA WHARVES & R.R. YARDS
6. MITSUBISHI STEEL & ARMS WORKS
7. MITSUBISHI-URAKAMI ORDNANCE PLANT

  Our air and sea power has already greatly reduced movment of Jap shipping south of Korea and should in the next few months cut it to a trickle if not choke it off entirely. Hence, there is no need for seizing further positions in order to block Japanese communications south of Korea.
  General MacArthur and Admiral Nimitz are in agreement with the Chiefs of Staff in selecting 1 November as the target date to go into Kyushu because by that time:
  a. *If we press preparations we can be ready.*
  b. *Our estimates are that our air action will have smashed practically every industrial target worth hitting in Japan as well as destroying huge areas in the Jap cities.,*
  c. *The Japanese Navy, if any still exists, will be completely powerless.*
  d. *Our sea action and air power will have cut Jap reinforcement capabilities from the mainland to negligible proportions.*

Straight Flush was the name of Superfortress B-29-36-MO 44-27301, victor number 85 that participated in the atomic bomb attack on Hiroshima on 6 August 1945. Assigned to the 393rd Bomb Squadron, 509th Composite Group, it was used as a weather reconnaissance aircraft and flew over the city before the final bombing to determine if conditions were favourable for an attack. *(USAAF)*

Marshall went on to state that there were important considerations regarding the 1 November date rather than a later one - the weather and cutting to a minimum Japanese time to prepare defences. Delays much after the November date meant that the weather situation in the succeeding months could be such that the invasion of Japan - and hence the end of the war - would be delayed for up to six months.

He said that the Kyushu operation was essential to a strategy of strangulation and appeared to be the least costly worthwhile operation following Okinawa. 'The basic point was that a lodgement in Kyushu was essential, both to tighten a stranglehold of blockade and bombardment of Japan and to force capitulation by invasion of the Tokyo Plain.

Marshall then went on to describe casualties in recent operations and what could be expected in the invasion of the Japanese mainland islands:

'*Our experience in the Pacific war is so diverse as to casualties that it is considered wrong to give any estimate in numbers. Using various combinations of Pacific experience, the War Department staff reaches the conclusion that the cost of securing a worthwhile position in Korea would almost certainly be greater than the cost of the Kyushu operation. Points on tho optimistic side of the Kyushu operation are that; General MacArthur has not yet accepted responsibility for going ashore where there would be disproportionate casualties. The nature of the objective area gives room for maneuver, both on the land and by sea'.*

Marshall coldly presented figures that showed that during the Leyte campaign, the US suffered 17,000 casualties, either killed, wounded or missing. Against this there were an estaminated 78,000 Japanese killed or taken prisoner. This created a ratio of US to Japanese of 1:4.6. At Luzon, there were 31,000 US casualties against 156,000 Japanese. creating a 1:5.0 ratio. At Iwo Jima there were 20,000 US casualties with 25,000 Japanese, a ratio of 1:1.25. At Okinawa there were 41,700 US casualties against at least 81,000 Japanese, a ratio of 1:2. Against these Pacific theatre figures Marshal noted that US casualties for the first 30 days of the Normany campaign were 42,000 and that the record for General MacArthur's operations from 1 March 1944 through to 1 May 1945 was 13,742 killed compared to 310,000 Japanese killed created a ratio of 22 to 1.

General Marshall continued: *There is reason to believe that the first 50 days in Kyushu should not exceed the price we have paid for Luzon. It is a grim fact that there is not an easy, bloodless way to victory in war and it is the thankless task of the leaders to maintain their firm outward front which holds the resolution of their subordinates.*

He went on to say that the total American assault troops for the Kyushu campaign were shown to be 766,700 - and that the opposition was expected to be eight Japanese divisions of of around 350,000. He stated that divisions were still being raised from the civilian population and that reinforcements from other areas of Japan was possible.

Marshall also read out a telegram from General MacArthur: *'I believe the operation presents less hazards of excessive loss that any other that have been suggested and that its decisive effect will eventually save lives by eliminating wasteful operations of nondecisive character. I regard the operation as the most*

The Great Artiste B-29-40-MO 44-27353, victor number 89, assigned to the 393rd Bomb Squadron, 509th Composite Group, that participated in the atomic bomb attacks on both Hiroshima and Nagasaki. Flown by 393rd commander Major Charles W. Sweeney, it was assigned to the Hiroshima mission, as the blast measurement instrumentation aircraft. On the mission to bomb Nagasaki it was to have been the aircraft carrying the bomb, but the mission schedule had been moved forward two days because of weather considerations and the instrumentation had not yet been removed from the aircraft. To avoid delaying the mission, Sweeney traded aircraft with the crew of Bockscar to carry the Fat Man atomic bomb to Nagasaki. (USAAF)

economical one in effort and lives that is possible. In this respect it must be remembered that the several preceeding months will involve practically no losses in ground troops and that sooner of later a decisive ground attack must be made. The hazard and loss will be greatly lessened if an attack is launched from Siberia sufficiently ahead of our target date to commit the enemy to major combat. I most earnestly recommend no change in OLYMPIC. Additional subsidiary attacks will simply build up our final total casualties'.

When it was General Eaker's turn to speak he said that he agreed completely with the the statements made by General Marshall in his digest of the memorandum prepared for the President. He had just received a cable in which General Arnold also expressed complete agreement. He stated that *'...any blockade of Honshu was dependent upon airdromes on Kyushu; that the air plan contemplated employment of 40 groups of heavy bombers against Japan and that those could not be deployed without the use of airfields on Kyushu. He said that those who advocated the use against Japan of air power alone overlooked the very impressive fact that air casualties are always much heavier when the air faces the enemy alone and that these casualties never fail to drop as soon as the ground forces come in. Present air casualties are averaging 2 percent per mission, about 30 percent per month. He wished to point out and to emphasise that delay favored only the enemy and he urged that there be no delay'.*

The Americans were very concerned about the Japanese code of Bushido, meaning 'Way of the Warrior', a Japanese code of conduct and a way of the samurai life, loosely analogous to the concept of chivalry. Since the build up to World War Two, Bushido was pressed into use for militarism, to present war as purifying, and death a duty. This was presented as revitalizing traditional values and 'transcending the modern'. Bushido would provide a spiritual shield to let soldiers fight to the end. As the war turned, the spirit of Bushido was invoked to urge that all depended on the firm and united soul of the nation. When the Battle of Attu was lost, attempts were made to make the more than two thousand Japanese deaths an inspirational epic for the fighting spirit of the nation. Arguments that the plans for the Battle of Leyte Gulf, involving all Japanese ships, would expose Japan to serious danger if they failed, were countered with the plea that the Navy be permitted to 'bloom as flowers of death'. The first proposals of organized suicide attacks met resistance because while Bushido called for a warrior to be always aware of death, but not to view it as the sole end, but the desperate straits brought about acceptance. It was expected that if the Americans were to invade the Japanese mainland islands, then its military and political leaders would invoke Bushido and every man, woman and child would fight to the death for their homeland and their Emperor.

Clearly there was both political and military concern about losses on both sides that would also include a high proportion from the Japanese civilian population. There was also the political and military will to bring the conflict with Japan to as swift a conclusion as possible.

The first test of an atomic bomb took place on 16 July 1945 at Alamogordo in the New Mexico desert. The news was immediately given to President Harry Truman, who was at the time at the Allied conference at Potsdam. He immediately

OPERATION CENTREBOARD

informed Winston Churchill and Chiang Kai-Shek of the success, but told Stalin only that the United States had developed a new and powerful weapon for use against Japan. However, Soviet agents in the USA had already passed the word to the USSR about the Manhattan Project, and Stalin was fully aware of what was going on. On 26 July the Allies issued a joint declaration which called for the unconditional surrender of Japan, indicating that the only alternative was prompt and utter destruction. Exactly what this meant was not specified, The fate of the Emperor was also left ambiguous, and was not mentioned in the declaration.

On 24 July a directive was sent to General Carl A. Spaatz ordering the 509th to deliver its first atomic bomb as soon as weather would permit. The cities of

Above: *Enola Gay* is pushed back over the pit in the special area at Tinian so that the *Little Boy* atomic bomb, numbered LII could be hoisted into the bomb bay. The bomb itself had been previously placed into the pit as seen on the left.

Many reports say it carried no markings, but it can be seen that it did carry '*LII*' and the original picture shows that it also carried a number of scribbled messages. The arming plugs, exchanged in flight are seen to the right of the single suspension lug. *(both USAAF)*

Hiroshima, Kokura, Niigata and Nagasaki were potential targets. Truman gave his final go-ahead from Potsdam on 31 July.

Project *Alberta*

Project *Alberta* was established within the Manhattan Project in March 1945, although its functions had been performed by various Project offices for months. Project *Alberta's* purpose was to deploy the bomb into the combat zone, and to ensure that it was ready for delivery at the earliest possible moment. That meant training bomb assembly teams and technical support personnel, providing logistic arrangements for the 509th's special weapons, and assembling and testing weapons and practice devices in the forward area.

The 509th Composite Group was deployed overseas in the spring of 1945. The 509th was formally a part of XXI Bombardment Command based in the Marianas. By July, the bombers were established at North Field on Tinian, which had just been completed for the 313th Bombardment Wing. Some of the 309th's aircraft were fitted with Curtiss electric propellers which had reversible pitch to reduce the landing run and carried special blade cuffs to increase the flow of cooling air into the R-3350 engines.

Deployment of key people to Tinian, including Parsons and Ramsey, was completed by the third week of July, and the first *Little Boy* practice bomb, L1, was assembled and dropped on 23 July. Four more *Little Boys* were assembled and test-dropped before the Hiroshima mission on 6 August. The first test *Fat Man*, F13, was dropped on 1 August. Three additional *Fat Men* were dropped before the Nagasaki mission on 9 August. In addition, the 509th carried out many practice missions, both over nearby waters, and against Japanese targets using the pumpkins.

The cruiser *Indianapolis* had delivered the *Little Boy* guns and bullet assembly to Tinian on 26 July. C-54s delivered the three separate pieces of the *Little Boy* target assembly, and other C-54s delivered *Fat Man's* initiator and plutonium core. Three B-29s left Kirtland, each carrying a *Fat Man* high-explosive pre-assembly. These did not arrive until 2 August.

In the early afternoon of 2 August Paul Tibbets and his bombardier Tom Ferebee arrived at LeMay's heradquarters on Guam to complete the details which Tibbets had been unable to incorporate in the draft mission order he cut the day

Paul Tibbets and the crew of *Enola Gay* return to Tinian after the first atomic attack. *(USAAF)*

before. LeMay had just been promoted to Chief of Staff of the Strategic Air Forces, so was in a good mood. Discussions took place on which would be the primary target; eventually Hiroshima was decided upon,with Kokura and Nagasaki as alternates. Hiroshima was chosen because intelligence reports had indicated that no Allied POW camps located there.

Legend has it that LeMay asked bombardier Ferebee to select his own aiming point - he unhesitatingly put his finger on the T-shaped Aioi Bridge shown on the air reconnaissance photograph. LeMay nodded, and Tibbets agreed, supposedly saying *'It's the most perfect aiming point I have seen in this whole damned war'*.

Operation Centreboard
The two atomic strikes on Japan - code-named Operation *Centerboard* - have been well reported. *Little Boy*, weapon number L11, was dropped on Hiroshima on the morning of 6 August; *Fat Man*, weapon number F31, was dropped on Nagasaki three days later. *Fat Man* F32 was held in reserve for the third strike, should President Truman direct its accomplishment, and 20th Air Force targeteers were reportedly preparing for a night-time strike on Tokyo when the stand-down order arrived. The records are not entirely in agreement, but there is some evidence suggesting that the nuclear core for F32 was dispatched from Albuquerque on the evening of 12 August, and that the aircraft was half-way to Hawaii when it received the return order. Fortunately, no further strikes were necessary.

Two months earlier, at a Los Alamos conference, one of Deke Parsons's staff had proposed 'arming' the bomb in flight. Groves and Robert Oppenheimer had opposed the idea, believing it would be too easy for something to go wrong. Nevertheless, Parsons, increasingly troubled by the spate of crashes on Tinian, had decided to insert the conventional explosive and its detonator into the rear of the bomb after the aircraft was airborne.

The first atomic strike was set for 6 August, and Col Tibbets was to command the attacking B-29. *Enola Gay* was not the only aircraft participating in the atomic bomb mission. Tibbetts assigned three B-29s to serve as weather scouts taking off one hour ahead of the main force. Major Claude Eatherly's *Straight Flush* would go to Hiroshima; *Jabbit III,* commanded by Major John Wilson, would fly to Kokura; the *Full House,* piloted by Major Ralph Taylor, was given Nagasaki.

Enola Gay turns off the taxiway to the 509th CG parking area after landing from the attack on Hiroshima. *(USAAF).*

Charles Sweeney's *Great Artiste*, and victor 91, commanded by Major George Marquardt and carrying photographic equipment, would accompany Tibbets to the actual target, whose final selection would still depend on the weather reports radioed back by the scouting B-29s. If all three cities were ruled out by weather conditions, *Enola Gay* would return to Iwo Jima, after Parsons had 'disarmed' the *Little Boy* in the air.

The seventh B-29, *Top Secret*, commanded by Captain Charles McKnight, was assigned to fly to Iwo Jima and park on the guarded apron by the specially constructed pit in case of any problems with *Enola Gay* after take off. Top Secret would wait here, and the bomb exchanged if needed.

Everything went smoothly, the weather scouts did their job and *Enola Gay* arrived over Hiroshima. Paul Tibbetts: *All that was necessary, upon reaching the I. P., was to fly the predetermined heading, with calculated allowance for the direction (170 degrees) and velocity (8 knots) of the wind. Since we were flying under visual conditions, the problem was simplified. The three-minute run gave Ferebee time to kill the drift and establish a perfectly stable platform for release of the bomb.*

Deke Parsons came forward and looked over my shoulder and so did Van Kirk, who was exchanging conversation with Ferebee in the nose of the plane. Navigator and bombardier compared notes and agreed that our ground speed was 285 knots (330 mph) and the drift to the right required an 8-degree correction. Adjustments were made to the bomb sight, which was now engaged to the autopilot for the bomb run. Ferebee, Van Kirk, and I were working as a team, as we had many times before over Europe and North Africa. As we approached the city, we strained our eyes to find the designated aiming point.

From a distance of 10 miles, Ferebee suddenly said, "Okay, I've got the bridge." He pointed dead ahead, where it was just becoming visible. Van Kirk, looking over his shoulders, agreed. "No question about it," he said, scanning an airphoto and comparing it with what he was seeing.

Van Kirk's job was finished so he went back and sat down, hooking up his

General Spaatz and his staff, together with Rear Admiral W R Purnell and Brig Gen Thomas F. Farrell, await the return of the *Enola Gay* to Tinian. *(USAAF)*

OPERATION CENTREBOARD

Maj. Thomas W. Ferebee on the left was bombardier of B-29 *'Enola Gay'* which atom-bombed Hiroshima, Japan. On the right is Maj. Monahan, Public Relations Officer from Washington, D.C.

This shows just how quicly the project changed from being highly secret to full public access. *(USAAF)*

safety belt and getting on the interphone. Now it was up to Tom and me. We were only 90 seconds from bomb release when I turned the plane over to him on autopilot.

"It's all yours," I told him, removing my hands from the controls and sliding back a bit in my seat in a not very successful effort to relax. My eyes were fixed on the center of the city, which shimmered in the early morning sunlight.

By this time, Tom Ferebee was pressing his left eye against the viewfinder of the bomb sight, using a headrest we had devised at Wendover to make sure that he was always in the same position.

"We're on target," he said, confirming that the sighting and release mechanism were synchronized, so that the drop would take place automatically at a precalculated point in our bomb run.

At 17 seconds after 9:14 A.M., just 60 seconds before the scheduled bomb release, he flicked a toggle switch that activated a high-pitched radio tone. This tone, ominous under the circumstances, sounded in the headphones of the men aboard our plane and the two airplanes that were with us; it was also heard by the men in the three weather planes, which were already more than 200 miles away on their return flight to Tinian.

Exactly one minute after it began, the radio tone ceased and at the same instant there was the sound of the pneumatic bomb-bay doors opening automatically. Out tumbled "Little Boy," a misnamed package of explosive force infinitely more devastating than any bomb or cluster of bombs ever dropped before.

By my watch, the time was 9:15 plus 17 seconds. In Hiroshima, it was 8:15. We had crossed a time zone in our flight from Tinian.

With the release of the bomb, the plane was instantly 9,000 pounds lighter. As a result, its nose leaped up sharply and I had to act quickly to execute the most important task of the flight: to put as much distance as possible between our plane and the point at which the bomb would explode.

The 155 degree diving turn to the right, with its 60 degree bank, put a great strain on the airplane and its occupants. Bob Caron, in his tail-gunner's station, had a wild ride that he described as something like being the last man in a game of crack-the-whip.

When we completed the turn, we had lost 1,700 feet and were heading away from our target with engines at full power. Midway through the turn, with its steep bank, it was necessary to back off on the ailerons (other pilots will understand this) to avoid the danger of a roll. I was flying this biggest of all bombers as if it were a fighter plane.

At the moment we released the bomb, the bomb-bay doors of Chuck Sweeney's plane also opened and out fell three instrument packages, whose purpose was to measure the effects of the detonation in terms of shock waves, radioactivity, and the like. These instruments, which sent back the results by radio, were suspended from parachutes that opened soon after their fall began. Their appearance accounted for an early erroneous report, from Japanese witnesses, that the bomb had been dropped by parachute.

General Eaker - at the head of the table, facing the camera, leads the debrief of Paul Tibbet's crew after the first A-bomb attack. (USAAF)

OPERATION CENTREBOARD 139

For me, struggling with the controls, the 43 seconds from bomb release to explosion passed quickly. To some in the plane, it seemed an eternity. Jeppson was quoted as saying that he had counted down the seconds in his mind, apparently too fast, and had the sickening feeling that the bomb was a dud.

Whatever our individual thoughts, it was a period of suspense. I was concentrating so intently on flying the airplane that the flash did not have the impact on my consciousness that one might think, even though it did light up the interior of the plane for a long instant.

There was a startling sensation other than visual, however, that I remember quite vividly to this day. My teeth told me, more emphatically than my eyes, of the Hiroshima explosion.

At the moment of the blast, there was a tingling sensation in my mouth and the very definite taste of lead upon my tongue. This, I was told later by scientists, was the result of electrolysis—an interaction between the fillings in my teeth and the radioactive forces that were loosed by the bomb.

"Little Boy" exploded at the preset altitude of 1,890 feet above the ground, but Bob Caron in the tail was the only one aboard our plane to see the incredible fireball that, in its atom-splitting fury, was a boiling furnace with an inner temperature calculated to be one hundred million degrees Fahrenheit.

I continued my course from the target, awaiting the shock wave, which required almost a minute to reach us. We were racing eastward away from Hiroshima, as was Chuck Sweeney in The Great Artiste. Sweeney had made a similar 155 degree turn, but to the left, as soon as he had dropped the instrument packages. Because his plane was charged with the photographic assignment, Marquardt had lagged behind, with movie and still cameras poised to make a record on film of the historic scene.

We must have been 9 miles from the point of the explosion when the shock wave reached us. This was the moment for which we had been bracing ourselves. Would the plane withstand the blow? The scientists were confident

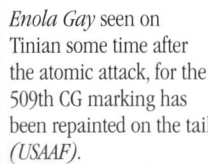

Enola Gay seen on Tinian some time after the atomic attack, for the 509th CG marking has been repainted on the tail. (USAAF).

that it would, yet they admitted there were some aspects of the nuclear weapon's behavior about which they were not quite certain.

Before Caron could warn us to brace ourselves, the wave struck the plane with violent force. Our B-29 trembled under the impact and I gripped the controls tightly to keep us in level flight. From my experience of flying through enemy flak over targets in Europe and Africa, I found the effect to be much like that produced by an anti-aircraft shell exploding near the plane.

Now that I knew we were safe from the effects of the blast, I began circling so that we could view the results. The giant purple mushroom, which the tail-gunner had described, had already risen to a height of 45,000 feet, 3 miles above our own altitude, and was still boiling upward like something terribly alive. It was a frightening sight, and even though we were several miles away, it gave the appearance of something that was about to engulf us.

Even more fearsome was the sight on the ground below. At the base of the cloud, fires were springing up everywhere amid a turbulent mass of smoke that had the appearance of bubbling hot tar. If Dante had been with us in the plane, he would have been terrified! The city we had seen so clearly in the sunlight a few minutes before was now an ugly smudge. It had completely disappeared under this awful blanket of smoke and fire.

Such was the damage caused, it was impossible to state with any degree of accuracy the loss of life and property. It was estimated that between 75,000 and 78,000 people were killed with a further 130,000 casualties. Between 48,000 and

Many pictures were taken after the first atomic attack - Paul Tibbetts made sure that the ground crew were not forgotten, as he is seen here with the 'other men of *Enola Gay.*' (USAAF)

OPERATION CENTREBOARD

70,000 buildings were destroyed and over 176,000 were made homeless. In that instant, the lone B-29 carrying a 9,000 lb bomb had delivered the equivalent power of the average bomb load of 2,000 conventional B-29s.

President Truman announced the dropping of the atomic bomb to the nation. At first, the Japanese did not know exactly what had happened, and poor communications between Tokyo and the devastated Hiroshima did not help. Even in spite of the bomb, there were still some Japanese officers who wanted the war to continue on to the bitter end. On 8 August Foreign Minister Shigenori Togo informed the Emperor that total destruction awaited Japan if it did not accept the terms of the Potsdam Declaration and surrender. The Emperor agreed with this gloomy assessment and Togo dispatched the Emperor's message to the Prime Minister, Baron Kantaro Suzuki, who was unable to convene the Supreme War council until the next day.

While the Japanese government was debating its options, there was no letup with the conventional B-29 raids. B-29s from the 58th, 73rd, and 313th BWs hit the Toyokawa Arsenal the next day. On the night of 7 August, the 525th BG dropped 189 tons of mines on several different targets. On 8 August, the 58th, 73rd, and 313th BWs dropped incendiary bombs on targets at Yawata in the southern island of Kyushu. At the same time, the 314th BW hit an industrial area of Tokyo. The Japanese defenses were still effective enough to down four B-29s during the Yawata raid and three at Tokyo.

In the meantime, since there was still no official reaction from Japan, the Americans felt that there was no alternative but to prepare a second atomic attack. The plutonium bomb *'Fat Man'* was loaded into a B-29 known as *Bockscar* (Martin-Omaha built B-29-35-MO serial number 44-27297), named after its commander, Capt Frederick C Bock. However, on this mission, the aircraft was flown by Major Sweeney, with Capt Bock flying one of the observation aircraft. The primary target was to be Kokura Arsenal, with Nagasaki as the alternative.

Original caption: Major Charles W. Sweeney, pilot of the B-29 'Bockscar' which dropped the atomic bomb on Nagasaki, Japan, 9 August 1945, is shown before his mission shaking hands with Colonel Paul W. Tibbets. On the right is Capt James F Van Pelt, Major Sweeney's navigator. Through a curious error, caused perhaps by the removal of the names from the planes, the official communique stated that 'The Great Artiste' carried the bomb on 9th August. However, the aircraft serial numbers in the mission report, as well as verification from Capt Frederick C Bock, the pilot of 'The Great Artiste' which was flown as one of the observation planes on this mission, proves the fact that 'Bock's Car' actually dropped the atomic bomb on Nagasaki. (USAAF)

BOEING B-29 SUPERFORTRESS

Crew labels on photo, left to right: M/S.J. KUHAREK, SGT. A. DEHART, 2ND. LT. F. OLIVI, S/S.E. BUCKLEY, CPT. K. BEAHAN, MAJ.C. SWEENEY PILOT, S/S. R. GALLAGHER, CPT. J. VAN PELT, 1ST LT. C. ALBURY, CPL. A. SPITZ

2ND ATOMIC BOMBER CREW
AUG 11, 1945

Interestingly both B-29s that dropped atomic bombs in anger have suffered from 'mis-identity' over the years. Many commentators call Tibbets' machine *The Enola Gay,* which is clearly was not, and also refer to Sweeney's aircraft as *Bock's Car,* which also is wrong.

Bockscar took off on 9 August with *Fat Man* on board. This time, the primary target of Kokura was obscured by dense smoke left over from the earlier B-29 raid on nearby Yawata, and the bombardier could not pinpoint the specified aiming point despite three separate runs. So Sweeney turned to the secondary target, Nagasaki. There were clouds over Nagasaki as well, and a couple of runs over the target had to be made before the bombardier could find an opening in the clouds. At 11:00 AM, *Fat Man* was released from the aircraft and the bomb exploded. The yield was estimated at 22 kilotons.

Paul Tibbets: *On Tinian the next day, I went ahead with plans for the second atomic mission. LeMay assumed that I would be flying this one also, but I had decided otherwise. I told him that Chuck Sweeney would drop the second bomb. Since his own plane, The Great Artiste, had been outfitted with special instruments for the Hiroshima flight and would play the same role on this mission, Sweeney was assigned to fly Bockscar.*

That mission came close to being a fiasco, through no fault of Sweeney. Everything went wrong, starting with a fuel pump malfunction that made it impossible to use 600 gallons of fuel in the bomb-bay tanks. At the rendezvous

Charles Sweeney and his crew after the second atomic attack. It is thought that the aircraft is 44-27297 *Bockscar,* despite the lack of nose markings. Left to right: M/Sgt J Kuharek, Sgt A Dehart, 2/Lt F Olivi, S/Sgt E Buckley, Cpt K Beahan, Maj C Sweeney, S/Sgt R Gallagher, Capt J Van Pelt, 1/Lt C Albury, Cpl A Spitz. *(USAAF) point south of Kyushu, one of the accompanying planes failed to show up and 45 minutes were lost. Kokura was the primary target, but visibility was poor.*

Sweeney circled for almost an hour before giving up. The result was another loss of precious time, particularly serious when his fuel supply was limited. Finally, the bomb was dropped on Nagasaki, the secondary target, under conditions that were less than ideal. It missed the Aiming Point by a wide margin, but the damage was extensive nevertheless. Returning with a marginal supply of gasoline, Sweeney managed to make an emergency landing on Okinawa with nearly empty tanks.

Approximately 35,000 people died at Nagasaki in the immediate blast.

That very same day, the Soviet Union declared war on Japan, and launched a massive invasion of Manchuria. The Emperor ordered that the government accept the Allied terms of surrender at once. It took time for the full details to be worked out, and there was a very real danger that some elements of the Japanese military would still not accept surrender and would attempt a coup even against the Emperor. In the meantime conventional bombing of Japanese targets still continued, with a record number of 804 B-29s hitting targets in Japan on 14 August. On the morning of 15 August, the Emperor broadcast word of Japan's surrender in an address to his nation. Most of his subjects had never heard his voice before.

All further offensive operations against Japan ceased after the Emperor's broadcast. After that time, most of the B-29s in the Pacific were diverted to missions

Bockscar as it was in later years when it was flown to the USAF Museum for display on 26 September 1961. *(USAF)*

of mercy, dropping food and clothing to thousands of Allied prisoners of war held in Japan, China, Manchuria, and Korea. 1066 B-29s participated in 900 missions to 154 camps. Some 63,500 prisoners were provided with 4470 tons of supplies These flights cost eight B-29s lost with 77 crew members aboard.

The surrender was formally signed on 2 September aboard the battleship *Missouri,* bringing the Pacific War to an end.

Silverplate postwar.

After the war, the USAAF demobilised so rapidly that, within a year, it had become virtually ineffective as a fighting force. So debilitated had long-range bombing units become, that in early 1947 Strategic Air Command found itself unable to identify the precise location and condition of all its *Silverplate* aircraft. As a result, inspectors were sent out to track down and physically examine all the aircraft remaining in the *Silverplate* fleet. So many modifications and changes - some documented, others not - had been made that no two aircraft were identical. Drawings and paperwork had been discarded or misplaced, and new engineering materials would have to be drawn up from scratch before further improvements could be incorporated. Even the very name *Silverplate* had become compromised through over-use and carelessness. To mark renewed emphasis on security, the USAAF's atomic weapon programme ceased to be called *Silverplate* on 12 May 1947; henceforth, a new codeword, *Saddletree*, would take its place.

PEACE - AND A 'POLICE ACTION'

The arrival of V-J Day in September of 1945 resulted in the cancellation of orders for 5092 B-29s. However, a limited number of B-29s still on the production lines at the end of the war were allowed to be completed. The last of 3627 B-29s was delivered on 10 June 1946.

Vast numbers of B-29s were placed in storage. Unlike the B-17 and B-24, B-29s were not declared surplus and released to the commercial market. This is the primary reason why so few B-29s survive today.

B-29s that remained flying after the end of World War Two formed part of Strategic Air Command (SAC). By 1947, as a result of postwar reductions, only six B-29 bomb groups remained in service with SAC, with only the 509th Group being equipped for the delivery of nuclear bombs.

SAC had evolved out of the 'Continental Air Forces' (CAF) that had been established on 13 December 1944 and activated two days later. On 21 March 1946, CAF was disestablished as part of a major reorganization of the USAAF. Within the United States, the USAAF was divided into three separate commands: Tactical Air Command (TAC), Air Defense Command (ADC), and Strategic Air Command (SAC). Airfields formerly assigned to CAF were reassigned to one of these three major commands.

SAC's original headquarters was at Bolling Field, the headquarters of the

Under the name of 'Project Cocoon' hundreds of B-29s were stored for future use, as seen here on 11 July 1946.. The aircraft were coated with 'Spraylat', a peelable protective system. *(USAF)*

RB-29 44-61727 of the 31st Reconnaissance Squadron, somewhere over Korea. Note the legend 'United States Air Force' on the forward fuselage amd 'USAF' on the wing. (USAF)

former Continental Air Forces in Washington, DC. The headquarters organization of CAF was designated Strategic Air Command. Its first commander was General George C. Kenney. SAC HQ moved to Andrews AFB, MD on 20 October 1946.

Strategic Air Command was created with the stated mission of providing long range bombing capabilities anywhere in the world. But because of multiple factors including the massive post World War Two demobilization and Kenney's unhappiness with being assigned to SAC, for the first two years of its existence, SAC existed mainly on paper. During this period, the United States Air Force itself was established on 18 September 1947. The situation began to change when on 19 October 1948, Lieutenant General Curtis LeMay assumed leadership of Strategic Air Command, a command he would continue to hold until June 1957. Soon after taking command, on 9 November LeMay relocated SAC to Offutt AFB, south of Omaha, Nebraska. It was under the leadership of LeMay that SAC developed the technical capabilities, strategic planning and operational readiness to carry out its stated mission of being able to strike anywhere in the world. Specifically, during LeMay's command, SAC embraced and integrated new technological developments in the areas of in-air refuelling, jet engines, and ballistic missiles into its operations.

By 1950, B-29s were no longer seen as the sophisticated, ultra-moden aircraft that they were some eight years earlier, and had been reclassified as 'medium' bombers, their long-range strategic mission having been taken over by the B-36. At that time, the USAF inventory included 1787 B-29 bombers and 162 RB-29 reconnaissance aircraft, either in storage or in service with eight Bomb Groups and one Strategic Reconnaissance Group.

However, B-29s were soon to be in action again. On 25 June 1950, the armed forces of the Democratic People's Republic (North Korea) under Premier Kim Il Sung, backed by the Soviet Union crossed the 38th Parallel and invaded the republic of Korea (South Korea) under Dr. Syngman Rhee, ostensibly backed by

PEACE - AND A 'POLICE ACTION'

the USA. On 27 June the UN Security Council voted to assist the South Koreans in resisting the invasion. President Harry Truman authorised General Douglas MacArthur, the commander of the US occupying forces in Japan, to commit units to go to the defence of Syngman Rhee's embattled troops.

MacArthur ordered General George E Stratemeyer, CIC of the Far Eastern Air Force (FEAF) to attack North Korean targets of opportunity between the front lines and the 38th parallel, particularly troop concentrations and supply dumps. At that time, the 22 B-29s of the 19th Bomb Group stationed at Anderson Field on Guam were the only aircraft capable of hitting the Korean peninsula, and this unit was ordered to move to Kadena air base on Okinawa and begin attacks on North Korea. These raids - effectively using the B-29 as tactical support machines for the South Korean Army, something for which they had not been designed for - began on 28 June. Next day, clearance was given for B-29 attacks on airfields in North Korea. The B-29s were frequently diverted into tactical attacks against advancing North Korean troops.

On 8 July a special FEAF Bomber Command was set up under the command of Major General Emmett O'Donnell, who established his headquarters at Yokata, Japan, and in addition to the 19th BG, was given two Bomb Wings - the 22nd and 92nd - transferred temporarily from SAC on 3 July by USAF Chief of Staff General Hoyt S Vandenberg. These aircraft, along with six RB-29 long-range reconnaissance aircraft belonging to SAC's 31st Strategic Reconnaissance Squadron on Okinawa, 24 weather-reconnaissance WB-29s and four SB-29 'Superdumbo' rescue aircraft, gave O'Donnell a theoretical strength of approximately 100 aircraft. Unfortunately his first brief came from MacArthur, who directed him to use them north of the Man River, principally against targets of opportunity on the battlefield - a role which should have been carried out by fighter bombers.

Original caption: 'B-29s of the U.S. Far East Air Forces speed to dump tons of bombs on the Chinese Red's military targets. In round-the-clock attacks, these bombers are carrying the bittter taste of war home to the Communist hordes'. (USAF)

Original Caption: *'When members of the United Nations Forces moved north over the 38th Parallel into the well-known industrial cities, they found gutted buildings and mounds of twisted steel that were formerly vital to Communistic Korea's military forces. Targets such as the large marshalling yards of Pyongyang, the oil refinery at Wonsan, and the key Kan-ni Arsenal near Pyongyang, are evidence of the efforts put forth by the U.S. Air Force B-29s flying the long air miles from bases in Japan and Okinawa. Upon request from the United Nations, bombardiers of the huge bombers paid close attention to pin-pointed military targets, and left surrounding civilian homes and business sections almost untouched. B-29s of the U.S. Air Force drop their 500-pound bombs on a strategic target in North Korea. These planes have devastated enemy North Korean supply lines, industrial areas and troop concentrations with their precision bombing.* (USAF)

The results were disappointing, and by 18 July Vandenberg was complaining to MacArthur that this was no way to treat the B-29s. MacArthur agreed and diverted the bombers to interdiction raids nearer the 38th parallel, designed to cut off the invading North Koreans in the south from their sources of supply. This was still not a worthy role for the strategic bombers, but at least it was a more formalised approach to their use. Interdiction Campaign No 1 was initiated on 4 August and O'Donnell was at last given definite target priorities. Between 4 and 10 August the B-29s hit a variety of marshalling yards and rail complexes in North Korea in an attempt to disrupt supplies, but once again the results were poor, because of a lack of pre-strike intelligence information. 47 aircraft hit the Cho-Sen Nitrogen Explosives Plant at Konan, and 39 B-29s attacked the Bogun Chemical Plant. As a result, between 12 and 20 August the emphasis was shifted to a number of strategic road and rail bridges north of the 37th parallel. Most of these were destroyed, even though they were of extremely strong construction, and the B-29s had to evolve entirely new combat techniques using unsatisfactory weapons. Both the 22nd and 92nd BWs, used to training for atomic strikes at very high altitude

PEACE - AND A 'POLICE ACTION'

Bombs Away-Regardless of the type of enemy target lying in this rugged, mountainous terrain of Korea, very little will remain after the falling bombs have done their work. This striking photograph of the lead bomber was made from a B-29 of the Far East Air Forces 19th Bomber Group on the 150th combat mission the 19th Bomber Group had flown since the start of the Korean war.

With his head covered by a fur parka reminiscent of the men of the great Northwest, 1st Lt Carl L Hinchey, 1207 Grand St, Duncan, Okla, a US Air Force B-29 "Superfort" pilot with the 98th Bomb Wing in Japan, was ready, in his protective clothing, for another high-altitude bombing attack against Communist targets in North Korea. (both USAF)

and equipped with B-29s which were only capable of delivering 500lb bombs, were not really suited to the tasks; although capable of carrying 1000 and 2000 lb weapons, the crews experienced tremendous problems. One particular railroad bridge at Seoul, assigned to the 19th, took three weeks to knock down, with strikes arranged every single day. Nevertheless by the end of August, O'Donnell could report the complete destruction of 37 of the 44 bridges involved in the campaign, with the remaining seven unusable.

USAF mission planners were unhappy with this emphasis upon tactical strikes, preferring a proper strategic bombing campaign against North Korean industry, something which was initially pressed for in early July. Vandenberg sent two more SAC Bomb Wings to Japan, the 98th and 307th, and in late July he was authorized to begin the necessary planning. SAC Intelligence, using RB-29s of the 31st SRS, earmarked five major industrial centres for attack: the North Korean capital of Pyongyang - a source

Original Caption: *'Combat infantrymen must know how to do a flat crawl, hugging the ground to avoid being hit. Combat airmen must also know how to maneuver horizontally, only they often do it high in the night skies over North Korea. This U.S. Air force B-29 gunner coming through the 35-foot tunnel connecting forward and rear pressurized compartments on his 'Superfort' is A/2C James J. Prater, Beaver Creek Drive, Powell, Tenn. Wearing parachute and 'Mae West' life preserver adds to the close sqeeze in negotiating the tunnel which runs through the big aircraft's twin bomb bays. Airman Prater flies nine-hour, 2,000 mile roundtrip missions from his 98th Bomb Wing base in Japan, to attack key Communist targets in North Korea.*

Original caption: *'20TH AIR FORCE, OKINAWA -- A/2C Don W. Murray of Mazon, Ill., flashes a victory smile from the gun blister of his U.S. Air Force B-29 "Superfort" after shooting down a Communist jet fighter. Airman Murray shot down the enemy jet during a pre-dawn strike against a Red staff school on the west coast of North Korea, October 8. Sighting the enemy fighter approaching from the rear, Murray fired as it attempted to sneak into the bomber stream. After five bursts, the jet broke away and exploded. Murray is a left gunner with the 307th Bomb Wing, based on Okinawa.*

KOREAN B-29 OPERATIONS - HOW THE PRESS SAW THEM

Original Caption: *'IN HIS ARMOR. Normally a good-sized man, Captain Melvin E. Jarvis, 1318 Roberta Street, Salt Lake City, Utah, pilot of a B-29 "Superfort" of the 307th Bomb Group, based on Okinawa, looks gigantic after donning over 105 pounds of flight gear necessary for combat missions. Captain Jarvis is shown at the controls of his B-29 just prior to take-off on a mission on Communist positions in North Korea. (USAF)*

PEACE - AND A 'POLICE ACTION' 151

of armaments and aircraft as well as an important rail centre; Wonsan, which had oil refineries around a major sea port; Hungnam for its chemical and metallurgical industries; Chongjin, for the iron foundries and rail yards and Rashin, which was a major naval base with oil storage facilities. Other targets of secondary importance included five east-coast hydroelectric power complexes. Clearly there were enough targets to justify a strategic campaign, particularly as the majority were conveniently concentrated in the northeast. It looked as if the B-29s could be used in their proper role.

The raids began on 30 July, when the Hungnam industrial complex was flattened, and this success was maintained against the other primary targets as enthusiasm for the venture grew in Washington and Tokyo. In early September O'Donnell was able to report the destruction of all known industrial facilities in the North with the exception of those at Rashin which, after one B-29 raid, had been deleted from the target list by Presidential order. Rashin was only seventeen miles from the Soviet border so it was thought that even a slight bombing error could cause a weapon to stray across the border. These raids proved the value of the B-29 when correctly assigned, so justifying the USAF insistence on correct planning. O'Donnell was already moving on to his secondary targets - the first raid in fact took place on 26 September against the Fusen hydro-electric plant - when the entire course of the war was dramatically changed. For a number of reasons the B-29s were never again to hit strategic targets.

The cancellation of the strategic campaign occured when most of the targets in North Korea were captured by UN forces in October 1950. An amphibious landing at Inchon and an advance eastward to Seoul in late September threatened to cut the North Koreans off from their homeland. An Allied offensive from Pusan created more pressure and the North Koreans began a retreat which, harried by constant air strikes, degenerated into a rout. South Korean forces crossed the 38th parallel on 1 October, Pyongyang fell eighteen days later and a UN advance toward

A pair of probables claimed by B-29 crews. These railroad bridges cross Kum River about 10 miles north of Taejon were hit on 6 August 1950. On near bridge: left approach out; right line out; direct hit on bridge structure. On far bridge, direct hit. *(USAF)*

Original Caption: Ten tons of bombs from Air Force B-29 Superforts of the FEAF Bomber Command sever these two important railroad bridges near Pakchon, 40 miles north of Pyongyang, in North Korea in an attack made on July 27, 1950. As Captain Meterio Montez of Gardner, Colorado, lead bombardier, released his bombs, the Superforts in the formation did likewise. Montez was in the B-29 piloted by Captain Leslie Westberg, Spokane, Washington. Military supply traffic from North Korea formerly routed over these rail lines to the battle zone will be affected by this phase of the U.S. Air Force's interdiction plan. (USAF)

the Chinese border on the Yalu River met little opposition. Stratemeyer diverted many B-29s to tactical strikes in what everyone thought was the dying moments of a successful land campaign; strategic bombing became unnecessary and FEAF Bomber Command was disbanded on 27 October, with the 22nd and 92nd BWs returning to SAC duties in the USA. Victory seemed assured.

Nothing could have been further from the truth - the war in Korea was soon to take a different and far more dangerous turn. China had repeatedly warned MacArthur against crossing the 38th Parallel, and in October, Chinese forces had begun to enter North Korea in response to the advancing UN forces. On 1 November Chinese MiG-15s appeared in battle for the first time, and Chinese forces were encountered in ground fighting in and around the Yalu. This forced FEAF Bomber Command to be hastily reactivated to face the new threat. Because of political considerations, B-29 attacks against strategic targets in China were forbidden, and B-29 raids had to be restricted to tactical targets on the Korean peninsula. Between 8 and 25 November, B-29s hit the southern approaches to a number of bridges crossing the Yalu river, since attacks on the northern spans would have been an attack on Chinese territory. Sinuiju, Hyesanjin, Uiju, Manpojin and Chongsonjin were all attacked and O'Donnell reported a 65% success rate, but it was all an illusion; many of the broken spans were quickly replaced by pontoons which were only used at night. The bombs used in attacking these spans were too small to do significant damage, and the Chinese buildup of supplies and troops continued unchecked. In addition, the B-29s began to suffer casualties, with one shot down and several damaged.

On 25 November Chinese troops intervened massively in the war, rapidly pushing the UN forces back below the 38th parallel. Any chance for the forced reunification of Korea had been lost. The B-29s flew close support missions in an attempt to slow the Chinese advance. It was not until the end of December that the line had stabilized. However, this time daylight bombing flights, which had

PEACE - AND A 'POLICE ACTION'

previously been unopposed, now began to experience flak and air opposition. Lavochkin LA-7 and La-9 and Yakovlev Yak-9P fighters began to appear, later supplemented by large numbers of MiG-15 jet fighters.

It was not just Soviet and North Korean aircraft that came up to investigate the B-29s. On 28 July 1950 a flight of Supermarine Seafires from a British aircraft carrier was vectored to investigate a 'bogey', which turned out to be several B-29 Superfortresses. One of the B-29s opened fire on the No.3 Seafire, as he passed the B-29 at about 300 yards range; the British pilot rolled his Seafire onto its back, and bailed out, the fuel tank having been hit. The sea was too rough to pick him up with the Sea Otter amphibian, and he had an hour's wait before the USS *Eversole* rescued him.

MacArthur and 'the bomb'

In an attempt to slow the Chinese advance, MacArthur ordered the bridges across the Yalu to be bombed. After due consultation with his advisors, Truman declared that he would not approve of such an action, and the Joint Chiefs cancelled the order. When MacArthur protested, the President and the Joint Chiefs authorised the bombings, subject to the caveat that Chinese air space not be violated. Major General Emmett O'Donnell would later cite this to the Congressional enquiry in MacArthur's replacement as an example of undue political interference in military operations. The Yalu River had many bends, and in some cases there were very restricted lines of approach without overflying it. This made life easier for the Communist anti aircraft gunners, but correspondingly less so for the aircrew. Within weeks, MacArthur was forced to retreat, and both Truman and MacArthur were forced to contemplate the prospect of abandoning Korea entirely.

With this oncoming defeat a distinct possibility, talk of using atomic bombs

B-29-50-MO 44-86340 *Wolf Pack* of the 345th BS, 98th BG based at Yokata on Japan seen over the clouds on its way to Korea. *(USAF)*

A B-29 crew parades before their aircraft in Japan as part of the standard pre-flight checks before another mission to Korea. (USAF)

was making the rounds of Washington. General Hoyt Vandenberg, speaking for the Air Force, suggested they were prepared to use them.

On 5 November 1950, the Joint Chiefs of Staff issued orders for retaliatory atomic bombing of Manchurian military bases if either their armies crossed into Korea or if the Peoples Republic of China or the Korean Peoples Army bombers attacked Korea from there. The President ordered the transfer of nine Mark-4 nuclear capsules '... *to the Air Force's Ninth Bomb Group, the designated carrier of the weapons, and signed an order to use them against Chinese and Korean targets'*.

There is some controversy wether MacArthur demanded or suggested a plan to use numerous atomic bombs. Legend has it that MacArthur insisted he be given the sole right to use fifty atomic weapons as he saw fit. In later years in his testimony before the Senate Inquiry, he said that he had never recommended their use. In 1960 he challenged a statement by Truman that he had wanted to use nuclear weapons, and Truman issued a retraction, stating that he had no documentary evidence of this claim, and it was merely his personal opinion. According to Major General Courtney Whitney, MacArthur did at one point consider a bizarre plan to use radioactive wastes to seal off North Korea, something originally proposed in a 1950 study by Louis Johnson, the United States Secretary of Defense.

At a press conference on 30 November 1950, Truman was asked about the use of nuclear weapons:

Questioner: *Mr. President, I wonder if we could retrace that reference to the atom bomb? Did we understand you clearly that the use of the atomic bomb is under active consideration?*

Truman: *Always has been. It is one of our weapons.*

Questioner: *Does that mean, Mr. President, use against military objectives, or civilian?*

Truman: *It's a matter that the military people will have to decide. I'm not a military authority that passes on those things.*

Questioner: *Mr. President, perhaps it would be better if we are allowed to quote your remarks on that directly?*

Truman: *I don't think—I don't think that is necessary.*

Questioner: *Mr. President, you said this depends on United Nations action. Does that mean that we wouldn't use the atomic bomb except on a United Nations authorization?*

Truman: *No, it doesn't mean that at all. The action against Communist China depends on the action of the United Nations. The military commander in the field will have charge of the use of the weapons, as he always has.*

The implication was that the authority to use nuclear weapons had been handed over to MacArthur. Truman was forced to issue a clarification that *'...only the President can authorize the use of the atom bomb, and no such authorization has been given'*.

On 5 April 1951, the Joint Chiefs of Staff drafted orders for MacArthur authorising attacks on Manchuria and the Shantung Peninsula if the Chinese launched airstrikes against his forces originating from there. Next day Truman met the chairman of the United States Atomic Energy Commission, Gordon Dean, and arranged for the transfer of a number of nuclear bombs to military control. Dean was apprehensive about delegating the decision on how they should be used to MacArthur, who lacked expert technical knowledge of the weapons and their effects. The Joint Chiefs were not entirely comfortable about giving them to MacArthur either, for fear that he might prematurely carry out his orders.

MacArthur insisted on bombing the Yalu power plants with multiple strikes by B-29s. A state of affairs was rapidly going from bad to disastrous. Supposedly, in

A B-29 of SAC's 98th Bomb Wing salvos both bomb bays at the same time over a North Korean target on 13 July 1951. *(USAF)*

the war room Vandenberg dismissed the idea of further reprimands to MacArthur. *'What good would it do? He won't obey the orders'.* General Ridgway exploded. *'You can relieve any commander who won't obey orders, can't you?'*

MacArthur again requested that the Pentagon grant him a field commander's discretion to employ nuclear weapons as necessary. He wanted them stockpiled in Okinawa; it seems that despite what he was later to claim, there was a plan to drop between 30 and 50 atomic bombs strung across the neck of Manchuria from the Sea of Japan to the Yellow Sea. The Russians, MacArthur claimed, would be intimidated by this and do nothing.

With all American forces in full retreat, some of the decisions made by MacArthur were accused of accelerating the crisis. MacArthur rejected any type of negotiated settlement. He had derailed the US initiative which was actually a dare for China to continue the fighting, as he had always wanted a war with China.

MacArthur not only meddled with the use of the B-29, he also interferred with policy at the highest level. On 1 December, MacArthur was asked by a reporter if the restrictions on operations against Chinese forces on the far side of the Yalu River were *'...a handicap to effective military operations'.* MacArthur replied that they were indeed *'...an enormous handicap, unprecedented in military history'.* On 6 December Truman issued a directive requiring all military officers and diplomatic officials to clear with the State Department all but routine statements before making them public and to *'...refrain from direct communications on military or foreign policy with newspapers, magazines, and other publicity media.'* Despite this order, MacArthur made similar remarks in press statements on 13 February and 7 March 1951. On 23 March, he issued a public statement to the Chinese that spoiled Truman's opportunity to present the Chinese with a cease-fire proposal. Instead, MacArthur issued an ultimatum:

'Of even greater significance than our tactical successes has been the clear revelation that this new enemy, Red China, of such exaggerated and vaunted military power, lacks the industrial capability to provide adequately many critical items necessary to the conduct of modern war. He lacks the manufacturing base and those raw materials needed to produce, maintain and operate even moderate air and naval power, and he cannot provide the essentials for successful ground operations, such as tanks, heavy artillery and other refinements science has introduced into the conduct of military campaigns. Formerly his great numerical potential might well have filled this gap but with the development of existing methods of mass destruction numbers alone do not offset the vulnerability inherent in such deficiencies. Control of the seas and the

Occasionally B-29s used RATOG (Rocket Assisted Take Off) to get airborne. *(USAF)*

An Armourer prepares another bombload in the bomb bay of a B-29 in Japan. *(USAF)*

air, which in turn means control over supplies, communications and transportation, are no less essential and decisive now than in the past. When this control exists, as in our case, and is coupled with an inferiority of ground firepower in the enemy's case, the resulting disparity is such that it cannot be overcome by bravery, however fanatical, or the most gross indifference to human loss.

These military weaknesses have been clearly and definitely revealed since Red China entered upon its undeclared war in Korea. Even under the inhibitions which now restrict the activity of the United Nations forces and the corresponding military advantages which accrue to Red China, it has been shown its complete inability to accomplish by force of arms the conquest of Korea. The enemy, therefore must by now be painfully aware that a decision of the United Nations to depart from its tolerant effort to contain the war to the area of Korea, through an expansion of our military operations to its coastal areas and interior bases, would doom Red China to the risk of imminent military collapse. These basic facts being established, there should be no insuperable difficulty in arriving at decisions on the Korean problem if the issues are resolved on their own merits, without being burdened by extraneous matters not directly related to Korea, such as Formosa or China's seat in the United Nations.'

The Pentagon received his message, which infuriated many high ranking officials. Truman had considered firing MacArthur many times previous to this, but this was the last straw. MacArthur's leadership could no longer be tolerated. A meeting was held with Truman to determine how to get rid of MacArthur. Truman is said to have insisted *'I'm going to fire the son of a bitch right now'*. MacArthur was ordered to turn over his command to Lt General Ridgway. General Bradley warned Truman that if MacArthur heard about the orders before they reached him officially he might resign in a fit of arrogant pique. Truman exclaimed *'The son of a bitch isn't going to resign on me, I want him fired'*. So MacArthur's dismissal was announced on late night radio: *'I have decided that I must make a change in command in the Far East. I have, therefore, relieved General MacArthur of his command and have designated Lt Gen Matthew Ridgway as his replacement'*.

Truman would later report that *'I was ready to kick him into the North China Sea, I was never so put out in my life.'*

He said of MacArthur's statement: *'This was a most extraordinary statement for a military commander of the United Nations to issue on his own responsibility. It was an act totally disregarding all directives to abstain from any declarations on foreign policy. It was in open defiance of my orders as President and as Commander in Chief. This was a challenge to the authority of the President under the Constitution. It also flouted the policy of the United Nations. By this act MacArthur left me no choice—I could no longer tolerate his insubordination'.*

USAF planners continued to search for a definate B-29 targetting policy so as to ensure that the enormous strike potential of these bombers could be concentrated against the enemy. In February 1951, a series of interdiction raids began against Chinese supply lines in the northwest of Korea. Up to early 1951, in the absence of organised defenses, B-29s had been able to make bombing runs at altitudes as low as 10,000 feet without any danger. However, on 25 February four B-29s on a raid against Sunchon were attacked by eight MiG-15s. Suddenly, these unescorted raids at low altitudes became extremely dangerous. Consequently, the missions were now flown at 20,000 feet, defensive formations were used, and fighter escort was provided by F-80C Shooting Stars and F-84E Thunderjets. Unfortunately, these fighters were

A Tarzon bomb is loaded under a 19th BG B-29. *(USAF)*

ineffective against the MiG-15, and coordination between the bombers and fighters was often poor. On 1 March a Superfortress formation was jumped by nine MiGs. On 12 April, a force of 48 B-29s attacking the railroad bridge linking Korea with Antung, Manchuria was attacked by dozens of MiGs, and three B-29s were shot down and seven were damaged. Because of these losses, General Stratemeyer called off these raids and diverted the B-29s to close-support raids against Chinese targets further south around the 38th parallel.

Radio-controlled bombs known as 'Razons' - first used in World War Two - were tried out from B-29s against bridges in late 1950 and early 1951. They were released from the bomb bay and then guided onto the target by remote control from the bombardier. They were named 'Razon' because the controller could alter RAnge and AZimuth ONly once they left the aircraft. They were moderately effective, but had the disadvantage of weighing only 1000 pounds. Their successors were known as 'Tarzons', and weighed 12,000 pounds each.

The ASM-A-1 Tarzon, also known as VB-13, was a guided bomb developed by the United States Army Air Forces during the late 1940s. Mating the guidance system of the earlier Razon radio-controlled weapon with a British 'Tallboy' 12,000-pound bomb, a weapon that was used to great effect by RAF Lancasters against German targets, including the German battleship *Tirpitz* in the latter part of World War Two, the ASM-A-1 saw brief operational service in the Korean War.

In addition to the 12,000 pounds nominal weight of the 'Tallboy' it was based on, the annular wing and control sufaces boosted the weight of Tarzon by an additional 1,100 pounds. The size and weight of the ASM-A-1 were such that the weapon would not fit inside the bomb bay of a Superfortress; instead, the weapon was carried in a semi-recessed mounting, half the weapon being exposed to the airstream. This increased drag on the carrying aircraft, in addition to causing turbulent airflow that could affect the handling of the B-29.

Limited testing was conducted during 1948 and 1949; additional testing at Alamagordo, New Mexico in 1950 led to the Tarzon being approved for operational service in the Korean War.

Tarzon saw its first combat use in December 1950, the ASM-A-1 replacing the Razon in operational service. Used solely by the 19th Bomb Group, the first Tarzon drop in combat took place on 14 December 1950.

Tarzon was used in strikes against North Korean bridges and other hardened targets, its improved accuracy over conventional 'dumb bombs' leading to the confirmed destruction of at least six high-priority targets during approximately six months of combat use; these included a hydroelectric plant, proving the effectiveness of guided weapons against conventional targets as well as bridges.

Thirty Tarzon missions were flown between December 1950 and March 1951; the weapon's success led to a contract for the production of 1,000 additional ASM-A-1 missiles. On 29 March 1951, however, a Tarzon strike against Sinuiju went awry; the group commander's aircraft was destroyed as a result of the

The size of a Tarzon bomb is ably shown in this picture. It was based on the Royal Air Force 'Tallboy' weapon in the Second World War. *(USAF)*

The B-29 was a big aircraft and occasionally it had to be moved from areas and circumstances to which it was not designed. The USAF came up with this connected half-track pair of vehicles that could also jack up the aircraft for removal from soft ground. *(both USAF)*

premature detonation of the bomb when, the aircraft suffering mechanical difficulties, the weapon was jettisoned in preparation for ditching. The thirtieth, and as it proved final, mission, three weeks following the Sinuiju mission, also suffered an unintentional detonation of a jettisoned, supposedly 'safe' bomb, although this time without the loss of the aircraft.

An investigation proved that the fault lay in the construction of the bomb's tail; breaking up on impact, a 'safed' bomb would have its arming wire removed, rendering it 'unsafe' and detonating the weapon. Modifications were made to solve the problem, but the damage had been done; safety issues, increased maintenance costs compared to conventional bombs, the fact that the bomb's guidance system required clear-day use only, rendering the bombers vulnerable to enemy fighters, required that the weapon be released at a prime altitude for the aircraft to be in danger from enemy flak. These combined with the weapon's poor reliability – only six of twenty-eight bombs dropped successfully destroyed their targets – to result in the production order being cancelled by the USAF; following this, the Tarzon program as a whole was terminated in August 1951 and the search continued for a viable B-29 role. Even so, in March 1951, *The West*

PEACE - AND A 'POLICE ACTION'   161

Above: On 27 October 1951, B-29 *Command Decision* flew on a strike against rail bridges at Sinanju, North Korea. On this mission, the crew shot down their fourth and fifth MiG-15 (they shot down the other three on 17 October). A MiG-15 cannon shell caused serious damage to *Command Decision's* flap on the 27 October mission.

Left: *Command Decision* had nose art on the left side showing its five MiG kills. Each painted bomb represented a mission. The right side artwork depicted characters from Walt Disney's *Snow White and the Seven Dwarfs*

Below: Capt Donald M. Covic makes a 'command decision' by flipping a coin, just like the artwork on his B-29. *(all USAF)*

Australian newspaper reported that: *'The American Air Force has been using a radio-controlled Tarzon bomb in Korea since last August, it was officially announced today. Weighing 12,0001b., the bombs are 27ft. long and are controlled from a radio transmitter in the launching aircraft. Bombardiers track the flight of the bombs by flares attached to the tail-fins and a special bombsight. They say they have excellent control of the bomb during its descent'.*

In October 1951, USAF planners decided to concentrate on the destruction of Chinese air power in northern Korea before trying a more vigorous bombing policy. In a move that was reminiscent of the 8th Air Force in Europe during 1943, the B-29s were to launch attacks on Chinese air bases in north Korea. They were acting as bait, hoping to lure MiG-15s into battle, where they could be destroyed by F-86 fighters. However, the MiG squadrons had been widely dispersed, making it difficult for USAF intelligence to find them, and B-29 losses were heavy. By 27 October five B-29s had been lost and 20 more heavily damaged.

These raids were suspended and replaced by night attacks using B-29s equipped with SHORAN (SHOrt RANge) navigation radar that was able to pinpoint small targets with great accuracy. The 98th Wing was the first to be equipped with SHORAN, followed by the 19th and 307th. The first SHORAN-equipped nighttime raids began in November of 1952, and continued throughout the remainder of the Korean War. However, night fighters and radar-controlled defences did cause some losses. For example, on 10 June 1952 four SHORAN-equipped B-29s suddenly found themselves illuminated by radar-guided searchlights over Sinuiju. Night

Superfortress bombs blanket the runway at Saamcham, about 50 miles north of Pyongyang. B-29 units regularly attacked North Korean airfields to deny the communists their use. *(USAF)*

A low level photographic sortie reveals the bomb damage to this railway bridge north of Pyongyang. *(USAF)*

fighters were directed in to attack, and two bombers were shot down.

In August and September 1951, a decision was made to concentrate attacks on North Korean rail lines, with B-29s hitting bridges at Pyongyang, Sonchon, Sunchon, Sinanju, and Huichon. However, the damage was often quickly repaired or bypassed, and little disruption of the supply lines was achieved. For 44 days beginning on 26 January 1952, B-29s along with other aircraft attacked the village of Wadong, where the lateral rail route of North Korea entered a a cutting. The B-29s did enough damage with this new policy so that it was formalised in March under Operation Saturate, but once again, heavy losses linked with Communist ingenuity - plus a lack of suitable targets negated the effects. A role for the B-29 still had not been found after two years of conflict.

In April 1952 approval was given for raids against hydro-electricity facilities at Sui-Ho, Fusen, Chosin, and Kyosen. SHORAN-equipped B-29s were to attack during the night, and USAF and Navy fighter bombers from Task Force 77 off the coast of Korea were to attack during the day. These began on 24 June and by the 27th, it was estimated that 90% of North Korean power supplies had been destroyed.

This success led to the adoption of a more general bombing policy, based upon concentration and co-ordination. It was thought that if selected targets of military importance could be located and then destroyed in a storm of aerial assault, then the Communists might agree to an armistice, the negotiations for which had been going on for nearly eighteen months.

The first and the biggest of these raids took place on 11 July against thirty different targets in Pyongyang and the campaign continued over the next few weeks with intensive strikes against Choshin, Sungho-Ri, Sindok and Sinuiju. The B-29s contributed to most of these and their gradually-improving nighttime techniques were shown to good effect on 30 September when 45 aircraft destroyed the Namsan-Ri chemical plant. As the raids continued, between November 1952 and January 1953 five B-29s fell victim to night fighters and three more were severely damaged. Only after the deployment of USAF night fighters, especially

A Boeing B-29 Airborne Early Warning aircraft, originally B-29-80-BW 44-87599. *(USAF)*

Marine Corps F3D-2 Skynight, did losses decrease. Even so, it was clear that the B-29 could never mount a campaign against North Korea on its own.

By the late spring of 1953, the emphasis was again on Chinese airfields and bridges in the north. The objective was to keep these fields unserviceable since tentative truce terms had allowed for a twelve hour free period between the signing of the truce agreement and the time it became effective, which could have given the Communist side enough time to move in massive numbers of aircraft to the ten major North Korean airfields.

During the Korean Conflict, three B-29s were modified in mid-1951 during a full-scale development programme for the concept of Airborne Early Warning (AEW) aircraft. The forward upper fuselage was extensively modified to house an AN/APS-20C search radar and the aircraft interior was extensively modified to house radar and electronic counter measures equipment.

This development programme was of interest to Strategic Air Command and Air Defense Command and led to the procurement of operational radar picket aircraft including the RC-121 (later EC-121). These aircraft were an aerial extension of the Distant Early Warning Line flying patrol missions off the coast of the continental United States and South East Asia.

When the Korean armistice came into effect on 27 July 1953, the B-29s had flown over 21,000 sorties, nearly 167,000 tons of bombs had been dropped, and 34 B-29s had been lost in combat (16 to fighters, four to flak, and fourteen to other causes). B-29 gunners had accounted for 34 Communist fighters (16 of these being MiG-15s) probably destroyed another 17 (all MiG-15s) and damaged 11 (all MiG-15s). Losses were less than 1 per 1000 sorties.

Its contribution to the United Nations' cause was undoubtedly significant, but clearly the B-29 was an obsolete weapon. This was partly due to a lack of strategic targets caused by the restraints of limited war, but it was also a result of tremendous advances in aerial technology which left the B-29 behind. The aircraft belonged to the 1940s, to an age before the jet fighter, radar-controlled defensces and superpower confrontation. It had more than justified its development in 1945 over the skies of Japan, but by 1950 it was almost an anachronism, awaiting retirement and totally unsuited to the rigors of another war.

WASHINGTONS AND TANKERS

In order to meet postwar British nuclear-capable bomber needs until the English Electric Canberra could be delivered in quantity 87 B-29s were loaned to the Royal Air Force in 1950 as the Boeing Washington under the American Military Aid Program. Serials were: WF434/448, WF490/514, WF545/574, WW342/355, and WZ966/968.

Royal Air Force Marham in Norfolk had been used as a base by several USAF bomber units in the two years 1948-50 for periods of from two to four months of TDY (Temporary Duty). The B-29 and B-50 squadrons found Marham's new runways and taxiways ideal to operate from, and when the RAF took delivery of the B-29 Marham was selected as the base for the Conversion Unit.

Equipping heavy bomber squadrons of the RAF with the Washington was intended to be an interim measure to replace the Avro Lincoln with a more modern, nuclear-capable aircraft and to fill the gap until the Canberra and V-bombers came into service. The Washington offered the RAF a modern aircraft straight off the shelf, with proven systems and no development costs.

The first aircraft arrived at Marham on 22 March 1950 for a ceremonial hand-over attended by the British Secretary of State for Air, the Rt Hon Arthur Henderson, the AOC-in-C Bomber Command, Air Marshal Sir Hugh P Lloyd, and the Commander of the USAF Third Air Division, Major-Gen Leon W Johnson. The RAF and USAF each provided Guards of Honour.

After all the ceremonial the first crews were converted to the aircraft by USAF instructors, and then became the nucleus of the Washington Conversion Unit, which was formed at Marham in April 1950 under Sqn Ldr B H B Foster DSO DFC. The course lasted eight weeks and in all nine squadrons were converted.

The first squadron converted was 115, back at Marham after eight years and its first resident Washington squadron from June 1950. 149 Sqn was next, going to Coningsby when conversion was complete in October, then 90, which joined 115

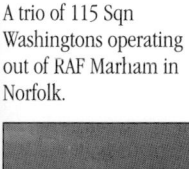

A trio of 115 Sqn Washingtons operating out of RAF Marham in Norfolk.

RAF Washington WW352 with its serial written very large on the vertical fin. (Simon Peters Collection)

at Marham in December 1950. Three more squadrons destined for Coningsby, 15, 44 and 57, completed the conversion between November 1950 and June 1951. In May 1951 207 Sqn arrived at Marham to start conversion and stayed as a resident squadron and in September 1951 the WCU was renamed 35 Sqn, which became the fourth resident squadron at Marham. 35 Sqn then became known as the Washington Training Squadron and acted as the OCU, training, amongst others, crews of 192 Sqn, which operated the type from Watton.

Once established, the squadrons trained up to a high degree of efficiency with their new aircraft. Flying consisted principally of bombing training, air firing, cross-country exercises and the usual familiarisation sorties.

During May the establishment of the squadrons was increased from six to eight aircraft - the Station supplied nine Washingtons during the month for a Bomber Command 'Bullseye' exercise. In August two crews of 44 Sqn participated in operation 'Beehive', the longest cross country exercise flown by the Squadron since converting to the Washington. As 1951 approached its end the training schedule of all three squadrons began to reach a peak. In October all three squadrons participated in operation *'Pinnacle'*, an exercise designed to test the air defence of Great Britain, and the squadrons had by this time begun carrying out fighter affiliation exercises with Southern Sector, Fighter Command.

Training also continued in high level bombing, radar fighter affiliation and air-sea firing as well as GCA and ILS practice. All three units were now supplying crews for the monthly 'Bullseye' exercises.

Operating procedures were modelled on USAF rather than RAF practices, this being a condition of the agreement when they were purchased. The squadrons took part in a series of defence exercises in the UK, in which they were able to achieve good

WF582 photographed at an airshow, showing the more standard small RAF serial on the rear fusleage. (via Paddy Porter MBE BEM)

WASHINGTONS AND TANKERS

An overview of the Royal Review at Odiham with three of the twelve RAF Washingtons in the flypast visible. There were four more in static display on the ground.

results against the jet fighters of Fighter Command. 90 Sqn won the Bomber Command Bombing Competition held in July 1952, and was presented with the Laurence Minot Trophy for visual bombing and the Sassoon Trophy for gunnery in October. The Laurence Minot Trophy was won by 115 Sqn in 1953.

On the down side, a few nasty accidents occurred to Marham's Washingtons. One of 35 Sqn's aircraft crashed near Swaffham on 14 December 1952, killing three of the crew; one from 90 Sqn crashed in Wales on 8 January 1953, with the loss of all ten of the crew; and one from 115 Sqn crashed into the sea on its way back to the USA on 27 January 1954, seven crew members losing their lives.

As was only right and proper, the Marham Washington squadrons were well represented in the Coronation Review of the Royal Air Force on 15 July 1953. Four aircraft for static display, one from each squadron, were sent down to Odiham, and a formation of twelve aircraft led by Wg Cdr H N G Wheeler DSO OBE DFC took part in the flypast by 641 aircraft. The flypast was the culmination of weeks of practice; a few months later the squadrons relinquished the Washington as they moved into the Jet Age.

ELINT Washingtons

192 Sqn acquired three RB-29As as replacements for its three Lincolns in 1952. The first two aircraft, WZ966, WZ967, arrived at Watton in April and were joined by WZ968 in June. All gun turrets and bombing equipment were removed, the rear observation blisters were faired over; the rear pressurised compartment was converted for Elint use with six Special Operators; the installation of two radomes under the rear fuselage for direction-finding antennae and the fitting of a number of other external antennae.

These machines were to intercept, analyse and plot the positions of Soviet radar stations, and intercept Soviet radio communications including transmissions between

WZ966 of 192 Sqn at Watton. Note the addional 'lumps and bumps' under the rear fuselage and lack of rear gun blisters. *(via Paddy Porter MBE BEM)*

Soviet GCI stations and fighters. The six Special Operator positions comprised two VHF communications intercept positions; two metric radar intercept and D/F positions; and two centimetric (X-band and S-band) radar intercept and D/F and positions. Wire recorders were carried to capture signals for later analysis.

During the first half of 1953 192 Sqn devoted its efforts to training Washington crews and to the installation and trials of equipment in the aircraft. The programme was helped by the acquisition of an unmodified Washington, WW346, in April, primarily for pilot continuation training. The squadron took advantage of Exercise 'Jungle King', a NATO naval exercise in March 1953, to fly a series of Elint sorties using all three Washingtons to locate and track the 'enemy' fleet using radar and voice intercepts.

The first Washington Elint mission - Operation Reason – was carried out during 1953 to intercept the new Soviet cruiser *Sverdlov* just north of the Shetlands following its visit to the UK in August 1953. This highly successful operation revealed the presence of X-band fire control radar on the ship.

In October 1953 two Washingtons accompanied by WW346 as a support aircraft were detached to Nicosia on Cyprus. Two Elint flights were carried out, probably over the Black Sea.

During the next four years the Washingtons flew three types of Elint operation. The first was the routine Border sortie. These were daylight missions over West Germany, flown 15 miles or so from the East German border. The second type of operation was the shadowing of Soviet naval units. These were flown on an opportunity basis and occasionally required the diversion of aircraft from pre-planned Elint sorties. Strict rules governed these flights, limiting how close the Washington could approach the Soviet vessels. The third type of operation, and the most risky, were Elint sorties flown in neutral or international airspace along the borders of the Soviet Union and its allies. The main area of operations for these flights were the Baltic Sea, flown from Watton or Germany; the Black Sea - flown from Cyprus - and the Caspian Sea, flown from Iraq. The Washingtons normally operated in conjunction with the squadron's Canberras, the Washingtons standing off a minimum of 70 miles from Soviet territory and monitoring reactions to the Canberras, which approached to within 30 miles of the border. Each of these sorties was reviewed and authorized by the British Foreign Minister before it was flown. Although they were flown in international airspace at a respectable distance from

WASHINGTONS AND TANKERS   169

Soviet borders they still risked a hostile reaction. To minimize the risk they were always flown in absolute darkness during the period of the new moon. Since few Soviet air defence fighters then carried AI radar this offered some protection from interception.

Early in 1956 Washington WZ966 carried out the first RAF Elint sortie into the Barents Sea. This 18 hour flight was made even more arduous by the failure of the aircraft heating system and the loss of one engine 12 hours into the mission. Following this operation the Barents Sea was added to the list of regular operational areas. However, subsequent sorties into the Barents Sea operated from Norwegian airfields.

In the autumn of 1956 a single aircraft was detached to Malta to compile an Egyptian electronic order of battle prior to the joint UK-French operations to reclaim the Suez Canal.

Maintenance of the 192 Sqn Washingtons was complicated by the withdrawal of the type from Bomber Command service in the early 1954. This made spares harder to obtain and as a result the aircraft were sometimes flown with non-essential equipment inoperable. The autopilot seems to have been an early victim of the spares situation. Mainplane corrosion problems were also encountered.

The Elint suite in the Washington was continually improved during the aircraft's service. The main problem was the accuracy of direction-finding, and thus the accuracy with which Soviet radar stations could be plotted. A number of improvements were made to the ARI 18021 equipment, and also to operating procedures; the ARI 18021 was later supplemented by the addition of US-built APA-17 direction-finders. Provision was also made for an alternative fit of additional HF and VHF receivers to enhance the aircraft's communications intercept capability.

Above: Boeing B-29 Washington WW349, which was based at Wisley from 1952 to 1955 taking off with a one-third scale Red Rapier missile test round under the fuselage.

Left: Vickers crew with B-29 WW349. (Left to right): Don Bowen (Navigator), George Errington, Eddy McNamara (pilot), Unknown, Frank Cox, John Whetmore, Pat White (Trials Engineers), Pat Toll (RAE Flight Engineer), Spud Murphy (Captain).
(via Peter Skinner/John E Forbat)

Left: B-29 WW353 with a one-third scale Red Rapier test round, which took part in trial drops at Woomera in Australia during 1953-4.

Below: The nose of B-29 WW349 after Valiant WP203 collided with it on the Wisley apron on 29 July 1955. The B-29 was so badly damaged that it was written off. *(via Peter Skinner/John E Forbat)*

The end for the Washington came in December 1957 after the maintenance situation had deteriorated to the point where it was considered unlikely the aircraft could successfully complete a sortie without some major unserviceability. As a result all three operational aircraft were stood down.

In September 1952 the Ministry of Supply loaned two Boeing B-29s Washingtons WW349, (formerly 44-61968) and WW353 (formerly 44-62049) to Vickers Aircraft Ltd to carry unpowered one-third scale models of the Vickers 825 'Red Rapier'. Twelve of these scale models were built at Weybridge to be dropped at Woomera from the Washingtons. Red Rapier was a 45 feet long flying bomb with a 500 lb warhead (presumably nuclear) powered by three Rolls-Royce Soar small turbojets, each with 1,750 lb thrust, which would be launched from a catapult, but this was also cancelled in 1954. These two Washingtons are also thought to have been involved in the testing of the Vickers 'Blue Boar' family of TV-guided, un-powered glider bombs with extending wings, which would allow

WASHINGTONS AND TANKERS

One of the Washingtons on loan to Vickers Wisley for test on the *Blue Boar* TV-guided missle flies low down the runway before landing. *(via Peter Skinner/John E Forbat)*

a bomber a degree of stand-off, in the hope that a heavily defended target would not need to be overflown.

WW349 was damaged and subsequently written off following an accident on 29 July 1955 in a spectacular slow motion incident when Vickers Valiant WP203 had a total hydraulic failure while taxiing back to the apron, was unable to stop and circled around, colliding with Boeing B-29 WW349, bending its nose by thirty degrees and hitting the tail of another Valiant. Its partner, WW353, was flown to the Weapons Research Establishment (WRE) at Woomera, Australia as A76-1 in September 1952 to be joined by WW345/A76-2. The suriviving RAF Washingtons were all returned to the USAF by 1955.

Use as Tankers

Aerial refuelling, also called air refuelling, in-flight refuelling (IFR), air-to-air refuelling (AAR) or tanking, is the process of transferring fuel from one aircraft - the tanker - to another called the receiver while in flight.

The procedure allows the receiving aircraft to remain airborne longer, extending its range or loiter time on station. A series of air refuellings can give range limited only by crew fatigue and engineering factors such as engine oil consumption. Because the receiver aircraft can be topped up with extra fuel in the air, air refuelling can allow a take-off with a greater payload which could be weapons, cargo or personnel: the maximum take-off weight is maintained by carrying less fuel and topping up once airborne. Alternatively, a shorter take-off roll can be achieved because take-off can be at a lighter weight before refuelling once airborne. Aerial refuelling has also been considered as a means to reduce fuel consumption on long distance flights greater than 3000 nautical miles. Potential fuel savings in the range of 60% have been estimated for long haul flights.

The two main refuelling systems are probe-and-drogue, which is simpler to adapt to existing aircraft, and the flying boom, which offers greater fuel transfer capacity, but requires a dedicated operator station.

British aviation pioneer Alan Cobham bought a patent from David Nicolson and John Lord for £480 each and started development of the Grappled-line looped-hose air to air refuelling system, which while complex in operation, was the world's first practical air-to-air refuelling system, with which he gave many public demonstrations. The receiver aircraft trailed a steel cable which was then grappled by a line shot from the tanker. The line was then drawn back into the tanker where the receiver's cable was connected to the refuelling hose. The receiver could then haul back in its cable bringing the hose to it. Once the hose was connected, the tanker climbed sufficiently above the receiver aircraft to allow the fuel to flow under gravity. While today aerial refuelling is used exclusively by military aircraft, when Cobham was developing his system, he saw the need as purely for long range trans-ocean commercial aircraft flights.

In 1934 he founded Flight Refuelling Ltd. (FRL), and by 1938 had used the FRL's looped-hose system to refuel aircraft as large as the Short Empire flying boat *Cambria* from an Armstrong Whitworth AW.23. Handley Page Harrows were used in the 1939 trials to aerial refuel the Empire flying boats for regular transatlantic crossings. From 5 August to 1 October 1939 sixteen crossings of the Atlantic were made by Empire flying boats, with fifteen crossings using FRL's aerial refuelling system. After the sixteen crossings further trials were suspended due to the war.

During the closing months of World War Two it had been intended that Tiger Force's Lancaster and Lincoln bombers would be in-flight refueled by converted Halifax tanker aircraft, fitted with the FRL's looped-hose units, in operations against the Japanese homelands, but the war ended before the aircraft could be deployed. After the war ended, the USAF bought a small number of FRL looped-hose units and fitted a number of B-29s as tankers to refuel specially equipped B-29s and later B-50s.

Six B-29s were fitted with R-3350-CA-2 fuel injection engines and the revised nacelles that were intended for late production B-29As in a programme to service test these new engine installations. These aircraft were redesignated YB-29J. Some of them were used for photo-reconnaissance work as RB-29J. Two - 44-86398 and 44-86402 - were converted to aerial tankers under the designation YKB-29J as part of a test of the Boeing-developed boom aerial refuelling system that was introduced in the KB-29P program. However, these two aircraft retained their service test and J-series designations.

The designation B-29K had originally been assigned to the hose tanker conversions of the B-29 that were eventually produced as KB-29M. Since none of the tankers ever actually used the K suffix,

KB-29M refuels B-50A 46-010 *'Lucky Lady II'* during the first non-stop around the world flight in February 1949, along with detail of the hose mechanism retracted into its receptacle inder the tail. *(USAF)*

WASHINGTONS AND TANKERS

Operation *High Tide*, which saw the first aerial refueled strike missions, began in May 1952 when twelve F-84Es flew non-stop from Japan to bomb targets in North Korea. In the same year, aerial refueled *Fox Peter* operations began flying F-84s non-stop across the Pacific. *(USAF)*

it was reassigned to a single B-29-BW that was used as a cargo transport and designated CB-29K.

The designation B-29L was originally assigned to B-29s that were to be converted as receiver aircraft for the British-developed hose-based inflight refuelling system. However, the B-29 receiver aircraft were designated B-29MR instead.

The designation KB-29M was assigned to 92 B-29s that were converted to aerial tankers using the British-developed hose refuelling system. In addition, 74 B-29 aircraft were converted as receivers for this system under the designation B-29MR. In retrospect, this hose refuelling system was unbelievably awkward and cumbersome, and it is a wonder that it worked at all. That it was so successful is a testament to the courage and ability of all concerned. The primary goal of the project was to extend the range of the B-29 fleet to make it possible to attack targets in the Soviet Union with nuclear weapons.

The B-29MR conversion was carried out by removing all the B-29 gun turrets and their associated equipment except the tail turret. On some of the conversions, even the left and right gun sighting blisters were removed and replaced by small ten-inch diameter windows to cut down on the drag. The rear bomb bay was fitted with an extra fuel tank of 2300 gallon capacity, and the forward bomb bay was modified to carry an atomic bomb. In addition, extra rendezvous equipment was installed to help in the tankers and bombers to locate each other. The B-29MR had a refuelling nozzle receptor installed on the lower right side of the fuselage, approximately at the location where the lower aft gun turret had been located prior to its removal. The receptor was connected to plumbing that transferred fuel to the gas tank system. A 450-foot cable (known as the hauling line) emerged from the centre of the nozzle receptor. This cable was controlled by a hydraulic winch that was operated by a crewman sitting in the tail turret position. The end of the cable held a dish-shaped metal pan equipped with grapnel hooks. The winch operator had no way of seeing what was going on outside his immediate station, and had to rely on guidance by an observer (usually the radar officer) sitting in the tail gunner's position.

Similar changes were made to the KB-29M tanker aircraft. All the gun turrets were removed, including the tail turret. The bomb bay of the KB-29M was fitted with a separate fuel tank holding 2300 gallons. This tank was also plumbed into the normal aircraft fuel system so that fuel from it could also be transferred to the receiver aircraft. The KB-29M tanker aircraft carried a system of hoses, reels, winches and fuel pumps needed for the transfer of the fuel to the receiver aircraft.

A power-driven reel for the refuelling hose was installed in the rear fuselage at the position where the lower aft turret had been located prior to its removal. The KB-29M also had a cable and associated winch (known as the contact line) that was used to assist in the setup of the connection between the two aircraft.

This was the air-to-air refuelling system that *Lucky Lady II,* 46-010 commanded by Captain James Gallagher, used to make its famous first non-stop around the world flight completed on 2 March 1949, having covered 23,452 miles in 94 hours and 1 minute.

During the refuelling operation, the tanker aircraft flew in formation slightly above, to the left, and to the rear of the receiver aircraft. In order to initiate the contact, the tanker aircraft let out about 300 feet of contact line behind it. There was a 50-pound weight at the end of the contact line cable, so it hung almost straight down from the tanker. At the same time, the receiver aircraft let out about 300 feet of hauling line cable that extended from the refuelling receptacle located underneath the tail on the starboard side. With the grapnel pan at the end of the MR's hauling line, the cable trailed almost straight back from the aircraft. With both lines fully extended, the tanker aircraft would then cross over to the right side of the MR, and the two cables would make contact. The operator in the tail turret of the tanker aircraft would then pull in his contact line cable, and the grapnel hook on the end of the MR's hauling line would ensure that a positive connection was made. The tanker aircraft would pull the contact line all the way into the aircraft. With the end of the MR hauling line cable now in the tanker, the operator removed the grapnel pan from the end of the hauling line and attached the hauling line to the nozzle at the end of the refuelling hose. The operator in the

Republic F-84G and Boeing KB-29 during in-flight refuelling. *(USAF)*

WASHINGTONS AND TANKERS   175

Above: KB-29 44-88383 using a boom refuels a F-86. *(USAF)*

Below: Probe and Drogue KB-29M refuels a B-29MR modified with a nose probe. *(both USAF)*

tanker aircraft then began to let out the hose, and at the same time the winch operator in the MR receiving aircraft started to pull in the hauling line. The hose and nozzle would be pulled around a 300-foot curve trailing behind the two aircraft, the reel unwinding as the hose extended. Once the hose nozzle reached the MR, it was mated with the nozzle receptor and locked into place.

While the receiver aircraft hauled in the hose, there was a very critical sequence which if not followed correctly could - and sometimes did - result in loss of the hose. At the point when the hose was 'coming 'round the bend' the winching had to be accelerated to keep the hose from whipping. If severe whipping did occur, the entire hose system usually had to be jettisoned.

After the nozzle of the hose was firmly seated in the receptacle of the MR aircraft and locked, a signal was sent to the tanker aircraft (which was now above and behind the receiver) that contact had been made and that fuel could now be transferred. Fuel then flowed via gravity from tanker to receiver aircraft. Incoming fuel was usually directed into the 2300-gallon rear-fuselage tank, but it could also be directed into the other tanks in the regular fuel system.

Once the fuel transfer was complete, the MR operator unlocked the nozzle and started letting out his hauling line cable. The tanker aircraft reeled in the

BOEING B-29 SUPERFORTRESS

Two pictures of Boeing testing their In-Flight Refuelling boom with B-50 49-260 and mock-up of the tail end of a tanker in a somewhat ramshackle area at the north end of the field at Seattle in October 1949. Quite what the gentleman is doing apparently sliding down the zip line is unclear!

Legend has it that Curtiss LeMay, the famously crusty, cigar-chomping US Air Force general, traveled to Seattle to see the system being developed. With puddles of gasoline sloshed everywhere on the concrete test pad, any fire hazard was a distinct danger, and so uncomfortable Boeing officials were finally forced to tell the general it would be in everyone's best interest if he would please put out his cigar! *(USAF)*

entire length of hose, and the operator in the tanker aircraft disconnected the MR's hauling line from the hose and re-attached the grapnel pan. The pan and hauling cable were then pulled back into the MR aircraft.

The feasibility of the system was first demonstrated on 28 March 1948 by two converted B-29s. Water rather than fuel was transferred during this test, but full fuel-flow trials were made in May 1948. Encouraged by this success, the Air Force then ordered conversion of 92 B-29s to serve as tankers using this system under the designation KB-29M. Boeing's Wichita Plant 2 was reopened in 1948 to handle this conversion. As part of the programme, another 74 B-29s were modified as receiver aircraft for the KB-29M tankers. Initially, the designation B-29L had been reserved for this version, but they were designated B-29MR instead.

The hose refuelling system used by the KB-29M turned out to be extremely cumbersome and difficult to use in service. The time needed for tanker and receiver to make contact was usually quite long, the rate of fuel transfer was slow, and the aerodynamic drag imposed by the hoses limited the airspeed. Flight Refuelling Ltd realized that their looped-hose system left a lot to be desired and began work on an improved system that is now commonly called the probe-and-drogue air-to-air refuelling system.

Boeing went to work on the problem and came up with the flying boom technique which is still in use today. Basically, it replaced the tanker hose and its system of lines, winches, and reels with an aerodynamically-controlled swivelling and telescoping arm steered by an operator situated in an observation bubble that replaced the former tail turret. Aerodynamic control of the boom was managed by a set of rudders and elevators attached to the boom which controlled the azimuth and elevation. Extension and retraction of the nozzle was done hydraulically. The receiver aircraft had a receptacle on top of the fuselage to receive the nozzle, and

Republic F-84F-20-RE (S/N 51-1543) being refuelled by Boeing KB-29 (S/N 44-83922). *(USAF)*

during the refuelling manoeuvre, the operator would 'fly' the boom nozzle into the receptacle of the receiving aircraft. Once contact was made, the transfer of fuel could begin. When not in use, the flying boom was latched onto a cradle which extended behind the tail of the tanker aircraft.

The boom system had the advantage in that relatively few modifications were needed in the receiving aircraft. However, the pilot of the receiving aircraft did have to keep the nose of his plane within a certain envelope behind and below the tanker in order to achieve contact with the end of the boom. The pilot of the receiving aircraft was assisted in his task by a series of indicator lights along the belly of the tanker aircraft which directed the pilot to move right or left, up or down, forward or aft.

Although the boom system was primarily used for the refuelling of large aircraft such as bombers, it could also be used to refuel fighters. However, the probe-and-drogue system was found to be more useful than the boom system in the refuelling of smaller aircraft such as fighters. In this system, the tanker aircraft trailed a hose behind it, and a drogue at the free end of the hose was engaged by a probe on the nose of the fighter. A few KB-29P boom tankers were adapted to refuelling fighters by this technique, in which a short length of hose and a drogue was installed at the end of the boom.

In order to meet the demand for boom tankers, the remainder of the Renton plant (part of which had been opened for C-97A production) was reopened, and 116 B-29s were converted to KB-29P configuration in 1950-51. The first of these was was delivered to SAC in March 1950.

It was found that the boom refuelling technique introduced on the KB-29P tankers was not as effective in refuelling small jet fighters as it was in refuelling large piston-engined bombers. The probe-and-drogue system was found to be more effective for refuelling these smaller aircraft.

A close up of the business end of a Boeing Flying Boom on the end of a B-29. the pivot point on the aicraft, boomers 'window' in the extreme tail and support structure is particularly noticable. (USAF)

THE B-50

The Wright-powered B-29 had always been somewhat underpowered for its weight, and with time it became clear that the airframe could take substantially more engine power if it were available.

The programme began in mid-1943, when Pratt & Whitney proposed to the USAAF that the B-29 be modified with larger engines. In July 1944, a contract was signed and B-29A-5-BN 42-93845 was made available to P & W for development work and conversion as a testbed for the new four-row 28-cylinder Pratt & Whitney R-4360 Wasp Major air-cooled radial engine, which was rated at 3500 horesepower. Modification involved complete redesign of the four engine nacelles.

Because the aircraft was intended to be only a testbed for the engine installation, most of its defensive equipment was removed - only two machine guns in the rear fuselage.

First flying in May 1945, the XB-44 proved 50-60 mph faster than the B-29. Production of the re-engined bomber was initially planned as the B-29D, but it was decided to change the aircraft designation in military inventory because of the extensive airframe changes that would be required - design work that would have to be performed by Boeing. This was not performed on the B-44 prototype except for the engine nacelle rework. Officially, the aircraft's new designation was justified by the changes separating the proposed B-29D from its predecessors: new engines, new engine nacelles and engine mounts, larger vertical tail required for engine-out stability, wing reinforcing due to greater engine weight, revised routing for combustion and exhaust gases, upgraded armament-control equipment, increases in landing gear capability and added fuel capacity

The USAAF placed an order for 200 production examples under the designation B-29D in July 1945, but this was reduced to only 50 after V-J Day. In December 1945, the designation of the B-29D was changed to B-50A - apparently a ruse to win appropriation funding for the procurement of an aircraft that appeared by its designation to be merely a later version of an existing model that was already being cancelled wholesale, with many existing models being put into storage. Officially, the justification for the new B-50 designation was made on the

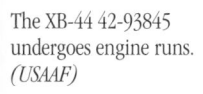

The XB-44 42-93845 undergoes engine runs. (USAAF)

basis that the changes introduced by the B-29D were so major that it was, in effect, a completely new aircraft. The strategy worked, and the B-50 survived the cutbacks to become an important component of the postwar Air Force.

The decision to produce the B-50 was confirmed on 24 May 1947. From the start, the B-50 was earmarked for the atomic bombing role. This decision was prompted by the uncertain future of the Convair B-36, the first long-range heavy bomber produced as an atomic carrier. A few of the B-29s that had been modified to carry the atomic bomb were still available, but they were nearly obsolete and would have to be replaced by a more efficient, atomic-capable bomber pending the availability of the B-36 or another bomber truly suitable for the delivery of atomic bombs.

The B-50 was externally quite similar to the B-29, but a glance was sufficient to tell the difference between the two aircraft. The traditional 24 ST aluminum structure of the B-29 was replaced by the newer 75 ST, which resulted in a wing that was 16 percent stronger than the wing of the B-29 and 600 pounds lighter. 3500-hp R-4360 Wasp Major engines gave a power increase of 59%. The new engine installation was the main external feature distinguishing the B-50 from the B-29, with the oil cooler being pulled further back on the lower part of the nacelle. Increased weight resulted in a requirement for larger flaps and a higher vertical tail. This was first tested on B-29-35-BW serial number 42-24528, which had been assigned to Seattle Experimental Flight Test. The tall vertical tail could be folded down to permit storage in standard USAF hangars. Other features included hydraulic rudder boost and nose wheel steering, faster acting undercarriage retracting mechanism, and electrical de-icing of the pilots' window through the use of conductive NESA glass. Wings and empennage were de-iced thermally by having the exhaust from three combustion heaters flow through hollow double-

B-50A under construction at Boeing's Seattle, Washinton plant. The streamlined version of the forward upper gun turret can cearly be seen. *(USAF)*

THE B-50

A B-50 with the Boeing name and B-50 script on its nose climbs out of the Seattle airfield. *(USAF)*

Boeing B-50A 46-010 'Lucky Lady II' of the 43rd Bomb Group, Davis Monthan Air Force Base, Ariz. Just visible on the lower nose is part of the word 'Kensmen' that was under a crest with the motto 'Ready, Willing and Able'. Assorted 'lumps and bumps' on the rear fuselage are noticable. *(USAF)*

wall structures in the leading edges of the aerodynamic surfaces. The propellers had a reversible pitch, which allowed the use of engine power as an aid to braking on short or wet runways. There was also some rearrangement of the crew. Despite the overall similarity of the two aircraft, only about 25% of the B-50 parts were interchangeable with B-29 parts.

The crew complement was typically eleven - pilot, copilot, engineer, navigator/radar operator/bombardier, bomdardier/navigator/radar operator, radio/electronic countermeasures operator, left side gunner, right side gunner, top gunner, tail gunner, and one extra crew member.

The B-50 was given the Boeing designation Model 345-2. The first B-50, 46-002, to be built was a production machine rather than a prototype and first flew on 25 June 1947. The first production version was designated B-50A, reflecting the new Air Force policy of assigning the A series suffix to the first production model of a new series. The B-50 was planned to have been built at Renton, but a change resulted in a move to Seattle Plant 2. 59 B-50As were built as standard bombers, with block numbers from -1 to -35. Although there was officially no prototype B-50, seven of the B-50As built were allocated to testing. The 60th and last example was held at the factory for modification as the YB-50C, which was intended as a prototype for the B-54A series, a further-improved version of the B-50.

The first B-50As were delivered in June 1948 to the SAC's 43rd Bomb Wing, based at Davis-Monthan AFB in Arizona. This Wing was assigned to be the primary carrier of the atomic bomb. SAC had come into existence in 1946 with about 250 B-17s and B-29s as initial equipment.

Production of the B-50A ended in January 1949. The B-50A remained in front-line service with SAC alongside the B-36 for several years. There were problems with cold-weather performance of the B-50A: one crashed in Alaska, and it was discovered that oil congealing in the small-bore tubing of the aircraft's manifold pressure regulator was to blame, and the regulators were modified. There were numerous engine malfunctions as the constant speed drive alternators were faulty. A deficient turbosupercharger resulted in a short period during which the aircraft was restricted from flying above 20,000 feet. Cracking of the metal skin on the trailing edge of the wings and flaps required additional modifications. Later, failure of the rudder hinge bearing caused the temporary grounding of all B-50As. Progress in fixing these problems was made, and the B-50A's performance steadily improved throughout 1949.

B-50A 46-026 is seen in flight *(USAF)*

THE B-50

The first production B-50B (47-118) was retained for special test projects and given the (Exempt) designation EB-50B. One EB-50B test project involved the modification of the landing gear. The caterpillar-type tracked landing gear proved inefficient and difficult to maintain and was never used on any production aircraft. The EB-50B was converted back to a conventional landing gear system and used for other test projects. *(USAF)*

After a short time in service, 57 B-50As were sent to Wichita to be modified as receiver aircraft using the British-developed hose tanker inflight refuelling system.

Eleven B-50As from the first contract were modified as TB-50A bombing-navigation trainers. They were primarily intended for use as training of the crews of the B-36.

SAC began phasing out B-50As in mid-1954, when the 93rd Bomb Wing finally began receiving its long-awaited B-47s. As obsolescence approached, all surviving B-50As and TB-50As were converted to KB-50J three-hose tankers.

The next production version was the B-50B, the Boeing Model 345-2. It was externally identical to the B-50A, all differences being internal. The aircraft had an increase in gross weight from 168,480 pounds to 170,400 pounds and was equipped with a new type of lightweight fuel cell.

A close-up of the 'front half' of of what is thought to be 48-096. Clearly the aircraft had been built with the front upper gun turret in its streamlined form, but the turret had been replaced by one of the earlier design. *(USAF)*

48-0121 was originally built as a B-50D-105-BO, but was later converted to WB-50D standards. *(USAF)*

The B-50B introduced a deviation into the Boeing production block number system. Instead of starting the block numbers over at -1 for the new series, the B-50B block numbers simply continued on from where the B-50A blocks had ended. Consequently, the first B-50B was B-50B-40 and continued on to -60. Subsequent B-50s continued this practice.

The first B-50B, 47-118, took off on its maiden flight on 14 January 1949 and was retained at the factory for test work under the designation EB-50B (E-for-Exempt) and was at one time fitted with a track-tread undercarriage in place of the conventional wheels. The wheels and tyres were replaced by a caterpillar-type track system. Tracked landing gear systems were installed on a wide variety of aircraft during the 1940s and early 1950s including the Curtiss P-40 and Convair XB-36. These systems were designed to reduce the overall pressure exerted on the ground by spreading the aircraft weight over a larger ground 'foot print'. This would, in theory, allow the aircraft to operate from more airfields and even unimproved strips.

All the other B-50Bs were sent to Wichita for conversion to the reconnaissance role under the designation RB-50B. This RB-50B featured four camera stations (supporting a total of nine cameras), weather reconnaissance instruments, and extra crew members housed inside a capsule housed in the

Boeing RB-50E serialled 0-70122, formerly 47-0122, that was originally B-50B-40-BO) at Jackson Field, Padua, on 27 Jan. 1964. *(USAF)*

Boeing RB-50F 0-70162, formerly 47-162, originally B-50B-60-BO, the last B-50B built as seen on 27 January 1964. It appears that all the armament has been removed. *(USAF)*

aircraft's rear bomb bay. The RB-50B was capable of being refuelled by the British-developed hose refuelling system, and could carry a 700-gallon auxiliary fuel tank under each wing.

In 1951, the RB-50Bs were again modified. There were three different configurations produced, which were later redesignated RB-50E, RB-50F, and RG-50G respectively.

Fourteen RB-50E conversions were undertaken for photographic reconnaissance and observation missions. According to the type of mission being flown, the left-side gunner could serve as a weather observer or as an inflight refuelling operator. Defensive armament consisted of 13 0.50-inch machine guns, housed in five electrically-operated turrets.

The 14 RB-50Fs were similar to the RB-50E but carried the SHORAN radar navigation system designed to conduct mapping, charting, and geodetic surveys. However, since SHORAN interfered with the RB-50F's defensive armament, it was housed in removable kits. The first RB-50F aircraft entered service with SAC in January 1951.

The RB-50G and Project *Half Track*

Electronic reconnaissance was the primary mission of the RB-50G which entered SAC service between June and October 1951. Fifteen RB-50G conversions were made and differed significantly enough from the RB-50E and F that they were assigned the Boeing Model 345-30-025 number. The RB-50G featured six electronic countermeasures stations internally, with external modifications to accommodate the radomes and antennae of the aircraft's new radar equipment. During the reconfiguration process, RB-50G was fitted with the improved nose of the B-50D, which had a large moulded plastic cone and an optically-flat bomb-aiming window in the lower portion. In contrast to the RB-50F, the RG-50G could use its defensive armament while operating its new electronic equipment.

The normal crew complement was sixteen: pilot, copilot, navigator, engineer, nose gunner, top gunner, left side gunner, right side gunner/radio operator, radar operator, tail gunner, plus six electronic countermeasures operators. Ten cameras could be carried - four K-38s with 36-inch lens, or two K-38s with 24-inch lens;

Not the best of images it is true, but then taking any pictures of any ELINT aircraft was almost a treasonable offence - here are two pictures of RB-50s used on ATRAN Missions The top picture is thought to be of RB-50 47-136 on the wash rack at Rhein-Main in April 1958, just before it was to depart the 7406th for its next assignment. Noticeable is the upper front turret with its four .50 cal guns.

The lower picture is of is 49-307 of the 7406th RB-50D in what was termed 'clean' condition - that is without armament - at Bovingdon, on 3 October 1957. *(both USAF)*

one L-22A or K-17; one A-6 motion picture camera; three K-17cs; one T-11 with 6-inch lens.

The 7499th Group was engaged in supporting the new Matador and Mace tactical guided missiles in Europe. The 7405th and 7406th Squadrons each flew a special kind of airborne collection mission - not traditional photo collection, and it certainly wasn't signals intelligence. It was imagery of a special sort, designed to support a tactical missile guidance system called the Automatic Terrain Recognition and Navigation (ATRAN) system, and the time frame was 1955-56.

In the early 1950s, the Air Force had fielded two versions of the Matador which depended upon positive guidance control by radar-directed ground controllers. The maximum range was about 200 miles, and they would be very susceptible to enemy countermeasures. So ATRAN was to be employed in the TM-61B version to correct those problems. The TM-61B was to evolve into the TM-76A Mace missile with a much-improved performance; this ATRAN-equipped Mace version was to stay in the Air Force inventory in Europe until September 1966.

The difficulty was how to get the required ground imagery to create the matching film. The main area of employment of these missiles was to be Western Europe, so collection would be in that arena. The hope was that reconnaissance missions and other intelligence sources would provide enough accurate data to be created and uploaded into the missiles. Headquarters US Air Forces in Europe (USAFE) at Wiesbaden, Germany, activated the Support Group at Wiesbaden in mid-1955. The 7499th Group would run its ATRAN missions under the project name 'Project Dream

Boat'. Two squadrons would have the ATRAN task among others. The 7405th Support Squadron would collect ATRAN material using a Douglas C-54D under Project 'Lulu Belle' - the 7406th Support Squadron would use three Boeing RB-50Ds and a RB-50G under Project 'Half Track'. Each of these aircraft would use specialised radar scope imagery, coupled with simultaneous regular photography, to get the required information. Each was limited to flying its missions over friendly territory, but this would enable the best possible accuracy for that part of a missile's flight path from launch until crossing into hostile territory.

The C-54 would be a very logical choice for ATRAN missions covering terrain underneath and near the air corridors to Berlin. Aircraft flying in the corridors were usually required to land at Tempelhof and would be subject to Soviet observation and probable complaints if they were perceived to be other than transport aircraft. Thus the RB-50s were disqualified on this ground as well being too large for the Tempelhof runways. Available photographs of the project C-54 show few protuberances to draw suspicion to it. The RB-50 might have been the best available choice for the missions over Western Europe because it could carry a heavier load of special equipment.

The RB-50D aircraft to be used in the Project Half Track part of ATRAN would seem an unlikely choice for low level intelligence gathering missions. Flying the huge modified bombers out of Rhein Main Air Base in Frankfurt, Germany, were crews of the 7406th Support Squadron which was activated in May 1955 and was to have two missions, both with RB-50s. One would be communications intelligence collection, with the RB-50G version, and the other was to be ATRAN route collection, with three RB-50Ds. The ATRAN aircraft were modified by Goodyear at Akron, Ohio, before being assigned to the 7406th. Problems at Goodyear delayed the arrival of the three aircraft (serial numbers 48-107, 49-307, and 49-312) until spring 1956. Finally all three were available, and the first ATRAN mission was flown 1 June 1956.

The 7406th Support Squadron memoirs describe the missions: *"The Half Track RB-50D aircraft had two pilots, two navigators, a flight engineer, a radio operator, two scanners/gunners, and a tail gunner... The "Half-Track" back-end crew consisted of two persons that were not members of the 7406th. These two sat in the scanner/gunner compartment, aft of the bomb bays, during take off and landings. During missions these two sat on a platform in the forward bomb bay...Low level flights commencing from points in Western Germany were flown to the East German border'.* They would fly as *'...straight a line as possible from middle Germany to the East/West German border at 500ft and 1000ft absolute altitude, and pull up at the border. At times an aircraft would return to Rhein/Main with tree limbs wrapped around the aircraft tail skid'.*

The 7406th flew about seven Half Track missions per week at first. Between July and September 1956, 52 more missions were flown. But then came the word that on 19 October 1956 the squadron was to be relieved of the Half Track ATRAN mission. Like the Lulu Belle C-54, the Half Track RB-50s were judged not able to produce the quality information needed. *'The equipment on the aircraft was not able to do the mission within specified tolerances. The same job would be done by synthetic methods.'*

More problems - more variants

Very early in the production run of the B-50B, a whole series of leaks in the new lightweight fuel cells caused their replacement. Pending the availability of new cells, deliveries of new B-50Ds were actually stopped. The new aircraft experienced fuel tank overflows, leaks in fuel check valves, failures of the engine turbosuperchargers, warped turbos and warped turbo bucket wheels. B/RB-50Bs also shared the B-50A's trailing wing cracking problem. The permanent solution to this problem was to use heavier metal in the fabrication of future wing flaps, but this took time to implement

The B-50C was an advanced version of the B-50, designed to obtain the maximum amount of performance from the basic Superfortress design. It was to be powered by four new R-4360-43 turbo-compound engines sometimes referred to as Variable Discharge Turbine (VDT) engines, a type that had also been considered for the B-36. The VDT engine concept combined the propeller thrust with the turbine engine exhaust acting as a 'jet assist' for additional power. These engines were being still being developed when the original order for the YB-50C was issued, but problems with the new engine system were never completely worked out and the VDT project was eventually cancelled. Without the new engines, the YB-50C project was cancelled also. The change to turbo-compound engines required a complete redesign of the airframe, with a wider wingspan and a longer fuselage. The takeoff weight of the B-50C was estimated to be 207,000 pounds, almost 50,000 pounds greater than that of most other B-50s.

An early B-50A, 46-061, was set aside to serve as a prototype for the YB-50C. The mockup of the B-50C was completed by November 1948 and 43 production aircraft (14 B-50Cs and 29 RB-50Cs) were ordered.

The most-produced version of the B-50 series was the B-50D, with 222 B-50Ds being built, primarily as a stopgap nuclear-capable medium bomber, pending the availability of the B-47.

The B-50D marked a major change in the B-50 series, which justified a new factory designation Model 345-9-6. The most noticeable outward change introduced by the B-50D was a revised nose with a single large moulded one-piece plastic cone and an optically-flat bomb-aimer's window in the lower portion which replaced the seven-piece B-29 unit that was used through the B-50B.

Boeing B-50D-120-BO '336' parked on a very dirty ramp, thought to have been after an airshow somewhere. *(USAF)*

THE B-50

Boeing B-50D-95-BO 48-096 in flight. The single piece 'blown' plexiglas nose glazing is clearly visible. (USAF)

Commencing with the 16th B-50D, receptacles were provided for the Boeing-developed boom-type inflight refuelling system. Two 700-gallon auxiliary fuel tanks could be carried on pylons underneath the outer wing panels. A new type of top forward turret was fitted. More efficient radar was installed, and the number of crew members was reduced from eleven to eight, with the typical crew comprising of pilot, copilot, engineer, radio/electronic countermeasures operator, left side gunner, right side gunner, top gunner, and tail gunner.

The B-50D first flew in May 1949, with deliveries to SAC starting in late June, the first units to receive them being the 93rd and 509th Bomb Wings. Initially, there were so many maintenance problems with the B-50Ds that SAC refused to accept any more until the defects could be corrected. Most of the B-50Ds were grounded during 1949-50 because of problems with main fuel cells, inverters, turbosuperchargers, alternators, generators, and cracks in wing trailing edges. There were also delays in the development of the boom-refuelling system, and neither the receiving end nor the feeding apparatus for the new equipment were actually fitted to most of the B-50Ds delivered, which led to a series of costly retrofits.

There were also problems in adapting the B-50D to carry atomic bombs. The B-50 was an adaptation of the B-29, which had been designed before the era of nuclear weapons. The bomb bay was really too small to house both the fairly large and heavy atomic bombs of the day plus the required accessory components such as arming controls, capsule insertion gear and other equipment needed for control, testing, and monitoring of the bombs. In those days, there was a high degree of secrecy surrounding the development of atomic bombs and there was little if any coordination between the USAF and the Atomic Energy Commission, which prevented information from reaching Boeing engineers who were assigned the responsibility for fitting these weapons inside the bomb bay of the B-50. This lack of communication resulted in the first few B-50Ds being delivered to SAC without having been adapted to carry both the Mark 3 and Mark 4 atomic bombs, so a costly and time-consuming series of modifications had to be done. This rapid development of nuclear bombs meant that new types of associated components would have to be fitted and the modifications would have to start all over again each time a new type of nuclear weapon was produced.

Incessant modifications required by the development of new types of atomic bombs severely strained the capabilities of both the Boeing factory and of the Air Materiel Command teams that were deployed to SAC bases. Special care had to be taken so that SAC's overall deterrent capability would not be seriously compromised by the seemingly never-ending series of B-50D modifications. The adaptation of 180 B-50Ds to accommodate the Mark 4 bomb's immediate successor had to be carefully scheduled, but there were some schedule overlaps and several serious delays. In March 1953, the Mark 4 bombs were finally taken out of service, which meant that all remaining B-50Ds would immediately have to be modified as well. By late 1953, SAC began to replace some of its B-29 and B-50 bombers with new B-47s, but there were serious delays in the delivery of B-47s.

Furthermore, the B-50D had been slated to receive the AN/APW-24, an improved bombing/navigation radar system, but this proved to be unsatisfactory because of lack of security, a high rate of malfunction, and a general inability to function properly in bad weather.

The last B-50D was delivered in December 1950. Some of SAC's five Wings of atomic-capable B-50Ds began to exchange their aircraft for B-47s in late 1953. The last B-50D, 49-330, from the 97th Bomb Wing at Biggs AFB, Texas was phased out of the active nuclear force on 20 October 1955.

Eleven B-50Ds were stripped of all armament and converted to TB-50D crew trainers. They were used for support duties, including the training of B-36 crews. Thirty-six B-50Ds were also stripped of their armament and used to replace weary WB-29s, which were beginning to suffer from extensive corrosionan. They were equipped for long-range weather reconnaissance missions using high-altitude atmospheric samplers, doppler radar, and weather radar, along with an AN/APN-82 Automatic Navigator, a radar navigation device capable of measuring drift and ground speed, the ANQ-7 temperature humidity indicator, the ML-313 Psychrometer, and improved altimeters and flight indicators. A bomb bay fuel tank was provided to extend the range, and these aircraft were re-designated WB-50D.

The modification contract for this work was assigned to the Lockheed Aircraft

Boeing WB-50D 48-115. Note the air sampling 'Bug Catcher' on the top aft fuselage. The display board by the nosewheel appears to show a parachute sonde. *(USAF)*

THE B-50

WB-50D 0-80108 is seen in flight, with a sampler on top of the fuselage and Military Air Transport Service titling. (USAF)

B-50J 49-350 of the 420th ARS seen at RAF Weathersfield in May 1959. (via John Hamlin)

Corporation. The new equipment proved more difficult to install than expected, and Lockheed could not meet the original schedules.

The first modified WB-50D flew on 20 August 1955, and the first example was delivered to the Air Weather Service in November. WB-50Ds served for a much longer period than expected. In 1960, after several fuel cells failed in flight, 28 WB-50Ds were temporarily grounded until they could be fitted with new or surplus fuel cells. One aircraft, 49-310, was given the temporary designation of JB-50D while being used for experimental work. WB-50Ds continued to serve well into the 1960s. Phaseout began in late 1963. 49-310, the last WB-50D was finally retired in 1967.

In the spring of 1951, the USAF cancelled the last 24 B-50Ds on the contract, ordering instead an equal number of TB-50H trainers. Boeing gave this version the Model 345-31-26 designation. The TB-50H was an unarmed bomber-navigation trainer intended to familiarise crews with the new 'K-system' radar bombing and navigation equipment developed for the B-47 Stratojet. Additional crew stations were provided for two students plus an instructor. The rear bomb bay was packed

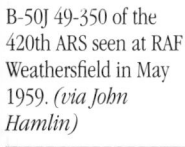

KB-50J '9391' seen on the ramp. Of interest is the detail shown in the open tip tank on the left. *(Hayes Corp)*

with electronic gear, but the forward bay could still carry bombs, but they were rarely dropped during training missions.

Since the training missions were of relatively short duration, there was no provision for inflight refuelling and no drop tanks could be carried under the outer wings. Because of its lighter 120,000 pounds loaded weight, the TB-50H was the fastest production B-50, with a top speed of 418 mph at 31,000 feet. Normal crew complement was twelve: pilot, copilot, engineer, bombardier, navigator instructor, left navigator trainee, right navigator trainee, right scanner, K-system trainee, K-system instructor, radio operator, and left radar trainee.

The first TB-50H was flown on 29 April 1952 and all were delivered between September 1952 and March 1953. They entered operational service with the 3236th Observer Training Squadron of the 3235th Observer Training Wing at Mather AFB in California. Operational service with Air Training Command was brief, the aircraft being phased out in June 1955. TB-50Hs were all later converted to aerial tankers under the designation KB-50K.

The Air Force planned that B-50s would be converted to aerial tankers, once they were no longer needed by the atomic bombing forces of SAC. All armament would be deleted, the outer wings would be reinforced, and equipment would be added that would make it possible for them to refuel three fighter aircraft simultaneously by the probe-and-drogue method.

0-80088 is a Boeing KB-50J in flight that was formerly 48-0088, originally built as a B-50D-90-BO of the 421st Air Refueling Squadron. *(USAF)*

With four turning and two burning this KB-50J is seen climbing out on another mission. *(USAF)*

The designation KB-50 was assigned to these conversions and the contract for the modification work was assigned to the Hayes Aircraft Corporation of Birmingham, Alabama. Additional fuel tanks were installed in the bomb bay and A-12B-1 refuelling drums were installed in the rear fuselage and in pods underneath each wingtip. The tail was lengthened by six feet. One hose was unreeled from the lengthened tail, and one hose was unreeled from a pod that was carried underneath each wing tip. The original B-50-type 700-gallon auxiliary wing tanks were retained. A refuelling operator's control station was added on each side of the fuselage aft of the pressure shell, with observation blisters.

Two B-50Ds, 47-170 and 48-046, were modified to serve as prototypes for later tanker conversions and were designated KB-50D. The completion date for the Hayes modifications was tentatively set for December of 1957, but the project proceeded so smoothly that it was completed ahead of time.

The first KB-50 flew in December 1955 and was accepted by the Air Force in

A good mixture of aircraft are seen in this picture - KB-50J 0-80114 trails it's hoses to for a North American F-100 Super Sabre and a McDonnell F-101 Voodoo. (USAF)

January 1956. By November 1957, Tactical Air Command's (TAC) KB-29s had all been phased out. By year's end, all of the command's aerial refuling squadrons had their full complement of KB-50s. TAC had nothing but praise for the new tankers; the KB-50s presented no serious problems, and their reliability was such that the command considered asking for more of them. Extra KB-50s would come 'cheap,' TAC calculated, if additional numbers of B-50s were added to the Hayes modification line. Nevertheless, the recommendation remained in limbo, which was just as well since the modification line had already been closed and the superior KB-50J was on the way.

Initially, no distinction was made between the different series of B-50s that had been modified; the tankers were all identified only as KB-50. However, the structural and equipment differences between different series made separation necessary for maintenance and operations, and distinguishing designations were eventually applied.

In 1956, the Air Force endorsed a programme to improve the performance of

KB-50J 49-9391 trails two of it's hoses while waiting for some trade. (USAF)

THE B-50

Above: A pair of F-104 Starfighters formate on KB-50J 0-90361 to take on more fuel. Note the angle of attack that the Starfighters are flying at!

Below: another mixed formation top up their tanks from KB-50J 0-80119. (both USAF)

the KB-50 aerial tanker fleet, brought about by the increase in performance in the next generation of jet aircraft. This performance enhancement was obtained by adding a 5200 lb.s.t. General Electric J47-GE-23 turbojet housed in a pod suspended from a pylon at the former location of each of the KB-50's auxiliary underwing wing tanks. The designation KB-50J was assigned to the conversion.

Flight testing began in April 1957. The aircraft made successful hookups and fuel transfers at higher altitudes, at greater gross weights, and at higher airspeeds than was possible with the KB-50. The jet engines increased the maximum speed to 444 mph at 17,000 feet at a gross weight of 179,500 pounds. In addition, the jet engines shortened the takeoff distance by 30%, and improved the time to climb

Getting up close and personal with KB-50J 48-391 with it's outer hose position about to deploy. *(USAF)*

to refuelling altitude by 60%. The KB-50J could maintain satisfactory refuelling speeds in level flight at altitudes which did not penalise the receiving aircraft.

The Hayes Aircraft Corporation converted 112 KB-50s to KB-50J configuration, delivering the first aircraft to TAC on 16 January 1958.

The KB-50J was considered as an interim tanker, pending the availability of the KC-135. Unfortunately, the KB-50Js began to deteriorate almost as soon as they were delivered, and TAC was forced to resort to cannibalization to keep some of the retrofitted tanker aircraft flying. The inner liner of KB-50 fuel cells began to crack, forcing Hayes to exchange fuel cells for new similar ones or for fuel cells that had been taken from B-50s that had been consigned to storage. Landing gear malfunctions were frequent, and many parts failure became common.

Following the withdrawal of the 24 TB-50H trainers from service, they were also modified as aerial tankers. Because of structural and equipment differences from earlier models, they were known as KB-50K, but were otherwise identical to the KB-50Js.

The tankers began to be phased out in 1964. Their pumping equipment and jet pods were transferred to KC-97L tankers serving with the Air National Guard. A few KB-50s were still around for the early stages of the Vietnam war, and were pressed into service to refuel jet fighters that were running low on fuel while still over enemy territory. Some of these refuellings were carried out at such low altitudes that they came under enemy fire from the ground. The last KB-50s were retired in 1965.

THE TU-4 'BULL'

The Tupolev Tu-4 was a piston-engined Soviet strategic bomber that served the Soviet Air Force from the late 1940s to mid 1960s and was a reverse-engineered copy of the Boeing B-29 Superfortress. 'Reverse engineering' is the process of discovering the technological principles of a human made device - in this case the B-29, its engines and all of its systems - through analysis of its structure, function and operation. It involved taking everything apart and analysing the workings in detail.

Just how the Soviets came to have any B-29s to be able to do this is a facinating story in itself. On 29 July 1944, B-29-5-BW 42-6256 *Ramp Tramp* of the 771st BS 692nd BG was commanded by Capt Howard R Jarrel. Because of problems with the auxiliary power unit, colloquially known as a 'putt putt', *Ramp Tramp* was the last aircraft to take off on the 1,650-mile mission; it took the crew almost two hours at a high-power setting to catch the rest of the formation, thus burning more fuel.

Capt Jarrell's aircraft made a normal bomb run on the Showa steel works at Anshan in Manchuria and may have been hit by a flak burst, but any damage was at most minor. When the pilot started his descent to cruising attitude for the trip back to Chengtu, the inboard right engine - the number 3 - ran away and could not be feathered. It had to be shut down and the increased drag of the unfeathered propeller made it obvious that the ircraft would not be able to return to Chengtu due to insufficient fuel.

As the aircraft was still over Japanese territory the crew began destroying all classified material on board including operating manuals, orders and instructions in case they were forced down in enemy territory. Small objects and shredded paper materials - flight manuals, checklists, placards, code books, etc - were dumped into the nose wheel well. In the meantime, the pilot headed toward the Russian base at Vladivostok to land the damaged aircraft in Allied territory. As the bomber approached a Russian airfield, a squadron of fighters was scrambled to 'escort' it. The Russian fighters fired near the B-29, but it was unclear whether they were trying to hit it, or force it down. After a few minutes a Russian fighter pilot motioned for the bomber to land. The B-29 began to head toward a field with a concrete runway, but the fighters started shooting again and indicated the plane should land at the grass fighter strip near Tavichanka. Although the grass field was too small for a B-29, Capt. Jarrell lined up to land since he had no choice. As he lowered the landing gear, all the shredded material in the nose wheel well streamed out and fell into the waters of Vladivostok Bay. The aircraft touched down at just above stalling speed and stopped before running off the end of the runway.

After landing, Capt Jarrell ordered the crew to stay aboard the B-29 while he left and tried to communicate with the Russian pilots, but none spoke English. A few hours later, the crew left the plane and joined Capt Jarrell who asked to be allowed to contact the American Consul in the city, but permission was denied. The Russian allies interrogated the crew for three day, trying to obtain operational details about the aircraft and its capabilities. The crew refused to divulge secret information. On the eleventh day after landing, the crew was finally able to speak with the Consulate. Unfortunately, the crew was not released to the consulate and remained prisoners of the Russians. Since the Soviet Union was not at war with Japan at the time, both the aircraft and Capt Jarrel's crew were interned.

On 20 August during a raid on Yawata staged out of the Chengtu bases, B-29A-1-BN 42-93829 - some sources say the serial was 42-93839 - commanded by R McGlynn of the 395th BS, 40th BG was forced to divert to the Soviet Union following flak damage. It crashed in the foothills of Sikhote Alin mountain range east of Khabarovsk after the crew baled out; again, the crew was interned.

On the night of 10-11 November 1944, B-29 42-6365 *Gen. H. H. Arnold Special* was damaged during a raid against Omura on Kyushu and was forced to divert to Vladivostok. Other reports suggest that Captain Weston H Price and his crew used up so much fuel fighting headwinds that they were forced to divert. It was followed on 21 November by 42-6358 *Ding Hao*. Again, both crews and both aircraft were interned.

Boeing B-29-15-BW Superfortress (s/n 42-6365) named *'Gen. H.H. Arnold Special'* from the 794th BS, 468th BG, 20th AF. This aircraft was lost when it was forced to divert to Vladivostok in the Soviet Union with battle damage on 11 November 1944. The crew was interned. This aircraft and two other damaged B-29s which fell into the Soviets hands were used to make the exact copy Tupolev Tu-4. *(USAAF)*

The co-pilot, John K 'Jack' Schaefer, recalls the flight: '"*The Ding Hao takeoff was uneventful. However, when I looked out my window, I could see a large fireball to the right and behind our plane.*" This was 42-6362, of the 792nd BS, commanded by Captain H.C. Maisch, who was unable to gain altitude after taking off, and headed for a grove of trees a half-mile beyond the south end of the runway. One of the propellers on the left side dipped a large tree, pulling the bomber into a steep turn and sent it cartwheeling into the ground.

The remaining B-29s continued on to Omura. Over Japan they met determined opposition from fighters and light bombers that dropped phosphorus explosives into the B-29 formations. Eight of the B-29s did not make it back to China. Among the missing was *Ding Hao*. Two weeks after the mission, on 7 December the War Department sent a telegram to the crewmen's families. Jack's parents in Michigan were informed that he was missing in action and that they would be promptly notified of any additional news as it became available. It would be some time before the Schaefers learned the story behind their son's disappearance. About 100 miles from Omura, Japanese fighters had attacked the B-29 formation. *Ding Hao* was hit by machine-gun fire from an enemy fighter approaching from below and to the side. *'Being hit by enemy fire was nothing new for the rest of the crew. They were on their ninth mission and this had happened before. It was new for me, but I was so busy doing my job that I didn't realize we had been hit until the engineer shut down no. 3. He advised the pilot that no. 4 was doubtful as well. I had been on several training flights where we had lost an engine, so I was not all that concerned. The pilot conferred with the engineer and the navigator and made the decision that we would not have enough fuel to get back beyond enemy lines. After reviewing our options, we decided to head north to Vladivostok in the Soviet Union'.*

'Most of the crew felt that the Russians would help us repair the Ding Hao and then give us enough fuel to get us back to China'.

Instead of being treated as comrades in arms by the Soviets, the *Ding Hao* crew received a decidedly cold welcome. As the bomber neared Vladivostok, four Yak-9 fighters intercepted it and fired tracer warning shots. The Soviet fighters forced *Ding Hao* to land on a small naval airfield south of Vladivostok. As they approached the runway Schaefer was surprised to see another B-29 on the ramp below. The approach and landing was very difficult because the runway was so short, but heavy snow on the ground helped slow down the aircraft.

Soviet military vehicles quickly surrounded the bomber, and the crew was ordered out at gunpoint. Made more complicated by the language barrier, the exchange was hardly the treatment one would expect from allies. While the Americans and Soviets were allies in the war with Germany, the Soviet Union was officially a neutral nation in the Pacific conflict. As a result, the Soviets said they were obliged to intern both the American combatants and their aircraft until the end of the war. The Soviet position was understandable given that they already had their hands full in an all-out war with Germany in the West, and the last thing they wanted was a war with Japan in the East.

After a brief stay in Vladivostok, the *Ding Hao* crew was transported by train 400 miles to the north, to Khabarovsk. There they met up with the crew of *Gen.*

'Ding Hao' was a chinese phrase that roughly translated into 'everything is ok'. (USAAF).

H.H. Arnold Special - the other B-29 on the ramp at Vladivostok - and a B-25 crew from the Aleutians.

On 3 December the 29 American servicemen departed by train on the Trans-Siberian Railroad for the central Asian city of Tashkent. The journey would take almost two weeks. On 16 December they joined 101 other US Army Air Forces and Navy internees being held in a compound outside Tashkent called Yang-Ul. This group included crews of other B-29s that had diverted to the Soviet Union.

The Americans were held in what had been a nobleman's estate before the 1917 Russian Revolution, but now it was not much different from a POW camp. Internees were given one blanket each and had very little food. It was the height of the Russian winter, and all suffered from the extreme cold.

Stalin was unsure how to handle the Tashkent internees. The USA was putting diplomatic pressure on the Soviets to release them, but the Japanese might view that as a violation of the Soviets' professed neutrality in the Pacific War. There was a potential solution: if the Americans 'escaped' from the camp, the Soviets could not be accused of supporting the US war against Japan.

Jack Schaefer: *'The escape was something we all really wanted badly. We had been cold and hungry for months and any kind of a rumor could get us talking about getting out. Unfortunately, the rumors were always just that until late January, when an emissary from the American Embassy in Moscow visited and told our senior officers that arrangements were completed for us to be spirited out of the camp and indeed out of the Soviet Union as well."*

After 45 days in the camp, Schaefer and the other internees boarded a train late at night on 25 January 1945, for a three-day trip from Tashkent to Ashkhabad and then on to Kizil-Arvat. They were transferred to Lend-Lease Studebaker trucks early on 28 January, under strict orders to remain silent. The trucks then drove out of the Soviet Union and into Iran.

Tu-4 'BULL' 201

On 30 January the internees were placed under control of U.S. security personnel outside Tehran. They were sprayed with delousing powder and instructed to take a shower. Their clothing was destroyed, and they were each issued a plain Army enlisted man's uniform, even though the group included both officers and Navy servicemen. U.S. embassy and OSS personnel debriefed them, telling the newly released servicemen that '...*officially they had never been in the Soviet Union'*, and that they were not to discuss their internment with anyone. Due to the extreme secrecy of their escape, the internees were referred to as 'War Department Special Group No. 2'.

All the released internees would be sent back to the USA and prohibited from participating further in combat. This was probably a stipulation of the release agreement between the USSR and the USA. The trip home took more than a month. They first flew in five C-46s from Tehran to Egypt, and then from Egypt to Naples, Italy, where they boarded the Liberty ship *Sullivan*. The members of War Department Special Group No. 2 were the only passengers on the voyage. *Sullivan* steamed to Oran, Algeria to link up with 35 other ships that would form a convoy. On 16 February the convoy headed for the Straits of Gibraltar. As it entered the Atlantic the next day, the convoy came under attack by German U-boats.

Sullivan anchored off New York on 5 March, but before the former internees could leave the ship next day they were once again reminded that they could not discuss their experience in the Soviet Union.

Discovering the secrets.

The Soviets were now holding three intact B-29s. Stalin was well aware of the need for a strategic bombing capability similar to that of the USAAF. In fact, he had ordered the development of a comparable bomber and also requested B-29s under Lend Lease, but the US refused to supply them. The Soviets kept the interned machines despite American demands for their return and Stalin tasked Tupolev with cloning the Superfortress. Soviet industry was to produce twenty copies of the aircraft in just two years.

In May 1945, Stalin ordered that the Soviet Union develop a copy of the B-29 for immediate manufacture. The design bureau of Andre N Tupolev was given

This picture surfaced from the former Soviet Union a number of years ago and is allegedly the *Gen. H.H. Arnold Special*, being slowly taken apart in Moscow on Stalin's orders.

While it could be a B-29, I remain to be convinced. *(Simon Peters Collection).*

responsibility for the airframe, while the engine bureau headed by Arkadii B Shvetsov was assigned the responsibility of copying the Wright R-3350 Duplex Cyclone engine. The Soviet version of the B-29 was assigned the designation Tu-4. The Shvetsov version of the Wright Duplex Cyclone was known as the ASh-73TK.

The three B-29s were flown to Moscow and delivered into Tupolev OKB. It has been reported in Russia that the *Gen. H.H. Arnold Special* was disassembled at the Central Aerodrome in Moscow. *Ding Hao* was the aircraft grounded as a reference machine and *Ramp Tramp* remained flyable. Supposedly *Ramp*

The Soviets put the Tu-4 to a number of uses.

Top: the 'basic' TU-4

The Tu-4 was also used as a launch vehicle in the same manner that the Americans used the B-29. This picture shows a pair of Samolet 346s - Soviet copy/developments of the German DFS 346 rocket powered aircraft.

A number of Tu-4s were modified as troop carrier with fuselage doors for paradropping. The Tu-4D also had large containers on underwing pylons carrying some of the troops equipment and weapons.

A small number of Tu-4s for use engine testbeds They were used to test engines such as the Kuznetsov NK-12 turboprop, Lyulka AL-5, AL-7, Mikulin AM-3 and AM-5 turbojets etc.

Tramp's engines were replaced with ASh-73TK's to make the aircraft more maintainable and it remained in-service for nine years.

Each of the B-29's 105,000 components had to be reverse-engineered by various design bureaus in Russia. There was difficulty producing the large tyres and landing gear, so agents were sent to the West to purchase them on the surplus market. In the end, the Tu-4 was only one percent heavier than the B-29.

When disassembling the *Gen. H.H. Arnold Special,* a plaque next to the bombardier's seat was found. It said: "*At the request of the workers of the Boeing plant in Wichita, Kansas, this B-29 is named the General H.H. Arnold*",

Tupelov engineers were under very heavy pressure to achieve an exact clone of the original B-29. Each minute alteration had to be scrutinized and was a subject to a lengthy bureaucratic process.

The go-ahead for the program was given before the end of 1944, and the Tu-4 project was well under way by the first quarter of 1945. A factory on the Volga was given the task of building 20 test and evaluation aircraft, and two factories behind the Urals were given the responsibility for full-scale production.

The Soviet Union used the metric system, thus 1/16th inch thick sheet aluminum and proper rivet lengths were unavailable. The corresponding metric-gauge metal was thicker; as a result, the Tu-4 weighed about 3,100 lb more than the B-29, with a corresponding decrease in range and payload. This went to extreme lengths in that because 1/16 inch nominal sheet thickness equals 1.5875mm, and no industry in the USSR was willing to take the responsibility to produce sheets with such accuracy.

The Soviets used a different engine, the Shvetsov ASh-73, which had some parts in common with the Superfortress' Wright R-3350 but was not identical. The remote-controlled gun turrets were also redesigned to accommodate Soviet 23 mm cannons. Engineers also had to lobby with high-ranking military officials even for the most basic common sense decisions. In another example, the Soviets reverse-engineered and copied the American IFF system and actually had it installed in the first Tu-4 built. As yet another example, Kerber, Tupolev's deputy at the time, recalled in his memoirs that engineers had to obtain authorisation from a high-ranking Air Force general in order to use Soviet-made parachutes for the crew.

At first glance, this is a B-29 - in fact it's a Tu.4 in one of the Russian aviation museums.

Two views of the Chinese AWACS version of the Tu-4 with Ivchenko AI-20 turbo-prop engines.

In spite of the end of the war, the Soviet Tu-4 program went forward with all deliberate speed. The first Tu-4 test aircraft was ready by the late summer of 1946.

Then in the 11 November 1946 issue of the Berlin newspaper *Der Kurier* there appeared claims that the Soviet Union was manufacturing a bolt-for-bolt copy of the B-29 in a series of factories located in the Urals. This report was widely disbelieved, since the Soviet Union was at the time thought incapable of manufacturing an aircraft as large and sophisticated as the B-29. However, the report was given more credence when it was revealed that some Soviet agents had been attempting to purchase B-29 tyres, wheels, and brake assemblies in the USA.

The Tu-4 first flew on 19 May 1947, piloted by test pilot Nikolai Rybko. Serial production started immediately, and the type entered large-scale service in 1949. Early test flights turned up problems with the electrically-actuated undercarriage, which forced several wheels-up landings. In addition, there were frequent runaway propellers. Many test pilots complained about the distortion of vision caused by the extensively-glazed nose.

During 3 August 1947 Aviation Day parade over Tushino Airport, Moscow, three four-engined aircraft which were obviously B-29s appeared during a low-altitude flyover. It was at first thought that these three aircraft might have been the same three intact B-29s known to have been in Soviet hands, but a fourth aircraft appeared which was obviously a transport conversion of the B-29, leaving no doubt that the earlier report of B-29 manufacture in the Soviet Union was completely accurate. The transport version was designated Tu-70, but it was only revealed later that the designation of the bomber was Tu-4.

Following the public debut of the Tu-4 in the Aviation Day parade, initial long-range trials began. Many teething problems with both the Tu-4 systems and the

Tu-4 'BULL'

Shvetsov ASh-73TK engines still remained to be resolved. The Tu-4 begin to enter service with the Soviet strategic bombing arm, the Dal'naya Aviatsiya (DA), in 1948, providing the Voennovosdushniye Sily (V-VS, the Air Forces of the USSR) with true strategic bombing capability. Series production Tu-4s suffered continuously from malfunctions in the remotely-controlled defensive armament system and in the crew cabin pressurization system. The reliability of the ASh-73TK turbosupercharged engines still left a lot to be desired. Quality control at the manufacturing plants had to be tightened up, and by early 1949, most of the more serious defects had been corrected. It was not until mid-1949 that the Tu-4s of the DA had achieved full operational capability. By the end of 1949, some 300 Tu-4s had entered service with the DA. In addition, a few Tu-4s entered service with the Aviatsiya Voenno-morskovo Flota (AV-MF, the Naval Air Force) as long-range patrol aircraft.

The Tu-4 was assigned the code name Bull in the NATO code naming system. Its entrance into service threw the USAF into a panic, since the Tu-4 possessed sufficient range to attack Chicago, Los Angeles, and New York with a worthwhile load on a one-way suicide mission. From seized airfields in Iceland, Soviet Tu-4s were even capable of hitting targets in New England, New York, Pennsylvania, and Ohio, and from bases in Greenland they could hit targets as far away as New Orleans or Denver. Since the Soviets now had a weapon capable of attacking North America, this forced the United States government to develop an extremely costly air-interception capability involving ground radar installations, a Ground Observer Corps, radar picket aircraft, Nike surface-to-air missiles, and a fleet of jet interceptor fighters. The development of the Soviet atomic bomb in 1949 gave the air defence programme a new urgency, since the United States was itself now in danger of a nuclear attack.

This prompted a somewhat interesting inter-air force co-operation exercise between the RAF and USAF in 1948 of which little is known. There is however an confidential RAF training film in existence that depicts the correct way to intercept American B-29s using Gloster Meteor IVs and De Havilland Vampires. Made with the support of the Central Fighter Establishment and the 92nd BG, part of the 3rd Air Division, it shows a group of RAF pilots being trained in methods to attack

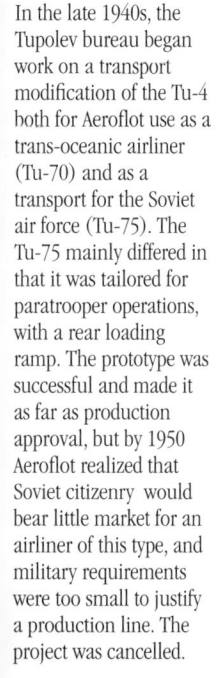

In the late 1940s, the Tupolev bureau began work on a transport modification of the Tu-4 both for Aeroflot use as a trans-oceanic airliner (Tu-70) and as a transport for the Soviet air force (Tu-75). The Tu-75 mainly differed in that it was tailored for paratrooper operations, with a rear loading ramp. The prototype was successful and made it as far as production approval, but by 1950 Aeroflot realized that Soviet citizenry would bear little market for an airliner of this type, and military requirements were too small to justify a production line. The project was cancelled.

squadrons of B-29s that were clearly 'standing in' for the threat from the Tu-4s.

Figures for production numbers of the Tu-4 vary widely; anything from 'around 850' to 'approximately 1200' Tu-4s are believed to have been built in the Soviet Union, with some going to China during the later 1950s when the Tu-4 was progressively withdrawn from operational service with the DA and replaced by more advanced types. These machines were then transferred to the air transport force, the Voenno-transportnaya Aviatsiya, to supplement the short-range Li-2s and Il-14s. As the Antonov An-12 turboprop transport became available, the Tu-4 was progressively withdrawn from the transport role. By the beginning of the 1960s, the Tu-4 was essentially also out of the inventory of the shore-based maritime patrol force. A few Tu-4s had been provided to China to provide that country with at least a token bombing force, and some of these were reportedly still in service in China as recently as 1968. Indeed, in 1967, China attempted to develop its first Airborne Early Warning aircraft, based on the Tu-4 airframe outfitted with turboprop engines. The KJ-1 AEWC was a first generation Chinese AEW (Airborne Early Warning) Type 843 rotordome radar fitted on top of a Tupolev Tu-4 bomber. The project was started in 1969 under the code name 'Project 926'. The prototype aircraft is currently on display at the Chinese Aviation Museum in Beijing. According to the Chinese governmental claim, a single Tu-4 AEW unit was equivalent to more than 40 ground radar stations, but production was stopped due to the Cultural Revolution. In the era of Chinese economic reform, the project was once again put on hold because economic development was the top priority. When the project was finally reviewed again for the modernization of the People's Liberation Army Air Force, it was already too late and outdated. Instead, China developed phased array radar for its KJ-2000 AWACS.

SPECIALS

XB-39

The XB-39 41-36954 *Spirit of Lincoln* was a modification of the first YB-29 which was turned over to General Motors for installation of liquid-cooled Allison V-3420 engines. The V-3420 was essentially two V-1710 engine spliced together with one crankcase and two crankshafts geared together. Normal output was 2100 hp at 25,000 feet, but the engines were not really ready for production. Aircraft speed increased to 405 mph at 35,000 feet, but the improvement in performance was not considered sufficient to justify production.

The XB-39 project was really nothing more than a proof-of-concept project to demonstrate performance with liquid-cooled 'Vee' engines. It was also insurance against shortages of the production engine. Only one XB-39 was built; it was delivered the US Army Air Force in early 1944 for testing. Most of the problems with the standard B-29 production version were corrected by mid-1944, and no orders for the XB-39 were placed.

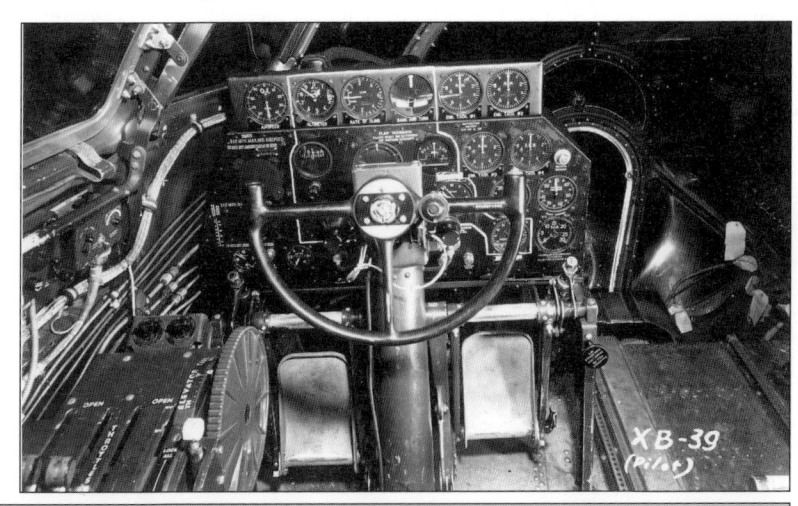

One of the very few photographs located on the XB-39 *'Spirit of Lincoln'* and the pilots position. *(USAAF)*

XB-29E

All of the series letters beyond D assigned to the B-29 were for modified earlier versions. XB-29E was the designation assigned to a B-29 that was converted for fire-control system testing.

The designation B-29F was assigned to six B-29-BWs that were winterised for cold weather testing in Alaska. They were all eventually converted back to standard B-29 configuration.

XB29G

A single Bell-built B-29B-55-BA, 44-24043, was modified as a testbed for General Electric jet engines and redesignated XB-29G. The engine was mounted on a cradle in the bomb bay which could be extended below the aircraft to test its operation in a fast airstream.

All armament was removed and engine test stations and instrumentation were installed. The bomb bay was used to house prototype jet engines which could be extended into the air stream for testing and retracted for takeoffs and landings. Tested engines included the Allison J35 and General Electric J47 and J73.

XB-29H and YB-29J

One B-29A was used for special armament testing under the designation XB-29H. Six B-29s were fitted with R-3350-CA-2 fuel injection engines and the revised nacelles that were intended for late production B-29As in a programme to service test these new engine installations. These aircraft were redesignated YB-29J. These engine nacelles had the oil coolers and intercoolers moved further aft, which gave them a 'chinless' appearance, so they became known by the nickname 'Andy Gump', who was a famous cartoon character of the period.

Boeing XB-29G 44-84043 airborne, left, and taxiing with an jet engine mounted on an extendable trapeze in the modified bomb bay. *(USAAF)*

SPECIALS

42-245528 fitted with 'Andy Gump' engine nacelles was used by Boeing to test electrical systems and the new, larger B-50 tail.

RB-29J and YKB-29J

Some of these YB-29Js were used for photo-reconnaissance work as RB-29J. Two machines - 44-86398 and 44-86402 - were converted to aerial tankers under the designation YKB-29J as part of a test of the Boeing-developed boom aerial refuelling system that was introduced in the KB-29P programme. However, these two aircraft retained their service test and J-series designations.

P2B-1S

On 14 March 1947 the US Navy took over four B-29-BWs for long-range search missions. The designation P2B-1S was assigned. They were assigned Navy Bureau of Aeronautics numbers as follows: 44-87766 as BuNo 84031, 45-21787 as BuNo 84029, 45-21789 as BuNo 84028 and 45-21791 as BuNo 84030.

One of the P2Bs (84029) was modified as the carrier aircraft for the Douglas D-558-II Skyrocket high-speed rocket-powered research aircraft. The P2B was named *'Fertile Myrtle'* and carried the NACA number 137. Its bomb bay was extensively modified to carry a D-558-II nestled underneath the belly. The research aircraft was dropped in flight from the bomb bay cradle, and the rocket engines were fired once the aircraft had fallen free of the P2B.

Boeing RB-29J *'Tiger Lil'* and crew from the 91st Strategic Reconnaissance Squadron, 91st Strategic Reconnaissance Wing. *(USAF)*

P2B 84029 *Fertile Myrtle* is raised on jacks with its tail buried into the hangar roof so that the Douglas Skyrocket can be towed underneath.

Left: the Skyrocket about to be launched from *Fertile Myrtle.(both NACA)*

The first D-558-II launch took place on 8 September 1950 with test pilot William B. Bridgeman at the controls of the research aircraft and George Jansen at the controls of the B-29. A series of Skyrocket launches took place over the next few years, each one further exploring the outer reaches of the flight envelope. The D-558-II exceeded Mach 2 for the first time on 20 November 1953 with test pilot Scott Crossfield at the controls. The last Skyrocket flight took place in December 1956.

'*Fertile Myrtle*' was eventually sold to a civilian owner, a museum in Oakland, California. This was the only example of a flyable B-29 ever being sold by the Air Force to a civilian operator.

EB-29 *Goblin* mother ship

Several B-29s were modified for various experimental purposes under the designation EB-29. Perhaps the most bizarre of these was the EB-29 used as the carrier aircraft for the McDonnell XF-85 Goblin parasite fighter in 1948. The rear bomb bay was modified to carry a special cradle from which the XF-85 could be launched and retrieved in flight.

SPECIALS

The XP-35 mock up in position with the EB-29 trapeze system rig. (USAAF)

This went back to 29 January 1944, when the Army Air Forces invited the aircraft industry to submit concept proposals for jet fighters capable of escorting its long-range heavy bombers. Since the first jet fighters were notorious fuel hogs, they promised to have insufficient range to escort the long-range B-35 and B-36 bombers then on the drawing boards. The USAAF proposed that one solution to the problem might be to revive the parasite fighter idea of the early 1930s and have the long-range bombers carry their protective fighters with them.

The McDonnell Aircraft Corporation of St Louis was the only company to respond to the proposal. They proposed a small fighter to be carried partially inside a parent B-29, B-36, or B-35 heavy bomber. However, the AAF rejected this plan in January 1945, concluding that the fighter would have to be carried completely inside the bomber. On 19 March 1945 McDonnell submitted a revised proposal - a plan for a tiny aircraft with an egg-shaped fuselage, a triple vertical tail, a tailplane with pronounced anhedral, and vertically-folding swept-back wings. The engine was to be a 3000 lb.st. Westinghouse J34-WE-7 axial-flow turbojet with a nose intake and a straight-through exhaust.

The USAAF liked the McDonnell proposal, and on 9 October 1945 ordered two prototypes - plus one static test airframe - under the designation XP-85. Conditional upon the results of flight trials with the XP-85, the AAF had intended to order an initial batch of 30 production examples, but before the completion of the first prototype this plan was shelved in favour of a more cautious approach in which only the two experimental aircraft would be acquired.

Since the XP-85 was to be launched and recovered from a retractable trapeze underneath its parent bomber, no conventional landing gear was fitted. A retractable hook was fitted to the fuselage in front of the cockpit. During recovery, the XP-85 would approach its parent bomber and the hook would gently engage the trapeze. Once securely attached, the aircraft would be pulled up into the belly of the bomber. If an emergency landing were necessary, the aircraft was provided with a retractable steel skid underneath the fuselage, and the wingtips were protected by steel runners.

Since no B-36 could be spared as yet for the project, 44-84111, a Bell-Atlanta-built Boeing B-29B-65-BA, was specially modified for use as the mothership in the initial testing. Redesignated EB-29B, it was fitted with a special launch-and-recovery trapeze that would be used for the first test flights of the XP-85.

In June 1948, the XP-85 was redesignated XF-85 when the USAF replaced the prefix P for Pursuit by F for Fighter. The first prototype XF-85 (46-523) was damaged at Moffett Field, California during wind tunnel testing, so it was the second aircraft, 46-524, that was used for the initial flight trials, which began on 23 August 1948. Initially, the XF-85 made captive flights suspended beneath the EB-29B at 20,000 feet above Muroc Dry Lake. The first free flight came on 28 August. The test pilot detached his XF-85 from the EB-29B and flew free for 15 minutes while he evaluated the handling properties of the new fighter. However, when it came time to re-hook, he ran into trouble. The XF-85 was caught in violent air turbulence underneath the parent aircraft. After ten minutes attempting to hook onto the trapeze, the XF-85 slammed up against the trapeze and the canopy

Above: EB-29 44-84111, nicknamed *Monstro* gets airborne with the XF-85 tucked half inside and half outside its belly. *(USAF)*

Later in the flight the XF-85 hangs suspended from the trapeze extended out of the EB-29. (USAF)

SPECIALS

The second Goblin parasite fighter, shortly after the first in-flight release on 23 August 1948. *(USAF)*

was shattered. Fortunately, the pilot was uninjured and he managed to make an emergency landing on the dry lake bed below.

Following repairs, 46-524 made three flights on 14/15 October 1948. Three successful recoveries were made, but each was a harrowing experience for all concerned. However, on the fifth flight, more trouble was encountered. The removal of the fairing around the base of the hook resulted in severe turbulence and loss of directional stability, forcing the pilot to make another emergency landing. Vertical surfaces were added to the wingtips in an attempt to improve directional stability while flying in the turbulent air underneath the EB-29B. However, this did not help very much, and the sixth XF-85 flight ended in yet another emergency landing on the lakebed. The same fate awaited 46-523 on 8 April 1949, when it made its first and only flight.

The Air Force reluctantly concluded that since the recovery operation was a difficult job for even experienced test pilots, it would probably be far beyond the capabilities of the average squadron pilot. In addition, it was projected that the performance of the XF-85 would probably be inferior to that of foreign interceptors that would soon enter service. The Air Force terminated the XF-85 programme on 24 October 1949.

XF-85 46-524 rises out of the pit at Muroc AFB and into the belly of the B-29. *(USAF)*

Above: the X-1A tucked inside mother ship 45-21800

Left: The Bell X-1 in flight

Below: The X-1-3 *Queenie* is mated to the EB-50A 46-006 at Muroc in November 1951. The operation was complex involving lifting the entire bomber as shown. This particular X-1 only flew twice before exploding and destroying both itself and the mother aircraft. *(USAF)*

SPECIALS

X-1 mother ship

Another famous aircraft was B-29-96-BW serial number 45-21800, which was used as the 'mother' aircraft for launches of the Bell X-1 rocket-powered research aircraft. On 14 October 1947, Capt Charles E 'Chuck' Yeager was dropped in his X-1 from the B-29 and became the first human to pilot an aircraft faster than the speed of sound. Though originally designed for conventional ground takeoffs, all X-1 aircraft were air-launched from a B-29 or B-50 due to the limited fuel supply and the hazard of fuel explosion during ground handling. The ground take-off was attempted only once. Having lit all four chambers, the X-1 accelerated so fast that the wing flaps blew off before the pilot was able to retract the undercarriage.

The B-29 and later a B-50 was adapted as mother aircraft. The X-1 was carried aloft in its bomb bay with no pilot onboard. A modified heavy bomb shackle was used as a releasing device. At an altitude of 8000 feet, the pilot would go down the small ladder, crawl into the X-1, seal the door, plug himself into all systems (electrical, oxygen, radio) and report being ready. After that the B-29 would climb a further 25000 feet before releasing the aircraft.

Each of the X-1s had its own carrier aircraft: B-29A 45-21800 was the mother ship of X-1-1 and X-1-2. This modified Superfortress was also designated JTB-29A. The X-1-3 was carried by EB-50A 46-006.

Project *Tip Tow*

The MX-1018 programme, code named '*Tip Tow*' sought to extend the range of the early jets in order to give fighter protection to piston-engined bombers with the provision for in-flight attachment/detachment of the fighter to the bomber via wingtip connections.

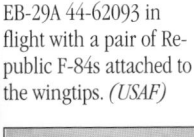

EB-29A 44-62093 in flight with a pair of Republic F-84s attached to the wingtips. *(USAF)*

US Air Force Republic EF-84D-1-RE 48-641 converted for use in Project Tip Tow in wingtip hookup with a Boeing B-29 shown here in a hangar, giving a close up view of the wing-tip coupling mechanism. (USAF)

Tip Tow aircraft consisted of a specially modified EB-29A 44-62093 and two EF-84B, 46-641 and 46-661. The bomber was fitted with booms installed at the wing tips onto which the F-84D's lance would be attached just before being withdrawn into the mother ship's wing to lock both planes together. The first hook-on trials were carried out on 21 July 1950 in the skies above Long Island, New York. With Major Clarence Anderson flying the starboard and Major John Davis running the port aircraft, the initial connecting test proved a resounding success. In the beginning both F-84Ds experienced heavy turbulence in their pitch and yaw while in the process of hooking into the booms, but after that the ride proved to be smoother than many anticipated. Restarting the Thunderflash's engine was also relatively easy and after several months the programme was ready for it next phase.

A number of flights were undertaken, with several successful cycles of attachment and detachment, using at first a single aircraft, and then two. The pilots of the F-84s maintained manual control when attached, with roll axis maintained by elevator movement rather than aileron movement. Engines on the F-84s were shut down in order to save fuel during the 'tow' by the mother ship, and in-flight engine restarts were successfully accomplished. The morning of 15 September 1952 marked another milestone in the project's life when the Thunderflashes made their first, long lasting link up with the bomber. That was followed by another 43 additional connections. After a brief inactive period, testing resumed in March 1953.

Wing flexibility of the B-29 as well as wing-tip vortices caused concern, and the mechanisms for attachment required modifications. The longest flight with all connected was on 20 October 1950, and lasted for two hours forty minutes. All these flights were accomplished with manual control of the F-84 aircraft. Republic received an additional contract to continue the experiments by incorporating an automatic flight control system. Meanwhile, as the modifications proceeded, additional test flights were made, including night flights. The automatic flight

SPECIALS

control modifications were ready for testing in March 1953, and a number of hookups were made with only one or the other of the F-84s while attempting to sort continuing electrical issues.

A month later, tragedy hit the programme. On 24 April 1953 during an engaging maneuver, Major Davis, flying in the left hand position, had his F-84D lose surface control when the the automatic system was activated, rolling upside down and hitting the upper wing structure of the EB-29A. Both aircraft plummeted into Peconic Bay with the lost of Davis and the entire bomber crew.

DB-50D

Early in 1951, one B-50D, 48-075, was converted as a drone director for testing the Bell XGAM-63 Rascal air to surface missile. The designation DB-50D was assigned.

The name 'Rascal' was actually an acronym that stood for RAdar SCAnning Link, so named for the guidance system that was used during the missile's dive onto the target. This guidance system was to be installed aboard the controlling aircraft. This system was to be developed jointly by Bell Avionics, Radio Corporation of America (RCA), and Texas Instruments.

The GAM-63 missile was powered by a Bell-designed liquid-fuelled rocket engine was made up of three vertical in-line thrust chambers developing a thrust of 4000 pounds. It had a launch weight of about 13,000 pounds and was 31 feet long with a body diameter of four feet. At a top speed of Mach 2.95, the missile could carry a 3000 pound nuclear warhead up to 100 miles.

Strategic Air Command was never very enthusiastic about the Rascal program, believing that the missile was far too complex, with a guidance system that was likely to be prone to frequent failures and which would be relatively easy for an enemy to jam. However, the Air Staff pushed hard for the Rascal concept, and SAC was forced to go along.

The Air Force had originally planned to activate two squadrons of Rascal-carrying aircraft, one of B-36s and the other of DB-50Ds. However, the Rascal-carrying DB-50Ds would have to operate from overseas because of the B-50's relatively limited range. Conversions of B-50Ds into DB-50D Rascal directors

It is thought that this picture is actually a montage of two images, for the angle of the missile and length of the rocket plume looks too close to the B-50!

The RASCAL project was cancelled in September 1958. (USAF)

were scheduled to start in June 1952, but deficiencies in the Rascal missile as well as other considerations altered these plans. In March 1952, it was decided that only the B-36 and the B-47 would carry the Rascal missile, and plans for a fleet of DB-50D Rascal-carriers were never carried out.

In spite of the cancellation of the fleet of DB-50Ds, a single B-50D was converted to DB-50D Rascal-carrying configuration for test purposes. The Rascal was carried on a special launch cradle which was lowered from the bomb bay of the DB-50D. The DB-50D carried out the first Rascal air launch on 30 September 1952 and continued flight testing of the Rascal until 1955.

It was later decided that only the B-47 would carry the Rascal, the B-36 being removed from consideration. A fleet of Rascal-capable B-47s was planned, and several such conversions were actually carried out. In the event, the Rascal concept rapidly became obsolete in the face of new developments in the field of air-launched missiles. The Rascal programme was formally cancelled on 9 September 1958.

SB-29

Fifteen B-29s and one B-29A were adapted for air-sea rescue duty after World War Two. Nicknamed 'Super Dumbo' and designated SB-29, these aircraft were modified to carry an air-droppable A-3 Edo lifeboat.

The A-3 lifeboat was developed by the EDO Corporation in 1947 for the USAF as a successor to the Higgins Industries A-1 lifeboat. The A-3 was a key element of 'Super Dumbo' rescue flights of the 1950s.

EDO built the lifeboat of aluminum alloy to be carried by the SB-29 performing air-sea rescue duties during the Pacific War. Approximately 100 of these lifeboats were built—their serial numbers began at 501 and continued in sequence. It was 30.05 feet long, it weighed 2,736 pounds when fully loaded and ready for attachment to the aircraft and could rescue fifteen people. It was powered by a four-cylinder four-stroke Meteor 20 gasoline engine made by the Red Wing Motor Company. With an Ailsa Craig propeller it was expected to give a speed of 8 knots under calm water conditions and carried 100 US gallons of fuel. The airborne lifeboat was dropped from the SB-29 on a single 100-foot parachute. Like previous airborne lifeboat designs, it was self-righting. The boat had a boarding ladder, and carried food and water for the rescued people.

SB-29 releases and Edo A-3 liftboat. The parachute is just about to deploy. *(USAF)*

SPECIALS

In March 1951, *Time* magazine reported that the USAF was testing a radio controlled steering device for the A-3 lifeboat. After the boat dropped into the sea, a radio operator aboard the rescue aircraft would start the lifeboat's engine remotely, then direct the boat toward the survivors to make it easier for them to reach it. After climbing aboard, the survivors could talk to the circling aircraft by two-way radio. A gyrocompass aboard the lifeboat would be set toward the nearest safe land, and the supply of fuel would allow for 800 miles (1,300 km) of range, with further range possible if additional water, food and fuel supplies were dropped along the way. The USAF expected all their A-3 lifeboats to be equipped with radio control by early 1952.

The primary mission of the SB-29 was rescue support for units flying long distances over water. It retained all the defensive armament of the production bomber with the exception of the forward lower gun turret, which was removed

Above: An Edo A-3 airborne lifeboat fitted to an unidentified SB-29. Note the radome replacing the front lower turret immediately aft of the nosewheel.

Right: An A-3 lifeboat 'dismounted', showing the interior contents, The lifetboat was dropped stern-first, with a detachable cover over the propeller. *(both USAF)*

to make room for the AN/APQ-13 radome just behind the nose landing gear. They served in the Korean War, and A-3 lifeboats were carried by Super Dumbos over the Yellow Sea and the Sea of Japan.

From the beginning of the Korean War, the A-3 lifeboat was kept shackled underneath an SB-29 waiting in constant readiness on the ground at each rescue airbase. However, rainwater could enter the boat and pool inside an open end of the parachute bag. After one air drop which failed because of water that had frozen at high altitude, trapping the parachute, the A-3 lifeboat was stored disconnected from the aircraft and with a rain cover in place.

The SB-29 remained in service throughout the Korean War and into the mid-1950s.

EB-29 Boom Reciever

While 116 B-29s were converted to KB-29s and equipped with Boeing's 'flying boom', only one aircraft, EB-29 as far as is known, was converted a 'boom receiver'. This machine, 44-62205, had a fuel receptacle fitted behind the cockpit and had a special application of white paint along the entire upper surface of the fuselage and vertical fin in order to show the flow pattern of any spilt fuel when using dyed water in refuelling tests.

YKB-29T

A single KB-29M (45-21734) was converted to a three-hose tanker that could refuel three fighters simultaneously by the probe-and-drogue system. One hose was installed in the tail, and the two others were installed on reels mounted in pods suspended underneath the wingtips. This aircraft was redesignated YKB-29T. This was the first triple-point tanker for the Tactical Air Command.

By now, the B-29 was thoroughly obsolete and was too slow to be compatible with the newer jet fighters, and only one of these YKB-29T conversions was built. However, a similar triple-hose system was later used on KB-50 tanker conversions.

The EB-29 Boom Reciever 44-62205 makes a test hook-up. The white painted top was to clearly show the flow patterns of any spillage of the dyed water they used for the transfer tests. *(USAF)*

B-54/B-54A/RB-54A

SPECIALS

A U.S. Air Force Boeing KB-29P tanker refuels three Royal Air Force Gloster Meteor fighters.(USAF)

The mock-up of the B-54A takes shape. The picture was taken on 24 November 1948, less than a year before the project was cancelled. (USAF)

In late 1948, the Air Force concluded that the B-50C was sufficiently different from the B-50A and B which preceded it that a new bomber model number of B-54 was assigned.

The standard Pratt & Whitney R-4360 engines of the normal B-50 had been replaced with R-4360-51 Variable Discharge Turbine (VDT) engines, the fuselage was lengthened by over 10 ft and the wingspan was extended by 20 ft which required the installation of outrigger landing gear in the numbers one and four engine nacelles. Large fuel tanks under the outboard wing section were required to carry an additional 3,000 gal of fuel to reach the intended 9,300 mile range. The outrigger landing gear required wider taxiways than those which existed at operating bases, and its introduction into service would require a massive programme of base reconstruction. It was also discovered that jet engines could not be installed on the B-54 without completely redesigning the wings. The new K-1 bombing system could not

Back and front of the B-54A mock-up.

In this view of the rear gunners position, the upper 'lance' is a gunsight with a radar dish below and finally a rotating, elevating turret.

As to the 'bulges' on the left hand side of the nose the smaller contains the gunsight while according to the drawing, the larger is the radome.
(both USAF)

be installed without sacrificing a belly turret or without a drastic alteration in the aircraft's fuselage.

Air Force Secretary W Stuart Symington and General Vandenberg supported the B-54 project, but General Curtis LeMay opposed it and argued for the cancellation of the B-54 in favour of more B-36s. However, Symington and Vandenberg were reluctant to terminate the B-54 since the loss of the B-54 and the procurement of more B-36s would alter the medium/heavy bomber mix that had been recently approved by the Joint Chiefs of Staff. As an alternative, Secretary Symington proposed that some additional B-50s be substituted for the B-54. General LeMay was unhappy with this proposal as well, and countered with an argument that if it were not possible to replace all programmed B-54s by B-36s,

Westinghouse and Glenn L. Martin employees pose in front of B-29 Superfortress 44-84121 used in Stratovision tests in 1948 or 1949. In the back row from left are Frank Gordon Mullins and C.E. Nobles. All others unidentified. *(Westinghouse)*

the best alternative would be to secure additional B-47 medium bombers. After balancing all factors involved, the Board of Senior Officers agreed with LeMay and recommended that the B-54 project be dropped and the project was cancelled in April 1949. The partially-built YB-50C was also cancelled.

Stratovision

One strange use that the B-29 was put to was something called 'Stratovision' - believed so called after the 'Stratfortress' name. In many ways this was the forerunner to satellite broadcasting we have today.

Television was just starting to become available in the 1930s. In the USA on 15 June 1936, Don Lee Broadcasting began a one month-long demonstration of high definition (240+ line) television in Los Angeles on W6XAO (later KTSL) with a 300-line image from motion picture film. The Federal Communications Commission (FCC) adopted NTSC television engineering standards on 2 May 1941, calling for 525 lines of vertical resolution. Other countries were conducting similar experiments and coming up with similar standards. For example, in the United Kingdom on November 2, 1936 the BBC began broadcasting a dual-system service, alternating between Marconi-EMI's 405-line standard and Baird's improved 240-line standard, from Alexandra Palace in London, making the BBC Television Service the world's first regular high-definition television service.

The outbreak of was saw severe cutbacks on TV development, especially in Europe where there were concerns that the Germans would 'home in' on the TV transmitters. In the USA, the FCC reduced the required minimum airtime for commercial television stations from 15 hours per week to 4 hours. Most TV stations suspended broadcasting. On the few that remained, programmes included entertainment such as boxing and plays, events at Madison Square Garden, and illustrated war news as well as training for air raid wardens and first aid providers. In 1942, there were 5,000 sets in operation, but production of new TVs, radios, and other broadcasting equipment for civilian purposes was suspended from April 1942 to August 1945.

B-29 44-84121 in flight with the extended aerial underneath and another on the tip of the fin. Even without the downward pointing aerial, the colour-scheme was striking!

With the coming of peace the TV industry slowly recovered. By 1947, when there were 40 million radios in the U.S., there were about 44,000 television sets with probably 30,000 in the New York area alone. Regular network television broadcasts began on the Dumont Television Network in 1946, on NBC in 1947, and on CBS and ABC in 1948. By 1949, the networks stretched from New York to the Mississippi River, and by 1951 to the West Coast.

Stratovision was an airborne television transmission relay system from aircraft flying at high altitudes. In 1945 the Glenn L. Martin Co. and Westinghouse Electric Corporation advocated television coverage of small towns and rural areas as well as the large metropolitan centers by fourteen aircraft that would provide coverage for approximately 78% of the people in the USA. This system has been used for domestic broadcasting in the USA, used by the US military in Vietnam and other countries, and unsuccessfully attempted by pirate radio operators.

Because the broadcasting antenna for Stratovision was usually hung beneath

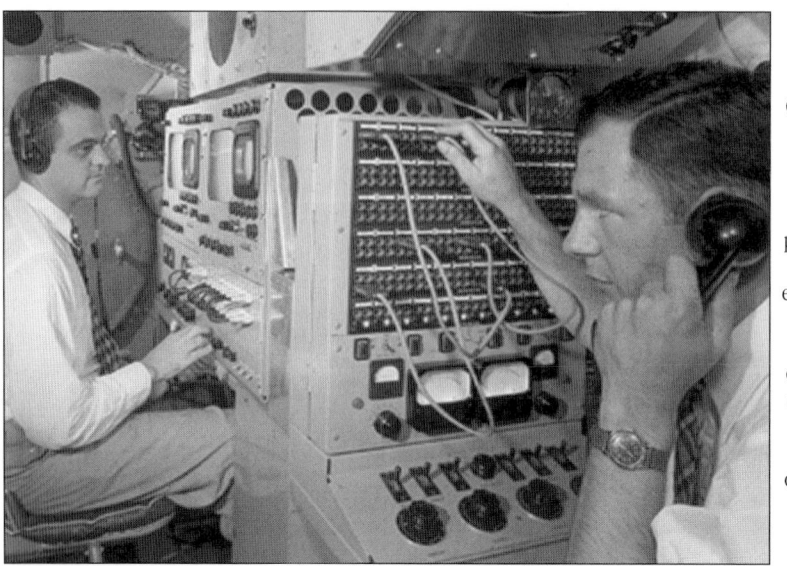

On board the aircraft - at the right Ben Carroll, Martin Stratovision project engineer, listens at the sound monitoring position. Nobles, 30-year-old Westinghouse engineer directed the first public demonstration of Stratovision tonight during which telecasts of the Republic Convention were rebroadcast from the east coast network over an area estimated a 525 miles diameter

SPECIALS

An on-board enginner winches down the main aerial aboard the Stratovision B-29. This aerial had to be lowered and raised during each flight.

the aircraft in flight, it naturally had a great command of a line of sight. Although transmission distances are dependent upon atmospheric conditions, a transmitting antenna 30,000 feet above the Earth's surface has a line of sight distance of approximately 211 statute miles.

A Stratovision 25 kW transmitter operating from 30,000 feet at 600 megahertz would achieve a field intensity of 2 millivolts per meter for a 30-foot high receiving antenna up to 238 miles away from the aircraft.

Stratovision tests were undertaken between June 1948 to February 1949. The first phase was undertaken by the Glenn L. Martin Co. and Westinghouse Electric Corporation using a twin-engined Lockheed PV-2 Harpoon aircraft flying at 25,000 feet that transmitted with 250 watts on 107.5 MHz and 5 kW on 514 MHz at Baltimore, Maryland so that broadcasts could be made at various locations ranging from Norfolk, Virginia to Pittsburgh, Pennsylvania and Boston, Massachusetts.

The second phase of testing was undertaken by these companies using a stripped-down B-29 Superfortress flying at 30,000 feet. The aircraft was equipped to receive a relay transmission from WMAR-TV, the Westinghouse television studios in Baltimore, Maryland which was then relayed over a 5 kW video transmitter and a 1 kW audio transmitter for reception on 82-88 MHz with a television set tuned to Channel 6.

The aircraft received its originating signals from circular dipoles attached to a streamlined eight-foot mast on top of the aircraft's vertical tail fin. The retractable 28 feet long broadcasting antenna hung vertically beneath the aircraft. It was composed of a two-element turnstile array for video and a single-element circular dipole for sound transmissions.

The receivers, transmitters and necessary air-conditioning were all powered by the aircraft's engines using three 15 kVA, 500 Hz alternators. Without air conditioning the transmitters in the interior of the aircraft would have generated a temperature of 134 degrees Fahrenheit (57 degrees Celsius) with an outside air

A 1948 Westinghouse advert for a B-29 based Stratovision service.

STRATOVISION TO HASTEN TELEVISION

The new Westinghouse Stratovision system—mounting transmitters and antennas in airplanes flying 30,000 feet above the earth—brings television and FM radio reception within the reach of everyone. This diagram shows how Stratovision overcomes line-of-sight limitation of ground stations by blanketing an area 18 times larger than is possible from a standard ground transmitter.

temperature of 25 degrees Fahrenheit (minus 4 degrees Celsius).

On 23 June 1948 the system's airborne transmitter rebroadcast the Republican National Convention, being held in Philadelphia, Pennsylvania, to the surrounding nine-state area during the 9 to 10 pm EDT time period. As part of the activity, a receiver was set up in a hall in Zanesville, Ohio, a small city on the outskirts of the broadcast area to demonstrate to the invited newspaper reporters that the system was capable of reaching small town and farm homes.

The tests were watched by many television viewers around the mid-west and east coast area, who sent in reception reports. From these reports it was calculated that Stratovision would require only eight relay planes to provide a transcontinental network and six additional planes to provide coverage to 78 percent of the United States. C.E. Nobles who was the head of Stratovision for Westinghouse said in his report:

'The major technical problems of the system have been solved, and the commercial development awaits only the crystallization of public demand for the expanded services offered by airborne broadcasting, application of the system by the radio industry to meet this demand, and the clarification of channel facilities available to make possible this application'.

Education by Stratovision

One of MPATI's DC-6s with the main transmission aerial in the deployed position.

In 1961 a nonprofit organization, Midwest Program on Airborne Television Instruction, commenced a Stratovision service from the airfield of Purdue University. The effort began as a three-year experiment funded by the Ford Foundation. The programme organized, produced and transmitted educational television programmes four days a week from a converted DC-6 airliner flying from Purdue University Airport in West Lafayette Indiana. One of the two aircraft would go aloft for six to eight hours at a time; take up a twenty-minute figure-eight station centered over Montpelier, Indiana, some 35 miles north of Muncie, Indiana at an altitude of 23,000 feet. When on station the aircraft would reduce speed, and then lower a forty-foot antenna mast that was gyroscopically stabilized so that the antenna always aligned from the aircraft to the center of the earth.

MPATI delivered its programmes to television channels 72 (call sign KS2XGA) and 76 (KS2XGD) in the UHF band, by transmitting videotaped lectures from the aircraft to an estimated potential 5,000,000 students in 13,000 schools and colleges. The aircraft were equipped with two 2-inch (51 mm) videotape machines and two UHF transmitters. By 1963, MPATI moved into its second phase where it relied totally on membership fees but it was never financially stable. MPATI found it difficult to get enough member schools to finance the organization. In its third reorganization, MPATI, unable to meet its expenses through membership fees, ceased producing and broadcasting courses in 1968 and became a tape library.

When MPATI signed on it used an 'Indian head' test pattern card which was shown for five minutes before and between programmes. Programming from the planes was totally canned; taped classroom instruction, test patterns and slates with canned music backing up the video. The service ended in 1968 when it became embroiled in legal action over their application of Stratovision in a controversy with the Westinghouse Company.

Pirate Television
A plan for an airborne television station to be called Caroline Television was announced in 1968 and the station was scheduled to go on the air by the spring of 1969. The proposed station was the brainchild of Irish businessman Ronan O'Rahilly. O'Rahilly had been the man behind Radio Caroline, which began broadcasting at Easter in 1964 from the *m.v. Fredericia,* a ship which had been renamed *m.v. Caroline.* Radio Caroline was anchored in International waters off the Suffolk/Essex coasts of the UK. O'Rahilly named the station after Caroline Kennedy,

daughter of US President John F. Kennedy. On a fund-raising trip to the US, O'Rahilly saw *Life's* photograph of Kennedy and his children in the Oval Office. Caroline Kennedy was playing and disrupting the business of government, the image he wanted for his station.

The programmes from Caroline Television were to have been beamed to the ground using Stratovision technology. Which aircraft were to be used still remains something of a mystery. Some sources said they were going to use civilianised Boeing B-50s, others said civilianised Boeing C-97s which were cargo derivatives of the B-29/B-50. Still other sources said that O'Rahilly was going to use a pair of Boeing Stratocruisers or maybe a pair of Lockheed Constellation airliners. Certainly there would be more space available in the C-97s and a number were then readily available, including some examples that had been at Stansted Airport in England.

Ronan O'Ralilly leaves one of his two pirate radio ships, the m.v. *Mi Amigo*.

Because the Stratovision concept was relatively unknown in Europe, many thought it was just at best a publicity stunt or worse, a hoax. The intention was to set whatever aircraft he was going to use on auto-pilot and fly them over the international waters of the Irish sea, although this was later changed to the east coast of Britain. The programmes were to have consisted mainly of recorded material bought from foreign countries.

A headline in the *Daily Mirror* newspaper of June 3 1970 stated '*Flying TV Pirates win a million dollar deal for adverts*'. The report went on to say that Caroline TV had won U.S. advertising contracts worth more than £400,000. The *Daily Mirror* report also said that advertising man Ted Page had sold Americans £8,000 a minute slots on the station.

Some sources reported that two Lockheed Super Constellation aircraft were purchased and taken to an undisclosed location - it may well have been Isreal Aircraft Industries - to be fitted-out for television broadcasts, but it is unclear exactly how much, or if any work at all was undertaken.

The shows were to have been broadcast from 6pm to 3am, mostly in colour on 625 lines and aimed at the high-population area in the south-east of England. The backing for the project was said to have come from foreign companies interested in the advertising potential of the station. Caroline Television's start-up cost was estimated at one million pounds, with offices in Canada and the United States set-up to sell air-time.

A statement relating to Caroline Television was made from the House of Commons on 16 February 1970 by the Minister for Posts and Telecommunications John Stonehouse. He said that concerted action would be taken by European countries against the operators, this included the withdrawal of aircraft registration and use of airports and legal measures against operators. The test broadcasts for Caroline Television were eagerly awaited, but no signals were ever received, and the project seemingly dropped.

OPERATING THE B-29

The B-29 was, in many respect the first of the modern aircraft. The operating proceedures, check-lists and details were covered by numerous manuals. It was probably also the first aircraft where the pilot was formally recognised as a 'management specialist' - indeed, one B-29 Manual, 51-126-4, laid out just what his duties, and those of the Flight Engineer was - in doing so it shows how complicated things had become. These extracts give a flavour.

You - the Aircraft Commander
The B-29 is a teamwork airplane, and you are the captain of that team Your success in combat and the safety of your crew and the airplane, depend n how well you organize your team and how well you lead it.

You are no longer just a pilot you hold a command post and all the responsibilities that go with it. You are flying an 11-man weapon. It is your airplane and your crew, not only when you are flying, but for the full 24 hours of every day.

Your crew is made up of specialists, every one an expert in his line. Each one contributes an important part to the whole. Know their capabilities as well as their shortcomings. Know their background, their personalities, their

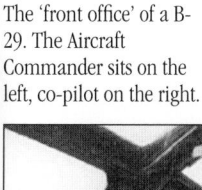

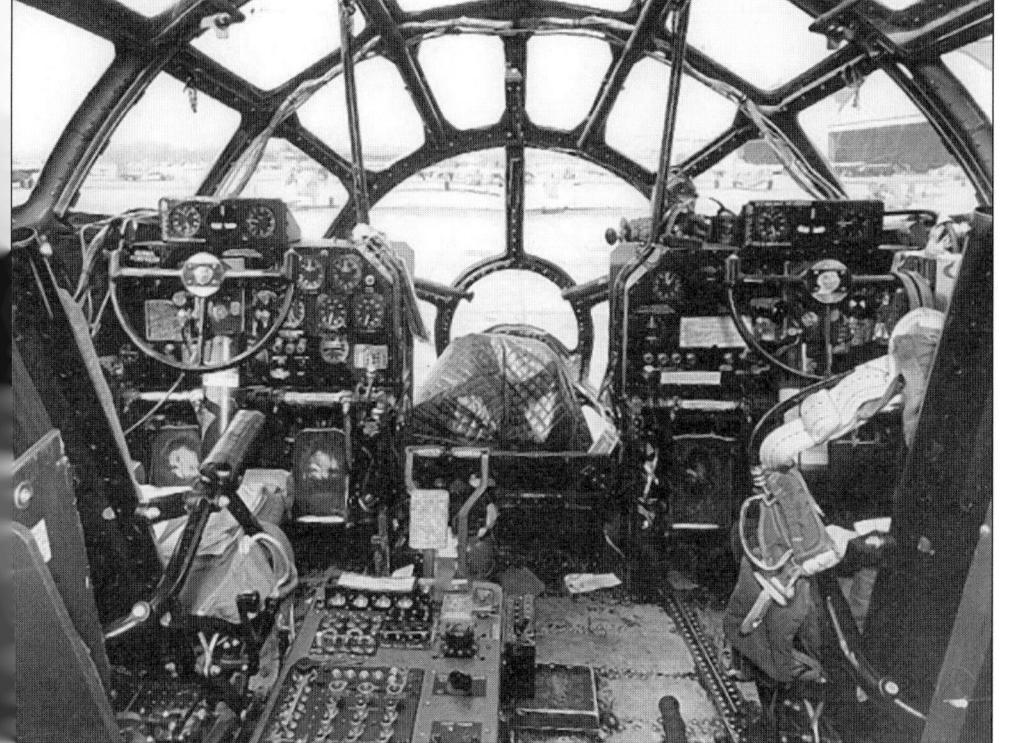

The 'front office' of a B-29. The Aircraft Commander sits on the left, co-pilot on the right.

individual problems, their needs for specific training.

You can't fly the B-29 alone. You need the full cooperation of your crew and you can get that cooperation only if the morale of your crew is good. You can help build that morale by taking the trouble to know just a little more than usual about your crew members. Find out who they were, where they lived, and what they did before the war. It gives a man considerable lift to have his commanding officer say something casually now and then about the town where he lived, his family, or the work that he once did Make a point of showing genuine interest in your men; it will pay big dividends in morale.

Make each crew member feel that he is an important part of the team Make a point of letting each man take a short turn at the controls during practice

Above: The Aircraft Commander's side control stand and below, the copilot's side control stand.

Both had throttle and trim-tab controls. (both *USAAF*)

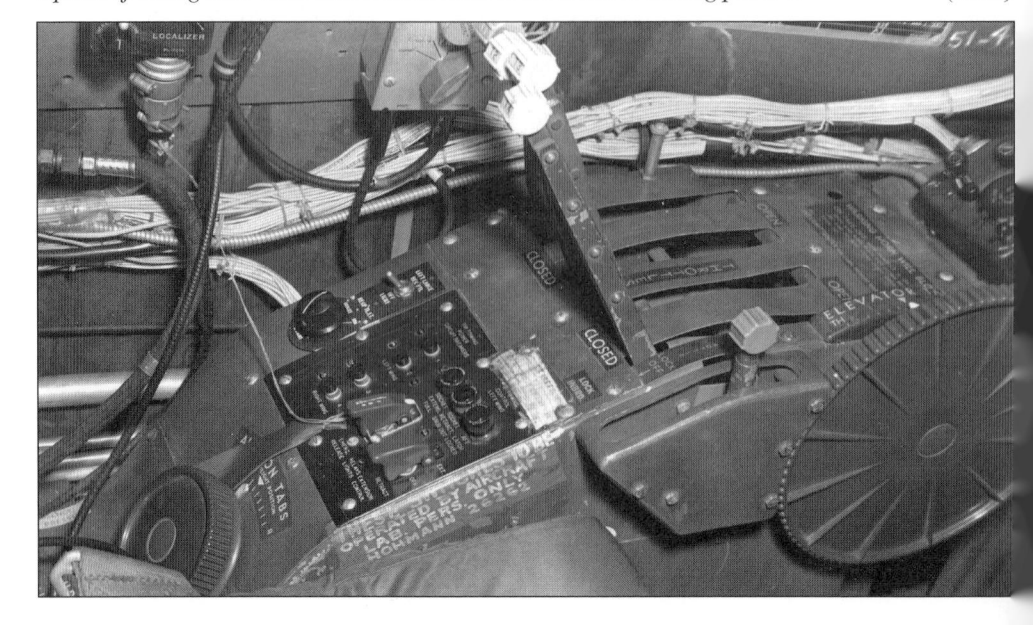

OPERATING THE B-29

SIDE AND CENTRAL CONTROL STANDS

Both Airplane Commander and copilot have individual control stands (and share access to a central control stand.

1. Throttles.
2. Elevator trim tab.
3. Aileron trim tab.
4. and rudder trim tab.
5. Emergency cabin pressure release.
6. Emergency bomb door release.
7. Emergency brake levers
8. Control surface lock
9. Landing gear switch
10. Emergency wing flap control switch
11. Wing flap control switch
12. Propeller feathering switches
13. Alarm bell switch
14. Propeller increase and decrease rpm switches
15. Phone-call signal light switch
16. Light switches
17. Propeller feathering circuit breaker re-set switch
18. Propeller governor circuit breaker re-sets
19. Turbo boost selector
20. C-1 automatic pilot controls
21. Pneumatic bomb door switches
22. Bomb salvo switch

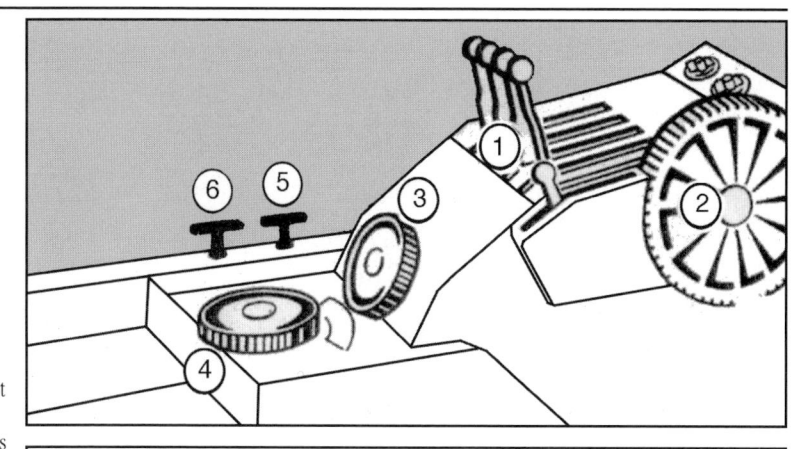

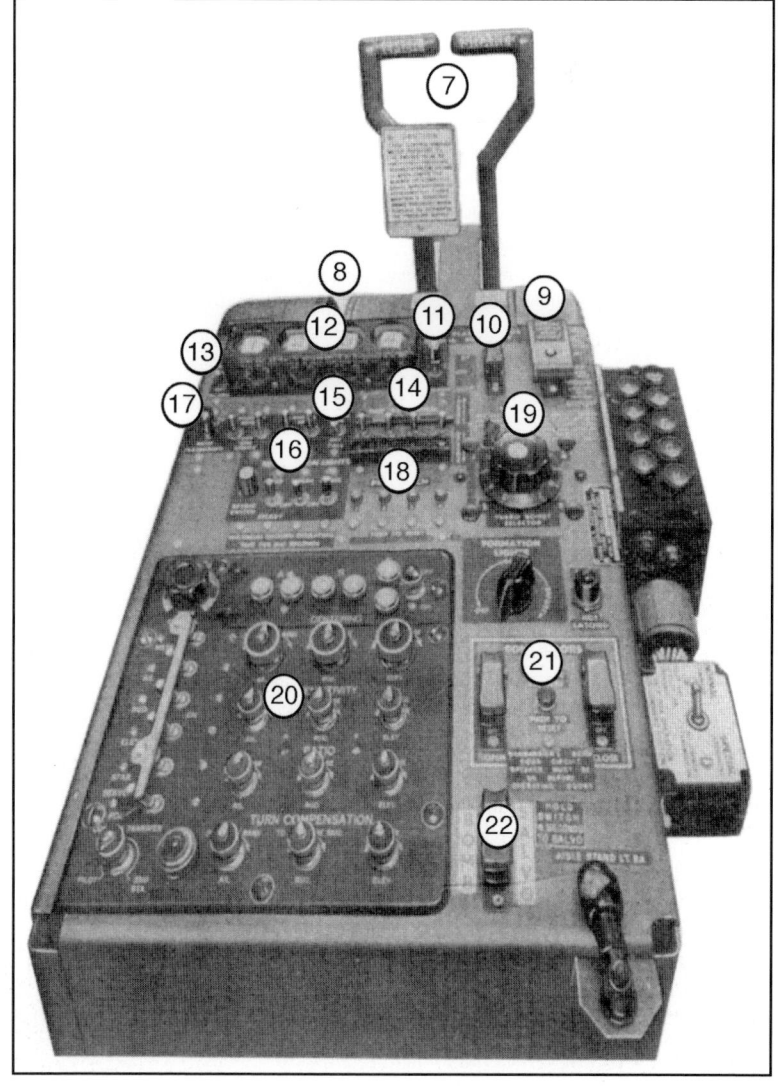

missions while you or the copilot stand by on dual. Make a tour of all stations at least once during every practice flight. Talk to the men, ask them questions about their duties, try to clear up any questions they may have. Make them want to have the best team in their squadron.

Train your crew as a team. Make teamwork their byword. Keep abreast of their training. It won't be possible for you to attend all courses of instruction with the members of your crew, but you should check their progress and their records constantly. Get to know each man's duties and help him to devise means for performing them quickly and efficiently. If knowledge Is lacking on some specific point, supply it.

Pair off your crew members and have them check and train each other. Simulate combat conditions and emergency situations and have each crew member describe his duties. Ask them what they would do under the following and similar conditions:

1 A designated crew member is seriously wounded.
2 A designated turret is out. of commission.
3 Gasoline or oil is leaking from a designated part of the airplane.
4 The airplane must be abandoned,
5 Bombs fail to drop.
6 Bomb bay doors fail to open.
7 Landing gear fails to operate.

Up in the bubble! The central fire control gunner's position in a Superfortress. *(USAAF)*

OPERATING THE B-29

8 You are forced to land in enemy territory,
9 You are forced to land on water.
10 Fire occurs in some part of the airplane.

A B-29 crew consists of airplane commander, copilot, flight engineer, bombardier, navigator, radar observer, radio operator, central fire control specialist gunner, left gunner, right gunner, and tail gunner.

As airplane commander you must:
1 Know your airplane and how it operates.
2 Be able to take off and land under adverse conditions.
3 Be able to fly under instrument conditions either with or without radio aids.
4 Be able to use blind-landing systems.
5 Be able to navigate and locate your position with the various radio and radar aids available.
6 Be proficient at formation flying, including the proper performance of evasive tactics at various speeds and altitudes.

The famous Norden bombsight installed in the nose of a B-29. *(USAAF)*

The bombardier position in a Superfortress. It must have been a 180 degree view around! (USAAF)

7 Be able to get the most out of your airplane under all conditions.
8 Know your crew.
9 Know yourself.

Your Bombardier
Your bombardier must:
1 Understand the bombsight, radar equipment, and automatic pilot insofar as they pertain to bombing.
2 Understand the normal and emergency operation of bombs, bomb racks, switches, controls, releases, doors etc.
3 Understand and be able to operate the computing RCT sight.
4 Be proficient at piloicige dnd dead reckoning.
5 Be proficient at target identification.

Your Co-pilot
Your copilot is your assistant the executive officer of your command post. He must be able to do everything that you can do so that he can assume full command should the occasion arise. You and he should be virtually

OPERATING THE B-29

235

AIRCRAFT COMMANDERS'S PANEL

Except for manifold pressure guages and tachometers, the instruments on the airplane commander's panel are all flight instruments:

1. Airspeed indicator
2. Altimeter
3. Bank-and-turn indicator
4. Rate-of-climb indicator
5. Turn indicator
6. Gyro-horizon
7. Pilot direction indicator (PDI)
8. Radio compass
9. Flux gate compass
10. Manifold pressure guages
11. Tachometers
12. Blind-landing indicator
13. Clock
14. Turret Wcirnmg lights
15. Bomb release indicator light
16. Vacuum warning light
17. Inverter warning lights

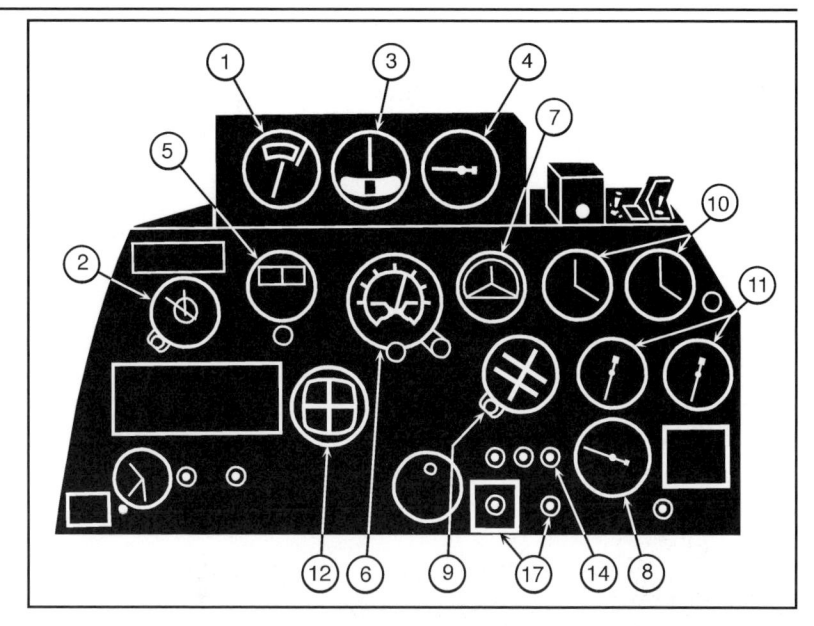

interchangeable. Let him handle the controls at least 30% of the time. Remember that your copilol is a potential airplane commander.

Your Navigator
Your navigator must:
1 Be proficient in pilotage, dead reckoning, radio, and celestial navigation.
2 Be familiar with all radar aids to navigaation. Understand and be able to operate the computing RCT sight.
4. Be proficient at pilotage and dead reckoning.
5 Be proficient at target identification.

CO-PILOT'S PANEL

1. Airspeed indicator
2. Altimeter.
3. Bank-and-turn indicator.
4. Rate-of-climb indicator.
5. Turn indicator.
6. Magnetic compass.
7. Gyro-horizon.
8. Flap position indicator.
9. Propeller rpm limit indicator lights.
10. Landing gear indicator lights.

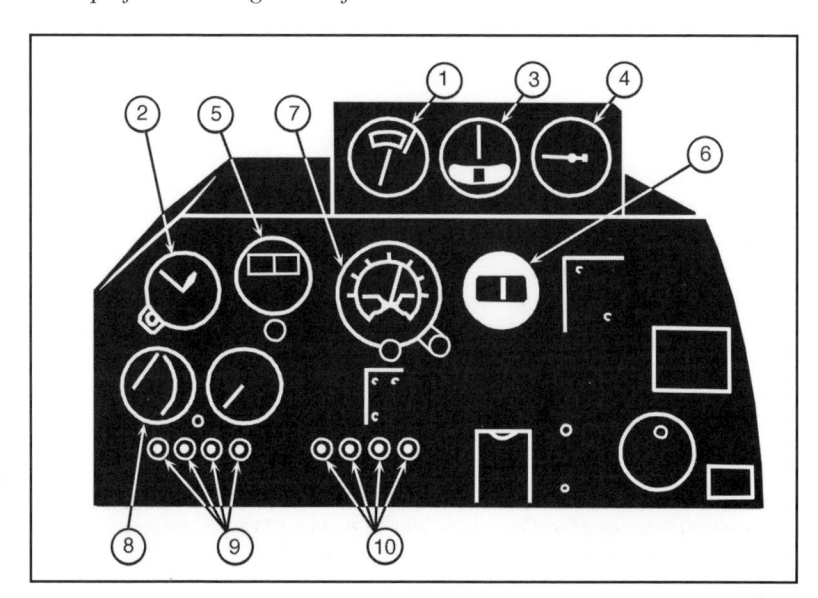

BOEING B-29 SUPERFORTRESS

OPERATING THE B-29

Besides throttles and mixture controls, the flight engineer's panel mounted the engine controls and guages.

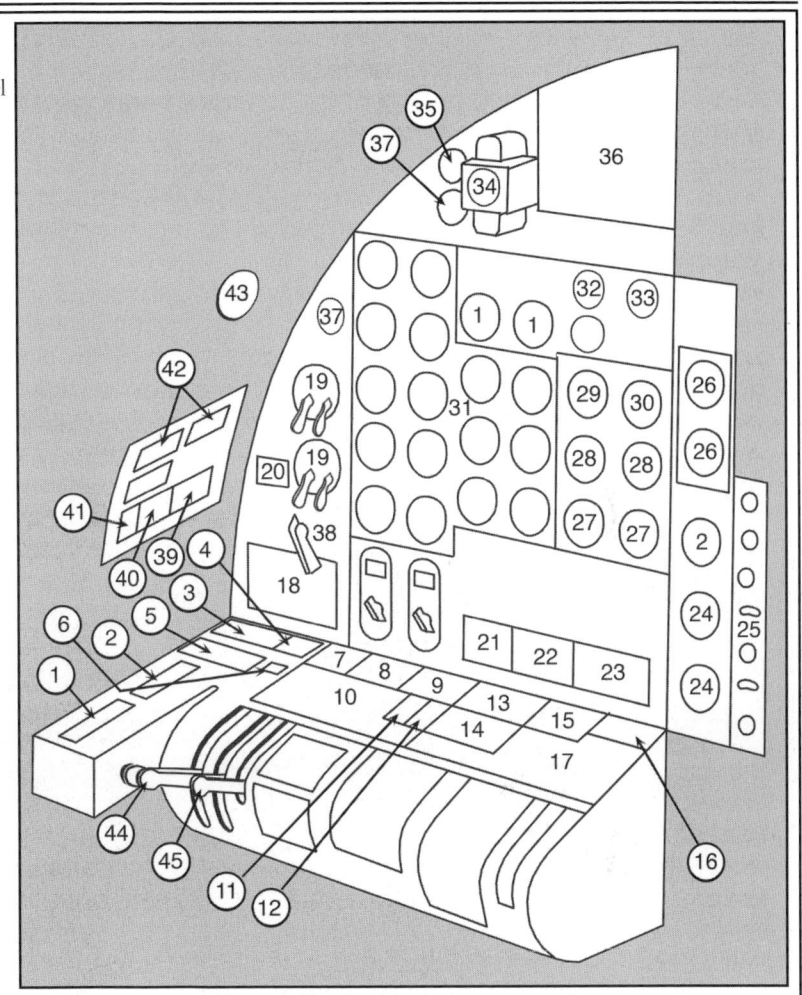

1. Cowl flap switches and indicators
2. Intercooler switches and indicators
3. Oil dilution switches
4. Starter switches
5. Oil cooler switches
6. Prop anti-icer and de-icer switches
7. Main tank shut-off valve switches
8. Engine shut-off valve switches
9. Manifold shut-off valve switches
10. Generator switches
11. Battery switch
12. Inverter switch
13. Fuel tank valve
14. Booster pumps switch
15. Pilot heater switches
16. Inverter switch circuit breakers
17. Hydraulic pump over-ride switch
18. Engine fire extinguisher controls and selector valve
19. Ignition switches
20. Putt-putt ignition switch and light
21. Engine primer switches
22. Fuel booster pump switches
23. Starter circuit breaker switches
24. Cabin air rate-of-flow guages (2)
25. Generator ammeters
26. Fuel Flow Meters (2)
27. Two rate of-climb indicators (outside and cabin)
28. Two altimeters outside and cabin)
29. Airspeed indicator
30. Cabin differential pressure gage
31. All engine, fuel, and oil gages
32. Clock
33. Cabin air temperature guage
34. Cabin air temperature rheostat
35. Suction guage
36. Circuit breakers for manifold transfer system
37. Main and emergency hydraulic system pressure gages
38. Emergency hydraulic system filler valve
39. Cabin air conditioning switches
40. Caibin pressure warning horn switch
41. Wheel well light switch
42. Fluorescent light rheostats
43. Free air temperature gage
44. Cabin air valve levers
45. Vacuum pump selector lever

A close up of the enginners position, complete with a couple of pencils and a pack of *Lucky Strike* cigarettes! *(USAAF)*

Your Radar Observer
Your radar observer must:
1 Be proficient at pilotage and dead reckoning.
2 Understand the operation of, and be able to use, all available radio and radar equipment for navigation and bombing.
3. Be able to perform minor maintenance on all radar equipment.
4 Be proficient at target identification.

Your Flight Engineer
Your flight engineer is an important member of your B-29 combat team. He runs your airplane while you and your copilot fly it. In actual flight, he relieves you and your copilot of many duties and responsibilities. On the ground, he is your chief liaison with ground crew maintenance. Check your flight engineer frequently to make sure he is on the job. He must:
1 Understand the operation and maintenance of all mechanical equipment.
2 Be thoroughly familiar with the engines and the fuel, oil, and electrical systems.
3 Be thoroughly familiar with the cruise control charts, weights and balance, and all operating procedures.
4 Be thoroughly familiar with the pressurized cabin system.
5 Be thoroughly familiar with the putt-putt and auxiliary electrical system.

OPERATING THE B-29

6 Be thoroughly familiar with the oxygen system.
7 Be thoroughly famiLar with all emergence procedures.

Your Radio Operator
Your radio operator must:
1 Be thoroughly familiar with the operation and maintenance of all radio equipment aboard the airplane.
2 Be thoroughly familiar with the use of all radio navigational aids.
3 Be proficient in transmitting and receiving.
4 Be thoroughly familiar with IFF procedures and equipment.
5 Understand the operation and care of the radio compass.
6 Be thoroughly familiar with AAF instrument approach procedures and the signal oper ation instructions (radio authentication, special codes for the day, weather codes, blinker codes, radio call signs).

Looking forward - the bombardier is working his Norden bombsight and is probably 'flying' the aircraft through it on their bomb run to target. *(USAAF)*

BOEING B-29 SUPERFORTRESS

A B-29 navigator working at his crew station. Compared to many other aircraft in the USAAF inventory, this was a spacious position.

From the lower picture it seems that long journies in the B-29 could be tiring! *(both USAAF)*

OPERATING THE B-29

Your Central Fire Control Specials Gunner.
Your central fire control specialist gunner should:
1. Be thoroughly familiar with the care, maintenance, and operation of the enure central fire control system.
2. Be thoroughly familiar with the loading and servicing of the turrets.
3. Be proficient in aircraft identification.

Your Career Gunners
Your career gunners must:
1. Know how to operate the computing sight.
2. Be thoroughly familiar with the central
fire control system.
3. Know how to load and repair turrets.

Watch your brakes!
The B-29 was, at the time of manufacture one of the few large bombers that had tricycle undercarriage. The manual took care in explaining this new phenomina:

'Like all tricycle-landing-gear aircraft, the B-29 taxis easily. The brakes are good and have four expander tubes per wheel. Rememeber, however, that the B-29 is big and heavy. It gains momentum rapidly and because of its size, you have to depend on your side and top gunners to act as observers to warn you of obstacles.

For all ground operations, set the props at 700-1000 rpm and the mixtruere in AUTO RICH. Never use AUTO LEAN for taxiing. If the carburetors are adjusted properly the engines idle as low as 550 rpin without loading up.

When taxiing uphill or in hot weather, 700 rpm may not keep the airplane rolling. Under these conditions, increase all throttle settings, but not more than necessary to continue taxiing. Always return throttles to 700 rpm when parked.

For maximum cooling and prevention of backfires, control both the speed and direction with brake alone. Entering a taxi turn with outside lhrottle doesn't save your brakes, in the long run, because the speed of the airplane accelerates quickly with this extra power and you must use the brakes to slow down. If you gain too much speed, bring the airplane almost to a stop, straight ahead, then stay off the brakes as long as possible to let them cool.'

Pre-flight walk-round and checks
The manual contains eighteen pages of details about checks that are to be completed - and this is before the aircraft is entered.

The aircraft Commander then entered the aircraft to double-check that all the ignition ignition switches were turned off. He would then signal the other crew members or the ground crew to pull the props through, provided the engines had been cut more than thirty minutes. The props had to be pulled through at least twelve blades, with not more than two men to a blade.

If the prop seemed to stick, remove plugs from bottom cylinders, pull the prop through to remove excess oil from the cylinders, install clean plugs and pull the prop through 12 blades. (Do not attempt to relieve a liquid lock by applying pressure or by pulling the prop backwards.)

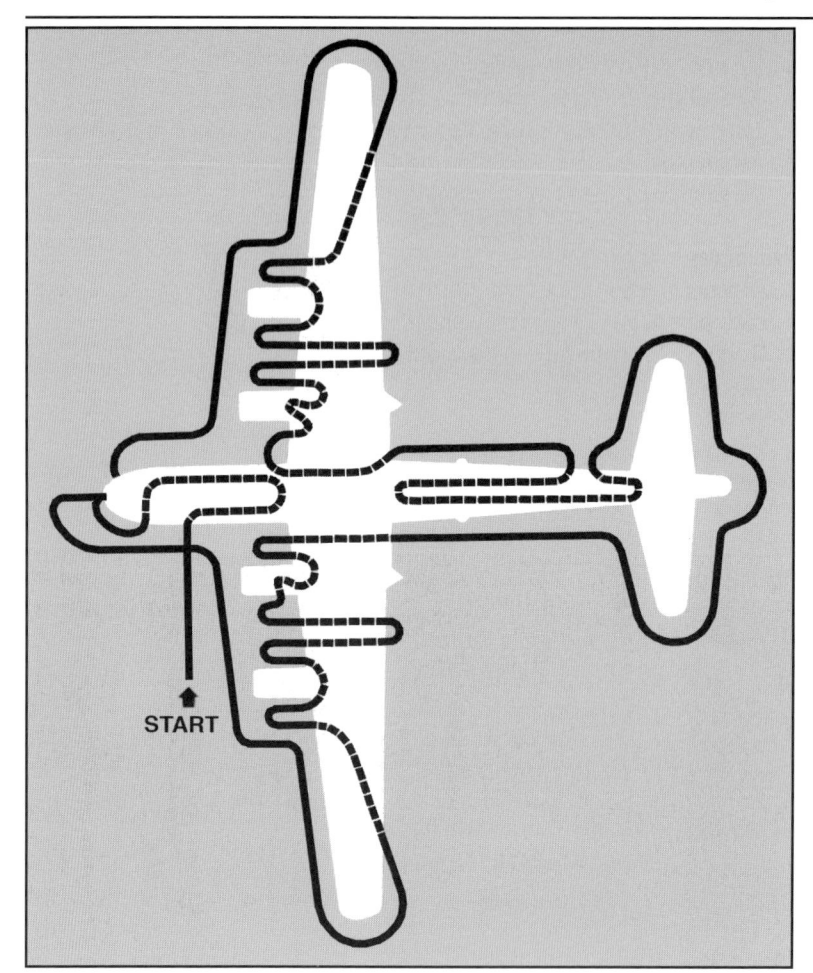

The walk-round for a B-29 was fairly complex, starting with an inspection of the flight crew and their equipment before moving on to the aircraft itself.

The manual went on: *'Airplane commander will then have crew line up to the left of the airplane's nose in the following order: copilot, bombardier, navigator, flight engineer, radar observer, radio operator, gunners, and passengers. Crew will then be inspected for physical condition and equipment, including oxygen masks, parachutes, flying clothing, and identification tags. (If dirty ramp conditions exist, crew members may place parachutes and other flying equipment hi the airplane during preflight. However, parachutes will be worn and all other flying equipment will be carried at crew inspection. It is definitely the airplane coniniander's responsibility to inspect the crew and all then equipment before flight.)*

Airplane commander will see that each crew member is familiar with his duties and with emergency procedures. After completing this inspection, crew members will enter the airplane and begin checklists for their stations.'

If flying was done 'by the book' then the manual set out a set of rules that had to be followed:

OPERATING THE B-29

Smoking:
a. No smoking in airplane at an altitude of less than 1000 feet.
b. No smoking during fuel transfer.
c. Never attempt to throw a lighted cigarette from the airplane Put it out first.
d. No smoking in tail gunner's compartment
e No smoking while on oxygen.

Parachutes.
a. All persons aboard will wear parachute harness at all times from takeoff to landing.
b. Each person aboard will have a parachute on every flight.
c. Have an extra parachute in front and rear pressurized compartments.

Propellers
a. No person will walk through the propellers at any time.
b. No person will leave airplane when propellers are turning unless personally ordered to do so by the airplane commander.

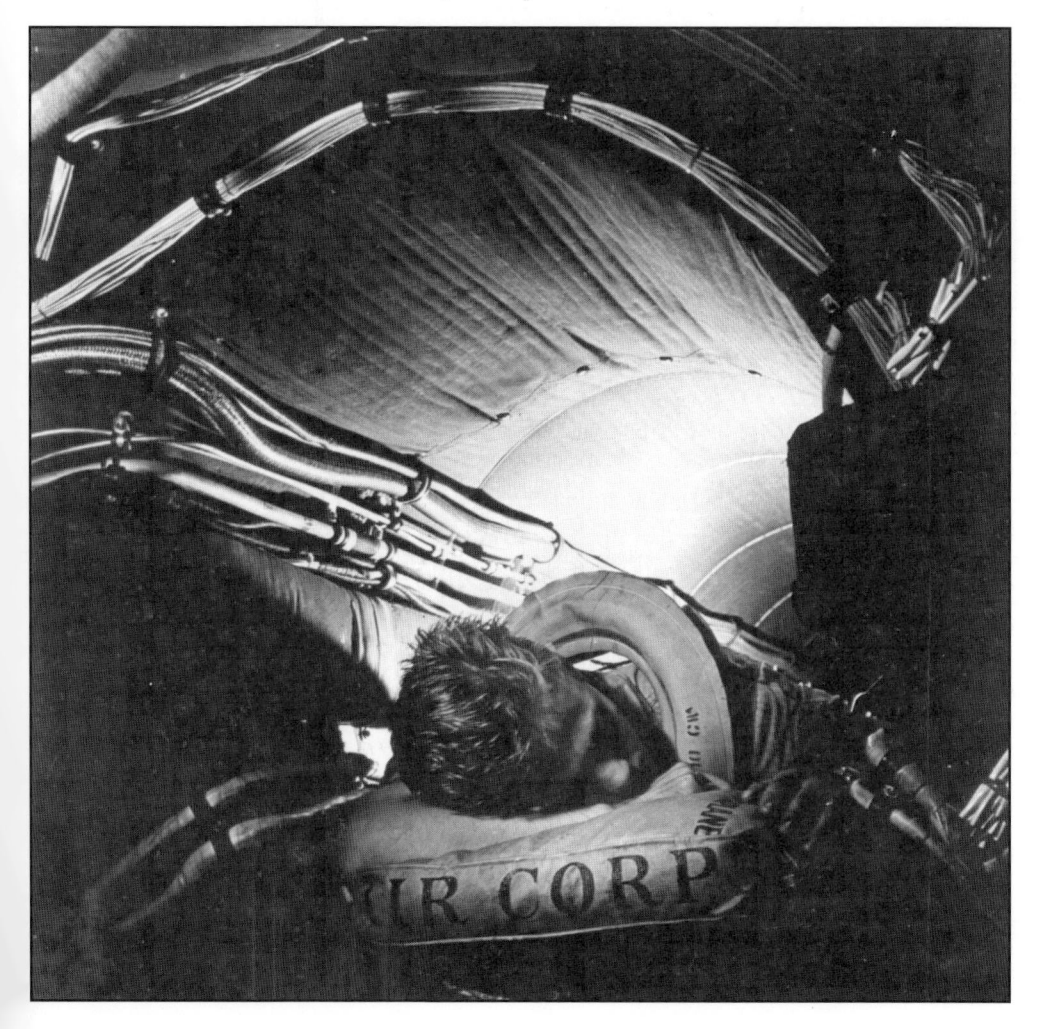

The tunnel connecting the front and rear pressure cabins of the B-29 was often put to good use as a rest area - as was an inflated lifevest! (USAAF)

Out on the Marianas, this B-29 crew don their parachutes and get ready for another mission over Japan. (USAAF)

Oxygen Masks

Oxygen masks will be carried on all day flights where altitude may exceed 8000 feet for more than 4 hours, and on all night flights.

Training

a. Tell youir crew the purpose of each mission and what you expect each member to accomplish.
b. Keep ihe crew busy inroughout the flight. Get position seporis from the navigator; send them out through the radio operator. Put the engineer to work on the cruise control and maximum range charts and require him to keep a record of engine performance. Give every crew member a workout. Encourage each to use his skill. A team is an active outfit.
c Practice all emergency procedures at least once a week bailout, ditching and fire drill.

Inspections

a. Check your airplane with reference to the particular mission you are undertaking. Check everything.
b. Check your crew for equipment, preparedness and understanding.

Interphone

a. Keep the crew on interphone. Require them to give immediate reports of all aircraft,trains, and ships ssighted with proper identification.
b. Require interphone reports every 15 minutes from all crew members in rear of airplane.

OPERATING THE B-29

The check-lists
Every 'crew station' had its own set of checklists for every stage of the flight. This is just the Pilot's and Copilots.

BEFORE STARTING

	AIRPLANE COMMANDER	COPILOT
1. PILOTS' PREFLIGHT	COMPLETED	-
2. FORM 1 A. LOADING LIST WEIGHT AND BALANCE	CHECKED	-
3. CREW INSPECTION	COMPLETED	-
4. LANDING GEAR DOWN LOCK	REMOVED	-
BOMB BAY DOOR LOCK	REMOVED	-
5. PARACHUTES	CHECKED	CHECKED
6. CLOTHING	CHECKED	CHECKED
7. LIFE PRESERVERS	CHECKED	CHECKED
8. SEATS AND PEDALS	ADJUSTED	ADJUSTED
9. PARKING BRAKES AND CHOCKS	SET, IN PLACE	IN PLACE
	LEFT	RIGHT
10. SAFETY BELTS	ADJUSTED AND FASTENED	ADJUSTED AND FASTENED
11 EMERGENCY LANDING GEAR DOOR RELEASE	IN PLACE	-
12 EMERGENCY BOMB RELEASE	IN PLACE	-
13. EMERGENCY CABIN PRESSURE RELEASE	IN PLACE	-
14 LANDING GEAR TRANSFER SWITCH	NORMAL	-
15 OVERCONTROL	ENGAGED	
16. LANDING GEAR SWITCH AND FUSE	-	SWITCH DOWN, FUSE CHECKED
17. BATTERY SWITCH	-	ON
18. HYDRAULIC PRESSURE	-	............PSI
19. FLIGHT CONTROLS	-	CHECKED
20. RADIO	CHECKED	CHECKED
21. ALTIMETERS	SET	SET
22. TURRETS	STOWED	-
23. LIGHTS	CHECKED	CHECKED
24 OXYGEN PRESSURE	............PSI	............PSI
25 PROPELLERS	HIGH RPM	-
26. TURBOS	OFF	-
27. FLIGHT ENGINEER'S REPORT	-	ENGINEER'S REPORT
28 STAND CLEAR—FIRE GUARD	CLEAR LEFT	CLEAR RIGHT

BEFORE TAXIING

1 VACUUM	-	CHECKED
2 GYROS	UNCAGED	UNCAGED
3. INSTRUMENTS	CHECKED	CHECKED
4. ALARM BELL	-	CHECKED
5. PHONE CALL SIGNAL LIGHT	-	CHECKED
6. COMBAT STATION REPORT	-	CHECKED
7. CHOCKS	OUT LEFT	OUT RIGHT
8. BOMB BAY DOORS		CLOSED
9. PARKING BRAKES	OFF	OFF - READY TO TAXI

10. EMERGENCY BRAKES   CHECKED   -

BEFORE TAKEOFF
1. NOSEWHEEL   -   STRAIGHT
2. ENGINE RUN-UP   -   -
3. WING FLAPS   -   SET TO 25°
4. TRIM TABS   NEUTRAL   -
5. AUTOPILOT   OFF   -
6 WINDOWS AND HATCHES   CLOSED   CLOSED
7. TURBOS   -   SET FOR TAKEOFF
8. PROPELLERS   -   HIGH RPM
9. CREW   -   READY FOR TAKEOFF
10. RADIO CALL   COMPLETED   -
11. THROTTLE BRAKE   ADJUSTED   -
12. FLIGHT CONTROLS   CHECKED   -

BEFORE LANDING
1 CREW   -   PREPARE FOR LANDING
2. RADIO CALL   COMPLETED   -
3. ALTIMETER   SET   SET
4. AUTOPILOT   OFF   -

In-flight catering - B-29 style!

Original caption: *Japan - meal time aboardthis B-29, with trays of vegetables, wasfancier tThan usual. Generally, crews were given sandwiches, cans of juice, gum, candy. They brought their own peanuts. (USAAF)*

OPERATING THE B-29

5.	TURRETS	STOWED	
6.	HYDRAULIC PRESSURE		.... PSI
7.	PROPELLERS	-	2400 RPM
8.	LANDING GEAR		DOWN, GREEN LIGHTS ON
9.	ENGINEER'S REPORT	-	GROSS WEIGHT ....LBS. PUTT-PUTT ON LINE — READY TO LAND
10.	STALLING SPEED	-	..........MPH
11.	WING FLAPS	-	AS REQUESTED
12.	TURBOS	-	SET

AFTER LANDING

1.	HYDRAULIC PRESSURE		- OK
2.	TURBOS	-	OFF
3.	PROPELLERS	-	HIGH RPM
4.	WING FLAPS	-	UP WHEN REQUESTED
5.	PARKING BRAKES	SET	-
6.	BOMB BAY DOORS	-	OPEN
7.	ENGINES		RUN-UP AND CUT
8.	RADIO	OFF	OFF
9.	CONTROLS	LOCKED	-
10.	CHOCKS	IN PLACE LEFT	IN PLACE RIGHT
11.	BRAKES	OFF	-
12.	FORMS 1 AND 1A	ACCOMPLISHED	-
13.	CREW INSPECTION		

Flying the beast.

The manual provides an insight into what it was like to fly a B-29:

'Even with its large size and weight, the B-29 has just about the same flying qualities as smaller aircraft. Large aircraft are usually slower m responding to the pilot's controls because of their greater inertia. But the control forces on the B-29 are light, and even at low flying speeds the combination of light forces with the high inertia of the airplane seldom gives the pilot any impression of sluggishness or lack of control. Just after taking off, and again during the interval of time while landing, the rudder and the aileron control response is slow but it is still positive. The controls are as good and in many ways better than those of many small aircraft.

Elevators - The elevator control is almost exactly like that on the B-17. The size of the horizontal tail is the same except that the B-29 elevators have a little more balance and the nose of the tail airfoil section is turned up so that the tail does not stall when making a power-on approach to a landing with the flaps full down. Elevator trim tab is extremely sensitive in high-speed dives, and you must be careful not to over-control the airplane when flying with the trim tab.

Ailerons - The ailerons are large and have a full throw of eighteen degrees up or down, so that the pilot has good control. The control wheel travel is greater than that of the B-17. This extra control is valuable if an engine fails just after takeoff or when, for some reason, fuel is used on one side of the airplane only and the other wing gets heavy. The effect of unbalanced amounts of fuel in the two sides is noticeable in the aileron control when flying straight and level. If you allow the speed to approach stalling, the amount of aileron needed to offset uneven wing weights increases rapidly. Don't attempt a landing when this unevenness exists until you check the aileron control in flight at the landing speed.

The aileron trim tabs are geared to move when the ailerons move. The shape of the wing airfoil is such that the part covered by the ailerons has a hollow on top and is full on the bottom. If the control cables are out during combat, the ailerons would ordinarily trim down because of this shape. To avoid this, the trim tabs are rigged down by one and a half inches at the trailing edge to trim the ailerons more nearly neutral if a cable is cut or broken.

Rudder - The rudder gives the maximum possible control and stability, yet it can be moved without the help of power boosts. The diamond shape of the rudder is the result of studies made to find a rudder which behaves normally under all flight conditions. A good rudder is one that can be moved with a small amount of effort when an engine fails at any speed and does not become overbalanced or locked. Don't be confused by the light B-29 rudder forces - they do not tell you what the rudder is doing to the airplane. In landing approach conditions, it is possible to get an appreciable amount of skid with slight effort. Remember, it takes a certain amount of time to skid a large airplane and also to stop the skid. Trim the rudder to center the ball.

Stability - The longitudinal stability of the B-29 is normal for all conditions. For good flying characteristics, however, the center of gravity (CG) must be

Take-offs in a B-29 was a critical time, especially with a full load. *(USAAF)*

OPERATING THE B-29

kept within the allowable limits. The forward center of gravity limits are fixed by structural strength, and the elevator control for these forward limits is good for all normal operations. The most rearward center of gravity limit is determined by the longitudinal instability which occurs at climbing power. Going aft of this limit makes the airplane difficult to fly and decreases safety in flight.

Make every possible effort to keep the center of gravity within the design limits and to keep the gross weight of the airplane to the absolute minimum for the mission to be performed. Use a weight-and-balance slide rule before and during every flight.

Stalls - The stall characteristics of the B-29 airplane are entirely normal. In practicing the approach to the stall (complete stalls are not practiced) use not more than 15" Hg. As the airplane approaches the stall, a noticeable lightening of the elevator loads occurs. It is necessary to move the controls an appreciable amount to get a response from the airplane. Remember that in a stall you lose aileron control before you lose rudder and elevator control. Just before the full stall is reached, a shuddering and buffeting of the airplane occurs. The airplane recovers from the stall normally and has no excessive tendency to drop off on one wing when the stalls are properly controlled. Power reduces the stalling speed, but in general has general has no effect upon the stall.

Never fly below the power-off stalling speed, since any loss in power when flying below this speed is likely to put the airplane into a violent stall. On all landing approaches, be extremely careful not to allow the speed to fall below the power-off stalling speed. Try power-off approaches whenever possible in order to become familiar with the airplane under emergency conditions. Never use power to reduce your landing speed.

When the airplane stalls, always recover by first nosing the airplane down and then increasing the power. Never apply power in the stall without first dropping the nose. In most aircraft, it is possible to obtain a high rate of descent by applying power during the power off stall without dropping the nose. Avoid these conditions in the B-29.'

Dead-Engine Characteristics - In straight and level flight, normal power with one engine feathered and power balanced, the flight characteristics of the B-29 differ little from those of normal 4-engine operation. When turning into a dead engine maintain a speed of at least 160 mph IAS.

If two engines on the same side are out, the airplane has a tendency to roll and yaw. To keep lateral trim, apply riirudder first and then aileron as needed. If turns are made into two dead engines, maintain a minimum airspeed of 160 mph indicated At low weights it is possible to fly with two dead engines with good control at speeds down to 150 mph. However, at slower speeds full rudder is necessary to control the crab. In general, always stay at least 10 mph indicated above the power-off stalling speed. Keep the drag of the airplane as small as possible At 100,000 lbs gross weight it is just possible to maintain level flight on two engines with two propellers feathered and with the landing gear down and 25 degrees of flaps.

BIBLIOGRAPHY

B-29 Photo Combat Diary - Specialty Press, 1996
B-29 Superfortress - John Pimlott; Bison Books, London, 1981.
B-29 Superfortress - Chester Marshall; Motorbooks International, 1993
B-29 Superfortress at War - David A Anderton; Ian Allan Ltd London 1978
B-29 Superfortress In Action - Steve Birdsall; Squadron/Signal, 1977
B-29 Superfortress Units of the Korean War - Mark Styling; Osprey Publishing Limited 2003
B-29 The Superfortress - Carl Berger; Ballantine Books, New York 1970
Boeing Aircraft Since 1916 - Peter M Bowers; Putman & Co London 1966
Carry Atomic Bombs - Richard H. Camp; McFarland & Company, Inc 2005.
Combat Aircraft of World War Two - Bill Gunston; Salamander Books 1978.
Detail & Scale Vol. 10, B-29 Production Versions - Alwin Lloyd; Tab Books, 1983
Detail & Scale Vol. 25, B-29 Derivatives - Tab Books, 1987
Final Assault On The Rising Sun - Chester Marshall with Warren Thompson; Specialty Press, 1995.
No Strategic Targets Left - F. J. Bradley; Turner Publishing Co.1999.
Point Of No Return: The Story of the 20th Air Force - W H Morrison; Time Books, 1979
Ruin From The Air - Gordon Thomas and Max M Whitts; Sphere Books, London 1978
Superfortress - The B-29 and American Air Power - General Curtis LeMay; McGraw-Hill 1988.
The Army Air Forces in World War Two - Kit C Carter and Robert Mueller; Combat Chronology 1941-45 Government Printing Office Washington DC 1975.
The Army Air Forces in World War Two Vol 5 - the Pacific Matterhorn to Nagasaki - Westley F Craven and James L Cate; University of Chicago Press 1953.
The Boeing B-29 Superfortress - Mitch Mayborn; Profile Publications, 1982
The Silverplate Bombers - Richard H Campbell; McFarland & Co Inc USA 2005
The Superfortress Is Born - Thomas Collison; Duell, Sloan and Pearce, New York 1945.
The Tibbets Story - Paul W Tibbets Jnr with Clair Stebbins and Harry Franken; Stein and Day, New York 1978.
The US Strategic Bomber - Roger Freeman; Macdonald and Janes, London 1975.

INDEX

A
A76-2 Australian B-29 serial: 171
ABC Television: 224
Aeroflot: Soviet airliner: 205
Air Defense Command: 145
Air National Guard (ANG): 196
Aircraft names
 Andy's Dandy: 72
 Black Magic: 87
 Bockscar: 124, 141-143
 Boeing B-50: 181
 Command Decision: 161
 Ding Hao: 198, 199, 200, 202
 Dauntless Dottie: 93, 95
 Eddie Allen: 84-87
 Enola Gay: 109-112, 123-125, 133-137, 139, 140
 Fertile Myrtle: 209, 210
 Full House: 135
 Gen. H. H. Arnold Special: 198, 201, 202, 203
 Gremlin Hotel: 47
 Gone With The Wind: 67
 Gunga Din: 71
 Katie: 85
 Kickapoo II: 73
 Last Resort: 86
 Little Gem: 92
 Memphis Belle: 93, 94
 Monstro: 212
 Nashville Express: 74
 O'Reillys Daughter: 79
 Pioneer: 57
 Queenie: 214
 Ramp Tramp: 197, 202
 Spirit of Lincoln: 207
 Straight Flush: 130, 135
 Stratovision: 223
 Tiger II: 209
 The Dragon Lady: 105
 The Flying Guinea Pig: 48
 The Great Artiste: 131, 136, 139
 Jabbit II: 135
 Wolf Pack: 153
Alberta project: 134
Albury, 1st Lt C: 142
Allen, Edmund T 'Eddie'; Boeing test pilot: 10, 14, 41-47,
Anderson, Maj Clarence: 216
Andrews, Brig Gen Frank M: 19

'Andy Gump' engine nacelles: 208, 209
Anserson, Capt Neils A: 62
Antonov AN-12 transport aircraft: 206
Archer, Sgt Robert N: 88
Armstrong, Brig Gen Frank: 107
Arnold, Gen. Henry H 'Hap': 19, 27, 47, 63, 66, 68, 76, 91, 93, 95, 96, 97, 114, 128
Atlanta, Georgia: 53, 54
Avro Lancaster bomber: 114, 159, 172
Avro Lincoln: 165, 172

B
B-17 Flying Fortress; Boeing bomber: 7, 8, 10, 11, 20, 34, 47, 49, 61, 62, 66, 90, 182.
B-19; Douglas bomber: 19.
B-24 Liberator; Consolidated bomber: 9, 14, 19, 20, 49, 24, 62, 69, 78, 90, 113.
B-25 Mitchell; North American bomber: 28, 49.
B-32 Dominator; Consolidated bomber: 5,
B-35 Flying Wing; Northrop bomber: 211
B-36 Peacemaker: Convair bomber: 180, 182, 183, 188, 211, 212, 217, 218
B-26 Marauder, Martin Bomber: 66
B-47 Stratojet; Boeing bomber: 95, 188, 189, 218
Bartlett, Capt: 99
BBC Television: 223
Beahan, Capt K: 142
Beall, Wellwood E; Boeing Executive: 10, 14, 19, 20, 26
Beehive operation: 166
Behrle, 2nd Lt Charles 84
Bell Aircraft Company: 26, 28, 53
Bell Avionics: 217
Bell, Lawrence E; Bell Aircraft: 28
Bendix Corp: 29
Berlin, Don R; Fisher Bodies: 28
Beser, Lt Jacob: 110
Biehle, 2nd Lt Charles E: 86
Bishop, Ronald: 13
Blanchard, Lt Col William: 62
Blue Boar missile:170, 171

Bock, Capt Frederick C: 124, 141
Boeing aircraft types:
 Clipper: 20
 Kaydet: 55
 Monomail: 20
 model numbers
  247: 20
  307 Stratoliner: 8, 10, 14, 20, 47
  316: 8, 11,
  322: 8, 12
  333: 13
  333A: 14, 15
  333B: 15
  334: 15, 16
  334A: 16, 17, 21
  341: 18, 20 - 23
  345: 22, 23, 24, 29
  377 Stratocruiser: 5, 228
Bolin, Sgt Claude L: 84
Bowen, Don: 169
Branshaw, Maj Gen C E: 56
Breech, Ernest; North American Aviation: 28
Bridgeman, George: 210
Briggs Corp: 28
Buckley, S/Sgt E: 142

C
C-46 Commando; Curtiss transport aircraft: 68, 201
C-54; Douglas transport aircraft: 134, 187
C-87 Liberator Express; Consolidated transport aircraft: 68, 69
C-97 Stratofreighter; Boeing transport aircraft: 5, 178, 228
C-109 Liberator tanker; Consolidated transport aircraft: 69
Canberra bomber: 165, 168
Caron, S/Sgt George R: 110, 112, 138, 139, 140
Carroll, Ben: 224
Carroll, Col Frank O: 19
Caroline, m.v.; ship: 227
Caroline Television: 227, 228
CBS Television: 224
Centerboard Operation: 109-144
Cessna Corp: 29
Chadwick, Roy; Avro designer: 114
Chapman, Col Thomas H: 66, 92,

Chennault, Gen Claire Lee: 61, 62, 68, 70, 80, 85, 88, 101,
Churchill, Winston, British Prime Minister: 91, 115, 133
Cobham, Alan: 171, 172
Cocoon project: 145
Collins, Fred B; Boeing Aircraft: 28
Constellation, Lockheed airliner: 228
Continental Air Command (CAC): 145
Continental Airlines: 67
Cook, Lt Col Frank: 19, 58, 59
Cook Brg Gen Orval: 56
Cover, Col Carl: 67
Covic, Capt Donald M: 161
Cox, Frank: 169
Craigie, Col William: 19
Crossfield, Scott: 210
Cruft Laboratory, Harvard University: 37
Crysler Corp: 28

D

Daily Mirror; UK newspaper: 228
Dansfield, Bob; Boeing Aircraft: 45
Davies, Brig Gen John H: 98
Davis, David R; designer of the 'Davis Wing': 14
De Havilland, Geoffrey: 13
Dean, Gordon: Atomic Energy Commission: 155
Dehart, Sgt A: 142
Detatchment operation: 98
Doolittle raid: 72
Drake, Col A M: 28
Dream Boat project: 187
Douglas DC-6 airliner: 227
Douglas Skyrocket: 209, 210
Dumont Television Network: 224
Duzenbury, T/Sgt Wyatt E: 110, 111, 112

E

Eaker, Lt Gen Ira C: 128, 132, 138
Echols, Col Oliver P: 19, 27
Eatherly, Maj Claude: 135
EDO Corp: 218
Edo A-3 lifeboat: 218, 219
Errington, George: 169
Estes, Col H S: 47
Evans, Capt Vince: 93
Eversole, USS: 153

F

F-80 Shooting Star; Lockheed fighter: 158
F-84 Thunderjet; Republic fighter: 158,
173, 174, 177, 216
F-86 Sabre; North American fighter: 162, 175
F-100 Super Sabre; North American fighter: 194
F-101 Voodoo; McDonnell fighter: 194
F-104 Starfighter; Lockheed fighter: 195
F3D Skynight; Douglas fighter: 164
Far Eastern Air Force (FEAF): 147, 152
Farrell, General Thomas F: 109, 136
Fat Man codename: 115, 116, 117, 119, 134, 135, 141, 142
Federal Communications Commision: 223
Ferebee, Maj Thomas W: 110, 112, 134, 135, 136, 137
Fisher, Col: 127
Fisher A J; Fisher Bodies: 28
Fisher, Edward F; Fisher Bodies: 28
Flight Refuelling Ltd: 172, 177
Fredericia m.v.; ship: 227
Frye Meat Packing Plant: 45
Forrestal, James V: 128
Foster, Sqn Ldr B H B DSO, DFC: 165

G

Gallagher, Capt James: 174
Gallagher, S/Sgt R: 142
General Electric: 29, 31, 34, 49, 50, 51, 55, 58, 107, 208
General Motors: 51, 207
Cleveland: 26
Detroit: 27, 28
Fisher Body Division: 26, 28
Gerrity, Maj Thomas: 56
Giles, Maj Gen B M 'Barney': 56
Glenn L Martin Corp: 28, 53, 223, 224, 225
Gonnella, Airo; Boeing Aircraft: 59
Goodyear Corp: 28
Grace, Flt Off Louis F: 84
Groves, Gen Leslie R: 112, 115, 123, 124, 135

H

Half Track project: 185-187
Harman, Col Leonard 'Jake': 30, 56, 58, 59, 63,
Hamilton Standard: 12, 51
Hansell, Gen Haywood Shepherd: 91-93, 95, 96, 97
Hansen, Maj Charles: 69
Hayes Aircraft Corp: 193, 196
Henderson, Rt Hon Arthur: 165
High Tide operation 173

Hills, Capt Alvin: 85
Hirohito, Emperor of Japan: 102
Hirschfeld, 1st Lt Herbert C: 84
Hitler, Adolf, German Reichchancellor: 7,
Hooker, Marvin P; Boeing Aircraft: 59
Hudson Corp: 28
Hunt, Leo F; Boeing Aircraft: 59
Hunt, O E; General Motors: 28

I

Indianapolis, US cruiser: , 134
Irvine, Col William: 19, 56
Isely, Commander Robert H: 91

J

Jansen, George: 210
Jarrell, Capt Howard R: 197
Jarvis, Capt Melvin E: 150
Jeppeson, 2nd Lt Maurice: 110
Johnson, Phillip Gustav; Boeing Executive: 9, 25,
Johnson, Maj Gen Leon W: 165
Johnson, Louis; Secretary of Defense: 154
Jungle King Exercise: 168

K

Kai-shek, Generalisimo Chiang: 61, 62, 63, 64, 88, 89, 91, 133
Kansas, Missouri: 26, 28
Kennedy, Caroline: 228
Kennedy, John F; American President: 228
Kenney, Lt Gen George C: 19, 28, 146
Ki.43 Hayabusa fighter: 69, 70
Kinderberger, J H; North American Aviation: 28
King, Admiral Ernest: 91
King, Fleet Admiral J: 128
Kranz, Sgt James: 99, 100
Kuharek, M/Sgt J:142

L

Lavochkin La-7 fighter: 152
Lavochkin La-9 fighter: 152
Lawrence, Dr Ernest O: 123
Leah, Fleet Admiral William D: 128
LeMay, Gen Curtiss: 55, 73, 76, 77, 87, 88, 97-102, 105, 134, 135, 146, 176, 222.
Lewis, Capt Robert A 'Bob': 110, 111, 112.
Little Boy codename: 116, 117, 119, 133-135, 137.
Lloyd, Air Marshal Sir Hugh P: 165

INDEX

Lockheed Aircraft: 190.
Lovett, Robert A; Undersecretary of War: 27.
Lord, John: 171.
Lustig, 1st Lt David M: 67.

M-
McBride, S/Sgt L E: 84
McDonnell Aircraft Corp: 211
McFarland, Brig Gen A J: 128
McGlynn, R: 198
McGuire, 1st Lt William R: 83
McKnight, Capt Charles: 136
Mcloy, John J: 128
McNamara, Eddy: 169
MacArthur, General Douglas: 89, 129, 130, 131, 147, 153, 154, 155, 156, 157, 158
Mahli, S/Sgt John J: 84
Maisch, Capt H C: 199
Manhatten Project: 63, 115, 133
Marietta, Georgia: 26, 49, 51, 58, 64, 65, 67, 107,

Marquardt, Maj Gen George W: 110, 136, 139
Marshall, Gen George C: 63, 128, 130-132
Mathews, Capt Ira: 84, 85
Matterhorn Project: 61-90, 92, 95,
Meigs, Merrill C: 28
Merrill, Elliott; Boeing Aircraft: 48
Meteor, Gloster: fighter: 205, 220
Meyers, Maj Gen B E: 56, 57
Mi Amigo m.v, ship: 228
Midwest Program on Airborne Television Instruction: 227
MiG-15 fighter: 152, 153, 158, 159, 161, 162, 164
Mineapolis Honeywell Corp: 34
Mitsubishi A6M 'Zero' fighter: 92
Mitsubishi G4M 'Betty' bomber: 92
Monahan, Maj: 137
Montez, Capt Metetio: 152
Morgan, Maj Robert Knight: 93, 94
Mullins, Frank G: 223
Murphy, 'Spud': 169

Murray, A2C Don W: 150.
Murray Corp: 29.

N
Nakajima C6N 'Myrt' aircraft: 92.
NBC Television: 224.
Nelson, Pfc Richard H, 110, 112.
Nicholson, David: 171.
Nimitz, Admiral Chester: 91, 129.
Nobles, C E: 223, 224, 226.
Norstad, Maj Gen Lauris: 96.
North American Aviation: 26, 28.
NTSC Television: 223.

O
O'Donnell, Gen Emmett 'Rosie: 91, 92, 93, 147, 148, 151, 152, 153
O'Keefe 1st Lt James 'Jim': 79, 84
O'Rahilly, Ronan: 227, 228
Olivi, 2nd Lt F: 142
Olson, Col: 47, 56
Omaha Nebraska: 28, 51, 53, 65, 118
Oppenheimer, Dr Robert: 124, 135

Despite their long range, many a B-29 ditched in the Pacific (USAAF)

Owens-Corning Fiberglas Corp: 38

P
P-51 Mustang, North American fighter: 106, 108
P-75 Eagle: Fisher Aircraft fighter: 28
PT-19A; Fairchild Aircraft trainer: 29
PV-2 Harpoon; Lockheed aircraft: 225
Page, Ted: 228
Parsons, Capt William S 'Deke': 110, 113, 114, 125, 134, 135, 136
Pearl Harbor: 25, 37, 61
Pinnacle operation: 166
Power, Brig Gen Thomas S: 102
Powers, Col E M: 28
Powers, Ron; journalist: 94
Prater, A2C James J: 150
Pratt & Whitney: 15, 179
Price, Capt Weston: 198
Pullman codename: 115
Purnell, Rear Admiral W R: 136
Putt, Lt Col Donald L: 19

R
Radio Caroline: 227.

RAF Serials
 WF434: 165.
 WF490: 165.
 WF565: 165.
 WF582: 166.
 WP203:170, 171.
 WW342: 165.
 WW352: 166.
 WW345: 171.
 WW346: 168.
 WW349: 169, 170, 171.
 WW353:170, 171.
 WZ966: 165, 167, 168, 169.
 WZ967: 167.
 WZ968: 167.
RAF Squadrons
 15 Sqn: 166.
 35 Sqn: 166.
 44 Sqn: 166.
 57 Sqn: 166.
 90 Sqn: 167.
 115 Sqn: 165, 166, 167.
 192 Sqn: 168, 169.
 207 Sqn: 166.
Ramsey, Dr Norman F: 113, 114, 134.

Rascal missile: 217, 218.
Razon bomb: 159.
Red Rapier missile:170.
Red Wing Motor Company: 218.
Reed, Al; Boeing test pilot: 41, 42, 46
Rhee, Dr Syngman: 147
Ridgeway, Gen Matthew: 156, 158
Robey, Col Pearl H: 56
Roosevelt, Franklin Delano; US President: 23, 47, 61, 63-65, 91, 115
Rybko, Nikolai; Soviet test pilot: 204

S
Saunders, Brig Gen LaVerne G: 62, 63, 66, 70, 73, 74, 87
Schaefer, John K 'Jack': 199, 200
Schairer, George S: Boeing aerodymanicist: 10, 14, 20
Schick, Rober; Boeing Aircraft: 59
Scott, Clayton; Boeing Aircraft: 48
Shepard, Col H A: 56
Showalter, N D; Boeing Aircraft: 20, 46, 47
Shumard, Sgt Robert H: 110, 112

The end of the line - a KB-50 meets the breakers blade out in the Arizona desert (USAF)

OPERATING THE B-29 255

Shvetsov, Arkadii B; Head of Tupolev Engine Bureau: 202
Sienkiewicz, S/Sgt S V: 84
Sims, Col Turner A Jnr: 19, 30
Sikorsky R-4 helicopter: 122
Silverplate codename: 115, 118, 119.
Silver Plated codename: 115
Spaatz, Gen Karl A: 133, 136
Sperry Corp: 29, 49
Spitz, Cpl A: 142
Stalin, Josef; Soviet leader: 133, 201
Steams, Richard H; Boeing Aircraft: 59
Stearns, Dr: 124, 127
Stewart, Jimmy: 95
Stiborik, Sgt Joe: 110, 112
Stillwell, Gen Joseph Warren: 61, 63, 68, 90,
Stimpson, Henry; Secretary of War: 128
Stonehouse, John, UK minister: 228
Strategic Air Command (SAC):145, 146, 152, 164, 178, 182, 189, 190, 217
Stratemeyer, Gen George E: 147, 152
Stratovision: 5, 223-228
Sullivan, Liberty Ship: 201
Sung, Premier Ill: 146
Supermarine Seafire fighter: 153
Suzuki, Baron Kantaro Japanese Prime Minister: 141
Sverdlov, Soviet cruiser: 168
Sweeney, Maj Charles W: 131, 136, 138, 139, 141-143
Symington, W Stuart: 222

T
Tactical Air Command (TAC): 145, 194, 196, 220
Tarzon/Tallboy bomb: 158, 159, 160, 162
Taylor, Maj Ralph: 135
Thin Man codename: 115, 116, 117
Thompson, T/Sgt Fred H: 84
Thompson, Kermit: 58
Tibbetts, Col Paul W Jr: 109-112, 118, 119, 125, 134, 135, 138, 140-142
Tip Tow project: 215-217
Tirpitz, German battleship: 159
Trans Canada Airlines: 9
Trans World Airlines: 8,
Truman, Harry, US President: 47, 132, 133, 141, 147, 153, 154, 155, 156, 157, 158
Togo, Shigenori, Japanese Foreign Minister: 141
Toll, Pat: 169

Tupolev, Andre N: 201
Tupolev OKB: 202

U
United Air Lines: 9.
USAAF/USAF/USN Serials
0-70122:184
0-70162: 185
0-80088: 192
0-80108: 191
0-80114: 194
0-80119: 195
0-90361: 195
84028: 209
84029: 209, 210
84030: 209
84031: 209
41-002: 26, 41, 45, 48
41-003: 42, 43, 46
41-18335: 46, 47, 48
41-20531: 29
41-39950: 49
41-35954: 49, 51
41-36957: 50
41-36959: 94, 95
41-36963: 58, 59
42-2444: 53, 54
42-6208: 27
42-6232: 73
42-6242: 52
42-6256: 197
42-6259: 115, 116, 119
42-6279: 74
42-6323: 74
42-6331: 65, 67
42-6344: 69
42-6358: 198
42-6362: 199
42-6365: 198
42-24471: 66
42-24504: 71
42-24528: 180
42-24579: 84-87
42-24582: 70, 86
42-24593: 99
42-24594: 95
42-24596: 92
42-245528: 209
42-24732: 67
42-63425: 105
42-43529: 77
42-63395: 75, 77
42-65208: 72
42-65209: 118
42-65216: 118
42-65217: 118

42-65252: 83
42-65275: 38
42-65312: 44
42-93845: 54, 179
42-93829: 198
42-93839: 198
43-46533: 122
44-27297: 124, 141
44-27301: 130
44-27353: 131
44-61968:170
44-62049:170
44-62093: 215
44-62205: 22
44-83922: 177
44-84043: 208
44-84111: 212
44-84121: 223, 224
44-86292: 112, 123, 124
44-86340: 153
44-86398: 172
44-86402: 172
44-87599: 164
44-87766: 209
44-96984: 100
45-21734: 22046-524: 213
45-21787: 209
45-21789: 209
45-21791: 209
45-21800: 215
46-002: 181
46-006: 214
46-010: 172, 174, 181
47-0122: 184
46-523: 212
46-641: 216
46-661: 216
47-118: 183, 184
47-136: 186
47-162: 185
48-0121:184
48-075: 217
48-096: 183, 189
48-107: 187
48-115:190
49-260: 176
49-307:187
48-391: 196
49-307: 186
49-310: 191
49-350: 191
49-9391: 194
51-1543: 177
USAAF/USAF Units
3rd AD: 205
14th AF: 85, 101

20th AF: 68, 74, 89, 96, 106, 198
421st ARS: 192
20th Bomber Command: 56, 58
XX BC: 66, 68, 69, 75, 76, 80, 84, 86-89, 91, 101, 106,
XXI BC: 91, 96, 97, 100, 105, 106, 123, 126, 128, 134
6th BG: 98, 123
9th BG:98
16th BG: 107
19th BG: 102, 103, 147, 149, 158, 159
29th BG: 96, 102
39th BG: 123
40th BG: 65, 67, 68, 70, 80, 82-84, 86-88, 198
43rd BG: 181,
62nd BG: 83
92nd BG: 205
98th BG: 153, 155
330th BG: 102
331st BG: 107
444th BG: 65, 68, 68, 80, 123
462nd BG: 65, 68
468th BG: 57, 65, 66, 68, 71, 72, 73, 75, 77, 198
472nd BG: 65
495th BG: 92
497th BG: 91, 95, 105, 123
498th BG: 91. 106
500th BG: 91, 100
501st BG: 107
502nd BG: 107
504th BG: 98, 118
505th BG: 98
525th BG: 141
25th BS: 68
44th BS: 68
45th BS: 68, 84, 87,
96th BS: 7
345th BS: 153
393rd BS: 118, 121, 130, 131
395th BS: 68, 77, 198
765th BS: 68
676th BS: 68
677th BS: 68
678th BS: 68
679th BS: 68, 77,
689th BS: 92, 95
768th BS: 68
769th BS: 68, 83,

770th BS: 68
771st BS: 68, 77
792nd BS: 68, 71, 73, 77, 199
793rd BS: 57, 68
794th BS: 68, 72, 198
795th BS:77
873th BS: 106
19th BW: 162
22nd BW: 147, 148, 152
43rd BW: 182
58th BW: 49, 57, 64-69, 77, 89, 106, 141
73rd BW: 66, 91, 92, 101, 123, 141
92nd BW: 147, 148, 152
93rd BW: 183, 189
97th BW: 190
98th BW: 149, 162
307th BW: 149, 150, 162
313th BW: 98, 134, 141
314th BW: 96, 102, 141
315th BW: 107
509th BW: 189
55th CBW: 123
509th CG: 116, 118, 119, 123, 130, 131, 133, 134, 135, 139, 145
323rd OTS: 192
3235th OTW: 192
7499th SG: 186
31st SRS: 147, 149
91st SRS: 209
91st SRW: 209
7405th SS:186, 187
7406th SS: 186, 187
320th TCS: 118

V

Van Kirk, Capt Theodore J: 110, 112, 136
Van Pelt, Capt James F: 141, 142
Valiant, Vickers bomber:170, 171
Vampire: De Havilland fighter: 205
Vandenberg, Gen Hoyt: 154, 156, 222
Volandt, Col W F: 25.

W

Walton, E C: War Production Board: 28
War Department Special Group No.2: 201
War Production Board: 28

Wedemeyer, Lt Gen Albert C: 90
Wells, Edward Curtiss 'Ed'; Boeing designer: 10, 11, 19, 20, 28
Weschler, Maj: 83
West, H Oliver; Boeing Executive: 9, 26, 29
Western Electric: 52
Westberg, Capt Leslie: 152
Westinghouse Corp: 29, 223, 224, 225, 226, 227
Wheeler, Wg Cddr H N G, DSO, DFC, OBE: 167
Whetmore, John: 169
Whisenhand, Col James F: 62
White, Pat: 169
Whitman, Ray; Bell Aircraft: 28
Whitney, Maj Gen Courtney: 154
Wichita, Kansas: 25-27, 29, 47, 49, 51-53, 55, 57, 58, 65, 94, 115, 119, 177, 183, 184
Wilson, Charles; General Motors: 28
Wilson, Maj John: 135
Wilson, Warren; Boeing Aircraft: 59
WMAR-TV: 225
Winborne, S/Sgt Samuel P:84
Winters, 1st Lt Robert A: 84
Wolfe, Gen Kenneth B: 28, 30, 47, 59, 63, 66, 68, 70, 73, 76, 87
Wood, Lysle A A; Boeing Aircraft: 20
Woodson, O L; Bell Aircraft: 28
Wright Aeronautical: 12, 15
Wright, T B, War Production Board: 28
Wright Field: 10, 17, 19-22, 24, 27, 30, 58, 115
Whitney, Edwin; Boeing Aircraft: 59

X

X-1 Bell research aircraft: 214, 215
XB-15; Boeing bomber: 7, 8, 39
XB-85 Goblin; McDonnell fighter: 210-213

Y

Yakovlev Yak-9 fighter: 153, 199
Yeager, Charles E 'Chuck': 215
Yoder, Sgt W J: 87

Z

Zedong, Mao, Communist leader: 88
Zuber, Joseph A; Boeing Aircraft: 59

Welcome...

*Ten authors invite you to join us in the
Twisted Legends Collection.*

These stories are a dark, twisted reimagining of infamous legends well-known throughout the world. Some are retellings, others are nods to those stories that cause a chill to run down your spine.

Each book may be a standalone, but they're all connected by the lure of a legend.

We invite you to venture into the unknown, and delve into the darkness with us, one book at a time.

TWISTED LEGENDS
AUTHOR SERIES

The COLLECTION

Vengeance of The Fallen - Dani René

Truth or Kill - A.C. Kramer

Departed Whispers - J Rose

The Labyrinth of Savage Shadows - Murphy Wallace

Hell Gate - Veronica Eden

Blood & Vows - Amanda Richardson

Under the Cover of Darkness - Emma Luna

Reckless Covenant - Lilith Roman

Bane & Bound - Crimson Syn

The Ripper - Alexandra Silva

Blurb

The first thing I'm warned about when I arrive at the girls' home is to stay away from the abandoned graveyard. Local urban legend claims it's host to a gate to Hell.

Then I was dared…

The legend is as real as the monsters I've summoned by activating the gate. Demons guard it, waiting for skeptical idiots like me to do the ritual. Three sinfully hot, dangerously powerful demons.

Valerian. Matthias. Alder.

Ruthless. Deadly. Terrifying.

The gate's three wicked protectors won't let me get away without paying their price.

Blurb

I'm at their mercy, fighting to survive them and the supernatural world they drag me into.
But none of us are prepared for what is awakening within me.

A long buried secret and hidden ancient magic will change everything.
The match is lit and together we're all going up in flames.

Hell Gate is a paranormal reverse harem romance. Due to dark themes, strong language, and graphic violent/sexual situations it is recommended for mature readers.

Content warning for mentions and brief depictions of past emotional/physical abuse from a foster parent, themes of abandonment and neglect, kidnapping, violence

Dedication

*Kiss the villains…
they know how to make us scream.*

Playlist

Gallows—Katie Garfield
The Tradition—Halsey
My Love Will Never Die—AG, Claire Wyndham
1121—Halsey
Bells in Santa Fe—Halsey
DARKSIDE—Neoni
Dancer in the Dark—Scratch Massive
Faith—CHVRN
All That I've Done—Levitate
Mumur—fantompower
please don't go—eevee
Strange Inside—Aimee Simone
dream of another way out—Visceral Design, anatu
Skin—Zarah Mahler
You—Lucy Daydream
i could be your goddess—CASHFORGOLD
Queen—CASHFORGOLD, Sidewalks and Skeletons
Lapse—Black Math
Royalty—Egzod, Maestro Chives, Neoni
Runaway—AURORA
As The World Caves In—Sarah Cothran

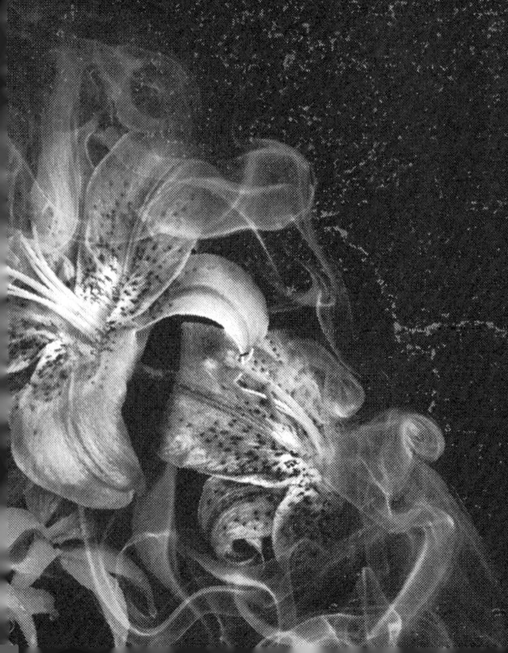

One
LILY

RAINDROPS SPLATTER THE WINDOWS OF THE ORPHANAGE matron's beat up station wagon, falling from the wet autumn leaves of sycamore trees lining the road. Mrs. Talbot, my new guardian, manages the girls' home we're on our way to. We haven't spoken for fifteen minutes since she picked me up in front of the tiny Amtrak station at the center of town. Dead air fills the car to the point I'm worried about suffocating.

The severely dressed woman took one judgmental look at my sharp winged eyeliner and thick thighs on display in a pair of fishnets beneath the black distressed shorts hugging my round ass and rolled her eyes.

Bitch. Sorry I don't subscribe to dressing in an

oversized shapeless sack to hide my body, because god forbid anyone else saw my curves. No one spontaneously combusts because they get a little self-conscious seeing a girl with big tits and a soft stomach confidently rocking short hemlines and low-cut tops. I wear what I'm comfortable in—screw anyone who has a problem with it.

My fashion sense is the one thing about me I still show the world.

It's not like I expected anything different, though. That's life in the system. Battered from riding the revolving door of foster homes to orphanages and never fitting in wherever I'm placed thanks to my history. They stopped sticking me with foster families years ago after too many…incidents.

Troubled, that's the word used most often in my file.

Lily is withdrawn…Lily is too much to handle…Lily got into fights at school…Lily started a fire again.

It's always the reason I ended up returned, like an unwanted Christmas present. A reject, that's me.

With stiff movements, I pull the cuffs of my burgundy sweater down over the scarred skin on the back of my clenched hands. The burns from the house fire healed, but they left my flesh ravaged by fine red and silver lines that run from my fingertips to my elbows. I don't remember everything about that night, only brief flashes of the worst parts.

The scars are my permanent reminder of it all—that terrifying night surrounded by deadly flames, the look on my foster brother's face, how there's something not right with me.

An uncomfortable lump thickens in my throat as I push my hands into my lap and trace the edge of my thumb along one of the scar paths through the sweater. For a moment, my vision blurs from the sting of tears. Pursing my lips, I blink them away and stare at the sad little town we drive through. I'll never let them fall again.

I don't have any way to explain it, but whenever I allow my emotions to get away from me, weird things happen. I've trained myself to be less—dull down everything about myself. This way I don't set myself up for failure and the pain of rejection.

The strange oddities that follow me everywhere scare people. Hell, they scare me. I have no explanation for the impossible things that happen around me when I'm out of control.

I've bounced from one group home to another for two years. I liked the one in Philadelphia, but thanks to overcrowding, I won the lottery to be shipped out of the city to Brim Hills, PA to make room for younger kids.

The town looks depressing as hell. One main road cuts through it with old red brick buildings sporting the cracked paint of faded business signs from when this place was in its heyday. That's got to be at least sixty years ago.

In Philly there were things to do. Bumfuck Nowhere, Pennsylvania seems to offer the scintillating options of a library, a movie theater running two movies from months ago, and a pitiful looking diner. Great. This is about to be the most boring month of my life stuck in this dead town stalled in the past.

By now I've accepted I'm going to age out of the system. There's no happy ending in a forever home, not for me, not after the fire. Whatever. My eighteenth birthday is soon. This is one more little bump in the long pockmarked road of my miserable life.

A month in the girls' home here is my final stop before I'm kicked out of the last place that is required by the state to take me in.

Then I'll be on my own.

Sink or swim.

I swallow. The haunting memory of my foster mom's voice is like a gut punch out of nowhere. Anytime I remember her favorite phrase, all I taste is the earthy well water the tub was filled with. A shudder threatens to overtake me, and I struggle to fight it off.

Mrs. Talbot flicks her eyes at me and her austere frown intensifies. She probably thinks I'm a junkie in need of my next drug fix. A lot of girls in the Philadelphia home have gone down that path. It's scary how easy it is to get your hands on any of it in Philly or the short train ride across the bridge to Camden. I won't touch the stuff. I'm already messed up and no amount of self medicating will fix me or numb whatever's screwed up about me.

We pass a sign stating the Brim Hills coal mines are permanently closed. It's a faded blue, tagged with graffiti.

"Why did the coal mines close?" I'm not sure what spurs me to ask. It's not like I really care. Simple curiosity to satisfy a bored mind.

She draws in a harsh breath and shakes her head, lips pressed so firmly together the wrinkled skin around her mouth pales. "Don't ask about the mines. Those damn death traps are cursed."

"Um, okay."

"Drove this town into Hell."

The hissed words seem to be directed at herself rather than carrying on normal conversation. She clutches the steering wheel in a death grip and her teeth grind.

I drop my head back against the seat with a sigh. "Sorry I asked."

She ignores me, which is fine by me. The main road ends and after a few turns, the station wagon pulls through a covered bridge onto a wooded road.

Tall, skinny pine trees reach high into the air like spindly fingers, connecting the canopy overhead that makes the eerie road dim and shadowed.

An overgrown abandoned cemetery catches my eye. The rusted iron gate declares it as Brim Hills Cemetery, but half the letters are missing.

It reminds me of a Japanese isekai manga I've read where the main character dies being hit by a car only to wake up in a different world entirely. The artist loved to use city ruins taken back by nature to contrast the main character's despair. I ended up enthralled by the story of discovering the hidden truth behind the world the main character was always meant to find. After reading it, I became addicted to isekai stories as my preferred escape from my harsh reality.

The cemetery disappears when we round the bend, then the tires hit a nasty pothole where the paved road is basically gravel. The car bounces and shudders through a turn down a driveway I almost missed.

"We're here," Mrs. Talbot announces.

Jumping for joy over here. Everything I take in on the short drive to the girls' home tells me the time I spend stuck here is going to suck. Creepy ass house in the woods? Check. Even more unsettling matching shed peeking out from beyond the house? Check. At least three miles to the nearest sign of civilization? Ding, ding, ding, we have ourselves a winner of a girls' home.

At this rate, I actually wish I could go back to live with the Clarks. Heat pricks my palms and I rub them on my thighs to stop the weird energy. Not now. Keep it together.

A brittle laugh catches in my throat before it can escape into the world. If I'd rather be there, it's official. I've finally lost it.

The car rolls to a stop in front of the three story house that looks like it was built by Wish-brand Quakers. One strong wind and this place could collapse. Weeds, ferns, and sapling sprouts create their own mini forest on either side of a damp mulch path leading up to the house.

"Get your bag and come inside. Don't dawdle," Mrs. Talbot orders as she exits the car and bustles away at a clipped pace.

One month. I scan the house again with a dejected frown. Absolute eternity.

Inside, I'm hit with a musty floral scent hanging in the air that I nearly gag on. I clap a hand over my nose and mouth. What is that, two decade old potpourri? Yikes.

Unaffected, she leads me to the second floor, down the narrow hall, then points to a door near the end. I pause in front of it, hiking the duffel bag stuffed with my meager belongings higher on my shoulder.

A piece of masking tape has *Lily Sloane* scrawled in marker beneath a more permanent black placard with white letters that reads *Marie Hawkins*. I stopped wishing for those cute little decorative name plaques for my door before I hit ten, but even this is a new low. A burning sensation stirs in my stomach. I rub it, yet it doesn't soothe the discomfort.

The matron raises her thin eyebrows. "It makes more sense to save resources and use something disposable. You're almost of age. You won't be here long."

Thanks, I don't say.

She opens the door to an empty room. It's set up much like a college dorm—two single beds pushed to opposite corners, matching desks, and two nightstands. My new roommate's side is tidy. There are a couple of posters pinned to the wall.

The sparse side of the room is mine. I dump my duffel on the faded floral quilt and wipe my clammy palms on my legs.

"House rules," Mrs. Talbot announces.

Oh boy, can't wait.

I keep my snarky non-enthusiasm to myself, as I do most things. People think I'm quiet and sullen, but I just prefer to play it safe. When I don't hold back, it's easier for me to lose my temper and things get away from me. When I lose control…

Well, it's not pretty.

I slump on the edge of my bed as Mrs. Talbot paces into the room.

"I was—informed of your need to act out," she begins with a hard glance in my direction.

Translation: she was *warned*. I'm used to it. Broken little Lily, desperate for attention. People stopped listening to me and looking for my side of things a long time ago. A wave of uncomfortable heat spreads across my chest. When my expression remains a bland mask, she continues.

"I'll have you know, I run a tight ship. Attitude and disobedience won't be tolerated here. You and the other girls are in my care, and I take pride in shaping each of you to the best of my ability during your time here." She assesses me with the same judgmental once over she gave me in front of the Amtrak station, lingering on the fishnets stretched over my legs. "Though you may not be under my roof long, I expect you to respect the rules here."

The weight of her stare follows another long pause. Begrudgingly, I mumble, "Ma'am."

"Good. In this house we wake at six sharp. First up is chores, then breakfast. After that, homeschool lessons." At the surprised sound that escapes me before I smother it, she turns from pacing to stand before me with her hands propped on her hips importantly. "You don't have your GED yet, young lady. Your time here is short, but you'll complete your lessons."

I cough in response and it seems to appease her. She drones on about lunch after homeschool. In the city, I was in my senior year for the second time, but what's the point? I'm not going to college. Once I've got the boot, I'm on my own.

My plan is to get out of here and find steady work. If I'm lucky, I'll land something that keeps a roof over my head and food in my belly. Too many kids are turned out onto the street when they age out, expected to fend for themselves with little help from the government funded program that cared for them up to that point in their lives.

"You're permitted to enjoy free time between lunch and dinner in the afternoons," Mrs. Talbot intones. "Do as you like, or work if you're inclined to seek a job. If you're home for dinner, we eat at six. If not, you're on your own. The fridge is stocked for such occasions and food is labeled accordingly." Her expression, if possible, turns even more strict as she speaks slowly like I'm an idiot. "Do not take from any container labeled for meal times. I specifically portion it out myself."

I nod dutifully, half-tuning her out. Jesus, Mrs. T. needs to get a grip. Or maybe let her bun down. From the corner of my eye, the door opens and my new roommate slips in. At first glance she's plain and lanky, but her fingernails are painted in a riot of color. She perches on her bed while our matron lectures me with the welcome speech.

Mrs. Talbot pauses again, scrutinizing my hair. I resist the urge to paw at my shoulder-length waves.

"If your hair is dyed that garish shade of red, you won't be allowed to use the bathroom for any home chemical kits."

"It's natural," I reply stiffly.

"I see." She sighs as if even my fiery red hair is an affront. "I've already told you about the mines. You're also to keep off the road that runs north of town. It connects to the underground coal fires still burning. Parts of the road disintegrate without warning."

Her words come out brittle and harsh. She flexes her hand, darting her glistening eyes to the window behind me. I look at the girl sitting quietly on her bed to get a hint if this is the norm with the matron or not. She's absorbed in her phone. It's a newer model than mine, which is so old it's practically a flip phone.

"Most importantly, stay away from the graveyard on the county road. It's the Devil's land. Poisoned ground. If I hear you've been there, you're out. It's absolutely forbidden." Mrs. Talbot stops talking, her face paling. She takes several deep breaths before she seems to regain her composure.

Her shaking hand motions toward my roommate. "Marie will help you for the next few days. Once you have your bearings, I expect you to be prompt, attentive, and obedient."

With that, she leaves, closing the door harder than necessary behind her. A skeptical frown tugs at my lips.

"What's up with that?"

Marie shrugs. "Don't worry. It's nothing—just an old wives' tale she likes to spread to scare us all into submission." She rolls her eyes. "At least you got The Talk, as we like to call it, at your age. I had to get it at twelve and was terrified she was going to give me a sex ed lecture."

My mouth slowly curves into a lopsided smirk. The shape of the barely there smile feels foreign. "Does that crone even know what sex is?"

She grins, hitching her shoulder. "Possibly. She had a son."

"Had?"

"Yeah, he died in some crazy accident when he was a teenager." She glances at the door. "We're not supposed to know about it, but she talks in her sleep sometimes and calls his name, begging him not to go somewhere."

Chills break out across my skin and guilt for laughing at Mrs. Talbot hardens into a pit in my stomach. Life sucks. I know that fact better than most.

"Anyway, I just came in for this." She grabs her purse and heads for the door with a wave.

I don't ask where she's going or see if I can go with her. It's not my business. I've learned it's best to keep to myself. There's no point in making friends with girls who could forget about you tomorrow.

Flopping back on the bed, I wriggle to get comfortable on the lumpy mattress, turning my attention to the window outside. There isn't much of a view, only an old tree closer to death than life.

I can survive a month here. I've lived through far worse than a group home in the boonies with an uptight matron.

The second I'm on my own, I'm out of here. I don't know if I'll catch a train back to Philly, or head somewhere else. As long as I put Brim Hills behind me.

Two
LILY

Twenty minutes after Mrs. Talbot shouts lights out and climbs to the third floor for the night, my new roommate shines her phone flashlight as she slips her shoes on. She's fully dressed in dark clothes.

I am too, but it's because I haven't mustered the motivation to unpack yet. I haven't moved from this spot all afternoon. Mrs. Talbot wasn't happy that I skipped dinner on my first night. I'm off to a great start with this whole punctual obedience thing she thinks she'll get out of me.

"Come on," Marie says when she catches me watching from my sprawl across my lumpy mattress.

"Isn't there a curfew?" I mutter.

She scoffs. "Yeah, you really seem like the type

of girl who follows the rules. Come on. We do this all the time." She crosses the room and tugs on my arm. "She sleeps like the dead and always goes to bed early so she can get up before sunrise. She's got a thing for the newspaper delivery guy, but don't mention it, or you'll piss her off."

My brows lift. That's a different picture than she painted earlier of our stern matron.

An owl hoots in the tree outside the window by my bed. At least I hope it's an owl. I'm not used to all this nature shit. The quiet stillness of this place is unsettling as hell compared to the constant noise, motion, and lights of city living. Without all that, I hear too many of my own thoughts. It'll take me at least another two hours to exhaust myself into sleep in this unfamiliar bed.

A light tap sounds on our door, followed by two slow taps, then a final tap after a beat of silence. Marie kneels next to her bed at the signal and rummages deep beneath it. She emerges with a long box and a bag.

Dusting herself off, she glances at me. "Seriously, last chance to come with us, or we're leaving you here."

I swallow, playing with the edge of the floral quilt beneath me. Left behind and left out, like always. No one asks me to go anywhere with them once they think they know my story. Mrs. Talbot must not have told the girls here what's in my file.

Thanks for the solid, Mrs. T.

This won't last. As soon as they find out I'm a freak, they'll want nothing to do with me. Just like everyone else.

"Fine." I feign indifference while a bubble of anticipation expands inside me at being included.

"Wear something you don't mind getting dirty." She gestures at herself.

I examine my fishnets, shorts, and low-cut sweater. After mulling it over, I dig through my duffel for a zip up hoodie, throwing it on over my outfit.

Marie holds a finger to her lips once I'm ready and motions for me to follow her into the hall. It's empty. I guess whoever knocked on the door went ahead of us. At the stairs, she points to a step before skipping over it carefully. There are four more on the way down she avoids. They must creak.

We quietly sneak through the house until we meet up with the others outside on the mulch path. Marie hands off the long, thin box and her bag to the shorter girl.

The rain let up, but it left the air dense and foggy. Cold moisture clings to my legs and cheeks. I cram my hands into the pockets of my hoodie, eyeing two other girls I haven't met yet because I avoided leaving the room once I arrived.

"That's Jessica and this is Violet," Marie whispers, pointing to each of them.

Unlike Marie, Jessica has on a full face of makeup with dark winged liner like mine. A beanie slouches over her loosely braided black hair. Violet is shorter than all of us and is the only one in hiking boots and sweatpants. Both of them are around sixteen. Between the three of them and me on the brink of aging out of the system we make a nice little reject pack.

The only difference is they still have that look in their eyes, the one holding on to hope that someday they'll find a family to take them away from this. The hope I gave up on so many years ago, I barely recall what it felt like to wish for a forever family.

"Are you warm enough?" Violet asks.

"I'm fine."

"Seriously?" Jessica's eyes drop to my legs. "It's freezing."

Shoulders tensing, I burrow my hands deeper in my pockets and shift on my feet. "I run hot. Always have. Did you drag me out of bed to break curfew just to stand in front of the house, or what?"

"You'll see. Come on." Marie goes to hook her arm with mine and I startle, breath gusting from my lungs harshly as I use my elbow to break away from her side. "Whoa, sorry. I didn't know you weren't a hugger."

I almost laugh. Normal people aren't huggers. I'm far from normal. It's better if I don't touch people. It's not like anyone wants to touch me, anyway.

They might not know my story, but I'm doing a great job of letting them see what a head case I am. This might be a new record for me.

Without another word, I turn to go back inside, teeth clenched, crushing the bubble of anticipation that had no right to grow.

"Chickening out?" Marie cuts me off, standing in my way with her hands up and an apologetic smile.

I glance between the three of them with my guard up. She still wants me to go with them? I don't get it.

"We're wasting time," Violet complains in an undertone. "I'm leaving your asses. See you there."

For a girl so short, she's speedy, scuttling into the woods, high ponytail bobbing and weaving. The tension ebbs from my body, leaving me unsure how to act when I'm used to keeping to myself.

Jessica rolls her eyes. "Let's go before she trips again."

I follow silently, keeping my eyes on the path they take so I know where to step. All three of them make their way through the moonlit woods with familiarity. Even paying attention, I stumble a few times where it's too dark to see.

Not long after, the dense weeds and overgrowth opens up to a lumpy clearing dotted with trees. Wait, no, not a clearing. Squinting, I scan the ground until the stone shapes make sense.

Gravestones. My brows jump up. We're in the abandoned cemetery. The place Mrs. Talbot warned me to stay away from.

Moonlight pierces the clouds, illuminating the fog blanketing the graveyard. From here I see the gate at the entrance down a small hill. Violet is nowhere in sight.

"It circles behind Talbot House," Marie says. "It's huge."

"This is all there is to do for fun around here?" The unimpressed mumble isn't meant to be heard, but Jessica grins at me.

"Everyone comes here." She points to the remnants of a stone building at the top of the hill. "Think you've got the guts to enter the chapel? It's haunted. I saw a ghost last time we snuck out here."

I shrug. "Only one way to find out."

Without waiting for them, I trudge across the damp ground, not bothering to avoid headstones half-sunken into the earth. I pass a weeping angel statue with part of her face missing.

If the matron finds out about this little transgression on my first night after she explicitly told me not to come here, will she kick me out? She's state-appointed to act as my guardian for the next month. I don't care if she tries to get rid of me. It's the same old song and dance I've been stuck repeating for years.

My fingertips skim over thick ivy vines creeping up one of the few headstones that remains upright. A strange sensation swirls in my stomach. It's almost like recognition. For this spot. This person, maybe? Tilting my head, I attempt to read the engraving, but the elements have deteriorated the name beyond legibility. The best I can guess is the year this person was laid to rest, over two hundred years ago.

The longer I stand there, the stronger the nagging tug at the back of my memory grows. There's something about this place that feels oddly nostalgic. I can't put my finger on it and push the feeling aside with a frustrated noise, done with myself.

I've spent too long aching for a place to fit in that abandoned graveyards have started to feel downright homey.

A bitter snort escapes me as I skirt around a mausoleum. *Someone get this girl into therapy, stat.*

Why would I know this graveyard? That makes no sense at all. According to my file, I was abandoned as an infant in the Pine Barrens, left on a doorstep not far from the Leeds house—notorious home of the Jersey Devil, if you're a cryptid enthusiast. I'm not.

What's left of a small stone chapel stands on top of the hill, the bell tower caved in with the bell missing. A set of crumbling stairs to an upper floor hug the side of the ruins, ending abruptly in a short drop to the ground with no destination. A small archway sits beneath the steps, just tall enough for a person to fit through.

For a second I think the air inside the arch shimmers. I blink, trying to see it again. I shake my head. It's the fog playing tricks on my eyesight.

Violet emerges from within the chapel holding a lit candle when I reach it. "Did you feel it?"

"Feel what?" My tone is guarded and I watch her warily.

"I don't know, like something wants out?" She laughs, shrugging. "The others swear they can't, but every time we've come out here I get goosebumps."

"Maybe it's just adrenaline," I offer logically. "You're psyching yourself out and looking for something that isn't there."

Jessica and Marie come up the hill. They whisper to each other.

I turn to them. "What's the deal with this place? Why is it off-limits?"

Mrs. Talbot's warning about the cemetery being poisoned ground doesn't track. I haven't seen anything out of the ordinary tonight. This place is just old, and other than being rude to stomp all over the resting places of the dead, I don't see why she's superstitious about it to forbid her wards from coming here.

"It's where we commune with the beyond," Jessica drawls in a suspenseful tone. "Did you get everything set up?"

"Yeah. The board is ready to go," Violet says.

"Good." Jessica holds up a box and smirks. "Who's ready to get our seance on?"

"She's totally legit," Marie murmurs to me as we head inside the ruins lit by the candles Violet set up around the room. "She once did a tarot reading and that week another girl got adopted by the family in town that runs the hardware store she was working at."

Sounds more like the girl met her new family on her own to me. I nod, faking interest while glancing around the cramped room. The amber glow of candlelight paints sinister shadows on the damp stone walls. A chill lingers in the room that makes me shiver. It's warmer outside in the open air.

In the middle of the room there's a blanket and a ouija board. It's aesthetic—even my dead inside ass can admit that. It has a black background and white writing with an illustration of a badass reaper on it. The piece that goes in the middle depicts a sun and moon. The girls sit in a circle around it, then look at me expectantly.

I shift my weight on my feet before joining them. I'm not really into this kind of stuff. I might enjoy manga about reincarnation from a mundane life into fantasy worlds, but I don't believe in magic. Ever since the Clarks fostered me at a young age, I've been disillusioned of anything that classifies as occult or supernatural.

My foster mother's rotten voice echoes in my head. *You're unnatural. The Devil sent you to test me. I'll sink you before you pull me down.*

A bolt of searing heat shoots through my stomach at the memory. She's gone. She can't hurt me.

The girls touch the heart-shaped piece sitting on the board. I don't follow suit immediately, curling my fingers into my palms.

"Have you ever done this before?" Marie asks.

No. Do I admit that? Also no.

"Of course. Who hasn't?" My voice is stiff and forced as I mirror them.

Nothing occurs for several moments. The knot of tension eases in my shoulders. My hands brush Marie and Violet's, and absolutely nothing is happening. No one is getting hurt. No one is screaming.

I hold my breath, glancing up at them. "So...?"

Jessica closes her eyes. "Spirits, hear my call. If

you're listening, my sisters and I welcome you to communicate with us. We open ourselves as your vessels."

"You're moving it," Marie hisses.

"No I'm not," Violet swears.

Am I pushing the heart-shaped piece slightly? Maybe. I didn't mean to nudge it. We stare—them in awe and me in skepticism—as the four of us track it across the board in a suspenseful drag. I focus on keeping the pressure of my fingers light while one of them probably moves it. They each lean in as their anticipation rises until the whole thing seems to end.

Violet gasps. "No way."

"We've never had such direct activity with the board before." Jessica lifts her eyes to meet mine. "Usually the spirits here are shy. I knew I caught vibes off you."

"Okay?" I peer around the circle. "What do the deadbeats want? The Netflix password to cure eternal boredom?"

Marie grins. "Cute, but no. They spelled *go home* and started another word but stopped at L. They have to mean you. Your name is the only one that starts with an L."

Oh. I see. They're just messing with me. I play along. It's better than ending this now and spending the next month with three pissed off housemates because I couldn't take a joke.

"Cool," I say belatedly.

"Ask them something," Violet says. "Why do they want you to go home?"

Resisting the urge to roll my eyes, I turn my attention to the board. "You heard her, spirit dudes. What gives?"

Jessica clears her throat. "Spirits typically need you to be really specific with your questions. Communicating can be difficult for them. How would you feel if you were disembodied energy?"

Considering I feel like disembodied energy most days, I think these fake ghosts and I would get along great.

Letting out a small sigh, I try again to appease her. "I've lived in a lot of places. Which home should I go back to?"

The candles flicker, though no breeze moves through the stone ruins. Violet and Marie exchange a wide-eyed look. Again, the wooden piece we touch moves across the board. The girls hunch over to watch, spelling out the message as the heart tip points to each letter.

"O…r…i…g…i…n," Marie finishes with a pinch in her brows. "Origin? Where are you originally from?"

Officially? No idea.

Licking my lips, I give them a smirk. "Technically Child Protective Services was called when I was found in the Pine Barrens."

Jessica's gaze sharpens with interest. "The Jersey Devil is in the Pine Barrens according to urban legend."

I don't need her knowing I was basically found on Bat Boy's doorstep, so I play it off. "You know your cryptids."

She taps her chin as she studies me. "Did you know Brim Hills has its own legend?" At my blank expression, she grins. "We're sitting in the very spot where it was born. This chapel burned down because of it."

"I get chills every time you point that out." Violet hugs herself and shudders.

"Brim Hills is host to a gate to Hell," Jessica announces.

A sharp laugh punches out of me. "Sorry, a what?"

"A gate. A pathway to Hell. The legend marks this cemetery as the spot where the gate is located."

"Come on."

"I'm serious. They're all over the world. This one first earned its reputation during the Revolutionary War. It's said that the gate is hidden, but can be opened with a ritual to call on it." Jessica plays with the end of her braid, another proud smile tugging at her lips. "But once it's opened...your fate is sealed. There's a demon guarding the gate that claims the soul of anyone who dares to call on it."

I snort. "So why bother? That sounds like a really shitty deal."

"That's the history of the gate." Violet shrugs. "People come from all over to do it. It's a test of courage."

"Have you tried this dumb death gate?" I counter.

She shakes her head, then prompts, "So are you brave enough, Lily?"

"What?"

"Open the gate. We dare you to try it." Her tone shifts from challenging to simpering. "Unless you're too scared?"

Everything clicks into place. I purse my lips. This was why they wanted me to come out here. Why they made up all that stuff about the ouija board. Classic mean girl shit. Jessica wanted to ensure the pecking order remains in place with a new girl here. She's clearly top dog amongst these three.

Part of me wants to tell her to go screw herself, resigned to spending my time in Brim Hills labeled as the uptight bitch who can't take a joke.

Then there's the other side of me. The one so tired of always making myself less for others. What—they think they can scare me with this?

The acrid phantom taste of well water in my mouth makes me swallow hard. I've survived worse than some made up legend.

Climbing to my feet, I dust off my shorts and stand over Jessica with crossed arms.

"Fine. I'll open the gate or whatever." It's not like anything will actually happen. The legend they told me is total bullshit. "Tell me what I have to do."

Three
LILY

VIOLET LEADS US OUTSIDE AFTER GATHERING THEIR STUFF into Marie's bag.

"We'll watch from down there." Jessica points to the iron gate by the road. "Good luck."

I narrow my eyes, a bolt of heat simmering in my gut. "If I survive," I say with air quotes emphasizing what I think of all this, "what will you give me? Don't think I'm doing this for nothing. I don't give a shit about what you think of my bravery."

She considers me for a moment. "A hundred bucks."

I slide my lips together. Cash would come in handy. My own stash is dwindling from what little I've scraped together in savings from my time in Philly. A month won't be long enough to get a decent job around here. No one wants a flight risk. What she promises will go toward my ticket out of here when my time is up.

"Deal."

Marie lingers as they start down the hill, dancing between the headstones like fools. "Start at the top of the steps, then descend backwards while counting to thirteen. At the bottom, you go through the archway."

She hesitates and I grow impatient. "That's it? What's supposed to happen next?"

"Once you pass through, it opens the gate to Hell." She glances out at the cemetery and plays with the zipper on her jacket. "If you see into it, the legend says you'll die before the night is out. If you survive, then you'll suffer seven nights of misfortune to drive you to madness. From what I hear, no one has made it to the seventh night without going out of their mind or dying. Either way, the gate will claim what it wants."

I chew the inside of my cheek. "Ominous."

"You'll be fine." She sounds like she's reassuring herself rather than me.

"Anyone you know done this?"

"Well… Jessica dared me to do it when I got here four years ago." She ducks her head. "I told her I did, even though I didn't. But Mrs. Talbot's son. Supposedly he did it, and that same week he got in a horrible accident. A sinkhole opened up on the road north of town and his car crashed into the crevice. One of his friends confessed to her at his funeral service that they'd been out here smoking."

"That's a really sucky coincidence."

A niggle of sympathy for Mrs. T pulls at me. To live next to this reminder of her son's last activities before he died must be a heavy weight to bear.

"All I'm saying is, I won't tell the others if you pretend to do it like I did."

"Thanks," I shoot back, not bothering to hide the bite in my tone.

She offers to cover for me, but she's still part of this, still in on the joke against me. Jessica was whispering to her before they climbed the hill—for all I know, it was her idea in the first place to dare me to run around wiggling my ass at the ruins.

Marie pulls away from me with a spurned expression. Frowning, she trudges down the hill to follow the others.

"Time to get this over with," I mumble.

Surveying the stone staircase to nowhere with disinterest, I begin to walk up them. The worn stones are slippery with soggy moss. A breath punches out of me halfway up when I lose my footing. I catch myself on the wall of the chapel ruins, stomach churning. The drop from the top step isn't too far, but it would hurt to hit the ground and crack my skull open on the large stones dotting the ground below.

If other people tried this after a rainy day like I am, I bet they slipped and fell to their death. That's probably how the legend got started.

At the top, I scuff my boot over the crumbling edge. Tiny pebbles rain down. Sighing, I spare a glance behind me and start my descent with my arms out for balance. As I go, I count to thirteen in my head. Near the bottom, the trees stop rustling, the air going dead. I can't hear the girls or anything else. The graveyard is silent except for the thud of my boots hitting the last few steps.

My gut twists. These are the types of weird occurrences that follow me everywhere.

I don't know if I'm supposed to keep up the backwards thing to go through the arch, and my last fuck has just gone missing. I'm ready to get out of here. Spinning around, I lift both middle fingers while I pass through.

As I suspected, absolutely nothing happens. I scored a hundred bucks for doing it, though.

"There," I shout to the bottom of the hill. "I did your stupid test. Happy?"

Wait. I search the graveyard again, stomach tightening. The girls are nowhere to be found. I'm alone.

A sigh gusts out of me. I knew it. I bet they're

already back in their beds laughing about getting me to do the dumb ritual. Even Marie. I'm sure she's only been nice to get me to drop my guard, but being friendly isn't enough to deceive someone with zero ability to trust others. I burned that away long ago in the fire that incinerated the Clarks' house with Mrs. Clark still inside.

For a second, I thought things could be different.

Stupid. This is what I get for going out on a limb and thinking I was worthy of trying to fit in with people. What the fuck ever. I know better and let myself get played anyway.

An odd, faint sensation tugs at me as I step away from the gate, as if an invisible tether cinches tighter around my middle the further I move.

The strange sense of déjà vu from earlier returns, like part of me recognizes the mossy clumps I've trampled beneath my feet. It's unshakeable. Violet said she could feel it, too. That to her it was like something trying to get out.

As I glare at the stone arch beneath the crumbling staircase, the shimmering air I thought I saw earlier happens again. Small, barely perceptible silvery lines that look like static electricity flicker across the gap in the stones. Then all at once they disappear and my ears pop. My hands fly up to cover them and I blink slowly several times. I imagined that, right?

I've got myself half-convinced it's all in my head until the stillness breaks with a haunting cry that causes all the hair on my body to stand on end. It sounds like someone calls out to me.

I whip around. "Hello?"

The voice sounds again, but the words are garbled, almost sounding like a different language. It's not one I understand. The words drag like a needle skipping on a warped record.

"Marie?" Silence. "Guys? Okay, haha. Very funny. I hope you filmed my reaction, because that's the last time you're getting it."

A branch snaps to my left, jolting my heart rate. The breeze picks up, the trees overhead rustling. A low, monstrous growl pierces the foggy darkness, then a hot gust moves over the back of my neck. I dart down the hill, officially less than chill.

I catch a whiff of smoke and choke on the rush of fear that clogs my throat. Not again. Please. Not now.

My sweaty hands claw at my neck. Memories of the fire assault me in sharp flashes. There's no fire. I'm in control. I repeat it to myself with each rushed step until I believe it.

Near the base of the hill, I pull up short with a harassed yelp. Three guys step out to block my path. One seems around my age, the other two maybe a little older. The girls could know them from town.

Have they been hiding out the whole time, watching from the woods?

They're tall and give off an air of danger. The shortest of them with disheveled white blond hair props a foot on one of the headstones that came to just above my knee, making it seem like it's matchbox sized next to them. He gives me a cocky wave.

His companions have a couple inches on him, the biggest of the group also the most muscular. He screams military vibes with his stiff posture, though his brown hair is longer on top and trimmed on the sides.

The last of them has thick tousled black hair and tattoos that run down his neck, continuing beneath his clothes. He licks his lips, cocking his head to the side.

One thing stands out that they have in common—their eyes. They almost seem to glow in the darkness, each a different shade of blue, green, and gold. But that's impossible. I'm not sure how they manage the effect. Maybe special contacts?

Wait—that's it. They're part of this. The girls got them to jump out and scare me after the dare. A scorching buzz builds beneath my skin. Shit. No—I have to keep myself in check.

My heart thuds as I consider my odds of making a break for it. They said the cemetery grounds circle behind Talbot House. I could run past the chapel ruins and find my way back through the woods once I lose these jerks.

"Oh." The blond guy sounds pleased, checking me out with a lingering once over. He rakes his teeth over his lower lip with a dirty groan roughing up his tone. "A girl. It's been a while since the gate's been disturbed by a woman. Hi, pretty thing. I'm going to enjoy every minute with you."

He winks and my head jerks. Horny Fuckboy taps his buddy on one of his massive arms.

"Irrelevant," the big guy barks.

The force of his voice makes me shudder. I dub him Scary Asshole.

The third guy remains quiet. Observant. He catalogs me from head to toe with a fierce scowl. His baleful gaze moves past me dismissively, sweeping the cemetery with disdain. A muscle flexes in his chiseled jaw.

"You," the brooding man clips out in a smooth British accent that feels out of place in this area. His long dark coat sweeps over the ground when he steps forward. I press my lips together, not about to talk to any of them. "You are found unworthy of the gate's secrets."

Horny pulls a face. "Why is it always you who says it?"

"Shut up, brother." Scary cuffs the back of his head.

"How about you three stop, and I'll save you the trouble," I call. "I'm out of here."

Scary Asshole shoulders past the other two, stalking toward me like I'm a bug he's eager to squash. He looks like he could annihilate someone with his foreboding glare alone. His broad muscular frame is formidable, and I can't help falling back a step when he navigates the crooked decayed headstones separating us with inexplicable speed. He must know the area well. All three of them avoid tripping over the lumpy ground while I shuffle backwards, stumbling every other step.

"Your soul is forfeit," he grits out through clenched teeth.

Ice spears through me. I ball my fists. He's certainly committed to the act. This trio of dicks are out here to freak me out. As much as I hate to admit it, they're succeeding.

"Fuck you!" The yell flies free and I forget about my efforts to keep my thoughts to myself.

They exchange eerie smirks at my snarled response, then advance on me as one, Scowly Bastard and Horny Fuckboy flanking Scary Asshole. A tremor builds in my chest until my entire body shakes with each retreating step. I keep my wide eyes locked on them. My gut tells me if I look away, things will get worse.

"That's enough. Congratulations, you hazed

the new girl in town, and scared the shit out of her in the creepy ass graveyard. Can you just—"

My blustering false bravado cuts off with a yelp when I tip over a knee-high angel statue that's half-unearthed, my ass planting hard in a damp patch of weeds. I wince, grinding my teeth against the pain of a small pebble bruising my soft thigh. Fucking *ow*, that's going to be pretty tomorrow. Lifting my fuming gaze, I find the three chucklefucks studying me with interest.

"Can we just what?" The slow curve of Horny Fuckboy's full lips is downright sinful. So is the heat brimming in his strangely bright hazel eyes as he flicks them down to the swell of my tits.

He saunters closer and crouches beside me. The scent of a snuffed out campfire tickles my nose. I don't recall smelling any firewood burning when the girls led me out to the graveyard. Minus the douchebag behavior designed to frighten me, he's handsome with a square jawline, a mess of icy white hair that swoops across his forehead, and gold contacts that are luminous in the dark, foggy night.

I lean away when he hums and strokes a long, pale finger down my cheek. His touch should make my skin crawl, yet it doesn't, stirring a strangely pleasant burst of warmth in my chest—a warmth that doesn't make me frightened of losing control.

What the—?

His mouth stretches into a smug grin and he tosses his head with a raspy laugh that twists my insides. "Get on with it? Love to. I'm as eager to have a taste as you are to be eaten, lost girl."

My lip curls, unimpressed. I'm finding it hard not to let my true feelings out, my reactions slipping free without my permission.

I don't get what's so funny to him. What's up with these jerks? Is small town, middle-of-nowheresville Pennsylvania life so boring that preying on girls at night to scare the hell out of them is their only form of entertainment?

The big guy emits a deep growl and turns to Tall, Dark and Scowly. "We need to finish her and be done with it. I hate being in this realm."

My stomach bottoms out and a wheezing breath gusts from my lungs. Finish me? What are they planning to do with me? I picture myself enduring one horrible thing after another if I don't get away, ending up chopped to little pieces sent floating down a backwoods creek in a trash bag.

Before my racing thoughts get far, strong hands lift me to my feet. Horny helps himself to feeling up my ass as he pretends to sweep dirt and grass off my shorts. He hooks a finger in my ripped fishnets and snaps them against my thigh with a pleased hum. I smack his wandering hands away, forgetting about my effort not to touch others. It's his and his cohorts' fault I fell in the first place.

He's lucky. No freak accidental burns harm him when I touch him, as they have when others catch me off guard. I need to get out of here. I'm not in the mood to play games.

Undeterred, his arms circle my waist and haul me against his firm body. A gasp slips free at how warm he is, the heat of his body enveloping mine like an embrace. It melts through his flannel shirt into my hoodie and another answering burst of foreign warmth rises in me. I stamp out the weird flutter in my stomach.

No, body. We don't get the warm fuzzies for someone when we're in danger, dummy.

"You're never any fun, tough guy." He shoots a dismissive look over his shoulder at the other two, brushing off the comment to finish me. "I want to play first. It's been too long since we've been topside. She's ours for seven nights before duty calls."

"Your lack of respect for our orders is growing old, Matthias," Scary growls across the cemetery. "I'll make good on my threats to report you for it."

"I still get the job done." Horny—Matthias—dips his nose against my neck, inhaling. I flinch, squirming to get away. Despite being leaner, he's still way stronger than he looks, easily keeping my arms pinned in his hug. "Damn, you smell really fucking good. Like toasted cinnamon. Do you taste as good, too?"

A strangled shriek works its way out of me when I feel the swipe of his hot tongue trailing a path up my throat. Is—is his tongue split? Another sinful groan rumbles out of him, vibrating against my neck. My stomach dips, clashing with my desire to get out of this. The strength of the mixed reaction leaves me dizzy and confused.

"Delicious. I love that shot of fear mixed in. It makes your blood sing." He lifts me up like I weigh nothing and I struggle, fighting him with my elbows and nails. It's futile as he drags me over to the others. "She tastes incredible."

My pulse rushes in my ears as they circle around me, closing me in on all sides. Ragged panting is making me lightheaded, draining my energy. My grip on my self control is fraying.

Up close, the other two are equally handsome. A short, hysterical laugh rips from me. Three sinfully hot assholes have me at their mercy.

Scary inhales sharply, tensing. "Valerian, she's—"

"Impossible." Even as Scowly mutters the refusal, he grabs at me, tugging sharply on my hoodie to pull me in his direction.

"I'm not done yet," Matthias says in a firmer tone, his languid joking around ceasing. "The first taste wasn't enough."

Three sinister growls reverberate around me. The sounds are gravelly and primal.

"Mine," Scary rumbles.

Horror twists my features as an answering noise like a goddamn pleased purr catches in my throat. I stop it before it escapes, snapping my wide-eyed gaze back and forth. Something in the air shifts and they cage me in until I'm bumping between three hard chests, their hands roaming my body as they please.

"Alder, hold her. I want to—" Valerian's order cuts off as a surging panic takes hold of me.

Sink or swim. Hands holding me down. Well water choking me, burning, burning, burning.

"No!" I scream.

The three of them fall back as if something pushes them hard and hot air swirls around me, leaving my skin buzzing. Oh no. Did I cause that somehow?

Valerian parts his lips, giving me a calculating once over. While his companions stare at me, stunned, he keeps his wits about him.

Before any of them have the chance to make a move, I bolt for the tree line. Heat billows in my chest and tingles in my palms. My lungs burn and overwhelmed tears prick my eyes, but I don't stop. A stray grave marker almost takes me out. I manage to keep my balance and run at full speed into the woods. Branches snag on my hoodie, my fishnets, and my cheek. I grit my teeth against the flash of pain from tiny scrapes.

The only thing that matters is getting away.

Once I'm deep enough, I hide behind a tree to catch my breath. Knees shaking, I peer around it, squatting to keep out of sight of anyone tracking me.

But they're not. No one follows behind.

With a heavy sense of foreboding, I make my way back to the house, my mind rejecting everything weird that happened tonight. Those guys were there to scare me by playing up the local legend. That's all.

Four
LILY

THE DAYS THAT FOLLOW ARE FULL OF ODD SHIT, EVEN by my skewed standards. While doing Mrs. Talbot's assigned chores, I swear hands and arms reach beneath the door to the cleaning closet to swipe at me, their limbs made of smoke and shadows that disappeared when I jumped back. Marie won't come on my side of our room, swearing I speak a freaky demonic language in my sleep. And I keep catching whispers that sound like my name. I'm sure it's Jessica being a bitch.

I haven't died or gone crazy yet, so it's a win in my book. Or maybe I'm just built different, too stubborn to let it all get to me like the other idiots in Brim Hills who mess with the supposed gate to Hell. It's all in my head. As long as I remember that, it will be okay eventually.

The weirdness will stop. I just have to ignore it like always.

On the third day after the night in the graveyard, I go to bed pissed off because Jessica refuses to cough up the hundred bucks she owes me for doing the dare. She'd better watch it; I'm not above stealing if I need to. Sleep brings no relief. As soon as I'm unconscious, I'm pulled into a terrifying prison my overactive imagination has cooked up every night since I ran from the cemetery.

The dream has been the same each night. It starts me inside the chapel ruins. Except when I leave, I'm not in the graveyard, I'm in a dark fairy tale realm.

Fire rages across the strange landscape surrounding me, yet it doesn't burn when I swipe my hands through it. The chapel sits on top of a rocky hill. Above the flames that can't hurt me, the violet sky is speckled with swirling clouds and a blood red moon. Across a ravine connected by narrow bridges made of ruddy clay and vines sits a city with architecture that pierces into the air above it. The heart of the city almost looks like a forbidden castle, the highest central tower emanating a bright orange glow.

There's something about this place that feels familiar. Maybe I've had this dream before. A different version where I'm closer to the underworld-like city in the distance. Or maybe it's the effect this dream has on me, instilling a sense of history I remember when I'm stuck here.

I'm over the isekai my subconscious has made up. Lucky for me, all I have to do is step off the hill to leave the fake fantasy world. Unluckily, it sends me into another part of the dream that forces me to relive a version of the worst night of my life. I tug at the long, regal skirt of the gown I'm dressed in, scuffing my toe against a rock. I watch it tumble down the hill into the ravine. I can't stand dreams like this, being aware and retaining my memory of being through the dream before, but unable to change it or get myself out without moving forward.

Balling my fists in the fine material of the dress, I take a running leap into darkness. Uncomfortable pressure chokes me from all sides until I fight my way up from beneath the hot water in the tub. Mrs. Clark's fingers dig harder into my skin.

"It's not right. Unnatural. I have to fix it. Have to fix it," she wails before shoving my small head under again.

I splutter through frantic tears, limbs flailing to get her off me, clinging to my will to survive. Everything is too hot, burning, burning, burning. It hurts, the ache to breathe like a cavern dug out of my tiny chest.

At last, I'm out of the bathtub. The water

bubbles, steam filling the room. My skin is pink and I'm quaking all over. My foster brother, Mrs. Clark's son, shakes me by my shoulders, shouting unintelligible words my brain can't decipher while asleep. Then he freezes as his skin bubbles and puckers until it melts off his arms, leaving behind sinewy muscle tissue and exposed bone. He glares at me like it's my fault.

Then the dream shifts and I'm outside alone, watching the Clarks' house burn to ash, swallowed by roaring flames.

Jolting awake, I scramble to a seated position and scrub my flushed face with a trembling hand as ragged breaths scrape my throat. My heart races and I question if I really am going crazy. Three fucking nights in a row I've endured that hellish vision.

The way it plays out in the dream isn't what happened. He did stop her, but the fire was after. One minute I was screaming hysterically, the next fire spread out from my feet to swallow everything in its path. We made it out. She never emerged from the inferno. And he didn't glare at me. His look of fear is one of the only things permanently carved into my mind from that night.

Swallowing hard, I check the clock on Marie's side of the room. It's a little past four. My roommate sleeps peacefully like she didn't have a hand in fucking me over, her features lax and a string of drool trailing from the corner of her mouth. My brows flatten. There's no way I'll sleep after that unpleasant trip down memory lane. Might as well get up now.

Screw waiting the full seven days. I'm sick of getting myself so worked up I have to keep reliving my worst nightmare.

I keep myself occupied for the next two hours once I creep downstairs, the creaky steps memorized after that first night we all snuck out. The library doesn't open until eight. First I'll need to deal with Mrs. T.

She pokes her head in the kitchen with a suspicious squint at ten to six and finds me on my hands and knees scrubbing the floor with vigor. This is above and beyond my assigned chores on the rotation schedule. It's also the only way I can erase the feeling of my foster mom's bony fingers digging into my skin, the hard floor and stringent chemicals stinging my nose reminding me where I am.

"What are you doing?"

"Exactly what it looks like. Chores."

She allows a beat of silence. "Why?"

"Couldn't sleep."

She doesn't question me further, skirting around me to make coffee. She sets an extra mug on the counter and leaves it for me before she goes to make sure the other girls get up. I don't touch it. Not because I don't like it, but because I've learned time and again never to trust anyone's random acts of kindness. They don't exist. They're more myth than the stupid local urban legend.

Five
LILY

Mrs. Talbot lets me out for free time early with far less pushback than I expected. Whatever she saw in me in the early hours, scrubbing the floor so hard my arms are sore, she's left me alone today.

While the other girls are stuck in the house enduring the matron's homeschooling, I walk along the side of the sun-dappled road to head into town. I've skipped my fishnets today for knee high socks, a flared tan corduroy miniskirt with suspenders, and a black v-neck shirt that makes my cleavage look amazing. The sleeves are long enough to hide my scarred hands if I want to.

These are my comfort clothes, my own brand of armor that helps me feel empowered and in control of my life—what little control I can take for myself.

When I feel good about the way I look, it gives me the courage to take on the judgmental as fuck world.

I give the rusted iron gate to Brim Hills Cemetery the middle finger on my way past and cross the road at the next bend to walk through the red covered bridge. As far as I'm concerned, the night I met those three guys there after completing my dare was a cruel prank. I refuse to even acknowledge the strange things that happened as anything more than a psychological break born of the potent high of adrenaline combined with fear. The girls hyped up a legend and my mind played right into it to create a hellish night of terror. Same goes for the nightmares and things I've seen from the corner of my eye in the last few days.

Today I'm getting some damn answers to put it all behind me. I need reassurance to confirm my past troubles aren't returning to haunt me.

The main street in town is just as desolate and depressing when I arrive as it was my first day here. At least the early October crispness in the air feels good against my flushed skin. I haven't quite cooled down from my crack of dawn self care cleaning session, despite showering. My body has always run hot and once it warms up, it's difficult to regulate my temperature. One of my foster placements told me it must be a redhead thing, because no one else she knew would go around in shorts in the middle of an upstate New York winter.

Crossing the road at the movie theater with more empty display posters than filled, I enter the library. It's a cramped, single-floor establishment that has a stale scent hanging in the air. One librarian sits at the counter by the door, though I'm not sure if he's a real person or a gargoyle statue. The temptation to wave a hand in front of his face for a reaction makes me pause.

I scan the shelves, wondering if they stock any manga. In a backwater place like this, I doubt it. If I'm lucky, maybe they carry Naruto. It's not my style, but since I'm stuck here I'll take anything. Pressing on my toes, I frown when I find the stacks only go three deep. Sighing, I go to the computer cubicles in the back corner, missing the city's bigger libraries.

There are three ancient desktops that look older than I am. I'm talking birth of the Internet-era hardware. I take the middle one, considering that it could be worse. At least they have computers.

Booting up takes forever. Once I'm logged into a guest account, I open a search engine and type in *Brim Hills Cemetery*. Results bombard me—news stories for disappearances that span decades, the graveyard being condemned, even a paranormal activity study. The link near the bottom of the page claims to be a full detailed history of the town.

I skim over the article's introduction explaining

the town was founded by Quaker settlers and the boring details about the small, close-knit population. It goes on to describe the town's notoriety centering on the urban legend that gained attention and earned its spot on the list of death dares like the legends of Bloody Mary and the Candy Man popular amongst teens.

Those said to disturb the gate to Hell in Brim Hills Cemetery will suffer fiery visions and psychological torment. Several deaths and disappearances are claimed to be linked to the condemned site.

"Yeah right," I mumble, reading on.

Brim Hills was originally named for the smell of brimstone early settlers claimed blanketed the town. They marked it as a bad omen, but remained in the area. In 1929, a sulfur pocket was discovered in the nearby hills. This underground pocket connects to the coal mine system.

Backing out, I pick another article that talks about local fires spreading across central Pennsylvania. This one talks about Centralia, a town not far from here.

The mine fire in Centralia is situated on a coal seam and has been burning underneath the borough since 1962. The fire's original cause is still debated. Many mines and roads have been closed due to the dangers of deterioration. This seam runs at least an 8 mile stretch and connects to the now closed mines of Brim Hills.

Well, that explains a lot. I haven't noticed the

sulfur smell, but I did pick up a smoky scent in the graveyard. These coal mine fires could be what inspired all of the stories about the Hell gate legend.

Getting an idea, I type *gates to Hell* in the search bar. Jackpot. At least ten other so-called Hell gates pop up and tout themselves as *the* doorway to the Devil. There's another version of the legend in Alabama, Colorado, Indiana, New York, and Washington. They're all over.

Some of the stories are way more fascinating and complex than the ritual I did. I get sucked into reading about the debate between the Devil picking one supposed spot because of witch hangings or because the graves of his children are there.

"Visitors are greeted by a ghost, then pushed down and left with the mark of the Devil? People are so imaginative."

I jump at the cool accented voice behind me. Angling my head, I find Valerian towering over me, tattooed hands braced on either side of my cubicle, looking very gothic prince standing in the middle of the small town library in dark clothes with his textbook bad boy trench coat sweeping the ground. His dark hair falls across his angular face, lips twisted in a mercurial frown.

"Do you mind? It's rude to look over people's shoulders," I snap.

He lifts a brow. "I do mind. You're wasting my

time."

I match my expression to his. When he doesn't move, I shoo him, growing agitated that he has the nerve to stroll up to me after what he did. "Then leave me alone. I don't want to see you or your asshole friends again."

I press my lips together. What is it about them that makes me unable to control my tongue or hold back my true thoughts and reactions?

He shakes his head. "I told you the consequence for opening the gate. You've sealed your own fate, just as others have before you. It's your price to pay."

His grip flexes on the cubicle walls and he leans over me to cage me in further. His handsome features shift from annoyance to something intense and hungry. God, those impossibly blue eyes are striking. In the light of day I can tell they aren't trick contacts, they're simply that brilliant, unique color. The raspy sound that catches in his throat makes my insides coil tightly. I hold my breath, pressing my thighs together against the flood of liquid heat.

This is different from the odd, instinctive sensations that teased my body the other night, less primal and wild. I'm in control. Yet I still don't want to feel any attraction towards this pompous bastard.

Shoulders tensing, Valerian moves one tattooed hand as if he's going to touch my hair, then drops it, his expression shuttering with precise control. "The sooner I'm rid of you, the better."

Damn him for being a total jerk because his British accent is like a smooth caress, even when he's irritated.

"The feeling's mutual," I grumble.

At least whatever weird Stockholm Syndrome I experienced at the cemetery isn't happening now. The heat from a moment ago fades as my anger at him returns. I'm glad. Out of everything, that was the strangest part of the night. I might not have any clue what I'm doing when it comes to guys, but I never expected to practically melt the first time one touched me. Seriously, yikes at myself for—for—I won't even name my reaction while faced with the precarious situation I was in.

"If you want to get rid of me, you can start by backing off. I'm leaving." I lift my chin, giving in to the urge to speak my mind instead of keeping my thoughts chained in place as usual. "In fact, just wait until Halloween in a few weeks. As soon as I turn eighteen, I'm leaving Brim Hills in the dust."

A dark, amused huff leaves him. "You think I'll let you escape? Go ahead. Run. Wherever you go, we'll find you."

Narrowing my eyes, I push up from my chair, satisfied when he inhales sharply and gives up his ground rather than touch me. That's more like it. I sock him in the arm, shoving aside the flash of fear that tells me bad things happen if I touch others. He makes another humored sound. It's creepy to see him laughing, his brooding sneer turning into a vicious smirk.

"Was that feeble attack meant to hurt me?" He tilts his head so his tousled dark hair falls in his face. "None of you ever learn."

"That's for the other night. Fuck you and your buddies for the trick you played on me. Did the girls at Talbot House put you up to it?"

I shut down the computer, ignoring the press of his eyes on my back. In the reflection of the monitor, I find his attention locked on the swell of my round ass. Gritting my teeth, I shove past him and make for the exit. I got the explanation I came here for. No more nightmares for me. The corner of my mouth lifts until I register Valerian's smoky, slightly bitter scent and the thud of his boots.

"Are you still following me?" I imitate his accent and moody tone. "I thought you wanted to be rid of me."

He waits until we're on the cracked sidewalk in front of the building, almost sounding like it costs him to admit, "You…smell different than most humans. It's the only thing that's earned you our mercy so far. A mere curiosity we wish to satisfy before fulfilling our duty."

Great, now he's insulting me. Is he kidding me?

I smell?

"Sorry for offending you," I sneer. "The deodorant provided by group homes is the cheapest the state budget can skate by with."

His brow furrows as he stares at me. I get the vibe that he's the brains between the three of them, the type who doesn't get surprised easily because he's already thought of every possible outcome of a situation. For all I know, I've crossed a small-time gang that believes they run this town. A bit out of place for middle of nowhere Pennsylvania, but the powerful way he holds himself fits, like he doesn't believe anyone can go up against him and win.

"You're impossible." His mutter seems to be meant more for himself than in response to me. "Such a strange black cat. I will figure out what you are."

Impossible. The same thing he said in the graveyard.

Oddly, the word resonates, colliding with me like a brick to the chest. I swallow past the lump that lodges in my throat and whirl to tell him off for being the world's biggest douche. Except—he's gone.

The words die on my tongue as I glance around. How did he muffle his footsteps? Whatever. I don't care.

I smirk, continuing down the main road while picturing him scurrying away to keep the mysterious illusion that he can simply vanish. He probably squeezed his sexy, emo ass down one of the tight alleyways that run between the shops.

A curiosities storefront catches my attention. I missed this during the drive in. Stopping, I peer at the items on display. It's interesting until I spot something that makes me roll my eyes—a homemade pamphlet on the cemetery. The headline reads *open the gate…if you dare.* Ugh, stupid legend crap.

"Hey, pretty thing," a charming voice says behind me. "I missed you. Couldn't stand watching from afar anymore. Are you on an adventure today?"

I spin to face another guy from the graveyard. Matthias, the flirty fuckboy with handsome boyish features. He leans against the brick exterior, messy white blond hair moving in the wind and full lips curved in an easy, lopsided smile complete with a damn dimple.

Small fucking town. I resign myself to the torment of running into the guys who pranked me for the next few weeks until I ditch this place.

Unlike his morose counterpart, Matthias wears a distressed band t-shirt that looks vintage and stretches perfectly around his biceps, black jeans with the knees sliced open, and a flannel shirt tied around his hips. It gives me a good view of the tattoos decorating his arms. The ink is a collection of styles and trends, everything from a badass lunar moth to a bright blue dolphin that would seem random if the rest weren't also such an eclectic mix.

Shit. If I didn't hate him for taking part in the prank on me, I would totally be into him. Compared to the others, he gives off a more approachable vibe, and the mischief dancing in his golden eyes entices me.

This day is shaping up to suck big time. What have I done to deserve this?

Existed, a poisonous corner of my mind whispers.

I huff to dispel the sting piercing my throat. "Watching from afar? Stalker. Why are you following me, too?"

The side of his mouth tugs higher as he checks me out without bothering to hide the sensual drag of his gaze. "Why wouldn't I? You're a knockout."

"I know I look good." I lift a brow at his grin. No, not every curvy girl spends her days lamenting her body image, thanks very much. "How about the real answer?"

Matthias strokes his chin, his playful demeanor sharpening to seriousness. He glances around as if he's making sure we're alone before he murmurs, "I'm drawn to you. The taste I got wasn't enough. It will never be enough."

When the words leave him, my heart gives a strange flutter and my chest tightens. His gaze holds mine, those gold eyes brightening as if they're glowing. But that's impossible. A trick of the light reflecting off the glass. I can't look away, my heartbeat thudding.

The moment passes when he pops off the wall, relaxed once more. "It must be the thrill. I haven't been topside in years. Come on." He plucks on the suspenders of my skirt with a cheeky wink and nods down the street. "There's a record shop at the end of this block. Every time I go in, I find gold."

No. I should definitely turn around and go the other way.

He can't win me over with that cocky smile after pranking me with his friends. Even if he did, it would end. He's definitely a player that can't be tied down, and I'm not keeper material. *Lily the reject.*

Yet I go with him, because I'm a glutton for punishing myself with the things I'll never have. Has it come to this? My desperation for any scrap of attention someone's willing to throw my way is so bad, I'll go along with a cute boy—one that was mean to me—just for a moment of *what if*. Whatever, I have to, anyway. Talbot House is that direction.

He ducks into the record shop and I hesitate on the threshold before following, expecting him to flip the switch and be a dick again any second. At least with the other two it's easy to hate them—with him, his open flirtatiousness with a dash of golden retriever energy throws me off from how he acted in the graveyard. I watch him carefully, waiting for the switch to flip back to asshole mode.

"Does anyone even listen to records anymore?" I trail after him, tapping my fingertips on the cardboard sleeves while he eagerly thumbs through a punk rock section.

"If they don't, they're idiots. Vinyl is the superior medium." He picks one, flipping it over to scan the back. His broad grin steals my breath. "It produces the best sound. Here. Like this."

He captures my wrist and tugs me to an old school record player set up with headphones. The side of his full lips curls up and he flashes me an impish glance, disheveled blond hair covering one of his eyes as he sets up the record. When he puts the headphones on for me, his gold eyes bounce between mine, nimble fingers moving through my hair. I'm trapped in his stare while the record starts, my pulse thrumming.

The song he picked is about a pair of runaways looking for something to make them feel alive. His grin grows while I listen, eagerly watching my reaction.

"See? It's unbeatable. The lyrics, the melody, it all sounds better and makes you want to hit the road." He brushes his fingers over my chest, and I let him, not pulling back when I'd usually jerk out of reach. "It resonates here."

I push the headphones off, skin still tingling from the contact. "Or I could just listen to as many songs as I want on my phone instead of keeping this cumbersome stuff."

He mutters something about MP3 players until I take my phone out. The thing is ancient, the touchscreen cracked, but it works. I don't get a data plan, so any public wifi is a blessing. After three days here, I've learned that this town barely understands what wifi is.

My phone catches his attention and he grabs it from me, ignoring my miffed protest. He turns it back and forth, tapping the apps and making a delighted noise with each one he opens. I slide my lips together, fighting off the thought that he's kind of adorable. Each one of those excited sounds causes something to unfurl in my chest.

"These things have come far. Last time I was here, they folded in half."

Clearing my throat, I raise a brow at the strange remark and snatch it back. "Well, everything about this place seems stuck in the past. There's nothing to do, the wifi is nonexistent and—" I squash the expanding sensation in my chest and give him an unimpressed glance. "—the people are pretty shitty. Basically, it blows here."

"Welcome to Brim Hills, lost girl." Matthias

chuckles darkly, swiping his tongue along his lip. I don't know why I thought it was split before. It seems normal now.

My eyes narrow as he returns to flipping through the bins of records in the musty shop. "Why the hell do you keep calling me that? You and your buddies each decide on a nickname to keep hazing me with?"

He shrugs lazily. "Dunno. You feel lost."

It hits too close to home, leaving me unsettled. I worry my lip with my teeth and back away. I should go, but each time I take a step toward the door an odd instinct stops me, pulling me back.

There's something about him that makes me think he would understand what it's like to feel so lost all the time. I don't know why, but watching the way he lights up at little things like finding a record by a band he likes makes me want to know more.

Toying with the edge of a record sleeve, I grapple with the urge to drop my guard, to give up something about myself. When I do that, I leave myself raw and vulnerable, and every time I end up hurt. It's why I've learned to keep my walls up and dull myself for self preservation.

The minute I start to respond, Matthias stiffens with a frown. Setting his jaw, he shoots a glare through the window of the shop. I don't see anything on the street to put him in a mood.

He nods curtly. "Fine." With a tetchy sigh, he abandons the records he picked out and heads for the door. "Sorry to cut this short."

The corners of my mouth tighten, holding in what I was going to say. There's the flipped switch. It comes every time without fail.

I follow him out. "Yeah." My voice is back to being flat. "I have to go, too."

"See you soon, lost girl. I wish…" The smile he gives me this time is tinged with a hint of regret. He laughs, shaking his head. "Nah. Never mind. It's a shame it's not meant to be. Alder would maim me. And then Vale would finish me off."

A beat up truck rolls by with its sad excuse for a muffler rumbling. I watch it chug down the road, gathering my courage. It's the first time in so long I've wanted to keep a conversation going. I open my mouth to ask what he means, but just like his broody partner in crime, he gives me the slip by the time I turn around.

This time it leaves an empty feeling hollowing out my chest and a burning sensation in my stomach. Always left behind. Always unwanted.

Not meant to be, like he said. At least the others are upfront with being shitty. He's more dangerous because he made me think for a second that I could actually let my guard down. He's still toying with me, the prank in the cemetery not enough to entertain him. Fuck them all. And double fuck him.

I blink away the tears that blur my vision, bitter hatred reigniting not just for Matthias, but for everything and everyone that's ever come and gone in my life.

The walk back feels twice as long, everything less vibrant than this morning—the autumn leaves on the sycamore trees, the red paint on the covered bridge, the satisfaction of finding the answers I wanted.

The entire way it feels like someone—some*thing*—watches me.

Six
LILY

WHEN MY EYES SNAP OPEN IN THE MIDDLE OF THE night, my pulse races. I lay still beneath the floral quilt in the dark, trying to get my brain to work. I wasn't having a nightmare. After I went to the library two days ago, I stopped having the same dream of the fake fantasy world my mind invented.

So why…?

Movement from the corner of my eye makes my heart stumble violently. A gasp catches in my throat as the huge shadow moves into the moonlight.

A large hand covers my mouth before I release the scream building in my lungs.

"Hush."

It's Alder. The last of my shadows.

I grab his wrist and squeeze hard, digging

my nails in. He brings his face close to mine, near enough that I can make out his unaffected smirk in the faint light filtered through the curtains. Forcing out a pissed breath through my nose, I react without thinking, attacking hard enough to break skin.

He flexes his grip, giving my jaw a little shake before he lets go without even a grimace of pain. I want to scream just to spite him. Sitting up, I press my back against the wall, bringing my knees up.

"What. The. Fuck?" I hiss. "Are you psychotic? How did you get in here?"

How long was he there watching me before I woke up?

Alder emits a gravelly rumble, jerking his chin at the window. I gape, eyes sliding from his massive build to the tiny window.

"You've got to be shitting me," I whisper-shout.

Across the room, Marie snuffles in her sleep and rolls over. My death grip tightens on the blanket. Oh god, if she wakes up—

"She will not wake," he mutters. "No one will while I'm here."

Is that a cryptic and creepy way of telling me he killed everyone else in the house? Dosed them? What is wrong with him? This is taking their odd obsession with messing with me too far.

My chest tightens. Even if I report him for breaking in, no one believes me when I'm in trouble.

Sharp sensations prickle across my palms.

Licking my lips, I fight to control my rapid breathing. He can't hurt me. He *won't*. If he tries anything…I'll lose control, like I always do when I let go of my emotions.

"How did you even find me?" My eyes widen. I knew I felt someone's gaze on me the other day. "Did you also follow me? Have you been watching me?"

He crosses his arms, making his rugged muscles appear bigger. "I tracked you by your scent, little stray."

My shoulders go rigid. What the fuck?

Pursing my lips, I subtly run my fingers through my hair and angle my head to take a sneaky whiff, checking if I stink. His friend insulted the way I smell, too.

"What are you?" he rasps. "Vale was right, your scent is…"

His gruff words trail off. Leaning in, he touches my hair, thick fingers sliding through it until he gives the short ends a light tug. Nothing about it is threatening. It feels sort of nice, which pisses me off. With an uneven breath, I lift my hand to bat him away. He grabs my wrist, his touch hot against my skin.

"Scars." I shudder at the fierce way he says it, the deep, angry rumble vibrating through my body.

"Burns," I correct harshly, even though scars is right.

Clenching his jaw, he examines my hand and follows the old wounds from my childhood up my arm. His piercing green gaze is intense and inescapable when it meets mine once more, even in the dark when I shouldn't be able to discern the vibrant color.

Each tiny movement I make, Alder tracks with the hunger of a predator, a hunter. If I run…he'll chase me until he catches me. Maybe push me face down into the dirt, wrap his huge hands around my hips and—

I slam down on the direction of my thoughts, chest heaving. When Valerian dared me to run, it sounded sinister, a challenge I would accept just to piss him off, but thinking about being hunted by Alder sends fire into my veins. The idea of doing anything with a man I hate should repulse me, but it has the opposite effect, my nipples pebbling beneath my camisole. He watches that too with a gleam in his hypnotic eyes and a ghost of a smirk tugging at the corner of his mouth.

"Stop it." I wrench my wrist from his firm grip. Screw my last few weeks as a ward of the state in the system. I don't want to stick around if it means living in close proximity to them. "I'm over this game. If you guys don't stop stalking me, I'm out of here."

"I'll always know how to find you. I'll enjoy it every time I have to hunt you down until we fulfill our duty and take what's ours." He frowns, backing away. He holds my gaze a beat longer, as if he wants to memorize me before tearing his attention away. "Time is almost up."

A shiver races down my spine at his deadly tone. I search for something to throw at him without taking my eyes off him. Marie's clock is too far, and my pillow won't make a satisfactory weapon. Phone it is. Gritting my teeth, I reach for it beneath my pillow. He watches, completely unthreatened.

Oh yeah?

With a vicious grunt I lob it right at his head, crowing in triumph when it clocks him across his brow. His head jerks and he allows my phone to clatter to the floor. Regret fills me immediately when he's unharmed. I probably just broke my phone for nothing.

"Shit," I bite out, scooting to the edge of the mattress to rescue my phone.

When I look up, Alder has vanished, melting into the shadows like a fucking creeper. Just like the others. I sit up all night, unable to go back to bed in case he comes back and decides to smother me in my sleep after all once he's finished sniffing me.

The seventh day comes and goes and I'm still here, so take that legend. I knew it was all fake.

Each day that passes helps me breathe easier.

It's not until halfway through the following week that I realize between my encounters with all three of them that I talked more to those assholes—and didn't hide the sarcastic remarks I'd normally keep to myself—more than I have in years. It's noticeable because I've spent the last four days practically silent around Mrs. T, Marie, and the other girls in the house. A new girl arrived this week, the youngest out of all of us, and Mrs. T is already marking the days on the calendar until I'm gone so the newbie can have my bed instead of the pullout couch.

The sooner my birthday comes on Halloween, the sooner I can get out of this town. Two more weeks. I can make it through that.

It's dark when I'm done poking my head in every single shop on the main street looking for part-time work. They all turned me down. I figured, but I had to try. I really need money to get me started once I age out.

"That hundred bucks you're gatekeeping is mine, Jessica." I cross my arms over my chest and ignore the sidelong looks from an older couple passing me.

I mull over my options. I could try the diner again. Diners always need help. I'd rather do that than hustle home to make it for Mrs. Talbot's house dinner.

When I turn to head back the direction I came, hands grab at me, yanking on my cropped hoodie and my high-waisted shorts. Before I so much as flail or scream, they cover my mouth. I'm lifted off the ground and carried down one of the narrow alleys between the buildings with my legs kicking. I suck in stinging, forceful breaths through my nose and aim a merciless elbow jab at the guy holding me. He grunts.

"I warned you, Lily Sloane," Valerian growls in my ear. "Time to pay the price. For all the trouble you've caused us, your soul is going to taste so fucking sweet. No more mercy, no matter what you are. You're done."

Oh shit. Oh *shit*.

My struggling becomes more frantic, survival mode kicking in. He sounds way too serious, making me uneasy. This doesn't feel like it's about a stupid prank. I thought I'd escaped and they'd knock it off. We're well past the seven nights crap they mentioned in the graveyard to freak me out. The anxiety I kept at bay when they taunted me for a week floods back in a dizzying rush.

How does he know my name? Alder creeping into my room in the middle of the night last week springs to mind. I bet anything he scoped out my name taped to the door.

No matter how hard I kick and flail, I can't get free. Valerian holds me with minimal effort, moving further into the shadowy alley. Once he's satisfied, he dumps me on my feet and slams my back against the wall. I wince, smothering a pained sound.

"Fucking bastard," I spit.

"Hold her," he commands.

I freeze when he steps away, Matthias taking his place when he melts out of the darkness. He grasps my waist, pinning me in place with equally little effort while Valerian leans against the brick wall beside us, watching with an infuriating cunning gaze. It probably helps that I stopped struggling, too stunned to process what's happening like a dumb bitch inviting death and worse things by not fighting my way out of this.

Snapping out of it, I blurt out the first thing that comes to mind. "What about vinyl?"

"Duty calls." Matthias' mutter is detached, void of his typical carefree spirit. The hard glint in those gold eyes that were so warm when he looked at me in the record shop squeezes my heart. "Even though your scent's got us curious, you opened the gate. That's not a fate I can save you from. It is what it is, lost girl."

What, are they part of a cult that kills people and covers it up with the urban legend of the gate?

"No." I shake my head, flinching as he massages my waist. "No, it's not real. You're being crazy. It was a dare. A stupid fucking prank."

He nods with a sigh, pressing a quick kiss to my forehead. I pound my fists against his chest, hatred welling in me until it feels like I'll burst. My palms prickle with a needle-like sensation and I swear the ground beneath us tremors. Fear rockets through me, making it difficult to breathe.

"You're sure? No take backs." Matthias directs the question at Valerian, studying my face in wonder. "You feel that, right? Because that's not me."

"I knew I should've brought Alder instead," Valerian grits out. "Just end the girl, collect her soul, and be fucking done with it. This fascination has run its course. We're over the limit. If we don't return to our guard posts, we're in a heap of shit with the council."

End me. Take my soul. Those are not euphemisms.

This is definitely not a mean joke to haze me. They're serious. Who the hell are they?

"I know how this works, Vale. Shut up."

"Then stop stalling."

They argue as if I'm not here and the topic isn't

take Lily's miserable soul. I guess it doesn't matter if I hear.

"My vote is hell fucking no," I screech. "Get off me!"

Matthias closes his fingers around my throat and croons to me like I'm a frightened animal. It's not as soothing as he thinks because I'm still riding high on terror and adrenaline.

I gulp as he buries his face in my neck and inhales. "Mm, toasted cinnamon. Double shot of fear." He licks, the sensation of his tongue being split back, just like that night. "Delicious."

Releasing a shrill yell, I aim a shot at his groin with my knee. He deflects it with a low chuckle, pinning me to the wall with his body so I can't move. My heart beats so fast my head swims. I gulp for air, mind racing for a way out of this.

Valerian bats Matthias' hand away, replacing it with his own. He wrenches my face to look at him. Out of the corner of my eye, the ink covering his skin moves of its own volition along his forearm, slinking beneath his pushed up sleeves. Freaked out and sure my brain has broken, I try to look at his tattoos. Both of them hold me in place, pinned between the wall, Matthias' body plastered against mine, and Valerian towering at my side to block my view of the alley.

"I told you, darling." His dangerous rasp fans over my lips, those haunting blue eyes dipping to my mouth. Transfixed, he drags his thumb along it. "There's no escape. Be a good girl and die for me."

His command sends a shiver through me, my fear sliced through by the shot of arousal ignited by his crisp, domineering order. Twisting free of his grasp, I spit. Saliva splatters his face, hitting him across his mouth and chin.

He stills. Trapping me in his penetrating gaze, he licks his lips, tasting my saliva. I gulp at how wrongly attractive it is when he does it. He lets go of me and swipes the rest away. The veins on his hand stand out prominently against his tattoos.

"Slit her throat," Valerian orders.

"I have a better idea." Matthias' teeth scrape my neck, making me jolt at how sharp they are. His words take on a musical quality that echoes around me as if I'm in a dream world. My rapid pulse slows from a frantic rush, my fear overtaken. His voice sounds so nice, it makes me want to do anything he says. "What if I fuck her to death? You can watch."

The arousal intensifies at his suggestion, spilling through me. My mind short-circuits and a strained gasp tears past my lips. I hate them, but—

"Look at you, pretty thing. You like that idea? Your cheeks turned such a delicious shade of pink." Matthias' eyes are so bright, the gleaming gold ensnaring me so I can't look away. I need to fight him off, but I can't remember why. All I'm aware of is how much I want is his devious mouth on every inch of me. "Which part? Vale watching? Riding my cock until your very last breath?"

With each lilting, oddly echoey question, he brushes a kiss lower and lower down my throat until he reaches the crook of my neck. A dizzying inferno of desire builds inside me. Yes. *Yes*. I want to do what he suggested. He swipes his tongue out to taste my flushed skin, then brings his lips to my ear to release a rough, filthy groan of pleasure that makes me shudder.

"You taste so good," he murmurs.

This is insane. I need to get away. Scream. Run. Anything.

My limbs don't obey. Why can't I move? Why am I so into this? Do I have a death wish after all?

Darting a look at Valerian, the corners of his mouth twist with a sinister smirk like he can read every thought flitting through my head. The press of his gaze has me burning up while Matthias drags his hands down to my hips and grinds the hard ridge of his dick against my stomach.

Matthias buries his face in my neck again, lips brushing my sensitive skin. "Fuck, I want to split your pussy apart with my cock, lost girl. Split you in pieces."

My core throbs. I smother the cry that tries to escape me, arching into him. His sinful, smoky words have the opposite effect on me than I expect when I'm not sure if he's talking in the literal sense or not. They ignite an inexplicable need in my veins stronger than I've ever known, one as strange as that purring noise I made in the graveyard when the three of them circled me. It comes on hot and fast, intensifying when he chuckles in approval. Hooking a hand beneath my thigh, he wraps it around his body and angles his hard bulge between my legs, right against my center.

Stars explode and my head tips back against the brick at the divine friction. What he's doing to me feels amazing. My hips move, my throbbing clit seeking more as my insides wind into a tight knot.

"Oh god," I choke hoarsely.

"No gods here, darling," Valerian says. "Only demons."

He's transfixed on my exposed neck. He brushes his tattooed knuckles down my overheated skin, eliciting another embarrassing, needy whimper from me while Matthias slides a hand beneath my cropped hoodie. He licks his lips with measured precision and I swear the tip of his tongue is forked like a snake. Matthias latches his mouth onto one side of my neck and Valerian dips his head, hot breath coasting over my thrumming pulse. He pauses before his lips connect with my skin and my body is hyperaware of the small distance he keeps between us.

For the first time ever, I'm burning up without being afraid of the explosion, without being afraid of whatever freakish thing will happen. I don't care, all I need is more of this. The world around me can burn to ash if I can have more of this.

Lifting his head, Valerian catches my chin and watches the shift of pleasure across my features, the parting of my lips and fluttering of my eyelashes as Matthias torrents my neck.

"Are you going to come for him?" Valerian asks.

"Please." I crave what comes next, needing more. I don't want this to stop.

A wild thought crosses my mind that sends another wave of heat spiraling through me—both of them touching me. Matthias taking me against the brick wall, but instead of watching, Valerian's mouth claiming mine in a heady, heart-stopping kiss while Matthias fills my pussy.

The cry that bursts from me is out before I can stop it. There's no fighting what I'm feeling, nothing to stop this crazy pull winding tighter. Matthias' touch is like a drug and with Valerian watching intently, I'm close to shaking apart, the tightly-wound coil of need about to snap and tip me over the edge into oblivion.

My heavy-lidded gaze drops to Valerian's lips. He emits a rough, dominant rumble, hovering his mouth over mine. Another rock of Matthias' hips makes my breath hitch. I'm so close.

"Christ, I can smell how wet you are. How much you need it, pretty girl. Doesn't she smell incredible, Vale?"

"These need to come off." Valerian tugs at the waistband of my shorts.

I gasp at how sharp Matthias' fingers feel against me beneath my hoodie, his fingertips becoming points that tease my bra. The same sharpness traces my hip. Dropping my attention to Valerian's hand, I freeze. His fingers shift before my eyes, lengthening into coal colored talons. When Matthias pulls away from my neck to grin at me, I gape at the pointed teeth in his smug, hungry smile.

Fangs. Glowing eyes. Absurd strength. Moving tattoos. *Claws*.

My heart beats hard, awareness slicing through some of the thick haziness keeping logic at bay.

"What the fuck?" I whisper.

There's no way to fool myself to explain what I'm seeing. These aren't magic tricks. I just watched them transform, changing from human to—to— monsters. I was about to fuck a legit monster.

If monsters are real, that means the legend is true. All those things I didn't want to believe I saw actually happened.

No gods here, darling. Only demons. Oh god. An

unpleasant tingle spreads across my body. Demons. That's what they are.

"Matthias." The curt urgency in Valerian's tone erases the last of my daze.

"Damn it," Matthias grumbles. "Now? It was just getting good."

My head pounds as the aftereffects of whatever hypnotic shit he did to me ebbs away. I screw my eyes shut to block out everything I don't want to handle right now. One of them—Matthias, I think—murmurs goodbye and caresses my cheek.

When I open them, I'm alone—again. They let me go, vanishing into the night.

This time, I don't know if I hope to never see them again, or if I wish they'd finished what they started. They didn't kill me. Doesn't mean they won't try again.

My jaded, scarred heart gives a painful throb. It's not like anyone would miss me if they succeeded. The world will be glad to be rid of troubled, difficult Lily Sloane. Maybe I'll get a cool do-over in a different kind of world like in my favorite isekai manga.

I sag against the wall to remain upright. The comedown from whatever Matthias did to me with his glowing gold eyes is a bitch, leaving me dizzy and thirsty. My mind is still twisted up in how into it I was, how I was moments from letting them do anything they wanted with me. Why do weird as fuck things have to follow me everywhere I'm bounced around?

A scuffle against the concrete makes me jump. I whip my head to the other end of the alley. A shopkeeper with a grizzly beard dumps trash at the back end of the alley and peers around. Spotting me in the shadows, he takes a step in my direction.

"Alright, miss?" he asks.

"Yup." Nope.

He takes another step. "Why don't you come inside?"

Are his eyes a little too bright, or am I still reeling from the adrenaline rush from an encounter with demons?

"No thanks. I've got to go."

Gathering all my strength, I push off the wall and hurry back to the main road. My heartbeat doesn't slow down, my thoughts a racing mess I can't make sense of.

I never should have gone to the graveyard and done the dare.

Seven
LILY

My long skirt swishes around me as I make my way down a long hall with pillars and an arched, intricately carved ceiling. The obsidian floor reflects the flickering orange flames dancing in my palm. I smirk at my pretties, curling my fingers around the fire. Double doors open at the end of the hall, and someone inside calls a name that isn't mine.

Wait.

This isn't right. Am I dreaming again?

The thick dark fog surrounding me shifts once I'm aware of it. I come out of the vision of another world, waking up to a dark room with a muffled yell.

What the—? My mouth is cottony and I gag

unable to swallow, unable to close my mouth because there's something stuck in it that makes my jaw ache. I want to rip it out, but my hands are stuck behind me, tied to the chair. Yanking, I get nothing but stiff limbs.

What's going on? Was I drugged?

Lifting my head, I blink several times, taking in the unfamiliar room. This is wrong. I went to bed at Talbot House, finally passing out after staying up for twenty-four hours reading the books on demon lore I borrowed from the library. I should be in it right now. It feels like I've barely been asleep, though my breathing turns harsh when I spot the date on the busted, flickering clock. Two days? No way.

Disorientation leaves my mind like sand pouring through an hourglass. It's the same unpleasant comedown I had after the hypnosis in the alley wore off. Bit by bit, the thick, abnormal fog seeps away, allowing flashes of what happened when I went to bed to rise to the surface of my memories.

They melted out of the shadows. Grabbed me. I fought, my elbow throbbing with the tenderness of crashing against rock hard muscles. My captors argued. Then came the order to knock me out.

If I close my eyes, I can still sense the large warm hand brushing my forehead with his thumb before the unnatural darkness claimed me.

Grinding my teeth against the fabric gag tied

around my head, I recap what I've learned in the last sixty seconds since waking. I don't know where I am, but I'm guessing it's a shitty motel going off the hideous, dated furnishings and the faint stench of nicotine hanging in the air. I'm bound and gagged, still wearing the oversized t-shirt I went to bed in. Judging by the twinges in my stiff body, I've been like this for most of the two days missing from my mind.

Alder, Matthias, and Valerian are dead for fucking kidnapping me. Chest heaving with fury, I squirm against the restraints to loosen them. My muscles are sore from being locked in the same position, but I savor the throbs of pain, feeding each one to my hatred. Once I get out of my bindings, I'll kick their teeth in.

The door opens and I catch a brief glimpse of a dark parking lot lit by the neon glow of a motel sign. Then my three asshole stalkers stride in.

Demons, my mind supplies helpfully. My stomach clenches. There's no denying what I saw in the alley. Their fingers that changed into long, terrifying claws. It's not normal. Not human.

I can't believe the gate to Hell is real. I can't believe I convinced myself they were going to leave me alone after that shift from danger to…something far more potent in the alley. They've each said they can't let me go. But kidnapping? Seriously?

Drawing in a deep breath, I launch into a tirade that's unintelligible with the gag blocking my mouth. They don't acknowledge me, too wrapped up in their own conversation. I rock back and forth on the chair, yelping when I nearly overbalance the damn thing.

Alder comes close enough to right my chair prison before it topples, scooting me with a forceful shove so I'm wedged between the ratty bed and the nightstand. Once he ensures I'm not going to tip the chair over, his focus returns to the other two men without sparing me another glance.

That's how we're playing this? Fine. Fuck. Them.

Huffing, I drop my head back and stare at the ceiling.

"Killing her was a total fail. We couldn't— hurt her," Matthias argues in a confused tone. "She looks the part, but I don't think she's human. Not completely. You felt it, didn't you? The pull is intense."

Fuckboy say what? I tune back into their conversation, no longer ignoring them out of spite.

Valerian waves dismissively. "We have more pressing problems and need to act quickly before we entertain our theories. The demon council won't buy it much longer with only one of us posted at a time. It's a risk for all three of us to come here."

"We have to make a decision," Alder cuts in. "We've made her disappear, but it's not enough."

"Uh-m, heh-oh? Ahh-hullth!" My agitated words come out completely garbled by the gag. I go for the loudest scream I can manage instead, satisfied when two of them turn their attention to me.

Alder takes a step in my direction first, but it's Matthias who beats him to me and touches the gag.

He lifts his brows. "No screaming. Deal?" I narrow my eyes. He huffs in amusement and holds up his hands. "If you scream, Alder will have to put you under again. You can punch me as much as you want if I take off the gag. Does that sweeten it for you?"

Put me under. It was definitely his large, rough hand that caressed my head before the darkness trapped me in that vision.

After considering, I nod curtly, flexing my jaw in relief when the soggy material leaves my mouth. I tense as he massages my cheeks before undoing one of my arms.

He gives my arm the same treatment, working the sore muscles with his skilled hands. "Sorry for this. You almost woke up twice already, so it had to be done. Better?"

Without missing a beat, I wrench my arm free, ball my fist, and drive it into his arm as hard as I can.

He barely moves, humming a little laugh that rakes across my frayed nerves.

"For the record, it was Alder who felt up your fantastic tits when we had to knock you out," Matthias adds.

Alder's expression darkens with outrage. "I carried her. I didn't—"

"Enough." Valerian interrupts Alder's response.

I shoot Alder a death glare, mouthing *I hate you, shithead*. In turn, he glowers at Matthias, fists flexing with the promise of violence.

"Why did you kidnap me?" I spit venomously, the ire for my enemies giving me courage to stand up against demons.

I've faced plenty of vile people. Demons can't be much worse.

"I don't see the need to repeat myself endlessly," Valerian says.

"People will know I've gone missing. The matron at the girls' home will call the police."

With a rough, scornful rumble, he stalks over and grabs my chin, giving me a glimpse of the whorls of ink that move across his knuckles before he angles my head up. "Think. You're close enough to the age humans cast you out of the system that grants you shelter. It was quite easy for us to stage your disappearance. Will anyone care to look for you, or will they believe you ran off on your own?"

Even I know it would be a stretch for anyone at Talbot House to bother. I only had another week and a half left there. Mashing my lips together, I level him with a scowl that gives the broody bastard a run for his money. He narrows his eyes and cocks his head, grasping my jaw with more force.

"Not such a mouthy little thing now, are you?" He serves me a cruel smirk. "If you didn't want to be captured by demons, you shouldn't have summoned us by calling on the gate."

Demons. My mind still attempts to shy away from the truth.

I push out a tight breath and jut my chin against his hold. "You still haven't killed me. What do you plan to do with me?"

Heat melts down my spine and coils in my core when I think of what happened when they tried to murder me in the alley. Valerian's nostrils flare, his blue eyes sweeping over me.

"If only it were that easy," he says with caustic bite. "We'd all be better off without you."

I try to hide my flinch at his callous remark, my walls against the constant rejection the world throws at me no longer as strong with splintering cracks in them. One little taste of being wanted and my heart can't withstand his dismissal.

He works his jaw, cutting his gaze away. "There's something about you. Something we can't stay away from."

Every word of his admission sounds like he's fighting to hold it in and keep it to himself. Matthias told me right away, much more open about what made him curiously fascinated by me. For some reason, they're drawn to me. Something that feels like a faint thread pulling in my chest echoes when I have the thought.

"You dragged me into this mess. You could've just left me alone." My throat clogs. "Or if you were worried about people wondering if the legend was still real, you could've just told me to get out of town. It's not like I was planning on sticking around."

"Humans missing you aren't the problem. The demon council is. They expect a soul."

"But you won't kill me," I say slowly.

"*Can't,*" Alder cuts in with a glare. He scrubs his brown hair. "And we want to know why. We've never failed."

Valerian strokes my chin with his thumb, the tip barely edging against my lower lip. I lift my eyes to his, stomach dipping at the way the bright blue darkens. After what I know now, and what happened the other night I should be disgusted by his touch. Except disgust doesn't describe the way my insides flutter. His mouth curves, showing the hint of fangs.

"Perhaps once we understand what's different

about you, then we'll find a way to feast on you," he croons.

I shiver, picturing their sharp, monstrous teeth against my bare skin. Okay, so maybe I'm down to fuck monsters. I would never trust them, but a whisper in the back of my mind wonders what it would be like. The way it felt when Matthias touched me, when I wanted Valerian to kiss me, was unlike anything I've ever experienced.

Valerian's cunning gaze is inescapable, watching as my lips part and my cheeks flush. A gravelly sound vibrates in his chest when he leans over me, tipping my face up.

"Let's fake it."

Matthias' suggestion breaks the moment between us as he sprawls on the bed to my side. He winks at me, trailing a finger down my arm and teasing the bottom edge of my shirt, unbothered by the way Valerian invades my space while he does it.

"Fake it?" Alder questions, posting himself with his bulky arms crossed by the nightstand at my other side.

"Her death," Valerian clarifies, his eyes narrowing in thought.

With all three of them crowding me at once, the air grows thick and hot around me. I strain to draw breath. The alley was bad enough with two of them caging me in, but this...I squeeze my thighs together, mortified by my reaction to their proximity. What is wrong with me? Why am I getting so turned on by the three men I hate? By my kidnappers? By demons?

Get it together, I scold myself. These are my enemies.

Shaking my head to clear it, I ignore Matthias' cocky stare. Whatever sinful, dirty thought is in his head, I don't want to know it.

"Would that work to fool your overlords or whatever?" I ask. "And how?"

"Demon council," Alder corrects with pride coloring his tone. "They oversee the different factions of demons. There are many like us—warriors, guards, hellhounds, and soul reapers. Those that can cross between the realms. Our king, Lucifer, rules the underworld and the council is like his right hand." His proud expression turns conflicted. "Disobeying our sworn duty to the council is as good as spitting in the king's face."

Color drains from my cheeks. "Don't piss off the Devil's lackeys in Hell. Got it."

It feels weird just saying that with a scrap of seriousness. Demons are real. The Devil rules over Hell in the underworld. Yeah, not getting used to that anytime soon.

"You oversimplify our realm. It would be too difficult for you to understand," Valerian mutters.

"This is why humans have such skewed knowledge when it comes to the underworld. Hell is only one part of our realm."

I scoff. "Politics suck no matter what. Doesn't seem that hard to grasp."

The corners of his mouth tighten. He starts to respond, then they all freeze, heads cocked like they're listening. One of them curses.

Matthias slides off the bed, his languid nature replaced by someone that moves with efficiency. He slinks to the window, flicking the curtain carefully to peer out.

My shoulders tense at seeing him so serious. "What is it?"

Alder and Valerian exchange a glance.

"Too late," Valerian says. "They've come for you."

"What?" I yelp in alarm.

Matthias closes the curtains. "They're circling the parking lot."

"It's a scout group," Alder says.

Without another word, Valerian kills the lights. The three of them take up positions in the shadowy corners around the room to conceal themselves while I'm left out in the open. I snap my head back and forth. What's the plan?

"Hello! Tied up still over here!" I jerk against the restraints, using my free hand to yank on them. I can't reach the knot. "I'm not playing bait!"

"You are," Valerian shoots back. "You'll only get in the way or run off the first chance you get because humans are all stupid, fragile creatures. Stay there."

"Are you fucking kidding me?" My muscles strain with my attempt to wriggle free. "I hate you. I hate all of you so damn much."

None of them are listening.

I freeze as the doorknob glows red-hot and melts, dripping down the door. It swings open with an unsettling creak and a tall figure steps inside, silhouetted by the lights from the neon motel sign and from the parking lot that stream in. Thick horns curl back from his angular face, his skin is stretched tight over cheekbones, giving his features a gruesome appearance. There's no mistaking him for human—he's a demon.

He speaks to the dark room in another language, chuffing in croaky amusement when no one responds. With each step he takes toward me, my heart climbs higher in my throat. Sharp pains cramp my stomach and stab my palms as terror ratchets higher.

Any minute now, guys.

They don't move from their hiding spots.

Don't let me die, assholes.

The light from the open door illuminates his face better when he turns toward me and I suck in a breath. His eyes snap to me, intent and eerily bright. I know him. I've seen him somewhere, without the horns.

My eyes widen when it hits me. It's the same grizzly beard. He was in the alley! "Wait—aren't you—?"

The not-so-human shopkeeper releases a horrible, ear-splitting screech and flings a ball of fire at the spot I last saw Matthias. With a grunt, Matthias dodges and the curtains ignite, the burst of flames licking up the fabric to reach the ceiling in a matter of seconds. Putrid smoke chokes me, the fast-spreading fire flinging me back into all my worst memories.

Alder charges the demon from behind, his huge arms encased in fire. Before he catches him, two more gremlin-like monsters rush through the door, one going high and the other sinking low, their leathery red clawed hands splayed to attack. While Alder is forced to split his attention to defend himself, the shopkeeper's fists bloom with more flames and he launches himself at Valerian when he darts out of the shadows.

They clash together, sending another burst of fire and ash into the air. The darkness flickers away with collisions of their dueling fiery fists grappling for the upper hand. My heart plummets when the shopkeeper gets hold of Valerian's neck and lifts him off the ground. He spits something in another language and flames erupt from his hand, burning Valerian's neck. Valerian lets out an awful, choked sputter, struggling against the vicious move.

Matthias comes to his aid, jumping on the shopkeeper's back and shooting fire into his face from the hand he slashes across it. The shopkeeper's fire sputters out. Growling, the demon reaches back and flings Matthias off. He turns while holding Valerian by his throat and punches a fireball through the air.

"No!" I scream.

My heart seizes as the blow knocks Matthias against the wall before he collapses to the floor. He doesn't get back up.

Valerian's chiseled features morph in rage, his transformed hands dragging across the shopkeeper's face while planting his feet in the demon's chest and forcing a gust of smoke and hot air with a push of his palms to break away. His opponent doesn't give up ground, raking a flaming hand down his side before he lands on the floor. He lets out a roar that makes me want to fly out of my chair and do something to help.

Alder isn't faring much better. Even with his massive size, he doesn't have much advantage over the two demons double teaming him. They're faster, using their quick moves to get in his blind spots and swipe at him. What's left of his shirt hangs in tatters from his body, showing the angry red welts and oozing cuts from their attacks no matter how many volleys of fire he blasts at them from his clenched fists.

Each panicked breath I drag in is tinged with smoke. I cough, tears welling in my eyes. I can't get out of the chair no matter how hard I struggle.

One of the demons Alder is dealing with peels off and jumps on the bed, peering down at me with a sickening fanged grin. The demon's claws recede and he grabs me by my hair. Gritting my teeth against the searing pain in my scalp, I shrink away instinctively, knowing it does nothing to protect me. Instead of worrying about how I'm about to get sliced to pieces, my focus shifts to the others.

This is bad. The fierce desire to help them screams at me. I hate the three of them…but they're better than the monsters attacking us.

If I hadn't done the dare, we wouldn't be in this mess. I would go on living my miserable life and they would still be guarding the gate to Hell.

Valerian was wrong. The demons haven't come for me. They've come for all of us. To kill me *and* them.

Eight
LILY

My throat closes as I accept death. The demons beyond the gate I opened expect a soul, and they're succeeding. At least my shitty existence will end in an epic way. No isekai hit and run or falling down the stairs, I'm going all out with a paranormal attack. I close my eyes.

A fierce, guttural roar across the room makes them snap open again.

"No!" Alder bellows. "Don't touch her!"

He has the other demon he's fighting incapacitated in a hold, brawny muscles flexing. He snaps the demon's neck with inhuman force, dropping the crumpled body before barreling across the room to stand between my attacker and me. There's barely any room for his huge frame, but he wedges between us, acting as my shield.

My heart clenches painfully. No one has ever cared about my safety. Never, not even as a small girl.

The demon on the bed screeches, fisting my hair tighter and yanking hard. A pained scream tears from me.

Seething, Alder slams his bright red smoldering fist down on the demon's arm to weaken the hold on my hair. The fucker doesn't budge, tearing some strands from my scalp. I grit my teeth while Alder grabs the demon's limb, digging in hard. From the corner of my eye, I gape in disbelief as the demon's arm melts, the leathery flesh bubbling and oozing pus as Alder's unyielding molten hot grip burns through tissue until he reaches bone. Once he does, he bares his fanged teeth with a growl and closes his fist with a stomach-churning *crunch*, destroying the bone with insane strength.

Holy shit.

The counterattack earns him a few seconds. Instead of pressing the advantage while the demon is down, writhing in pain, he reaches back and grabs my restraints, putting my safety before his own. With a sharp tug, his claws slice through them, freeing me from the chair. I spring to my feet and back away, fighting the urge to hug the guy who was prepared to kill me the night we met for saving me.

"Stay down and behind me." The second the clipped words leave him, the demon is up on his feet, ready with another attack despite missing an arm. "You won't have her."

Something cinches tight in my chest at his protective tone. His back muscles ripple as he takes up a fighting stance. The Henley shirt is nothing but scraps of fabric dangling from his body. My gaze flies down his body, taking in the wounds he's sustained. Something else catches my eye, illuminated by the fire eating away at the motel room. Markings cover his torso and arms.

Scars.

The air in my lungs punches out of me. They look similar to my burn scars. Is this why he was mad I had them? Because he knows? An ache pangs in my chest, questions tugging at me. I wonder how he got them, if they bother him.

An ugly painting decorating the room crashes to the floor from its hanging spot on the wall, snapping me out of it. The room is still very much on fire and we're still in the midst of fighting demons that want to kill us. I don't have time to think about this now.

Focus.

Darting a look over my shoulder, I'm relieved to find Matthias on his feet again, swiping his mouth with the back of his hand. His playful boyish features take on a brutal edge to match the callous glint in

Valerian's eye as they circle the shopkeeper. An icy chill arrows through me when the shopkeeper gives them a hideous smile in anticipation.

Flames spread down Valerian's arm in a coil almost like a whip. His gaze flicks to Matthias. Signaling him with a nod, they both move together, Valerian using his fire to encircle the demon and hold him in place. He fights against the binding while Matthias forges the fire springing from his palms into a pointed tip, using it like a dagger. The demon throws up his arms to block, then grabs hold of Valerian's coil.

A niggling sense bolts down my spine out of nowhere with some kind of recognition of what's about to happen when he yanks Valerian closer with it.

"Watch out!" I shout.

They both fall back from the burst of hot hair the shopkeeper puts off with another screech that pierces me to the bone. I drop to a knee, slapping my hands over my ears.

By the time my head stops pounding and I scramble to my feet, the fighting seems dire.

None of the guys can get an edge over the shopkeeper or the other remaining demon. Blow for blow, they're matched and overpowered. Matthias takes a hit to the side that slows him down, pain written across his contorted face. Alder can't catch the smaller, quick demon keeping out of his reach before darting in when he can't block to carve his claws into his skin. Valerian is backed against a wall, glaring at the shopkeeper pining him with a rush of fire shooting from his hands.

No, no, no.

Oh god. It's not enough. They're all going to die because of me.

As the harrowing thought enters my mind, I gasp from the sensation of being squeezed by an invisible force.

The pressure becomes unbearable. I reach for Alder, gasping for air. My vision blurs. Shit, I can't breathe. Panic trickles over me, my senses bombarded by smoke and heat. I feel as though I'm being compressed from all sides. Is the shopkeeper doing this?

Sparks prick along my nerves, racing down my arms. The energy builds in my palms, growing hotter. Static blocks out my hearing, then a sharp *pop* makes me wince as the sensation ceases, flowing away in a rush. It leaves my hands tingling with the aftereffects.

Bright electric sparks rain over the open door to the parking lot, followed by a loud explosion that shakes the building from outside. It distracts the attackers. I think a transformer blew because the lights outside cut out, leaving the room lit by the orange glow of the fire.

Everyone freezes, glancing suspiciously at each other. Valerian uses this to his advantage, recovering while the shopkeeper isn't paying attention. His merciless uppercut snaps the shopkeeper's head back and he grabs him by his horns.

"Now," he barks.

Matthias crosses his hands in front of him, gold eyes flashing bright. He tears the demon's throat with his claws while Valerian traps him. The shopkeeper's black eyes bulge and he gurgles. Dark, tar-like blood seeps from his ravaged neck, staining his chest.

"Oh my god," I choke.

Alder finally grabs the smaller demon and releases a chilling growl. With one forceful yank, he rips the demon's body in half like it's made of paper. Blood and other gross innards spill from each severed half, coating Alder and the bed. My pulse thunders and inexplicably I think of beefy lumberjacks who rip tree logs in half with their bare hands.

When the shopkeeper's body slumps to the floor, the blaze engulfing the room sputters out, leaving it stinking of sulfur. Part of the drywall has burned away, the beds are destroyed, and the TV is cracked in half, toppled to the floor.

"I don't think you're getting your security

deposit back." The mumbled words are the first to jump in my head.

Matthias smirks, rubbing his side. "Not our problem." He winces. "Damn, we're out of shape. Alder, you good?"

He grunts in response, dumping the demon remains on the trashed mattress before shredding the scraps of his shirt clinging to his glistening muscles. I swallow thickly, unable to move from the center of the room.

We won. My demons beat the other demons, each of them reveling in their violent triumph. Valerian slowly wipes away the shopkeeper's blood, lips curling into a ruthless smirk. Matthias releases a laugh that's more than a little unhinged, grabbing the shopkeeper's slack face and shaking it. Alder's chest heaves with rumbling breaths, more beast than man at the moment.

My heartbeat thrums with relief, fear, and something warm and fluttering I don't want to name as my gaze moves between the three of them.

When I move, my limbs feel stiff. My hands skitter over Matthias' side first. "Are you guys okay?"

"I'm better now," he murmurs.

I ignore the brash smirk he gives me before I move to Alder, hovering my fingers over the fresh welts covering his existing scars. Valerian clenches his jaw and gives me his back.

"Not now." Alder takes my wrist and tugs me with him. "We need to move before more come."

Outside, I spot the smoking transformer that blew, the plume of smoke rising high into the night sky. My palms tingle with the phantom sensation I felt before. Rolling my lips between my teeth, I curl my hands into fists to dispel the tingles.

Valerian is the last to leave the destroyed motel room as we circle the long strip of rooms to the edge of the building. A sleek, black muscle car is parked there. Matthias pulls out a set of car keys. Before I learned the truth, I wouldn't blink twice. Knowing he's a demon, it trips me up.

"This is your ride? Where did you get a car?" I blurt.

Matthias grins. "Stole it."

"Get in," Valerian demands as he takes the keys.

"Where are we going?" I question as Alder hustles me into the backseat.

"Our gate," Valerian says. "We need to contact the demon council to find out what's going on."

My brows pinch. "Is that a good idea?"

Alder distracts me for a moment while Valerian pulls onto the road. He pets the top of my head with a big palm. My breath catches. Whatever he's doing helps soothe the dull throb lingering from having my hair ripped out. I want to melt against his warm side and beg him to never stop running his hand over my head like that.

Biting my lip to smother a sigh, I focus on my questions. "I mean, did the council put out like a burn notice or something for not killing me?"

Matthias twists from the passenger seat with a smirk. He understands human references much better than the others.

"They don't operate on whims without a deliberation to pass judgment," Valerian says. "Even if a human escapes death by a gate guard's hand, there's an order to these things."

"It's not just that they attacked us unprovoked that's a red flag," Matthias explains. "They broke our laws by potentially exposing our kind to humans. Big fucking no-no."

I smack the back of his headrest. "Then what about people like me who fuck with your gate? You revealed yourself then."

"Humans who summon the gate fall under a different classification than the general populace," Alder says. "They are destined for death, so it's not necessary to hide our true nature from them."

The car falls quiet as I process what they've told me. According to the dash, it's almost three in the morning.

"That guy spoke to you before he attacked us." I frown. "It was in another language. What did he say?"

Alder shakes his head. "He accused us of being traitors to our king. It doesn't make any sense."

Unease churns my stomach. "So why send scouts if they think you're traitors?"

"That was not a fucking scout group," Valerian grits through his teeth. "Who gave the order to the warrior guild to come topside? The council would never go to such extreme measures for a mere human."

"And us," Matthias reminds him.

Valerian's grip tightens on the wheel and he steps on the gas. The sign for the Brim Hills town limits comes into view.

Nine
LILY

IF I WERE A MERE HUMAN, THIS WOULD BE OVER ALREADY. Before their kidnapping plan went tits up because of the attack on the motel, Valerian said there was something different about me. The impossible thought clangs around in my head as the car rolls to a stop in front of the abandoned Brim Hills Cemetery. I've been told there's something wrong with me my whole life and have fought to run from it.

"I saw that demon in town before all this." Valerian and Alder freeze at my confession, turning expectant gazes on me. I avoid their eyes. "Um, in the alley. Without the horns, obviously. Before you and Matthias left."

Heat spreads through me when I recall what they were doing to me, how close they had me to exploding in pleasure before something made them leave.

"That was the scent I picked up." Valerian mutters a curse and slams the car door when he climbs out. "Stay alert. If they've been watching that long, something isn't right."

"Got it," Matthias says.

I poke my head out of the car and Alder blocks my path. "Stay here."

"Um, how about fuck no. You three kidnapped me. You're not leaving me behind to sit in the car with potential murder demons on the loose." I point at myself. "I'm not bait."

"Very well."

Sighing, he stands aside and allows me to enter the cemetery, keeping close behind me. The dead grass crunches beneath my bare feet. My gaze drifts to the woods that lead to Talbot House. If I run, he'll catch me easily. Part of me wants to test them to see, but it's fleeting. My curiosity keeps me moving up the hill with everyone.

I haven't stepped foot inside the graveyard since my first night here. It's not lost on me that the last time we were all here together I was running from them in terror, believing they were playing a cruel prank on me. Now the three of them position themselves around me while we navigate the headstones as if they want to keep me safe.

At the top of the hill, Valerian approaches the chapel ruins. He recites some kind of lilting incantation, frowning when the air crackles. The others tense. If I squint, I can make out the static electricity in the stone arch beneath the staircase, fainter than when I thought I saw them before.

"What's supposed to happen when you do that?" I ask.

"Not that," Matthias mutters. "As guards of the portals between realms, we have a connection to our gate. It's like a unique key."

"So the door is locked?"

"They've been here," Alder says.

"Yes." Valerian blows out a breath. "They've blocked our exit back to Hell. We have to abandon our post."

Without another word, he starts down the hill. Alder lingers, touching the side of the arch. The tightness at the side of his mouth and eyes draws a pang of sympathy from me.

I place a hand on his arm. "Are you okay, Alder?"

"Fine," he responds gruffly.

"Roadtrip. I call shotgun." Matthias drapes an arm over my shoulder, steering me back to the car. I don't miss the cautious glance he sweeps the area with as we walk through the cemetery. "Give the big guy a minute. He takes his orders seriously. Vale's been guarding this gate the longest, but Alder's the one who lives to serve our king. Abandoning our post is as good as treason to him."

I peer back at Alder. "I mean, they did try to kill us. I think we're past that."

"It will be difficult to prove we aren't traitors by leaving," Alder says behind us. "We've never failed our duties before."

"Better than dying," Matthias says.

"I could just go back to Talbot House." I motion to the trees with no intention of stepping off the path I've been dragged down to return to my miserable life. "It's right there through the woods."

Matthias drags me closer. "Nah. We've captured you. We're not letting you go yet, lost girl." He plays with the ends of my short hair. His tone shifts, becoming more intense. "You're ours."

I huff, grasping for sarcasm to cover for the weird tug low in my stomach at his words. "I guess I'm stuck with you. Woo. My safe word is meatloaf."

He snorts, but this reference seems lost on him. I explain the lyrics being the perfect fit for when things are over the line and his golden eyes light up. I want to kick myself for ever thinking they were special effects contacts as a way to convince myself otherwise and ignore everything I saw, because that luminous flare of color is pure magic.

His knuckles brush my cheek and my stomach

dips. "Clever little thing."

The wind rustles through the trees, making me shiver. My gaze darts to the woods again. "So, uh. Do I have time for some B and E? I don't want to go around barefoot in the t-shirt I wore to bed. Hopefully Mrs. T hasn't donated my clothes yet."

His crooked grin stretches into something wolfish and he tugs on the hem of my shirt, sending a cool breeze higher up my thighs the more he exposes them. "I dunno, I'm really digging this on you. It has easier access than that hot little pair of shorts you had on."

Alder smacks the back of his head as he passes us with long strides. "We took your bag when we stole you. Made it look like you ran off on your own. It's in the trunk."

"How thoughtful," I say cynically. "Thanks for leaving me unconscious for two days without pants on."

The warm, rich scent of woodsmoke and maple tickles my nose. I glance between Matthias and Alder, trying to decipher which of them it belongs to. Matthias' expression is too open, but a muscle in Alder's jaw jumps and he flexes his hand at his side.

Valerian is behind the wheel and has the car idling by the time the rest of us reach it. Alder lifts me without warning and carries me to avoid broken glass at the edge of the road. He deposits me in the backseat, then goes to the trunk and thumps his fist on it twice. Valerian pops it and Alder brings me my beat up duffel bag held together by duct tape and a prayer.

"Thanks." I quickly rummage for a pair of leggings and shimmy them on while the car whips around to head back the way we came.

"You're the source of the power surge we felt during the attack." Valerian's accusation slices through the silence in the car.

I glare at the back of his head. "Excuse me?"

"It wasn't power from the three of us." His haunting blue eyes flick to the rearview mirror to meet mine, narrowing. "We've been together long enough to recognize the feel of each other's power signature. It came from you. Care to share what you haven't told us?"

"You're crazy. That wasn't me." I cross my arms. "I don't have powers. It could've been the demons that attacked us."

Matthias barks out a sharp laugh from the passenger seat. "They couldn't take out a transformer without touching it."

Alder shakes his head. "The warrior's guild is powerful. Yes, those demons were high ranked, but no one in the guild is capable of producing that surge of energy without more demons to pool their powers together."

"No way," I insist hoarsely.

My breathing turns shallow and strained as flashes of memories assault me. The haunting pieces of my past I've run from and ignored.

Fires I've never been able to explain.

Flickering lights when I got yelled at. My palms prickling with sharp pains when my emotions were too much to cage inside me.

Even the time the whole street went dark, the street lights bursting on my way home after a teacher kept me late. The touchy feely old bastard thought that because I was a group girl no one would believe me. Except, when he went to grope me, I grabbed his wrist and burned the hair right off his arm. He took me to the principal and had me expelled.

"I believe this is why you've triggered these strange instincts in us." Valerian says instincts like it's a curse. He works his chiseled jaw. "Why you don't smell like a human should. Instead it's more like a scent escaping through the cracks, like something is masking what you really are."

Not human. I feel human. How could I not be?

With a thick gulp, I tuck my hands between my thighs, as if hiding the worst of my scarred flesh makes it disappear. "It's not like I hit puberty and sprouted horns I never knew about. My body is normal."

"Your body is gorgeous," Matthias chimes in.

"One hundred out of ten would smash."

Alder strokes his chin, studying me intently. "Still, what we felt… It was far more powerful. Something on the king's level almost."

I blanche. "The king—as in like, Lucifer? The Devil?"

"Smooth motherfucker himself. I've seen it firsthand. About a century ago, at an orgy at the palace." Matthias bites his lip, his chuckle depraved. "I swear he was commending my form. Anyway, his power feels like that, like it could choke you and you'd thank him for it."

I smother the angry pinch of jealousy in my stomach and skip right over the tossed out *century* comment. "I don't have powers."

"Whatever you say, pretty girl." Matthias winks over his shoulder, reaching back to squeeze my knee.

"We'll discuss it later when we get somewhere safe," Valerian mutters.

The sharp, bitter smell of smoke chokes the car. It's coming from one of them. Their scents seem to shift with their emotions.

Plucking at the seatbelt, I slide my lips together. More questions burst free after a short silence. "What are the gates? Why do they exist if you're not supposed to show yourselves to humans? You look human enough, until you go all Wolverine hands and Human Torch with the fists of fire."

Valerian's expression shutters and his grip tightens on the wheel. There's a beat of tense silence before Matthias breaks it.

"They weren't always a secret. Humans used to know about them." He ignores the severe scowl Valerian shoots at him, acting like he's setting the stage for an epic tale. "Not as urban legends, but as altars."

"Altars?" My stomach clenches.

"For sacrifice." Alder's no-nonsense confirmation doesn't make me feel any better. "The humans sacrificed an agreed upon number of souls willingly to feed the demons and keep the king of the underworld from razing the mortal territories to the ground when we all existed as one realm."

"Oh god," I whisper.

Valerian scoffs and catches my eye in the mirror. "God," he mocks. "Humans have told themselves such twisted lies. What you understand of Hell and the underworld is mostly wrong. Your folklore is born out of an ancient war that split the realm between the demonic fae beings in the underworld and the humans."

My fingers tighten on the seatbelt and my voice shakes. "I'm not a religious person, but I know the Bible doesn't talk about anything like that. I don't think any other religion does either."

What he's saying is nothing like the books I read

on demon lore.

"Exactly," he sneers. "The humans are left to have their own ideas. There is only a semblance of truth when in reality, our kind has existed far longer than yours, descended from the primordial gods of the heavens and the underworld. Humans wouldn't be able to fathom the truth now."

I wait, disbelief ricocheting around my head, but he doesn't elaborate. "Okay, so why do you guard the gates if you're just going to kill the people who find one?"

"To keep humans from wandering into the underworld on their own, as they used to. It's part of the treaty between fae and mortals in the aftermath of the war that divided the realms," Alder says. "The gates are still used for hunting grounds as part of the old sacrificial quota."

"And bridges between the mortal and underworld realms," Matthias adds. "They're our only access points. We can't just blip back and forth wherever we want. There's a barrier that separates our realms."

"Yes. But they've become a secret, another myth," Valerian interjects in an acidic tone, his hatred unmistakable. "To ward off humans too smart to meddle where they should keep away from predators. The number of souls consumed has dwindled because of this change. Don't look so nauseated. This is how the world works. There's nothing you can do about it, no saving the humans from what awaits them. It's not as though your kind are endangered. They are the prey and we are the predators."

I hate that he's right. The world sucks—I know it better than most.

"Humans can't be your only food source." I hope they're not.

"No, we eat and drink regular food." Matthias laughs, tipping his head back against the headrest. "Most demon fae aren't all like blood suckers and incubi that need to feed on specific things to survive, though we're definitely the best looking of the bunch. Souls bolster our strength. We're closer to our hellhound cousins with the ability to shift some of our appearances. Only difference is they can fully turn into beasts to hunt for damned souls marked for Hell."

"Vampires are real?" I choke. "What's next, aliens?"

My love of fantasy and isekai manga has only helped me process the existence of more than one world with magical beings so much. I rub my pounding temples. Alder reaches across and pinches the back of my neck, his fingers warmer than normal as he massages a pressure point that helps with my stimulation overload headache.

Between the three of them, Alder and Matthias can't stop touching me, finding little excuses to brush against me or put their hands on me. I'm not used to the feeling at all, but it's…

Well, I don't hate it. No one will catch me admitting it out loud, though.

Maybe I'm already addicted to the odd tingling thrill that runs through me whenever they do it. I tuck away the thought, not willing to unpack how pathetic I am for buckling to the first sign of attention after going so long without it. This is temporary. It's not like they'll stick around when their place is in the underworld.

Needing another distraction, I ask, "Do you have horns? Is this just some skin suit you put on for my sake to blend in?"

Matthias snorts. "This is how we look. Most of us stick to a fully human appearance when we're topside. Makes humans easier to hunt. Demon fae aren't all red little monsters humans depict us as. Different bloodlines have different traits. Tails, horns, scales—there's a she-demon I know with wings. The three of us just have claws, fangs, and these ears." He rakes his blond hair back and his ear shifts, extending into a pointed one like an elf's. He smirks, eyes dancing. "It means our dicks are huge."

"Matthias," Alder grouses impatiently. "It's a mark of our strong bloodlines, you imp. Different appearances like horns come from crossing bloodlines with other underworld beings. The original demon fae were made in the old gods' image."

"That's enough," Valerian says. "We still don't know what she is. Until we do, we can't trust her."

His callous words slice into me, leaving a hollow space in my chest. He's the only one who stops himself from creating a connection between us when he reaches for me. It shouldn't upset me because I hate him right back, yet I can't stop the flood of disappointment.

"I'm right here, dick."

He ignores me. With a huff, I lean against the window and stare at the town we're leaving in the dust. Leaving Brim Hills was my goal, though I never planned to do it with company.

My heart skips a beat when we pass the faded sign that says *now leaving Brim Hills, come back soon*.

They've pulled me into a world I never knew existed. Somehow in the span of a couple hours I've gone from reject orphan to kidnapping victim to a fugitive soul on the run with my enemies, bound together as allies until we find out what's different about me, and why it matters to the demons beyond the gate.

Ten
LILY

WE DRIVE UNTIL SHORTLY BEFORE DAWN, STOPPING AT another motel outside of Manhattan on the New Jersey side. I wake with my head pillowed on Alder. All he says in response to my raised eyebrow is that he didn't want my neck to cramp from how I fell asleep. When I ask why we're stopping here, Valerian says he wants somewhere to lay low and blend in with human scents. The denser population of the cities masks their distinct scents.

They let me sleep until early afternoon in the stuffy motel room. I'm surprised I managed to sleep at all, not used to letting my guard down around those I can't trust. As I peel my eyes open groggily, I groan at the dull ache throbbing in my temples.

"I told you I should've helped her sleep,"

Alder's deep, rumbling voice comes from the corner of the room. "She needs rest."

"She'll be fine. It wouldn't have worked anyway. She came out of it on her own when you knocked her out." Valerian stands over me. "Up."

I give him the finger. There's something about his pompous attitude that pisses me off even more when he's being demanding in his crisp British accent. "Are your manners crammed up your ass next to the barbed stick stuck there?"

He disregards my snarky remark, his chiseled features impassive. "It's time to test what you are, if not human." Leaning over the bed with a hand planted on either side of me in the sheets, he narrows his eyes, his smoky scent changing from sharp to something smooth and spiced. "Stop being a petulant brat. Get out of the fucking bed, or I'll drag you out myself."

I freeze, trying not to breathe in his scent and failing spectacularly. It's alluring, making my mouth water. An ache builds between my legs. Oh god, his scent is turning me on. I have to hold on to my hate for him, not wish for him to close the distance and crash his full lips against mine.

His blue eyes flash brighter, then the color disappears, his eyes darkening with unmistakable, heady lust. He clenches his fists in the sheets as his gaze searches my face like he's savoring the flush of my cheeks, my parted lips, the movement of my throat when I swallow thickly. His face lowers another inch, his mouth practically touching mine. My stomach dips and I rub my thighs together, barely aware of anything outside of his inescapable stare.

"Get out of bed, Lily," he rasps. "Now. Before I—"

"Fine. I have to pee anyway." He continues caging me for another beat before backing off. Huffing, I fling the covers away, tugging my sleep shirt down from where it rode up to my soft waist. I use the excuse to fly through the motel room, pushing past a smirking Matthias into the bathroom. Locking myself in, I brace against the door. "What is wrong with me?"

Crap, I'll have to walk back out there in just a t-shirt. I ditched the leggings on the floor between the beds when I crashed.

A knock sounds on the door.

"I brought your bag in from the car. I'm leaving it here," Matthias says. "Alder went out for breakfast."

"It better not be another human," I mutter through the crack in the door when I open it. "If any of you assholes try to kill someone, I'll stop you."

"Donuts and coffee."

I press my lips together. Begrudgingly, I admit to myself that while Valerian is still an asshole, Alder and Matthias are tolerable. Sometimes. It's hard to hate someone that brings you donuts.

"Fine. How do any of you have money to pay for the motel and food?"

His face appears in the small opening as I grab my bag. His attention flicks down like he's trying to see if I'm naked yet. I glare and he holds his hands up with an amused tilt to his mouth. "I told you. I love coming topside. A human I met a long time ago insisted on investments being the way to go. He opened a bank account for me and now I apparently have a lot of money."

I shower in record time under ice cold water that makes me groan in relief from how overheated my body is. I resist the urge to play with my hardened nipples and relieve the thrumming pulse in my clit. No way in hell will I touch myself while thinking of Valerian's sharp jaw, piercing blue eyes, or his demanding accent whispering filthy things to me with his fangs grazing my skin. Nope, nope, nope.

The harder I try not to think about it, the more my mind drifts down a dangerous road contemplating if demon dicks are different. Am I getting into the tentacle porn arena? A delirious laugh bubbles out of me. These demons make themselves appear human-like, yet I've seen their claws, their fangs. I've felt their forked tongues.

Pushing my face into the frigid spray, I shudder,

my hand gliding down my torso, slipping between my thighs. At the first touch, my eyes fall shut. I bite my lip hard to keep silent while I indulge my fantasies.

By the time I dress in a killer pair of red leather shorts I found at a secondhand shop and a black cropped bleach-dyed t-shirt, Alder has returned with food. Matthias pushes the box of donuts across the small table we congregate around, his gaze intent, almost as if he can somehow see what I did in the shower written all over me. I avoid his smoldering stare and dig in.

"What's the game plan?" I ask once I've downed two sugar dusted donuts and half a cup of coffee.

"We'll stay on the move for now in case scout groups are tracking us." Valerian props a shoulder against the wall, folding his arms. The black button down shirt he changed into stretches taut against the curve of his biceps and defined forearms, his abstract tattoos peeking out from the collar and sleeves. "Once you're finished, Alder found an alley we can use to test you."

"I didn't know there'd be a test," I deadpan. "I didn't study."

The corner of Matthias' mouth hitches up. "Not that kind of test, lost girl."

"Quit it," I grumble. "I'm sick of you calling me that."

It hits too close to home, picking at all my insecurities of being rejected and left alone. Their theory that I'm not even human exacerbates those feelings. I don't want to think about having powers because then it validates every horrible thing ever said about me. *Sink or swim*.

"Do you prefer pretty girl instead?" He chuckles at my blush.

"We talked while you bathed. We believe the reason you smell so damn g—" Alder cuts off and clears his throat gruffly. "Your scent could be different because you truly belong to the underworld. A demon trapped inside a human body. It's the only thing that fits. These instincts to protect you wouldn't be triggered otherwise."

He doesn't mention the way the three of them nearly fought over me the first time they caught my scent and circled me in the graveyard, or bring up what happened with Matthias and Valerian in the alley, assuming he knows. Protecting me isn't the only thing they're interested in.

We're not talking about it. The thing that happens whenever they're too close to me, like earlier with Valerian, or when one of them touches me for too long. The invisible pull that I don't understand. A force that defies logic and overrides any hatred we harbor for each other, almost like fate forcing us together. I shut down the ridiculous thought. It's an off-limits topic and I'm happy to keep it that way.

I purse my lips to the side. "I've lived here in the—the mortal realm my whole life. I didn't even know all this supernatural stuff was real outside of the books I like to read."

There's the strange things that happen when my emotions are out of control. The buzz of energy beneath my skin. The inexplicable incidents. Everything I've ignored and run from.

"I think there's some kind of seal blocking you to make you and everyone you encounter believe that. Both your power that is seeping through the cracks and possibly your memories." Valerian surveys me, stroking his chin in thought. "If there is one, I want to know why. We'll break it to see if it gives us an answer to what you are."

"Great," I say dully around a mouthful of a third donut. The burst of sugar on my tongue is the only thing keeping me from going insane at this conversation. After licking the remnants of sugar from my fingers, I wiggle them at the guys. "Let's get this over with so you can let go of the idea of me with powers now."

Three sets of otherworldly, luminous eyes are trained on my mouth.

Our motel is situated in an industrial district with the New York skyline peeking over the top of the squat warehouses. I pause to look at it. I've been bounced around this area, but I've never been to Manhattan.

Matthias catches my hand. "If we had time, I'd take you to the Lower East Side. There's a killer burlesque club there. It's an unforgettable experience."

"You've been to New York?" My attention shifts back to the towering buildings across the river.

"I've been all over. I make a point to see as much as I can when I'm in the mortal realm." He shoots me a smirk. "I love humans. They're all so fascinating and inventive."

"But you also kill people."

He shrugs. "Death is a fact of life."

"Yeah, if you get sick or in an accident."

"I'd say summoning demons and challenging the power of Hell is in the same category of people that die climbing mountains. There's an acknowledged risk involved."

"Not if they don't know the danger, like me."

Matthias ruffles his hair, making it more disheveled. "Not our fault if people are nonbelievers."

"No, just some dumb ancient treaty that stole the knowledge this world used to have, according to you guys. That's not fighting fair."

"Life isn't fair, baby."

"Don't I know it," I mutter.

The guys lead me down an access road behind the motel to a wide alley between the buildings backlit by the afternoon sun. It has a gravel lot at the back of the dead end road.

"This will do. Stand over there, Lily," Valerian instructs.

"This is a waste of time," I mutter while I stand in the middle of the alley.

After Valerian does a strange circular gesture in the air with his hand toward the mouth of the alley, he positions himself beside Alder a short distance from me while Matthias moves to the stairs jutting off from one of the warehouses.

Voices drift over. Two men in utility uniforms pause at the end of the alley as they talk. They haven't noticed us.

"They don't know we're here," Valerian says dismissively.

"Barrier." Matthias props his elbows on the metal railing and leans back. The sun makes his messy white blond hair shine. He wiggles his fingers. "They can't sense the ward magic. And if they did, I'm very persuasive. They won't bother us."

I wonder if he means like Alder's ability to put people in a deep sleep, remembering when his big hand brushed my head before the strange fog overtook me. Matthias seemed to hypnotize me in the alley. Do all demons have a unique parlor trick like that up their sleeves on top of the fire they control? I have no idea what else these guys are capable of. If he can pull tricks on the mind, I bet he's the one who fed me all those visions that tormented me the week after I called on the gate.

Everything I've ever thought about demons is wrong. They're real, for one. Instead of twisted souls of humans or fallen angels, they're actually supernatural beings from a different world with magic.

And they believe I have powers sealed away in me. Because they think I'm not human. That I could be from the underworld somehow.

It's difficult to wrap my head around. I've spent a lifetime rolling with it for the sake of shoving down the weird stuff that happens around me. I've never wanted to face it. Stuck on the run for our lives with them, I have little choice other than to go along with it all.

I flex my hands at my sides. "What am I supposed to do?"

The three of them exchange glances. Alder speaks up, extending his arm. "Visualize what you want. The energy will build." A swirl of fire and smoke dances in his palm before he closes his fist to snuff it out. "You harness it with your will."

Oh, good. Just will it, even though I wasn't aware I was capable of it. Piece of cake.

"Here goes nothing."

I hold both hands in front of me, imagining a fireball expanding between them. My fingers strain as I stretch them as far as they can reach and my tongue sticks out from the corner of my mouth. I feel like an idiot trying to follow Alder's advice.

After several minutes, it's clear it's not working.

I scrub my face, my words coming out muffled. "Look, I don't know, guys. I have no clue what I did before."

"Don't sweat it, petal."

My head jerks up at the new pet name from Matthias. At least he listened about not calling me lost girl anymore. He saunters over and stands behind me, tracing his fingertips up my arms. I suppress a shudder.

The curve of his grin presses against my ear when he dips his head. "No one gets it on their first go. Here, put your hands on mine. I'll show you."

Sighing, I allow him to lift our arms in front of me, palm to palm. His skin is warm against mine, then grows warmer as he emits tiny sparks between our hands.

"Oh." I startle. "That kind of tickles."

He chuckles and leans his head against mine. "See? It doesn't have to be a big power move. Start small."

He lowers his hands and the sparks ignite into flames. I start to yank my hands away but he stops me.

"Wait. I won't hurt you. It's a bit strange, but I feel like I could never consider hurting you again. The thought of you hurt is…" He pushes out a stilted laugh, unlike his usual relaxed nature. "Painful."

Angling to glance at him from the corner of my eye, his flirtatious smile tinges with regret for a moment before he pulls it back. As open as he's been with me, this feels like the first truly genuine glimpse he's allowed me to see. Ducking my head to hide my smile, I keep my hands in place, surprised when the fire doesn't burn me. Biting my lip, I swipe my fingers through it.

"How are you doing that? It doesn't burn."

He pauses in consideration before answering. "It becomes instinctive, like breathing. If I focus on it, then I can picture the well inside. Once you tap into that, you'll be able to do it, too. Try it. Give me some sparks, baby."

I huff sardonically at the double meaning he injects into his request. "I don't think we need to pour anymore gasoline on those sparks. Things already get out of control with the barest provocation."

Like me being fully okay with him fucking me in the alley, if it got that far. I smother the urge to press my thighs together and give myself away, though he seems to know the direction my mind goes.

"I disagree." His voice lilts and he brushes the top of my head with his lips as he steps closer so I can feel every firm line of his body against my back, the hardness he nudges against my ass. "I think you'd ignite the hottest inferno. I want to burn up in your fire."

An unsteady breath hisses out of me. Licking my lips, I try not to think about the flutter of need he stirs in me and try to replicate the sparks he showed me. Come on, internal well. Help me out here.

Nothing. Again.

I blow out another sigh. "This is pointless. I can't do it. I don't have the powers you think I do."

Matthias snuffs out his flames and wraps his arms around me. "We'll figure it out. Don't worry."

His embrace is tight and comforting, the calming scent of a campfire surrounding me. He hugs me like he never intends to let me go. My chest constricts.

Don't get attached. Temporary, I remind myself. I don't get to stay with them. I shouldn't even want that.

"Let me try to help you." At Alder's offer, Matthias returns to leaning against the railing. "Young demons coming into their powers often need exercises to assist them until they understand how to control their power on their own. Give me your hands."

My fingers rub together for a beat in hesitation before I place my hands in his. A jolt of energy shocks me when we touch. His grip tightens with a forceful rumble when I try to pull away. When the feeling fades, he turns them over.

"Stay still. When I pass hellfire to you, just maintain it."

"Easier said than done," I say.

"Focus."

With no effort at all, his hands glow like molten heat flows beneath his skin, then fire engulfs his hands. His thumbs stroke the sides of my palms and his green eyes catch mine, holding my gaze.

"Look, you're doing it," he says with a hint of pride and wonder.

My eyes widen. Oh my god, I'm doing it. The fire he transferred to me dances above my skin without scorching me. I have power. Which makes me not as human as I believed. This is unreal.

I can feel the energy constantly shifting, swaying as it seeks freedom. It challenges my feeble control, wanting more, wanting to explode.

In the few seconds I manage to hold his fire in my palms, my stomach rolls as reality overlays with the buried memory of my childhood resurfacing from the tight mental prison I locked it away in. I drop my hands and the flame dissipates. It doesn't take my harrowing memories with it.

I remember that feeling, the sensation of something taking control of me, to stop the pain and fear of my small head being pushed under the bath water. That night, after my foster brother pulled me from the tub, it whispered to me and promised to take away my hurts. While he yelled at his mom, it erupted from me before I understood what would happen. It lied.

People were right to fear me. Those strange things that follow me…I cause them all.

My shaking scarred hands cover my face. I'm unable to stop hyperventilating. An awful noise of despair tears free.

All three demons rush me.

"Breathe, sweet blossom." Alder keeps murmuring to me, his lips brushing my forehead as he gathers me in his arms before my knees buckle. "Breathe for me."

Within a few minutes, he helps me calm down. I sniffle, listening to the steady beat of his heart until I stop trembling. His embrace feels safe, wrapping me up and sheltering me from the world. He won't let the fire or anything else hurt me. I can fall apart and for once there's someone there to catch me.

"You know it won't burn, so why panic?" Valerian scrutinizes me. I bury my face in Alder's chest. "You've done that before."

It's not a question. Alder strokes my back. Gritting my teeth, I nod.

"You're blocking yourself," Valerian says. "Instead of panicking over whatever your mind is telling you, you need to face it. Access that side of yourself."

"Enough testing your theories for one day, Vale." Alder plants himself in front of me to shield me. "We confirmed her power. She needs a break."

I step around him, shaking out my hands as I pace. "I'm fine. Just—give me a minute."

Valerian gets in my face, moving too fast for me to track. I gasp at his proximity, aware of the intense press of Matthias and Alder's gazes. They don't stop him, despite Alder's admonition a moment ago.

"Come on, Lily."

His growl is demanding, the rough way he says my name making my mind snap to this morning when he practically covered my body with his in bed. He grabs my waist and hauls me closer. My hands fly up on instinct and rest against his chest. His heartbeat is thundering like mine. I should push him away, but the feel of his hard body against mine makes me hesitate.

"Fight me off," he commands, then lowers his voice to a sensual rasp as his nose grazes my cheek. "Blow us away again like you did last night, little flower."

A strangled cry lodges in my throat. The tight hold I keep on my emotions shatters, already shaky from facing my memories and unable to withstand the way my chest blooms at his words, leaving me caught between anger—at him, at myself because some part of me wants him to keep pushing me, to take this further—and the force of my desire.

My forbidden thoughts that taunted me, tempted me in the shower an hour ago flood back without my willpower to compartmentalize it all. They're the absolute last thing I should be thinking about in this situation.

A burst of hot air and a blinding stream of sparks knock him back when I shove against his chest with a fierce yell for making me face this. The familiar tingling in my palms lingers. My eyes grow wide. I did that. That—that power came from me.

Valerian regains his footing several feet from me across the alley. Staggering back another step, he swipes at his mouth with an intrigued glint in his eye. "I see. Strong emotions allow you to get past the seal. It's a start."

Shit. It's true.

My dazed attention falls to my scarred hands. They turn blurry before me as overwhelmed tears gather in my eyes.

All those incidents that frightened my guardians in the system, the fire at the Clarks', the things they brushed under the rug and explained away as me being a troubled, dangerous, uncontrollable kid.

I have powers. And I've been running from them all my life.

Eleven
LILY

THE NEXT WEEK BLURS TOGETHER AS WE STAY ON THE move from those hunting us while they work with me to use my powers. To think that only a few weeks ago I was counting down the days until Halloween. I'm pretty sure it's this week, though now I'm not sure if my birthday is even real. If I'm a trapped demon caged by some magic seal, I have no idea how old I really am. For all I know, being a demon could make me hundreds of years old, like the guys seem to be going off their casual comments talking about centuries like they're nothing.

I'm losing track of where we are and where we've been from the constant cycle of motel hopping, and training to connect to my powers. Since the first moment I accessed them, an uneasy worry sets up camp in the back of my head. I haven't got a decent night's sleep since. That could also be because we don't stay in one place for more than a full day, and when we do stop, the guys rotate guard shifts, one of them resting in the second bed while the other two keep watch.

Though they eat regular food, they don't need as much sleep as I do, my practice sessions leaving me even more drained. They assure me once I learn how to wield the power hidden within me that it won't tire me out so much every time I call on it.

I squint at the overcast sky behind today's training grounds. The condemned roadside pizza shop provides cover while Alder and Matthias encourage me to set a pile of sticks on fire. My boot nudges the pile I haven't succeeded in igniting. Not even a sizzle.

"I'm not your walking, talking matchstick," I complain. "And being here makes me crave pizza."

If I focus on that instead of the large pond behind the building, I don't have to think about Mrs. Clark. Letting the past in leads to me losing my shaky hold on the magic fire I manage to produce.

"Stop deflecting. You'll never gain control if you're not serious." Valerian is a tyrant during these little training sessions, impossible to fool. Every time I get frustrated, he pushes my buttons to throw me off before I can compartmentalize my emotions. He pushes off the counter and circles me, the long black trench coat he wore the first night we met sweeping my legs. "If you continue to cower in fear every time you use your power, it will only fail you. That power is yours, Lily. Take it. Use it. Bend it to your will."

Working my jaw, I prop my hands on my hips. "I'm getting tired of these lectures."

He stops behind me, hot breath fanning over my exposed shoulder from the cut of my flowy shirt tucked into my fitted high-waisted skirt. "Tough shit. I'll keep giving them until you show me you can do it."

I roll my eyes and try again when he steps away. Reaching for my powers is finicky at best. I don't know if young demons deal with this, but it's annoying as fuck to feel so inept at the simplest tasks.

"You can do it, babe." Matthias gives me a supportive smile from his cross-legged perch on top of a table.

Okay, inner power well thing. Time to make you my bitch.

Concentrating on the pile of sticks Alder crouches beside, I picture the flow of energy, the build of heat from smoking to the first spark to the flame catching, visualizing the odd sensation of painless fire twisting around my fingertips. It's close, but not there yet. I shift my stance, sinking to one knee across from Alder, holding my hands above the sticks.

Wrong move. The pond snags my attention when it enters my periphery through the open door. My mouth floods with the imagined taste of metallic water and a gasp rips from me. *Sink or swim*. That awful, deranged voice taunts me from my memories even though she's gone.

I lose it as a burst of erratic power knocks me on my ass on the dusty, dirty cracked tile. The pile of sticks implode, burning hot and fast until they're nothing but cinders.

Controlling this is a struggle. I either produce inconsistent spikes of energy that are too much power, or end up with a sputter that's far too little.

"Damn it."

"Better. Again." Valerian's order brooks no room for opposition. He makes a demand and expects me to obey. "Get out of your head next time. You're the one holding yourself back."

The laugh that punches out of me isn't humorous. I wipe soot from my arms and frown at the snag in my fishnets. They caught the edge of a busted tile. Better my tights than my pencil skirt, I guess.

Alder offers a hand to help me up. I smile in thanks. He doesn't let go, drawing comforting patterns on my scarred skin. His musky woodsmoke scent surrounds me.

"You will learn to control this, but it only comes with practice." He dips his head. "Understand?"

"Yes."

At my determined exhale, he smiles, hypnotic green eyes hooding. "Show me what I know you can do."

His steadfast belief in me feels like something I stole. It makes me want to get this right.

Clearing my mind, I shut my eyes to visualize better. Instead of following every change in the energy that tingles beneath my skin, I picture their displays of power. Their faces spring into my head. Their gazes, smoldering, predatory, and penetrating.

The heat in my palm expands with an incandescent rush that spreads throughout me with insurmountable speed, touching every part of me.

I hold my breath, staring in awe at the perfectly formed flame cupped in my hand. It's beautiful.

"I did it! It worked this time!"

I beam at Alder first, then Matthias. Their smiles, both proud and happy, fill me with a glow I've rarely experienced. I seek out Valerian last, and my heart thuds at the way he looks at me, the satisfaction and hunger sending a bolt of excitement down my spine.

"Well done, little flower," Valerian praises in a smooth tone.

The approval washes over me, opening me up

further. It makes my heart drum, pushing me to go to him.

I take a step toward him, unsure why, but giving in to the intense tug drawing me closer. One of them rumbles as I take another. He pins me with his gaze and my nipples harden, every inch of my body strung tight. I want—

A splash in the pond outside snaps us all out of the heady trance. I blink, mortified at how badly I wanted to close the short distance between us to throw myself at him. It worries me that the onset is happening quicker and without us touching now, like an invisible force pushing me together with one of them. With all of them. Thanks for the save, duck.

The three of them don't relax, their stances tense and alert. Valerian nods to Alder and he takes up a position at the back door. Matthias unfolds himself from sitting on the table and moves to my side in seconds, wrapping a protective arm around me.

"Be ready to run if I tell you, okay?" he murmurs, expression guarded.

Oh crap. Was it not a duck? My stomach turns.

"No matter what happens, get her out," Valerian commands. "We'll meet you at the car. If we're not there by the time you get it started, go."

"Wait—"

Before I get out any protest, an attack strikes the window, shattered glass raining across the floor.

Matthias yanks me against him, shielding me as his arm sweeps through the air to send a fiery burst slashing through the air at the demon. Valerian doesn't give the tall, vicious-looking woman the chance to retaliate, punching a continuous streaming blaze like a flamethrower. Her slicked back high ponytail whips around as she spins to block it. They trade blows back and forth, neither of them landing a hit.

Alder's grunt of pain wrenches my focus to him. At the back of the small abandoned building, he grapples with another demon. She's mid-shift, but instead of the claws and fangs I expect, her jaw lengthens into the maw of a beastly, black dog-like creature that snaps her terrifying teeth at his neck.

"No!" I fling my hand out before the decision fully forms. The badass torrent of flames I visualize comes out of my fingertips as nothing more than sparks. "Fuck, not now. Come on!"

I hate not being able to help him, my gut churning as he jerks his head away from the beast's jaws. It knocks him off balance, massive paws pinning him to the floor.

Before the demon Valerian fights shifts her form, he catches her around the throat. His fingers lengthen, claws sprouting forth.

"She'll never be queen," the demon garbles. "You've already lost."

Valerian growls, gouging his elongated clawed fingers deeper into her throat, ripping it out mercilessly. Her body slumps to the ground, choking and spluttering as her blood pools around her and her hands slip against her skin to stem the bleeding.

"What are you waiting for? Get her out of here," he snaps.

Matthias' arm tightens around me. "Time to go."

"Wait—no! Not without them!" I push against his chest, but it's futile. The three strong demons have no trouble manhandling me. Matthias lifts me when I drag my feet. "Not yet! We can help!"

"Sorry, Lils." He doesn't sound too sorry.

I yank on his hoodie and pummel his back. It's futile. Before I know it, his long strides reach the spot we stashed the car. He stows me in the back seat, grabbing my chin to force me to look him in the eye.

"You won't leave this car." His voice has a musicality to it that sounds so good. "Okay?"

That sounds like the best idea. I nod. With a relieved sigh, he gets behind the wheel and starts the car.

Wait. My face scrunches. There was a reason I wanted to get out of the car. It's important.

Alder and Valerian aren't in the car. My ears pop and I grab a fistful of Matthias' hoodie.

"Don't leave without them," I scream.

"How the fuck did you break through that quickly?" Matthias grits his teeth, revving the engine. "Petal, it's to keep you safe."

"No! I'll—" I trip over my threat to kill him if we leave the others behind, the word sticking in my throat. A sharp pain stabs into my chest, pricking my racing heart. I claw at my shirt, panting. "Don't fucking leave yet."

"Two minutes. Max, baby. They're my brothers, but protecting you is more important."

I grind my teeth, plastering myself against the back seat to watch. Every second we're separated while they face danger feels like an unbearable eternity.

At last, Valerian's dark tousled hair and sweeping trench coat come into view, followed by Alder, his muscles straining as they sprint toward the car. A plume of smoke rises into the treetops behind them.

"Go!" Valerian shouts once he has the passenger door open. "The second one won't be down for long in her shifted form."

Alder barely has time to throw himself into the back with me, the car rocking with the force as it rolls into motion.

"Fucking hellhounds," Matthias snarls as he floors the gas, the tires kicking up dirt in our wake.

"If the hounds are tracking us, it's bad." Alder surveys his scraped up arms. "There could be anyone hunting us."

Heart twinging, I touch his forearm, careful to avoid where he's hurt. "Shit, are you okay?"

"It's nothing." He pauses to smirk at my fussing. "Truly, I'll be fine. Are you alright?"

She'll never be queen. The fuck was that supposed to mean?

I tuck my hands between my thighs and the seat. "Yeah, just rattled."

"They won't get you," he says fiercely.

"We need to put miles between us and them," Matthias says. "If we're lucky, they'll lose our trail."

The car ride knocks me out, surprisingly. I didn't think I could sleep after we were discovered, but I wake up warm in a drowsy daze as we pull into a rest stop. Closing my eyes again, I snuggle further into the charcoal-scented pillow. It shifts beneath my cheek, then an arm cinches tighter around me. I lift my head so fast I almost crack my skull against Alder's jaw.

He pulls back with a soft smile, watching me. "I was just about to wake you."

"Let me guess, you were worried about my neck

cramping again." I surreptitiously check the snug fit of his t-shirt for drool spots.

The scrapes he sustained have vanished, his defined, veiny forearms back to normal with the faint red and silvery scars that crisscross across his skin.

He caresses my hair and cups my cheek. "Sleep on me whenever you need."

My lips roll between my teeth and I try not to nuzzle my face into his palm for more of the sweet touch. "Thanks."

Matthias parks at a gas pump in front of a convenience store. "Let's stock up while we're here."

"Is it safe to stop for that long?" I ask.

"As long as we're quick," Valerian answers. "They're pack creatures. First they'll wait until they've recovered enough to hunt together. They won't catch up on foot, even in their hellhound forms."

Once Matthias sets up the gas pump, he grabs my hand, dragging me inside. He heads straight to the snack aisle. He plucks packs of powdered donuts, gummy bears, and cheddar potato chips from the shelves. I watch, twisting my fingers, not wanting to assume he'll help me when I have no money to pay for any goodies I might want.

"Don't you want snacks?" He nabs the pack of chocolate-covered pretzels I've looked at three times while he saunters up and down the aisle.

Damn him. He plays up the carefree act, but he's perceptive.

I pat invisible pockets on my skirt. "No money."

The few bucks I scraped together before leaving Philly for Brim Hills are back there, stashed between the mattress and box spring of my bed. I never keep money in my bag when I have it, too conditioned by life in group homes.

He shoots me a wink. "Get anything you want. If you don't pick something, I'll pick for you." Putting the bag of pretzels in my hand, he grasps my chin, leaning into me. "Anything you want, I'll give you, Lily."

Excitement flickers to life gradually until it drowns out my skepticism. Matthias wants to treat me. To take care of me.

Putting my trust in someone else to care for me after a long, hard life of only being able to rely on myself for survival is foreign. The hurdle shouldn't be so easy to overcome, yet something instinctive tells me I can trust him.

Picking out the first colorful package that catches my attention, I swallow back the lump that forms in my throat. No need to get so emotional over some snacks. No one's going to steal them or tell me I can't have any. I get into it the more I scan the selection. A bag of spicy nuts with a cute flaming pepper character calls my name.

"These sound good."

He pauses, watching me with a tender, charming smile that makes me glow inside. "What do you like better? Salty or sweet?" He grabs some beef jerky. "Maybe a little bit of savory to break it up so you don't get a stomach ache. Why limit ourselves, right?"

"I...don't really know what I like," I mumble. "I've never really tried any of this because there wasn't a point."

Matthias halts. "A Twinkie?" I shake my head. "Sour gummy worms? A cherry-raspberry mixed Icee? Why?"

Even a demon from another realm knows more about this than I do. "My foster placements were all frugal, and any time I was on my own in a group home, it was harder to find money. There was a bakery in Philly that donated day-old stale donuts, but that's about as wild as things got for me."

Matthias' smile tightens at the corners of his mouth, his golden eyes shifting over my shoulder. "I'll go get you one. We'll split up, cover more junk food bases. Sound good?" I nod and he plants a quick kiss on my forehead. "Remember, anything you want."

I laugh, my heart swelling. "Got it."

A shadow moves into my peripheral vision

when I go to the next aisle. I angle my head to look back at Valerian lurking behind me.

"Still a stalker," I joke.

His lips twitch. My eyebrows shoot up in surprise.

The amused expression drops off his face as quickly as it appeared. I smirk. He must have realized I made him show a sign of humor before he shut it down.

With a growl, he pins me to a pillar halfway down the aisle. It effectively tucks us between the shelves, hiding us somewhat from anyone passing by unless they came down this aisle. His sharp, narrowed gaze cuts back and forth, searching for something. His guard is up.

"Wh—? Vale," I breathe. "They found us?"

"No, different scent," he clips out. "Definitely demon, though. There are too many people in here to fight them. Play along. We need to blend in."

"People don't really, uh, do this in convenience stores." I grip the lapels of his trench coat so I don't wrap my arms around his neck.

"They won't know that."

"What about the people here who do?" I hiss.

"Christ, Lily." His grasp on my waist flexes.

I hold back a shocked cry as he leans in, gaze intent like he might kiss me. He diverts at the last second, burying his face in my neck. It could appear like we're kissing to anyone that spots us.

He speaks against my neck in a gravelly voice that shoots heat straight to my core. "For once, just do as I say without arguing about every little thing."

"You're infuriating," I shoot back hoarsely.

"Likewise, little flower." He nips my neck, the prick of his fangs teasing my skin. A strangled noise tries to escape me. "If I could be rid of you, reject you somehow, I would." I flinch, the sentiment of rejection cutting me deep. He soothes me with a rumble, petting my sides, pressing us closer together in contradiction to what he's saying. "Then I could kill you, perhaps. Rip this pretty throat out with my teeth and enjoy the sweet taste of your blood on my fangs. Maybe that would end this obsessive need to keep you near, to keep you for myself."

I forget why he pinned me to the pillar in the first place, too overcome by the needy ache pulsing between my legs. A faint groan sounds from him, his fingers sinking into my hair. I crave the feel of him crushed against me, but he keeps some distance between our bodies.

Warm, smooth hickory twines around me, the same as I picked up on in the motel room near New York. Is this his scent when he's aroused? I know the threat is empty since they admitted they're unable to kill me. Instead of fear, I'm captivated by his dark allure, wanting to learn if his touch would be as rough and intense as his callous words.

"Don't move." His fingers dig into me. "Sell it."

Oh. Demons, right. My head swims. Focusing is nearly impossible when everything in me is screaming to wrap my legs around the tall, brooding bastard and beg him to fuck me in the middle of a rest stop. The fact that sounds so wrong doesn't even register to my clouded brain.

Then I smell it—sulfur. Brimstone.

I strain my ears, squeezing the material of Valerian's jacket. He moves his head like we're locked in a passionate kiss. I mimic him with stilted, clumsy finesse. For good measure, I fake a moan. His grip turns bruising, a deep, sexy rumble vibrating against my neck.

My eyelashes flutter. Oh, shit. Okay, moaning was too much. We're both dancing on the precarious edge of control as it is from our close proximity. Faking intimacy is only fanning the flames.

The unpleasant scent drifts closer. Shit, it's not working! The demon's on to our act.

"Hey! The machine is on the fritz back here. It's spitting frozen drink everywhere, man." Matthias' voice sounds from the back corner. The demon changes course. "Is anyone around to fix this?"

"Move." Valerian nudges me in the opposite direction, toward the exit.

Seconds after we exit, Alder pulls the car up.

Valerian herds me into the back seat, keeping his grip on my nape. Matthias bursts out of the store, whipping off his blue-stained hoodie. He takes shotgun.

"Floor it. Blue raspberry isn't going to distract him for long," he says. "Too many humans around to kill him. I just made it look like he slipped and hit his head."

"Was it another hellhound?" I ask.

"No," Valerian says. "This was a low-rank reaper. Possibly one in training.. It was a bad coincidence he wandered in at the same time. We need to change tactics. If there are so many demons in the mortal realm, it will be difficult to avoid them in populated areas while you learn to use your power."

His bitter smoke scent chokes the car, blending with the sharp and musky scents the other two put off as Alder drives away. I pick his out as the same scent the last two times we were under attack, using it to read his frustration. It's far different than the warm hickory scent whenever he has me pinned at his mercy.

Valerian's grip on my nape doesn't fall away, even several minutes after we get away.

Twelve
LILY

NEAR DUSK AND TWO STATE LINES LATER, WE FINALLY stop when we find an abandoned theme park Matthias knew of in Maryland. Alder melts a hole in the fence for us to slip through. Past the *KEEP OUT* signs, the rusty attractions with chipped-paint inside the park are partially swallowed by wild overgrowth.

"I've always wanted to go to an amusement park. I walked by a small carnival one summer when I was growing up." They stop when I linger in front of a kiddie coaster. My reminiscent smile falters. "That foster placement was one of the few I thought would stick. The following week, they sent me back because I had another nightmare and they decided I was too much to deal with. Just like the others."

The three of them flash me fierce looks that stir a flutter in my chest. It expands into a hum in my blood that wants to split me in three different directions. Shaking my head to clear it, I move on, craning my neck to look up at the ferris wheel.

"Think any of these still work?"

"Doubt it." Matthias scratches his stomach, pushing up the black t-shirt he threw on when we were far enough away from the last demon we encountered. While it was off, I got an eyeful of his trim, tattooed body. I watch while trying not to. He catches my eye with a dirty smirk. "But I'll take you on as long of a ride as you want, babe. We won't stop until you're screaming."

"Matthias," Alder growls.

He dodges with a cocky laugh when Alder swipes at him. We continue walking through the park. I picture it lit up and bustling with people rather than the eerie silence interrupted by the tread of our feet on the pavement.

"Think we'll be safe here?" I ask.

"Long enough to rest and regroup," Alder says. "We'll remain on guard until then. No training while we're here. I think the hellhounds found us because of the strength of your magical signature. The more you use your power, the stronger it is to sense. Let's not find out if I'm right tonight."

"Good with me."

I press my fingers against my eyes, rubbing weariness away before raking my fingers through my hair. I'd kill for a shower, my short red locks feeling too greasy for my taste. We've been on the go nonstop and I didn't expect two demon encounters in the same day throwing us off our planned course. I'll have to endure it because I doubt there's running water here, and I'm not touching any standing body of water.

Alder motions to a faded striped tent. We duck inside, taking in the worn wooden floor strewn with straw and the tiered benches that circle the space. It must have been used for a small circus show.

"Rest," Alder says. "I'll go set up a perimeter to ward off anything that could be in the area."

I sit on a bench, plucking at the snag in my fishnets from when I fell in the pizza shop earlier. Hard to believe that was this morning. "Never thought I'd miss the shitty motels you guys picked out. We don't have to go full off-grid, right?"

Valerian studies me with a sidelong glance. He's kept close after we got out of the car, hovering over me. "We need to plan out our next move. You're not in control of your powers, so we can't go to the underworld yet."

"We're going there?" My head jerks up. He towers over me, the corners of his eyes tight.

"Eventually. We can't run forever from those hunting us. We don't belong here. Neither do you."

I twist the material of my fishnets around my fingers. The one thing I've kept at bay in my mind after learning I have a secret power hidden away inside me is that they were right about me. I'm not human. If I'm not human, then the mortal realm isn't my place. It's not like I've ever fit in. I never imagined it's because I wasn't part of this world to begin with.

Matthias sits next to me, offering one of his charming dimpled smiles. "You'll like it. Our home is unlike anything you could ever imagine. The shifting mountains of the Whispering Highlands that reach so high you can see for miles across the realm when they appear. Vast caverns lit by magic gemstones that create kaleidoscopes on the cave walls. Midnight falls that spill into pools of starlight beneath the blood moon." His eyes crinkle at the corners and he covers my hands, stopping me from worrying my ruined fishnets. "After we've sorted this mix up with the demon council, I'll take you there."

My heart stutters, then beats harder at the way he says *our home*. Like I could belong there without question. A long-buried wish for my own place to fit in rises from the depths where I hid it.

There's also something familiar about what he

describes, like in the dreams I had the week after I opened the gate.

I tuck my hair behind my ears, peeking at both of them through my lashes. "How will we get there? The Brim Hills gate is blocked."

"First, we must find out how to break the seal that's kept your power buried away." A muscle jumps in Valerian's cheek when he clenches his jaw. Some of his dark hair falls in his face as he gazes down at me. "There are many gates. It's harder to access them without being the guard with the incantation key, but we'll deal with that when we get to it."

I take in the troubled shadows in his drawn face, resisting the desire to reach up and smooth the rigidness in his features until they're gone. "Do you miss your gate?"

"No." His curt response is immediate and for the first time since he pinned me to the column in the rest stop, he turns his back on me, his spine rigid.

Something Matthias told me when we were first flung into our life on the run surfaces in my mind. "It's okay to grieve it. You guarded it for a long time."

"There's nothing to miss about a cursed assignment to punish me for my mistakes," he growls. "I'm going to check the perimeter is secured with Alder."

I jump to my feet as Valerian stalks off.

Matthias catches my hand to stop me, grip firm. "Stay with me." His gaze cuts away, the bright gold color dimmed. "Let the broody bastard go. He gets like this sometimes without Alder around to distract him from getting lost in his rage. They used to be at each other's throats when Alder was appointed to keep him in check. By the time I was assigned to guard the gate with them, I was sure they'd kill each other and I'd wind up with a sweet gig all to myself."

I watch the tent flap, wishing to go after him, but not wanting to leave Matthias' side when he asked me to stay. "Why?"

"The three of us have been together a long time. Over a century for me, even longer for them. In all that time, we've never really forged friendship. We tolerate each other at best." He chuckles, ruffling his hair. "Alder used to say it was because he had no respect for a disgraced knight and a guy like me who doesn't take anything seriously. He's a buzzkill yes-man who follows his orders no matter what. Guarding the gate isn't what he wanted, though. I think he was just pissed he was taken away from a warrior guild to become a guard."

"Valerian was a knight?" I picture him as if he's a character from one of the fantasy worlds in my manga, cutting a brooding yet handsome figure with a cloak and armor.

I can see it, though I prefer the trench coat I first teased him about in my head. There's something more roguish and dangerous about him now that's far more appealing.

"Yeah, highly decorated, one of the top fighters among Lucifer's knights. The king trusted him implicitly. He was lined up to become commander of the demon knights until he screwed up and lost the charge he was supposed to protect."

"Oh."

It helps me understand why Valerian got so uptight about today's encounters. He doesn't want to fail protecting another person he's promised to keep safe.

"The council decided instead of paying for his failure with his life, he would spend eternity guarding the borders between the realms."

"So if Alder only took the guard position to follow orders and Valerian had no choice, how did you end up there?"

"The urban legend was drawing too many people for them to handle alone. The only good part was free rein to discover how interesting the human world is, and even that was starting to lose its appeal. This is much more exciting. Being on the run with you." His mouth tugs up at the corner and his fingers thread through mine. "You came along and somehow you're the glue that makes us work together."

"Come on," I scoff. "We're all dysfunctional. Forced together because the alternate option is dying. I'm sure you'd all survive just fine without me."

He steps past me, tugging on my hand. "Let's go explore. You said you've always wanted to go to a theme park." Some of his upbeat energy returns. He's been odd since our close call at the rest stop. He shoots a kid-in-a-candy-store grin over his shoulder. "We're not passing up the opportunity."

I laugh and allow him to lead me out of the tent under the twilight sky. My worries and stress slip away as he lifts my spirits.

When we reach the carousel, he helps me untangle myself from a thorny vine that snags my clothes. I rest a hand on his shoulder for balance. "A pencil skirt is definitely not the right outfit for exploring abandoned rides."

"Want to trade?" Matthias' smirk is mischievous. He pinches the hem of his t-shirt to flash me his abs. "You'd look way better in my shirt."

I fight back a smile at his flirting, glad that he's back to his normal self. It breaks free anyway, and he hums, offering me a hand to help me step onto the carousel platform. I spin around when elastic snaps against my thigh, lifting my brows at his mask of innocence. He hooks a finger in one of the holes of my tights and flicks his gaze up to meet mine.

"I'll get your bag from the car when we go back to the tent so you can change."

"Thanks," I say sardonically. "My hero."

His teeth rake over his lip and he waggles his brows. "As long as I get to watch, babe."

A soft, husky laugh leaves me. Grabbing the pole of a faded white horse, I swing away from him. "It sucks we can't get this thing working."

"Pick one." He follows me as I weave through the carousel. "We'll close our eyes and imagine it."

It's like I have permission to let go of everything that weighs me down when we're alone. He reminds me I deserve to have a good time rather than the bitterness I've internalized for years. I have more fun with him than I've ever had.

I circle the entire first tier of the ride, ending up back at the horse where we climbed on. Matthias brushes against my back, grabbing my hips. A squeal slips out of me as he boosts me onto the chipped seat.

"Here, beautiful." He has a small wildflower he twirls between his fingers. "I found this on the other side for you. A flower for my petal."

Cheeks flushing, I accept it. "Thank you. What's this for?"

"Because I love your smile and I'll do anything to earn it," he murmurs.

The carousel horse puts me eye to eye with him. A warm glow fills my chest that breaks through the walls I built up around my vulnerable heart when the world made me believe I was troubled, difficult, and unlovable. He always accepts me without judgment.

"I get the sense you haven't done a lot of smiling while you've been stuck in the mortal realm."

I tear my gaze away. "Not really."

"Then it's my job to make up for all the smiles you've missed out on. I promise to make you smile every day."

He braces a hand on the horse's rump and caresses the outside of my thigh. The fear that used to make me wrench myself away from allowing anyone to touch me vanishes around him. I bite my lip as his touch trails up to my hip, his eyes bouncing between mine when I'm brave enough to meet them.

"You're the perfect height now."

Matthias dips his head and captures my lips. My stomach bottoms out and my fingers twist in his shirt.

The press of his mouth is sweet. He cups my cheek, swiping his tongue along my lips. Startled by the feeling of the fork in his tongue, I gasp into the kiss. He swallows it, deepening the kiss with a groan. I follow his lead clumsily until kissing him becomes natural. That devious tongue wraps around mine and he *sucks* it into his mouth, ripping a moan from me. Things go from sweet to sensual and wild, heating up with the filthy way he claims my mouth.

He ends it before I'm ready. I chase him, eager for more. He swoops back in with a depraved chuckle, kissing me until my lips feel swollen. Stroking my hair, he breaks away, leaving me breathless.

My heart thuds as I bring my fingertips to my tingling lips. That was my first kiss. And my second.

He gives me a soft, crooked smile. His golden gaze brims with affection as he traces the corner of my mouth with his thumb. My stomach dips and a shaky breath leaves me. I'm not used to anyone looking at me like this, like I'm the only thing they need in the world.

"Wow. You're even more stunning after you've been kissed, petal." His eyes roam every inch of my face greedily. "I've wanted to do that for weeks."

"You have?" I breathe.

"Since the first moment we met. One hit of that toasted cinnamon scent and I was a goner. Vale ordered us not to touch you after we let you run away. He doesn't think we should let the pull your scent has on us control us, but fuck that." His forked tongue peeks out to trace his lower lip, captivating me once more with the split shape. Sinking his fingers in my hair, he rests his forehead against mine and groans. "Your scent is so intoxicating, Lils. It's euphoric. Even just holding you like this makes me want you. All of you."

My chin quivers. I don't have any experience with this. He's so good at getting past my defenses, making me want to trust what he's saying. Wanting to believe he won't rip away at any second and reveal it's all a joke, because how could anyone want me, the reject?

"When I saw Vale all over you at the rest stop, all I could think was *mine*." His embrace tightens and his hot breath fans over my lips. I strain closer, hoping for another kiss. "I don't care what Vale or Alder want, Lily. I'm fighting for what I want—fighting for you. I'm done holding back when everything is screaming at me to make you mine."

His. I like the sound of that, my heart beating faster.

"I want to take care of you no matter where we end up. It's not just that I find everything about you sexy as hell. This pull I feel—" He puts my hand over his heart. He's breathing almost as hard as I am, his tone heartfelt. "It means something important. That you're mine to cherish, if you'll let me."

Every time I've felt a moment of tension between us and held myself back from more was because I've been setting myself up for disappointment and loneliness as usual. A lump forms in my throat as I struggle not to fall apart at his promise that this isn't temporary, that someone could want me. My heart swells, echoing the sentiment. I want that, too. I want to be with him.

Guilt at choosing passes over me for a moment, but I'm happy as long as I get to stay with one of them. It's not like Alder or Valerian have feelings for me outside of the strange thrall of sexual tension my scent triggers in them. Something inside me fights against that belief, but I push it down. In a short span of time, they've each become important to me. I can't imagine what life would be like without them. When we've figured all of this out, at least I don't have to go back to being alone.

"I feel it, too," I stammer.

His head lifts, surprise written across his face. "You do?"

I nod, throat constricting. "I've felt it for a while. In the alley, when you..." I trip over my words, sliding my lips together. "I wanted you to. Even though Valerian was right there watching, even though you were threatening me, all I wanted was more. I needed you to kiss me, to keep touching me, or I thought I would die before you could make good on your threat. Isn't that insane?"

A rough noise falls from his lips. "Right here?"

His other hand covers my heart and my eyes fall shut. The invisible tug around it at his touch draws me closer to him. I don't admit I've felt this sensation for all three of them whenever they're close or touching me, terrified that if I do, he won't want me anymore.

"Do you know what that means?" At the shake of my head, he presses his lips to my forehead. "That's a bond you feel. They only happen when you're near the connection it wants to make. It means I'm your fated. That I'm yours and you're mine. In the underworld, a fated bond with your demon mate is considered a sacred gift."

When he says *mate*, I cry out, clinging to him as something cracks open inside me, sending a strange pulse thrumming all over my body.

This is crazy. The kind of thing that only happens in the fantasy stories I read, not real life.

It's an instinct I've ignored and shut down until now. The whisper at the back of my mind I've pushed aside because I didn't understand it and it overwhelmed me. Yet it feels so right once I acknowledge it. He's someone who would never reject me, the one meant for me. My soulmate.

"Damn." He sways against me, dipping his nose to rest in the crook of my neck. He inhales, wrapping his arms around me, his erection grinding against my legs. "I think I'm literally high on your scent right now."

I snort at his slurred observation. It helps cut through the frenzied need that crashed over me a moment ago. The ache between my legs doesn't quiet completely, though I feel more in control of myself.

"Mine," he repeats in a smoky rasp.

I shudder, my head swimming from his enticing scent. "Yours."

Matthias grasps my chin, tipping it up. The bright gold in his eyes darkens to a warm, sultry shade of honey. "If you look this gorgeous after a kiss, I have to know…"

"What?"

His hands drag down my back, trailing down the sides of my skirt before he pushes beneath the hem, massaging my thick thighs. "What you look like when you come. I have to get another taste of you. I'm going insane imagining it all the time."

An acute, heady fire spreads through me once more, burning hot in my core as he slides my skirt up my hips, exposing me to the chill of the night. I nod, wrapping my arms around his shoulders. A sinful, pleased rumble vibrates in his chest and he rips a new hole in my ruined fishnets to get at me.

He kisses me again, each swipe of his tongue and nibble of his teeth dizzying and addictive. His fingers trace the edges of my panties, teasing me. I squirm, desperate for his touch on my pussy.

"Please." The breathy plea comes out mumbled between kisses. "I need—"

"I've got you, petal," he swears in a sinful tone. "I'm going to make you feel so good. Fuck you with my fingers and eat your sweet cream from them when you come. You taste so perfect everywhere. I knew you would."

I moan, digging my fingers into his shoulders. His mouth moves to my neck, sharp fangs scraping my sensitive skin, followed by the flick of his forked tongue. My hips buck, my clit throbbing with the rush of pent up desire. I've only allowed myself quick relief in secret when I shower. It's not enough. I need him.

His fingers slip into my panties, wrenching the material aside. My thighs squeeze together on instinct, and he blocks me, pushing my legs wide for him to step between. He glides his fingers through my slick folds and presses a filthy sound against my ear.

"So wet already, petal." Matthias leans back, encouraging me to look at him. His gaze burns into me as he lifts his fingers to his mouth, tasting me. "Mm, so damn sweet and perfect. I can't wait until your pussy soaks my cock."

My lashes flutter, panting breaths tinged with little moans of pleasure when he circles my clit. I open my mouth to tell him what I like, but the words die out, his touch skilled perfection. The tingling sensation of sparks bursting and causing vibrations against my clit and folds rips a startled cry from me.

"Oh my god." I whimper. "What are you doing? That feels... Oh, shit."

"You liked it when I showed you these sparks before. This is what I was imagining doing to you," he rasps. "Oh yeah, you like that. You're grinding on my hand, baby. Making such a gorgeous mess, getting my fingers all wet and sloppy. You need them filling your pussy?"

"Yes," I hiss.

My head falls back, spine arching as he teases his sparking fingers around my entrance. We've barely done anything and I'm already close to shattering, faster than any time I've made myself come.

"Tell me, Lily. What do you want right now?"

A ragged breath rushes out of me. "Please, Matthias."

"Tell me and I'll give it to you."

"I want—I want your fingers inside me. Fuck me with them."

His hooded gaze traps me. "You want to come all over my hand?"

I nod. "Please."

A whimper spills from me as he pushes a finger inside. I've only ever touched myself, and this feels like so much more, so much better than when I do it. The further he sinks inside, the more my core throbs, the tight coil ready to snap.

"Christ, you look good like this."

I like the roughness tinging his voice, like he's seconds from losing control. Illuminated eyes flashing brighter, he adds a second finger, curling them deep inside my pussy with each thrust. His thumb circles my clit.

The sparks grow more intense and I can't hold on. His power sends me over the edge with a shudder. I bite my lip, burying my face in his shoulder as the eruption of oblivion ripples through my core.

"Fuck, pretty girl. Look at you coming for me." Matthias kisses my temple. "Such a good girl."

He keeps going, still amplifying things with his sparks, thrusting inside me until the sound is obscene. It tips me from one orgasm right into the next.

"That's it. Cream all over my fingers. Give me a good taste."

Once my body stops shivering, he pulls free, making sure I watch as his forked tongue licks his fingers clean. His wicked gaze ensnares me. *Mine.* The thought echoes in my head and the corners of his mouth hitches up.

"What about you?" The words slip out before I'm able to stop them.

I duck to hide my blush as I reach for the bulge in his jeans. I came twice and still clench around the emptiness without his fingers inside me.

Am I being too greedy to want more? Too much too soon? I don't know what I'm supposed to do, only able to follow the thrumming instinct of the bond. Using my palm, I map the thick hardness of his dick and rub him.

"Shit, babe." He grinds against my touch for a moment, features slack with pleasure.

My brows furrow when he pulls back. "Don't you want to come?"

He grins, cupping my cheek. I lean into his palm, savoring how good it feels, the affectionate touch filling me with a warm glow.

"I do, baby, so badly. But I can sense the others making their way back, and they'll be pissed if they find out I've stolen you away to ravage you. You should get some rest. Let's head back and take a nap to recharge before we have to hit the road again." He winks. "You can use me as a pillow. I can't promise I won't feel you up while you sleep, though."

"Okay." It comes out through a laugh. I've never laughed so much in my life, but with him I feel light and free.

Matthias helps me down from the ride and fixes my skirt before stepping away. My heart gives an unsure, panicky thump at the distance. The worry that he's done with me rears its ugly head, despite everything he promised.

It calms down when he reaches for my hand. My

world feels a little less askew as I take it, quieting the fear that I'll be discarded.

Thirteen
LILY

After our secret night together, I feel torn in two. The pull I feel with Matthias settles after he claimed me as his fated mate a couple days ago, yet it doesn't go away around Alder and Valerian. If anything, it's more intense, stronger without them coming as close. If they look at me, the sensation acts up, begging me to go to them. When Matthias wraps his arms around me and brushes kisses along my neck, the unruly thing within me calms, content in his embrace.

I'm happy with him. I shouldn't want more, yet…

Can someone have more than one soulmate? I thought it would go away after what happened with Matthias.

The confusion has today's training session off to a rough start. I have yet to successfully block Alder's mild ranged attacks and Valerian's patience is growing thin. The next one catches me off guard and knocks me to the dead pine needles covering the sandy floor of the woods we're in. They sizzle as I stare up at the tall trees.

It's been eighteen years since I've been back to the Pine Barrens. Jersey Devil territory, where I was found as a baby. If this is where I was, I wonder if there is a gate to Hell near the Leeds house. I prod at my mind, searching for a memory clouded by the magic that trapped my powers until they broke free, but there's nothing there to tell me how I got from the underworld to here.

"Are you going to daydream the next time a hellhound or warrior attacks as well?" Valerian mutters coolly. "Because you'd be dead by now. Pay attention, or you'll never learn to defend yourself in combat."

"I am. This is still weird for me." Climbing to my feet, I wave my hands. A burst of wild steam rises from them into the trees at my untamed emotions. "I didn't grow up knowing I could do this. I was terrified every time a fire was blamed on me because it meant I was a freak and I'd be booted from a foster home placement again. It's hard to tap into this when I haven't been doing it as long as you all have."

It's still a lot to wrap my head around—a demon trapped inside a human body. I don't even know how I can withstand my powers in this form, unsure if this body is mine or if I'm like the others, able to shift to a true form behind the human appearance. I flex my smoking scarred hands. If I'd known how to control this, maybe I wouldn't bear the mark of the horrors I've been through.

Before I admit more than I want to about my past, I snap my jaw shut. Valerian narrows his eyes, gesturing for me to go again before crossing his arms, his rolled up sleeves straining around his strong forearms inked with tattoos that shift with his moods.

Arms wind around me from behind and Matthias surrounds me with the scent of a campfire shot through with warmed chestnuts and maple. The frustration that consumed me a moment ago melts away at his soothing embrace. I hum, my pleased smile slowly curling the corners of my mouth.

"Hey."

"I'm attacking you, babe." His breath tickles. "Fight your way out of my arms. I like it rough, so don't hold back."

"Matthias, get the fuck out of here," Valerian grits out. "You're distracting her. Go check the wards along our perimeter."

Alder and Valerian have doubled up on the

magical barriers they erect around us when we stop. They believe it will help mask the magnitude of my power and keep us from being tracked. It's worked so far while we keep moving.

Matthias presses the curve of his smile against my ear. "Turn around, baby."

That tone is all mischief. I spin to face him, sucking in a breath when he cradles my face and kisses me deeply. I meld against him. It's over too soon and I already crave the next one.

The other two growl, their stances rigid. Valerian scowls and Alder glares at Matthias. Both of them shift their focus to me and I gasp at the desire filling their penetrating gazes. It's almost like they're jealous. My stomach tightens at the thought, the pull confusing me again when it wants me to do the same with them even though I love kissing Matthias.

We haven't hidden anything from the others, though this is the first time he's kissed me in front of them. For the most part, we've spent the last two days holding hands and sticking close together once we moved on from the amusement park before dawn.

"I'm not hiding or stealing moments with you," Matthias says. "You're mine. They'll learn to deal with it."

Biting my lip, I nod, the tiny glow inside my

chest expanding every time he claims me like that.

"Matthias," Alder pushes out through clenched teeth.

"I'm going. Check the wards, got it." He smacks my ass affectionately and takes my chin between his thumb and finger. "I promise to keep you safe so you can figure your shit out."

I huff, rolling my lips between my teeth to keep from snickering. Giving the others a challenging stare, he saunters off through the trees.

"Get back in position," Valerian says roughly.

Sighing, I follow his orders. After Matthias shed some insight on his past, it's not hard to miss that he's used to being in command of those around him.

"At the ready," he says. "Though in a true fight, you won't have the heads up. It's best to remain prepared."

"Oh shit!" I throw my hands up too late when Alder's next attack—a spiraling stream of steam and flames—barrels at me with more force than he's used all morning. The fire singes a hole in my sweater, plunging the neckline deeper where the yarn melts away to reveal more of my cleavage. I flick at it, then glare at him. "What's your deal?"

"Training," Alder grumbles. "If you didn't want to ruin your clothes, you should've worn something else."

"Maybe I'll borrow one of your shirts and see if

you still want to fuck up my clothes."

Alder quiets, his green eyes gleaming with the silent promise that he definitely would as his focus dips to my chest. I falter, picturing it. His oversized t-shirt hanging off my curves, the way his fire would burn through it, leaving me bare for him to devour me.

"I've removed the dalliance driving you to distraction, so what's the problem now?" Valerian stalks toward me, ignoring the daggers Alder glares at his back when he doesn't stop until he's in my face, drowning me in his spiced smoky scent. I stand my ground, fighting the heady stir of lust at my forbidden fantasy. "Or do you think this is a game we're enjoying?"

"Fuck you."

Valerian smirks when I push against his chest. The pull inside me becomes taut, almost unbearable. Both of us breathe hard, our scents mixing together. Hickory and cinnamon. It's the first time I smell what they sense. His eyes are almost black, blown pupils swallowing up the blue as he grips my elbows to keep me in place.

"Vale," I choke out.

A deep rumble vibrates in his throat at his name falling from my lips. "Do I have to keep pushing you until you break, little flower? I will. If that's what it takes, I'll keep pushing until you beg me."

His head dips closer. I strain, caught between closing the little distance left between us and remembering that I belong to another.

Alder grabs me by the arm and breaks us apart. Valerian sighs, releasing me as Alder draws me away. I find no relief from the invisible force inside me, struggling with the same insistent push toward him.

"Step away." I flinch at the hardness riding his tone. His fingers dig into my arm almost to the point of bruising, contradicting his words. "Do it, Lily. Please. Before I do something you don't want. I can't—when you smell like this, it's difficult to resist."

Thinking of Matthias' affectionate smiles and how much I need them, I wrench free with a pained cry. Alder's fist closes around nothing as I stumble away, scrubbing at my face. This bond shit isn't fair. Why is it tormenting me like this after finding my mate?

Once I no longer feel like ripping my clothes off and demanding one—or both—of them take me, I lean against a tree. Valerian has stalked far away, his attention locked on me. Alder sits on a rotted out log, bracing his forearms on his legs, veins prominent when he clenches his fists.

We need a break. I call on a small fire, pushing the limits of what I've learned to control without my power failing me or exploding free. It dances in my palm, not scorching me.

"Why doesn't it burn my skin?" I ask without looking away from the orange glow.

"Our own powers don't hurt us," Alder says. "It's innate, a part of us. It comes from within you."

"Then why…" I force out a tight breath. Talking about this terrifies me, but I have to know. He would understand. It gives me the courage to let them in. "There was a fire when I was little. It burned down my foster home after something bad happened. I think—it came from me."

"Is that why your hands are scarred?" Valerian's dangerous voice is closer.

I nod. "I was in the hospital for two weeks once I was back in the state's custody." I pass the flame back and forth between my marred hands. "I don't know exactly what happened. I blocked a lot of it out. After that, I learned to suppress my emotions. If I didn't feel too much, I would be safe."

Valerian's boots enter my peripheral vision. "Do you know what a changeling is?"

"They're in fairy tales and mythology. A stolen child swapped for another." My eyes widen. Oh. I was found as a baby. "Is that what I am? How I appear human, but…I'm not?"

"I believe so. Your demon was magically sealed in this form. You're trapped. It's possible that the force of your mature powers were too much to handle before your human vessel aged to adulthood." His voice hardens. "Whoever brought you here and sealed you like this most likely expected your powers to kill you."

My shoulders sag. So this might not be my body. Lily Sloane doesn't exist. I'm nothing.

I smell smoke before I sense something—off, like a strange shift in the air. It's not a familiar scent from one of the guys. Alder and Valerian tense, searching the woods. The three of us whirl to a rustling bush. Alder rushes to guard me, pulling me behind him.

Matthias tears through the bush, alert, fanged teeth bared. "Do you sense it?"

"Someone's approaching," Valerian confirms.

A deep laugh echoes around us, seemingly from all directions. Valerian instinctively reaches for his hip, closing his fingers around air. He curses under his breath.

A moment later, a demon materializes out of thin air on a small incline above us with a broad grin. "I see it's still impossible to sneak up on you, Vale."

"Rainer," Valerian says flatly, still on edge.

"Hello, old friend. It's been a long time."

"Almost three centuries," Valerian mutters.

Rainer looks every bit like a knight, his dark leather attire outfitted with a sword hilt attached at his hip beneath his cloak. He has thick sandy hair that reaches past his shoulders, half tied back, and a trimmed beard. Like my demons, the only indicators he's not a human messing around cosplaying a fantasy knight in the woods are his glowing eyes and the serpent-like tongue poking out from the edge of his smile, keeping his other demon features hidden. His friendly eyes are a deep amber that match the shade of mine. He said three hundred years, but only looks in his late twenties at most.

He jumps down from the incline, surveying us. "I found you. As soon as I heard, I set out to search for you. I have news—"

Valerian cuts him off. "Not here." He sweeps our surroundings with a calculating gaze. "If you can get past our perimeter without tripping it, so can others."

Alder keeps himself positioned between Rainer and me as we head for the dinky motel we're staying at on one of the isolated backroads that cut through the Pine Barrens. Matthias puts his arm around my waist, almost lifting me off my feet from how tightly he holds me. Even Valerian serves as a barrier when Rainer glances at me.

The walk to the motel isn't far once we make it to the road from the trail we took into the woods. Valerian remains alert until we're inside the dim, musty room.

I crinkle my nose, looking forward to getting out of here. I grab the first stray shirt I find—Alder's, making my stomach dip—and slip into the bathroom to change out of my ruined sweater. His shirt reaches the ripped knees of my jeans. Tying it in a knot at my hip, I dust the sand and a leaf stuck in my hair before returning to find my three demon companions blocking Rainer from entering the room further than the small chair posted by the door.

Smirking past their shoulders at me, he takes a seat.

"So what the fuck is going on?" Valerian folds his arms. "It's been a shitstorm up here. Demons are crawling all over the realm."

"The underworld is in chaos as well." Rainer sighs, gesturing flippantly. "No one can get to the king to seek an audience and find out his wishes. The council is acting on his behalf. You've been labeled as traitors. It's come down directly from the council."

"The council?" Alder barks. He pushes his large hands into his brown hair. "How? What did we do that warrants this?"

"The official report is grim. It details your plot to harbor a fugitive to overthrow the crown and take the throne for yourselves."

Valerian scoffs. "That's ridiculous. If I was going to do that, I would've been better off doing it with Lil—" He cuts off, sharp jawline working as he collapses to sit on the end of the bed I'm standing beside. It's the first time I've seen him so weary. He glances at me. "I was in a better position to stage a fucking rebellion when I was a knight. I don't have any interest in that. My loyalty has always been to Lucifer. Why would I wait until now, festering away guarding a gate portal?"

"I'm only telling you what the council claims. I don't believe them for a second. Though it's been a long time, I still know you, Vale." Rainer shifts his curious gaze to me. "They say the girl is powerful."

The three of them close rank around me with feral warning growls. Valerian pulls me into his lap while Matthias and Alder square off with Rainer. My heart thuds, startled by the speed they moved. Valerian's arm slides around my waist, his palm spread on my soft stomach to keep me in place.

"Don't look at her," Matthias says viciously.

The force of Valerian's answering growl vibrates against my back, his chin dipping over my shoulder. In my periphery, I can see his fangs as his lip curls back. Alder's fists are poised to punch, his tense knuckles smoking with his impending flames at the ready.

Rainer sniffs the air and laughs. "I see. Quite the predicament you've ended up in, old friend."

"Why are you here?" Valerian demands.

Rainer holds up his hands. "To repay the life debt I owe you. And because you still have people's trust. Allow me to be your eyes and ears in the underworld."

The three of them exchange glances. Alder stares at my shirt, seeing me in it for the first time. Matthias lingers on the way Vale holds me, but doesn't show Rainer any cracks in our unified front.

Alder nods in agreement. "We need to understand what's going on instead of running blind."

"Very well." Vale's fingers twitch, giving my stomach the barest caress. "Update us when you can."

"I will." He holds out his hand.

Valerian seems reluctant, like he's torn between letting me go and allowing Rainer any closer. His exhale blows my short hair and he shifts me off his lap, rising when Rainer does. They clasp arms, Valerian's tattoos swirling across his forearm.

"Thou who seeks to bind in loyalty and allegiance. *I consentio relligo*," Valerian intones.

"Thine pledge is my fealty, given in honor. *I conveniunt ad nervo*," Rainer responds.

Their skin glows with an intricate red design that matches up where they touch. The magic light becomes brighter, then burns off in a flash of smoke and ash. The only evidence left behind is a small circular mark with the same pattern on both of their wrists. Rainer mutters something in another language, dragging two fingers across the mark. It vanishes, melting into nothing on his skin.

"Whoa." I lean forward. "What was all that?"

"A masking spell and a Demon's Pledge," Rainer explains. "It's a binding promise forged between your brethren. It'll allow me to communicate with Vale across vast distances."

My brows jump up. "Even across the realms?"

"That's more difficult, but possible. Only bonded mates and very strong demons are capable of such feats."

My gaze seeks Matthias. He's already watching me, gold eyes hooded and a dimpled smirk playing at the edge of his mouth.

"So we don't have to keep running? We can do something about this. Fight the council."

Alder frowns. "It's suicide to go against the council."

"They're the Devil's right hand," Valerian says.

"We have to try. Otherwise we'll be running forever. I don't want to run." I slide my lips together, shocked by my own fierce burst of confidence. "If we can get Lucifer to listen, we can convince him to call off this hunt."

A muscle jumps in Valerian's cheek. "You think you hold so much sway that the king of Hell would grant you an audience, little flower?" His cold gaze cuts away. "He is merciless."

I narrow my eyes. "Then we'll go without you."

"You'll do no such thing," he grits out.

Matthias pulls me away from Vale by my hand, wrapping me in his arms. Alder reaches out, touching the shirt I stole from him.

Rainer chuckles, patting Valerian on the shoulder. "I should be off before my presence upsets the balance among you. Be careful, old friend. I only tracked you because I understand how your mind works after fighting alongside you, but the hellhounds are circling the area. Witches are keeping them at bay."

"What do you know of the local covens?" Valerian slides into strategy mode. "I'm seeking them out to find one that can break a powerful magic seal."

"They're to the east along the coastline. Ask for Juniper."

Valerian nods. Before Rainer leaves, he clasps his shoulder. "It's good to see you. After so long."

"And you." Rainer gives him a smile that's sad and fond. "It will not be so long next time."

Valerian nods, his throat bobbing. A pang hits me in the chest at the display of emotions he keeps locked up tight. It makes him look younger when he's not scowling.

Fourteen
LILY

After Alder brings back lunch, Matthias takes my hand with a mischievous glint in his eye. He gives me a playful wink.

"Come on."

"I thought I had to finish learning how to block?"

Valerian left shortly after his knight friend to look for any witches nearby, leaving orders for me to continue the interrupted training session. Alder expects me to follow him back out to the woods in fifteen minutes.

"Skip it. You deserve a break and I want to take you out." He draws me closer, kissing me. "I can see you're about to go crazy if you don't get away from this for a little bit. You think you're hiding it from us but you're not as good at it as you think."

It's odd that he can read me so well when I've spent my life hiding my thoughts and opinions, dulling myself for the sake of others. Odd and nice. With the guys, I don't have to do that anymore. I can be my real self, the girl I've never fully shown to anyone else.

"I won't let anything hurt you." He traces my nose with the tip of his, white blond hair brushing my forehead. "I might not be a warrior like Alder and Vale, but I know how to fight."

"Always trying to slide in as my hero," I tease. "You already got the girl."

"That's right, baby."

"Fine." My beaming expression gives me away. "Let me change first."

I take my bag into the bathroom, hesitating with my grip on the bottom of Alder's shirt. If I'm going out with my demon boyfriend, my—my mate, I shouldn't be wearing another man's clothes. His shirt smells so good, woodsy with hints of charcoal. Shaking my head, I peel it off. Instead of leaving it for him to find, I stuff it deep in my bag and pick an outfit I think Matthias will like. Once I'm dressed in the leather miniskirt that hugs the curve of my wide hips and a loose crop top with skull hands that appear to hold my breasts, I swipe on some mascara and red lipstick I stole.

"Bombshell." Matthias rakes his teeth over his lip, taking me in with a heated gaze. His arm drapes across my shoulders and he leads me out to the car Valerian didn't take, swinging the keys around his finger. "I want to make it up to you that we missed out on your first rest stop junk food feast. I found a spot nearby I think you'll like."

I tilt my head curiously, brushing my fingers against his chest as an excuse to get closer. "What is it?"

The corner of his mouth lifts. "It's a surprise."

"Surprises generally aren't a good thing for me."

With a hum, he brings his lips to my ear. "Then I'd better get to work on showing you how enjoyable they can be."

The shiver I attempt to hide makes him snicker. He opens the passenger door for me with a grand sweep of his arm. A laugh bubbles out of me at his antics and the spark of excitement flickers to life as he pulls away from the motel with the windows down. The cool autumn air blows my hair back from my neck and shoulders. He rests one hand over the wheel and stretches the other out to thread through my hair before he drops it to my lap, tucking it between my legs. The casual, possessive move makes my insides twist pleasantly.

"When Alder finds out we bailed on him, he's

going to kill us," I say.

Matthias squeezes my thigh. "He'll be more pissed he didn't think to take you out first."

As much as I like how that sounds, I bite my lip. "I don't have a lot of experience. Well, none, if I'm honest. And I'm pretty terrible at expressing myself because I've spent a long time keeping quiet. But I'm yours." It leaves me breathless every time I say it, feeling more important and permanent each time. I placed a hand over my fluttering heart. The invisible cord around it hums with a gentle squeeze. "I'm yours."

He smiles, thumb stroking the top of my leg. "I know, petal. I love that you're mine."

The back roads of the Pine Barrens almost make it seem like we're the only two people in the world. More houses and farms break up the trees as we reach a main road. We're not on it long before he pulls into a farmers market stand.

"Here's our first stop." He takes my hand and urges me to the faded blue and white stand boasting fresh fall pies and cider donuts.

"Is it open? We're the only customers."

"It is. Do you like apple or pumpkin?" He holds up two different pies. "Or both. We don't have to choose between them. You can have everything you want. Everything your heart desires. If you feel the urge, take it."

There's something about the way he says it that makes me pause, looking up from the basket of fresh apples. The bond stirs in my chest, the faint tug in the opposite direction ever-present. Are we still talking about pie?

"Both? I don't know, I've never had any."

For a moment, his mouth tightens and his golden eyes flash. He covers with a nod. "We'll have to fix that, won't we? Both it is. Anything to spoil my pretty girl."

I blush, moving along to the huge pile of pumpkins. "The cider donuts sound good, too."

"You know we're not leaving without donuts, Lils. Some for now and some for later."

I play with the bottom hem of my top. This date isn't grand or fancy, but it's perfect. Once we're stockpiled and Matthias pays, we get back in the car.

"This was fun." I rub my fingers together before reaching for his hand. He twines our fingers together and kisses my knuckles, drawing a soft smile from me. "I don't think the others would care, but this is more than anyone has ever done for me. Thank you."

He watches me from the corner of his eye. "They would care. And we're not done yet. The best part about getting pie is enjoying it."

"We're driving in the opposite direction from the motel."

"It's just up ahead. Found it while I was scouting past our perimeter last night."

I shake my head. "Do any of you actually sleep?"

"We can go a long time without it." He shoots me a wink. "We have excellent stamina."

Heat bolts through me at his sexy tone and I lick my lips. Matthias grins without looking at me. He lifts his chin and inhales, eyes hooding.

"Fuck, you smell good. When you're wet, my mouth fucking waters and I can't wait for my next taste. Just hold on a little longer, petal."

"W-what?" I cover my mouth, hissing through my fingers. "You can smell when I'm—turned on?"

His grin stretches. "That's right, mate. Your scent is better than the sweetest sin."

"Oh my god." I press my legs together while the bond practically purrs in my chest from the praise of my fated mate.

The car pulls into a parking lot with a sign for hiking trails. He hops out of the car and produces a sheet from the trunk.

"Is that from the motel?"

He waggles his brows. "Yeah, I swiped it. We're having a picnic."

I bite my lip around a warm smile. "I've never had a picnic."

We grab the donuts and pie, strolling along the wide sandy trail. Matthias teases me by bumping against me and pretending he didn't do it. He switches sides, blowing on the back of my neck, avoiding my eye with a playful smirk. I get him back by flicking sand at him with my boot. He retaliates by smacking my ass with a deep laugh.

"I'll get you back for that," I promise.

"Don't drop our pie," he taunts.

My attention falls to his tattooed arms. He has a geometric wolf and a badass lunar moth on his biceps. The one that makes me most curious is the random dolphin.

"How does a demon have tattoos? The ones you got here, I mean."

He smirks. "Who says I got them in the mortal realm?"

"Come on, I can't picture a demon tattoo artist inking butterflies and swallows on people. Plus, Valerian's aren't like yours. His move."

"You're right. He got his in the underworld." He shrugs. "I like these."

"I like them, too." The charming crooked smile he gives me makes my chest expand with a soft glow. "What about the random ones?"

"They're my expression of self. None are random."

"The bright ass dolphin?"

He laughs, cheeks coloring as he scratches his nose. "Ah, it was the nineties. It was the thing to get."

The trail opens up and my good mood evaporates. I freeze in terror at the edge of the trees. The lake would be beautiful and peaceful to anyone else. To me, it makes my stomach cramp and my limbs turn to statues. The pie box crinkles between my death grip.

"Lily?" Matthias turns serious, scanning the area for a threat. "What's wrong?"

"The lake," I whisper hoarsely.

"Did you see someone there? A demon?" He moves in front of me, fingers lengthening into claws.

"No." Fuck, will I ever escape this? I press my face against his back, trembling. "I'm sorry. I'm ruining this."

"Tell me what's got you so spooked?" Realizing there's no actual danger, he turns and wraps me in his arms. His claws recede and he strokes my hair. "It's okay."

I take deep gulps of his scent. "I…" My throat constricts. I hate this stupid fear. "I don't like water."

His embrace tightens, the pie probably getting squished between us. "I didn't know. I'm sorry." He rests his cheek on top of my head. "I wanted to surprise you and show you a good time."

"It's not your fault." I squeeze my eyes shut.

"Will you tell me why you don't like water?" he murmurs.

I try, but the words won't come. I blink away tears and soak in his gentle touches. "When I was a kid I had a bad experience."

It's an understatement, a mere shadow of the truth, yet he doesn't push me for more. He just holds me, helping me breathe easier. "I'm sorry." He presses his lips to my forehead and speaks against my skin. "Let me make it better."

"How?" I've tried so many things to get over my fear.

"We'll overwrite your bad memories of water with something good."

My lips slide together. The fact he wants to erase my bad memories touches me, calming the racing beat of my heart. The bond tightens with the hug he gives me.

"Do you still want to have our picnic?"

I lean back, frowning at the pie box. "It got kind of crushed."

His expression softens and he massages the back of my neck gently. "It's okay. Or we can go. Anything you need."

Matthias only wanted to take me on a date. He did this for me and I ruined it.

"I don't want to go. I want to stay here with you."

His tender, protective gaze bounces between mine. "I'll be with you anywhere we go. You never have to worry, mate. I'm with you."

At my nod, he guides me along the edge of the tree line, keeping us separated from the lake. I can still see it, but it's better we're not on its banks. We find a spot with a small clearing and he spreads the stolen sheet.

He kicks off his boots and sprawls across it, patting the spot beside him. "Come here, pretty girl." I follow suit, accepting his encouragement to lean into his side. "Is this okay?"

"Yeah. This is nice." It's a relief that I haven't messed up our date and driven him away. As long as he's with me, I can survive sitting near the lake.

"Good." He kisses the top of my head and we sit like that, listening to the rustle of orange leaves overhead until my heart stops beating so hard. Sensing I'm more relaxed, he plays with my hair. "Ready to try your first bite of pie?"

"Yes."

"Close your eyes."

I tilt my head back and do as he asks. The scent of a campfire and maple gets stronger, winding around me like a phantom caress from my mate. I swallow thickly, waiting. A low, pleased rumble sounds right in front of me and his fingertips touch my lips.

"Open for me, Lily," he rasps.

I part my lips, gasping at the first buttery sweet taste melting on my tongue. It's so good, the tartness of apple spiced with cinnamon and the sugary flakes of crust making me moan. He traces my lips reverently.

"You like that." His mouth captures mine, kissing me deeply. "Keep your eyes closed. Now try this."

Matthias feeds me another piece, this one smooth, less sweet, but just as delicious. "What is that?"

"Pumpkin pie." I lick some of it from his fingertips, mouth quirking at his groan. "Hold on. I want you to taste this."

His sugar coated fingers bump against my lips and his breath fans across my cheek as I accept it, sucking on his fingers. The cider donut is good, but his skin tastes even better. His lips trail across my jaw, his searing, open-mouthed kisses moving down my neck as he grasps my waist.

"So good," I murmur.

"Yeah? Not as good as you taste." He nudges me until my back hits the sheet, covering my body with his. "Like here." His forked tongue swipes between my breasts. "Mm, so sweet."

I open my legs and he settles between my thighs, rocking his hardness against my core. He grins at my gasp, guiding my arms overhead. Pinning them there, he nips at my neck, grinding against me until the tight coil inside me snaps, sending a ripple of pleasure through me.

"That's it, baby. Let me make you feel good."

"More."

The whisper feels illicit, yet I don't want to stop. Not with him. I want everything.

I want to squash my fears and remember the divine sensation of his lips on my skin instead. Overwrite the bad memories with his touch.

Matthias slides his hands beneath my shirt, groaning when he finds no bra. Going without was worth it for this. My back arches as he plays with my nipples, pushing my shirt higher to expose me.

"Watch," he rasps.

With effort, I snap my eyes open, meeting his heady gaze. He closes his mouth around one and sucks, tongue swirling. A gasp tears from me and I wrap my legs around his hips. I'm burning up, filled with a delicious, frenzied heat that I don't want to end. I need to feel him, my core aching for it.

"I want you," I choke out.

"Shh, I've got you," he murmurs, kissing his way back up my neck to my lips, speaking between kisses. His tone shifts to something filthy and rough. "Is this what you want?"

He grabs my hips and thrusts against my pussy, making me cry out. Panting, I nod. With a feral sound, he shoves my skirt up and all but claws my underwear down. When he strokes his fingers through my folds, I buck my hips. He spends a moment teasing me, then sinks a finger inside me.

"So wet, pretty girl. I want to worship you. Take my time and savor every sound you make. Taste you all over." He growls as I clench around him and spears me with another finger. "I can't promise to go slow right now. Your scent is driving me crazy. I'll be gentle later. Right now I need to claim you and make you feel me after."

"I want it. I want to be yours," I beg, as swept up as he is, the heat overtaking my body. My hips move with his fingers as he fucks me with them, heightening my pleasure by giving me jolts of his power with small, sparking vibrations that push me to the edge. "Please, Matthias."

Removing his fingers, he braces over me, pinning me under his sultry gaze as he licks the slickness from them. Without breaking eye contact, he reaches back to peel his t-shirt off, then drops his hands to pop the button on his jeans. He takes them off and I gasp at the sight of his cock.

The curiosity crossed my mind before. My imagination didn't prepare me and my chest collapses with my exhale.

His cock is big—longer than a human's, enhanced with two rows of ridged bumps along the top. The ache in my core intensifies and arousal spills through me.

Matthias watches me with a primal glint of amusement in his eyes, circling his fingers around the thick base. He strokes it, spreading the precome leaking from his tip until his length is slick with it. He settles between my hips, the big tip of his dick teasing between my folds.

"Oh," I breathe. "It's big. Will it fit?"

His rumbling chuckle is downright dirty. "It will fit. This pussy will take it all and beg me for more."

He concentrates his power, hitting my clit with tingling sparks from his cock. A moan slips out of me and my back bows as pleasure races through me. My fear of the lake is completely forgotten, swallowed by my need for him, for my mate to claim me as his.

Lining up, he kisses me hard. "Burn with me, petal."

His cock sinks into me with a long thrust, somehow fitting every dizzying inch. My lips part and he swallows the cry that escapes. He stills, allowing me to feel him inside, bracing on an elbow to roam my face with primal hunger for my reaction. I wrap my arms around his shoulders as he claims me, the size of him overwhelming as the ridges rub deep inside me, filling me, stretching me to the brink. It's intense, the sensations making me lose control.

"Oh god," I whimper. "Matthias, it's too much."

"Fuck, your pussy was made for my cock." He drops his head to mouth at my neck, nibbling on a sensitive spot that makes my vision hazy. "You take it so well. Listen to those pretty sounds you're making."

I moan, half-delirious as an orgasm hits me out of nowhere, the ecstasy exploding from my core. My nails scrape his back as his pace picks up. A strangled noise catches in my throat when he slides his fingers into my hair, then maneuvers his other hand between us to rub my clit, fingers releasing intermittent sparks, echoing them inside me each time he buries his cock inside me. He keeps me riding the wave of pleasure, extending it each time I'm about to recover.

"Fucking gorgeous," he praises. "Gorgeous and mine."

The possessive growl against my neck comes as a blaze spirals through me, sending me over the edge once more from the heat building between us. With a ragged groan, his cock throbs inside me as he comes.

Something expands in my chest, bright and hot, the light touching every part of me and engulfing him. He covers my heart with his hand and kisses me.

I feel him everywhere as I'm shattered and remade, no longer a broken, unloveable girl. Inside me. In my heart where the bond connecting us thrums. Holding me. Marking me as his forever in every way.

"You belong to me, petal," he breathes against my lips, fingers tightening in my hair. "I've claimed you as mine. You'll always be mine, mate."

Those words burn into my very soul with the promise I'll never be alone again.

Fifteen
LILY

WE TAKE OUR TIME GETTING BACK, LINGERING IN the moment while we giggle about feeding each other slightly squashed pie. When we finally get dressed and return, Valerian waits outside the motel room with a surly expression. I steel myself for his anger, not in the least bit sorry for enjoying the afternoon with Matthias instead of training. I can still feel him between my legs, inside me, the glowing warmth in my chest at his claiming vow emanating from within me like a beacon.

The anger doesn't come.

Valerian stares at me for a long beat, something unreadable shifting across his chiseled features. He inclines his head, his black tousled hair falling in his face. "Get back in the car. We have to go south."

Alder comes out of the room with my bag and heads for the car. He pauses halfway there, spine rigid as his head jerks in my direction. There's no way he or Vale can tell that we had sex, right? I hope they can't smell it on us like Matthias said he could smell when I was aroused. I avert my eyes from Alder, heart pounding.

"Did you find the witches?" Matthias steers us around, rubbing my back in soothing circles.

"Yes, but they couldn't do what I want without calling on other covens to join them at their sabbath. We can't wait that long. They suggested another coven and contacted them on my behalf. It's a long drive."

So much for showering. Not that I'm in a rush to wash away what happened.

Once we're on the road, my mind has free rein to roam. I curl against the door in the back, watching the scenery speed by. Alder and Valerian mutter to each other up front while Matthias dozes, arm outstretched across the seat so his fingers brush against my hip.

An hour into the drive as we're leaving the state, my stomach tightens at the thought of what awaits me when we find a witch powerful enough to undo the binding trapping me as a human.

What will happen if it's broken?

The guys think I'm a changeling, my true

demon form locked away. But what if that demon is different? What if the person I am now disappears, erased once the memories of my demon life are free?

A harsh breath blows past my lips as I wring the hem of my loose skull hands crop top.

If I'm not me, will I still be Matthias' fated mate? I bite the inside of my cheek to stave off the panicky beat of my heart. No. I felt it earlier by the lake—his words touched me to the core of my being.

Yet the niggle of worry only grows, as it always does once the thought enters my head, the ugly whisper that I'll be alone.

I don't even know what it means to be a changeling. There's a chance that breaking the magical seal might destroy this body to reveal my demon. It occurs to me again as my thoughts turn in circles that I might not be the age I think I am depending on what my life was before I was brought to the mortal realm from the underworld. My head jerks with a bitter snort. All the years I've spent dreading and hoping for my eighteenth birthday to escape the system that never helped me, yet I might have aged out ten times over.

She'll never be queen. The hellhound's vicious snarl surfaces in my head along with Rainer's report about the council labeling Valerian as a traitor for the treasonous rebellion he's plotting.

They can't mean me. I'm no queen.

"Come here." Matthias moves to the middle of the seat and pulls me into his lap. "I can hear those gears turning in your head. Steam's about to blow out of your ears from thinking so hard. What's bothering you?"

The panicky internal crisis slows down once I'm in his embrace. I focus on the calm beat of his heart against my back.

"I'm fine. Just nervous I guess." I twist my fingers in my lap. He covers my hands, squeezing them comfortingly. "We don't know what will happen if the witches can break the seal."

"Let me take your mind off it." His tone lowers and he shifts against my ass so I feel his erection. "You still smell like me."

My cheeks flush and I dart my eyes to the front. Can they smell it?

"It's making me want you again," he whispers against my ear. "Can you be quiet?"

I angle my head to give him a *what the fuck* look. Smirking, he releases my hands and slips his fingers beneath my shirt, tracing the edge of my breast. I smother a shaky breath as he ignites a new burst of heat in me.

He lifts his brows in question—continue or stop? Rolling my lips between my teeth, I give a small nod.

This is wrong. We shouldn't, not when Alder

and Valerian are right there in the front seat. Yet I don't stop him from caressing my hips and teasing the hem of my short skirt with a barely there touch. Part of me wants them to see, wants them to hear what it sounds like when I come. A pulsing hum fills my chest at the thought, urging me on.

He brushes light kisses along my shoulder, tracing maddening circles on the inside of my thighs. Then he stops until I wriggle, rubbing them together to help the throb in my clit. His mouth curves against my neck and he massages the softness of my legs, encouraging me to open for him. When I do, he rewards me by sneaking his hand up my skirt to stroke a knuckle along my pussy through my panties.

"So wet still," he breathes against my ear so the others won't hear.

My heart stutters as he pushes past them and strokes me. My legs spread wider and a soft sigh rushes out of me before I realize it. I swallow thickly as he slowly tortures me.

"Can you stay quiet while you take my fingers?" he whispers. "What about my cock? Do you think you could ride my cock without them knowing?"

A strangled noise catches in my throat as he pushes two fingers inside my pussy with little resistance, my body still loose from when he claimed me in the woods. Cursing under his breath, he curls them deep inside me, making my chest rise and fall as my hips roll, seeking more.

I forget about staying quiet when it becomes too much, clamping my legs around his wrist as my pleasure implodes in my core.

There's no hiding what he's doing to me anymore. We're going to get caught. The bond wriggles in my chest and I clamp down on the dirty little thing dancing in excitement at the idea of Valerian and Alder watching this.

"S-stop," I hiss. My head tips back on Matthias' shoulder and my eyes slam shut against the sensation of his fingers stroking my folds. "Please. This is—they can hear…"

"Not just hear. Your scent is telling them everything about how good you feel right now," he murmurs against the side of my neck, mouthing at my flushed skin with a hint of his fangs. His fingers circle my clit and I feel the curve of his grin branded into my throat when I shudder. "I'm not stopping until you're soaking my hand, petal. I want you dripping for me, baby. I want you so wet you ruin the leather so none of us ever forget it."

"Oh god." I arch into his sinful touch, lost to the headiness of his filthy demand.

The game is over. It was over before we began. We both knew there was no way to hide this, no way I could be quiet. I forget about stopping, shuddering as he rubs the spot inside me that lights me up.

A rumble catches my attention. I look at Valerian, but he's glaring ahead at the road, knuckles white on the wheel, the ink that normally covers them retreating up his wrists. My gaze slides to Alder and I gasp. He's staring between my spread legs like I'm a feast waiting for him, intently fixated on every movement of Matthias' hand. He reaches out and hesitates before placing his big hand on my knee, encouraging me to open my legs wider. My body quakes and another cry escapes me.

This is insane. I'm letting Matthias fuck me with his fingers in the back of the car while Alder gets a front row seat to the show—literally. But god, I can't stop. It's too good, too intense, too hot to ever stop.

"Slow down." Alder's deep rasp causes a pulse in my clit until his words register.

Matthias stops and I nearly whine. He soothes me with a sweet kiss to my jaw. "Hush, petal. I've got you."

"She's too close. Draw it out. Tease her." Alder lifts his hypnotic green eyes to meet mine and my stomach clenches. "Make her beg for it."

Fuck. Oh *fuck*.

Matthias' mischievous laugh vibrates against me. "You dirty fucker." He follows Alder's directions, fingers playing with my pussy almost absently. "How many more times do you think I can make her come? I already wrung one out of her."

"Don't stop until she's crying."

Air punches out of my lungs and I bite down hard on my lip when Matthias thrusts a third finger into me without warning. The sound they make from how wet I am is obscene. In the mirror, Vale's nostrils flare, but he remains silent while his demonic buddies have me at their complete mercy.

Instead of feeling ashamed and wanting to hide, a powerful thrill shoots through me. I feel beautiful, the sense chasing away the horrible voice in my head that whispers I'm not enough and makes me believe everyone will leave me alone.

But my demons won't. Matthias claimed me, swearing I belonged to him. Alder watches me with desire filling his gaze. Valerian promised I'd never escape him.

They won't leave me.

I don't stop the moan that bursts from me as Matthias' power vibrates inside my pussy while he teases my clit. He murmurs praise in my ear, taking me higher to teeter on the brink of falling.

"The whole fucking car smells like her." Alder growls, his fingers shift and his claws dig into his seat.

"Smells like a beautiful sin," Matthias purrs. "Ready to come again? C'mon, you can do it." I shake my head, panting raggedly. It's too much. If I come, I'll split apart at the seams. "Yes you can. Do it for me. For us. Come for us, petal."

His thumb presses down on my clit and he plunges his fingers deep within me, hitting the spot that makes me shatter with a stronger burst of sparks that ignite into a flame stroking me until I fall apart. The noise that tears from me doesn't even sound human. All I know is sweet oblivion and the pleased murmurs from Matthias as I shake apart with another orgasm.

"Good girl," Alder rumbles.

"Mm, so good for us," Matthias says.

The heated flush spreads like wildfire across my skin, engulfing my body in the erotic flames of ecstasy from what they're doing to me. My fantasies are overlapping with reality.

Matthias pulls his fingers free. They're glistening and he chuckles, curling his tongue around them to taste me.

The serpent-like forked tip still sends a jolt through me and a rush of air hisses past my lips. How would that devious, otherworldly tongue feel buried between my legs? In me? The thought drives me crazy. As if he can read the sensual places my mind goes, his warm gold eyes flare, the radiant flecks glowing to make them brighter.

Alder watches with hunger burning in his hardened green gaze. His own forked tongue flicks his lower lip, sending an answering thrum of desire to my core.

Another low laugh vibrates against my back and Matthias hikes my leather skirt higher, bunching it around my hips. I'm completely exposed like this. Alder's chest collapses with the breath he forces out, focused on the way Matthias strips my panties the rest of the way off. He flings them and my face is seconds from spontaneously combusting because they arc through the car, landing up front.

"Where'd they land? Please tell me I got the gear shift. Twenty bucks if I did."

Vale mutters something in an acidic tone I can't decipher, too caught up in the depravity pricking my senses. I don't want to stop though, lost to the aching need for *more*.

"Prop her foot on the seat," Alder demands. He yanks on his seatbelt, the distinct sound of the taut material tearing audible as he shifts around for a better viewing position while Matthias complies, hitching my leg up.

"Not done yet, babe." Matthias presses a trail of hot kisses over my jaw, teasing my ear with his wicked tongue. He uses the heel of his palm against my swollen folds, groaning when I rock against it for more. "Fuck. You make me want to drive my cock into you again and make you scream."

Alder growls from the front seat. I guess he's

fine with watching his friend finger me, but he doesn't want to see how Matthias fucks me.

"Fine, fine. But christ, I'm going to fuck you so good later. I'm going to rearrange your goddamn guts, baby."

Matthias' hard cock digs against my ass as he buries his fingers inside my pussy with a thrust that tears a frayed gasp from me. He fists my hair while he grazes his fangs over my throat. I arch against him, riding his fingers.

He nips my skin. "You want that, petal? You want me to bend you over and split you open on my dick?"

"Yes!" I'm too delirious to manage any coherent response other than begging for everything he wants to give me.

Somehow my eyes flutter open and lock with Vale's in the rearview mirror. His eerie blue gaze burns into mine. My core spirals tighter with his eyes on me, piercing through me as senses are overwhelmed by the smoky scents filling the car from all three of them.

Is he picturing what Matthias said he'll do to me later? Does he imagine it's him bending me over instead? Liquid heat fills my core as my own imagination takes off with that thought. My heart stammers just as Matthias presses deeper and triggers another orgasm that shakes me to the bone.

I'm lost to wave after wave of heady, mind-blowing pleasure, the thrum in my chest going crazy. For a moment, my world isn't tilted off its axis, the echo of rightness panging inside me.

When I stop quivering, Matthias uses the corner of his shirt to dab at the beads of sweat on my face and fixes my skirt before nestling me on his lap so I'm sideways, resting against him. His lips brush my forehead.

"Does she need water?" Alder asks.

Whoever decides to answer, I miss it, but no one shoves a drink in my face. I'm grateful for it because I don't want to move. Matthias is comfortable and I'm pretty sure I'm a puddle. A chill moves over my leg and I feel the remnants of his ministrations dripping down my thigh. A tired smirk pulls at my lips at the thought of the car permanently stained with this memory.

"You did so good for us, pretty girl." Matthias' tone is affectionate and proud. It envelops me, igniting a glow of happiness in my chest. "Sleep now, petal."

"We'll wake you when we get there," Vale says.

His voice is strange. Rougher and thicker than the detached iciness I'm used to from him. I like it.

Low murmurs fill the car, but I drift in a hazy toneless cloud, too wrung out to even worry about what had my thoughts racing before Matthias and Alder's wicked game. I burrow further into Matthias' arms and smile when they tighten around me. This is where I belong, the place I've searched for my whole life.

Sixteen
LILY

"So... can I have my underwear back?" I keep my voice low, but Alder hears my whisper to Matthias anyway when we climb out of the car later that night somewhere in Virginia.

"If you continue to taunt us because you're the one who gets to have her, I'll kill you," he growls.

"No!" My outburst is loud and fierce, cutting through the night.

Fire springs forth to cover my hands, his threat to kill my mate the only thing that registers.

The precise control over my powers startles all of us. I've never managed to call something of this level on my own.

Matthias tucks me under his arm and kisses my cheek. My fire snuffs out at his touch, smoke rising from my arms. "It's okay. He's not serious."

Valerian pockets my underwear and goes into the motel office. A heated flush pricks at my cheeks and my stomach twists with the illicitness of his actions. Did that asshole seriously just—?

It should piss me off that he stole my panties, yet the thrum circling my chest likes the idea of him carrying them around, knowing I'm bare beneath my miniskirt.

He returns a few minutes later with keys to a room. "Don't go anywhere unless it's to work on your defensive moves."

"Where are you going?" Alder prompts.

"The coven. They're expecting me. I'm going to find out if they have a witch that can access the seal, or at least tap into her memories to find her true identity."

"This late?" I question.

"It's the witching hour," he says plainly.

His gaze falls to the possessive arm Matthias has around my shoulders and a muscle jumps in his cheek. A sting spears through my chest when he turns his back on me without another word.

Once he drives off, Alder catches my wrist, tugging me away from Matthias' side. "We're not done. You're finishing your training for the day."

"What? Are you kidding?" My skin warms beneath his firm hold, tingling pleasantly. I bite my lip, his gruff words while he watched Matthias finger fuck me filtering through my head. "It's late. All I want to do is shower and go to sleep."

"I'm not joking. You're not escaping this."

His grip presses into my skin, unwilling to let me go. A thrill shoots through me, much like the way I felt when he touched my knee to spread my legs wider to expose my body for his own devious pleasure. I make no move to free myself.

Heat throbs between my legs. I'm bare beneath my skirt.

He tosses my bag at Matthias, dragging me across the damp pavement reflecting the purple neon glow of the motel sign. "Meet us out back. I'll find a spot to work."

We head around the side of the motel. A small slope leads down to a narrow creek. I suck in a breath at the sight of murky water trickling across dead leaves and sticks. Alder pauses, giving me a sidelong glance.

The fear isn't as potent as it usually is. Closing my eyes, I picture Matthias' kisses in the woods by the lake earlier until I breathe easier, a relieved smile twitching my lips. His effort to replace my bad memories with a better one worked.

Alder shifts directions, heading for a copse of trees. "Here will do. There's not as much room as we had at our last location. We'll work on close range."

He finally drops my wrist, only to wrap his arms around me from behind. "Breaking a hold is about understanding balance and reserving your energy to utilize against your attacker efficiently."

The circle of trees feels as though it blocks us off from the world, interrupted only by the faint sounds of cars passing on the nearby road. His palms skate across my stomach, toeing the edge of decency when he moves up and takes the hem of my shirt with him, dangerously close to revealing the bottom curves of my tits. My chest rises and falls, my awareness shrinking to the feel of his rough hands on my body and the drum of his heartbeat against my back.

"Alder," I whisper.

"When you can't protect yourself, I will be there to keep you safe." Sighing, he locks his arms around my shoulders, effectively pinning my arms at my sides. He speaks against the top of my head. "But I'll teach you to fight like a warrior. I sense she's within you."

My stomach dips and I brush my fingertips against his sides, the heat of his embrace captivating my senses. His gravelly rumble reverberates against my back, surrounding me. I know he's teaching me, but I don't want to move from this spot, from his steadfast embrace.

"To get out of this, you have two options. Drop your center of balance lower than mine, then use the force of your power to push the advantage by attacking the inner knee or groin. I want you to focus on this method."

"What about the other way?"

"Your other option is if your hands are pinned like this, call on your fire to punch up through the hold, then turn and drive with all your might toward your attacker's chin. With enough strength behind your counter attack, you can knock them back and even blind them. We'll run through it so you understand the basic maneuver first, then do it with hellfire in the mix."

He mutters gruffly, talking me through what he wants me to do, guiding my movements. Once I have the basic idea down, he instructs me to try on my own.

My attempts only lead to him tightening his hold. "How am I supposed to break out of this if you know what it takes to do it? When I go to drop low, you just hold me tighter."

"Escape," he urges, his low tone fraying. "I won't go easy on you and let you go."

An insistent pulse echoes inside me.

Slow down. Make her beg for it. Don't stop until she's crying.

My lashes flutter as I try to clear my head. Licking my lips, I rein myself in. The car was a fluke. It was the pressure of life on the run living in close proximity with them blurring the line. A dirty fantasy come to life that we're not likely to repeat. I should focus on what he's teaching me instead of getting horny.

The problem is that I don't want to get out of his hold, enjoying the feel of his firm chest plastered to my back.

I barely let myself look at other boys growing up, too worried of how much deeper their rejection would cut. I have no defenses against this deep well of desire I've uncovered in myself, too addicted to these stolen touches healing years of isolation that have left me starved for any touch.

"Do it, Lily," he orders roughly, as affected by our proximity as I am.

Gulping, I get it together. His directions run through my head. I fake dropping my weight, then drive my elbow back hard. He grunts. I doubt I actually hurt him, but it's enough of a distraction to catch him off guard when I drop a second time. Crouched low, I charge my shoulder against his knee until he stumbles backwards a few paces.

I freeze, a smile breaking free. Getting up, I launch at Alder. He catches me and I hug him. "I did it."

"You did." He hesitates, then returns the hug with crushing force. "Well done, sweet blossom."

A laugh bubbles out of me. "Let's do it again."

He releases me and I turn around.

My concentration is occupied by repeating the moves he showed me. I don't hear the swift footsteps moving through the trees until Matthias appears before me with a mischievous smirk. Before I react, he pushes me back against Alder's chest, pinning me by my shoulders.

"What are you going to do, Lils?" he murmurs. "Now you're trapped between the two of us."

My brain short circuits, everything Alder showed me flitting away as they press against me, sandwiching me between them.

"Hold her," Matthias says.

Alder growls in warning, yet he grabs me by my upper arms with more strength than a moment ago. Escaping this hold is too difficult. I don't attempt it, not interested in moving from between them, drowning in their smoky scents blending together. An intense throb thrums in my clit.

Matthias swipes his tongue along his lip, then kisses me. It's not sweet or soft. The kiss is urgent and sensual, scorching me in a matter of seconds with each slide of his tongue against mine. He owns me with it, reminding me I'm his. He doesn't let up, sweeping his palms down my sides, pushing beneath my shirt to caress my skin. I forget about training, chasing his wicked tongue for more.

"Mm, petal, I love it when you smell like this. So

fucking delicious, so needy." His touch skates down, nudging between my legs, cupping me beneath my skirt. "You have no idea how much I want to feast on you until you can't stand without Alder holding you up."

A hoarse cry escapes me. I feel Alder at my back, grinding his hard cock against me at the dirty picture Matthias paints of him on his knees before me while I melt against Alder's embrace. I struggle for air. He feels even bigger than Matthias is.

"Oh, damn. You just got wetter," Matthias murmurs against my lips as he teases between my legs. "Is that what you need right now? Alder helping you ride my face until you make a gorgeous mess?"

I blink as shock filters through my arousal. It's almost like he wants me to be with Alder, too. Is he serious? If he is, could it mean he wouldn't be mad if my heart was pulled in another direction than only him? My pulse speeds up at the possibility.

"You want that?" I push out.

"Baby, I want everything," he croons. "I know you'd look so beautiful coming apart, submitting to your pleasure. Just like earlier while he watched. You liked that?"

I nod, my stomach dipping pleasantly. "Yes."

His eyes flare. "I want to give you all of that. Let us take care of you. Both of us."

Both. My head swims from the force of the bond trilling in my chest.

Alder stills, then presses against me more insistently. My head tips back and he dips his face to my neck with a feral sound, his touch searing with a divine heat that spreads across my body. I arch as Matthias kisses a path down my throat.

"This isn't defense training." Valerian's cutting tone penetrates the sensual fog of desire I'm lost to. If Alder wasn't supporting me, I'd tip over and collapse. Valerian steps out from behind a tree, jaw clenched. "Enough. Time for her to rest. Matthias, you're on watch."

Matthias pulls away, smiling at me unapologetically as he tucks my hair behind my ears. "I'll finish this later." He plants a quick kiss on my lips. "Sweet dreams, my pretty girl."

Alder is more reluctant to release me, keeping me in place when I try to step away. His nose grazes the top of my head, inhaling faintly. A beat later, he lets go. I hug myself, but it's not the same.

"Tomorrow you're coming with me to meet the witch," Valerian says.

※

My demons surround me on my throne carved from jagged obsidian in a large room with high stone arches and burning sconces. Alder kneels before me, taking my hand, and Matthias perches on the arm, brushing a knuckle along my cheek while Vale grasps my chin to guide my eyes to him on my other side. Contentment fills me as they dote on me. I don't want this moment to end, happy to stay like this forever with them by my side.

But something is wrong.

One by one my men are stolen from me by cloaked figures with gruesome claws. They fight to escape, and I'm powerless to help, a chain locked around my ankle to keep me on the throne. I don't want this. I never wanted to be the queen ruling Hell.

Hellfire explodes from my hands to destroy the chain. As soon as I'm free, I run, searching the long halls, my crimson gown getting in the way. I fling off the crown atop my head, the studded spiked halo weighing me down.

"She will never be queen!" The demons hunting me shout it over and over.

"No!" I scream.

But it's no use. They capture me without my handsome demon knight to guard me.

Their claws slice into me, shredding my gown, pushing me down to the gleaming dark floor. Their red eyes spew fire and they bare their fangs at me. The floor swallows me, the water sloshing over my head. I flail hard, unable to break free. I sink further into the abyss and death calls to me.

The stale air in the dark motel room chokes me as I snap my eyes open with a harsh gasp. I press a trembling hand to my throat, my lungs searing as I drag in air. I'm not drowning.

Squeezing my eyes shut, I wrench the neck of my sleep shirt—the one I stole from Alder and put on after a shower—up to my nose, dragging in deep gulps of his scent.

My bed shifts, drawing another freaked out wheeze from me. Who the—? Matthias has been sleeping in bed with me, but tonight he's out on watch. I went to bed alone when Alder and Valerian stepped out to talk.

Large hands grab me as I struggle, a deep voice hushing me. The scent of smoldering charcoal and woodsmoke registers when I'm pulled against a broad, muscular chest. *Alder*.

"Shh, sweet blossom." He pets my hair. "What's wrong?"

It takes me a moment to calm my harsh breathing and find my words, the horrible tendrils of the dream clinging to my mind. "Nightmare," I choke out. "You're here?"

"I'm here. You're safe," he promises. "You were tossing and turning. Something agitated you. When I laid next to you, it seemed to settle your restlessness."

"I feel better like this," I admit. "Your scent is nice. It makes me feel protected."

A brief pang of guilt plagues me. I shouldn't say it, even if it's true. I belong to Matthias.

He gives a gravelly hum in response, his embrace cinching tighter. My heart swells. Why does it feel so right in his arms?

"I'll hold you as long as you need," he promises. "Nothing can hurt you."

My throat stings and I burrow against his chest, tucking my nose into the crook of his neck. His strength and support are everything to me. From the first time we were attacked after they kidnapped me from my bed, he's guarded me with unwavering dedication. He's stopped my training whenever I'm too tired or over emotional. He makes sure I rest.

When I feel like I'll fall apart, he lets me. I don't have to hold myself together on my own as long as he's there to catch me.

"Thank you," I mumble.

Alder cards his fingers through my hair and massages my neck and shoulders with power warming his touch. I melt against him, allowing him to ease away my nightmare. He's patient while he comforts me. We exist in a bubble, just the two of us.

After a while, he traces my scars. He's not as relaxed as he was a few moments ago.

"Who hurt you?" The jagged demand slices through the quiet. He guides my chin so I face him instead of hiding. His mouth presses into a thin line. "Tell me what humans did to make you lose control and let your power out like this?"

I freeze. My throat constricts and I shake my head.

"I want to hunt them all down and rip them limb from limb for hurting you. Since I first saw them, I knew you had known pain no one should suffer," he growls. "They don't deserve to live another day for this."

My heart beats harder, a band tightening around my chest. I don't talk about this. He squeezes my hand and I think of his own scars. If he can turn out so strong and bear those scars, maybe I'll grow strong, too. Gulping, I tell him the truth.

"She's dead. She died in the fire I started." I close my stinging eyes as he brushes the pads of his thumbs across my marred skin. "It's only her memory that hurts. I was a monster all along, just like she always believed."

He makes a fierce noise refuting my words. "You are not a monster. I've known many monsters and you aren't one of them." He doesn't stop me from touching the red marks that crisscross his forearms. "My father. I descend from a line of demon warriors with a long-standing reputation. He wanted to uphold it. Forced me through harsh training, not understanding the importance of control."

My throat closes in sympathy and the cord in my chest draws me closer to him. I want to shield him from the pain of his past. Without a second thought, I lift his hand and press a kiss to his knuckles.

"You're nothing like that."

Our eyes meet and something snaps taut within me, tethering me to him. I can't fight the pull anymore. There's no way to resist what every part of me wants—him.

"Ald—" I begin to murmur his name urgently, but he captures my lips in a searing kiss.

It's over far too soon when he breaks it off. His harsh exhales fan over my skin in the small space that separates our mouths while his hands roam. He traces the shape of my jaw, down my neck, his inescapable gaze reverent.

My breath hitches when he traces the collar of the shirt I wore to bed, tugging on it. Neither of us acknowledge that it's his shirt, his scent wrapped around me that I slept in rather than the other clothes in my bag.

His hand trails lower, brushing my pebbled nipples through my shirt, mapping the softness of my stomach, my hips. At the edge of the shirt draping over my thigh, he keeps blurring the line. He takes a meandering path along my thigh, skimming higher.

I can't help squirming, silently urging him on, too afraid to speak and break this spell.

He stops short of where I'm aching, not going any further. Lowering his head, he mutters against my temple. "I should let you sleep."

The simmering heat in my body is unbearable and the pull in my chest won't be silenced.

"No," I whimper. "Please. Please touch me. I need you—"

I don't finish before he releases a rough noise and destroys the line drawn between us. The first stroke of his fingers against me makes me quiver and bite back a moan. He rubs my clit more firmly, with more purpose than Matthias' teasing. I like it just as much, writhing in his arms. It's exactly what I need right now.

"More," I demand.

He wrenches my underwear aside and sinks two thick fingers inside me. My back bows and he holds me steady. His fingers alone fill me, stretching my body to accommodate him.

"Matthias got to have you first, but I will be the first to taste you here." His fingers curl inside me. "The first to feel you come on my tongue."

"Wait." It bursts from me. He goes rigid, then begins to pull away. I put a hand on his chest, pressing closer as my pelvis rolls to grind on his hand to chase the pleasure he's giving me. "Ngh.

No, not—I don't want to stop. Please. I want to taste you, too."

His hypnotic green eyes gleam, cutting through the darkness to capture me. "Have you ever done that?"

I shake my head. The corner of his mouth lifts, the curve of it belonging to the same predator that once promised to chase me until he caught me. My heart stutters and my thighs clamp around his forearm, enjoying that look on him, a spark of pride racing through me because I put it there. The muscles flex as he plunges his fingers deeper inside me.

"Lay back," he says.

I watch while he peels my underwear down and discards them off the side of the bed. He wastes no time stripping out of his clothes, kneeling before me naked and unashamed, every inch of his muscular body on display. I stare at his huge cock, eager anticipation spiraling through me as liquid heat spills into my core. His hungry gaze tracks my tongue as I lick my lips.

Like Matthias, his cock is lined with two rows of ridged bumps, the tip leaking a copious amount of fluid that he spreads down his endless length while he works himself. If possible, his dick thickens more while he leers at me. Jesus. There's no chance of fitting even half of it in my mouth, let alone inside me. Still, a sensual thrill runs through me at the thought of trying and an answering thrum pulses in my chest to encourage me.

When I reach for the hem of my shirt, he catches my wrists. "Leave it. I want you to come wearing it."

I bite my lip. He's going to make me come while I wear his shirt.

Alder lays on his side next to me, his body turned the opposite way. His thick, long cock strains toward me. He hooks a hand under my knee to draw my thigh closer, nibbling a path up my sensitive flesh. Again he stops before he gets to where I want him so badly. A whimper escapes me.

"Open your mouth."

Bracing on an elbow, he cradles my head, threading his fingers into my hair. When I part my lips, he rumbles, attention fixated on my mouth as he guides the tip of his cock inside. Closing around it, I give a tentative suck. The velvety skin is hotter than the rest of his body, the tip smooth against my tongue when I press against it. I like the weight of it and the shape of the ridges, angling my head to take more in my mouth.

"Fuck. The sight of you with my cock in your perfect mouth will be permanently seared into my mind." His smoky scent grows muskier. Tightening his grip on my hair, his hips give a little jerk when I tongue the underside of his head. "I'm going to fucking devour you."

He lowers his face between my thighs, covering me with his mouth. The first swipe of his forked tongue makes me release a garbled cry. He pins my hips, sucking on my throbbing clit. I try to focus on sucking his cock, but what he's doing is too much, too good. Before I know it, I fly off the edge while he laps at my pussy, my core clenching as the ripples erupt from deep within me.

"Oh god," I hiss. "Oh my god, Alder. It feels so good."

"Not done yet." His tone is feral, stoking the wild flame within me.

With a deep growl and a yank on my leg, he pulls me on top of him, spreading my thick thighs wide and squeezing the globes of my ass while his mouth and tongue bring me the sweetest, most sinful pleasure imaginable. With his grip on my backside, he encourages me to rock on his face. He licks and sucks me without care for his need to breathe, entirely focused on heightening my pleasure. I'm consumed by the simmering heat spreading through me.

My fingers wrap around the base of his thick cock and I suck on it, moaning each time his tongue flicks across my clit. He's leaking into my mouth and I swallow his taste. Fitting his entire hard length is impossible, but a determined part of me that's high on this moment, enthralled in erotic abandonment wants to give him as much pleasure as he's giving me.

He tenses, fingers digging into my flesh. With a filthy groan, his cock twitches and come floods my mouth. It's all I can do to swallow some of it, the rest leaking out of my mouth when he doesn't stop eating me until I shatter again.

"You are every dream I've ever had come true," he whispers against my thigh while I tremble. "My stunning blossom."

My heart drums as I collapse on top of him. I'm distantly aware of him petting my thighs and tracing my spine. Time feels strange inside the hazy cloud of passion being with him has left me tangled in.

Once we catch our breath, he rearranges us so we're beneath the covers, dragging me back into his arms. I can barely function and I'm grateful for how he takes care of me.

All I know is how right this feels, my head on his bare chest as his thumb caresses my cheek, catching the remnants of his release I didn't manage to swallow. Drowsiness takes over, keeping my thoughts at bay. This is all that matters—the safe warmth blanketing me in Alder's arms.

"Sleep now, sweet blossom," he says gruffly. "I'm here. I won't let you go."

The bond feels more at ease in my chest as I drift off, my off-kilter world shifting closer to alignment.

Seventeen
LILY

It's official—I've cracked. I'm sure of it. Between being dragged into a supernatural world I'm somehow part of, life on the run from other demons, learning to use powers I didn't know I had hidden inside me, and finding a demon that is my fated mate I've grown greedy, wanting to live my life instead of watching it pass me by. Maybe it's Matthias' encouragement and determination to ensure I indulge and live in the moment.

This girl who doesn't tamp down on her emotions, who won't let what she wants slip through her fingers is unrecognizable. But I think I like her.

I want more.

Specifically, I still can't stop my heart from fluttering or my pussy from throbbing every time

Alder or Vale are near. And last night I gave in to the tempting desire, letting the pull I still feel towards my other demons have what it wants.

It's not possible to have more than one fated mate…is it? I'm still getting used to the idea that one person is destined to love me. The idea—the fleeting, impossible hope—that there could be more than one fated match for my heart is too good to be true.

Alder is still asleep, though another part of him is very much awake and pressed against my stomach. I admire his features, his stern practical nature softened in sleep. Despite his habit of getting the minimum amount of rest they need and taking the most watches, he stayed with me, holding me close the rest of the night. My heart pangs. I allow myself one more moment of resting in the cradle of his strong arms before I slip free.

I sit on the edge of the bed, reliving a dream where I didn't have to choose between the three demons who stole me away. They surrounded me in the dream, all of them touching me without hesitation, as if I'm someone they cherish above all else. It was like last night, Alder's head between my thighs, devouring me while Matthias held me in his lap, pinching my nipples to get me to arch as Vale grasped me by the throat and kissed me for an eternity. The three of them sharing me, devoted to me.

Want crashes over me so fast and strong that it steals my breath away, the insistent thrum in my chest expanding like it needs to break free.

My thighs slide together and a husky sigh leaves me. I wait for guilt to tarnish the incredible fantasy that played out in my dream, to berate me for what happened last night without stopping to think of Matthias, but it doesn't plague me. The bond purrs in my chest, wrapping around my heart like a supportive hug.

Maybe in Hell and the other underworld realms it's not a big deal to be with more than one person. I twist my fingers in Alder's shirt as hope rushes through me. I should ask Matthias and tell him about what happened with Alder last night while he was on guard. He let Alder watch in the car, and if Valerian hadn't interrupted, things might have gone further while I was pinned between them. I hold onto my suspicion from yesterday that he almost wants me to be with Alder, too.

Still, maybe I shouldn't have allowed the insatiable pull urging me on last night to control me without asking my mate if he was okay with it first. Things happened so fast, the pull so demanding that it was impossible to withstand. I don't want Matthias to decide that I'm not worth the trouble, fated mate or not.

My grip on the shirt becomes rigid. He won't hate me or decide he's done with me. I know he won't. I repeat it to myself until the side of me so ready to accept that people will throw me away fades into the depths of my mind.

"It's time to go."

Valerian interrupts my thoughts, making me startle and fall off the edge of the bed. I rub the plump curve of my ass, glaring at him. He lurks in the small alcove leading to the bathroom.

"Why did you have to sneak up on me?"

He lifts a brow, melting out of the shadows to stand over me. I squeeze my thighs together, remembering I'm bare beneath the shirt. My underwear is on the floor between us.

"You were the one enjoying a languid morning lie in." His smooth accent carries a bite to it that makes me hot all over. His eyes flick to the bed, the corners of his mouth tensing. "Both of you."

Cheeks prickling, I scramble to my feet. "Not that I have to explain myself to you, but I had a nightmare. He helped calm me down."

He doesn't answer, his cunning gaze moving over Alder's shirt hanging off my body in a sensual slide. His eyes flare, then he scoffs. "Calming you from a nightmare. That's why you stink of him." Expression hardening, he folds his arms, the abstract black swirls on his exposed forearms shifting in agitated movements beneath his rolled up sleeves. "Shower. I'm not getting in the car with you smelling like that again. You have five minutes."

Rolling my eyes, I shove past the broody bastard.

The ride to the witch is strained and silent. I'm miffed Valerian forced me out the door before I got to see Matthias, stating that we'd be late if he allowed me to get distracted again. It's the first time we're truly alone together. Since we first crossed paths, Vale's been careful to avoid being alone with me other than the one time he tracked me down at the library.

His demanding words stick in my mind, refusing to leave me alone. There's no way he was jealous to find Alder naked and holding me in bed, but the more his crisp accented words repeat in my head, the more I'm struggling to refute the jealousy in his tone.

The animosity between us has waned, yet it's not truly gone. It's no longer rooted in anger and contempt, but neither of us give up an inch when it comes to fighting with each other. Mainly because he knows exactly how to get under my skin and make me fly off the handle whenever he pushes my buttons and prods at my weaknesses. I don't despise him anymore, but when he challenges me I have a tendency to fight back before thinking. It's not like that with Alder and Matthias; with Vale, I think he finds enjoyment in trading barbs with me.

Looking at his scowling brows, the sharp slope of his nose, the shape of his frowning lips, I can't deny he's handsome. Devastatingly so. The side of me that allows him to get to me, that goads him because I enjoy testing him, does it on purpose because I think I crave his attention. The thought of those haunting blue eyes looking at anyone but me pierces my heart.

My attention slides to Valerian's pocket. I think he still has my other pair of underwear. I couldn't find them anywhere, not in my bag or left out in the room when I snatched up the pair Alder all but ripped off me last night. Vale's wearing the same dark pants and black button down he wore yesterday, the sleeves rolled up, tempting me with his tattooed forearms on display.

Warmth creeps up my neck as I picture my underwear draped on the gearshift between us. I wonder how debauched I looked spread on Matthias' lap, bared for Valerian and Alder. Peeking over my shoulder, I scan the leather for any inkling of what happened, for proof that I had all three of them contributing in some way to my orgasms.

If things had been different and Valerian had my

body spread and at the mercy of his whims, would our passion feel different?

Yes. I sense the truth of it without a doubt.

When I fight with Vale, the fire he ignites in me is hotter, the burn more intense. I know it would consume us both if we gave the tension between us free rein.

As the journey continues, I judge the distance to our destination by Valerian's shoulders growing tenser and the sharpness of his smoky scent pressing in on me from all sides. The wheel begins to smoke beneath his rigid grip, fingertips glowing with smoldering embers of his power leaking out. He never lacks this much control over himself. It sets me on edge that he's worried enough for it to show, his brooding no longer able to hide his emotions.

"What will happen if the witch succeeds and breaks this seal binding me in this human body?" I bite my lip as soon as the words are out, stomach cramping at letting him witness my vulnerability. It's worth the risk because the nerves are about to eat me alive. "Will I still be me?"

He takes a long beat to answer, eyes narrowing on the winding road leading up the rolling hills. "I can't say for sure. You're the first changeling I've encountered."

The lack of reassurance that this version of me—Lily Sloane, a stubborn girl learning there's a fighter within her wanting to be let out and take on the world—won't be destroyed to make way for the demon I truly am doesn't bode well. Is anything about me real? A bitter thought surfaces. My love of isekai manga might even be born of some part of me longing for another world I'm meant to return to. Anything I've ever liked in life could be attributed to the person trapped by the magic seal.

I could be temporary. Fleeting and easily forgotten. Replaceable.

Acid churns in my stomach and I shift uncomfortably. I should be used to it by now. I've been rejected, returned, and replaced my whole life. A hot sting slides down my throat. I don't want to go. Don't want to leave Matthias or the others. Don't want to be forgotten and left behind.

Vale studies me, his dark blue gaze penetrating. "No matter what, keep your guard up. Don't divulge information unless I give you permission."

I cross my arms. "It's my body. My power trapped inside me. Why are you suddenly the boss of it?"

He gives me a hard look. "Because it's my duty to protect you and I won't fail it. Demons and witches have a shaky relationship in the mortal realm at best. We are natural enemies. They summon us through rituals and trap us within their sigils to siphon our power."

My mouth drops open. "Then why is the witch agreeing to help?"

Before responding, he turns into a mulch driveway under an ivy-covered arch of woven sticks and vines. The air here feels different. Even inside the car, it seeps through the steel and glass, twisting around me.

"Hallowed ground." His mouth flattens. "She's blessed her land to ward off those that mean her harm. It's testing you."

Stones capped with dried moss line the driveway and damp dead leaves blanket everything. A small creek runs alongside us and circles around a cottage. When we stop, he gets out, scanning the area with a calculating sweep.

"I thought demons couldn't step foot on hallowed ground?" I stretch my stiff legs and adjust my distressed shorts from rolling up.

"Another myth humans adapted to convince themselves they were safe from the predatory fae who hunt them. One the priests borrowed from the very witches they burned at the stake, if I'm not mistaken." He steers me by his grip on the back of my neck, halting before we enter the covered porch. "If I give you an order, follow it. Understand?"

My nape tingles where he squeezes firmly, leaving me slightly lightheaded as my stomach dips. "Fine."

He pounds a fist on the door. "Witch!"

The door opens a few moments later and an unimpressed woman with crow's feet at the corners of her freckled face eyes us, giving Valerian a shrewd once over. "Demon." She narrows her eyes, then waves an arm in invitation. "My name is Lane."

"Hi, I'm Lily. Thanks for your help."

I glare at Valerian when he clamps on my neck hard, ignoring the burst of heat throbbing in my core. What harm is there in giving my name? It's not world-ending information.

Lane's wavy brown hair is tied back and shot through with streaks of silver, though she doesn't appear burdened by age. She moves spryly through her house as we follow to a kitchen with a worn round table and dried herbs hanging from the exposed beams. Like the rest of the cottage, her kitchen is cluttered at first glance, every worktop covered in repurposed tea tins, candles, and an eclectic mix of knickknacks. I get the sense she's a woman who enjoys spending her time in nature and working her land.

"My sisters assured me you'd pay well for my help." She wipes her hands on an apron and gestures to a chair. "Sit."

"And they assured me you're the best at dealing with spells of a binding nature." Valerian positions himself behind me, bracing his hands on the high back of my seat. "Your payment depends on that skill."

"Best on the east coast," Lane says airily. "Let me get a sense of you, Lily."

She lights a stick of cloying incense and brings it to the table, wafting it around me. Vale releases a low growl in warning when she grasps my chin. She ignores him, turning my face from side to side before taking my hands and closing her eyes.

"Oh," she murmurs.

"Is something wrong?" he demands.

"No, it's just—the pain. It's overwhelming."

I duck my head, face flaming. He didn't mention the witch would be able to see through me in under thirty seconds.

"What about the seal?" He presses closer, his torso brushing against the back of my head. There's an urgency I've never seen from him bleeding through his sternness. "Can you sense if her memories are there?"

"I need to put her in a meditative state to get a better sense of the binding. It's strong. Though I'm able to discern that she's stronger." Lane hums and creases her brow. "This feels as though she was forced into a rebirth. If that's true, there's a chance there aren't memories to find locked in her head. She may only have echoes and fragments left of her past life."

I exchange a glance with Vale when she moves away. The corners of his mouth are downturned in thought. A knot forms in my stomach. What's rebirth for a demon? Did someone kill me and reincarnate me?

Another awful thought pops in my head. He seems to care about the demon inside more than me. If I don't live up to his expectations, he'll abandon me as a lost cause that upset the balance of his life as a guard for nothing.

"Here." Lane returns with a tray of crystals, a small green bottle, and a hammered bronze dish stacked with orange marigolds. "Drink the potion."

Before I bring it to my lips, Vale snatches it, giving it a whiff. He glares at Lane. "Poison."

"No. It's a small dose of belladonna to encourage the meditative trance. It's not enough to poison her." Lane places an amethyst in one of my hands and clear quartz in the other, sitting them face up on the table. "The quartz will act as a vessel to take on the energy scribed to it, keeping you grounded. The amethyst will promote mental clarity to help us navigate your mind and find the path to the magical seal binding you. And for distrustful demonic minds, the calendula flowers are for me. They bring positivity to the spell."

"Sounds legit," I say.

She huffs in amusement, casting a baleful

glance at Valerian. "That's because it is. Now, take the potion and close your eyes while I chant the incantation to guide you into the trance state."

"Bottoms up." I toast Vale and down the slightly sweet concoction.

The trickle tingles down my throat, spreading outward gradually until my fingers and toes feel numb. Everything is heavy. Lifting a finger takes effort. My head lolls back and Vale stares down at me with concern, cradling my face. He strokes my cheeks, mouthing my name. I can't hear him clearly over Lane's chanting, like I'm underwater. The thought sends a spike of panic through me, and he brushes his knuckles down my cheeks when Lane waves a hand at him.

The last thought to cross my mind before the darkness at the edges of my vision takes over is that he looks nice with his tousled black hair falling in his face like that.

Eighteen
LILY

"Vale," I mumble.

"—here. Right here, little flower."

The soft touch to my cheek feels so good. I nuzzle into it, seeking more.

A bright flickering light to my left distracts me. I'm not in Lane's kitchen anymore, but the hall from my dream with obsidian floors and stone arches. I turn my back on it, not interested in visiting the throne room. Although—the guys could be there. The need to see them crashes over me.

My demons, my heart tethers, my home.

I pick up the gauzy material of my skirts and hurry down the halls, passing columns lit from the floor by pools of eternal hellfire flames. The closer I get, the longer the hall stretches. That's not right. I know this wing of the demon king's castle.

"Matthias?" I call. "Alder? Valerian!"

My voice echoes off the high walls. An inky swirl of black smoke rises from the floor to my right, circling faster in a churning frenzy until it forms a portal. The king—?

Red eyes glow within the magic and the demon's clawed hands snatch me. Something pushes me back hard.

When I blink my eyes open with a wheezing gasp, Lane's face is pale, her attention locked on a bowl of water that bubbles and turns black.

"My wards." It's the only thing she gets out before Valerian wrenches me from the seat, sending both of us crashing to the floor as the back door blasts open in a rain of fire.

"Go!" he commands.

Four terrifying cloaked demons charge through the door with impossible speed, short, deadly black horns, and white hair. Two of them converge on Lane. Horror traps me in place when they grab her by her hair and slash her neck before she can do any magic to counter them. The sachet clutched in her hand falls to the ground and her eyes bulge in shock. Then her body drops to the floor, severed from the head the demon grips by her hair.

An ear-splitting scream rips from my lungs.

Grunting viciously, Valerian pushes to his feet.

His tattoos shift as hellfire erupts from his fists. He punches the first demon he rushes, throwing up an arm to block the second that goes for him. He's a sight to behold when he fights, his speed and ruthlessness unmatched. His black elongated talons spear one of his opponents under their wide jaw while he holds the other back with a wall of firepower.

The other two turn their attention on me, dropping Lane's head. Opening their fanged maws, they both let out chilling growls. They advance on me and I scramble back, banging my head on a cabinet. My flames spark along my arms and sputter out at my fingertips, blocked by the fear coursing through my veins.

Valerian's demanding voice fills my head. *Don't panic. Control it.* It's followed by Alder's gruff encouragement. *The power is yours, blossom. It's not something you need to fear.* Then Matthias' warm tone wraps around me. *You're more amazing than you realize, pretty girl.*

I can do this. I can help fight against our attackers.

This is my power. My life that's been toyed with, stolen, and locked away from my access. Whoever the hell the demon is trapped inside me, these fuckers don't get to kill her or me.

They come for me as a unified force, undeterred by the ball of flame I morph between my palms. I fling it and curse when the one on the left dodges while I scramble to my feet. The demon's yellow eyes flash like he's mocking me. As I gather tingling energy in my hands to form another blast, they draw swords, dragging their claws along the blade with an awful screech. Fire licks along the weapons and they raise them.

Oh god. I'm not as fast as them. How do I block a fucking flaming sword?

"Lily!"

Valerian's hoarse roar cuts through the terror freezing me in place as the demons' swords arc down. He throws himself in front of me, directly in the line of attack. My mind splits in two, the scene overlaid with a strange vision—instead of his black shirt, he wears a knight's attire like Rainer's.

The swords find a new mark, slashing into his sides as he blasts them back with a strong wave of flame and hot air before he staggers on his feet and falls to one knee with a groan.

"No! Vale!" My chest aches as if the blades pierced my heart.

This is my worst nightmare come to life. The sight of him hurt, crouched on the floor in pain because he protected me unlocks a fathomless well inside my chest that demands retribution. It's the same fierce feeling that erupted from me when Alder threatened to kill Matthias.

A savage noise bursts from me and my power explodes like a furious star. Bands of fire lash out from me, my arms spread and my head thrown back. They whip around the room, claiming the neck of each demon. I choke them, my flames forcing down their throats. Their legs kick as I lift them into the air, their strangled sounds of pain not enough to pay for what they've done. Baring my teeth, I eviscerate them, burning their bodies to ash from the inside out.

Blood rushes in my ears and I collapse, the power retreating. I gasp for air from how much it drained my energy, taking in the destruction surrounding me—Lane's wrecked kitchen, her dead body, and what little remains of the demons.

My heart leaps into my throat when I lock eyes with Valerian. He's propped against the cabinets, intense gaze trained on me. Straining against my dizziness, I rush to his side.

He stares at me in astonished reverence. "Lili—" He cuts off, gritting his teeth and pressing a hand to his side. His hand comes away bloody. "Damn it."

Grabbing his wrist, an agonized breath catches in my throat. His dark blood soaks the tattered black shirt, the deep gashes visible through the holes. "You're hurt. Don't move."

I swallow the painful lump clogging my throat and scrounge around the kitchen in search of medical supplies, casting an apologetic glance at Lane. This is my fault. Her death, the attack, Vale getting hurt.

"Sorry Lane."

There's nothing I recognize, only herbs and unmarked bottles. A floral tablecloth in the next room catches my eye. With a sweep of my arm, I knock the contents from the table and shred strips off the tablecloth. Kneeling at his side with a bowl of water and the makeshift bandages, I grimace at how much blood there is. I've never seen any of my demons this badly injured.

"There's no first aid kit. This will have to do." I shove aside everything around us and focus on him.

He remains surprisingly quiet while I fuss over him, obliging without argument when I unbutton his shirt and help him out of it. I wet my lips, sparing a moment to admire his physique while I carefully dab a damp cloth to his sides to clean them.

The abstract ink on his arms moves in reaction when I brush my fingertips over his abs for balance to reach his other side. Intrigued, I repeat the touch, lower and the tattoos shift faster. I keep working diligently until it's clear he's not going to die if I don't stop the bleeding. Curiosity gets the best of me and I trace the whorls covering his arms, the smoke-like ink morphing into shadowy outlines. The tattoos respond to me, fascinating me when they seem to curl around my touch.

I tilt my head. "What does that feel like? Can you control the movement, or is it just part of magic tattoos?"

He remains silent, nostrils flared as he scents the air. There's an unreadable look in his eye when I chase one of the smoky shapes to the inside of his elbow, a thrum echoing inside me when I catch it. His chest expands with a deep, shuddering breath. I tear my hand away, worried I've hurt him. Biting my lip, I resume tending to his injuries.

"This is pointless." Other than the mild interjection, he does nothing to stop me, tracking everywhere I touch him like he doesn't want to miss a second of it.

"Why? Don't tell me some bullshit about being too stubborn to accept help." I drop the bloodied cloth in the murky water, frowning at how bad the wounds look. "Just shut up and let me repay the favor of saving your life, asshole."

His lips twitch at the almost fond way the derogatory term comes out. I clear my throat, busying myself with wrapping his torso with bandages.

"I'm not going to die. Demons have the ability to heal. This drained my energy, that's all." He rests his head against the cabinet. "It will take some time to replenish my strength."

"How can you replenish your strength?" I pull a face. "You don't strike me as the bed rest type.

Should I get you Powerade or something?"

The smile he gives me is feral, fangs peeking out. He leans closer, erasing the small distance between us. "When in the mortal realm without access to the natural power that sustains us in the underworld, two ways. One, consuming souls."

Usually the thought pisses me off, but the way he traps me in his stare sparks a wildfire that grows from an ember and quickly engulfs me. Gulping, I whisper, "And two?"

Vale's hand skates over my hip, traveling up my side, thumb brushing the edge of my breast while his attention falls to my parted lips. This time I'm the one that inches closer, our hot exhales mingling.

"Feeding on another kind of energy," he rasps, tracing the curve of my breast maddeningly slow. His fingers dig in. "Like what you feel between you and—your mate."

Matthias. Or does he mean Alder? My mind flickers between both of them. He lifts his hand and wraps his fingers around my throat, wicked gaze promising me sinful bliss if I give in to the temptation. It's happening again. The invisible force tied around my heart drawing me closer, and in different directions. I want this. I want to kiss Valerian.

No, I need to kiss him. More than I need my next breath. My entire being urges me to close the scant gap.

Before our lips touch, he stills, then glances around. *We need to go. We should get back to the others. I smell the blood of the witch's coven on these demons. They're from the assassin's guild.*

I blink. His voice filtered through my head, but his mouth didn't move. "Did—Did you just talk inside my head? Like, telepathically?"

Shock flits across his face before he nods sternly. "Alder can control consciousness. Matthias has the ability to persuade the mind. My gift is communicating without speaking aloud. Come on. It's not safe to stay here."

"Wait, can you read my mind?"

"It doesn't work like that." He takes my hand to help him to his feet, clenching his jaw. "Only with a special bonded connection, like the one between fated mates, is capable of creating a true mental link."

He pauses at the door to pass a devious look over me. A moment later, my mind floods with the mental image of exactly how I looked from his point of view in the back seat of the car, riding the fingers Matthias buried inside me with abandon.

"Dude," I hiss.

He smirks. "As you can see, I can push thoughts into your head." He stops me from patting him down for the keys. "No. I'm driving. Get in."

I'm too occupied with the buzzing warmth spreading through me at the image he put in my head to argue. Once we get off Lane's property, he floors it. I'm not a religious person, but I glance back and offer another silent apology for getting her killed.

"Why didn't you talk to me that way before?"

His hand moves from the gearshift, reaching for me. It falls short and he balls his fist. "I had no interest."

The curt brush off feels forced. This hidden skill explains how the three of them seem to get by with few words sometimes. When they've fought off the demons after us, they move as a unit despite how different they are.

As we race away from the cottage, part of me wishes we could have stayed in that stolen moment longer so I could know what it's like to kiss him.

Nineteen
LILY

Once we reach the others, we don't sit around. Valerian decides motels aren't safe anymore. Within minutes, we're in the car speeding away in a winding path to the nearest city, circling around and trailing in a different direction. At certain points of our meandering journey, he makes us get out to purposely leave a trace of our scents before we're on the road again.

Then at random, he directs Alder to pull in when we pass a remote cabin in the middle of the Appalachian Mountains. It looks like a vacation home. The quaint house has a dead garden and stale dust coating everything when we get inside after me and Matthias find a rusty spare key hidden under the porch.

The garden makes me think of Lane again. She didn't deserve to die because of me. I hug myself, wishing I could've saved her.

"There's practically no human scent here," Matthias says. "Should be safe enough with the scents we left to throw them off. We'll triple the barriers on our perimeter to be sure. The gates in this area are far off. The nearest one feels like it's at least two hours away."

"As long as they're unable to track us after we doubled back to the mountains from the opposite direction. They're not likely to expect us to return to the same area near where they attacked you," Alder mutters. "Now, tell us what the hell happened? Did the knight set you up?"

We only gave a brief picture of what we went through at Lane's cottage, Valerian unwilling to divulge more details until he was sure we were safe.

He sets his jaw. "No. Rainer owes me a life debt. Besides that, he wouldn't betray me. He's one of the few that believed losing my charge wasn't my fault."

His gaze seeks me out. It's the same strange look he had in the cottage. I cover the insistent thump of my heart with a hand.

"We were attacked by assassins. The Shadow Vanguard, going by their white hair and swords," Valerian says. "They have to be tracking the witches because I could smell the blood of the coven I met with that sent me to this witch."

I cast my eyes down. More blood on my hands. Alder said I'm not a monster, yet I'm feeling the label fits right now.

"Damn. That highly classed? They only go after the priciest bounties." Alder scrubs the top of his head, tugging on the longer brown locks on top. "That was smart since the hellhounds haven't been able to keep on us. How did you fight them off?"

"Lily. It makes more sense to me now." Valerian studies me. "She has an incredible amount of dormant power at her fingertips. More than we sensed. She took all four assassins down with one attack. Her demon is someone important, high ranking—high *value*. Someone that others would benefit from by getting rid of her with the level of power she has. It's more than enough to rival the Devil's and must be why the demon council has every faction hunting us to protect their seats."

The reverence and respect coloring his tone recounting how powerful my counterattack was when he was injured catches me off guard.

"Do you know who?" Alder asks.

Valerian hesitates. He covers it quickly, but I don't miss the flicker in his eyes. "Not yet."

"Did the witch break the seal?" Matthias grasps my chin, bringing his face close to study me. "You don't look any different, pretty girl."

Needing him, I close my fingers around his wrist and press on my toes to kiss him. *Oh*. My heart swells at the swipe of his tongue. I missed this. Missed him. He wraps me in his arms with an affectionate hum that chases away my guilty sadness for the witches.

As long as my demons are okay, I'll be okay.

"No," Valerian answers. "The only answers we got are that she might have been forced to reincarnate."

Alder releases an unhappy rumble, pressing against my back while Matthias strokes my hair. Between them I'm safe and warm. Could it be this easy to have them both? To share their love and fit them both into my heart? An empty void tells me I still have room for more in my hungry heart.

"No demon I know would challenge our laws like that." I lift my head and Alder elaborates for me. "It's forbidden. Reincarnation is a gift from the fae gods demons descend from. Forcing it is sadistic torture, keeping the demon from healing, on the edge of death until they trigger the regeneration."

I shudder, picturing the swirling black portal that swallowed me whole. Is that what awaited me on the other side?

"The witch put her in a meditative spell to access the seal, but we were interrupted before we could find out for sure," Valerian says.

"It felt like something pushed me out." I frown.

"I thought maybe it was because her concentration broke, but could it be the seal keeping me out?"

"Yes." Matthias touches my temple. "The mind is a complex thing. Like when you broke free of my persuasive thrall to stay in the car. It can be swayed, but for the complete block of a binding seal, the magic has its own layer of protection to convince the mind to stay away."

"What did you see when you entered your mental plane?" Valerian asks.

"I was in a castle. It had an eerie gothic vibe, like Dracula would definitely live there." Matthias snorts, kissing my forehead. "It also felt...familiar. I knew the hall I was in would lead to a throne room."

The three of them exchange a glance. Alder squeezes my shoulders. "That's Lucifer's castle at the heart of Hell in the Towering City."

I nod slowly in acceptance. There isn't any running from this or ignoring it.

"I've dreamed of it before today. I knew my way around. At Lane's, I was going to the throne room to see if you guys were there like in my dream. Before I got there some kind of—portal, I think? Smoke gathered from the floor and swirled around. Someone grabbed me through it."

Valerian braces against the back of the sofa, staring out at the sun setting behind the mountain view through the door that leads to the deck.

"Alder."

"Right." His nose touches my crown and he inhales. "I do not wish to leave you, sweet blossom."

"What?" Whirling around I grab two fistfuls of his fitted t-shirt. "Don't go."

"We need to set the protective wards so we can settle here for the next few days," Valerian says. "After that, I need to find Rainer."

Alder nods. "We should check if the demons hunted the other witches down. We can keep muddying our trail so we're harder to track, too."

Valerian pushes off the couch with a faint flinch of pain. "Agreed. Matthias, you'll guard Lily."

"With my life," Matthias says.

"Are you insane?" I release Alder, ignoring the crack in my heart to block Vale's path. "You're still hurt!"

"I'm fine. It's faster if the two of us go alone." The tip of his serpent-like tongue traces his lower lip. "You can play nurse later. Stay put. I mean it."

He uses his most demanding tone and cups my face, throwing me right back to the moment we almost kissed. The tether in my chest strains with the desire to crash against him and taste his lips. His blue gaze flares brighter.

The tense beat breaks when he nudges me into Matthias's waiting arms. The scent of maple and roasted chestnuts surrounds me.

"I'll take care of you, mate," Matthias says against my ear in a rough tone that makes me shudder.

Vale holds my eye. "We won't be gone long. Before the night's out, we'll return."

The pull in my chest tugs as I watch two of my demons leave me behind. Even Valerian's promise doesn't soften the fractures splintering my heart.

It's been too long. I'm sick of pacing, my stomach tying itself in knots. Matthias isn't faring better, his usual easy nature tinged with restless agitation.

"I can't take this." I scrub my face. "I don't like not knowing what's going on or if they're okay."

"I know. Come here, petal." He pulls me into his arms and flops us on the thick chaise cushion of the L-shaped couch with me resting on his chest.

Guilt clangs around inside me for a moment. Matthias hasn't left my side, indulging my need to keep moving. He's done everything to keep my mind occupied to steer me away from spiraling into an anxiety-induced panic. As soon as the guys left, he suggested we explore the house and check if the hot tub on the deck worked so we could try to relax. It didn't, unfortunately. We did find a questionable shrine to Mothman in the basement, complete with totally Photoshopped blurry photos of the cryptid, a hand-sewn costume, and some sexy Mothman fan art.

"I just hate waiting," I mumble into his neck.

He plays with my hair, combing through it soothingly. "Want to see if there are any movies? I didn't see a VHS player, but hopefully they've got something."

"It's all on disc now. DVD. It's more compact."

He makes an inquisitive sound. "Such clever creatures. So what do you say, babe?" He claps his hands on my plump ass and squeezes. "Let's pretend the world doesn't exist for a minute and we've escaped for a lover's holiday. We'll act like we're watching the movie until we can't keep our hands off each other. I'll eat your pussy until the credits roll and you're crying for me to stop because it's too much."

"That's called Netflix and chill now." I giggle at his quirked eyebrow.

"There's that smile I love so much." He kisses me, keeping my laughter going when he attacks my face with more light kisses.

This is what I like about being with Matthias. He does everything to make me smile and make me feel worshiped. He also reminds me life doesn't have to be so serious. With him, I can laugh even when the world around me feels like it's about to fall apart.

"Sometimes I forget you're older than you seem until you remind me you're basically stuck in the 90s." I give him a wry smile, shyly tugging on a lock of his hair. "How old are you really? You seem younger than the others."

"Not by much. Vale is the oldest, but age is relative to us. Demons don't celebrate the way humans do." He pretends to chomp on my finger, grinning around the digit and coiling his tongue around my knuckle until I squirm. "If I seem young, it's a personality flaw for a trickster demon like me. Chaos is addictive."

"Yeah, you give off that vibe." I smirk. "When we first met, I called you fuckboy in my head."

He waggles his brows. "Before I became of age, I kept sneaking through the gates. The demon academy had a hell of a time controlling me. It was decided that I'd be assigned as a gate guard. They thought it was a lesson in restraint, but I lived my best life every time I got to go topside."

I shake my head, smiling easier than I have all night. "You showed them."

"You know it, babe." He cups my face. "I think I was so drawn to this realm because I've been searching for you."

Our bond hums, twining around my heart in contentment.

"Okay, so if not a movie, what would you do,

then? Pretend we're not on the run. Hit me with your ideal day." The corner of his mouth lifts. "I promise to make it happen because you deserve the world, my pretty girl."

A warm glow fills my chest when he talks like that, like he cherishes me. I guess a fated mate is wired to love the one they're bonded to, but I still have trouble believing he feels that way for me.

I blush, licking my lips. "I doubt Vale and Alder would let us do that."

Matthias brushes my cheek with his knuckles. "Pretend the underworld isn't in chaos and our lives aren't at stake. What would make you happy?"

"I don't think anyone's ever asked me that," I admit. "People in my life were always more focused on how messed up they believed I was."

His smile falters and he draws me down for a kiss. "You never have to face that again. I'm asking you now, so tell me."

I roll my lips between my teeth as I open up a part of my mind I've kept closed off and neglected. What I want... Scenes from my isekai manga pop into my head.

"I've always dreamed of seeing the world. The foster system bounced me around, but I've never been to the beach. If I could do anything, I'd want to do that."

"And swim in the ocean?" he asks cautiously.

"I'm surprised after your reaction at the lake."

"Oh. Well, I know the ocean is saltwater. I think I would be okay. It's just freshwater that makes me think of—"

I blow out a breath. I can tell him. It's scary, but I have him and the others to protect me now. I'm not alone anymore.

"Of the well water. The taste, the smell. It makes me relive what I'm afraid of."

"We'll rewrite all the bad memories with good ones. I promise."

Relief spills through me at his lack of judgment. "You'd really take me to the beach?"

"I'd take you anywhere you want to go." His serious expression clears and he winks to lighten the mood. "Plus, I love sex on the beach."

I pinch him. "Matthias!"

He smirks. "I could put on the costume we found downstairs and we could indulge in a sexy role play game to cure ourselves of going stir crazy."

"I'm not a monster fucker, you dick."

"Just demons, then?" His dimpled grin is unapologetic. "You do bring out the beast in me, mate. I can be more monstrous for you. Anything you need, baby."

When I sock him in the side, he snickers, forked tongue poking out from the side of his mouth. I kiss him to cut off his laugh, chasing that mischievous tongue. He threads his fingers in my hair and rolls us over, pinning me to the couch while he claims my mouth. The kiss turns hot fast, fueled by our anxiousness and uncertainty. We both need to feel right now.

Matthias slides a hand under my shirt and we break apart so he can whip it off. My bra follows and I arch with a moan as his mouth captures my nipple while he palms my other breast. He trails his way down my body, worshiping every curve, every dip and fold with sultry kisses, murmuring how beautiful and soft I am.

I gasp as he drags my shorts and panties off. "I need—"

"I know, pretty girl." He gets on his knees and tugs me to the edge, settling between my spread thighs. Blond hair falling across his forehead, he peers up the length of my body, snaring me in his sultry golden gaze. "I can smell how badly you want my cock, and I'm going to give it to you, baby. But I'm fucking starving for you. I need to feast on your first."

"Oh god." The first swipe of his tongue is heaven.

Like the kiss, the glide of his mouth on my pussy heats up quickly. He doesn't draw it out to tease me with sweet torture, but insists I come on his tongue. He devours my pussy. When his tongue pushes inside me, I whimper, grabbing hold of his hair. He groans against my slick folds as my hips undulate.

Then I shatter for him, the tidal wave of pleasure rolling through me for long moments. He releases a gravely noise as he positions his thick cock at my entrance and thrusts inside, filling me with his dizzying length. I gasp, nails scrabbling on his back. The ridges on his cock rub the sensitive spot still throbbing from my first orgasm, another one racing up to steal my breath as he sets a hard, wild pace.

"Fuck, your pussy feels amazing, petal. So good for me, squeezing my cock so tight. Is this what you needed? My cock destroying your pussy, making you come all over it?"

All I can do is push out a breathy moan and hold on, engulfed in the molten heat between us. His thrusts have so much divine force, each one scoots me up the chaise until he climbs onto the cushion, covering my body with his. He hooks an arm beneath my knee and wraps my other leg around his hips, positioning me so I feel him even deeper when he drives his cock inside me. My mouth falls open on a scream of pleasure.

It doesn't register that the door opened until the blended scent of woodsmoke and rich hickory hit my nose.

They're back.

Matthias doesn't stop, pinning my wrists over my head. There's no break in his pace as Alder and Vale come into view past his shoulder, the hot press of their gazes making me writhe in sinful ecstasy.

Alder's eyes darken with desire at the sight of Matthias fucking me with wild abandon without stopping. I meet his fiery green gaze and cry out, clenching on Matthias' cock. Matthias groans, burying his face in my neck, nibbling at my flushed skin.

He braces over me, giving me a filthy smirk. "You like the audience, petal? You're getting wetter by the second. They're watching you, Lily." A hot, dirty chuckle falls from his lips as my core throbs and tightens around him. He glances over his shoulder at the others, then looks at me with a challenge in his hooded golden eyes. "Show them how gorgeous you are when you come on my cock."

Alder rumbles, coming closer. Valerian hangs back, leaning against the wall. God, he's staying to watch instead of leaving. A strangled moan catches in my throat as Alder kneels next to the chaise, his breath ghosting over my neck before his lips connect. Matthias grins, adjusting to give Alder room to fondle my tits as his tongue licks a stripe up my pulse point, taking over pinning my wrists in one big hand as they wrench pleasure from me.

"Show us, Lily," Alder rasps. "I want to see you

come. Soak his cock."

With a choked gasp, I flutter my eyes open and seek out Valerian, burning up from the intensity of his attention locked on every move I make. I tear my eyes away with effort, meeting Alder's smoldering stare as he drinks me in and teases my nipples. Then Matthias grasps my chin and steals my focus, his eyes flooding with lust at the obscene sound of his cock driving into me from how wet I am, the slickness dripping down my thighs.

This is so much more intense than what happened in the car. The thrum in my chest sings in harmony as I come hard with all three of their gazes trained on me.

"That's it, petal. So beautiful when you cream my cock like that." Matthias reaches between us, touching where my body is stretched around his hardness. He brings his glistening fingers to his mouth and groans. "You taste so fucking sweet. Here, you need to taste her right now."

Matthias grabs Alder's arm and guides him to do the same. His thick fingers skate over my folds, rubbing my clit. A low growl vibrates in his chest as I tip my head back, lips parted. I pant under his unwavering stare as he brings me to the brink again. When I fly off the edge into oblivion, my pussy fluttering around Matthias' dick, Alder swipes my wetness and sucks his fingers clean without breaking eye contact.

He dips his head to capture my lips, letting me taste my own pleasure when his tongue pushes into my mouth to glide against mine in a searing kiss. I wrap my arms around his shoulders, clinging to him while they both stoke the inferno blazing within me. He swallows my gasp when he surprises me by shifting his fingers into claws, grazing my skin. Matthias does the same, teasing my hips with light scrapes that have me shaking apart with a breathless moan.

If it's this unbearably good with two of them, what would it be like if I was with all three of them at the same time? I wish Vale would come kneel on my other side and give me the kiss I wanted so badly earlier.

Movement in the corner of my eye snags my attention. Valerian moves to the kitchen, ignoring the depraved scene at the edge of his periphery. He raids the cabinets with meticulous focus, pulling down a forgotten, half full bottle of whiskey. He doesn't bother with a glass, swigging straight from the bottle.

My chest clenches, then loosens at Matthias' croon in my ear. "Do you think this pretty little pussy could take two of our cocks at once if we shared you?" He hums when my core flutters. "Good girl. Soon, petal. Soon we'll both fill you at once and show you that you belong to us."

"Yes," I whimper.

The orgasm that crashes over me at his possessive, claiming words is intense and all-consuming, pulsing through my body in time with the thrum of the bond in my chest. Matthias braces above me as his dick throbs, swelling even thicker inside me on the next thrust. I lose my breath at the full sensation, the stretch overwhelmingly good. My head lolls and my vision swims as sparks of ecstasy race through me.

"Are you knotting her first after you also had her first, you bastard?" Alder growls.

"Can't help it," Matthias grits out. "Fuck, she feels so good."

I'm aware of Alder smoothing my hair back, of Matthias brushing his lips across mine, the place where we're connected, and the shivers of blissful passion racking my body. Everything else fades away as I drift in and out for a long stretch, my heart beating hard and the bond in my chest reverberating with an incandescent glow.

"It's okay, sweet blossom. We've got you," Alder murmurs. "You're doing so well. Taking your mate's knot is intense the first time, especially for a human body. Just let go and let us take care of you."

Twenty
LILY

WE PLAN TO MOVE FROM THE CABIN AS SOON AS Valerian heals. The morning after, I was surprised by how much better the wounds looked when I caught him shirtless, a towel wrapped low on his waist while he made coffee in the kitchen. He turned at my sharp inhale, meeting my eye with a smirk when I muttered I was glad he wasn't on death's door.

Neither of us brought up what happened when he returned with Alder and caught Matthias fucking me.

The memory of how it ended is still hazy. I came back to myself in a warm bath, resting against Alder's hard chest while Matthias gently washed away the mild soreness between my thighs. The adoration in his bright gold eyes made my heart float all day.

But it doesn't dull my frustration that the answers are out of reach because of the attack. It eats at me. I throw myself into training while we're at the cabin, determined to improve. I'm at it day and night, pushing my powers to obey my command until my legs shake, ready to buckle from draining my energy. Alder tries to stop me the first day, but Vale intervenes and tells him to let me do what I want. I've lost track, the hours bending together, sunsets becoming sunrises.

I'm getting sick of running. I have to get better so we can stop this insane hunt for our heads before it gets us killed.

Training this hard also means I have an excuse not to talk to Matthias about Alder and Vale. It's shitty of me, but when I see his affectionate smile, my chest constricts. I'm terrified my mate will look at me with hatred like every other person that was supposed to love me. Choked by the fear he'll be angry because I have feelings for the others. I couldn't bear it, but I'm powerless to stop what I feel.

It's not just Alder and Matthias I'm torn between. It's Vale, too. Almost losing him made it clear that I don't want a world without him in it, challenging me, pushing my buttons, igniting my need to fight back.

Matthias said I belonged to both of them, yet I can't quiet the fear lurking in the back of my mind that he'll reject me.

I shove everything stressing me out from my mind, bracing my hands on my hips as I catch my breath. My panting clouds the night air in the woods behind the cabin where I've cobbled together my practice area.

Gritting my teeth at the ache in my arms, I lift them and force my hellfire to spill into my palms. The lid I pulled off the broken hot tub—my makeshift target—has holes singed in it. This time I'll hit a bullseye. My focus zeroes in on the spot I want to go. I push with all my might, the fireball bursting from my hands.

The force knocks me back and my twinging legs give out.

"Fuck!" The fireball skews to the left, taking out a bush as I tumble backwards, landing on my ass in the dirt.

"Stop shifting your center of balance to compensate for pushing yourself to the point of exhaustion." I jump at Alder's stern tone. He steps out of the trees behind me, shirtless, wearing only a pair of gray sweatpants that make my mouth water with the memory of his dick filling my mouth. "You're training too hard. Control isn't just about hours of practice, Lily. It comes when you learn to rest, too."

I climb to my feet, rubbing my sweaty face with the back of my hand. "How long have you been watching?"

"Every night you've snuck out here after pretending to fall asleep." He frowns at my crappy form when I prepare to try again, nudging the inside of my knee for a sturdier center of gravity and tucking my elbows. "I didn't appreciate the sight of you leaving me alone in bed. I'm sure Matthias hasn't enjoyed it, either."

I falter, screwing up my fireball blast before the flames have swirled into a mass. They sputter out as I whip around, my throat stinging.

His stoic expression softens and he smooths his hands over my shoulders, massaging the aches and pains from my overworked muscles with magic heat emanating from his touch. I wobble on my feet with a feeble moan, ready to sway into him. He hushes me, working out the kinks in my tired body until blissful tingles spread throughout it.

"Why are you so stubborn?" He doesn't seem to expect an answer, talking more to himself. "You don't have to do this alone. You have me. Matthias. Vale, in his own way. We'll take care of you, blossom. You only need to ask."

I give up my fight with gravity, leaning against him. He supports me without question, adjusting his embrace to keep me upright while massaging the back of my neck. My eyes flutter. God, this feels incredible. Safe, warm. All the things he reminds me I have now.

"I'm sorry," I mumble with my head against his chest. "I just want to get better. I don't want to fail again if it means any of you getting hurt trying to protect me."

"It's alright. We swore to protect you, Lily. I understand your desire to be your best." My heart thumps with his promise. I wind my arms around his waist, hugging him. He sighs. "I don't want to see you push yourself as hard as my father pushed me. You'll only end up hurting yourself. I won't allow it."

A smile twitches my lips, cutting through my waning exhaustion. "Yes, sir," I sass. "Are you going to punish me for being such a brat?"

He stills, then adjusts his embrace. His woodsmoke scent grows thicker, snaking around me with a heavy swirl of charcoal mixing with it.

The air between us shifts, crackling with tension as he catches me in a hold we've been practicing. Our bodies are plastered together, his grip tightening on my arm to tug me against him, making the invisible tether in my chest flutter. The hard ridge of his dick grinds against my spine.

"Get away," he challenges.

"I thought I needed rest?" My words are light and breathless, too distracted by the throbbing heat building in my core.

"You need something else. No more holding back."

His nose grazes my neck, inhaling with a low, pleased rumble. I rub my thighs together. Can he smell how wet I am? How much it turns me on to be trapped by him?

"I've grown tired of Matthias' teasing. He doesn't get to keep you to himself anymore," he rumbles. "I won't wait around for him to share you."

The flutter in my chest ricochets around my heart. "Alder—"

"Break out of my hold, Lily." His gruff tone makes it hard to deny his wishes.

Focusing on what to do is a struggle with the distraction of his scent and every place we touch. I drag in a breath, wanting to earn one of his proud smiles when I get things right. Wriggling my shoulders to fake a struggle, I wedge my hands into position and drive them up in the circle of his arms with a tight spiral of flames to add to my force while stomping on his foot.

Breaking away, I whirl with a satisfied grin. It feels badass when I execute these moves. Size and shape don't matter. Only technique and understanding balance. Alder taught me that and with his lessons, he's giving me something even more powerful—the ability and confidence to defend myself.

I open my mouth to go off about my success, but the words never come.

Our eyes meet. My breath hitches at the primal darkness in his piercing stare.

"Run," he orders.

I fall back a step, eyes widening. Is he serious? I can barely stand. He'll catch me in no time and—*oh*. I lose my breath in a rush. He'll catch me, like the wicked promise he gave me at Talbot House in the middle of the night.

A thud drums against my ribcage. I want Alder to catch me. I want to be hunted by him until he pins me in the dirt and takes what I desperately want to have with him.

His chin dips, his predatory hooded gaze trained on me. "Run, sweet blossom. *Now*."

My pulse races as I take off, stumbling on a root. I feel it everywhere—my heart, my neck, my clit. Every pumping beat sends lust and a thrilling shot of anticipation coursing through my veins.

At first he crashes through the trees behind me, a deadly beast on my trail. Then as I brace a hand against a tree to catch my breath, I can't hear him anymore. His scent drifts on the air, tickling my nose, letting me know he'll never stop. My stomach twists into a pleasant coil of desire. His hunting becomes silent, stalking his prey for the right moment.

A threatening growl echoes to my left. The dangerous sound should strike fear in me, but all it does is steal my breath and make me crave the moment he'll catch me. I push off again, circling around to double back.

"I would've thought catching me would be easy, big guy," I call teasingly. "You said you'd always be able to hunt me do—*oof*!"

A heavy mass of brawny muscle and alluringly scented smoke collides with me, catching me off guard from the opposite direction I expected him. His strong arms lock around me, taking the brunt of our fall. His sweatpants are gone, discarded somewhere while he hunted me.

Rolling over, he pins me face-down beneath him in the dirt, gathering my arms and pinning my wrists at the base of my spine. I writhe, not willing to give in so easily. He grinds his cock into my ass the size of it spreading between my cheeks. I gasp, twisting to rest my flushed cheek against the cool ground, then press back against his erection with more purpose. My core clenches, aching to feel him inside.

Alder releases a feral sound, digging his fingers into my hip to keep me still. "I don't care that Matthias claimed you first. All that matters is that you're mine."

"Yes," I whimper.

He fists my pants and shreds them with a brutal yank. I squirm beneath him in the dirt, small needy sounds slipping out. My shirt goes next, the back of the tank top split from the neckline. The chilly night air teases the sides of my breasts as he caresses his palm down my bare spine. His grip around my pinned wrists flexes, then he destroys my panties, tearing the material like it's paper to bare me to him.

"Beautiful girl."

He guides me to kneel with a jerk of my hips, leaving my chest against the ground. Cupping between my thighs, his thick fingers glide through my slick folds, using it to massage my entire pussy.

"So wet," he praises gruffly.

My legs threaten to give out as he torments my clit with firm rubs that make me race to the edge of oblivion. "C-close," I whine. "Alder, please. I want to come."

"I know. You will." His lips brush the small of my back with a tender kiss. "You'll come so hard on my cock you'll never forget."

"Forget what?" I breathe.

He stops playing with my clit right before I reach my orgasm and I cry out, wriggling against his uncompromising hold to seek out the friction I need. He chuckles when I shut up at the feel of his thick head rubbing against my entrance. "Forget that you're mine."

My nipples tighten to hard peaks at those words falling from his lips in a jagged and steely tone. At the same time, he grabs my hip and pushes inside with a forceful thrust that makes me see stars. My breath comes in ragged puffs as he fills me so deep, stretching my body to accommodate his massive size, the ridges on his length lighting me up with each inch he buries further within me.

It's so intense, awakening the raw need inside me for him to make me irrefutably his, to carve his name into my very soul and claim me in every way.

"Please." It's the only word I can form, my core ravaged by our passionate flames.

"So fucking tight." He strokes my back, giving me a moment to adjust to his size once he's buried to the hilt.

His fingers trace down to dip between my ass cheeks. They disappear for a moment, then return wet with spit as he circles the hole with a teasing lightness that grows more insistent until one of his thick fingers sinks inside to the first knuckle.

"Oh!" My back bows at the sensation of his cock filling my pussy while he plays with my ass. He starts to move, his thrusts growing sharper as my body opens for his huge cock. "Fuck, that's—that feels really good."

"Yes, blossom." The rough possessiveness in his tone sends a shiver down my spine. "I'll have you in every way imaginable."

I moan at the promise, flooded with want for whatever he'll give me.

A savage sound rips from him and he releases my pinned wrists to wrap his arms around me, lifting me against his chest. A scream catches in my throat as the position seats him so deep it pushes me over the edge without warning, the eruption of ecstasy exploding from my core. I scrabble at his muscular arms banded around me as he fucks me harder, our scents blending and heightening my pleasure.

"Mine," he growls.

All I can do is nod. More than anything, I want it to be true. I want to be his too, because this feels too good, too right to be wrong.

My nerve endings burst all over my body, the insistent thrum in my chest singing in harmony with my aroused moans. His forked tongue swipes at the crook of my neck and his lips close on my pulse point, sucking hard on my sensitive skin. As I reach oblivion again, he slams deep inside my fluttering pussy, rugged muscles tensed as a feral sound tears from him. His cock pulses within my core as he comes.

His release leaks from where we're joined, dripping down my thighs. My lips part and I tilt my head back, angling to kiss him. He captures my mouth, hips pumping with tiny movements that make me gasp into the kiss. He swallows every sound, lips curving against mine.

As his hand coasts down my soft stomach to splay across my lower abdomen, his chest reverberates with a rumble. My eyes pop open and I break our kiss as something urgent occurs to me.

"Will I get pregnant? I don't think there are condoms big enough in the human world for you and you definitely didn't pull out."

Not that I wanted him to. I love the feeling when he spills inside me. I gulp, realizing I haven't used protection with Matthias, either.

He shakes his head, sighing. "Though I would love nothing more than to see your belly swelled with our child, beautiful, you won't be able to conceive like this. The seal that binds you keeps your true form trapped."

I sag against him. "Okay. I'm not ready for that."

I might never be. After the life I've had, I'd no doubt screw a kid up. My heart twists, thinking of how many kids in the system go for so long wishing for a family to pick them.

"We would never push you to do anything you don't want," he assures me. "But I do like this."

His hand dips lower, caressing my swollen pussy and touching my stretched entrance. Gathering his come leaking out of me, he pulls out slowly and uses his fingers to force his come back inside. I clench around them, feeling empty without his cock buried in me.

"Next time I want to knot you," he rasps. "Then after it's gone down, spend the rest of the night pushing my come back into your pussy with my fingers before I fuck it back into you with my cock."

My thighs clench and a ragged breath hisses out of me. His chuckle is warm and tinged with a dirty air he's kept hidden from me. I like this side of him. He continues playing with me, fingering me gently until I'm writhing once more. He's not satisfied until he wrenches another orgasm from me, leaving me fucked out and on the edge of delirium.

"It's time for bed." He kisses me deeply again, laying his claim and possessing me with his mouth. "This time you'll stay put by my side. If you try to sneak out again, I'll chase you, sweet blossom."

"I don't know if that's a bad thing." I laugh at his warning look. Biting my lip around a smile, I nod. "I want to stay with you."

Alder sweeps me into his arms, leaving my tattered clothes behind. I'm glad, because this time I really am past my limit. I'd never be able to stand after that. We're covered in dirt and worn out, a sweet ache lingering between my legs. He carries me through the woods, back to our cabin.

His lips brush my forehead and his comforting scent twines around my heart as it bursts with the unfamiliar happiness of being completely taken care of.

Twenty One
LILY

My heart sits in my throat all day from the moment I wake up in Alder's arms near noon. Last night, I was powerless against my desire, influenced by the strong pull to him. I have to tell Matthias. Fear ingrained from so much rejection locks around my heart.

After I snuck into the shower, then found my bed empty, Matthias convinced me to take a break from training. We walked a nature trail he found, weaving around the cabin in the cool autumn breeze while he conjured dazzling little light shows with his illusion magic and pretended to be a tour guide to get me to smile. I opened my mouth at least a dozen times, the confession about last night ready to burst free, yet unable to escape. Each time he cast a worried look my way when he thought I wasn't paying attention, my heart wedged tighter into my throat.

He treats me to the sweetest day, showing me consideration no one's ever given me before. It underlines the fact I can't hide from him any longer.

Our day-long date ends with dinner on the balcony watching the moon rise.

We sit on a blanket overlooking the moonlit Appalachian mountains, surrounded by candles and the dinner he put together for me. It's a beautiful night and I'm with the one my heart is fated to. He's done everything to spoil me today and I can barely taste the food because my stomach is in knots. I'm a terrible mate.

"Okay." Matthias wipes his mouth and draws me against his side beneath his arm. "You have to tell me what's on your mind, or I'll—"

"I had sex with Alder." I blurt it out with way less tact than the million other ways I thought of to tell him. Closing my eyes to avoid seeing his disappointment, I push the rest of my confession out. "Twice. Alone. Not like—not like what we've done before. It was last night, and at the motel last week."

I tense, waiting for his rejection. My heart fractures at the thought of my mate rejecting me. Even fate doesn't save me from the eventual moment everyone leaves me behind because I'm not enough.

Matthias chuckles. "Is that all, petal?" My eyes fly open and he lifts my chin. "Did his cock make you cry out in that beautiful way I love so much?"

My lips part. He grins at my flustered expression.

Raking his teeth over his lip, he sighs. "Fuck, I wish you'd let me watch, mate. Bet it was so hot. I want to see him fuck you and hear every sexy sound you make while you take his cock."

I sit in stunned silence for a beat, heat spreading through me. "You're not mad?"

"No, baby. Trust me, if I wasn't willing to share you with my brothers, I'd never let them see you. But they're the only two I'll ever let touch my mate. If anyone else dares to look at you, I'll carve out their eyes with my claws." He kisses my forehead when I shiver at his casual possessiveness. "I'm relieved you followed your heart. I was worried you'd deny yourself. Tell me this, did you want him?"

"I—yes." My cheeks are inflamed. "I did. I… do."

"Then that's all that matters. Your happiness is what makes me happy." I swallow the lump in my throat. He covers my heart with his hand. The bond reacts to his touch, emanating a soft glow. "You feel it? You belong to me. But you also belong to Alder, too."

"How?" I breathe.

"The bond's magic doesn't allow us to look at anyone who isn't our fated mate. If you didn't feel it for him, he wouldn't be able to seduce you away from me."

His explanation opens a whole new world to me. Reawakens the hope I hardly allowed to take flight—that I could have more than one fated mate. The tugs I've felt in three directions aren't trying to tear me apart. I didn't betray the bond with my mate and he's not casting me aside after finding out I was with Alder. The stress I've battled all day ebbs.

I cover his hand with mine, my lashes brushing my cheeks at the feel of our bond filling me. "That's really possible? I could have more than one bond?"

"Of course, petal." He frowns at me in concern. "We thought you knew once your bond with me took shape. I'm sorry. I would have explained it better to you instead of dropping hints."

I shake my head. "It's okay."

"It's rare. We're as shocked by it as you are, but I told you we feel it, too. Your scent is what triggered the bond and helped it form. Outside of hellhounds, only powerful demon lines have more than one fated mate."

Relief spreads through me. "I was so afraid you would hate me when I told you."

"Never, Lily." He cradles my jaw, tilting my face. His eyes gleam with affection. "You don't have to choose between us. You're our mate, and we're yours."

I shudder at those words. The truth in them echoes through me, my bond growing as I stop fighting my feelings out of fear of rejection.

Matthias kisses me deeply. Every brush of his lips and tongue feels like a promise to love me. The cracks that formed in my heart with my worries mend.

"Did you like your birthday dinner?" he asks when he ends the kiss.

"Wait, what?" My brows pinch. "You told me demons don't celebrate birthdays. Besides, mine isn't even real."

"You grew up here. We wanted any excuse to celebrate you, Lils. Birthday girls get spoiled in the mortal realm and I want to spoil you forever, mate."

I gasp against his mouth when he swoops down to give me another scorching kiss.

"It's belated. I think the mortal's Halloween was a week or two ago." He pulls a face, then shrugs. "But we put this together for you. The day off, this dinner. The rest of tonight is up to you."

My heart skips a beat. "We?"

"All of us." He winks. "It was Vale's idea and I ran with it. He saw you training so hard. He'll be back later when Rainer relieves him from watch to guard us all tonight."

For the longest time, I thought I'd spend my eighteenth birthday walking away backwards from the group home with both middle fingers raised. One final *fuck you, goodbye* to the system that screwed me over time and again.

Instead, I spent it on the run and forgot about it. Tonight has turned into the most perfect one I could imagine out of all the times I wished for someone to celebrate me growing up. My real age as a demon doesn't matter right now. What does is that they did this for me. They gave me today—gave me permission to exist. It's the greatest gift of all, the one I've longed for the most.

Tears of gratitude well in my eyes. The way the three of them meet my needs heals me from years of crushing abandonment.

"Thank you," I whisper. "This is... No one's ever done this for me. I've always spent my birthday alone."

"You'll never be alone again." He traces the shape of my lips with his thumb. "For now, why don't we go inside and find Alder?"

"Yes." My breathless answer makes Matthias chuckle.

As soon as he suggests going to find my second mate, need arrows through me. I have to see him. Have to tell him how I feel.

We find him sitting on the first step, rugged

arms braced on his thighs and his stare locked on the door as we come back inside. He sits up straighter and my heart gives a drumming beat when our eyes connect.

"Any longer and I was about to come out there," he grumbles. "I shouldn't have agreed to your plan. You just wanted her to yourself all day."

"It's what she needed. I'll put her needs first above any of ours every time." Matthias takes me by the shoulders from behind and brings his lips to my ear. "Go to him."

My breath comes in short bursts. Each inch of distance between us is unfair. *Mine*. The rough, feral tone he used last night crashes over me, knocking the wind from me.

"Alder." He shoots to his feet at my strained murmur. I rush him when he opens his arms, squeezing my eyes shut when he catches me and lifts me off the ground. "Mate."

"Yes, sweet blossom," he rumbles into my neck. "You're mine."

"And mine." Matthias makes no move to intervene in our moment. "Ours."

"Ours." Alder's embrace tightens.

It feels so right, the tender light in my chest brilliant, more settled. When he lifts his head, I kiss him, my heart opening for him. His chest reverberates with a deep, gratified rumble and he braces my back against the wall. The ardent, claiming kiss is full of smoldering heat that burns me with the sweetest passion.

I pull back with a gasp. "Can we go upstairs?"

Alder grabs me beneath my thighs and hauls me higher, wrapping my legs around his ripped torso. His strength leaves me lightheaded. I rest my hot cheek against his shoulder. Matthias follows as Alder carries me upstairs, kneading my ass the entire way.

In the bedroom, I glance between them, then strip until nothing separates me from them. The burn of their gazes on my body fills me with confidence and makes me feel incredibly beautiful. Alder reaches back to tug off his shirt first, then Matthias does the same. They leave their boxer briefs on while I'm bare.

It's not that I want to have sex with both of them right now. The bond is making me crave skin on skin contact. The intimacy of feeling their heartbeats directly against mine.

"Whatever you want," Matthias reminds me.

I nod and take both their hands, inviting them to get in bed. They sandwich me between them, their arms draped over my waist and stomach. I face Alder and Matthias drags my hips back, my ass snug against his erection. Neither of them push me, allowing me to take this bond with them both at my own pace.

Tucked between them, I feel like I've found my place for the first time in my life.

I'm at a loss for what to do next, reluctant to end this blissful moment wrapped in their arms. It could've been like this from the first moment we felt the bond if I hadn't resisted what I was too scared to hope was real.

Part of me is glad we could take it slow. If I'd realized they were my fated mates in the abandoned graveyard, before I knew I'm really a demon, it would have freaked me the hell out. I wouldn't have believed it, too broken to think the demons who threatened to kill me were destined to love me, the unlovable, troubled orphan.

"What's going through your head?" Alder cups my cheek with his big hand.

A soft sigh leaves me at the touch and I rub my face against his palm. "Imagining how this would've gone down between us if we realized the night we met in Brim Hills." I smile wryly. "Not only would I not have believed for a second you wanted me, but the whole we're here to kill you thing would've made it awkward."

Matthias snickers. "We resisted the pull, too. None of us understood why it was happening. It was hard to focus because you smelled so fucking good."

I marvel at how easy this is now, to be free to map the hard planes of Alder's chest while Matthias traces teasing circles on my stomach. "When did you realize what it meant?"

"For me, the moment we were attacked. When the demon was going for you, I couldn't bear it. I needed to protect you without regard for my life or my brothers'," Alder says.

"At the rest stop when I saw Vale all over you." Matthias huffs. "Vale's probably known this whole time. I bet it's why he was so resistant to letting us seek you out alone."

A comfortable lull stretches. I bask in their soft touches and indulge the urge to touch my mates. Each exploratory caress opens a bottomless well of hunger in me, leaving me starved for this to stretch on forever, to always feel the profound joy that glows in me at their touch.

"God, this all had me so stressed." I press my face into Alder's chest. "I'm sorry I didn't say something sooner. We could've had this instead of me keeping us apart because I was afraid."

He pets my hair. "As long as you know you're ours now. You'll always be ours, sweet blossom."

"I'm not used to having anyone to rely on. I don't know how to do—this. Love. Relationships, magically ordained or otherwise. Even friendship is foreign to me."

The vitriol people have directed at me my entire life runs across my mind. Perhaps it's because they sensed the demon hidden in me that instinctively terrified them, but I endured it all, focusing on making myself less and less to keep my emotions from lashing out at their hatred.

My teeth sink into my lip and I push myself to be open with them. "I've spent a long time keeping my thoughts and emotions to myself. Trust in others doesn't come easily for me when I've been feared and rejected all my life by the people who believed I was different. That girl couldn't dream of finding one person fate chose to love her, let alone more than one."

When my choked words break off, Alder growls, holding me closer. Matthias echoes the fierce sound. Both of them show me with their embraces that I'll never face that kind of cruelty again.

Alder speaks against the top of my head. "I want to destroy any human who has ever made you feel this way."

Matthias kisses my shoulder, squeezing my waist. "And the ones who stole you from the underworld and put you through this. They'll pay for this."

A shuddering breath leaves me. Their acknowledgement alone that I shouldn't have been treated the way I was, shouldn't have been made to endure the abuse of the people that were supposed to shelter me splinters the thorns I grew around my heart.

Alder catches my hand and kisses every burn scar, then does the same to my other hand. He showers each marred expanse of skin that I've always hated with tender brushes of his lips.

"Every mark you bear is proof of your survival," he rasps. "You made it through that. It didn't break you permanently, and you'll never be alone again. Our hearts and souls will never be separated now that we've found you, Lily."

"You have us forever," Matthias adds.

I sniffle, burrowing against Alder and reaching for Matthias' hand. He scoots closer so there's no space between the three of us. The only thing that would make it better would be if Valerian were here, but for now this is enough. Understanding that I'm not being forced to choose by the fated magic connecting us is enough.

They cocoon me in their warmth and devotion. Every loving touch is a balm directly to my battered soul. It's almost overwhelming how the simplest caress of their fingertips following the roundness of my cheek or their fingers carding through my hair lights me up with an incandescent glow, almost drunk on their affections because I've never known the kindness of a hug. Between my mates, I'm enveloped in tenderness that makes my heart swell with euphoria.

The tears that spill down my cheeks aren't born of sadness. Neither of them say anything, maybe understanding how I feel better than I can voice myself. They simply hold me, showing every curve, every scar, and every invisible crack in my heart that they cherish me.

Twenty Two
LILY

After I doze for a while, I wake from my nap with a soft whimper. A sinfully delicious heat engulfs me, and when I open my eyes, I find Alder's head between my legs, massaging my thick thighs as his tongue plunges inside me.

Matthias smooths my hair back and grins when our gazes lock as I dance on the edge of falling. He traces my lips, then presses more insistently until I grant him access, allowing him to slip two of his fingers into my mouth, arching against Alder's divine ministrations as Matthias strokes my tongue.

I catch the rich scent of hickory and seek Vale out, my chest constricting when I find him seated in a chair by the bed. Watching. Out of the four of us, he's the only one fully clothed, the others stripped as bare as I am.

They're all here with me. All focused on me. A harmonious hum reverberates in my chest. Valerian's scent teases me while Matthias bends to capture my lips, swallowing my moan when Alder pushes me over the edge, crashing into a sea of pleasure.

"So gorgeous when you come." Matthias' golden gaze darkens, fixated on my mouth as he pushes his fingers in again, keeping my tongue occupied. My cheeks prickle from how much I like it. He pulls free and grasps my chin. "What do you want, pretty girl? We're going to take care of you."

Clashing emotions clog my throat. Gratitude, desire, and my newfound confidence that these men treasure me chase away the nasty voices in my head that have spent my lifetime telling me I'm unworthy of this. Of being loved and taken care of. It's not true, not anymore. Because I have my mates.

It's difficult to think, the pleasure about to pull me back under as Alder continues devouring my pussy with unwavering concentration. Not yet—this is important.

"D-don't go," I say to Vale.

Whatever he hears in my plea, he nods. I relax against the bed, relieved he won't ignore me again.

Alder's rumble vibrates against my sensitive folds and he buries his face harder against my center, drawing a ragged sound from me.

"Like that?" Matthias smiles, kissing my forehead. "Like when Alder feasts on your sweet pussy? Come for him again, petal. Soak his tongue and give him a good taste before he fucks you."

A deep pulse beats in my core at his sultry croon. Alder looks up the length of my body, the pupils of his hypnotic green eyes blown. He spreads me wider and spears me with his wicked tongue, then makes an obscene slurping sound as he sucks and laps at the slickness coating my pussy.

"Ah!" The coil in my core snaps and I ride the waves of my orgasm, hips rocking against his face.

Alder soothes his palms up my sides, then crawls over me, kissing his way up my body. "I want to be inside you."

I nod eagerly. His arms slip around me and he rolls us, grinding his hardness against me. I spread my legs to straddle him, planting my hands on his chest to push up. Reaching between us, he lines up and my head falls back as I sink down his enormous length.

He grips my hips and guides our pace. Matthias stretches out beside us, watching with a heated gaze as he strokes his cock. The press of his gaze and Valerian's makes my blood sing as I ride my mate.

"Fuck." Vale's wrecked mutter cuts through my haze of pleasure.

His legs fall open and his hand squeezes the

hard bulge tenting his pants. The evidence of his arousal turns me on even more.

A pang of sadness hits me for a moment. I know what I feel for him is the same as what I feel for my mates. I wish he'd join, melt me with his touch. But he's here, watching. He's not leaving. As long as he doesn't leave, it's okay.

He catches my eye and holds my attention. "Alder. Turn her around. I want to watch her tits bounce while you fuck her on your cock."

I shiver. He smirks, his hooded blue gaze smoldering as it slides over every inch of me straddling Alder's hips.

Alder props on his elbows, grasping the back of my neck to drag me down for a searing kiss before he lifts me off his lap and repositions himself to sit on the edge of the bed. We'll be facing Valerian, giving him a complete show. My chest collapses with a dizzying exhale and Alder tugs me into his lap, mouthing at my nape. He grips beneath my thighs and spreads me wide open. Vale's gaze is a sinful caress while Alder lifts me with ease and lowers me onto his length once more.

My eyes flutter as he fills me and sets a pace that makes me moan with each thrust. I reach back to hold on to his head and clutch one of his muscled arms supporting me with my free hand.

I swallow as Valerian takes out his cock. It's

big—not as thick as Alder's, but it has to be about as long, also enhanced with the row of ridges that feel incredible stroking my inner walls. A shiny dribble of precome drips from the tip, rolling over each tantalizing ridge along his length. He makes sure he has my attention as he takes himself in hand. My core clenches as I imagine what it would feel like inside me and Alder grunts.

Matthias stands in front of me and dips his head to kiss me, making me gasp as he teases my nipples. He skates his free hand down my soft curves to circle my clit with his fingers.

"You look so gorgeous riding Alder, Lils," he murmurs. "Mm, I want to know how tight you'll be if you take us both at once."

"Both? I don't know if I could," I push out. "You wouldn't fit, you're huge."

Alder slams me down harder, his chest shaking with amusement at my scream. I lean back against his broad chest, pussy clenching around him. The erotic sound of how wet I am is obscene.

"You were made for us," he says. "Made to take our cocks."

His praise arrows through me. The thought of taking both of them is enticing.

"Our pretty girl," Matthias says.

His fingers sink into my hair and he kisses me, nipping at my lips. I chase his kiss when he pulls away. He gives me another, smiling into it before leaning back.

His grip tightens in my hair and his eyes hood. "I need to fuck these tits, baby."

Biting my lip, I nod, arching my back. He plays with my breasts, thumbs teasing my nipples in maddening circles that spread electric tingles to my core.

"Please," I beg.

As Matthias holds the base of his cock and trails the leaking tip over my skin, Alder licks a stripe up my throat. The weight of Matthias' hardness rests between my breasts and he gathers them, squeezing around his length. I gasp at the friction when he snaps his hips. The slide of his hot, velvety skin as he tightens his hold on my tits stirs a throb deep in my core. His precome slicks the tight channel he makes thrusting between my cleavage until he secretes so much he glides against me as easily as he sinks into my pussy.

With Alder fucking me and Matthias using me for his own pleasure while Valerian watches the three of us, touching himself, I lose myself to the sensual experience.

Matthias curses, head tipping back with a grunt. His come splashes across my tits as his hips keep bucking, his dick sliding through it. I moan as some of it hits my chin, wishing to know what he tastes like.

I feel utterly marked, *claimed* by his come coating my skin while Alder fucks me and sucks another possessive mark into my neck.

"Mine." Eyes gleaming, Matthias draws a heart on my messy cleavage, then catches some of it and flashes me a mischievous grin before he smears it across my lips with his thumb and pushes it in my mouth.

I suck it from his thumb greedily, enjoying the tangy taste of him as much as I enjoyed Alder's.

His. Theirs. And they're mine. The thoughts bowl me over. I never thought I could be so happy.

Alder slows down his pace, dragging out my pleasure with even more intensity as he makes me feel every inch of his huge cock each time he guides me down on it. My eyelids fall to half mast, my lips parting as he lifts me and drives into me again slow, slow, slow, the ridges on his length sending heady shocks of pleasure racing through me.

Matthias falls to his knees before me, working around Alder. He gets Alder to hold my legs open even wider, my back bowing at the new angle the slight change causes as he spears me on his thick length. Then Matthias flicks his forked tongue across my throbbing clit and I shatter, one orgasm drifting right into the next when he sucks on it with a filthy chuckle, enjoying every second of ecstasy he wrenches from me.

"Oh god!" I whimper.

Alder groans, his grip flexing on my thighs as my pussy clenches. "So tight."

"Keep going, Matthias," Vale orders. "Make her cream his cock so much that it leaks out of her cunt from having her clit sucked so good while she gets fucked."

A choked gasp slips out of me as Alder and Matthias match their pace, the rhythm of Matthias' tongue synced with Alder hitting a spot deep inside me that is so overwhelmingly good, tears spring to my eyes as I come hard, dropping a hand to grip Matthias' disheveled white blond hair, overtaken by a greedy, primal desire to keep him *right there*.

"That's it, little flower. You're fucking beautiful like this, taking what you want," Valerian croons in his smooth accent. "Ride his face. Grind your needy little clit on his tongue while you take your mate's cock."

"Fuck, fuck, fuck," I hiss.

I collapse back against Alder's broad chest. He buries his face in my neck, his fangs grazing my sensitive skin. How would it feel if he bit me? Marked my skin with a lasting reminder of this moment, of his claim on me? My head spins with how much I want that.

As though they sense my thoughts, Matthias

rises from his knees. He sits next to us and threads his fingers through my hair, tilting my head back to expose my throat. Three approving rumbles sound around me. Lips and teeth move on both sides of my neck. One of them mutters *mate*. I can't pick out who, though an answering flutter beats in my chest.

"You feel it, sweet blossom?" Alder laps at my throbbing pulse point.

I nod, unable to verbalize the sensation thrumming in the bond. A purr escapes me. I'm trapped in Valerian's sensual stare, his blue eyes burning bright and hot as he strokes his cock.

"You're ours," Matthias rasps.

"Yours. All yours," I echo with a cry, needing my mates to know.

Alder's fangs scrape my neck again and Matthias brushes my cheek with his knuckles. Swallowing, I wish for Valerian, the bond snapping like a vibrating chord in my chest.

"Please."

Vale makes a rough sound from his spot, watching intently. He staggers over, tracing my parted lips.

A glow lights me up from inside. "All yours."

"Yes," Vale whispers raggedly, his come spilling over his fist.

My vision grows hazy when Alder groans and tenses. Part of his cock swells thicker, stealing my breath. His chest shudders with a wild exhale and he gently lets my legs down, wrapping his arms around me as our bodies lock together with his slower, rocking thrusts. Every small shift of his hips brings me unbelievable pleasure and I exist in an endless tide of orgasmic bliss.

"I've got you," he says. "You were made to take my knot, my beautiful blossom."

The intensity leaves me in a daze. I'm distantly aware of Alder's fingers touching the place we're joined, tracing the edge of my pussy stretched around the swollen base of his dick buried inside me.

"Look at you, petal." Matthias splays his palm across my soft stomach. "So pretty and full. Shit, I can't decide if it's sexier to knot you myself or watch you take my brother's."

Valerian grasps my chin, his thumb tracing the shape of my lips. I press a kiss to it and my heart stutters at the reverence shining in his eyes. My name falls from his mouth in a hoarse whisper. "Lily."

Alder's arms tighten around me and with another low groan, his cock throbs deep inside as he finishes. The pulse of his come filling me makes me clench around him, shattering once more with a frayed, overstimulated whimper.

I don't fully return to earth until Alder and Matthias have me cleaned up and nestled between them in bed, surrounded by their warmth. Their gazes are full of devotion that touches me to my soul. The thrum in my chest is a quiet, content hum, no longer constantly pulling in different directions.

The chair near the bed creaks, the sound stabbing through my chest.

My head pops up and a sound of distress snags in my throat. Valerian catches my hand and sits back down, his chair scooted closer to the bed.

"I'm not leaving, little flower," he says. "None of us will ever leave you."

Tears blur my vision. "Okay."

Alder and Matthias draw me back to rest between them. Once again, the bond is at ease, settled knowing I have the three of them with me.

My past in the mortal realm is painful, and I can't remember my life in the underworld. Those memories might be lost forever. I focus on who I am now because it feels like after everything I've endured, I have a real future as long as I can stay with my three demons that have stolen my heart piece by piece.

I needed each of them more than I knew. With them, I have someone who understands my painful scars and protects me from getting hurt, someone who makes me smile and reminds me to be myself, and someone who challenges me and sparks my fighting spirit to life.

For so long, I've suppressed my ability to love because the world didn't want me. I learned not to open up and give myself to others because I only ended up spurned and hurt. Opening up for my mates is like opening a floodgate. My wounded heart expands bigger than I ever thought it was capable of, no longer afraid of being abandoned.

Somewhere along the way, my enemies became my lovers. My fated mates. I've fallen for them. My heart is irrevocably theirs. Every broken, damaged shard of me belongs to all three of them because with them I've found the thing I've always longed for—my true home.

Twenty Three
LILY

In the morning, I smile without opening my eyes, sandwiched between Matthias and Alder in bed. It's a tight fit, yet I wouldn't change a thing. As long as I'm surrounded by them, I'm happy.

The bond dances in my chest. I trace my fingers over my heart, so relieved to understand it better. Now I get that it was never about making me choose between what I feel for my three demons, but attempting to guide me to the fated connection I share with each of them.

Stretching, I savor the pleasant ache between my legs from Adler's knot. His stoic features are softened in sleep, I gaze at him, my heart brimming with the rightness of being his. A soft snore at my back makes me roll over to snuggle beneath

Matthias' chin, smiling fondly at his smoky maple scent. They shift to accommodate me, even in sleep they naturally drift closer to wrap around me.

It's so simple to just lay here and feel high on absolute bliss.

"You're awake."

I twist and pop my head up to see past Alder's wide shoulders, blinking at the sight of Valerian in the same spot as last night. He didn't go. "How long have you been there? All night?"

"For most of it." He smirks at my blush. "I relieved Rainer of his watch at dawn. No demons have tracked us here. It seems we remain safe for the time being, so I can be indulgent."

I bite my lip, wondering if the indulgence he means is watching me sleep. Hope trickles through me.

As amazing as last night was, I don't know where we stand. The bond is happy when I'm near Vale and I know I want to be with him, too. He stayed all night, but I'm not sure if I'm allowed to touch him as freely as I can with my other two demon mates.

Before I gather the courage to ask, he stands. "Come on. I need to talk to you."

My stomach clenches. Leaving the safe bubble of this room is daunting.

"What about…"

"They'll wake soon and join us. For now, let me have you to myself." He pauses at the door. "I know who you are. Your demon."

My heart stops, then thuds hard. Reluctantly, I leave Matthias and Alder in bed, grabbing one of their discarded shirts to slip into. I duck into the bathroom quickly, halting at the sight of my neck covered in hickeys. My lips twitch as I prod at them.

Downstairs, Valerian offers me a steaming mug of coffee and leads me out to the balcony. The early morning sun cascades through the trees. We lean against the railing side by side, his wrist ghosting against my arm.

"I've suspected who you could be for a while," he starts. "Part of me might have always known, but I thought it was my own past mistakes twisting my mind into seeing you. I told myself it was impossible. That I'd lost you."

"You knew me?" My eyes roam the sharp lines of his profile, wishing he'd look at me. "This is from when you were a knight."

It's a guess. He nods stiffly, blowing out a breath.

"Since I had myself convinced it was wishful thinking, I've ignored the other signs. I should've recognized your hellfire right away. And only the most powerful demon lines are known to have more than one fated mate." A tingle spreads through me when he says *mate*. "I should've known from the moment I first caught a hint of your faint scent seeping through the cracks in the seal binding you. You've always smelled of toasted cinnamon."

My brows furrow. "At Lane's cottage, did you know then?"

"It was when I first let myself believe. Even without your memories to confirm it, I know you. I feel you where I thought I never could again." His throat bobs and he rubs at the center of his chest. "The forbidden bond that almost formed between us doesn't lie. It didn't fully form before, but now…"

"Forbidden?" I swallow and pull his hand to my chest by his wrist. His fingers fist the material of my shirt, yanking me closer. My coffee sloshes over the edge of my mug. "Whoever I was, I'm not letting anything come between us."

The corner of his mouth lifts. "Always so stubborn. I'm glad your fiery spirit isn't lost."

Before I demand he stops dragging this out, he pushes an image into my mind—a memory that isn't my own playing out. It's…me, but not. The way my dream self is me, though slightly different. In the memory, I have pointed ears, small black horns peeking from longer red hair, fangs, and vibrantly glowing amber eyes. Familiarity tinges the scene as I get in a demon knight's face, jabbing a pointed, bright crimson claw in his chest.

"You think you get to boss me around and keep me

contained? Tough shit. If I wish to go somewhere, you can't stop me." I smirk. *"And if you think you can, by all means, challenge me. I have no qualms fighting the king's knights. I relish whooping your asses every chance I get."*

Valerian laughs. "Are you tormenting my knight's guard yet again, Lilith?"

My smirk stretches into a playful grin when I realize he's there. "Always. It's only my favorite pastime. They think they can order me to stay within the castle's boundaries when everyone knows I prefer to spend my time adventuring throughout the underworld."

"Dismissed," Valerian says to the guard who tried to stop me from leaving the courtyard. Once he's gone, he offers a smirk to match mine. "If you sneak off on one of your adventures, it's my duty as the knight assigned to guard you to follow."

My eyes flash with mischief. "Then catch me if you can, Vale. I won't go easy on you."

"Always." He glances around to check if we're alone before stepping closer. "I like it when you give me a challenge."

I blink as it fades away. *Always.* The warmth in his tone echoes through my mind.

He inclines his head. "Lilith."

My lips part. "That feels like I know it."

"It should. It's your name." He steps closer, repeating it in his crooning accent. "Lilith."

The way he says it makes my knees go weak. I

clutch at the railing. His gaze darkens with a hint of deviousness at my reaction.

"Your disappearance three hundred years ago was shrouded in mystery. You were just—gone." He clenches his teeth. "On my watch. I thought you were just out exploring the realm, but I couldn't find you. No one could. We never thought to look in the mortal realm. The king was furious. You were meant to become the queen of Hell and rule alongside Lucifer as his bride."

Everything in me revolts at the thought of being married to the Devil, the bond bucking uncomfortably. *She'll never be queen*. I inhale sharply. That's what the demons meant. Why they're out to kill me.

"This hasn't been about you betraying the underworld," I say slowly as my gears turn. "They didn't want me to become queen. Whoever kidnapped me is pissed I'm still alive."

"I think so, yes. They're covering it up by labeling me the leader of a rebellion to unseat the queen Lucifer did marry. If he finds out people in his court conspired against him, it would mean true death for anyone involved." His eyes roam my face and his tone turns gravelly. "They were right to suspect I'd recognize you before long."

Relief spirals through me. The Devil hasn't spent three centuries looking for a lost queen he intends to wed. It doesn't matter if my true identity is Lilith, I don't want to be queen or marry anyone besides Alder, Matthias, and Valerian. I abandon my coffee on the railing to wrap my arms around his waist, breathing in the spicy sharpness in his smoky scent.

His fingers sink into my hair with a low growl. "They stole you away from me."

More images flash in my head—glimpses of how dedicated he was in protecting me, watching me wherever I went, the way we danced around each other but never acted on the spark between us. He shows me wielding my powers with deadly skill in some kind of tournament. Sneaking out of the castle to ride a beastly underworld creature and him tracking me down, but not forcing me back to a castle that makes me restless right away. Stolen moments of *what if* where our eyes would meet across the room.

Each memory he sends into my mind is tinged with the strength of his feelings for me, illicit yet inescapable. I can tell that much from the small flashes he allows me to see of our past. The depth of his love feels like it's spanned years, carried in his heart.

With a rough, broken noise, he pulls my head back by my hair and his mouth collides against mine. It's everything he's held back. The kiss is a passionate storm, all-consuming and wild. A claiming demand on my mouth, my heart, my very soul, telling me I'm his and will always be his. A cry escapes me and he drinks it in, his grip on me tightening as he devours my mouth.

Vale wrenches away, pressing his forehead to mine with a jagged breath that breaks my heart. "I failed you once before. The thought of ever losing you again terrifies me to the depths of my being."

He pulls back and a panicked noise leaves me at the thought of him retreating behind his brooding walls after that. I push on tiptoe and kiss him, unwilling to let him go. He clutches me to him as we kiss again, and again, and again until my heart feels ready to burst.

"I found you," he says against my mouth. "I won't let you go this time."

I shake my head, pressing so close I think I'm trying to climb inside him so we're never parted again.

Once my racing heart slows, I'm able to think more clearly. The others come outside, Alder sitting on the edge of the empty hot tub and Matthias hopping up to sit on the railing. Vale squeezes me like he doesn't want to share, but lets me slip out of his arms. I shyly fit myself between Matthias' knees to kiss his cocky smirk away, ending up smiling into our kiss. Then I go to Alder and give him a soft kiss, humming when he pets my hair.

He grazes my nose with his. "You're radiant."

My cheeks tingle and another smile breaks free. I return to Vale, leaning back against him. His tattooed arms move around me without the hesitation he's had with me before. At last my world's axis finds its alignment with all three of them.

"You said you had something important to discuss today," Alder says. "Are we ready to move?"

"Soon now that I'm healed. I know who Lily is." They both lean forward in anticipation. I trace his inked fingers interlocked around my waist, the abstract whorls shifting and curling around the places I touch. "Lilith."

"Lilith? *The* Lilith?" Alder's brows hike up.

"Shit," Matthias breathes.

"Shit indeed," Valerian mutters. "It brings the entire chain of command for the last few centuries into question. The council serves both as the overseers of the factions, and as royal council to Lucifer. We don't know which members are behind this other than speculating based on who benefited most in power."

The amount of time my demon has been missing stumps me. "If it was that long ago, how am I here now? I was found as a baby."

Alder crosses his arms, his muscles bulging. "Your bloodline is royalty amongst the demon fae. All demons descend from the primordial fae gods and the original Lilith is said to be one of those goddesses who reincarnated herself to become a demon because she fell in love. Every she-demon born to your bloodline inherits the original goddess' gifts. You are the daughter of a line that has never been broken, one of the strongest the underworld has. It's why you were destined for the throne."

Jesus. My gaze falls to my scarred hands. After everything I've been through, that's what awaited me in the place I truly come from? Respectfully, fuck that.

"That's some heavy shit," I mumble. "Still doesn't answer my question."

"Remember when I explained the laws surrounding reincarnation?" At my nod, he continues. "With your bloodline descending directly from our gods, it would take an immense amount of dark power to force you to reincarnate. It's likely they kept you on the brink of death for centuries wherever they had you hidden away before they were able to force you through it to bind you."

"Fuck," Matthias bites out fiercely.

Alder's expression hardens. "By weakening you enough to trap you in a changeling form, they probably thought their plan was complete since they never had anyone watching you. They kidnapped you. Tortured you. Then left you to die in the mortal realm by the humans' neglectful hands or by your own volatile untrained powers being too great for a human form to withstand."

Twenty Four
LILY

Learning the truth leaves me torn. I thought finding out the identity of the demon trapped inside me would make things clearer. It only leaves me conflicted.

Do I belong in the underworld realm I've forgotten, sitting on a throne I don't have any desire to take?

Am I Lilith? Or will she destroy me when we find a way to break the seal imprisoning her within me? I have her power, but a small corner of my mind still fears that who I am as Lily Sloane is only a stand-in shell born of her need to survive the mortal realm until her demon knight could rescue her. Someone who took the brunt of abuse while she remained hidden behind the magic seal trapping her inside me.

My throat tightens. Then why do I have a fated mate connection to all three of them? Is that hers, too? Would she have eventually found my warrior and trickster demons destined to love her?

No. The bond pulses in my chest in refusal. Fuck that. These demons are my home. My fate. No one will take them from me. They're the only good my rotten life has granted me.

They've given me so much already. I've experienced more life with them than I was ever allowed the privilege of before. I belong with them, allowed to take up space instead of being shunned and tossed aside.

I hold on to hope that we are one in the same, needing to believe I won't be separated from the three men who fill my heart.

"If this hadn't happened, would I have found you?" My throat constricts. "Vale knew me, but… How would I have found you guys if I was supposed to get married?"

"It's possible the reincarnation rewrote your magic. You're a rebirth of the Lilith I knew, and we never…" Valerian's forearms flex, his tattoos shifting restlessly with his thoughts. "The witch was right. You might not have most of your memories of your past life after going through hundreds of years of torture and surviving as a changeling that was likely meant to be your final death sentence."

"I've seen the underworld in my dreams." I slide my lips together, unsure why I'm trying to reassure him when I'm afraid he's only interested in *her* and not me. "Maybe it's not all gone. And…her memory lives on in you."

"What was between us was a possibility. This bond—" His palm splays over my heart and our bond swells to brush against his touch. His own heartbeat thumps against my back. "—is fated. You needed us and we needed you to bring us together. No one in the underworld would deny that as this incarnation Lilith, we are the mates fate chose for you."

Alder and Matthias come over and place their hands over Valerian's, the three of them circling me where they belong. The bond dances in my chest, the glow of warmth emanating through my skin. Fascinated, I turn my translucent, glowing hand back and forth.

"You're ours, Lily." Matthias takes my hand and brings my scarred knuckles to his lips.

"Fate brought us together. That's all that matters." Alder tucks my hair behind my ear. "Loving you is a gift bestowed upon us by the gods."

"Ours." Vale's embrace tightens with his rough echo.

"Yours," I murmur. "All of yours."

Three pleased rumbles sound around me. A happy, light laugh escapes me.

We stay like that for several moments until I think about everything standing between us and what I want—to be with them wherever our lives take us. We can't have that until we stop the corruption in the underworld that wants us all dead.

"So what will we do? As much as I'd love to ignore all of this, we can't stay here forever in our perfect bubble at the cabin."

Matthias jokes around with a scandalized gasp. "Don't let the Mothman shrine in the basement hear you talk about leaving him behind."

I give him a flat look. "No. You're not bringing that costume with us."

He grins. "I totally am, petal. I'll make Alder pin you down while I wear it and feed my cock to these gorgeous lips."

Maintaining my stern expression is hard when the mental image stirs a throb of desire in my core at the thought of Alder holding me down for Matthias to torment me with sinful pleasure. Damn him.

He laughs at my expression and leans in to kiss me. "Such a dirty girl. I love making you blush like that."

"She's right." Alder's gruff tone is thicker, his green eyes darkened with interest by Matthias' teasing. "We need to move and decide what to do."

I lift my head, my mouth set. "I don't want to keep running. I'm sick of it."

"We'll find out who did this to you, little flower," Vale promises. "And then we'll make them fucking pay."

The others echo his vengeful sentiment. It sends a shudder of adoration through me, leaving me weak in the knees.

"I'll call Rainer back before he gets far and meet up with him," he continues. "We'll strategize the best gate to use to sneak into the underworld. They blocked us from using ours and we wouldn't want to risk going through it if they've set up anyone there to capture us, but if we retrace our steps to an area they already tracked us it should provide enough cover to get to Hell."

"What about me?" A spike of anxiety hits me. "They've spent this long keeping me out of the underworld. We could go through the gate and it could destroy me."

Valerian crushes me against his chest and the others mutter unhappy sounds of refusal. "You are a powerful demon," Valerian says firmly. "Even though your kidnappers bound you, you chipped away at the seal, allowing your power to seep through. The portal's magic will recognize your place is in the underworld and grant you safe passage."

"Humans have come through the gates before," Alder reminds me. "As guards, we're meant to deal with them, but they have crossed over from the mortal realm. You'll also go through with us surrounding you as extra protection."

His reassurance that they won't make me go through this alone helps.

"Once we're in the underworld, I think we'll be able to break the seal by getting you back where you belong," Valerian says. "The energy of the realm will restore you to your full strength rather than keep you in this starved state. You'll have the power to break the seal on your own, shattering through the cracks to free yourself."

"I don't know. You really believe I can do that?" I push out of his arms to face the three of them, holding up my hands. "Guys, I've barely learned to control this in the last few weeks."

Alder steps forward to cradle my face. "You can do it. Trust in your own strength. And if you can't do that, then trust in us. When you falter, we're here to catch you. We believe in you even when you don't, mate."

My throat clogs and my eyes glisten as I stare back at him, then shift my attention to Matthias and Vale. Their solemn gazes choke me up even more. They believe I can do this. That for them, I'm enough.

Their support lends fortitude to my own tattered

belief in myself.

The ones who kidnapped me wanted to kill me and they almost succeeded. What they didn't know is that every time I've been knocked down, abused, rejected, tossed aside and forgotten, I've gotten the fuck back up and kept going. I survived and I'll keep fighting for my right to exist, to live on in spite of those who would rather see me dead.

Blinking away tears, I nod in determination. Alder kisses my forehead.

"I'll go find Rainer. Once I'm back, we'll leave and start our journey back up the coast," Valerian says.

Matthias gives me a crooked smile when Alder steps away and kisses me. Before I'm ready, I'm tugged away, Valerian's mouth claiming mine. He murmurs my true name against my lips like a prayer.

"I'm going to squeeze some practice in," I say.

"I'll be out shortly to join you," Alder says. "Don't overdo it."

"Yes, sir," I sass with a mock salute.

His scorching gaze sweeps over me and I smirk.

Matthias tugs on a lock of my short wavy hair as he passes, winking at me. "I'm going to pack up and see what I can scrounge up. If we're stocked longer, we'll only need to stop for gas."

"Don't even think about taking anything from that creepy ass shrine, Matthias," I warn.

The devious grin he flashes over his shoulder tells me he's absolutely going to do that. A soft, fond laugh leaves me.

Once I change into a pair of leggings and find a forgotten hair tie in the bathroom to secure my hair half up, I head out to my makeshift training course. Part of me is going to miss this cabin when we have to go. It's been our safe haven, and I'll always remember it as the place where my mates forged a deeper connection with me. Where I chased what I wanted and let them in.

Practice starts off rougher than I'd like as anxiety creeps back in. Even if we make it to the underworld without getting caught, what will it mean for me if I can break the seal?

I frown as the fire whip I visualize sputters out pitifully, nowhere near as badass as the whip Valerian wields. Switching to fire blasts, I start jogging, punching my shaky balls of flames through the air, imagining them hitting targets on the move.

My thoughts plague me while I continue to work. If I die, is that it, or will I reincarnate again? Or worse, when the seal breaks, will I return to my true form as Lilith and forget everything about myself as Lily? I don't want to give my fears life, but the second they flit into my head, they take flight, sweeping through me.

An unnatural explosive sound, followed by a

roar of pain, cuts through the woods and makes my heart stop. I swear that was Alder. It didn't come from the direction of the cabin. Forgetting about training, I cast a frantic gaze around to search for the source. Another yell that sounds like Matthias pierces my heart.

"Lily!" That angry, agonized bellow comes from Vale.

They're in trouble.

I take off, following the sounds of powers clashing as my pulse races. The steeper incline nearly trips me with uneven roots and the underbrush I crash through in my need to get to my mates. My heel slips on muddy leaves and I lose my balance. The wind knocks out of me when I land and slide down the hill for several feet, twigs and rocks jabbing my legs, my hair tie snagging and pulling free. Gritting my teeth, I push to my feet and keep going.

Three snarling howls echo around me, the familiar noises gutting me. I falter, my bond aching.

No, no, no. How did our enemies find us? This morning Valerian said there weren't any traces of demons in the area. Could they have masked their presence with magic and carefully planned an attack while we thought we were safe?

It doesn't matter. I have to get to them and help.

They are my everything. The matching shards

of my heart and soul that bind together to make us whole together. They're where I fit and I'm terrified of losing it and being isolated again without my fated mates.

I can't think straight. Can't breathe as terror settles like a leaden weight in the depths of my stomach.

Reaching the base of the hill, I burst out onto a backroad. An abandoned strip mall is across the street with the windows blacked out and half the buildings covered in graffiti. A crash inside an arcade at the end spurs me into action.

My ragged breaths scrape my throat and with a vicious slash of my hand, fire wraps around my fist. The locked handle melts beneath the searing heat covering my fingers and I shoulder my way inside.

"No!" I scream as I rush forward.

A frighteningly large demon with dark brown coiffed hair in a white suit oversees everything with a bored expression while several other thin, monstrous looking demons jump around the room chaotically, their features twisted in chilling fanged grins that stretch their skin. A woman in tight leather and a cloak shifts over to keep me at bay.

My worst fears play out before me.

Valerian, Alder, and Matthias fight the laughing demons that have them bound in chains. Valerian bares his fangs while Alder's claws spark against their bindings. Matthias' eyes glint with fury as he jerks against the restraints.

They won't break. They must be infused with magic to drain their strength because they're not using their flames.

Instinctively, my power takes over, fueled by my fury at seeing my mates hurt. Except when I push out to rain an attack on my enemies, the flames sputter out, stealing my breath as unbearable pain lances through my chest.

No. Not now. Don't fail me when I need to save them.

I try again. Again. *Again*.

Nothing. My powers won't obey while my mates are tortured before my eyes.

One of the demons stabs Matthias in the chest, right through his heart. Ice spreads through me, the stab echoing in my own chest as if those claws carved through my heart by stabbing my mate.

A wail wrenches from me as our eyes meet. He mouths my name before his eyes go dark. I freeze as his head slumps.

"Matthias!" The others fight harder at my shriek, calling for him to get up.

The demons make sure I'm watching as they position themselves behind Alder and Vale next. They struggle, but can't escape before the laughing demons rip their throats out with their teeth.

Raw power races through me as I fall apart with heavy sobs. It scalds me from the inside out, unable to unleash like I want it to. Like I need it to in a vengeful, raging torrent of hellfire for daring to hurt my mates. My power razes me instead of my enemies.

I keep trying until my arms sear with pain and I struggle to breathe, my skin cracking and burning like paper, embers eating away at my flesh. Ignoring the agonizing scorch of flames, I push myself harder because I can't lose them.

My failed attempts makes the demon near me peel back her blood red lips in a chilling, satisfied grin. "You should've died years ago," she hisses. "You're more trouble than you're worth. We won't have you wrecking our meticulous planning."

Two tall, thin demons flanking her release sinister, shrieking, high-pitched hysterical laughter. They dance around, relishing my increasing panic when nothing works. They remind me of Matthias—tricksters, but purely evil.

I can't break past an invisible barrier that kept me from running to them. Kicking dusty posters and a rotting piece of cardboard away from the floor, I gape at the eerie white glowing symbols circling around me. The bitchy demon and her minions laugh as I pound a fist weakly against the spell keeping me from getting to them.

I'm bound to a magic prison. They baited me. Lured me here after capturing my mates to force me to endure the agony of their deaths.

Twenty Five
LILY

*L*ILY. VALERIAN'S VOICE IN MY HEAD CUTS THROUGH MY anguish. *Hold on, little flower. We're coming. I know it hurts. We sensed it. We're almost there.*

I stagger, clutching a pinball machine within the boundary trapping me. He's alive. They're all alive and they're coming for me. The cracked open cavern in my chest throbs, the cord connecting me to them pulled taut in the opposite direction.

The demons lured me with a trap, but it's not real. They've messed with my mind. Preyed on my worst fears with the cruel illusion of my mates in trouble.

With the last of my strength, I push a thought to him, hoping it reaches him. *I'm sorry*.

I believed I was coming to their rescue, but I

only fell for the trick. Now they could truly be in danger needing to rescue me. My vision is woozy from trying to use my power.

Hold on for me, Lily.

"What are you waiting for?" The demon in the suit unfolds his arms. "She stepped in the curse circle. Kill her now, Petra."

"Yes, sir." Petra approaches me with a gleam in her yellow eyes.

"Hell no, bitch," I wheeze. "I didn't survive sink or fucking swim just to die here."

Her brows furrow, not getting my meaning. It doesn't matter because the darkened windows shatter behind us and a strong gust of humid air knocks over the cluttered arcade games. My sweaty, blistered grip slips on the pinball machine as a relieved sigh escapes me at the sight of my guys charging through the broken window.

Alive.

I push through pain and exhaustion to drink in the sight of them, my faint heartbeat echoing as I bounce my gaze between them. Fresh tears well in my eyes, and I hate them for the few seconds they take away my ability to see my guys clearly.

"Petra?" Alder barks. "Cessair?"

"You understand duty best, warrior," the sinister demon in a white suit drawls. "If you stand down now, I'll show you mercy. My brothers and sisters on the council only demand Valerian's head for his betrayal to the demon court."

"No. The council is wrong. You will pay for attacking my mate!" Alder's bellow shakes the building.

"Then you die alongside the she-demon," Cessair says.

"You fucking bastard." Valerian's eyes flash a cold, deadly shade of blue, then he rushes Cessair.

Alder and Matthias flank him, their assault coordinated without speaking. Valerian clashes against a wall of flames Cessair erects while Matthias deals with the laughing demons, pinning one under his knee before he uses his claws to slice it from the corner of its jaw to its chest, black blood oozing out. Three of the demons vanish as if they never existed.

"I see through your shitty illusions, old man," Matthias grits out. "They're not as good as mine."

Alder has Petra by the throat after knocking her away from me with a fireball. His grip digs into her neck without mercy. My warrior is stronger than her and her eyes bulge as he squeezes with such force her throat collapses with a nauseating crunch. Not satisfied, he locks an arm around her body and twists her neck until her flesh tears, her head dangling from his white-knuckled grip.

"Cessair!" he shouts as he joins Valerian's fight.

The three of them trade fiery blows while

Matthias creates his own illusions to distract and give the others an advantage over Cessair. Several doubles of my guys materialize to join the fight.

Though I'm in excruciating discomfort, I see the difference. If he hadn't announced his were illusions, I'd believe these doubles of the three of them were real compared to the ones Cessair conjured to torture my mind with. Cessair's versions lacked the right details—the shades and length of hair off, their eyes not as bright—that Matthias perfectly nails in his. I only missed it because I was so fraught by the belief they were captured.

I try to keep my eyes open. My lids grow heavier with each labored, rattling breath I take. Darkness ebbs at the edge of my vision, the shadows encroaching until I'm unable to fight them off.

Someone yells my name as I collapse to the musty floor while the cacophony of fighting rages on.

"Is she alive?" Alder's gruff question sends a sharper needle of agony through me than the sweltering fire I wake to.

Did they burn the building down around us? My eyes refuse to crack open. It's so hot and my tongue sits heavy in my mouth.

Matthias lifts my upper body. I'm out of it, consumed by pain, but I recognize the comfort of his scent. It's sharper, tinged with anger.

He curses when he touches my scorched arms with shaking hands and draws a strangled noise from me. "Barely. She's all burned up and overheated. She needs to heal now."

I hold on to the fact I'm in his arms as he carries me. Then I'm passed off with a curt command, Valerian's bitter smoke scent twining around me.

"I've got you." His accented words are tight and cracking. He presses his lips to my temple. "My flower, my flower, my flower."

Each frayed whisper feels like he's pleading with me. Whatever he wants, I'll give it to him. He has me always and forever.

Everything aches with an acute, stinging throb. It's difficult to draw a full breath as if my lungs have seared away from the inside out.

"Fuck, that trickster demon's curse trapped her hellfire inside. It could've burned her internal organs without any outlet." Alder peels back my eyelids when Valerian sets me down.

It's soft, yet cold. Leaves? The treetops blur overhead. Still in the woods, then. Better than burning alive in the arcade, except I get no relief from the humidity compressing me in the open air.

"—re…safe?" My feeble voice cracks. "'m s'rry."

"Shh, petal." Matthias wedges in beside Alder, his expression fraught with worry. He tries to give me a smile and it crumbles. "You'll be okay. I promise."

I swallow thickly, hating the tremor in his voice. It's my fault it's there. If I hadn't been an idiot, if I hadn't fallen for the illusion that invaded my mind, he wouldn't be upset. Another fiery wave of pain passes through me and I grit my teeth to smother a scream.

"We don't have time," Valerian snaps.

Alder nods gravely and drags Matthias away. He fights, struggling to stay by my side.

"I want to stay with her, too," Alder barks. "But we have to keep her safe by guarding them while he saves her life."

Matthias wrestles away and lifts my hand to his face. A shuddering breath punches out of him. My tears spill over, stinging down my heated cheeks.

"Don't let our mate die, Vale," Matthias orders in a solemn, fractured tone.

"Never," Valerian snarls.

The only thing that soothes the misery of Alder dragging a reluctant Matthias away is Valerian's fierce kiss. I drown myself in it, focusing on him instead of everything else. Every glide of his lips and tongue against mine sends a spark along the invisible tether connecting us.

If this is the moment I die, then at least I'll go with the memory of his kiss on my lips.

He growls. "You're not fucking dying, Lily. I won't let you." He holds my jaw and deepens the kiss. "Keep surviving for me. For us."

I nod, clinging to him. I want that. I want to be with them always.

Valerian strips out of his clothes in record time and pulls me onto his lap. His fingers twist in my brittle hair and his jaw clenches.

The next kiss sweeps me away. Despite the blistering pain, I move against him, grinding against his hard length. My need comes on strong with a life of its own like the bond in my chest. A feral sound reverberates in his chest and my bond hums in response to my mate. I need him.

Let me in. Valerian's voice is warm and demanding in my head. *Give yourself to me, mate. I will make it all better.*

A piercing noise tears from me. *Yes. Please.*

That's it, little flower. He hears my unspoken plea.

Valerian growls, shredding what's left of my singed clothes with his claws to bear me for him. I grit my teeth. With a swift, brutal thrust, he enters me. My back bows and a cry lodges in my throat.

"Fuck," he rumbles. "Hold on. I know it hurts, but I swear to you it won't for much longer."

He sets a quick pace that steals my strained breath. The rough way he takes me reminds me I'm alive. The will to keep living for him, for Matthias and Alder, for *me* burns through me with flames that don't hurt.

Within moments, my heart beats stronger. He's right. The agony begins to subside.

The pleasure overtakes my pain, the heat between us erasing the discomfort, replacing it with a passionate hunger fueled by a wildfire. Our bond rewrites the hurts within me, the injuries covering my body, healing me with each kiss, each caress, each thrust that joins our bodies. The inferno moves from his body to mine and swirls around us, the flickering sparks creating rings of fire at the edges of my awareness.

As the building sensations crest, his tattooed fingers grasp my jaw. "You are mine. You hear me, Lily Sloane? *Mine*, and no one else will ever dare take you from me again. That includes you. Don't you dare retreat. You'll burn bright and vibrant, as the descendent of the fae goddess Lilith should. Promise me."

I nod frantically, my throat clogging. He sees me. He wants *me*. I am his Lilith.

The rings of fire race faster while we collide over and over like exploding stars, then burst in a rain of sparks that send up tendrils of smoke from the ground.

We moan in unison as his cock throbs inside me, the deep pulses triggering my orgasm. The bond goes crazy in my chest, heightening the intensity of everything—the sensation of fullness from his length buried in me, the heady mingling of our scents, both spicy and sweet, the thrumming in my chest that feels like I could reach out and touch the fated threads that tie our hearts together.

"My flower," he rasps. "My Lily flower."

There are no walls left between us. Though he held himself back from me the longest, my love for him overwhelms me.

My arms shake, no longer plagued by the searing, tight pain of my wounds. The burn marks fade as I lift them from his chest to wrap around his shoulders.

"It's not enough." He holds me against him, our hearts beating as one. "You need more."

It takes him several moments to pull out. When he does, he maps a path across my body with his mouth, guiding me to my back on the ground as he moves lower, settling between my legs. He leers up at me as he lowers his head, making sure I'm watching as his mouth covers my pussy.

I gasp as he devours me, his tongue stirring a new wave of arousal. He's relentless, his mouth moving on me mercilessly to bring me pleasure.

Before my thoughts fully form for what I need, he reads me through our bond and makes me come so hard my screams of ecstasy pierce the treetops above us and send birds flying through the air.

The fiery rings no longer surround us, yet the flow of energy along the tether connecting us continues as he worships my body. This is what he meant in the witch's cottage, the energy mates could share to replenish their strength, to heal each other.

An insistent throb pounds in my core. My fingers tug on his tousled black hair. I want him inside me again more than I desire my next breath.

"Vale. I need you. Please, I'm burning for you."

He understands, his piercing blue gaze smoldering as he gathers me in his lap again, our bodies moving together in anticipation before his hard cock sinks into me once more. A shivery moan slips out of me and my head tips back. This time the pace isn't as fast and urgent, the slower build even more intense, spreading tingling sparks through me.

He takes me by the throat with his inked fingers and squeezes slightly, dominating me with each hard thrust. "Ride my cock, mate. We're not stopping until you make a fucking mess on it."

My body bends to his will, the need in me growing more dizzying the more he takes control. I grab his wrist, holding his hand against my throat as my hips move, chasing the sweet oblivion building inside each time I slam down on his cock. When I come, I clench around him, greedy to feel this pleasure forever. He groans, fixing his mouth to my shoulder, sucking fiercely to leave proof I'm his on my skin. He releases my throat to grip me by the nape, hauling me closer.

Valerian teases my fevered skin with his fangs again as his knot swells within me. He buries a groan in the crook of my neck and I answer him as he fills me completely, our bodies locked together and our souls entwined.

The urge has come before and this time it's stronger than ever.

"Do it," I demand. "Mark me. Bite me. Make me yours."

My head tilts to give him better access and he releases a rough, primal sound at my neck on display, fingers digging into me. His cock pulses within me, stroking me so deep, the knot thickening even bigger. Groaning out a curse, he sinks his fangs into my skin.

We both tense at the breathtaking resonation in the bond between us. My fingers scrabble along his glistening muscles and he bands one arm around me, crushing me against his chest. His other hand drops to my ass and grabs it with bruising force.

Panting, he draws back, lapping at the bite with his forked tongue. Shudders rack my body, my sensitive nipples dragging against his firm chest. His luminous eyes collide with mine, full of enraptured possessiveness. His mouth curves into a feral grin, taking my hand and placing it over his drumming heartbeat.

"Mine," I whisper.

Twenty Six
LILY

It takes a few minutes for Valerian's knot to go down. This is the first time I've managed to remain awake through the experience, the sensation of his cock returning to normal as delicious as the stretch of the knot when it grows. When it's fully down, he pulls out, the flood of his come oozing out of me. He releases a filthy, satisfied sound and keeps me on his lap, his movements lethargic.

Exhaustion tugs at me, but I keep my eyes open, not willing to lose a second of basking in his arms wrapped around me. I have lost time to make up for and want every greedy moment with him I can get.

Even feeling his heartbeat against my breast, the unbearable sight of his throat being ripped out remains vivid in my mind. I shift as close as possible, needing to feel his skin on mine to reassure myself he's alive.

"I'm sorry," I whisper. "I didn't think—I couldn't. I thought you were in trouble and it killed me."

"It's not your fault. We should have protected you better. Shouldn't have left you alone." The scorn in his tone directed at himself makes my heart ache. He sighs harshly and strokes my back. "You're safe now. That's the only thing that matters."

His hands continue to wander my body and he kisses me endlessly. I like that he's so handsy with me. Affection glows in my chest for the side of himself my broody disgraced knight kept hidden behind his caustic barbs and abrasive attitude.

"We can't go again," I sass against his lips with a tired laugh.

He bucks against me, massaging my plump ass. "Even if I didn't have the strength to, I would, little flower. If you want my cock, then I'll give it to you until you can't take it anymore." He claims my mouth again with a rumble. "I need to make up for all the times I resisted the desire to do this. And this. This."

Valerian rains kisses on me, each one as devastating as the last, laying his claim to my heart and soul.

"How is she?" Matthias calls as he and Alder

return to check on us. My heart clenches at his voice. "We're clear, but if she's okay, we should move as soon as we can. I've got the car ready."

Alder kneels beside us, clasps my nape, and steals my breath with the force of his kiss. "We thought we'd lost you," he rasps.

He's no longer the stoic man of action, allowing his emotions to bleed through to engulf me. I swallow, pressing closer for another kiss to tell him how sorry I am to frighten him by putting myself in danger.

Matthias slots in behind me, ignoring the fact I'm still straddling my other mate's lap, completely nude in the woods. His heartbeat thumps against my back and his hands still tremble, moving over me gently. I lean against him, craving being near each of them to settle the echo of fearful despair in our bond.

He kisses every inch of skin he can reach, brushing his lips over the claiming bite Valerian marked me with. My breath catches. It's sensitive. I want the others to do the same with their own claiming bites to match it so I carry the marks of my mates.

"I shared enough energy with her through the bond to heal her internal wounds and external wounds to keep her from succumbing to the worst of it." Vale caresses my arms. "Let's go before we're found again. Lily, if you feel anything wrong, you tell us immediately, understand?"

I nod, still exhausted but feeling more of my strength return.

"If need be, we'll stop where we can and give her more of our life force," Alder says.

Inhaling sharply, I grab at him. "What?"

"I told you, little flower." Valerian rests his forehead against mine. "Demons can heal. I'll give you as much energy as you need."

I knew it was shared energy through the bond, but I didn't think it was his life force. Is that why he seems tired?

I shake my head. "What if it's enough to kill you?"

Alder hushes me, squeezing the back of my neck comfortingly. "It's not. The bond wouldn't allow you to kill your mate by absorbing their energy. Come on. I don't want to linger here any longer than necessary."

※

I'm in and out of consciousness on the drive, still recovering from the curse. At some point, I remember waking in Matthias', then Alder's arms, sprawled in the back seat wearing only the shirt Alder had on earlier. They each give me energy through the bond,

Matthias burying his head between my thighs, lapping at me gently for over an hour until I can't take another orgasm, then Alder fingering me with the same steadfast dedication for an endless stretch that leaves me floating in delirious bliss. Their touch restores my strength, soothing away my exhaustion and any lingering aches.

When I wake again with my head in Matthias' lap, the windows are down, fresh salty air whipping through the car. He has a hand out the window, surfing the wind while stroking my hair with the other.

"Feeling better?" he asks when I curl against the pillow of his leg.

"Yeah. A lot better." I sit up and lean into his side.

The lines etched around his tense mouth relax, his gaze softening as it roams my face. He drapes an arm over my shoulder and kisses the top of my head. "Good. I'll never accept seeing you hurt or losing you."

"Where are we?"

His warm chuckle trickles over me and a smile tugs at my lips. "We're almost there. The place you've wanted to see."

A seagull cries somewhere outside and I peer through the window curiously. My eyes light up at the sight of a bay when we drive across a bridge, the hazy coastline beyond it visible past the barrier islands separating the bay from the ocean. This water doesn't frighten me like the lakes, creeks, and ponds we've come across. The ocean smells fantastic.

"The beach?" A buzz sings through me at his broad smile. I'm not sure if it's my excitement feeding to him or his emanating from our bond. "I thought the plan was to retrace our steps to get to a gate?"

"We are," Alder assures me from the front, reaching back to touch my knee. I take his hand. "We were near here. This beach is closer to the gate we'll use."

"You said you wanted to go to the beach, pretty girl." Matthias kisses my temple. "And after this is over, we'll hit every beach topside and the shores of the underworld realms. You want beaches? We'll give you all of them."

A laugh bubbles out of me. "Thank you." *I love you. I love you all so much.*

They see me. Understand me. Care for me in ways I never dreamed to hope for. Happiness overflows in my chest, despite everything at stake, the hardships we've faced, and the attacks of our enemies. They still found a way to take me to the beach.

We roll the windows up and I take in the small beach town we drive through. It's quiet this late in the fall. The only stores open are a tiny supermarket and a flower shop with baskets of mums decorated with wooden turkeys and pumpkins. The car turns down a road one block from the ocean and I crane my neck to see past the dunes at every intersection.

"We'll go through the gate as soon as we're sure your strength is fully restored." Vale catches my eye in the rear view mirror, sending heat zipping down my spine at his leer. "Once we get to our destination, I'll contact Rainer and let him know to meet us when we're prepared. Cessair likely went back to the underworld after he retreated. I'll have Rainer track his movements to learn what we can before we face him in the underworld."

"That suit guy." I frown. "You all knew him. And the other demon with him."

"Petra," Alder growls. "Another warrior demon. She was a dedicated leader to her warrior clan and was always close with the council. Never a match against me, though."

"Is she, uh... Coming back from what you did? You said before the hellhounds could keep getting back up to track us."

"No, they're different. Arguably the hardest to put down. Cessair left Petra behind. Even immortal demons capable of reincarnation can be seriously wounded and killed in the mortal realm if they don't return to the underworld as quickly as possible.

Only the bond of a mate could have kept her alive long enough to heal from that. The assassins you killed when you were attacked at the witch's place, and the ones that attacked us at the motel outside of Brim Hills also met their ends."

Unlike Lane, I don't feel remorse that Petra died at Alder's hand. She's our enemy and he was protecting me. The three of them kill for me without mercy, even back when we hated each other, and I'd do the same for them.

"And Cessair is a trickster like me," Matthias says. "He's our boss and one of the oldest members on the council. Gate guards report directly to him."

"He's behind this." Vale's tattoos shift across his stiff knuckles. "Corruption is poisoning the council. If he's involved in it, then it might not have been a mere demotion when I was assigned my gate in Brim Hills."

Alder's grip clenches my hand. I soothe my thumb across his knuckles. "What makes you think that?"

Valerian works his jaw. "He was…aware of my interest in Lilith. That it went beyond what a demon knight should feel for the king's betrothed he's sworn to guard. I think he wanted to keep me distracted from looking for you and keep a close eye on me to ensure I never did." He releases a sharp laugh. "He underestimated you because you survived and found us instead."

"They're all like that," Matthias grumbles. "Old farts with superiority complexes the size of Texas."

I snort. "Do you know what you're saying?"

He shrugs, shooting me a lopsided grin that makes my heart flutter. "I've always wanted to use that one."

"He's not wrong," Alder says. "The demon council is made up of the oldest bloodlines. They're powerful and experienced."

The light mood in the car evaporates. They exchange glances, then Vale stares at me from his reflection.

"What?" I narrow my eyes. "New rule. No mind speak if you're going to exclude me. I hate being left out."

Valerian's lips twitch. "It's for your protection."

I hang my head, chewing on my lip. Honest vulnerability bleeds into my voice. "Don't keep me out of the loop. Please."

Alder twists to face me with a repentant expression. "They won't be easy to fight. Less so to kill."

"You'll need your full power for us to stand a chance against the council." The steering wheel creaks beneath Valerian's grip. "We're worried because Cessair alone almost killed you."

"The seal..." I trail off, pushing aside my

doubts about being able to break it myself. His gaze sharpens and I inject confidence into my tone to cover so he can't read my feelings so easily. "We just have to believe our plan will work. When we get to the underworld, I'll break it and bring the pain."

Matthias chuckles when I sit up and punch my fist against my palm, sending a gust of smoke and sparks into the air. "Our fierce little fighter."

"We're here," Valerian says.

A crumbling lighthouse stands at the end of the road. The car rolls to a stop at the gate with a dangling CONDEMNED sign. Alder gets out and wrenches the gate open with brute force, his muscles flexing. He trails after the car as we follow the sandy driveway to a small caretaker's house at the base.

"How did you know about this place?" I climb out and pause at the salty breeze shifting my hair and the distant sound of waves crashing beyond the lighthouse.

"The gate is inside the lighthouse," Alder says.

I smirk. "Oh, so when you said near our destination, you meant we're camping out right at the door to Hell."

"It's seldom used," Valerian says. "It's a one-way portal rather than one that grants access both ways, like in Brim Hills."

I follow them inside the tiny abandoned beach house, marveling at the glimpses of the shoreline through the windows. "Can I go down there?"

Alder catches me in his arms before I make it to the door. He cradles my face. "Do you still feel any pain?"

"No, I'm good as new. Look." I flash my hands back and forth. Only the scars of the fire from my childhood remain. "Please?"

"Someone go with her," Vale says. "She's not to be left alone for a second."

"I'll do the ward spells." Alder kisses my forehead and I hug him, enjoying his warm bare chest against my cheek. "Then I'll join you."

Matthias plops my beat up duffel on a rickety chair and coughs at the cloud of dust. "Do you want something warmer to wear before we go out, Lils?"

I pluck at Alder's shirt. "I'm good in this."

He flashes me a wink. "If you get cold, I'll be with you to warm you up, babe."

Valerian sighs behind me. He winds his arms around me and I spin to face him. The openness of his expression takes me by surprise. His mouth presses to mine in a fierce crush and he breathes me in like he's committing me to memory.

"I'll return to you," he promises.

"I'll be counting the seconds until you do," I murmur.

He steals another kiss before he leaves to meet Rainer. A piece of my heart goes with him, the hole left behind waiting for him to come back to me and make me complete again.

Matthias takes my hand. "Ready to see the beach? I wish we could take you to a nicer one as your first experience, but—"

"Yes." The corner of his mouth kicks up at the excitement brimming in my tone. "I don't care. I just want to see it."

"Let's go then, pretty girl." He kicks off his boots and leaves them behind.

We make our way through the back door that has a small deck and steps leading down to the sand. I freeze, staring past the break in the dunes protecting the old house from the tide.

"Wow," Matthias breathes.

"Yeah." I blink, realizing he's staring at me instead of the ocean. A blush colors my cheeks. "Come on."

The first touch of the chilly sand against my bare feet startles me. A delighted laugh slips out as I squish my toes in it. Matthias smiles at my joyful reactions. We move onto the beach and I pick up a shell. He holds out his hand and tucks it in his pocket for me.

It's beautiful. The beach is wild and unmaintained, but it's so perfect.

I watch the waves crash against the shore, the long drag as the saltwater rushes back out to sea, leaving its mark behind on the wet sand. Clumps of seaweed dot the sand and seagulls glide on the wind overhead.

This is amazing. I made it to the beach.

We stroll hand in hand along it. In the distance past an inlet that separates this part of the beach from the rest of the island, I spot a pier with a lone fisherman.

"Thank you," I murmur throatily. "This is the best gift."

"Anything for you." He grasps my chin and kisses my nose.

Beaming, I pull his face down for a kiss.

Twenty Seven
LILY

ALDER JOINS US ON OUR WALK BACK, HIS SMILE SOFT AND tender as I dip my toes in the water. Matthias splashes me first and I shriek at the frigid cold. He hides behind Alder and I scoop water into my hands and fling it at both of them to get him back. Alder glances between us with a lethal smirk and the two of us dash away as he chases us.

I laugh hard enough my belly cramps. His brawny arms catch me around my waist, lifting me. We're both soaked from the splash fight. I kick and scream as he wades deeper into the freezing waves, shirtless, strong, and unbelievably sexy.

"Truce?" I wriggle around to plant kisses all over his square jaw, licking away the salty droplets.

He adjusts me in his arms, supporting me so

my legs wrap around his waist. "It'll cost you a kiss, sweet blossom."

I grin. "I always want to kiss you."

His raspy laugh cuts off as I press my lips to his. A wave breaks against us, his rugged body not moving a muscle against it. I shiver, gliding my tongue against his.

"You're cold," he says.

"Not with you here to keep me warm." I glance back to the shore where Matthias picks out more shells. "Take me back to the beach?"

When we come out of the water, I hop down and race to Matthias, colliding with him with a happy yell. His arms circle me automatically and he laps at my damp skin with a playful growl.

"Did you like your swim?"

"It was short lived." I rub against him, my chilly damp shirt clinging to all my curves. "The water's cold as shit."

"Your nipples are like icicles." He touches my lips. "No more swimming, though. Even with you running a little warmer than a human should, I don't want you to catch a cold."

"Not without one of us taking you." Alder scrubs at his damp brown hair when he reaches us. "The current is strong."

"Here, I picked this one out for you." Matthias offers me a beautiful shell. The pearlescent shimmer has swirls of orange. "It reminded me of you."

I trace the wavy fan shape. "I love it."

Alder takes it and puts it in the pile we've collected, abandoning his soggy shoes. Matthias threads his fingers with mine and walks me back to the edge of the water. Our toes sink in the sand as the water rushes over our feet.

I wish Valerian was here with me, where he belongs. I want to enjoy our life together with only the four of us and no worries in the world.

He's coming back, I remind myself. He promised.

"Hey." Matthias holds my face, his golden eyes bounce between mine. "I love you more than anything. I just want you to know that."

My heart stutters recklessly. His soft smile grows, the tips of his fangs peeking out.

"I love you."

The words come out soft, stolen on the wind. I've never given them to anyone. Once they're out, I want to give them to Alder and Vale, too.

His thumbs sweep across my cheeks. "I know, baby. We all feel how big your love is. Here." He touches his chest. "Today, I was really scared of losing you."

"Me too."

He kisses me, the first gentle press of our lips quickly becoming more. Alder appears behind me while I make out with him.

Matthias burns me up with his kiss, warming me from the cold beach until I'm panting. He holds me close, mapping my curves with his clever sparking fingers. They tease higher, beneath the hem of my borrowed shirt. His tingling touch buzzes as he kneads my ass, then sinks between my cheeks.

I moan with wild abandon, hips bucking against the vibrations. Matthias swallows it as he teases me. Alder rumbles at my back, tracing my hips while he nibbles my shoulder. Being pinned between them is heaven.

Breaking away from Matthias, I face Alder and stare into the green depths of his handsome eyes. "I love you."

He presses his forehead to mine. "And my heart beats for you and you alone, mate."

I sense Vale's return before I see him. A hum lights up the bond and I gasp. Turning, I find him standing on the deck, his tousled dark hair whipping in the wind and his focus honed in on me. I need him. I need all of them.

"Come on." Alder scoops me up and carries me up the beach, back to my other mate.

Inside the house it's warmer, though it's not a natural warmth. It's coming from the four of us. From the desire growing from a flicker to a strong blaze now that we're here together. They take me upstairs. The bedroom is dusty, but I don't care. I don't need fine things and clean sheets—I only need my mates.

Alder sets me down and I immediately go to Valerian. I trace his sharp jaw. "You came back."

"Nothing will keep us apart again," he says roughly.

"Never," I echo with a swallow. "I love you."

He stills, his blue eyes flaring. "I've waited to hear those words from your lips for so long."

"I love you. I love you, I love you." The words won't stop coming, tinged with emotion after being locked up inside me, waiting and wishing to be let out for someone that loves me back.

I have the connection I've always longed for with my demons.

Valerian strokes my hair. "You are the only reason I exist, Lily. To love you for all eternity."

A whimper escapes me and I crash against him. He fists my hair and captures my mouth in a scorching kiss. *I love you*, he says reverently in my mind.

I grew up an orphan desperately aching to be loved. I never imagined I'd have three fated mates that match me so perfectly.

The room fills with my favorite scents. Woodsmoke and charcoal. Campfire roasted chestnut and maple. Rich, spiced hickory. And my own cinnamon scent dances with each of theirs. I want to be as connected to them as our scents are, the bond urging me on.

Alder strips out of his drenched sweatpants while Valerian stops kissing me long enough to divest his clothes, then tugs me back against him. Air rushes past my lips in anticipation. We don't need to say anything, not even through Valerian pushing thoughts into our heads. We all ride the tidal wave of desire crashing over us.

"We'll break the bed if we all climb on," Matthias says.

"Hold her up," Valerian suggests.

Alder peels my wet shirt off, baring me for them. Three leers drink me in. The wet shirt plops to the floor as Alder cups my breasts from behind me.

He bends and guides my arms around his neck. "Hold tight."

I do as he says and he stands tall, lifting me by my thighs. He opens my legs, and Valerian and Matthias freeze, their hot gazes dragging over me. Every time they look at me like that, I feel like the most gorgeous woman in existence.

"Fuck, I love the sight of you spread like that." Matthias discards his pants and fists his cock. "You're the most beautiful vision, petal."

"Agreed." Valerian strokes the insides of my thighs. "So soft and perfect."

"Fuck me," I beg. "Someone. Please."

They chuckle and Alder's grip flexes on my legs. Valerian nips at my lips and glides the tip of his cock through my slick folds. I strain my hips, but Alder won't let me have what I want.

"Please."

"You want my cock, little flower?" Vale rumbles.

My lashes flutter and I tip my head back on Alder's shoulder. "I need you inside me. I want all of you." A sharp cry escapes me when he stops teasing me and thrusts inside. "Yes. Please."

"We've got you," Matthias croons in my ear.

"You want all of us?" Alder murmurs.

I nod, gasping as Valerian pulls back and snaps his hips, filling me to the brim. My nipples tighten with a sweet ache. Matthias hums, playing with them.

"Give her to me," Vale orders. "Matthias, open her ass for Alder."

"With pleasure," Matthias says in a sinful tone.

A moan slips out of me as Alder guides my legs around Valerian's waist and lets him support me, his cock sinking deeper with every hard thrust. I cling to his shoulders, my nails digging into his inked skin. Matthias' touch skates down my spine, sending tingles straight to my core with the sparks buzzing in his fingers from his power. Just as he did earlier, he teases my ass, circling my hole. My pussy clenches on Valerian's cock and he groans, gathering me closer.

Matthias spreads my cheeks. "Spit, big guy. Let's get her nice and wet for you."

Alder kisses his way down my back as he bends and instead of spitting, his tongue drags across my tight hole. A throb pulses in my core and my breath hitches.

Valerian smirks and slams into me again. "She likes that. Her pussy is getting wetter."

"Next time," Alder promises. "I'll devote an entire day to feasting on every inch of you."

A thick glob of spit hits my asshole and I shiver as Matthias rubs his buzzing fingers through it. "Relax," he instructs. "It'll make it easier."

"I trust you." I mean it wholeheartedly.

It's not bad. The heat he warms his fingers with helps me ease open for him. Before I know it, my hips push back for more.

Alder shifts to watch as Valerian fucks me with slow, unrelenting precision and Matthias fingers me open to get me ready to take him. He jerks his massive cock, gathering the precome leaking from the tip. Stepping closer, he spreads my ass cheek more and adds his slickness to the spit Matthias uses to lubricate me.

I feel full already, the stimulation in my pussy and ass sending me right to the brink. My hazy gaze meets Valerian's and my lips part at the gleam in his eye.

"You're fucking beautiful like this," he rasps. "Getting fucked by your mates."

"Yes," I whimper.

"Are you ready for Alder to fuck you, petal?" Matthias kisses my shoulder. Cheeks hot, I nod fervently. "Good girl."

He moves out of the way, stroking his cock while he watches us. Valerian holds still, fluttering kisses up my neck as Alder spreads me to spit on my stretched hole again, then lines up. Even with Matthias' preparation, the first nudge of Alder's huge cock steals my breath.

"Open for us, my sweet blossom." Alder mouths at my neck. "I promise I won't hurt you."

"They'll feel so good filling you up, both of them at the same time." Matthias circles my nipples with his fingers, giving me electric jolts of ecstasy that throb in my clit. "And whoever finishes first, I'm taking their place to keep you so full you'll feel us everywhere for days. Because you're ours, mate. Ours to fuck. Ours to worship. Ours to pleasure. Every one of your sweet sounds when we make you come belongs to us."

"God, yes," I cry. "I belong to you. I'll always be yours."

I lose my breath again when Alder takes my

hips and sinks inside inch by inch, stretching my body further than I thought possible to fit his cock. Matthias fondles my breasts and draws my face to his for a kiss while Alder takes his time working his cock into my ass.

"Lean back against me." His arm wraps around my shoulders to guide me back against him. "Just feel."

He starts to move and my eyes roll back as he pulls out and pushes his cock back in. Then Valerian does the same. They work into a rhythm that leaves me lightheaded between their ridged lengths filling me at once.

It's overwhelming, but good. My senses are on overdrive, drunk on the blend of our arousal feeding through the bond between all four of us.

The connection between us sings in every inch of my being to the depths of my soul.

When my orgasm explodes from the slow build of taking them both, my body locks up and I scream. It's so intense, the erotic wave smashing through my core over and over. They support me while they fuck me, keeping me pinned between them. Alder holds me up, tethering me while my cresting pleasure threatens to sweep me away.

"Such a good girl, coming for us," Matthias praises. "So pretty when you fall apart."

I want him, too. My fingers reach for his cock and

he steps within reach. He slides his fingers between me and Vale, finding my clit. My chest heaves as he hits me with intermittent jolts of sparks to tease me over the edge again while the others fuck me. His cock leaks on my fingers continuously as I jerk it, his length growing slick with precome. I bring them to my mouth and taste him, wishing I could take him in my mouth.

"Let me taste you with me on your tongue." He tugs my hand back to his cock and leans in to kiss me with a groan.

I break away with a strangled cry as Valerian thrusts harder.

"Fuck." He tenses, burying his throbbing cock deep in my pussy as he comes.

Alder rumbles against my ear when my back arches and my muscles clamp on his length. "So tight."

Valerian trails biting kisses along my jaw. "Take good care of our girl."

The moment he pulls out, Matthias makes good on his promise to keep me full while Valerian steps back to watch. He sinks in with one smooth glide that sends a ripple of heat through me.

"So good," I whimper.

"Yeah, baby?" Matthias caresses my thigh wrapped around him and grinds deeper. "You love taking it."

"I do," I breathe. "Fuck me."

When they groan in unison as Matthias drives into me, my back arches. I never want this to end. It feels so right to have my mates inside me and I want more.

"Mark me. I want you both," I urge.

Alder releases a feral sound when I bare my neck. The scrape of his fangs on my skin is divine. His claiming bite makes my mouth part on a silent cry at the sensations racing through me from the bond. After he laps at it, he moves back and Mathias gives me a crooked grin. He kisses me, then trails his lips down my jaw, my neck, and sinks his fangs into me with his claiming bite, doubling the intense pulse from the bond.

The fated magic cord signs in harmony, connecting the four of us together. I shatter, falling into oblivion in my mates' arms. They have me. They'll never let me go.

This is how it's always meant to be. The three of them surrounding me, their bite marks left on my skin a permanent reminder that I'm irrevocably theirs.

Alder releases a deep groan and his cock pulses, filling my ass. It sets Matthias off and both of them dig their fingers into me while the three of us ride out our orgasms. We stay joined like that, panting and trembling.

Valerian tips my chin up for a soft kiss. "Are you okay?"

I nod, shivering with aftershocks. Alder pulls out first. I whimper at the loss and Matthias hushes me as he carefully does the same.

"You did so good, petal." He rests his forehead against mine.

"That was amazing." My smile is drowsy in a good, *no thoughts, only orgasm coma* way.

They've left my body singing, floating in a blissed out ebb and flow.

I can barely move after my last release. All I know is Matthias is holding me. Alder says something about a bath and a delirious laugh bubbles out of me. "This place is abandoned. I doubt there's a nice bathroom, let alone running water."

Yet it didn't occur to me that we're demons. He finds a basin and hauls it to the bedroom while Matthias massages my lower back with heat emanating from his hands. Valerian helps Alder fill it with seawater and in no time they have a steaming bath ready for me.

Valerian swirls his tattooed arm through the water. "What was that about doubting our ability to care for you, mate?"

"I'll never doubt you again." I stick my tongue out at him as Matthias helps lower me in, giggling when Valerian gives me a wry look and pinches my ass beneath the water.

The hot saltwater feels great against the ache between my legs and in my backside. I relax, closing my eyes as Valerian cards his fingers through my hair. Matthias perches on the other side of the basin and Alder kneels near my feet, reaching into the bath to massage my limbs.

They stay with me.

A smile tugs at my mouth. I have the missing pieces of my heart that have made me whole. Nothing will take this away from me.

Twenty Eight
LILY

AFTER TWO DAY'S REST AT OUR PRIVATE LITTLE STRIP of beach at the lighthouse, I grow antsy and announce I'm ready. Valerian doesn't want to hear it, but I argue with him that we're giving Cessair and the other dicks on the council more time to play kings with their home.

"Our home." Alder speaks firmly, getting between us before our fighting gets out of hand. "Yours and ours, Lily."

I rest a hand on his chest, over his heart. "My home is wherever I go with you three."

"You should rest more," Valerian grits out.

"No. You said it yourself. We're out of time." I sigh, moving around Alder to cup Valerian's jaw. He clasps my wrists. "We can't put this off. They've stolen enough from me."

A muscle in his cheek twitches and his grip digs into my wrists. "I know." He exhales jaggedly. "Forgive me for being selfish."

"I love that about you," I whisper, then press on tiptoe for a bittersweet kiss.

My fear of this slipping out of my grasp rears up. I shove it back down and bury it inside.

The flame burning inside me that kept me fighting to survive was almost snuffed out by the time fate guided me to cross paths with my mates. They stoked the flame back to life, feeding it to a roaring inferno.

They are my reason to fight. To survive. For them and for myself. For everything I've been denied being stuck on this earth destined to suffer until I found the ones who healed the jagged shards of my heart.

No more. I'm terrified of going through that portal, but I won't be less for anyone else ever again.

Vale's gaze bounces between mine. I feel echoes of his own fear of losing me again. I press closer to reassure both of us that it won't happen. Nothing will keep us apart.

"Lily," he says roughly.

"It's time," I say. "Those bastards thought they got away with this for the last three hundred years."

He grits his teeth. "Very well."

"Same plan?" Matthias leans against the wall. "We need to outsmart Cessair and whoever else is on Team Asshole. You know Cessair isn't calling the shots. Leadership isn't his style. He prefers to let someone else do the heavy lifting while he reaps the benefits."

"I know how he thinks. Sneaking back in under cover is out. All isn't lost, though." Valerian paces the small room, stroking his angular jawline. Alder's arms band around me and tug me against his broad chest. "This gate will put us close to a wellspring in the underworld."

My stomach turns. "A well?"

"Not necessarily a physical well," he answers. "Hell has many natural pockets of energy that provide the demon fae with their restorative power. It's how we can heal, even when we're in the mortal realm."

"River Styx?" Matthias' brows pinch. "Yeah. Cessair won't expect us to come through Hell where the human souls crossover."

"The waters will help undo the unnatural curse binding her," Alder says.

My nose wrinkles. "There will be souls in the water?"

"We're not making you eat souls, though it would help you regain your full power faster," Valerian says.

"Hard pass."

"The waters have absorbed the latent power of the souls that are ferried to their afterlife. We'll have to worry about any soul reaper demons and hellhounds in the area, but otherwise it's the nearest natural pocket of energy we can get you to. Once there, you'll be able to break the seal."

"And then we go for the council." The brittleness in Alder's tone is shocking. Compared to the demon I first got to know as someone who respects his orders and the chain of command, he sounds ready for bloodshed. "They'll pay for all they've made you endure. They're the ones who put you in the hands of the humans who harmed you."

I shiver at the vow of violent retribution bleeding into his words.

Valerian touches his wrist and murmurs, activating the glowing red symbol of his Demon's Pledge connecting him to Rainer. Concentration lines his sharp features to reach the demon knight across the realms, testing the limits of the spell. "The time has come, old friend."

Rainer's voice filters in Valerian's head, and he pushes it through to the rest of us with his telepathic gift. *I tracked Cessair as you asked. He returned to the council's wing of the castle. Most of the underworld is under their rule. They've been acting in place of the king and queen, not just on Lucifer's behalf, but with their own agenda in mind*.

"Do they believe they have the power to dispose of Lucifer to take the underworld for themselves?" Valerian frowns. "Their greedy hunger for power has gone to their heads."

Lucifer has yet to stop them. He's still nowhere to be found, Rainer answers. *I'll make my way to you.*

Valerian nods. "It's decided. We'll leave at dusk and set out to break Lily's seal."

That gives me a little over an hour to hide how much I'm freaking out. We have to do this. The council won't get away with what they've done to me and my mates. We're going to the underworld to kick ass so we can be left the hell alone.

"I'm going to change," I say.

And I need a minute alone to prepare for what awaits us.

"Not keen to rock up wearing nothing but your mate's stolen shirts, barefoot and commando beneath?" Matthias wriggles his fingers teasingly. "That's the way we like you. Easy access."

I level him with a sardonic expression. "Well, you dickheads kept shredding my clothes with those claws, so yeah, your shirts are offered up as acceptable sacrifices. I don't have much, but I fought with my elbows out to score my small collection of vintage pieces from secondhand shops."

He pops off the wall and threads his fingers in

my hair, tugging lightly. "I'll buy you new clothes, babe. You'll never want for anything ever again."

I nuzzle against his wrist with a soft sigh. I can't lose this.

"Okay. Be right back, I have to go get hot as shit for going to war." My clothes have always been my armor. My source of confidence.

"That's my girl." Matthias smacks my ass and makes me laugh on my way up the rickety, worn steps in the lighthouse caretaker's house we're squatting in.

I pick through my bag, smirking as I remember the first time Matthias saw me in my suspender skirt, how much Alder's found an appreciation for my crop tops, and how Vale's gaze flares when I'm in fishnets.

Cessair and his accomplices put me in this body, but it's mine. Every curve, every dimple, every roll. It's beautiful and fierce, and with this body they intended to be my downfall, I've survived.

I change into a tight red crop top, a leather jacket, and high waisted black distressed shorts. The fishnets aren't exactly practical for battle, yet they're a necessary part of the metaphoric armor I pull around myself. The difference between now and who I was when I stepped off the train into Brim Hills is that I'm no longer alone.

Leather boots finish off my outfit. I check the

cracked mirror and set my jaw at my reflection. How would the previous Lilith like this look? In my past life, I seemed so restless stuck in those gowns, but full of confident spirit. Drawing a breath, I search for that version of me in my mind.

The dreams I've had of another world are all that remains. Who knows what's locked beyond the magic seal?

Don't screw us, Lilith. I love our mates, and if you grant me your strength, I'll share them with you. Help me break this seal without destroying who I am now.

My amber eyes glisten in the reflection.

Rainer arrives by the time I return downstairs, looking every inch a roguish demon knight. He tips his head in greeting with a smirk. "Princess. I see you've sorted the balance between them since we last met."

"It's not princess anymore," I say. "Just Lily."

Matthias slips his hand into mine. His clever golden eyes see through the brave face I put on. "If you're not ready, we don't have to do this."

Damn it. I thought I was masking it. "I am. And we do."

Alder appears at my other side, squeezing the back of my neck. "We'll protect you no matter what."

"Let's go." Valerian meets my eye, trapping me in his astute gaze.

I keep hold of Matthias' hand and push past

him before he asks about why I'm barely keeping it together under the surface. It's all I can do to keep the worries plaguing me at bay, trying to stop my anxieties from feeding along the bond tethering me to my mates.

The climb up the rusted iron spiral steps in the lighthouse is only making it worse. To distract myself, I voice the first stray question that pops in my head.

"Does this Hell gate have an urban legend, too?" I crane my neck to look at the top of the lighthouse past the point the steps have deteriorated.

"Nailed it." Matthias brackets his hands on the railings on either side of me, climbing right behind me. "Locals claim it's haunted with steps that lead to nowhere and don't reach the top. The portal is past that point, but since it's a one-way trip it's less active."

The closer we get to the top, the more my breathing becomes strained. "And how do we activate it?"

"You'll feel it. This one doesn't have a ritual. It will recognize demons," Alder calls back from a few steps above us.

Rainer is ahead of him. Vale brings up the rear. Alder and Matthias are going to hold my hands, surrounding me as we go through together like they promised. It doesn't stop me from picturing being rejected by my true place.

"See you on the other side," Rainer says.

Shimmering static electricity like I saw in the Brim Hills graveyard crackles through the air above the broken steps. It looks like he needs to jump into it. My heartbeat drums erratically and my palms smoke as my emotions fray. He flashes a grin and steps on nothing—on air—and vaults himself through the portal that ripples around him with a flash of light.

Valerian pushes up to join me. He pins my hips against the cool brick wall. Alder plants himself at the top and Matthias blocks the path down. The three of them surround me, forcing me to face them.

"Don't lie to us, mate. We sense your fear. You can't hide it from the bond," Valerian rumbles. "Say the word and we call this off."

"We can't," I push out hoarsely.

"We'll do anything when it comes to you," Matthias says.

Alder cups my cheek and angles my face to his. He swipes the teardrops spilling over. "What are you afraid of?"

"Losing you." A shuddering breath hisses out of me. "Of being separated from you forever when I break the seal. I—I'm afraid that I don't exist. That the real Lilith is waiting to break free."

Valerian growls, getting in my face. "You

are Lilith, little flower. You. You're our mate. Our goddess incarnate."

The others make fierce noises of agreement. I swallow past the lump in my throat.

"We'll never be separated again. Right?" Vale gives me a hard, heart-stopping kiss.

"Never." I clutch his arms.

They study me for another beat. I nod, harnessing the flickering fire within me. This body is mine. This life is mine. Their love is mine. No one can take any of it from me—not even my past self locked behind the seal.

"Okay," I say.

"You can do this," Alder says. "You're a survivor."

"Our little fighter," Matthias adds fondly.

"And you're not alone." Valerian's knuckles graze my jaw. "With us, you'll never be alone."

Their belief in me twines around me, chasing away my doubts. When I falter, they're there to catch me. It's the reminder I need, the push that keeps me going.

We face the crackling air of the portal together. Anticipation of the unknown flutters through my stomach. Is this what the moment in isekai manga where the main character faces their new world feels like? Uncertainty, yet pulled in by the allure of the unknown? The thought stirs a rush in me. I always dreamed of that moment and this is my chance to live it as I step back into the place I truly belong.

"Ready?" Alder asks.

My chin dips in determination. "Let's do it."

Vale steps behind me and the others take my hands. We climb the last available steps. A faint wind blows through the portal that is much warmer than the damp, chilly air at the beach below. It feels nice.

Before I step through the gate, the hardest moments of my life flash through my mind. Mrs. Clark's wariness of how unnatural she claimed I was. The kids that bullied me because they were afraid of me. The times the world looked down on me and drilled it into my head I was not enough.

I am enough. I've always been enough.

Gritting my teeth, I jump into the shimmer in the air, Matthias and Alder squeezing my hands tight. My stomach plummets when it feels like we'll fall to our deaths before we're compressed on all sides and sucked through dark clouds of smoke. The sensation knocks the wind out of me. For a moment my panic spikes, remembering the black smoke portal in the castle.

The only thing keeping me upright when we hit hard ground is their grip on me.

"Sorry. We should've warned you the landing can be rough," Matthias says.

Valerian lands nearby in a swirl of smoke with

more skill than me. He comes to my side, grasping my chin to check me over.

"I'm fine."

Rainer, now sporting short horns, gets up from his perch on a rock and shakes his head with a smirk. "Thought you'd gotten lost. The area's clear. Hellhounds are up in the canyon's caverns, but I don't sense any soul reapers."

To underline his warning, a bone-rattling howl splits the balmy air.

Now that we're no longer in the mortal realm, my guys have dropped the small glamorous that masked their demon traits, their ears pointed and their eyes more luminous. Maybe it's the effect of being in the underworld, the natural power in tune with them.

My lips part as I take in our surroundings. We did it. We're in Hell. Some part of me recognizes it, unfurling inside me like a flower in bloom. It's strange to recognize a place I've only seen in my dreams and fragmented memories, to not feel the ever present ache of being out of place, yet have no idea what lies ahead.

At first glance, we could be at the base of any craggy ravine, but the sky above is a deep hue of red twilight with violet clouds that no sunset could create. Steps carved out of the dark colored stone rise in the distance, the top shrouded in fog. I wonder how far we are from the Devil's castle in the city reaching into the otherworldly sky.

"We should move before the hellhounds pick up our scent," Alder says.

Valerian gestures behind us to the mouth of a cave. Blue light like the kind put off by bioluminescent organisms casts a soft glow on the walls coming from a small stream weaving a meandering path through it white smoke bubbles from its surface.

"This way," he directs. "It's the fastest route to the river from here."

Twenty Nine
LILY

We remain alert on our journey through the cave. The deeper we go, the more faint whispers and the occasional eerie moan echoes off the cave walls.

"What is that?" I hiss when it sounds closer.

"Souls trapped in the waters. Well, what they've transformed into. A soul that cannot crossover because it follows the offshoots of the river becomes…lost." Alder crouches to pass a hand through it and shimmering apparitions race against the current for his hand with chilling screeches.

"Watch out!" I yank his arm. "What the hell, Alder?"

He chuckles and wipes his hand on his leg. "They won't hurt me. They're nothing more than mindless creatures that swarm when they sense stronger beings to leech from."

"Jesus," I mumble. "What a terrible fate. I thought demons eat souls for their power. Why let any get away?"

"We do," Matthias answers. "But fresh ones. We can't consume the ones in River Styx. It was one of the stipulations of the treaty the old humans made with the demon fae, granting safe passage to the afterlife as the gods always had."

"There's nothing to help the lost souls get back?" I frown at the bright blue water. For a long time, I was as lost as they are. "That's depressing."

"That's life," Vale says. "Keep moving. We don't have time to sightsee."

"But after." Matthias grins. "I'm starting a list. It will be an epic tour of beaches first, then the sights of the underworld realm I'm dying to show you. I can't wait to watch you experience it all."

He lightens the tense mood, helping me breathe easier. Despite the fact we're here to face our enemies, every moment I spend here lifts a weight off my shoulders. Little by little, Hell seems to seep into my bones, directly into my being through the soles of my feet from the damp stone.

Is this what Valerian meant by the natural restorative energy in the underworld? We haven't reached the wellspring yet, and I already feel—

something. Stronger. More in tune with the power thrumming inside me. I'm even able to sense the bond with my fated mates better, and beneath those threads connecting us, the hazy shape of the seal forms in my mind.

I halt, eyes unfocused. It's intricate, the symbols similar to the curse circle trap Cessair set in the arcade connected by the gnarled roots of a tree. They're a tangled mess, interwoven through the magic binding. An unwanted weed that took root and choked out everything else, growing a forest's worth of unruly vines.

"Lily?" Valerian rests a hand at the small of my back.

I wave him off. "I can...visualize the seal."

He inhales sharply, glancing at the others. "I was right. You're stronger here. Your scent is growing more potent." Grasping my jaw, he demands my attention. "Now you smell like a demon, little flower."

"Your eyes are glowing," Matthias says. "And you smell even more delicious, mate."

"Do you feel the source of your power?" Alder prompts.

I lift a palm and with much less effort than it takes me in the mortal realm, I create a dancing flame. Fascinated by how my power feels completely under my command, I add a ring of sparks to spiral around the flame, eyes widening when it works.

"Holy shit," I whisper. "I'm doing it."

"Good," Alder says. "This is a promising sign. Your power is coming through the cracks you've made in the seal with more ease because you're here where you've always belonged. The birthright of your goddess ancestor is flowing into you."

"They never could have kept you weak in the underworld. Not when twenty minutes has this effect on you after two decades away to emaciate your power," Vale says.

"The cave splits ahead. It's not far to the main river once we reach the other side," Rainer says.

I don't let my flame dissipate when we continue, marveling at its beautiful form. A thrill shoots down my spine. This is working. Our plan is going to work.

For the first time, relief creeps through, no longer shrouded by doubt about breaking the seal. Being in the underworld fills me with a breath of life that leaves me eager for more, to shed the cursed shackle binding me as a changeling and claim what's rightfully mine—my place here.

But not as Lucifer's bride. A smirk twitches my lips.

I could be useful in other ways. Carve my own path. In the memories Valerian shared with me, I seemed to have the same hunger for life. Possibility opens on the path of my future, waiting for me to chase it.

First I have to break this seal. I'm ready to see if I can form my own claws and use them to hack through the unwelcome roots keeping the seal magic in place.

The end of the cave lets out into a misty forest that thins as we make our way through the trees. The stream widens and flows down a waterfall into an underground pocket. More whispers follow us and I can't shake the sense we're being watched. I scan the trees, swearing small sets of glowing yellow eyes track us.

I catch up to Alder and lean into his side. "More lost souls?"

Valerian shakes his head. "The lesser beings of Hell. They're recognizing a superior power. Yours."

I slide my lips together. "Let's hope their gossip doesn't spread before I break the seal. We wouldn't want the council to find out we're sneaking in before we're ready to take them down."

"It's far too late for that, Lilith."

Fuck.

Our group tenses, whirling at Cessair's nasty voice. He appears through the trees, materializing out of thin air much like Rainer did the first time he found us when he drops the spell to hide his presence.

Cessair is joined by four others in matching

pompous white suits. One is stout with large horns curving back from his head, his sagging face in a permanent moe of sadness, and another with long, pointy gray horns has a venomous air about him, wrapped on his broad shoulders like a cloak. His thick lips curl back, baring his fangs at us.

"Shit," Rainer utters. "Brone and Samael."

Cessair defers to the tallest of the four, a man with pale skin stretched over unsettling angular features. His translucent skin is cracked with thin black lines that spread from his short, sharp red horns and around his fathomless dark eyes. His long white hair parts for pointed ears. The sight of him sends a chill down my spine.

"Alastor?" Matthias hisses. "You? But—you're Lucifer's closest friend! How could you betray him like this?"

Alastor's mouth forms a grim, hateful line. "It's simple, boy. I want what he has. Hell should be mine, not the arrogant, spoiled king's."

Valerian growls. "You aren't fit to rule the realms, you scheming bastard. None of you are."

"And yet we have the people's trust." Brone, the stout one, gives us a smile that's more of a grimace. "We have been at work putting the pieces into place. You won't stop what's in motion."

"We're primed to take our prize after centuries of planning," Samael says in a harsh, terrifying voice.

"Cessair." Alastor waves him forward with a clawed hand.

"You thought I let you win because you came to her rescue? We had spies watching you once I left the mortal realm."

Cessair holds out a hand and the whispers around us increase. The air crackles with static electricity and a small creature with delicate fairy wings materializes, landing in his palm. It's not cute or pretty like the fairies in my fantasy stories—its bared teeth are like needles and its fish-like eyes glow a sickly green.

"We've been waiting for you to arrive so we can end this as we should have long ago. It was clever of Valerian to think of the soul river. It probably would've worked. You've proven to be quite difficult to be rid of, Lilith. Even after we separated your body piece by piece until you were finally weak enough to bind, it seems you've still managed to fight your way past it instead of dying like a good little bitch."

My mates growl dangerously. Gritting my teeth, I surge forward, desperate to attack the bastards who did this to me. Alder's arm blocks me, tucking me behind him. They knew. They've been waiting, ready for us this whole time to stop us from reaching the river.

Keep them talking. Vale's voice echoes through the bond in my head. Matthias and Alder give barely perceptible nods, shifting in front of me while he moves behind me.

"You've broken sacred laws to satisfy your own ends," Alder says darkly.

Alastor laughs, the sound brittle and disconcerting. "Laws only stand in the way of those too weak to take the power they seek." He snatches a creature from a low hanging tree branch and crushes it in his fist without mercy. "We have no use for them. We've done whatever was necessary. Once we take Hell from its weak ruler, we'll restore the underworld as it should have always been. The treaty never should have existed."

"You can't mean destroying the barrier separating us from the mortals?" Matthias jerks his head in disgust. "That would be chaos."

"Precisely," Samael says.

"We won't allow you to continue," Alder counters.

Lily, get to the river. It's right past the trees. Valerian's urgent order enters my head while the others distract the council members. *We'll hold them off.*

"No," I hiss. "I'm not leaving you."

He fists my jacket and mutters against my ear. "Damn it, Lily—"

"I won't," I vow firmly. "I'll never leave you alone."

"Then you need to do it now without the river. Break the seal." His grip tightens and he hauls me closer. "You can do it. You have to."

"You won't be enough to stop us," Cessair boasts. "You've only escaped death thus far because we wanted to know why she survived."

"Yeah? Well we've killed everyone you've sent after us." I pull free of Valerian's grasp and push past Matthias. Alder grabs my jacket, freezing when I hold up a hand. "So far all I've heard is a bunch of douchebag men patting themselves on the back. I'm sick of it."

Alastor's mouth curls into a malevolent grin. "Just like your mother before you centuries ago. She met her end at my hand, and so shall you. The only mercy I'll grant is a swift end because you've already taken more than enough of my time."

My chest twinges and a sharp tingle spreads throughout my body. This demon has taken too much from me. I won't let him steal anything else—I'm done letting anyone decide my fate.

"No fucking way."

Flames spill down my arms into my hands. My nails lengthen into short red claws with the fierce anger coursing through my veins. My guys flank me, ready to go to war with me.

"This ends here," Valerian says.

The forest creatures hidden amongst the mist in the trees screech when I move for the first attack, creating a cacophony while the flames I push at our enemies clash against the twirling fire Brone wields to defend the group. Our hellfire illuminates the forest in violent bursts of light and oppressive heat.

Valerian and Alder charge Alastor while Matthias goes against Cessair. Rainer draws a sword and takes on Samael, and I fling another rush of flames at Brone.

This is nothing like the fights we've faced so far. It takes all my concentration to block Brone's rapid fireball attacks, my speed not as fast as his. Despite his stout stature, he's not slow. I barely have time to check on the others, too busy dodging like Alder taught me.

Rainer fights Samael, coating his blade in flames. They dance around each other in close combat, Rainer's sword and fist challenging Samael's powerful fiery hits matching him blow for blow. I think it's only Rainer's experience as a demon knight that keeps him on his feet as Samael gains ground, punching and slashing with burning fists to land vicious hits.

Matthias conjures fire and illusions to keep Cessair at bay, confusing him with doubles mimicking each move he makes so it's unclear where the true source is. His flames race to circle them, licking up the trees, and from those flames dog-like creatures made of molten stone and smoke burst free. Cessair smirks, unthreatened and counters with a fearsome flash that torches a path straight for Matthias, picking him out from the magic dopplegangers.

I yelp, moving mere seconds before Brone's spiraling fire molded like a spear catches me in the chest, knees skidding in the dirt. Heart pounding, I push to my feet and swing my arm to protect myself with a rush of hellfire. Though it's a strong burst, the flames sputter out before they reach him. He smirks, his sagging cheeks gruesomely folding over his mouth.

Don't panic. Break the seal, Valerian urges. In the corner of my eye, I watch in horror as Alastor rains endless hellfire on him and Alder. He splits his attention between the demon he fights and me, using his fire whip to force Alastor back several steps.

Don't let them win, Lily. Undo what they've done to you. We know you can do it.

My throat stings. We need to do something. My heartbeat stutters as I dodge another bout of blistering flames from Brone, flattening to the ground. How am I supposed to concentrate on breaking the seal by myself while fighting off the demons who did this to me?

They believe in me. It has to work.

Closing my eyes, I seek the seal in my mind, stomach plummeting at the thick roots and vines twisting through the ancient magic. I imagine claws to slice through the mess. Small pieces chip off, but I don't get far. The glowing symbols mock my inability to put a dent in my magic prison.

I gasp, eyes flying open at Alder's grunt of pain. Alastor has him by the throat, talons piercing his corded muscles. With a terrible bark of laughter, he throws my strong warrior aside against a thick tree trunk and turns his attention to Valerian.

"It's time for you to die," Alastor says.

"No!" I yell.

It's not enough. *I'm* not enough to save us—to save my mates. The harrowing truth I've always battled with shreds my heart.

We weren't ready. I can't break the seal and all the training they gave me isn't a match for the old, powerful demons corrupting Hell.

Dark smoke springs from Cessair's fingers like marionette strings, trapping Matthias in a magic swamp. He grunts, blocking the monstrous, skeletal creation Cessair pulls out of it, controlled by smoke, while trying to get his legs free. He's sinking and more illusions surface in the swamp, slashing at him, swarming him. They're too many for him to handle alone. He needs help.

"Matthias!" Alder calls hoarsely.

Valerian's flame whip catches Alastor's wrist and he wrenches. In the spare moment he gains the advantage in the fight, his gaze snaps to Matthias. Alastor knocks him back and pins him to the ground, claws slicing through his skin. Gritting his teeth, he struggles, raking his claws through the forest floor.

There's no curse circle trapping me this time. Before I make a move, Brone blocks my path to my mate, circling me with a ring of fire.

Cessair's grin is triumphant as Matthias chokes in pain when a creature sinks its teeth into his neck and pulls him deeper into the murky water. His golden eyes hold mine, their bright glow brimming with despair, with regret, with bittersweet love.

This isn't one of Cessair's cruel illusions. This time my worst nightmare is real.

"I'm sorry. Remember me, petal." Matthias' wry tone echoes with the melodic magic of his gift, trying to ease my mind, to convince me to believe this is okay, but it only carves deeper canyons in my aching heart when I don't allow his magic to sway my mind.

My mate's head disappears into the mucky swamp.

No. My heart stops. Frantic sounds escape me as I abandon my fight, leaping through the flames, ignoring the sear of pain, forcing my way to him. *No, no, no*. Please. I can't—I can't lose him. Not any of them.

Thirty
LILY

"MATTHIAS! NO!" MY ANGUISHED, PIERCING screams send a pulsing wave of hot air out, knocking Brone away from me and blasting Cessair back from the magic swamp Matthias drowns in. "You promised! You promised not to leave me!"

A piece of my heart breaks off, threatening my ability to live whole ever again without him. He's my light. My reason to smile, the one who makes me laugh. I can't do this without him. Without Alder or Valerian. I need them all—without one of them, I'm lost.

"Matthias," I choke through a painful sob, clawing at the mud as the swamp recedes from my flaming hands burning out of my control, drying it to steam and cracked dirt. "*Matthias!*"

"Lily!" Valerian's yell is raw and broken.

"Lily, move!" Alder begs.

He staggers to his feet and dives to block Brone's fireball from hitting me. The force of it breaks over his body. He falls to the ground and doesn't get up. Again, my bond clamors in my chest as another piece of my heart fractures. Alastor growls and pins Valerian with enough force the crack of bones cuts through the air, the sound twisting my stomach. I scream through a wrecked sob.

It can't be like this. We didn't come this far for our enemies to win. I have to do something now to save us before we all die. I frantically turn my attention to the seal binding me from my true self.

These bastards barred me from the underworld and cast me into the mortal realm as a lost girl. Alastor, Cessair, Brone, and Samael will pay with their lives for their sins. I don't care how hard immortal demon fae are to kill. I will make them suffer.

The roots don't matter. They're a distraction. Another illusion to keep me out. To convince me I can't take what's always been mine.

The cursed seal they bound me with doesn't imprison a demon ready to erase me. I am Lilith. Not two separate parts—all of me. The truth sings clear in my veins now. It has from the moment I stepped foot in the underworld. The reject, troubled girl too afraid of myself with the royal blood of a fae goddess descendent within her.

I am Lily Sloane, the new incarnation of Lilith and *no one* will hurt me or my mates ever again.

I was terrified of losing myself to Lilith, but we're the same. They couldn't stamp me out, couldn't drown me, couldn't steal my power like they stole my life.

Sink or fucking swim.

Clenching my teeth, I drive my hands into the ground, chest collapsing when I feel Matthias buried under the earth. "I choose swim!"

My head flings back and I unleash a screech charged with a fury that awakens the slumbering power of a demon goddess in my blood. The heat of my rage scorches through me in a wild blaze, searing through my skin and exploding from my mouth, my chest, my hands. It's like the instinct that overcame me when we were attacked at the witch's cottage, but with the full strength within my grasp.

Driving my claws into the ground, I grasp what I want. I feel the seal shatter as I rise into the air, pulling Matthias free. My power flows through me, no longer locked away, giving me the strength needed to stop the corrupt demons.

A sharp breath catches in my throat. I remember. Not all of it—I remember being kidnapped from the castle halls through the black smoke portal. I remember the endless pain I endured, trapped by so many curses I couldn't escape.

"Lily." Matthias croaks. "Get that bastard, baby."

He coughs, spitting a mouthful of wet dirt. He's out of breath and caked in mud, but alive. *Alive*.

I smash my mouth to his, praying the hasty kiss triggers the bond to feed him my life force. He clutches the back of my head, breathing easier. When I pull back, his eyes gleam and he springs to his feet.

"Did you think that was enough to put me down, old man?" Matthias prowls toward Cessair, fiery fists poised to strike. "Putting me in the ground won't end me. Only slow me down."

Cessair narrows his eyes and looks past him dismissively to catch my eye. "We bound you once, Lilith. We will succeed again."

"Not before we kill you for doing it the first time," Matthias grits out.

Alder has recovered from taking Brone's attack to shield me, to my relief. Our eyes meet and I feel the echo of his pride in me emanating through the bond. He gets to his feet and uses his formidable brute strength to tackle Alastor, freeing Valerian to get to his feet. Vale abandons strategy and barrels into Alastor's other side, gripping him by the lapel and punching him with a flaming fist. Alastor growls and grabs his face, cutting open fresh wounds with his claws.

"Her power!" Brone squawks at the others. "She's freed her full power!"

"That's right, asshole. *My* power. The one you tried to take from me." My lip curls back from the fangs that lengthen in my mouth. "You failed."

His eyes go round, beady with apprehension. Without the seal, I realize how much my life was dulled down, tamped by magic. It wasn't me that made myself less—it was the curse. My senses sharpen, hearing what I couldn't before while the fighting rages around me, my eyesight keener to take in the nervous sweat beading Brone's saggy forehead.

I bolt to him through the charred trees with newfound speed, my hellfire springing forth before I visualize my attack. The ground turns molten wherever I step, the heat coming off me explosive from being bottled up, ready to let loose.

Brone collapses to his knees. "Mercy, Lilith. I beg of you."

"You're pathetic," I growl. "You fold at the first sign you won't win. Spoiler alert, shithead: you won't."

Grabbing him by one of his curved horns, I rake my claws across his greasy face. They're sharper and longer now that I've broken the curse, my demon traits no longer locked inside. He shrieks, wriggling to escape.

"Samael! Cessair!"

"They won't help you," I hiss.

Kicking his chest, he flies back and crashes against a tree. I trace a circle in the air with my arms, calling on the natural power of the underworld feeding into the deep well of my power. It heeds my call, the ground splitting open with rattling fractures. A cloud of brimstone floods the misty air and fire rises from the depths of the underworld with molten earth to encase Brone against the tree.

His droopy features go slack. "That's not possible. No daughter of Lilith has power like this."

I clench a fist, then leap across the crevice separating us and drive it into his face. His head snaps to the side and I pull back again to throw another punch like Alder taught me. This one knocks him unconscious. And breaks his jaw, the bone crunching against my blazing knuckles.

I want to help Vale and Alder in their struggle against Alastor, but Rainer and Matthias are both fighting alone. Matthias is holding his own against Cessair, but Rainer has lost his sword to Samael.

When I join the fray, Samael's focus locks on me and he releases a hair-raising predatory sound. My heart pounds, recognizing it from the depths of my fragmented, lost memories. He was in charge of my torture, keeping me at the edge of death with curse upon curse.

Fucking bastard got off on every second of pain I endured.

My fire races to my fingertips, burning a bright, scorching blue. Panting, Rainer falls back a step from the sweltering heat coming off me. Blood trickles into his eye and his sleeve is torn.

"Go help the others," I say.

"And let you handle the fun on your own, princess?" He holds up his hands at the ferocious look I shoot him.

"I owe him a world of pain," I mutter.

Samael bares his teeth and sprints at me. I throw my hands up, dissipating the billow of flames he throws at me with my hotter ones, using them as my shield to get close enough to blast his head with an endless stream of blistering heat. He roars, skin burning. Jerking back, he swings a fist at me. The blow knocks me off balance. Alder's steady voice in my head reminds me to recenter myself to stay upright.

"You're twice as ugly now." I swipe the back of my hand across my mouth. "When Lucifer finds out what you've done, he'll charge you with treason and true death."

"He is a fool, hiding away in his castle. He practically handed the crown to us," Samael snarls.

"You're the idiots. You should've killed me

when you had the chance. Now I'm back and I'm pissed."

I launch myself at him, calling once more on the underworld to aid me. The ground melts at Samael's feet. His eyes widen and he sinks faster the more he thrashes to escape. I stop when he's up to his shoulders and wrench his head back by his hair.

"Hell and the underworld realms will never be yours," I spit before smashing his head down on my knee with ferocious strength repeatedly until he's unconscious.

Thirty One
LILY

ONCE I'VE DEALT WITH SAMAEL, I FIND ALDER, Valerian, and Rainer handling Alastor with unrelenting attacks. Matthias is still on his own against Cessair.

I narrow my eyes. They've got this, and I want payback for the arcade and for trying to kill Matthias.

Cessair and Matthias trade blows with their blazing fists, both of them fighting off dueling illusions while brutally attacking each other. Serpents wrap around Cessair's leg, constricting tighter to knock him off balance, while Matthias deals with a horde of the nasty fairies Cessair had spying on us, their spindly teeth tearing into his arms and neck.

Closing the distance between us, I jump onto Cessair's back, winding one arm around his neck and clapping a hand over his eyes. Furious energy buzzes through me and I push a torrent of savage blue flames through my palm. His skin bubbles beneath my grip. I hope I'm melting his goddamn eyes.

"Augh! Fucking bitch!"

His arms pinwheel, claws biting into my skin, scrabbling over the short horns I've sprouted. The injuries he inflicts on me are nothing—they heal within moments as my power beats through me with the rhythm of my pulse. I won't let go, vicious in my attack to blind him.

"Get off, you little cunts." Matthias growls and twists in a spiral, blasting the horde of malicious fairies away from him with a burst of flame and humid wind. He plucks one from the air and pinches its head between his fingers, squashing it. Turning his attention back to us, his lips curl in satisfaction. "You picked the wrong fight, old man. Our girl is unstoppable."

Cessair reaches back and grabs me by the hair. I grit my teeth, digging into his face harder with a renewed shot of heat. He groans and collapses, taking me with him. I roll his body over and straddle his chest, squeezing his throat hard enough to pierce his skin with my sharp talons. His boiled skin and the charred remains of his eyes aren't enough.

He hurt Matthias. He hurt the others. He hurt

me. He doesn't deserve to live. None of them do.

A strangled sound leaves me as I claw at his filthy, tattered suit, the material shredding beneath my furious swipes. I slice through skin and bone, panting through my unshakeable anger. He slaps me and Matthias bolts over with a dangerous growl, pinning Cessair's arms in the smoking dirt.

"I'm going to rip your fucking hands off for that. Finger by finger," he promises. "And then I'll force feed them to you."

When I stop thrashing Cessair's chest, I'm panting and blood soaks my hands. Through his broken ribs and ravaged chest cavity, his exposed heart beats. I wrap my trembling fingers around it.

"Tell me why," I demand. "You're going to die anyway. You're done."

Cessair bucks, but between me and Matthias he's unable to gain leverage. He collapses with a squelched gargle when I squeeze his heart.

"Why?" It comes out low, rough, and shaky.

"Power," he grits out furiously. "You were too unpredictable. Not—susceptible to the influence I tried to plant in your mind."

I squeeze harder, ready to fucking burst his heart between my fingers and roast it in blue flames for retribution. His mouth falls open with a choked gasp when heat builds in my hands and the stench of smoking flesh and blood rises into the air.

"When we realized—you needed to go, we wanted to put our own queen on the throne to manipulate Lucifer." His breathing is labored. "But—But the pawn queen wouldn't be-behave. We knew we had to claim the throne for ourselves."

"Your greed is your downfall," I growl.

All the pain, heartache, fear, and uncertainty I've battled filters through me. The unbearable sight of Matthias disappearing beneath the surface of the swamp. Of Valerian when he was severely hurt guarding me from the demon assassins. Alder's fierce protectiveness against the demons that almost sliced him to ribbons in the motel. The looks on my mates' faces when I almost died trapped by Cessair's curse.

Tears sting my eyes and spill over as the riotous energy of my power culminates to a breaking point in my palms. Fire explodes through my hands, burning Cessair's rotten heart. His body jerks and Matthias holds him down while he babbles. A wet gasp leaves me as I squeeze harder until the seared muscle in my hands bubbles to a liquid state, oozing between my fingers.

Cessair twitches, then slumps. His sticky dark blood stains my hands.

"I killed him," I whisper.

Matthias covers my bloody hand with his, squeezing in support. "If you didn't, I was going to do it. Or the others. Did you want to?"

I close my eyes. "Yes. Do you hate me for it?"

"No. Never." His tone is gentle. He leans in and kisses my temple. "Do you regret it?"

I shake my head. He fucking deserved it. He was going to kill me and my mates if I didn't end him.

"Let's see if the others need our help." He draws me to my feet. "I'm proud of you. We knew you could break the seal."

I don't spare Cessair's body another glance. He brought his fate on himself the moment he crossed me. My focus shifts to my other mates, to needing to help them end this.

Not far off, the others have Alastor on his knees. He's missing half an arm, the bloody limb on the ground, a scrap of Valerian's shirt clutched in the fist. My heart skips a beat and we rush to them.

"You have not won yet, Lilith," Alastor thunders. "You—"

I don't stop jogging, speeding up with a scowl. Alder yanks Valerian out of my path, pride glinting in his gaze as I coat my fist in ruthless blue flames and smash it into Alastor's face. His head snaps to the side from my punch and his chin slumps to his chest. The one hit knockout feels really damn good.

"Shut the fuck up," I grit out.

"Fiesty little princess." Rainer chuckles through

his exhaustion, slumping against a tree, using his sword to brace himself. "Consider our life debt repaid, old friend."

"Beautiful right hook," Alder praises warmly.

"Are you hurt?" Valerian grabs my wrist, examining my bloody hands.

I shake my head, leaning into his chest, covering his own torn up wounds. They mend beneath my touch. His arms close around me, speeding my own healing until I'm good as new. I bask in his embrace, breathing him in. He strokes my hair, holding me tight enough to let me know he's never letting me go.

When he lets me draw back, Alder takes me in his arms. I rub my cheek against his firm chest, passing my hands over him to check for wounds. He kisses the top of my head.

We did it. We're alive and we won.

I leave Alder's embrace to hug Matthias the hardest, still rattled from the threat of losing him. He lifts me and spins us around, face buried in my neck.

After he sets me down, the three of them close in around me, enveloping me in their smoky scents. Valerian catches my chin and draws it to him for a kiss while Alder's hug crushes me against his chest. I turn from Valerian to kiss Matthias. Alder's fingers move up my throat and he guides my head back to capture my lips for himself.

My heart flutters, brimming with love for my mates.

"If you four are going to fuck, can you give me a warning?" Rainer jokes. "The frenzy of battle does strange things to people. The comedown from all that adrenaline hits hard."

I laugh, pushing free of the circle. "Thank you for your help. You risked your life for us."

He smiles softly, patting my shoulder. "I would do it again. I owed Vale a debt, and more than that, he's my brother in arms."

"Will you be alright?" I eye Rainer's blood soaked sleeve, deep gashes from claws cover his skin.

"I'll heal soon." He smirks. "I don't have a mate bond to feed off of. Nifty trick."

I turn back to our defeated enemies with a frown. "What about any people that want them to rule? It can't be just them working alone for this long."

"I believe I'll take care of that," a new voice answers.

I whirl around, fire exploding around my fists, prepared to take on a new opponent.

"Your Highness." Rainer kneels, clasping a fist over his chest.

A moment later, Valerian and Alder do the same. Matthias remains on his feet, inclining his head with

a murmur of respect for the demon.
　　That means—Lucifer.

Thirty Two
LILY

THE KING OF HELL IS TALL, WITH DARK DISHEVELED HAIR, pointed ears, and angelically handsome chiseled features. With one smirk, I know he's a dangerous, intelligent demon. Like the council, he wears a sharp suit, black with intricate details woven into the silk. A fur-edged cloak perches across his shoulders and rings decorate his fingers.

He surveys the destruction around the misty forest, lingering on each of the demon council that plotted to overthrow him. The corners of his mouth kick up in a smirk.

"Thanks for doing the heavy lifting." He strolls up to me and touches my face. "Welcome home, Lilith."

All of us tense at the honeyed tone and the

sweep of his eyes roving over me. The guys shift restlessly. This is their king, but I sense through the bond that they're ready to take him on to fight for me. In the corner of my eye, Rainer clasps Valerian's shoulder, holding him back, muttering in his ear.

Lucifer's brow lifts and he glides his fingertips down my neck.

"Hey!" My head jolts back as my three mates surge forward.

"My, my. You charge at your king like that?" Lucifer laughs, holding up a hand.

They freeze as a ring of brilliant blue fire traps them, blocking their path to me. Each of them set their jaws, prepared and willing to walk through fire for me. My heart pounds and panic floods me.

"W-wait. Please." Lucifer's attention returns to me. "What do you want? I promise to do anything if you'll spare them and let them go."

"What I want?" Lucifer's smile grows. "What would you like, Lilith? Shall I break the bonds you've formed with these demons so you can become the queen of Hell ruling at my side, as you were meant to?"

I shove away from him, fire erupting along my skin hot enough to rival the flames he trapped my guys with. If he won't allow my mates to fight for me, I'll fight for myself.

"No!" My fierce refusal is echoed by three

growled responses from Alder, Matthias, and Valerian. They grow more restless, trapped by Lucifer's hellfire. "I never wanted to be your queen. That much I remember. You won't take me from my mates."

Lucifer laughs, unbothered by my threatening stance. "Good."

I snuff out my flames, eyeing him warily. "Good? I don't get you, dude."

My suspicious distrust delights him. "I knew you were unhappy at the castle. You were much more yourself when you slipped past your guards and ventured out into the realm." He drops the blaze keeping my mates at bay. "I needed to be sure. Though my queen will not be happy with me for offering, even if I had no intention of taking you. She's quite the fiery spirit. You'd like her, I believe."

Keeping an eye on him, I back up, feeling the tethers connecting me to my demons as a guide. They close the distance between us in swift strides until I hit Valerian's chest. His arms lock around me, Alder and Matthias flanking us and taking my hands. Together we're a unified front, us against whatever threatens to tear us apart.

"I hope you can forgive me for testing you." Lucifer's smile falls into a chilling sneer as he takes in the incapacitated demons. He pauses on Alastor, his angelic features twisting, darkening. "I can't be too careful. Even those I trust enough to call a friend are quick to stab me in the back to sate their own greed."

Rainer hauls Alastor's unconscious body up and drags him, wrists bound with the glow of a spell. He moves to Samael and Brone, pausing to consider how to remove them from the ground I encased them in. "At your word, I'll alert the royal guard to prepare three cells, sir."

"Three?" Lucifer's gaze flicks between his council members, landing on Cessair's body. "Ah. I see."

I tense, remembering Alder's explanation of the sacred laws demons abide. I killed Cessair.

Sensing my stress, my guys press closer. They won't let any harm come to me.

"They planned to overthrow you, Your Highness," Valerian says gruffly. "The charge from the council that we betrayed you—that I was planning rebellion—was a lie to cover their schemes. They kidnapped Lily, tried to kill her, and sought to take the realm from you."

Lucifer chuckles dangerously, his crimson eyes flashing. "Oh, I'm not so easily manipulated. I'm the king of Hell and many have tried to fool me. I suspected something was at work when I heard of this."

Valerian's chin dips, grazing the top of my head.

"Sir."

"Truly, the first inclination something was wrong was when Lilith went missing. At first I thought you'd staged your own kidnapping as a way out of our betrothal. You always chased your wild ideas." Lucifer frowns. "But you never turned up. Then this treasonous claim and demons flocking through portals to the mortal realm didn't add up. I used you as bait to draw out those that sowed their corruption while I protected my queen."

"I hate being bait," I mutter.

Alder huffs in amusement, squeezing my hand. "What happens now?"

"Rainer," Lucifer says. "We'll need a prisoner transport."

Rainer bows, placing his fist over his heart before nodding to us. "Until next time, old friend."

"Uh, alright peace out, then." I elbow Valerian to get him to move.

"You're different, yet still much like yourself. Your true feelings shine through. It's good to see." Lucifer's grin shows a peek of fangs. "Where are you off to in such a hurry?"

I open and close my mouth. Right. He's the king of the underworld. We probably need his permission.

"Are we allowed to go? We collected your trash, so we're good, right?"

Matthias coughs to cover his laugh.

"Are you three not guardians of a gate?" Lucifer squints at my guys. "If that's where you wish to return, by all means. Unless you'd like to be reinstated to the knights, Valerian. Seeing as how the charge you guarded is now your mate."

Valerian is at a loss for words. I twist to see his wide-eyed gaze locked on the Devil, tremors of reprieve running along our bond. He's no longer disgraced now that Lucifer knows the truth about my disappearance.

"We'll go where you order us to, Your Highness," Alder says respectfully on Valerian's behalf.

Lucifer studies me for a moment. "I relieve you three from your duty as guards. For your loyalty and service to Hell, you're free to come and go as you please." At my quick inhale of excitement, he tilts his head. "On the condition you'll accept positions on my council, seeing as I have open positions to fill."

It's Alder's turn to be speechless. This must be a big deal.

"Council seats are inherited by descendants of a bloodline," Valerian murmurs in explanation.

"As long as we join the council, we can do whatever we want?" I bite my lip, waiting for another rug to be pulled out from under me—a habit I picked up growing up in the mortal realm.

Lucifer nods. "I wish you the grandest

adventure, Lilith."

"It's Lily now." I stick out my hand. "Nice to meet you."

A huff leaves him and he takes my hand to shake. "Lily. It suits you."

"It does." Warmth infuses Valerian's low rasp. "Perfectly."

"Then I leave you here." Lucifer gestures to Brone and Samael's forged prisons. "They're my—trash, as you put it, to deal with."

A weight lifts off my shoulders as my guys lead me away from our battleground. We make our way to the edge of the misty forest, the sprawling landscape of Hell opening up before us. The underworld flows through me, present in every breath I take. It's part of me, welcoming me back to the place I belong with open arms.

I stop to touch a tree in silent thanks for lending me extra strength to defeat our enemies. The guys give me soft smiles that touch the content bond wrapped around my heart.

"Where to first?" Matthias prompts.

The possibilities are endless. All that matters to me is that we're together. We will be, forever. Nothing will keep me and my mates apart.

A smile breaks free. "Let's go to the beach."

Epilogue
LILY

Three Months Later

"YOU STILL NAPPING, PETAL? I FOUND YOU SOME more shells for our collect—oh." Matthias grins at the sight he walks in on in our tropical villa in Montego Bay, the third stop on our worldwide, multi-realm beach tour itinerary he planned.

Valerian has me on my hands and knees on the huge bed, taking me from behind. My sun hat is discarded by the door, my bathing suit bottoms hastily peeled down around my thighs, and my tits are spilling out of the flowy, off-shoulder sunflower print bikini.

Another strangled cry catches in my throat. I'm trying to be quiet, but Vale is making it his mission to make me scream after he challenged me to be quiet. My fists ball in the sheets as he drives into me harder with an audience.

His wicked chuckle lights me up, pushing me over the edge. "Shit!"

I press my face into the sheets to muffle a moan while I circle my hips, savoring the delicious glide of his cock filling me while my pussy flutters.

He fists my hair, drawing my head up. "No cheating. What's wrong, Lily? Can't you be a good girl and stay quiet?" He covers my back with his chest, bracing a tattooed hand on the bed. "Or does my cock make you scream?"

A breathy groan slips out of me. "You smug bastard."

"This is hot." Matthias grabs the instant camera he bought me when he announced the trip and snaps a photo. "Pull her hair again."

Vale complies, his hips snapping hard enough to make me see stars every time he slams into my pussy.

"Fuck," I breathe. "God, it's so good."

"I know, little flower."

"Hold that position. Yeah, like that. Mm, you're so sexy taking Vale's cock like that." He snaps another instant photo, the print fluttering to the floor for us to discover later. He tosses the camera to a bench and kneels on the huge bed, pushing his shorts down. "You look hungry, pretty girl."

Valerian lets go of my hair and grabs my hips for leverage. Matthias takes over, tugging a fistful hard enough my lashes flutter.

I lick my lips and open for him as he feeds me his cock. His head lolls back with a husky sigh and he pushes deeper into my mouth. I swirl my tongue, moaning around him when he thrusts, shallowly fucking my mouth.

Both of them fill me. I want to make them feel as good as they make me feel.

"Fuck, that's a sight, petal." Matthias cups my jaw. "Open wider. That's it. Shit, I'm not going to last. You're too fucking sexy like this."

He releases my hair and fists his dick, keeping just the tip resting on my tongue. His eyes gleam and his crooked smile shows a peek of his fangs before he grunts. His come shoots into my mouth. I swallow, some of it spilling down my chin. He catches it and pushes it back in alongside his dick. My tongue swirls around his finger and his cock, savoring the taste of him.

He pulls free, grasping my jaw to kiss me, swallowing every sound of pleasure I muffle into the kiss while Valerian picks up his pace and plays with my clit. I come with a gasp, burying my face in Matthias' neck, right where I've marked him with my own claiming bite. They each carry my possessive mark.

Valerian groans my name like a curse and a prayer rolled into one, slamming into me one last time as he comes. He presses a trail of kisses up my back, then pulls out. He spends a moment forcing his come back in me with his fingers before sprawling on the bed.

"You cheated again," he says in a rough, drowsy tone.

I flop onto my back beside him, chest heaving. "You never said I couldn't tag in outside help to stay quiet." My head turns on the pillow of Vale's arm to address Matthias when he stretches out on my other side. "Where's Alder?"

"Fascinated by swimming with sea turtles," Matthias answers. "He's going to be pissed when he figures out he's the odd man out."

A fond smile curves my mouth. "He's taking me stargazing on the beach tonight. I'm sucking his cock later. You two aren't invited."

Vale makes an unhappy sound, dragging me into his lap when he sits up. "We're invited if we want to be, mate. Maybe I'd like to watch these beautiful lips stretched for our brother."

"Agree to go parasailing with me," I barter. "I told you, I want it to be you. Then you can watch all night long."

His jaw clenches. "You drive a hard bargain."

I grin and kiss him. "Thank you. I'll hold your hand the whole time. We won't fall."

He grumbles until I kiss him again, then pats my thigh and gives me a wicked smirk. "I'm ordering Alder to fuck your throat raw tonight for this." My breath hitches and his luminous eyes glitter with satisfaction. "So perfect for us, mate."

Matthias takes my hand. "Come on. Let's head back to the beach. I want to make all the guys there jealous when I rub my gorgeous girl down with sunscreen. Then I want to show you the shells I scored for you."

Grinning, I slide my arms around his neck and kiss him.

Three Years Later

"Go, go, go!" I tap on Alder's shoulder to urge him on. The tattoos on my arm shift with my adrenaline, the lily flowers swirling into smoky shapes from my wrist to my elbow.

He cranes his neck, jogging down the narrow path we climbed to get here with me on his back. He's always been faster than me and grabbed me before I could move. "What made you think you could ride a wild isillion?"

"How was I supposed to know it would try to absorb me through its scales because that's where it keeps its extra teeth?" I shudder, reliving the moment my hand sank into a slimy mouth lined with sharp teeth. "I thought isillion were like dragons! I wanted to ride a dragon. Come on, that would've been badass if it worked."

Alder shakes his head and moves at an unmatched speed while the beast crashes out of its cave at the top of the mountain. "Next time you want to take some time off for an adventure, you're going to tell me exactly what your goals are so I don't have to relive watching you almost get eaten because you're obsessed with taming underworld beasts."

A laugh bubbles out of me and I hug him, kissing his cheek. "You love me."

"Old gods help me, I do, sweet blossom. With every fiber of my being. So much that I let my beautiful mate talk me into dangerous adventures for fun." There's a smile clear in his voice. He starts to laugh, deep and full of life. "The look on your face when you climbed on and it woke up."

My eyes widen as the huge creature takes flight, flapping leathery black wings beneath the blood moon rising in the sky. "I rode the smaller ones in Valerian's memories! I thought this would be the same."

"Those are the young!" He throws his head back and laughs harder. "We send warrior scouts into the mountains on missions to collect the eggs and raise them from hatchlings. They never open their scales and the teeth don't develop. You can't tame the fully grown wild ones at all, you crazy girl."

"Less talking, more running for our lives." I can't stop another giggle from escaping. "Vale's going to kill us."

"You're on your own there," he tosses over his shoulder as he twists to fling a fireball to deter the flying beast from snapping its deadly jaws at us.

"I thought you were my protector against all things?" I help him, conjuring a powerful whip made of flames to crack at the scaled isillion when it throws its antler-like horns at the cliff's edge.

"If he still lets me live after he finds out I let you come up here."

"I'll protect you, then." I crack my whip and tug on his shirt. "Stop for a second."

"Are you insane?" Alder slows, gesturing at the creature rearing back to attack us.

"Let me down."

"Lily—"

"For real, I've got this."

Reluctantly, he complies. I push up the sleeves of my sweater and adjust my tits. Alder rumbles at my side, prepared to jump in front of me. He doesn't yet, trusting me to handle myself. I send him reassurance that I know what to do along our bond.

When the dragon-like creature with antlers charges the cliff, I fling my arms out, sending a strong gale of flames and hot air arcing out. It forces the isillion back and burns holes in its wings.

"Do you know who I am, beasty?" It screeches, circling around to try again and I grin. "I am Lily, bearer of the goddess Lilith's blood. Now sit the fuck down."

I build a fireball in my hand that grows larger as I spread my hands. The corner of my mouth kicks up as I send it flying with perfect accuracy. It hits the creature in the chest with enough force to make it fall several feet in the air until it recovers. It retreats, flapping its injured wings with an angry groan. It leaves us alone.

"See?" I turn to Alder with a triumphant smile. "Be the bigger baddie."

He shakes his head, clamping the back of my neck and hauling me close for a hard kiss. "I love you, you wild, fierce girl."

"I know." I hum and kiss him again. "Can I still get that piggyback ride?"

Nine Years Later

Valerian's fingertips lightly tracing the inside of my wrist, playing with my shifting tattoos that match the abstract ones covering his arms, distracts me from the demon council's discussion. He doesn't miss a beat, smirking at me before he interjects with his thoughts.

"We should think about the future. It's always best to consider all possible outcomes rather than wait for seeds of doubt to sow. Anticipating those outcomes helps us foster peace throughout the underworld."

Lucifer chuckles, chin propped against his fist in his throne, overseeing the meeting. "Sharp as ever, Valerian."

"Your Highness." Vale bows his head.

Whatever is said next goes over my head when he continues drawing lazy patterns on my sensitive skin. It takes me another moment to realize it's letters.

I love you. Over and over.

I peek at him through my lashes while Alder and another warrior demon on the council carry the discussion. His lips twitch.

Finally caught on, did you? He sends the words into my mind. I duck to hide my smile from the council. The last time I was caught flirting with my mates during a meeting, Vale made a bet with me that I couldn't sit through a whole meeting without getting distracted by them.

This so doesn't count because you're distracting me, not the other way around, I sass through our bond. *Also, I love you.*

His mouth curves and he traces the secret message into my skin again.

When the meeting ends, Valerian takes my hand and the four of us return to our home in Hell. It overlooks a pearlescent lavender lake with a balcony terrace where we've spent many nights enjoying each other and the view. I no longer fear water and my past can't hurt me anymore. I've overwritten all my bad memories with thousands of good ones with my mates by my side.

Between my many bookshelves packed with manga and a vast collection of books, we've covered the walls with photos of our travels, the little camera Matthias gifted me with working overtime to capture our memories—adventures exploring the underworld realm, traveling the mortal world three times over, and perfect little moments in between of our life together.

I stop in front of the portrait of all four of us that Matthias got enlarged. It's much like a dream I had once where they surrounded me on a throne. I've never wanted to be the queen of Hell, but Lucifer and his wife goaded me into sitting there during one of their opulent parties. My guys surrounded me as they did in that dream, taking their places at my side always, never leaving me alone. It's the only way it should ever be.

Matthias squeezes my shoulders. "Want to sit out on the balcony? The stars are sparkling off the lake and I got you something."

I smirk, catching the hint of mischief in his tone. "What are you up to?"

He tucks my hand in the crook of his elbow and escorts me outside. Grasping my waist, he boosts me onto the stone banister and fits himself between my legs, plucking at the suspenders of my corduroy skirt.

"I still remember when I first saw you wearing this," he rasps against my lips.

Pulling away from the kiss, he produces a small, plastic-wrapped treat. I turn it over and lift my brows.

"A Twinkie?"

"I didn't forget my promise." He winks. "We never made it back to any rest stops, so I wanted to bring it to you. I still want you to experience everything, Lils. We're not done by a long shot."

I wrap my arms around his shoulders to draw him closer. He settles his hands on my thighs and I smile.

"Thank you."

The way he always thinks of me with big and small gestures, and his boundless desire to see me live life with abandon makes my heart swell. Each of my mates takes care of me in their own way, and together as a group they fulfill me completely.

"There's my favorite sight," he murmurs. "Your smile is more beautiful than all the stars in every realm combined."

He takes the treat and feeds it to me while we watch the lake sparkle.

An Endless Lifetime Later

Time as an immortal fae being is fluid. Entire years can pass, yet it only seems like it's moments later.

With my fated mates, I've experienced everything I ever longed for in life. They sate my needs in every way, granting me a life full of exciting adventures fit for the stories I used to read to escape my pain. We've traveled far and wide, amongst the mortals and the fae.

There are so many that never wanted to see me live as I have. So many cruel people that stole my happiness. They don't matter now. They haven't for a long time.

The stars are beautiful tonight. We're in the abandoned Brim Hills cemetery on Halloween. We've come back to the place we started countless times over the years, but this is the first time we've spent Halloween here.

It's in a much worse state than all those years ago when I came to this town. Talbot House no longer stands beyond the woods and Brim Hills eventually died out as a town. Now it feels like it's our secret hideaway in the overgrown graveyard reclaimed by nature.

"Come here, petal." Matthias offers his hand. "Dance with me."

My fingers slip into his and I grant him a tender smile. He guides me into his arms and we twirl in a slow circle to the melody of our entwined heartbeats. He strokes my cheeks with a captivating smile.

"What?" I ask.

"Nothing. I was just thinking you're just as stunning as the night we first met."

"I don't look much different," I tease.

"It's your heart that's beautiful, mate," he murmurs before brushing his lips across mine.

Alder taps him on the shoulder. "I'd like to cut in."

"Happy birthday, Lils." Matthias grazes his nose against mine and hands me off to him.

"I still don't get why you all make a point of celebrating today," I say sardonically. "We know as demons we don't truly have birthdays to celebrate."

"We need little reason to show you we love you," Alder rumbles. "You are our treasure."

He spins me beneath his arm and pulls me back against his chest, kissing the top of my head. Valerian watches, leaning against the arch beneath the crumbled stairs of the chapel ruins. I don't need the ritual to activate the gate now. It recognizes the power in us and comes when we call it to return us to Hell.

On the next spin, Valerian and Alder switch seamlessly. He draws my hand to rest over his heart, caressing the swirling ink on my skin as he gazes at me, my magic tattoos as attuned to his touch as his are to mine.

"We celebrate your birthday because without your rebirth, we wouldn't have you," he says. "You're ours, Lily. Our goddess."

I sigh in contentment, resting my head against his chest. "And you're mine. My knight. My warrior. My trickster. I love you."

My mates make me happy. In them I have everything I've ever needed—beyond that. My protectors. My challengers. My perfect matches.

"Let's go home," Valerian says against my temple.

I smile as they circle me. "I've told you all hundreds of times. It doesn't matter where we go. In every realm, my home is with you, always."

Thank you so much for reading HELL GATE! Enjoy a special bonus by downloading three scenes from Alder, Matthias, and Valerian's points of view. Download the bonus scene at: **bit.ly/hellgatebonus**

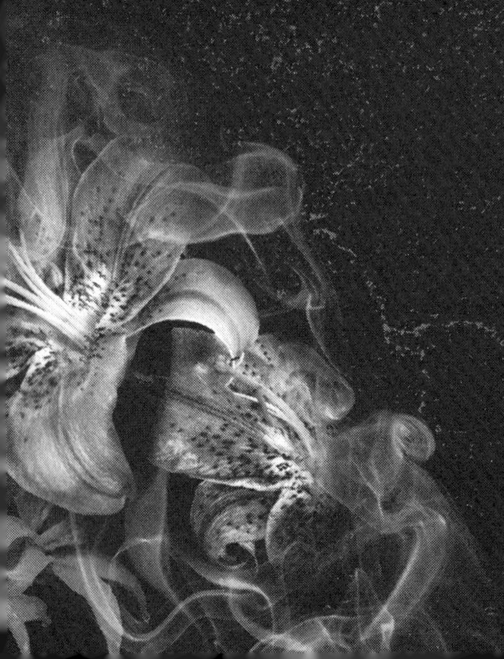

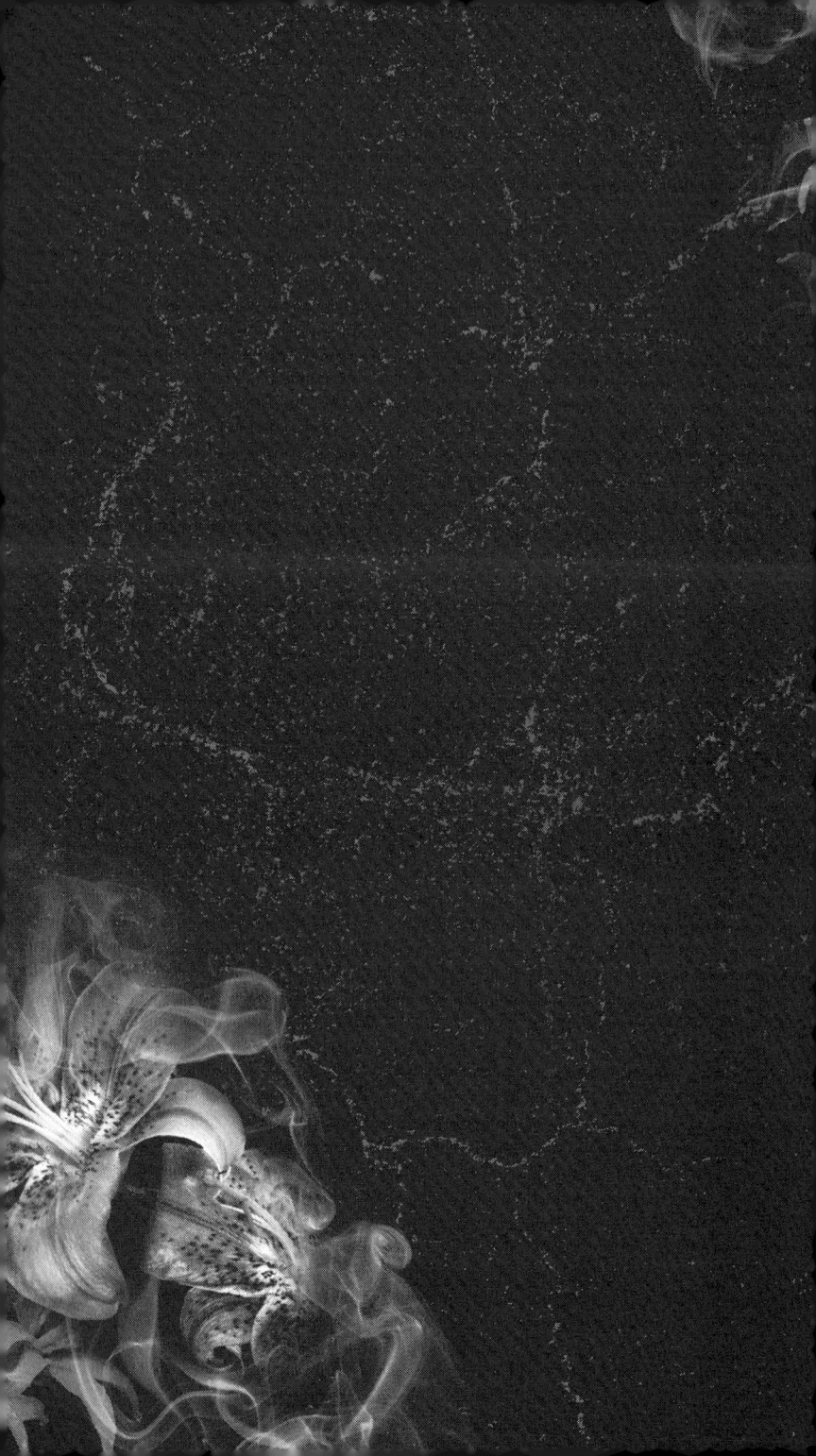

Thank You
WHAT'S NEXT?

Thanks for reading Hell Gate! If you enjoyed it, please leave a review on your favorite retailer or book community! Your support means so much to me!

Need more Hell Gate right now? Have theories about which characters will feature next? Want exclusive previews of my next book? Join other readers in Veronica Eden's Reader Garden on Facebook!

Join: bit.ly/veronicafbgroup

Are you a newsletter subscriber?
By subscribing, you'll receive exclusive content

and news about upcoming releases, and be able to download a special deleted bonus scene from the Crowned Crows world.

Sign up to download it here:
veronicaedenauthor.com/bonus-content

Thank You
ACKNOWLEDGMENTS

Readers, I'm endlessly grateful for you! Thanks for reading this book. Lily's story was so fun and special for me to work on. I fell so in love with this world, with her, with her guys, and I hope you enjoyed the magical adventure! It means the world to me that you supported my work. I wouldn't be here at all without you! I love all of the comments and messages you send and live for your excitement for my characters!

Thanks to my husband for being you! He doesn't read these, but he's my biggest supporter. He keeps me fed and watered while I'm in the writer cave, and doesn't complain when I fling myself out of bed at odd hours with an idea to frantically scribble down.

Thank you always to Dani, Becca, Ramzi, Sara, Kat, Jade, Sarah, Mia, Bre, Heather, Katie, and Erica for the supportive chats and keeping me arguably sane and on track until the end! And to my beta queens for reading my raw words and offering your time, attention to detail, and consideration of the characters and storyline in my books! With every book I write my little tribe grows and I'm so thankful to have each of you as friends to lean on and share my book creation process with!

To my lovely PA Heather, thank you for taking things off my plate and allowing me to disappear into the writing cave without having to worry. And for letting me infodump at you, because that's my love language hahaha! You rock and I'm so glad to have you on my team!

To my street team and reader group, y'all are the best babes around! Huge thanks to my street team for being the best hype girls! To see you guys get as excited as I do seriously makes my day. I'm endlessly grateful you love my characters and words! Thank you for your help in sharing my books and for your support of my work!

To Shauna and Wildfire Marketing Solutions, thank you so much for all your hard work and being so awesome! I appreciate everything that you do!

To Samantha & Brittni at Overbooked Author Services, thank you for your hard work and your booktok love!

To the bloggers and bookstagrammers, thank you for being the most wonderful community! Your creativity and beautiful edits, reviews, and videos are something I come back to visit again and again to brighten my day. Thank you for trying out my books. You guys are incredible and blow me away with your passion for romance!

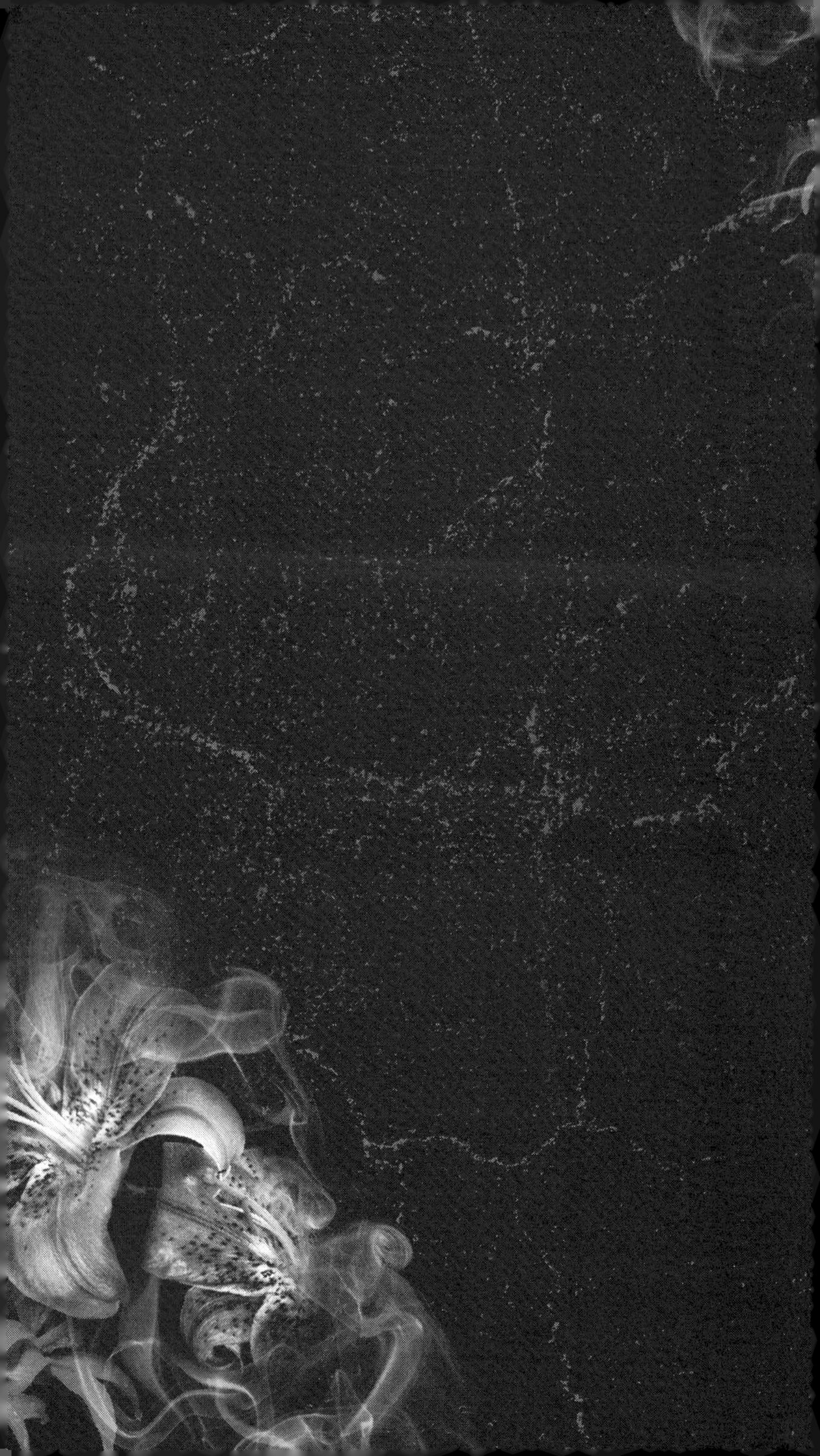

About THE AUTHOR

Stay Up All Night Falling in Love

Veronica Eden is a USA Today & international bestselling author of addictive romances that keep you up all night falling in love with spitfire heroines, irresistible heroes, and edgy twists.

She loves exploring complicated feelings, magical worlds, epic adventures, and the bond of characters that embrace *us against the world*. She has always been drawn to gruff bad boys, clever villains, and the twisty-turns of a morally gray character. She is a sucker for a deliciously swoony hero with a devastating smirk. When not writing, she can be found soaking up sunshine at the beach, snuggling in a pile with her untamed pack of animals (her husband, dog and cats), and surrounding herself with as many plants as she can get her hands on.

CONTACT + FOLLOW
Email | Website | Facebook Group | Amazon

Other books BY VERONICA

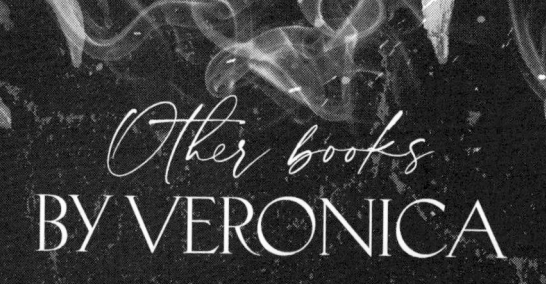

Sign up for the mailing list to get first access and ARC opportunities! **Follow Veronica on BookBub** for new release alerts!

Dark Romance

Sinners and Saints Series
Wicked Saint
Tempting Devil
Ruthless Bishop
Savage Wilder
Sinners and Saints: The Complete Series

Crowned Crows Series
Crowned Crows of Thorne Point

Loyalty in the Shadows
A Fractured Reign

Standalone
Unmasked Heart
Devil on the Lake

Reverse Harem Romance
Standalone
Hell Gate
More Than Bargained

Contemporary Romance

Standalone
Jingle Wars
Haze

Printed in Great Britain
by Amazon